ETHICS

Selections from
Classical and Contemporary Writers

NINTH EDITION

OLIVER A. JOHNSON
Late of the University of California, Riverside

ANDREWS REATH
University of California, Riverside

THOMSON
™
WADSWORTH

Australia • Canada • Mexico • Singapore • Spain
United Kingdom • United States

THOMSON

™

WADSWORTH

Publisher: *Holly J. Allen*
Philosophy Editor: *Steve Wainwright*
Assistant Editors: *Lee McCracken, Anna Lustig*
Editorial Assistant: *Melanie Cheng*
Technology Project Manager: *Susan DeVanna*
Marketing Manager: *Worth Hawes*
Marketing Assistant: *Kristi Bostock*
Advertising Project Manager: *Bryan Vann*
Composition Buyer: *Ben Schroeter*

Print/Media Buyer: *Karen Hunt*
Permissions Editor: *Sarah Harkrader*
Production Service: *Scratchgravel Publishing Services*
Text Designer: *Harry Voigt*
Copy Editor: *Toni Zuccarini Ackley*
Cover Designer: *Yvo Riezebos*
Compositor: *Scratchgravel Publishing Services*
Text and Cover Printer: *Webcom, Limited*

For more information about our products, contact us at:

**Thomson Learning Academic Resource Center
1-800-423-0563**

For permission to use material from this text, contact us by:

Phone: 1-800-730-2214
Fax: 1-800-730-2215
Web: http://www.thomsonrights.com

Library of Congress Control Number:
2003105423

ISBN 0155058649

Wadsworth/Thomson Learning
10 Davis Drive
Belmont, CA 94002-3098
USA

Asia
Thomson Learning
5 Shenton Way #01-01
UIC Building
Singapore 068808

Australia/New Zealand
Thomson Learning
102 Dodds Street
Southbank, Victoria 3006
Australia

Canada
Nelson
1120 Birchmount Road
Toronto, Ontario M1K 5G4
Canada

Europe/Middle East/Africa
Thomson Learning
High Holborn House
50/51 Bedford Row
London WC1R 4LR
United Kingdom

Latin America
Thomson Learning
Seneca, 53
Colonia Polanco
11560 Mexico D.F.
Mexico

Spain/Portugal
Paraninfo
Calle/Magallanes, 25
28015 Madrid, Spain

PREFACE

I am taking over the editing of *Ethics* from Oliver Johnson, who died in 2000 after a long and productive career in philosophy. The format of the last edition has been maintained, but there have been changes to many of the selected readings. In Parts One and Two, some authors included in the last edition have been omitted, and the selections from other authors have been slightly altered. Small additions have been made to Plato and Aristotle; more substantial additions were made to Hobbes, Hume, and Mill. The bulk of the changes come in Part Three, which has been completely revised and updated. One of my principal aims in redoing Part Three has been to include representative selections from some of the most important moral philosophers and problems in moral philosophy of the past three decades. Many of the introductions to the individual selections have been revised, and obviously, new introductions have been written for newly included authors. I have tried to make the new introductions more substantive by providing the reader with a brief overview of the issues with which the selection is concerned and the views developed by the author. The intent is to provide some orientation for the material that follows. Likewise I have rewritten the general introduction to Part Two and have written a new introduction to Part Three. Study questions have been revised throughout, and the selected bibliographies have been updated.

As in previous editions, Parts One and Two are organized chronologically. Some of Part Three is also organized chronologically, but strict chronological order seemed neither feasible nor desirable for selections written between 1971 and the present. However, the emphasis on the history of moral philosophy has been maintained. Much of the book remains a survey of representative selections from the most important authors in the history of western moral philosophy. The continuity between the history of moral philosophy and contemporary moral theory has been stressed by including many contemporary authors who work within the general framework of one of the historically important moral philosophers. Some of the connections between contemporary and historical authors can be seen in the "Topical Contents," which suggests a problem-oriented way of organizing the selections.

Several reviewers have contributed helpful comments: Lorraine Arangno, University of Colorado at Colorado Springs; Judith Barad, Indiana State University; Robert Halliday, Utica College of Syracuse University; Assya Pascalev, University of North Florida; and Anita M. Superson, University of Kentucky. I am grateful to them and to all who have helped on this edition.

Andrews Reath

CONTENTS

TOPICAL CONTENTS

Justice

Moral Relativism and Moral Absolutism

Morality and Self-Interest

Basis of Moral Obligation

Moral and Nonmoral Value

An Introduction to the Study of Ethics

What Is Ethics?

If the account given by Plato of Socrates' trial before the Athenian court is accurate, it is clear that Socrates could have avoided the death penalty. The jury almost certainly would have acquitted him if he had agreed to give up his practice of going about Athens interrogating its citizens concerning the ultimate questions of human existence. Socrates preferred, however, to run the risk of being sentenced to death rather than to abandon his way of life because, as he said, "The unexamined life is not worth living."

The kind of examination of life to which Socrates devoted himself is the branch of philosophy called "ethics" or "moral philosophy." In a word, ethics is rational inquiry into how to act and how to lead one's life. Ethics or moral philosophy—we shall use those terms interchangeably—is one of the oldest branches of philosophy, and over the course of its history it has encompassed many different questions: What are the proper aims of life at which we should direct our actions? What goods are truly worth having, and what kinds of actions and activities truly worth engaging in? What traits of character make a person good and make a life worth living? What are the principles that distinguish right from wrong? What principles should guide our treatment of others, and what limits do they impose on our pursuit of our own happiness and our personal goals? Where moral principles limit our pursuit of individual happiness, what reasons do we have for conforming to them? What is the source of their authority? And are there objective answers to questions such as these? Are there, for example, any universally valid moral principles that all people and all societies ought to accept?

Many areas of the humanities and social sciences are concerned with human conduct and values. But as you may be able to gather from the questions just posed, ethics or moral philosophy is a *normative* enterprise rather than a *descriptive* one. It is not concerned with how people actually act, but with how they ought to act. Social sciences such as psychology, sociology, and anthropology are concerned (among other things) with describing actual human behavior and explaining why human beings act the way that they do in the circumstances studied. They are descriptive and explanatory disciplines, concerned with the empirical facts of human behavior. Moral philosophy cannot ignore actual human conduct. It needs a realistic view of human nature and human motivation, and of how societies function. But its aim is not to describe people's actual behavior and goals, or even to describe the values that people actually accept—which, after all, may turn out to be flawed when subjected to critical scrutiny. Instead, moral philosophy attempts to develop a principled account of how we ought to act, what values we ought to

1

accept, and what kinds of goals are worth having. For this reason, it is perfectly legitimate for the moral philosopher to articulate ideals of conduct and character
that diverge from, and may even be deeply critical of, a society's accepted values
and practices. As a normative enterprise, moral philosophy may have an important
critical dimension. Likewise, as a normative enterprise moral philosophy is concerned with voluntary conduct. It assumes that people are capable of exercising
reasoned control over their actions and attitudes, that they are responsible for their
choices and the kinds of lives that they lead, and that they are capable of examining
their goals and values and changing them if they see reason to. Moral philosophy
examines what goes into choosing and living well.

We said earlier that ethics is a form of rational inquiry that aims at a principled
account of how we ought to act and lead our lives. It is a form of rational inquiry
because moral philosophers advance claims about values and principles of conduct
that can be true or false and for which they provide rational support. Does that
mean that there are uniquely right answers to the kinds of questions with which
moral philosophy is concerned? That is one of the questions of moral philosophy,
and it would be premature to attempt an answer here. Certainly any survey of
moral philosophy will reveal controversy and ongoing disagreement. But individuals engaged in moral philosophy proceed on the assumption that there are right
and wrong answers to the questions that they raise, and that some responses can
be rationally supported and others not. They are not merely expressing their "personal opinions," as that phrase is often understood now. People who engage in
moral inquiry and discussion of ethical questions do say what they believe. But
they are expressing the beliefs that they think are best supported by reasoned argument, and believe that the reasons that persuade them to accept these conclusions should have rational force for others as well. They are willing to defend their
conclusions by giving reasons that support them, but also to examine them critically and to reassess them should others find them unpersuasive or point out weaknesses in their views. Moral philosophy often takes the form of dialogue between
people who share many assumptions in common, but who nonetheless disagree on
others. But it is a form of rational dialogue in which people develop arguments intended to persuade others.

Because morality is not the only area in which we find normative principles
that govern conduct and choice, it may be useful to distinguish it from other normative domains, such as law, religion, and etiquette. There are similarities and connections among all of these areas. All contain rules of conduct that are to varying
degrees codified and socially reinforced. But morality should not be identified with
any of them.

Both law and morality function socially to control and to coordinate human
conduct and to make it possible for individuals with diverse and sometimes conflicting goals to live together. Law, like morality, defines certain actions as right and
wrong (i.e., as "legal" or legally permissible, "illegal" or legally wrong, and legally
required) and it defines rights and duties. To give some trivial examples of legal
rights and duties, we have a legal duty to register our cars in the area in which we
reside, and we have the legal right to contest a traffic ticket in court. Obviously law
is much more formalized than morality. We have elaborate and fairly explicit social

processes for making and changing laws, resolving ambiguities in the meaning or application of a law, enforcing penalties for violations of law, and so on. In law, for example, formal penalties such as fines and imprisonment are assessed for illegal acts, whereas sanctions for conduct that is morally wrong are limited to such things as the pangs of conscience and the disapproval of others.

Finally, some overlap exists between what is legal or illegal and what is morally right or wrong, but this overlap is partial at most. Illegal actions such as murder, theft, and fraud are also morally wrong. Certain important legal rights, such as the right of free expression, the right of political participation, or the right to a fair trial have a clear moral basis. And many writers argue that we have a general moral obligation to obey the law. But in general the aim of law is not the enforcement of morality, and there are several important ways in which the content of law and morality may diverge. First, actions that in themselves are morally innocent may be illegal, such as failing to register one's car. Would it make sense to say that I have done something morally wrong if I fail to register my car? Probably not, because that action seems morally insignificant by itself. Someone could only claim that it is morally wrong by citing the existence of a moral obligation to obey the law; if I am morally bound to obey the law in general, them I am bound to obey this one. But even that seems insufficient. If my failure to register my car is to count as a moral failure, it would have to be due, say, to intentional disregard of the law, rather than mere forgetfulness. Second, actions that are morally wrong may not be illegal. For example, it is not against the law to lie or to deceive people in one's personal relationships, but most people would agree that such actions are in most cases morally wrong. Third, laws can be unjust or immoral. Laws permitting segregation or discrimination based on race and gender were valid laws (in a legal sense), but they were unjust or morally wrong. Here it is important to realize that we can criticize laws from a moral point of view when they violate moral standards.

The connections between morality and religion are as complex as those between morality and law. Most religious outlooks include or support a moral code in the narrow sense of a body of principles that govern how one should regard and treat others. The moral code of a religion may also have implications for a person's attitudes toward God, nature, and so on. But many religious duties do not in and of themselves seem to be moral duties—for example, duties to engage in certain religious practices or rituals, or to engage in certain specific forms of worship. Of course, this is a complicated issue. Religious practices may take on a moral dimension within the broader context of a religious outlook. For example, if one believes in God and, because of the relationship between God and humankind, believes that one has duties of worship that are moral in nature, one may think that the practices of one's religion are morally obligatory. The duty to worship God may entail that one is morally bound to follow these religious practices.

Perhaps the most important point to make here is that, although morality is often given a religious basis, it need not be. A religious outlook may base morality in divine authority by understanding moral principles as divine commands, or as representing God's will for humankind. Religious beliefs may then provide the motivation to act morally. Furthermore, it may be part of a religious outlook to hold that the content of morality has been made known to humankind through divine revelation, for example, through the words of a prophet or sacred text. But the dominant trend in moral philosophy since the 17th century has been to find a basis for morality that is independent of religion and any conception of divine authority. Moral philosophers have argued in different ways that morality is based in reason—that human beings have the capacity to discover the content of morality on their own through the use of reason and that our understanding of these principles, in conjunction with normal features of human psychology, can motivate us to comply with moral principles. Moreover, given the diversity of religious and nonreligious outlooks in the modern world, many thinkers believe that it is extremely important that we find a basis for morality that does not presuppose a religious outlook.

Of course, one can accept a philosophical account of morality that bases it in reason while also thinking that it has a religious basis. There is no apparent inconsistency in accepting both. The claim that we can discover the content of morality on our own through reason can be, and historically often has been, incorporated into a religious outlook. And a religion can believe that morality has a basis in divine authority in addition to its having a basis in reason.

Etiquette, like morality, is a source of rules telling us how we ought to behave in certain circumstances whose overall aim is to promote social harmony and good relations between people. But certainly the "ought" of etiquette is not the same as the "ought" of morality. The rules of etiquette—such as rules that govern proper forms of greeting, dress, and eating or that specify how certain social rituals (weddings, funerals, and so on) should be carried out—are conventional. They are matters of social custom in ways that moral principles are not. We should expect variation in such customs between one society or historical period and another. As is the case with law, behavior that is morally innocent may be contrary to etiquette. It should be clear that etiquette and morality are different. At the same time, there may be connections between them. For example, a code of etiquette consists, in part, of conventional signs of respect, and most people would agree that showing respect toward others is morally obligatory. Thus, in many situations we fulfill this duty by observing the conventions of etiquette.

The Relevance of Ethics

Our quick survey of some of the questions of ethics should make it clear that the study of ethics is not merely a subject of academic interest. Although a person with an inquiring mind can lead a fulfilling life without ever delving into the fields of, say, linguistics, paleontology, or cosmology, one cannot in the same way avoid the questions of ethics. They are questions that any reflective person will encounter in the course of his or her life. Ethical issues arise in many areas of our lives. They include questions that we face as individuals—issues concerning our personal goals in life, personal relationships, and proper conduct in our interaction with others. As citizens of a democratic country we must face the pressing social and political issues that confront modern societies—issues of equality and basic civil rights; questions about what counts as discrimination based on race, gender, and sexuality and how past and present discrimination should be rectified; ethical issues arising out of new developments in science, technology, and medicine; environmental issues; questions of international justice; and so on. All are studied by scientists and social scientists, policy makers, religious leaders, and politicians, and we discuss them together as fellow citizens. All at root raise ethical questions.

Socrates' challenge to examine one's life and one's basic values is particularly relevant for those who are making the transition to adulthood and independence. Almost all of us have, without questioning, accepted the moral precepts and practices that we were taught while growing up. Perhaps this is as it should be. However, there comes a time when one begins to look critically at the moral precepts and values that one has always accepted. It may be that one is confronted with a novel situation or a social issue in which the principles that one has learned do not apply, or in which they either demand or permit an action that now suddenly seems wrong. Or perhaps one encounters people with very different backgrounds, or one begins to gain a deeper understanding of the complexities of the modern world, with the result that one begins to question values and principles that one had always taken for granted. For someone in this situation, the question is what to believe and why. What justifies the familiar conventional precepts that one has always accepted? Are they justified by more basic principles or should they be revised or abandoned?

The study of moral philosophy can provide one with tools for addressing a range of ethical issues. The ethical dimensions of current social issues are studied in philosophy courses or books on "applied ethics" or "contemporary moral issues." The focus of this book is more general. We concentrate on philosophical accounts of the nature of good and bad, or the basic principles of right conduct. This field is sometimes called "moral theory" or "ethical theory," as opposed to "applied ethics." Both fields are important. What one can hope to gain from the study of moral theory is an understanding of some of the different theoretical approaches to ethical questions that will enable one to think about a variety of issues with greater sophistication.

Some of the Main Questions of Ethics

In order to present a more informative characterization of the subject matter of ethics, let us distinguish two fundamental concepts—the good and the right. Two of the basic questions with which moral philosophers have been concerned are "What is good (or bad)?" and "What is right (or wrong)?" Answers to these questions provide the basis of a normative theory that can provide substantive guidance about the goods worth seeking in life and the basic principles by which we should govern our actions. What is the difference between these two questions?

When we say that something is good we are saying that it is in some way desirable. When philosophers talk about *the good* they generally mean that which is truly desirable or worth having for its own sake. An account of the good encompasses the proper aims or *ends* of action: Which of the kinds of goods that human beings tend to desire are truly worth having or pursuing for their own sake? What sorts of activities are truly worth engaging in? It is common to make a distinction between what is *good in itself* and what is *good as a means*. Something is good as a means, or good *instrumentally*, if the reason to seek it is that it is a means to something else. For example, we do not desire to go to the dentist for its own sake; it may even be quite unpleasant. We do it as a means to something else that we do value, namely the health of our teeth. By contrast, something is good in itself if it is desired or chosen for its own sake, and not as a means to anything beyond it. Goods of this latter sort, sometimes called *final ends*, might include happiness, self-realization or self-development, friendship, success, integrity, and so on. Philosophical discussion of the good is concerned with final ends, or what is good in itself. In most contexts, the good is understood as what is good for the individual—as the ultimate end (or ends) that individuals would choose for themselves under the direction of reason, possession of which is truly fulfilling or makes their lives worth living. The good in this sense is what each of us truly has reason to aim at. Philosophers differ in their views on the nature of the human good. Some have argued for the view known as *hedonism*, according to which the sole final end is pleasure. Others have argued that the good lies in some objective end or activity other than pleasure. Still others have concluded that the search for a single ultimate good is misguided, arguing that we must recognize a plurality of intrinsic goods and final ends, which are not reducible to any single good.

Discussion of the good tends to focus on what is good or bad from the point of view of an individual, but in some contexts it may focus on states of affairs that are good or bad in an "agent neutral" sense, or from everyone's point of view. For example, one might think that it is a bad thing if a child suffers—not just a bad thing for the child (or for the child and its parents), but a bad thing period—and that in consequence anyone in a position to relieve the child's suffering has a reason to. Here the child's suffering is viewed as bad from an agent-neutral point of view, that is, from anyone's point of view. Philosophers who think along these lines might argue that it is a good thing when human beings (or other sentient beings) flourish and a bad thing when they suffer, and that we all have reasons to act in ways that promote the flourishing and diminish the suffering of human (or other sentient) beings.

Whereas the good is concerned with the proper aims or ends of action, right and wrong are generally viewed as properties of actions themselves. When we are faced with a difficult choice and are uncertain about how to act, we ask what the right thing to do is. When we reach a decision we often express it by saying "This is what I ought to do." But the word "ought" is used in different senses, to which correspond different senses of "right" and "wrong." If one sells a stock that a week later doubles in price, one will likely say in retrospect that one made the wrong decision; one ought to have waited. Someone considering two different ways of achieving some goal, who suddenly discovers that the first way has substantial hidden costs, will decide that he ought to take the second way; that is the right choice under the circumstances. Someone torn between two very different career paths realizes after much reflection that although one involves certain risks, it is what she really wants to do. She decides that that is the right choice. In each of these cases, one decides what one ought to do by determining what will best satisfy one's desires or advance certain desired ends. But there is a special moral sense in which actions can be right or wrong that calls into play the idea of moral obligation and is not in any straightforward way a matter of whether the actions best satisfy one's desires or advance one's ends. Ethics is concerned with right and wrong in this sense—specifically, to articulate the basic principle or principles by which we distinguish right and wrong action and determine what our moral duties and obligations are.

When we say that an action is morally right, we mean that it is called for or required—that one ought to do it. When an action is judged to be wrong, one ought to refrain from doing it. In each case the moral "ought" expresses the judgment that there are especially weighty reasons for either performing or refraining from the action, which override or take priority over reasons based on one's desires and personal goals. One ought to perform or to refrain from the action whether one wants to or not, regardless of the effect on one's desired ends. Many people follow the 18th century German philosopher Immanuel Kant in thinking that moral reasons are "unconditional" in the sense that they bind us without appealing to our desires, interests, and ends. Principles of right conduct apply primarily to the proper treatment of others, and spell out our duties to others (although some thinkers hold that we can have duties to ourselves). Their role is to impose constraints on the pursuit of both personally desired ends and socially desirable goals, limiting both the ends that we may permissibly adopt and the means that we may take to our ends.

The fact that ethical requirements can set limits on the pursuit of our desires and personal ends leads to another question that has occupied philosophers since at least the time of Plato. Given the possibility of conflict between ethical demands and self-interest, why should we act justly or morally—especially in situations where we are required to refrain from some action that would contribute to our happiness or where we can profit from injustice? What is the relationship between morality and self-interest? What is the basis of moral obligation? Plato is concerned with demonstrating that only the just person can be truly happy, so that the ultimate reason to act justly is that it leads to true happiness. Thomas Hobbes, the 17th century British philosopher, argues that the reasons to institute and to comply with moral rules, and thus the basis of moral obligation, lie in long-term self-interest. Both thus hold that when we take the larger point of view, there is no real conflict between morality and self-interest. In contrast to Hobbes, the 18th century British philosophers Joseph Butler and David Hume, as well as Kant, base moral obligation in forms of motivation that are not self-interested—Butler in conscience, Hume in our natural capacity for sympathy, and Kant in reason.

Theories that attempt a systematic account of ethical thought will encompass both the right and the good, but a thinker's overall approach may be shaped by which concept is emphasized or by how these concepts are related. Ancient Greek philosophers such as Plato and Aristotle, as well as medieval thinkers such as Aquinas, tend to focus on the nature of the good. For them the basic question of ethics is what is the true human good, which they see as the final and overarching end at which all conduct should be directed. In these theories, the concept of a *virtue* becomes one of the key notions. The virtues are those traits of character

that are either conducive to, or form part of, the true human good—the characteristics that we need to develop in order to attain the highest good. Proper treatment of others is addressed by specific virtues such as justice and generosity. These
virtues may set limits to self-interested conduct, but they are nonetheless conceived to be part of the individual's good. As we will see, in the early modern period beginning in the 17th century, greater emphasis is placed on the notion of the
right, and duty and obligation become central notions. A common aim of the
thinkers of this period is to identify the basic principles of right conduct and to explain why we are obligated to follow them.

Within the modern period, we find two competing approaches to understanding right action that are distinguished by the ways in which the right and the good
are related. Many thinkers agree that it is a feature of common-sense moral
thought to accept a number of principles of right conduct that we should follow
for their own sake—simply because they are right, and not because doing so serves
some further end. Thus we think that we should keep our promises and agreements simply because we have made them. We think that individuals have certain
rights that ought to be respected, even in circumstances in which violating someone's rights might benefit others or serve some larger social end. Kant develops a
moral theory that derives principles of this sort from a more general principle of
respect for persons. According to Kant, persons, because they are rational agents,
have an absolute value that imposes inviolable limits on how they may be treated.
Certain ways of acting are required or impermissible as a matter of respect for the
persons affected. In a moral outlook of this kind, principles of right conduct are
defined without bringing in a conception of the good in the sense that the principles of right conduct identify reasons for action that are not based on the pursuit
of desired or desirable ends. The principles of right conduct are immediately binding and should be followed for their own sake. Furthermore, these principles impose limits on the ends that we may pursue and the ways in which we may pursue
them. An end has no value if it can be achieved only at the expense of violating a
principle of right conduct. (For instance, to use one of Kant's examples, my happiness is not really a good if I have achieved it by violating someone else's rights.) A
moral outlook in which the right in this way is prior to the good and serves to
limit what is good is referred to as "deontological," a term derived from the Greek
word for "ought."

The competing approach is called "teleological" (from the Greek word for
"end," *telos*) or "consequentialist" (referring to the importance of consequences).
The basic intuition behind teleology or consequentialism is that right action is directed at producing good results in the world and that the value of an action
comes from its consequences or the end at which it is directed. These theories
begin with a conception of what is good, and then define right action as the action
that will produce the most overall good, or has the best consequences. Different
forms of consequentialism are possible, depending on how one defines the good.
The most influential form of consequentialism, and the one represented in this volume, is a theory called "utilitarianism," which was articulated in the late 18th and
19th centuries by British philosophers Jeremy Bentham and John Stuart Mill.
Utilitarians define the good as human happiness and then define the right as what

maximizes happiness—not, of course, the happiness of the individual, but the total happiness of all people affected by an action.

As we can see, deontological and teleological or consequentialist theories are distinguished by the way in which they relate the right and the good. The driving intuition behind deontological theories is that certain ways of acting, or certain ways of treating persons, can be right or wrong in themselves. For the deontologist, principles of right are prior and they limit the kinds of ends and actions that are good. They give us reasons for action that are not based on the ends or the results of an action. In a teleological or consequentialist theory, the rightness of an action is a function of the good that it produces. The good is thus the prior notion, and the right is defined as what will produce the most overall good. The reason for doing any particular action is that it has better overall consequences—that it produces more overall good—than any of the alternatives.

Our brief overview of some of the main concepts and questions in ethics has identified three different approaches to normative ethics that have been influential in the western tradition—theories of the virtues, deontological theories, and teleological or consequentialist theories. But this is not merely a survey of some of the main currents in the history of ethics. It is also a partial guide to much contemporary moral thought. All of these approaches have contemporary representatives who build on and extend what they regard as the central insights of the historically important moral theories. One feature of moral philosophy that this book wishes to emphasize is the continuity between the history of moral philosophy and contemporary moral thought. There are many contemporary moral philosophers who believe that one of the historically important theories has captured an important part of the truth in ethics and provides a viable starting point for further reflection about the central questions of ethics. There is no better way to learn about moral philosophy than to study the major writers in the history of ethics and to see how their insights have been taken up and transformed by contemporary thinkers. That is the approach that we have taken in this book.

Normative Ethics vs. Meta-Ethics

To this point we have been surveying the field of normative ethics. A normative ethical theory develops a substantive account of the nature of good and bad, the basic principles of right and wrong, the nature of the virtues, and so on—in other words, a substantive account of how we ought to act and live. There is also an area of moral philosophy known as "meta-ethics" that was important in the 20th century, and that remains important today. We should mention it briefly here. Whereas normative ethics addresses substantive issues about value and about how to act, the subject matter of meta-ethics is, in a sense, normative ethics itself. Meta-ethics is about normative discourse and normative thought. It studies such topics as the meaning of ethical terms, the distinction between fact and value, or the justification of moral claims, without actually developing any specific account of good and bad or right and wrong. Probably the best way to clarify this distinction is to explain some of the questions of meta-ethics.

One question in meta-ethics has been the analysis of the meaning of ethical terms such as "right" and "good." Can terms such as these be defined? If so, can they be defined or analyzed in terms of purely descriptive or factual language? Or can they be defined only in terms of other ethical or value terms—that is, by using normative language such as "good," "right," ought," "rational," and so on? Another way to approach this issue is to ask what sorts of properties rightness and goodness are. Are they natural properties on a par with other empirically discernible features of the world that figure in scientific descriptions? Or do they contain an element that cannot be reduced to purely empirical properties? "Naturalism" is the view that ethical terms or properties can be understood in terms of purely natural properties. "Non-naturalism" denies this claim. Both naturalists and non-naturalists tend to believe that reasons can be given that justify ethical claims, and thus that they can be true or false and are claims of which we can have knowledge. Because they believe that ethical claims can be true or false and are objects of knowledge, they are known as "cognitivists." But there are also philosophers who believe that ethical claims are very different in nature from factual or scientific claims. They do not believe that ethical claims are kinds of statements that can be true or false, or rationally supported, and thus are not the sorts of things that can be objects of knowledge. They are known as "noncognitivists." A form of noncognitivism that was influential in the middle of the 20th century is "emotivism." Emotivists hold that ethical claims do not convey factual information of any sort. Rather, their function is to express the speaker's emotional attitudes (such as feelings of approval or disapproval) and to influence others to share these emotional attitudes. Because the function of ethical claims is to express and elicit emotional attitudes, they are not supportable by reasons.

A recent controversy in meta-ethics that has emerged from the debate between cognitivism and noncognitivism is the issue of "moral realism." Moral realists believe that there are moral facts—for example, facts about right and wrong that are not just facts about what a person or group of persons believes to be right or wrong. Moral claims are claims about moral facts, and the truth or falsity of a moral claim depends on the moral facts. By contrast, moral antirealists have trouble seeing how our current picture of the world leaves room for moral facts. They either deny that there are such things as moral facts, or believe that they are nothing more than facts about people's beliefs or their tendencies to respond to certain kinds of actions or states of affairs.

Much meta-ethics concerns the relation between moral thought and ordinary factual or scientific thought about the world. It tries to understand how the subject matter of ethics fits into our larger picture of the world. These issues are very complex and we cannot do justice to them here. The selections in this book for the most part are concerned with questions in normative ethics. Some of the selections from the contemporary era, however, explicitly take up meta-ethical issues, and meta-ethical questions often arise in discussing normative ethics. They are an important component of our overall understanding of the domain of moral thought.

We will conclude this introduction with a word of advice. We should not be surprised or discouraged to find a great deal of disagreement among the great moral theorists. In a subject as complex and subtle as moral philosophy, the truth is neither quickly nor easily attained, and disagreement is to be expected. In fact, that is one thing that makes moral philosophy so interesting. In studying the theories represented in this book, it is important both to give an author a sympathetic ear and to understand what the author is saying and why. But it is equally important to develop your own critical assessment of the author's views. To assess an author's views, it helps to begin by looking for the basic insights that drive a theory, and then trying first to understand, then assess, the arguments offered in support of the author's views. You should ask whether a theory coheres with your own intuitive convictions. You may find that an author is articulating in a more explicit way a view that you already accept. You may also find that there is a real conflict between your intuitive convictions and the basic tenets of the theory. In that case you have a decision to make: Either you can revise the convictions with which you began and accept the theory, or you can reject the theory and stand by your initial beliefs. Seeing the differences between the views of different philosophers also helps you to gain perspective. As you begin to understand the important disagreements, you can assess one author's views by setting them off against an alternative. Engaging the theories included in this book in this way can be a starting point for developing and articulating your own views.

As important as an author's conclusions are, the reasoning that leads to the conclusions is equally if not more important. You should not consider a theory any better than the reasoning used to support it and its overall ability to make sense of the area of moral thought with which it is concerned. Reading the theories with this in mind, you may conclude that none of the theories included in this book expresses the complete truth, but that all have grasped some part of the truth.

PART
ONE

———

THE CLASSICAL AND
MEDIEVAL ERAS

The classical and medieval eras in the history of ethics cover a long period of time; more than sixteen hundred years lie between the death of Socrates, a citizen of ancient Athens, and the birth of Thomas Aquinas, a professor in the medieval University of Paris. During these centuries Western civilization underwent many important changes. To mention only two of these: the center of culture moved from the shores of the Aegean and eastern Mediterranean seas, first to Rome and later to western Europe, and the character of religious belief was fundamentally changed, from the paganism of the classical world to the Catholic Christianity of the Middle Ages. Although it is doubtful that the geographical shift had any important effects on philosophy, the transformation in religious beliefs produced consequences of profound significance in ethical theories.

The most general change in ethical outlook consisted of a radical shift between ancient and medieval times in the way in which thinkers conceived the relationship between religion and ethics. In the selection with which this book begins, we find Socrates arguing with Euthyphro in defense of a view affirming the independence of ethics from theology; to find answers to ethical questions, Socrates maintains, we do not have to make any appeal to the gods. To the medieval Christian, however, such an independent outlook would be unthinkable. Although we may and *should* pursue our ethical inquiries as far as we can through the use of our reason and without reference to religious faith, ultimately we can find the answers to the deepest questions of human values only within a theological framework, which determines what these values must be.

Looking more closely at the differences between the moral perspectives of the classical and medieval worlds, we can discern two contrasted conceptions of human nature and value that separated the pagan from the Christian philosophers. The first concerns the place of humankind in the world, and the contrast lies between classical *naturalism* and Christian *supernaturalism*. The second concerns the nature of the highest good for humanity, with its contrast between classical *humanism* and Christian *otherworldliness*. Although these two differences in point of view are related to each other, they need to be distinguished, because their emphasis falls on different characteristics of the human condition.

13

In his *Antigone,* the great Greek dramatist Sophocles wrote, "Wonders are many, and none is more wonderful than man." In these words he expresses an appreciation of human nature generally shared by the classical philosophers. Nevertheless, although they believed humanity to stand at the pinnacle of the natural world, these philosophers almost without exception still considered us a part of nature. Like everything else that exists, we are the product of natural forces and must, therefore, be understood in natural terms. The Christian view of human nature is quite different from such a naturalism. Everything that exists, including human beings, is a product of God's workmanship, but we are absolutely unique, the Christians believe, in that God created us in his own image. We cannot be understood in purely natural terms because God, in creating us, endowed us with a supernatural component—a soul. Our soul, besides distinguishing us from every other created being, is incomparably our most important possession. It renders us truly "children of God."

The second contrast between classical and Christian thought flows directly from the first. If we are natural creatures, alike in kind to the rest of animate nature, our good must lie in this world, in the present life. Such a view of value, called humanism, was shared by most of the classical moral philosophers. For some the present life had to contain all the values that human nature can enjoy, for the simple reason that it is the only life we have. Epicurus reveals his commitment to such a view when he writes: "All good and evil consists in sensation, but death is deprivation of sensation." Aristotle would certainly agree with the Epicurean denial of personal immortality and although Socrates and Plato both believed in a life after death, they nevertheless sought the highest good for human beings in the life we are living here and now. About the nature of this highest good, there were, of course, differences of opinion. Epicurus, for example, found it in a pleasant life of health and mental tranquillity, whereas Aristotle found it in the successful development of our powers as active, rational beings. Nevertheless, the good to be sought, whatever it might be, was something to be gained in a natural way and during the present life. From the point of view of the Christian philosophers, however, such humanism is shortsighted. In their minds it is not the goods of this world that are important, but rather the supreme good to be found in another world, which lies beyond the grave. Our present life contains no intrinsic values, to be sought for their own sake; instead its highest purpose is to prepare us for the life hereafter. Only in its immortal state can the human soul enjoy the highest good, described by St. Augustine as "the eternal felicity of the city of God." Or, as St. Thomas described it, our ultimate happiness, which cannot be of this life, consists in "the contemplation of God."

Nevertheless, in spite of the fundamental differences in their views concerning the human condition and the highest good, the classical and medieval moral philosophers share an important assumption—a *teleological* orientation toward ethics. Although all of these philosophers devoted attention to the issues of right and wrong action, for them the fundamental question concerns the nature of the good, which they understood as the highest good for the individual. Thus their primary concern is with the ultimate end or goal at which rational conduct ought to be directed. The good provides the standard by which actions and states of character are to be assessed: They are good insofar as they contribute to the real-ization of this final end. On the classical side, this teleological orientation is exem-plified in the Plato's *Republic* with its ultimate emphasis on the Form of the Good, which is, according to the Platonic conception of the universe, the very heart of reality. Likewise, Aristotle's Nicomachean Ethics is an inquiry into the nature of the true human good—*eudaimonia,* or happiness. For Aristotle the virtues are those states of character that are conducive to or part of *eudaimonia.* Turning to the Christian writers, it is clear that both Augustine and Aquinas are concerned with final ends. In their opinion, the only goal truly worth seeking comes in an af-terlife in which the soul enjoys eternal felicity in communion with God. Aquinas believes that the virtues are prescribed by natural law, or divine law, and holds that we should act virtuously simply because that is God's command. But the aim of natural law is to direct individuals to their true end, or true happiness.

Among the writers from the classical and medieval eras selected for inclusion in this book, one is in clear disagreement with the general emphasis on the ends we should seek—the Stoic philosopher Epictetus. His *Encheiridion* is devoted to laying down rules about the way in which rational, moral beings should conduct themselves. Nevertheless, despite his concern with the *deontological* side of ethics, Epictetus was by no means oblivious to the teleological side. His rules, especially the most important of them—that one should always keep one's moral purpose in harmony with nature—were not laid down in a vacuum. Rather, Epictetus believed that following these rules was the only way by which we could attain the highest goods in life, which the Stoics considered to be happiness and freedom.

1

SOCRATES

———

Although written by Plato, the dialogue *Euthyphro* is generally considered by scholars to represent the thought of his mentor

> . . . *piety and what is pleasing to the gods are different things.*

Socrates (c. 469–399 B.C.) who himself wrote nothing but devoted his energies to questioning his fellow Athenians about the deepest problems of human existence in his perennial examination of life. Socrates roamed the *agora,* or marketplace, asking questions of the leading citizens of Athens. Unfortunately, the questions Socrates asked his fellow citizens embarrassed and enraged many of them, mainly because they could not offer satisfactory answers. Socrates became increasingly unpopular (particularly with influential Athenians) and was finally indicted on a capital charge of subverting the youth. The conversation between Socrates and Euthyphro, recorded in the following dialogue, takes place just outside the law court in which Socrates is going to stand trial for his life. Ironically, in light of the conversation between the two men, the main charge lodged against Socrates was that of *impiety* toward the gods.

Although the *Euthyphro* was written during an early stage in the development of ethical thought, it is concerned with a question that remains very much alive today. Socrates asks what makes an action "pious," which is roughly equivalent to an action's being right or righteous. Specifically, he asks whether an action is pious because it is pleasing to the gods or whether it is pleasing to the gods because it is pious. The dialogue raises issues about the connection between morality and religion and whether morality is based in the will of God, and if so how. Is an action right because it accords with the will of God—so that God's willing that we perform certain actions makes them right? Or does God will that we perform certain actions because they are right? In the first case, morality requires a foundation in religion, and we can only know what is right and wrong if we have knowledge of God's will through a scripture or holy text, the edicts of a religious authority, or some other form of religious revelation. If God's will makes actions right, we also have to ask whether God could have made any action right (murder, for example) by willing it to be right. On the other hand, if God wills that we perform certain actions because they are right, rightness is an independent feature of the action that explains why God wills that we act in this way. Morality is then independent of religion in the sense that we can determine principles of right conduct through the use of our own reason, without relying on religious beliefs or religious authority.

Although Socrates is concerned with the connection between morality and religion, his question also has a more general application. Viewing rightness as a feature of actions and goodness as a feature of ends or states of affairs, we can ask the following questions: Are actions right because we approve of them, or do we approve of them because they are right? Likewise, is a state of affairs or an end good because we desire it, or do we desire it because it is in some way good? In the first cases, rightness and goodness depend on our actual beliefs, desires, feelings, and so on. It is our having certain attitudes that makes an action right, or a state of affairs good. In the second cases, rightness and goodness are features that are independent of our actual beliefs, desires, and feelings, and that ought to guide and to explain these attitudes. The issue here is whether moral properties are *subjective* features that depend on our evaluative attitudes, or *objective* features that are independent of our attitudes and that, when we are thinking clearly and rationally, are the basis of our evaluative attitudes.

———

Euthyphro

Characters of the Dialogue

Socrates

Euthyphro

Scene—The hall of the King Archon

EUTHYPHRO   What in the world are you doing here at the Archon's hall, Socrates? Why have you left your haunts in the Lyceum? You surely cannot have a suit before him, as I have.

SOCRATES   The Athenians, Euthyphro, call it an indictment, not a suit.

EUTH.   What? Do you mean that someone is prosecuting you? I cannot believe that you are prosecuting anyone yourself.

SOCR.   Certainly I am not.

EUTH.   Then is some one prosecuting you?

SOCR.   Yes.

EUTH.   Who is he?

SOCR.   I scarcely know him myself, Euthyphro; I think he must be some unknown young man. His name, however, is Meletus, and his deme Pitthis, if you can call to mind any Meletus of that deme—a hook-nosed man with lanky hair and rather a scanty beard.

From *Plato: Euthyphro, Apology and Crito,* translated by F. J. Church, copyright © 1948, 1956 by The Liberal Arts Press Inc., reprinted by permission of The Bobbs Merrill Company, Inc.

EUTH. I don't know him, Socrates. But tell me what is he prosecuting you for?

SOCR. What for? Not on trivial grounds, I think. It is no small thing for so young a man to have formed an opinion on such an important matter. For he, he says, knows how the young are corrupted, and who are their corruptors. He must be a wise man who, observing my ignorance, is going to accuse me to the state, as his mother, of corrupting his friends. I think that he is the only one who begins at the right point in his political reforms: I mean whose first care is to make the young men as good as possible, just as a good farmer will take care of his young plants first, and after he has done that, of the others. And so Meletus, I suppose, is first clearing us off who, as he says, corrupt the young men growing up; and then, when he has done that, of course he will turn his attention to the older men, and so become a very great public benefactor. Indeed, that is only what you would expect when he goes to work in this way.

EUTH. I hope it may be so, Socrates, but I fear the opposite. It seems to me that in trying to injure you, he is really setting to work by striking a blow at the foundation of the state. But how, tell me, does he say that you corrupt the youth?

SOCR. In a way which sounds absurd at first, my friend. He says that I am a maker of gods; and so he is prosecuting me, he says, for inventing new gods and for not believing in the old ones.

EUTH. I understand, Socrates. It is because you say that you always have a divine sign. So he is prosecuting you for introducing innovations into religion; and he is going into court to arouse prejudice against you, knowing that the multitude are easily prejudiced about such matters. Why, they laugh even at me, as if I were out of my mind, when I talk about divine things in the assembly and tell them what is going to happen; and yet I have never foretold anything which has not come true. But they are resentful of all people like us. We must not think about them; we must meet them boldly.

SOCR. My dear Euthyphro, their ridicule is not a very serious matter. The Athenians, it seems to me, may think a man to be clever without paying him much attention, so long as they do not think that he teaches his wisdom to others. But as soon as they think that he makes other people clever, they get angry, whether it be from resentment, as you say, or for some other reason.

EUTH. I am not very anxious to try their disposition toward me in this matter.

SOCR. No, perhaps they think you are reserved, and that you are not anxious to teach your wisdom to others. But I fear that they may think that I am; for my love of men makes me talk to everyone whom I meet quite freely and unreservedly, and without payment. Indeed, if I could I would gladly pay people myself to listen to me. If then, as I said just now, they were only going to laugh at me, as you say they do at you, it would not be at all an unpleasant way of spending the day—to spend it in court, joking and laughing. But if they are going to be in earnest, then only prophets like you can tell where the matter will end.

EUTH. Well, Socrates, I dare say that nothing will come of it. Very likely you will be successful in your trial, and I think that I shall be in mine.

SOCR. And what is this suit of yours, Euthyphro? Are you suing, or being sued?

EUTH. I am suing.

SOCR. Whom?

EUTH. A man whom I am thought a maniac to be suing.

SOCR. What? Has he wings to fly away with?

EUTH. He is far enough from flying; he is a very old man.

SOCR. Who is he?

EUTH. He is my father.

SOCR. Your father, my good man?

EUTH. He is indeed.

SOCR. What are you prosecuting him for? What is the accusation?

EUTH. Murder, Socrates.

SOCR. Good heavens, Euthyphro! Surely the multitude are ignorant of what makes right. I take it that it is not everyone who could rightly do what you are doing; only a man who has already well advanced in wisdom.

EUTH. That is quite true, Socrates.

SOCR. Was the man whom your father killed a relative of yours? But, of course, he was: you would never have prosecuted your father for the murder of a stranger?

EUTH. You amuse me, Socrates. What difference does it make whether the murdered man was a relative or a stranger? The only question that you have to ask is did the murderer murder justly or not? If justly, you must let him alone; if unjustly, you must indict him for murder, even though he shares your hearth and sits at your table. The pollution is the same if you associate with such a man, knowing what he has done, without purifying yourself, and him, too, by bringing him to justice. In the present case the murdered man was a poor laborer of mine, who worked for us on our farm in Naxos. In a fit of drunkenness he got in a rage with one of our slaves and killed him. My father therefore bound the man hand and foot and threw him into a ditch, while he sent to Athens to ask the seer what he should do. While the messenger was gone, he entirely neglected the man, thinking that he was a murderer, and that it would be no great matter, even if he were to die. And that was exactly what happened; hunger and cold and his bonds killed him before the messenger returned. And now my father and the rest of my family are indignant with me because I am prosecuting my father for the murder of this murderer. They assert that he did not kill the man at all; and they say that, even if he had killed him over and over again, the man himself was a murderer, and that I ought not to concern myself about such a person because it is impious for a son to prosecute his father for murder. So little, Socrates, do they know the divine law of piety and impiety.

SOCR. And do you mean to say, Euthyphro, that you think that you understand divine things and piety and impiety so accurately that, in such a case as you have stated, you can bring your father to justice without fear that you yourself may be doing an impious deed?

EUTH. If I did not understand all these matters accurately, Socrates, I should be no good—Euthyphro would not be any better than other men.

SOCR. Then, my excellent Euthyphro, I cannot do better than become your pupil and challenge Meletus on this very point before the trial begins. I should say that I had always thought it very important to have knowledge about divine things; and that now, when he says that I offend by speaking carelessly about them, and by introducing innovations, I have become your pupil. And I should say, Meletus, if you acknowledge Euthyphro to be wise in these matters and to hold the correct belief, then think the same of me and do not put me on trial; but if you do not, then bring a suit, not against me, but against my master, for corrupting his elders—namely myself whom he corrupts by his teaching, and his own father whom he corrupts by admonishing and punishing him. And if I did not succeed in persuading him to release me from the suit or to indict you in my place, then I could repeat my challenge in court.

EUTH. Yes, by Zeus! Socrates, I think I should find out his weak points if he were to try to indict me. I should have a good deal to say about him in court long before I spoke about myself.

SOCR. Yes, my dear friend, and knowing this I am anxious to become your pupil. I see that Meletus here, and others too, seem not to notice you at all, but he sees through me without difficulty and at once, and prosecutes me for impiety forthwith. Now, therefore, please explain to me what you were so confident just now that you knew. Tell me what are righteousness and sacrilege with respect to murder and everything else. I suppose that piety is the same in all actions, and that impiety is always the opposite of piety, and like itself, and that, as impiety, it always has the same idea, which will be found in whatever is impious.

EUTH. Certainly, Socrates, I suppose so.

SOCR. Tell me, then, what is piety and what is impiety?

EUTH. Well, then, I say that piety means prosecuting the wrongdoer who has committed murder or sacrilege, or any other such crime, as I am doing now, whether he is your father or your mother or whoever he is; and I say that impiety means not prosecuting him. And observe, Socrates, I will give you a clear proof, which I have already given to others, that it is so, and that doing right means not letting off unpunished the sacrilegious man, whosoever he may be. Men hold Zeus to be the best and the most just of the gods; and they admit that Zeus bound his own father, Cronos, for wrongfully devouring his children; and that Cronos, in his turn, castrated his father for similar reasons. And yet these same men are incensed with me because I proceed against my father for doing wrong. So, you see, they say one thing in the case of the gods and quite another in mine.

SOCR. Is not that why I am being prosecuted, Euthyphro? I mean, because I find it hard to accept such stories people tell about the gods? I expect that I shall be found at fault because I doubt those stories. Now if you who understand all these matters so well agree in holding all those tales true, then I suppose that I must needs give way. What could I say when I admit myself that I know nothing about them? But tell me, in the name of friendship, do you really believe that these things have actually happened?

EUTH. Yes, and stranger ones, too, Socrates, which the multitude do not know of.

SOCR. Then you really believe that there is a war among the gods, and bitter hatreds, and battles, such as the poets tell of, and which the great painters have depicted in our temples, especially in the pictures which cover the robe that is carried up to the Acropolis at the great Panathenaic festival. Are we to say that these things are true, Euthyphro?

EUTH. Yes, Socrates, and more besides. As I was saying, I will relate to you many other stories about divine matters, if you like, which I am sure will astonish you when you hear them.

SOCR. I dare say. You shall relate them to me at your leisure another time. At present please try to give a more definite answer to the question which I asked you just now. What I asked you, my friend, was, What is piety? and you have not explained it to me, to my satisfaction. You only tell me that what you are doing now, namely, prosecuting your father for murder, is a pious act.

EUTH. Well, that is true, Socrates.

SOCR. Very likely. But many other actions are pious, are they not, Euthyphro?

EUTH. Certainly.

SOCR. Remember, then, I did not ask you to tell me one or two of all the many pious actions that there are; I want to know what is the idea of piety which makes all pious actions pious. You said, I think, that there is one idea which makes all pious actions pious, and another idea which makes all impious actions impious. Do you not remember?

EUTH. I do.

SOCR. Well, then, explain to me what is this idea, that I may have it to turn to, and to use as a standard whereby to judge your actions and those of other men, and be able to say that whatever action resembles it is pious, and whatever does not, is not pious.

EUTH. Yes, I will tell you that if you wish it, Socrates.

SOCR. Certainly I wish it.

EUTH. Well then, what is pleasing to the gods is pious, and what is not pleasing to them is impious.

SOCR. Fine, Euthyphro. Now you have given me the answer that I wanted. Whether what you say is true, I do not know yet. But, of course, you will go on to prove the truth of it.

EUTH. Certainly.

SOCR. Come then, let us examine our words. The things and the men that are pleasing to the gods are pious, and the things and the men that are displeasing to the gods are impious. But piety and impiety are not the same; they are as opposite as possible—was not that said?

EUTH. Certainly.

SOCR. And I think that that was very well said.

EUTH. Yes, Socrates, certainly.

SOCR. Have we not also said, Euthyphro, that there are quarrels and disagreements and hatreds among the gods?

EUTH. We have.

SOCR. But what kind of disagreement, my friend, causes hatred and anger? Let us look at the matter thus. If you and I were to disagree as to whether one number were more than another, would that provoke us to anger and make us enemies? Should we not settle such a dispute at once by counting?

EUTH. Of course.

SOCR. And if we were to disagree as to the relative size of two things, we should measure them and put an end to the disagreement at once, should we not?

EUTH. Yes.

SOCR. And should we not settle a question about the relative weight of two things by weighing them?

EUTH. Of course.

SOCR. Then what is the question which would provoke us to anger and make us enemies if we disagreed about it, and could not come to a settlement? Perhaps you have not an answer ready; but listen to me. Is it not the question of right and wrong, of the honorable and the dishonorable, of the good and the bad? Is it not questions about these matters which make you and me and everyone else quarrel, when we do quarrel, if we differ about them and can reach no satisfactory agreement?

EUTH. Yes, Socrates, it is disagreements about these matters.

SOCR. Well, Euthyphro, the gods will quarrel over these things if they quarrel at all, will they not?

EUTH. Necessarily.

SOCR. Then, my good Euthyphro, you say that some of the gods think one thing right, and others, another: and that what some of them hold to be honorable or good, others hold to be dishonorable or evil. For there would not have been quarrels among them if they had not disagreed on these points, would there?

EUTH. You are right.

SOCR. And each of them loves what he thinks honorable, and good, and right; and hates the opposite, does he not?

EUTH. Certainly.

SOCR. But you say that the same action is held by some of them to be right, and by others to be wrong; and that then they dispute about it, and so quarrel and fight among themselves. Is it not so?

EUTH. Yes.

SOCR. Then the same thing is hated by the gods and loved by them; and the same thing will be displeasing and pleasing to them.

EUTH. Apparently.

SOCR. Then, according to your account, the same thing will be pious and impious.

EUTH. So it seems.

SOCR. Then, my good friend, you have not answered my question. I did not ask you to tell me what action is both pious and impious, but it seems that whatever is pleasing to the gods is also displeasing to them. And so, Euthyphro, I should not be surprised if what you are doing now in punishing your father is a deed well pleasing to Zeus, but hateful to Cronos and Uranus, and acceptable to Hephaestus, but hateful to Hera; and if any of the other gods disagree about it, pleasing to some of them and displeasing to others.

EUTH. But on this point, Socrates, I think that there is no difference of opinion among the gods: they all hold that if one man kills another wrongfully, he must be punished.

SOCR. What, Euthyphro? Among mankind, have you never heard disputes whether a man ought to be punished for killing another man wrongfully, or for doing some other wrong deed?

EUTH. Indeed, they never cease from these disputes, especially in courts of justice. They do all manner of wrong things; and then there is nothing which they will not do and say to avoid punishment.

SOCR. Do they admit that they have done wrong, and at the same time deny that they ought to be punished, Euthyphro?

EUTH. No, indeed, that they do not.

SOCR. Then it is not everything that they will do and say. I take it, they do not dare to assert or argue that if they do do wrong, they must not be punished. What they say is that they have not done wrong, is it not?

EUTH. That is true.

SOCR. Then they do not dispute the proposition that the wrongdoer must be punished. They dispute about the question who is a wrongdoer, and when and what is a wrong deed, do they not?

EUTH. That is true.

SOCR. Well, is not exactly the same thing true of the gods if they quarrel about right and wrong, as you say they do? Do not some of them assert that the others are doing wrong, while the others deny it? No one, I suppose, my dear friend, whether god or man, dares to say that a person who has done wrong must not be punished.

EUTH. No, Socrates, that is true, in the main.

SOCR. I take it, Euthyphro, that the disputants, whether men or gods, if the gods do dispute, dispute about each separate act. When they quarrel about any act, some of them say that it was done rightly, and others that it was done wrongly. Is it not so?

EUTH. Yes.

SOCR. Come then, my dear Euthyphro, please enlighten me on this point. What proof have you that all the gods think that a laborer who has been imprisoned for murder by the master of the man whom he has murdered, and who dies from his imprisonment before the master has had time to learn from the seers what he should do, dies wrongfully? How do you know that it is right for a son to indict his father and to prosecute him for the murder of such a man? Come, see if you can make it clear to me that the gods necessarily agree in thinking that this action of yours is right; and if you satisfy me, I will never cease singing your praises for wisdom.

EUTH. I could make that clear enough to you, Socrates; but I am afraid that it would be a long business.

SOCR. I see you think that I am duller than the judges. To them, of course, you will make it clear that your father has done wrong, and that all the gods agree in hating such deeds.

EUTH. I will indeed, Socrates, if they will only listen to me.

SOCR. They will listen if only they think that you are a good speaker. But while you were speaking, it occurred to me to ask myself this question: suppose that Euthyphro were to prove to me as clearly as possible that all the gods think

such a death unjust, how has he brought me any nearer to understanding what
piety and impiety are? This particular act, perhaps, may be displeasing to the
gods, but then we have just seen that piety and impiety cannot be defined in
that way; for we have seen that what is displeasing to the gods is also pleasing
to them. So I will let you off on this point, Euthyphro; and all the gods shall
agree in thinking your father's deed wrong and in hating it, if you like. But
shall we correct our definition and say that whatever all the gods hate is impious and whatever they all love is pious: while whatever some of them love, and
others hate, is either both or neither? Do you wish us now to define piety and
impiety in this manner?

EUTH. Why not, Socrates?

SOCR. There is no reason why I should not, Euthyphro. It is for you to consider
whether that definition will help you to teach me what you promised.

EUTH. Well, I should say that piety is what all the gods love, and that impiety is
what they all hate.

SOCR. Are we to examine this definition, Euthyphro, and see if it is a good one?
Or are we content to accept the bare assertions of other men or of ourselves
without asking any questions? Or must we examine the assertions?

EUTH. We must examine them. But for my part I think that the definition is right
this time.

SOCR. We shall know that better in a little while, my good friend. Now consider
this question. Do the gods love piety because it is pious, or is it pious because
they love it?

EUTH. I do not understand you, Socrates.

SOCR. I will try to explain myself: we speak of a thing being carried and carrying,
and being led and leading, and being seen and seeing; and you understand that
all such expressions mean different things, and what the difference is.

EUTH. Yes, I think I understand.

SOCR. And we talk of a thing being loved, and, which is different, of a thing loving?

EUTH. Of course.

SOCR. Now tell me: is a thing which is being carried in a state of being carried because it is carried, or for some other reason?

EUTH. No, because it is carried.

SOCR. And a thing is in a state of being led because it is led, and of being seen because it is seen?

EUTH. Certainly.

SOCR. Then a thing is not seen because it is in a state of being seen: it is in a state of
being seen because it is seen; and a thing is not led because it is in a state of
being led: it is in a state of being led because it is led; and a thing is not carried
because it is in a state of being carried: it is in a state of being carried because it is
carried. Is my meaning clear now, Euthyphro? I mean this: if anything becomes
or is affected, it does not become because it is in a state of becoming: it is in a
state of becoming because it becomes; and it is not affected because it is in a
state of being affected: it is in a state of being affected because it is affected. Do
you not agree?

EUTH. I do.

SOCR. Is not that which is being loved in a state of becoming or of being affected in some way by something?

EUTH. Certainly.

SOCR. Then the same is true here as in the former cases. A thing is not loved by those who love it because it is in a state of being loved; it is in a state of being loved because they love it.

EUTH. Necessarily.

SOCR. Well, then, Euthyphro, what do we say about piety? Is it not loved by all the gods, according to your definition?

EUTH. Yes.

SOCR. Because it is pious, or for some other reason?

EUTH. No, because it is pious.

SOCR. Then it is loved by the gods because it is pious; it is not pious because it is loved by them?

EUTH. It seems so.

SOCR. But, then, what is pleasing to the gods is pleasing to them, and is in a state of being loved by them, because they love it?

EUTH. Of course.

SOCR. Then piety is not what is pleasing to the gods, and what is pleasing to the gods is not pious, as you say, Euthyphro. They are different things.

EUTH. And why, Socrates?

SOCR. Because we are agreed that the gods love piety because it is pious, and that it is not pious because they love it. Is not this so?

EUTH. Yes.

SOCR. And that what is pleasing to the gods because they love it, is pleasing to them by reason of this same love, and that they do not love it because it is pleasing to them?

EUTH. True.

SOCR. Then, my dear Euthyphro, piety and what is pleasing to the gods are different things. If the gods had loved piety because it is pious, they would also have loved what is pleasing to them because it is pleasing to them; but if what is pleasing to them had been pleasing to them because they loved it, then piety, too, would have been piety because they loved it. But now you see that they are opposite things, and wholly different from each other. For the one is of a sort to be loved because it is loved, while the other is loved because it is of a sort to be loved. My question, Euthyphro, was, What is piety? But it turns out that you have not explained to me the essence of piety; you have been content to mention an effect which belongs to it— namely, that all the gods love it. You have not yet told me what is its essence. Do not, if you please, keep from me what piety is; begin again and tell me that. Never mind whether the gods love it, or whether it has other effects: we shall not differ on that point. Do your best to make clear to me what is piety and what is impiety.

Study Questions

1. Is Euthyphro right to prosecute his father? Why or why not? How would you characterize his motives? Is he acting on principle, or for some other reason?
2. What is Socrates asking for when he asks Euthyphro to explain "the idea of piety which makes all actions pious?"
3. List the definitions of piety that Euthyphro gives. What are Socrates' objections to them? In particular, what problem does Socrates find with the definition that "what is pleasing to the gods is pious, and what is not pleasing to them is impious?" What does this lead him to conclude?
4. Is an action right because we approve of it, or do we approve of it because it is right?

Selected Bibliography

Allen, R. E. *Plato's "Euthyphro" and the Earlier Theory of Forms* (New York: Humanities Press, 1970). Commentary on *Euthyphro*.

Cornford, F. M. *Before and After Socrates* (New York/Cambridge: Cambridge University Press, 1993). Science and philosophy in classical Greek thought.

Gomez-Lobo, A. *The Foundations of Socratic Ethics* (Indianapolis: Hackett, 1994). Socrates' views on self-interest and morality.

Irwin, Terence. *Plato's Ethics* (Oxford: Oxford University Press, 1982), Chaps. 2–8. An account of Plato's ethical thought.

Plato. *Apology, Crito, Phaedo.* (Available in many editions.) An account of the events that followed the conversation between Socrates and Euthyphro.

Vlastos, Gregory, ed. *The Philosophy of Socrates* (Garden City, N.Y.: Doubleday, 1971), Essay 8. Socrates on the definition of piety.

2

PLATO

—

The *Republic* of Plato is one of the most influential books shaping the history of Western civilization. Although the reasons for its enormous and lasting influence are many, two, in particular, stand out. Beginning with a discussion of jus-

> *Goodness is not the same thing as being, but even beyond being, surpassing it in dignity and power.*

tice, the *Republic* proceeds to a consideration of most of the areas of deepest human concern—marriage and family life, education, economics, politics, ethics, religion, the nature of knowledge and reality, and human destiny. Furthermore, because of the profundity with which it treats all of these subjects, it has stimulated and challenged its readers throughout the ages. The *Republic*, although written by Plato, reflects in part the thought of his friend and teacher, Socrates. The question of how much of the *Republic* represents the ideas of Socrates and how much those of Plato is complicated by the fact that Plato makes Socrates the chief speaker. Although no absolute answer can be given to the question, scholars generally agree that the early part of the dialogue is Socratic in outlook and the latter part Platonic.

Plato (427–347 B.C.), the most famous of the disciples of Socrates, was planning a career in politics when the execution of his teacher convinced him that society could not be saved by political means but rather by the kind of wisdom displayed by Socrates. So he abandoned his political career to devote his life to philosophy. He did not, however, retreat into an ivory tower. Because he believed that philosophers have a duty to society, to help their fellow citizens in their search for wisdom, he established a school in Athens, the Academy. Plato's Academy, which remained open for more than nine hundred years, was forcibly closed by the Christian Emperor Justinian in A.D. 529 because it was a pagan institution. It ranks as one of the great centers of learning in Western history.

The selection that follows is made up of four passages from the *Republic*. To separate the issues and give continuity to the argument, they are given in a different order from the original. The selection begins with the "Ring of Gyges," which raises the issue of whether we have any natural desire to act justly. This leads to the more basic question: What is justice? Thrasymachus, who is Socrates' chief opponent in the dialogue, states his views about justice and then is questioned by Socrates. Thrasymachus takes a skeptical attitude toward justice and argues that the unjust person is better off than the just person. Socrates then argues to the contrary that the just person is better off and happier than the unjust person. The selection ends with Plato's conception of the Form of the Good as the supreme reality, concluding with his famous Allegory of the Cave.

———

Republic

(359c–360e)

Next [said Glaucon] men practise [justice] against the grain, for lack of power to do wrong. How true that is, we shall best see if we imagine two men, one just, the other unjust, given full license to do whatever they like, and then follow them to observe where each will be led by his desires. We shall catch the just man taking the same road as the unjust; he will be moved by self-interest, the end which it is natural to every creature to pursue as good, until forcibly turned aside by law and custom to respect the principle of equality.

Now, the easiest way to give them that complete liberty of action would be to imagine them possessed of the talisman found by Gyges, the ancestor of the famous Lydian. The story tells how he was a shepherd in the King's service. One day there was a great storm, and the ground where his flock was feeding was rent by an earthquake. Astonished at the sight, he went down into the chasm and saw, among other wonders of which the story tells, a brazen horse, hollow, with windows in its sides. Peering in, he saw a dead body, which seemed to be of more than human size. It was naked save for a gold ring, which he took from the finger and made his way out. When the shepherds met, as they did every month, to send an account to the King of the state of his flocks, Gyges came wearing the ring. As he was sitting with the others, he happened to turn the bezel of the ring inside his hand. At once he became invisible, and his companions, to his surprise, began to speak of him as if he had left them. Then, as he was fingering the ring, he turned the bezel outwards and became visible again. With that, he set about testing the ring to see if it really had this power, and always with the same result: according as he turned the bezel inside or out he vanished and reappeared. After this discovery he contrived to be one of the messengers sent to the court. There he seduced the Queen, and with her help murdered the King and seized the throne.

Now suppose there were two such magic rings, and one were given to the just man, the other to the unjust. No one, it is commonly believed, would have such iron strength of mind as to stand fast in doing right or keep his hands off other men's goods, when he could go to the marketplace and fearlessly help himself to anything he wanted, enter houses and sleep with any woman he chose, set prison-

From *The Republic of Plato*, translated by F. M. Cornford. Reprinted by permission of the Oxford University Press.

ers free and kill men at his pleasure, and in a word go about among men with the powers of a god. He would behave no better than the other; both would take the same course. Surely this would be strong proof that men do right only under compulsion; no individual thinks of it as good for him personally, since he does wrong whenever he finds he has the power. Every man believes that wrongdoing pays him personally much better, and, according to this theory, that is the truth. Granted full licence to do as he liked, people would think him a miserable fool if they found him refusing to wrong his neighbours or to touch their belongings, though in public they would keep up a pretence of praising his conduct, for fear of being wronged themselves. So much for that.

———

(336b–344d, 348c–349b, 350d–354)

All this time Thrasymachus had been trying more than once to break in upon our conversation; but his neighbours had restrained him, wishing to hear the argument to the end. In the pause after my last words he could keep quiet no longer; but gathering himself up like a wild beast he sprang at us as if he would tear us in pieces. Polemarchus and I were frightened out of our wits, when he burst out to the whole company:

What is the matter with you two, Socrates? Why do you go on in this imbecile way, politely deferring to each other's nonsense? If you really want to know what justice means, stop asking questions and scoring off the answers you get. You know very well it is easier to ask questions than to answer them. Answer yourself, and tell us what you think justice means. I won't have you telling us it is the same as what is obligatory or useful or advantageous or profitable or expedient; I want a clear and precise statement; I won't put up with that sort of verbiage.

I was amazed by this onslaught and looked at him in terror. If I had not seen this wolf before he saw me, I really believe I should have been struck dumb;* but fortunately I had looked at him earlier, when he was beginning to get exasperated with our argument; so I was able to reply, though rather tremulously:

Don't be hard on us, Thrasymachus. If Polemarchus and I have gone astray in our search, you may be quite sure the mistake was not intentional. If we had been looking for a piece of gold, we should never have deliberately allowed politeness to spoil our chance of finding it; and now when we are looking for justice, a thing much more precious than gold, you cannot imagine we should defer to each other in that foolish way and not do our best to bring it to light. You must believe we are in earnest, my friend; but I am afraid the task is beyond our powers, and we might expect a man of your ability to pity us instead of being so severe.

Thrasymachus replied with a burst of sardonic laughter.

Good Lord, he said; Socrates at his old trick of shamming ignorance! I knew it; I told the others you would refuse to commit yourself and do anything sooner than answer a question.

*A popular superstition, that if a wolf sees you first, you become dumb.—Tr.

Yes, Thrasymachus, I replied; because you are clever enough to know that if you asked someone what are the factors of the number twelve, and at the same time warned him: "Look here, you are not to tell me that 12 is twice 6, or 3 times 4, or 6 times 2, or 4 times 3; I won't put up with any such nonsense"—you must surely see that no one would answer a question put like that. He would say: "What do you mean, Thrasymachus? Am I forbidden to give any of these answers, even if one happens to be right? Do you want me to give a wrong one?" What would you say to that?

Humph! said he. As if that were a fair analogy!

I don't see why it is not, said I; but in any case, do you suppose our barring a certain answer would prevent the man from giving it, if he thought it was the truth?

Do you mean that you are going to give me one of those answers I barred?

I should not be surprised, if it seemed to me true, on reflection.

And what if I give you another definition of justice, better than any of those? What penalty are you prepared to pay?*

The penalty deserved by ignorance, which must surely be to receive instruction from the wise. So I would suggest that as a suitable punishment.

I like your notion of a penalty! he said; but you must pay the costs as well.

I will, when I have any money.

That will be all right, said Glaucon; we will all subscribe for Socrates. So let us have your definition, Thrasymachus.

Oh yes, he said; so that Socrates may play the old game of questioning and refuting someone else, instead of giving an answer himself!

But really, I protested, what can you expect from a man who does not know the answer or profess to know it, and, besides that, has been forbidden by no mean authority to put forward any notions he may have? Surely the definition should naturally come from you, who say you do know the answer and can tell it us. Please do not disappoint us. I should take it as a kindness, and I hope you will not be chary of giving Glaucon and the rest of us the advantage of your instruction.

Glaucon and the others added their entreaties to mine. Thrasymachus was evidently longing to win credit, for he was sure he had an admirable answer ready, though he made a show of insisting that I should be the one to reply. In the end he gave way and exclaimed:

So this is what Socrates' wisdom comes to! He refuses to teach, and goes about learning from others without offering so much as thanks in return.

I do learn from others, Thrasymachus; that is quite true; but you are wrong to call me ungrateful. I give in return all I can—praise; for I have no money. And how ready I am to applaud any idea that seems to me sound, you will see in a moment, when you have stated your own; for I am sure that will be sound.

Listen then, Thrasymachus began. What I say is that "just" or "right" means nothing but what is to the interest of the stronger party. Well, where is your applause? You don't mean to give it me.

---

*In certain lawsuits the defendant, if found guilty, was allowed to propose a penalty alternative to that demanded by the prosecution. The judge then decided which should be inflicted. The "costs" here means the fee that the sophist, unlike Socrates, expected from his pupils.—Tr.

I will, as soon as I understand, I said. I don't see yet what you mean by right being the interest of the stronger party. For instance, Polydamas, the athlete, is stronger than we are, and it is to his interest to eat beef for the sake of his muscles; but surely you don't mean that the same diet would be good for weaker men and therefore be right for us?

You are trying to be funny, Socrates. It's a low trick to take my words in the sense you think will be most damaging.

No, no, I protested; but you must explain.

Don't you know, then, that a state may be ruled by a despot, or a democracy, or an aristocracy?

Of course.

And that the ruling element is always the strongest?

Yes.

Well then, in every case the laws are made by the ruling party in its own interest; a democracy makes democratic laws, a despot autocratic ones, and so on. By making these laws they define as "right" for their subjects whatever is for their own interest, and they call anyone who breaks them a "wrongdoer" and punish him accordingly. That is what I mean; in all states alike "right" has the same meaning, namely what is for the interest of the party established in power, and that is the strongest. So the sound conclusion is that what is "right" is the same everywhere; the interest of the stronger party.

Now I see what you mean, said I; whether it is true or not, I must try to make out. When you define right in terms of interest, you are yourself giving one of those answers you forbade to me; though, to be sure, you add "to the stronger party."

An insignificant addition, perhaps!

Its importance is not clear yet; what is clear is that we must find out whether your definition is true. I agree myself that right is in a sense a matter of interest; but when you add "to the stronger party," I don't know about that. I must consider.

Go ahead, then.

I will. Tell me this. No doubt you also think it is right to obey the men in power?

I do.

Are they infallible in every type of state, or can they sometimes make a mistake?

Of course they can make a mistake.

In framing laws, then, they may do their work well or badly?

No doubt.

Well, that is to say, when the laws they make are to their own interest; badly, when they are not?

Yes.

But the subjects are to obey any law they lay down, and they will then be doing right?

Of course.

If so, by your account, it will be right to do what is not to the interest of the stronger party, as well as what is so.

What's that you are saying?

Just what you said, I believe; but let us look again. Haven't you admitted that the rulers, when they enjoin certain acts on their subjects, sometimes mistake their own best interests, and at the same time that it is right for the subjects to obey, whatever they may enjoin?

Yes, I suppose so.

Well, that amounts to admitting that it is right to do what is not to the interest of the rulers or the stronger party. They may unwittingly enjoin what is to their own disadvantage; and you say it is right for the others to do as they are told. In that case, their duty must be the opposite of what you said, because the weaker will have been ordered to do what is against the interest of the stronger. You with your intelligence must see how that follows.

Yes, Socrates, said Polemarchus, that is undeniable.

No doubt, Cleitophon broke in, if you are to be a witness on Socrates' side.

No witness is needed, replied Polemarchus; Thrasymachus himself admits that rulers sometimes ordain acts that are to their own disadvantage, and that it is the subjects' duty to do them.

That is because Thrasymachus said it was right to do what you are told by the men in power.

Yes, but he also said that what is to the interest of the stronger party is right; and, after making both these assertions, he admitted that the stronger sometimes command the weaker subjects to act against their interests. From all which it follows that what is in the stronger's interest is no more right than what is not.

No, said Cleitophon; he meant whatever the stronger *believes* to be in his own interest. That is what the subject must do, and what Thrasymachus meant to define as right.

That was not what he said, rejoined Polemarchus.

No matter, Polemarchus, said I; if Thrasymachus says so now, let us take him in that sense. Now, Thrasymachus, tell me, was that what you intended to say—that right means what the stronger thinks is to his interest, whether it really is so or not?

Most certainly not, he replied. Do you suppose I should speak of a man as "stronger" or "superior" at the very moment when he is making a mistake?

I did think you said as much when you admitted that rulers are not always infallible.

That is because you are a quibbler, Socrates. Would you say a man deserves to be called a physician at the moment when he makes a mistake in treating his patient and just in respect of that mistake; or a mathematician, when he does a sum wrong and just insofar as he gets a wrong result? Of course we do commonly speak of a physician or a mathematician or a scholar having made a mistake; but really none of these, I should say, is ever mistaken, insofar as he is worthy of the name we give him. So strictly speaking—and you are all for being precise—no one who practices a craft makes mistakes. A man is mistaken when his knowledge fails him; and at that moment he is no craftsman. And what is true of craftsmanship or any sort of skill is true of the ruler: he is never mistaken so long as he is acting as a ruler; though anyone might speak of a ruler making a mistake, just as he might of a physician. You must understand that I was talking in that loose way when I answered your question just now; but the precise statement is this. The ruler, insofar as he is acting as a ruler, makes no mistakes and consequently enjoins what is best for himself; and that is what the subject is to do. So, as I said at first, "right" means doing what is to the interest of the stronger.

Very well, Thrasymachus, said I. So you think I am quibbling?

I am sure you are.

You believe my questions were maliciously designed to damage your position?

I know it. But you will gain nothing by that. You cannot outwit me by cunning, and you are not the man to crush me in the open.

Bless your soul, I answered, I should not think of trying. But, to prevent any more misunderstanding, when you speak of that ruler or stronger party whose interest the weaker ought to serve, please make it clear whether you are using the words in the ordinary way or in that strict sense you have just defined.

I mean a ruler in the strictest possible sense. Now quibble away and be as malicious as you can. I want no mercy. But you are no match for me.

Do you think me mad enough to beard a lion or try to outwit a Thrasymachus?

You did try just now, he retorted, but it wasn't a success.

Enough of this, said I. Now tell me about the physician in that strict sense you spoke of: is it his business to earn money or to treat his patients? Remember, I mean your physician who is worthy of the name.

To treat his patients.

And what of the ship's captain in the true sense? Is he a mere seaman or the commander of the crew?

The commander.

Yes, we shall not speak of him as a seaman just because he is on board a ship. That is not the point. He is called captain because of his skill and authority over the crew.

Quite true.

And each of these people has some special interest?*

No doubt.

And the craft in question exists for the very purpose of discovering that interest and providing for it?

Yes.

Can it equally be said of any craft that it has an interest, other than its own greatest possible perfection?

What do you mean by that?

Here is an illustration. If you ask me whether it is sufficient for the human body just to be itself, with no need of help from without, I should say, Certainly not; it has weaknesses and defects, and its condition is not all that it might be.

---

*All the persons mentioned have some interest. The craftsman *qua* craftsman has an interest in doing his work as well as possible, which is the same thing as serving the interest of the subjects on whom his craft is exercised; and the subjects have their interest, which the craftsman is there to promote.—Tr.

That is precisely why the art of medicine was invented; it was designed to help the body and provide for its interests. Would not that be true?

It would.

But now take the art of medicine itself. Has that any defects or weaknesses? Does any art stand in need of some further perfection, as the eye would be imperfect without the power of vision or the ear without hearing, so that in their case an art is required that will study their interests and provide for their carrying out those functions? Has the art itself any corresponding need of some further art to remedy its defects and look after its interests; and will that further art require yet another, and so on forever? Or will every art look after its own interests? Or, finally, is it not true that no art needs to have its weaknesses remedied or its interests studied either by another art or by itself, because no art has in itself any weakness or fault, and the only interest it is required to serve is that of its subject matter? In itself, an art is sound and flawless, so long as it is entirely true to its own nature as an art in the strictest sense—and it is the strict sense that I want you to keep in view. Is not that true?

So it appears.

Then, said I, the art of medicine does not study its own interest, but the needs of the body, just as a groom shows his skill by caring for horses, not for the art of grooming. And so every art seeks, not its own advantage—for it has no deficiencies—but the interest of the subject on which it is exercised.

It appears so.

But surely, Thrasymachus, every art has authority and superior power over its subject.

To this he agreed, though very reluctantly.

So far as arts are concerned, then, no art ever studies or enjoins the interest of the superior or stronger party, but always that of the weaker over which it has authority.

Thrasymachus assented to this at last, though he tried to put up a fight. I then went on:

So the physician, as such, studies only the patient's interest, not his own. For as we agreed, the business of the physician, in the strict sense, is not to make money for himself, but to exercise his power over the patient's body; and the ship's captain, again, considered strictly as no mere sailor, but in command of the crew, will study and enjoin the interest of his subordinates, not his own.

He agreed reluctantly.

And so with government of any kind: no ruler, insofar as he is acting as ruler, will study or enjoin what is for his own interest. All that he says and does will be said and done with a view to what is good and proper for the subject for whom he practises his art.

At this point, when everyone could see that Thrasymachus' definition of justice had been turned inside out, instead of making any reply, he said:

Socrates, have you a nurse?

Why do you ask such a question as that? I said. Wouldn't it be better to answer mine?

Because she lets you go about sniffling like a child whose nose wants wiping. She hasn't even taught you to know a shepherd when you see one, or his sheep either.

What makes you say that?

Why, you imagine that a herdsman studies the interests of his flocks or cattle, tending and fattening them up with some other end in view than his master's profit or his own; and so you don't see that, in politics, the genuine ruler regards his subjects exactly like sheep, and thinks of nothing else, night and day, but the good he can get out of them for himself. You are so far out in your notions of right and wrong, justice and injustice, as not to know that "right" actually means what is good for someone else, and to be "just" means serving the interest of the stronger who rules, at the cost of the subject who obeys; whereas injustice is just the reverse, asserting its authority over those innocents who are called just, so that they minister solely to their master's advantage and happiness, and not in the least degree to their own. Innocent as you are yourself, Socrates, you must see that a just man always has the worst of it. Take a private business: when a partnership is wound up, you will never find that the more honest of two partners comes off with the larger share; and in their relations to the state, when there are taxes to be paid, the honest man will pay more than the other on the same amount of property; or if there is money to be distributed, the dishonest will get it all. When either of them hold some public office, even if the just man loses in no other way, his private affairs at any rate will suffer from neglect, while his principles will not allow him to help himself from the public funds; not to mention the offense he will give to his friends and relations by refusing to sacrifice those principles to do them a good turn. Injustice has all the opposite advantages. I am speaking of the type I described just now, the man who can get the better of other people on a large scale: you must fix your eye on him, if you want to judge how much it is to one's own interest not to be just. You can see that best in the most consummate form of injustice, which rewards wrongdoing with supreme welfare and happiness and reduces its victims, if they won't retaliate in kind, to misery. That form is despotism, which uses force or fraud to plunder the goods of others, public or private, sacred or profane, and to do it in a wholesale way. If you are caught committing any one of these crimes on a small scale, you are punished and disgraced; they call it sacrilege, kidnapping, burglary, theft and brigandage. But if, besides taking their property, you turn all your countrymen into slaves, you will hear no more of those ugly names; your countrymen themselves will call you the happiest of men and bless your name, and so will everyone who hears of such a complete triumph of injustice; for when people denounce injustice, it is because they are afraid of suffering wrong, not of doing it. So true is it, Socrates, that injustice, on a grand enough scale, is superior to justice in strength and freedom and autocratic power; and "right," as I said at first, means simply what serves the interest of the stronger party; "wrong" means what is for the interest and profit of oneself. . . .

Come then, Thrasymachus, said I, let us start afresh with our questions. You say that injustice pays better than justice, when both are carried to the furthest point?

I do, he replied; and I have told you why.

And how would you describe them? I suppose you would call one of them an excellence and the other a defect?

Of course.

Justice an excellence, and injustice a defect?

Now is that likely, when I am telling you that injustice pays, and justice does not?

Then what do you say?

The opposite.

That justice is a defect?

No, rather the mark of a good-natured simpleton.

Injustice, then, implies being ill-natured?

No, I should call it good policy.

Do you think the unjust are positively superior in character and intelligence, Thrasymachus?

Yes, if they are the sort that can carry injustice to perfection and make themselves masters of whole cities and nations. Perhaps you think I was talking of pickpockets. There is profit even in that trade, if you can escape detection; but it doesn't come to much as compared with the gains I was describing.

I understand you now on that point, I replied. What astonished me was that you should class injustice with superior character and intelligence and justice with the reverse.

Well, I do, he rejoined.

That is a much more stubborn position, my friend; and it is not so easy to see how to assail it. If you would admit that injustice, however well it pays, is nevertheless, as some people think, a defect and a discreditable thing, then we could argue on generally accepted principles. But now that you have gone so far as to rank it with superior character and intelligence, obviously you will say it is an admirable thing as well as a source of strength, and has all the other qualities we have attributed to justice.

You read my thoughts like a book, he replied.

However, I went on, it is no good shirking; I must go through with the argument, so long as I can be sure you are really speaking your mind. I do believe you are not playing with us now, Thrasymachus, but stating the truth as you conceive it.

Why not refute the doctrine? he said. What does it matter to you whether I believe it or not?

It does not matter, I replied. . . .

[In an omitted argument Socrates forces Thrasymachus to admit that the just man, rather than the unjust, is superior in character and intelligence.—Ed.]

Thrasymachus' assent was dragged out of him with a reluctance of which my account gives no idea. He was sweating at every pore, for the weather was hot; and I saw then what I had never seen before—Thrasymachus blushing. However, now that we had agreed that justice implies superior character and intelligence, injustice a deficiency in both respects, I went on:

Good; let us take that as settled. But we were also saying that injustice was a source of strength. Do you remember, Thrasymachus?

I do remember; only your last argument does not satisfy me, and I could say a good deal about that. But if I did, you would tell me I was haranguing you like a public meeting. So either let me speak my mind at length, or else, if you want to ask questions, ask them, and I will nod or shake my head, and say, "Hm?" as we do to encourage an old woman telling us a story.

No, please, said I; don't give your assent against your real opinion.

Anything to please you, he rejoined, since you won't let me have my say. What more do you want?

Nothing, I replied. If that is what you mean to do, I will go on with my questions.

Go on, then.

Well, to continue where we left off. I will repeat my question: What is the nature and quality of justice as compared with injustice? It was suggested, I believe, that injustice is the stronger and more effective of the two; but now we have seen that justice implies superior character and intelligence, it will not be hard to show that it will also be superior in power to injustice, which implies ignorance and stupidity; that must be obvious to anyone. However, I would rather look deeper into this matter than take it as settled offhand. Would you agree that a state may be unjust and may try to enslave other states or to hold a number of others in subjection unjustly?

Of course it may, he said; above all if it is the best sort of state, which carries injustice to perfection.

I understand, said I; that was your view. But I am wondering whether a state can do without justice when it is asserting its superior power over another in that way.

Not if you are right, that justice implies intelligence; but if I am right, injustice will be needed.

I am delighted with your answer, Thrasymachus; this is much better than just nodding and shaking your head.

It is all to oblige you.

Thank you. Please add to your kindness by telling me whether any set of men—a state or an army or a band of robbers or thieves—who were acting together for some unjust purpose would be likely to succeed, if they were always trying to injure one another. Wouldn't they do better, if they did not?

Yes, they would.

Because, of course, such injuries must set them quarreling and hating each other. Only fair treatment can make men friendly and of one mind.

Be it so, he said; I don't want to differ from you.

Thank you once more, I replied. But don't you agree that, if injustice has this effect of implanting hatred wherever it exists, it must make any set of people, whether freemen or slaves, split into factions, at feud with one another and incapable of any joint action?

Yes.

And so with any two individuals: injustice will set them at variance and make them enemies to each other as well as to everyone who is just.

It will.

And will it not keep its character and have the same effect, if it exists in a single person?

Let us suppose so.

The effect being, apparently, wherever it occurs—in a state or a family or an army or anywhere else—to make united action impossible because of factions and quarrels, and moreover to set whatever it resides in at enmity with itself as well as with any opponent and with all who are just.

Yes, certainly.

Then I suppose it will produce the same natural results in an individual. He will have a divided mind and be incapable of action, for lack of singleness of purpose; and he will be at enmity with all who are just as well as with himself?

Yes.

And "all who are just" surely includes the gods?

Let us suppose so.

The unjust man, then, will be a god-forsaken creature; the goodwill of heaven will be for the just.

Enjoy your triumph, said Thrasymachus. You need not fear my contradicting you. I have no wish to give offense to the company.

You will make my enjoyment complete, I replied, if you will answer my further questions in the same way. We have made out so far that just men are superior in character and intelligence and more effective in action. Indeed, without justice men cannot act together at all; it is not strictly true to speak of such people as ever having effected any strong action in common. Had they been thoroughly unjust, they could not have kept their hands off one another; they must have had some justice in them, enough to keep them from injuring one another at the same time with their victims. This it was that enabled them to achieve what they did achieve: their injustice only partially incapacitated them for their career of wrongdoing; if perfect, it would have disabled them for any action whatsoever. I can see that all this is true, as against your original position. But there is a further question which we postponed: Is the life of justice the better and happier life? What we have said already leaves no doubt in my mind; but we ought to consider more carefully, for this is no light matter: it is the question, what is the right way to live?

Go on, then.

I will, said I. Some things have a function; a horse, for instance, is useful for certain kinds of work. Would you agree to define a thing's function in general as the work for which that thing is the only instrument or the best one?

I don't understand.

Take an example. We can see only with the eyes, hear only with the ears; and seeing and hearing might be called functions of those organs.

Yes.

Or again, you might cut vine-shoots with a carving-knife or a chisel or many other tools, but with none so well as with a pruning knife made for the purpose; and we may call that its function.

True.

Now, I expect, you see better what I meant by suggesting that a thing's function is the work that it alone can do, or can do better than anything else.

Yes, I will accept that definition.

Good, said I; and to take the same examples, the eye and the ear, which we said have each its particular function: have they not also a specific excellence or virtue? Is not that always the case with things that have some appointed work to do?

Yes.

Now consider: is the eye likely to do its work well, if you take away its peculiar virtue and substitute the corresponding defect?

Of course not, if you mean substituting blindness for the power of sight.

I mean whatever its virtue may be; I have not come to that yet. I am only asking whether it is true of things with a function—eyes or ears or anything else—that there is always some specific virtue which enables them to work well; and if they are deprived of that virtue, they work badly.

I think that is true.

Then the next point is this. Has the soul a function that can be performed by nothing else? Take for example such actions as deliberating or taking charge and exercising control: is not the soul the only thing of which you can say that these are its proper and peculiar work?

That is so.

And again, living—is not that above all the function of the soul?

No doubt.

And we also speak of the soul as having a certain specific excellence or virtue?

Yes.

Then, Thrasymachus, if the soul is robbed of its peculiar virtue, it cannot possibly do its work well. It must exercise its power of controlling and taking charge well or ill according as it is itself in a good or a bad state.

That follows.

And did we not agree that the virtue of the soul is justice, and injustice its defect?

We did.

So it follows that a just soul, or in other words a just man, will live well; the unjust will not.

Apparently, according to your argument.

But living well involves well-being and happiness.

Naturally.

Then only the just man is happy; injustice will involve unhappiness.

Be it so.

But you cannot say it pays better to be unhappy.

Of course not.

Injustice then, my dear Thrasymachus, can never pay better than justice. . . .

————

[Later in the dialogue, Socrates continues his discussion of whether the just person is happier than the unjust person.—Ed.]

(580d–587, 588b–591d)

Very well, said I; that may stand as one of our proofs. But I want to consider a second one, which can, I think, be based on our division of the soul into three parts, corresponding to the three orders in the state. Each part seems to me to have its own form of pleasure and its peculiar desire; and any one of the three may govern the soul.

How do you mean?

There was the part with which a man gains knowledge and understanding, and another whereby he shows spirit. The third was so multifarious that we could find no single appropriate name; we called it after its chief and most powerful characteristic "appetite," because of the intensity of all the appetites connected with eating and drinking and sex and so on. We also called it money-loving, because money is the principal means of satisfying desires of this kind. Gain is the source of its pleasures and the object of its affection; so "money-loving" or "gain-loving" might be the best single expression to sum up the nature of this part of the soul for the purpose of our discussion.

I agree.

The spirited element, again, we think of as wholly bent upon winning power and victory and a good name. So we might call it honour-loving or ambitious.

Very suitable.

Whereas the part whereby we gain knowledge and understanding is least of all concerned with wealth and reputation. Obviously its sole endeavour is to know the truth, and we may speak of it as loving knowledge and philosophic.

Quite so.

And the human soul is sometimes governed by this principle, sometimes by one of the other two, as the case may be. Hence we recognize three main classes of men: the philosophic, the ambitious, and the lovers of gain. So there will also be three corresponding forms of pleasure.

Certainly.

Now, if you choose to ask men of these three types, which of their lives is the pleasantest, each in turn will praise his own above the rest. The man of business will say that, as compared with profit making, the pleasures of winning a high reputation or of learning are worthless, except insofar as they bring in money. The ambitious man will despise the pleasure derived from money as vulgar, and the pleasure of learning, if it does not bring fame, as moonshine. The philosopher, again, will think that the satisfaction of knowing the truth and always gaining fresh understanding is beyond all comparison with those other pleasures, which he will call "necessary" in the fullest sense; for he would have no use for them, if they were not unavoidable. In this dispute about the pleasures of each class and as to which of the three lives as a whole is not merely better and nobler but actually pleasanter or less painful, how is one to know whose judgment is the truest?

I am not prepared to say.

Well, think of it in this way. What is required for a sound judgment? Can it rest on any better foundation than experience, or insight, or reasoning?

Surely not.

Take experience, then. Which of our three men has the fullest acquaintance with all the pleasures we have mentioned? Has the lover of gain such an understanding of the truth as to know by experience the pleasure of knowledge better than the philosopher knows the pleasure of gain?

No, all the advantage lies with the philosopher, who cannot help experiencing both the other kinds of pleasure from childhood up; whereas the lover of gain is under no necessity to taste the sweetness of understanding the truth of things; rather he would not find it easy to gain that experience, however hard he should try.

In experience of both sorts of pleasure, then, the philosopher has the advantage over the lover of gain. How does he compare with the ambitious man? Is he less well acquainted with the pleasures of honour than the other is with the pleasures of wisdom?

No, honour comes to them all, if they accomplish their several purposes; the rich man is esteemed by many people, and so are the brave man and the wise. So the pleasure of being honoured is familiar to them all; but only the philosopher can know how sweet it is to contemplate the truth.

Then, so far as experience goes, he is the best judge of the three.

Yes, by far.

And the only one in whom experience is seconded by insight.

Yes.

Further, we agreed that the decision must be reached by means of reasoning; and this is peculiarly the tool of the philosopher, not of the money-lover or of the ambitious man.

No doubt.

Now, if wealth and profit were the most satisfactory criteria, the judgments of value passed by the lover of gain would be nearest to the truth; and if honour, courage, and success were the test, the best judge would be the man who lives for honour and victory; but since the tests are experience, insight, and reasoning—

The truest values must be those approved by the philosopher, who uses reason for the pursuit of wisdom.

Of the three kinds of pleasure, then, the sweetest will belong to that part of the soul whereby we gain understanding and knowledge, and the man in whom that part predominates will have the pleasantest life.

It must be so; in praising his own life the wise man speaks with authority.

What life or form of pleasure will this judge rank second?

Obviously, that of the warlike and ambitious temperament. It comes nearer than the businessman's to his own.

And the pleasure of gain will come last, it seems.

Surely.

So now the just man has scored a second victory over the unjust. There remains the third round, for which the wrestlers at the Great Games invoke Olympian Zeus, the Preserver;* and a fall in this bout should be decisive. I seem to have heard some wise man say that only the pleasures of intelligence are entirely true and pure; all the others are illusory.

That should settle the matter. But what does it mean?

I shall discover the meaning, if you will help me by answering my questions. We speak of pain as the contrary of pleasure. Is there not also a neutral

---

*At banquets the third libation was offered to Zeus the Preserver. This passage seems to imply that competitors at the Olympic Games had a corresponding custom. Plato is fond of quoting the phrase "the third (libation) to the Preserver," where his arguments culminate at the third stage.—Tr.

state between the two, in which the mind feels neither pleasure nor pain, but is as it were at rest from both?

Yes.

Well, you must have heard people say, when they are ill, that nothing is pleasanter than to be well, though they never knew it until they were ill; and people in great pain will tell you that relief from pain is the greatest pleasure in the world. There are many such cases in which you find the sufferer saying that the height of pleasure is not positive enjoyment, but the peace which comes with the absence of pain.

Yes; I suppose at such moments the state of rest becomes pleasurable and all that can be desired.

In the same way, then, when enjoyment comes to an end, the cessation of pleasure will be painful.

I suppose so.

If so, that state of rest which, we said, lies between pleasure and pain, will be sometimes one, sometimes the other. But if it is neither of the two, how can it become both?

I do not think it can.

And besides, both pleasure and pain are processes of change* which take place in the mind, are they not? whereas the neutral condition appeared to be a state of rest between the two. So can it be right to regard the absence of pain as pleasant or the absence of enjoyment as painful?

No, it cannot.

It follows, then, that the state of rest is not really either pleasant or painful, but only appears so in these cases by contrast. There is no soundness in these appearances; by the standard of true pleasure they are a sort of imposture.

That seems to be the conclusion.

You might be tempted, in these instances, to suppose that pleasure is the same thing as relief from pain, and pain the same as the cessation of pleasure; but, as an instance to the contrary, consider pleasures which do not follow pain. There are plenty of them; the best example is the pleasures of smell. These occur suddenly with extraordinary intensity; they are not preceded by any pain and they leave no pain behind when they cease.

Quite true.

We are not to be persuaded, then, that relief from pain is the same thing as pure pleasure, or cessation of pleasure the same as pure pain.

No.

On the other hand, the class of pleasures which do involve some sort of relief from pain may be said to include the great majority and the most intense of all the pleasures, so called, which reach the mind by way of the body; and the same description applies to the pleasures or pains of anticipation which precede them.

Yes.

---

*Plato is thinking specially of pleasures, like that of satisfying hunger, which accompany the physical process of restoring the normal (neutral) state, which has been depleted with accompanying pain.—Tr.

Here is an analogy, to illustrate their nature. You think of the world as divided into an upper region and a lower, with a centre between them. Now if a person were transported from below to the centre, he would be sure to think he was moving "upwards"; and when he was stationed at the centre and looking in the direction he had come from, he would imagine he was in the upper region, if he had never seen the part which is really above the centre. And supposing he were transported back again, he would think he was travelling "downwards," and this time he would be right. His mistake would be due to his ignorance of the real distinctions between the upper and lower regions and the centre.

Clearly.

You will not be surprised, then, if people whose ignorance of truth and reality gives them many unsound ideas, are similarly confused about pleasure and pain and the intermediate state. When the movement is towards a painful condition, they are right in believing that the pain is real; but when they are passing from a state of pain to the neutral point, they are firmly convinced that they are approaching the pleasure of complete satisfaction. In their ignorance of true pleasure, they are deceived by the contrast between pain and the absence of pain, just as one who had never seen white might be deceived by the contrast between black and grey.

Certainly; I should be much more surprised if it were not so.

Then look at it in this way. As hunger and thirst are states of bodily inanition, which can be replenished by food, so ignorance and unwisdom in the soul are an emptiness to be filled by gaining understanding. Of the two sorts of nourishment, will not the more real yield the truer satisfaction?

Clearly.

Which kind of nourishment, then, has the higher claim to pure reality—foodstuffs like bread and meat and drink, or such things as true belief, knowledge, reason, and in a word, all the excellences of the mind? You may decide by asking yourself whether something which is closely connected with the unchanging and immortal world of truth and itself shares that nature together with the thing in which it exists, has more or less reality than something which, like the thing which contains it, belongs to a world of mortality and perpetual change.

No doubt it is much more real.

And a higher or lower degree of reality goes with a greater or less measure of knowledge and so of truth?

Necessarily.

And is there not, to speak generally, less of truth and reality in the things which serve the needs of the body than in those which feed the soul?

Much less.

And, again, less in the body itself than in the soul?

Certainly.

And in proportion as the sustenance and the thing sustained by it are more real, the satisfaction itself is a more real satisfaction.

Of course.

Accordingly, if the appropriate satisfaction of natural needs constitutes pleasure, there will be more real enjoyment of true pleasure in such a case; whereas in the opposite case the satisfaction is not so genuine or secure and the pleasure is less true and trustworthy.

Inevitably.

To conclude, then: those who have no experience of wisdom and virtue and spend their whole time in feasting and self-indulgence are all their lives, as it were, fluctuating downwards from the central point and back to it again, but never rise beyond it into the true upper region, to which they have not lifted their eyes. Never really satisfied with real nourishment, the pleasure they taste is uncertain and impure. Bent over their tables, they feed like cattle with stooping heads and eyes fixed upon the ground; so they grow fat and breed, and in their greedy struggle kick and butt one another to death with horns and hoofs of steel, because they can never satisfy with unreal nourishment that part of themselves which is itself unreal and incapable of lasting satisfaction.

Your description of the way most people live is quite in the oracular style, Socrates.

Does it not follow that the pleasures of such a life are illusory phantoms of real pleasure, in which pleasure and pain are so combined that each takes its colour and apparent intensity by contrast with the other? Hence the frenzied desire they implant in the breasts of fools, who fight for them as Stesichorus says the combatants at Troy fought, in their blindness, for a phantom Helen.*

Yes, that is bound to be so.

Take, again, the satisfaction of the spirited element in our nature. Must not that be no less illusory, when a man seeks, at all costs, to gratify his ambition by envy, his love of victory by violence, and his ill temper by outbursts of passion, without sense or reason?

It must.

What then? May we boldly assert that all the desires both of the gain-loving and of the ambitious part of our nature will win the truest pleasures of which they are capable, if they accept the guidance of knowledge and reason and pursue only those pleasures which wisdom approves? Such pleasures will be true, because truth is their guide, and will also be proper to their nature, if it is a fact that a thing always finds in what is best for it something akin to its real self.

Well, that is certainly a fact.

To conclude, then, each part of the soul will not only do its own work and be just when the whole soul, with no inward conflict, follows the guidance of the wisdom-loving part, but it also will enjoy the pleasures that are proper to it and the best and truest of which it is capable; whereas if either of the other two parts gains the upper hand, besides failing to find its own proper pleasure, it will force the others to pursue a false pleasure uncongenial to their nature.

Yes. . . .

Good, said I. And now that the argument has brought us to this point, let us recall something that was said at the outset, namely, if I remember aright, that

*At *Phaedrus* 243 Plato refers to the legend that the poet Stesichorus, divinely punished with blindness for defaming Helen, regained his sight only by writing a recantation declaring that she never went to Troy, but was all the while in Egypt. Euripides' *Helen* is based on this story.—Tr.

wrongdoing is profitable when a man is completely unjust but has a reputation for justice.

Yes, that position was stated.

Well, we are now agreed about the real meaning and consequences of doing wrong as well as of doing right, and the time has come to point out to anyone who maintains that position what his statement implies. We may do so by likening the soul to one of those many fabulous monsters said to have existed long ago, such as Chimaera or Scylla or Cerberus, which combined the forms of several creatures in one. Imagine, to begin with, the figure of a multifarious and many-headed beast, girt round with heads of animals, tame and wild, which it can grow out of itself and transform at will.

That would tax the skill of a sculptor; but luckily the stuff of imagination is easier to mould than wax.

Now add two other forms, a lion and a man. The many-headed beast is to be the largest by far, and the lion next to it in size. Then join them in such a way that the three somehow grow together into one. Lastly, mould the outside into the likeness of one of them, the man, so that, to eyes which cannot see inside the outward sheath, the whole may look like a single creature, a human being.

Very well. What then?

We can now reply to anyone who says that for this human creature wrongdoing pays and there is nothing to be gained by doing right. This simply means, we shall tell him, that it pays to feed up and strengthen the composite beast and all that belong to the lion, and to starve the man till he is so enfeebled that the other two can drag him whither they will, and he cannot bring them to live together in peace, but must leave them to bite and struggle and devour one another. On the other hand, to declare that justice pays is to assert that all our words and actions should tend towards giving the man within us complete mastery over the whole human creature, and letting him take the many-headed beast under his care and tame its wildness, like the gardener who trains his cherished plants while he checks the growth of weeds. He should enlist the lion as his ally, and, caring for all alike, should foster their growth by first reconciling them to one another and to himself.

Yes, such are the implications when justice or injustice is commended.

From every point of view, then, whether of pleasure or reputation or advantage, one who praises justice speaks the truth; he who disparages it does not know what it is that he idly condemns.

I agree; he has no conception.

But his error is not wilful; so let us reason with him gently. We will ask him on what grounds conduct has come to be approved or disapproved by law and custom. Is it not according as conduct tends to subdue the brutish parts of our nature to the human—perhaps I should rather say to the divine in us—or to enslave our humanity to the savagery of the beast? Will he agree?

Yes, if he has any regard for my opinion.

On that showing, then, can it profit a man to take money unjustly, if he is thereby enslaving the best part of his nature to the vilest? No amount of money could make it worth his while to sell a son or daughter as slaves into the hands of cruel and evil men; and when it is a matter of ruthlessly subjugating all that is most godlike in himself to whatsoever is most ungodly and despicable, is not the wretch taking a bribe far more disastrous than the necklace Eriphyle took as the price of her husband's life?*

Far more, said Glaucon,** if I may answer on his behalf.

You will agree, too, with the reasons why certain faults have always been condemned: profligacy, because it gives too much license to the multiform monster; self-will and ill temper, when the lion and serpent part of us is strengthened till its sinews are overstrung: luxury and effeminacy, because they relax those sinews till the heart grows faint; flattery and meanness, in that the heart's high spirit is subordinated to the turbulent beast, and for the sake of money to gratify the creature's insatiable greed the lion is browbeaten and schooled from youth up to become an ape. Why, again, is mechanical toil discredited as debasing? Is it not simply when the highest thing in a man's nature is naturally so weak that it cannot control the animal parts but can only learn how to pamper them?

I suppose so.

Then, if we say that people of this sort ought to be subject to the highest type of man, we intend that the subject should be governed, not as Thrasymachus thought, to his own detriment, but on the same principle as his superior, who is himself governed by the divine element within him. It is better for everyone, we believe, to be subject to a power of godlike wisdom residing within himself, or, failing that, imposed from without, in order that all of us, being under one guidance, may be so far as possible equal and united. This, moreover, is plainly the intention of the law in lending its support to every member of the community, and also of the government of children; for we allow them to go free only when we have established in each one of them as it were a constitutional ruler, whom we have trained to take over the guardianship from the same principle in ourselves.

True.

On what ground, then, can we say that it is profitable for a man to be unjust or self-indulgent or to do any disgraceful act which will make him a worse man, though he may gain money and power? Or how can it profit the wrongdoer to escape detection and punishment? He will only grow still worse; whereas if he is found out, chastisement will tame the brute in him and lay it to rest, while the gentler part is set free; and thus the entire soul, restored to its native soundness, will gain, in the temperance and righteousness which wisdom brings, a condition more precious than the strength and beauty which health brings to the body, in proportion as the soul itself surpasses the body in worth. To this end the man of understanding will bend all his powers through life, prizing in the first place those studies only which will fashion these qualities in his soul; and, so far from abandoning the care of his bodily condition to the irrational pleasures of the brute and

---

*Eriphyle was bribed with a necklace by Polynices to persuade her husband, the seer Amphiaraos, to become one of the seven champions who made war on Thebes and of whom all but one lost their lives.—Tr.

**Thrasymachus has long since dropped out of the discussion.—Ed.

setting his face in that direction, he will not even make health his chief object. Health, strength, and beauty he will value only insofar as they bring soundness of mind, and you will find him keeping his bodily frame in tune always for the sake of the resulting concord in the soul.

———

(506b–509b, 509d–518d)

But, Socrates, what is your own account of the Good? Is it knowledge, or pleasure, or something else?

There you are! I exclaimed; I could see all along that you were not going to be content with what other people think.

Well, Socrates, it does not seem fair that you should be ready to repeat other people's opinions but not to state your own, when you have given so much thought to this subject.

And do you think it fair of anyone to speak as if he knew what he does not know?

No, not as if he knew, but he might give his opinion for what it is worth.

Why, have you never noticed that opinion without knowledge is always a shabby sort of thing? At the best it is blind. One who holds a true belief without intelligence is just like a blind man who happens to take the right road. Isn't he?

No doubt.

Well, then, do you want me to produce one of these poor blind cripples, when others could discourse to you with illuminating eloquence?

No, really, Socrates, said Glaucon, you must not give up within sight of the goal. We should be quite content with an account of the Good like the one you gave us of justice and temperance and the other virtues.

So should I be, my dear Glaucon, much more than content! But I am afraid it is beyond my powers; with the best will in the world I should only disgrace myself and be laughed at. No, for the moment let us leave the question of the real meaning of good; to arrive at what I at any rate believe it to be would call for an effort too ambitious for an inquiry like ours. However, I will tell you, though only if you wish it, what I picture to myself as the offspring of the Good and the thing most nearly resembling it.

Well, tell us about the offspring, and you shall remain in our debt for an account of the parent.

I only wish it were within my power to offer, and within yours to receive, a settlement of the whole account. But you must be content now with the interest only; and you must see to it that, in describing this offspring of the Good, I do not inadvertently cheat you with false coin.

We will keep a good eye on you. Go on.

First we must come to an understanding. Let me remind you of the distinction we drew earlier and have often drawn on other occasions, between the multiplicity of things that we call good or beautiful or whatever it may be and, on the other hand, Goodness itself or Beauty itself and so on. Corresponding to each of these sets of many things, we postulate a single Form or real essence, as we call it.

Yes, that is so.

Further, the many things, we say, can be seen, but are not objects of rational thought; whereas the Forms are objects of thought, but invisible.

Yes, certainly.

And we see things with our eyesight, just as we hear sounds with our ears and, to speak generally, perceive any sensible thing with our sense-faculties.

Of course.

Have you noticed, then, that the artificer who designed the senses has been exceptionally lavish of his materials in making the eyes able to see and their objects visible?

That never occurred to me.

Well, look at it in this way. Hearing and sound do not stand in need of any third thing, without which the ear will not hear nor sound be heard; and I think the same is true of most, not to say all, of the other senses. Can you think of one that does require anything of the sort?

No, I cannot.

But there is this need in the case of sight and its objects. You may have the power of vision in your eyes and try to use it, and colour may be there in the objects; but sight will see nothing and the colours will remain invisible in the absence of a third thing peculiarly constituted to serve this very purpose.

By which you mean—?

Naturally I mean what you call light; and if light is a thing of value, the sense of sight and the power of being visible are linked together by a very precious bond, such as unites no other sense with its object.

No one could say that light is not a precious thing.

And of all the divinities in the skies* is there one whose light, above all the rest, is responsible for making our eyes see perfectly and making objects perfectly visible?

There can be no two opinions; of course you mean the Sun.

And how is sight related to this deity? Neither sight nor the eye which contains it is the Sun, but of all the sense-organs it is the most sun-like; and further, the power it possesses is dispensed by the Sun, like a stream flooding the eye.** And again, the Sun is not vision, but it is the cause of vision and also is seen by the vision it causes.

Yes.

It was the Sun, then, that I meant when I spoke of that offspring which the Good has created in the visible world, to stand there in the same relation to vision

---

*Plato held that the heavenly bodies are immortal living creatures, that is, gods.—Tr.

**Plato's theory of vision involves three kinds of fire or light: (1) daylight, a body of pure fire diffused in the air by the Sun; (2) the visual current or "vision," a pure fire similar to daylight, contained in the eyeball and capable of issuing out in a stream directed towards the object seen; (3) the colour of the external object, "a flame streaming off from every body, having particles proportioned to those of the visual current, so as to yield sensation" when the two streams meet and coalesce (*Timaeus,* 45 B, 67 C).—Tr.

and visible things as that which the Good itself bears in the intelligible world to intelligence and to intelligible objects.

How is that? You must explain further.

You know what happens when the colours of things are no longer irradiated by the daylight, but only by the fainter luminaries of the night: when you look at them, the eyes are dim and seem almost blind, as if there were no unclouded vision in them. But when you look at things on which the Sun is shining, the same eyes see distinctly and it becomes evident that they do contain the power of vision.

Certainly.

Apply this comparison, then, to the soul. When its gaze is fixed upon an object irradiated by truth and reality, the soul gains understanding and knowledge and is manifestly in possession of intelligence. But when it looks towards that twilight world of things that come into existence and pass away, its sight is dim and it has only opinions and beliefs which shift to and fro, and now it seems like a thing that has no intelligence.

That is true.

This, then, which gives to the objects of knowledge their truth and to him who knows them his power of knowing, is the Form or essential nature of Goodness. It is the cause of knowledge and truth; and so, while you may think of it as an object of knowledge, you will do well to regard it as something beyond truth and knowledge and, precious as these both are, of still higher worth. And, just as in our analogy light and vision were to be thought of as like the Sun, but not identical with it, so here both knowledge and truth are to be regarded as like the Good, but to identify either with the Good is wrong. The Good must hold a yet higher place of honour.

You are giving it a position of extraordinary splendour, if it is the source of knowledge and truth and itself surpasses them in worth. You surely cannot mean that it is pleasure.

Heaven forbid, I exclaimed. But I want to follow up our analogy still further. You will agree that the Sun not only makes the things we see visible, but also brings them into existence and gives them growth and nourishment; yet it is not the same thing as existence. And so with the objects of knowledge: these derive from the Good not only their power of being known, but their very being and reality; and Goodness is not the same thing as being, but even beyond being, surpassing it in dignity and power. . . .

Conceive, then, that there are these two powers I speak of, the Good reigning over the domain of all that is intelligible, the Sun over the visible world—or the heaven as I might call it; only you would think I was showing off my skill in etymology.* At any rate you have these two orders of things clearly before your mind: the visible and the intelligible?

I have.

*Some connected the word for heaven (οὐρανός) with ὁρᾶν "to see" (Cratylus, 396 B). It is sometimes used for the whole of the visible universe.—Tr.

Now take a line divided into two unequal parts, one to represent the visible order, the other the intelligible; and divide each part again in the same proportion, symbolizing degrees of comparative clearness or obscurity. Then (A) one of the two sections in the visible world will stand for images. By images I mean first shadows, and then reflections in water or in closegrained, polished surfaces, and everything of that kind, if you understand.

Yes, I understand.

Let the second section (B) stand for the actual things of which the first are likenesses, the living creatures about us and all the works of nature or of human hands.

So be it.

Will you also take the proportion in which the visible world has been divided as corresponding to degrees of reality and truth, so that the likeness shall stand to the original in the same ratio as the sphere of appearances and belief to the sphere of knowledge?

Certainly.

Now consider how we are to divide the part which stands for the intelligible world. There are two sections. In the first (C) the mind uses as images those actual things which themselves had images in the visible world; and it is compelled to pursue its inquiry by starting from assumptions and travelling, not up to a principle, but down to a conclusion. In the second (D) the mind moves in the other direction, from an assumption up towards a principle which is not hypothetical; and it makes no use of the images employed in the other section, but only of Forms, and conducts its inquiry solely by their means.

I don't quite understand what you mean.

Then we will try again; what I have just said will help you to understand. (C) You know, of course, how students of subjects like geometry and arithmetic begin by postulating odd and even numbers, or the various figures and the three kinds of angle, and other such data in each subject. These data they take as known; and, having adopted them as assumptions, they do not feel called upon to give any account of them to themselves or to anyone else, but treat them as self-evident. Then, starting from these assumptions, they go on until they arrive, by a series of consistent steps, at all the conclusions they set out to investigate.

Yes, I know that.

You also know how they make use of visible figures and discourse about them, though what they really have in mind is the originals of which these figures are images: they are not reasoning, for instance, about this particular square and diagonal which they have drawn, but about *the* Square and *the* Diagonal; and so in all cases. The diagrams they draw and the models they make are actual things, which may have their shadows or images in water; but now they serve in their turn as images, while the student is seeking to behold those realities which only thought can apprehend.*

True.

---

*Conversely, the fact that the mathematician can use visible objects as illustrations indicates that the realities and truths of mathematics are embodied, though imperfectly, in the world of visible and tangible things; whereas the counterparts of the moral Forms can only be beheld by thought.—Tr.

This, then, is the class of things that I spoke of as intelligible, but with two qualifications: first, that the mind, in studying them, is compelled to employ assumptions, and, because it cannot rise above these, does not travel upwards to a first principle; and second, that it uses as images those actual things which have images of their own in the section below them and which, in comparison with those shadows and reflections, are reputed to be more palpable and valued accordingly.

I understand: you mean the subject-matter of geometry and of the kindred arts.

(D) Then by the second section of the intelligible world you may understand me to mean all that unaided reasoning apprehends by the power of dialectic, when it treats its assumptions, not as first principles, but as *hypotheses* in the literal sense, things "laid down" like a flight of steps up which it may mount all the way to something that is not hypothetical, the first principle of all; and having grasped this, may turn back and, holding on to the consequences which depend upon it, descend at last to a conclusion, never making use of any sensible object, but only of Forms, moving through Forms from one to another, and ending with Forms.

I understand, he said, though not perfectly; for the procedure you describe sounds like an enormous undertaking. But I see that you mean to distinguish the field of intelligible reality studied by dialectic as having a greater certainty and truth than the subject-matter of the "arts," as they are called, which treat their assumptions as first principles. The students of these arts are, it is true, compelled to exercise thought in contemplating objects which the senses cannot perceive; but because they start from assumptions without going back to a first principle, you do not regard them as gaining true understanding about those objects, although the objects themselves, when connected with a first principle, are intelligible. And I think you would call the state of mind of the students of geometry and other such arts, not intelligence, but thinking, as being something between intelligence and mere acceptance of appearances.

You have understood me quite well enough, I replied. And now you may take, as corresponding to the four sections, these four states of mind: *intelligence* for the highest, *thinking* for the second, *belief* for the third, and for the last *imagining*. These you may arrange as the terms in a proportion, assigning to each a degree of clearness and certainty corresponding to the measure in which their objects possess truth and reality.

I understand and agree with you. I will arrange them as you say.

Next, said I, here is a parable to illustrate the degrees in which our nature may be enlightened or unenlightened. Imagine the condition of men living in a sort of cavernous chamber underground, with an entrance open to the light and a long passage all down the cave. Here they have been from childhood, chained by the leg and also by the neck, so that they cannot move and can see only what is in front of them, because the chains will not let them turn their heads. At some distance higher up is the light of a fire burning behind them; and between the prisoners and the fire is a track with a parapet built along it, like the screen at a puppet show, which hides the performers while they show their puppets over the top.

I see, said he.

Now behind this parapet imagine persons carrying along various artificial objects, including figures of men and animals in wood or stone or other materials, which project above the parapet. Naturally, some of these persons will be talking, others silent.*

It is a strange picture, he said, and a strange sort of prisoners.

Like ourselves, I replied; for in the first place, prisoners so confined would have seen nothing of themselves or of one another, except the shadows thrown by the fire-light on the wall of the Cave facing them, would they?

Not if all their lives they had been prevented from moving their heads.

And they would have seen as little of the objects carried past.

Of course.

Now, if they could talk to one another, would they not suppose that their words referred only to those passing shadows which they saw?

Necessarily.

And suppose their prison had an echo from the wall facing them? When one of the people crossing behind them spoke, they could only suppose that the sound came from the shadow passing before their eyes.

No doubt.

In every way, then, such prisoners would recognize as reality nothing but the shadows of those artificial objects.

Inevitably.

Now consider what would happen if their release from the chains and the healing of their unwisdom should come about in this way. Suppose one of them set free and forced suddenly to stand up, turn his head, and walk with eyes lifted to the light; all these movements would be painful, and he would be too dazzled to make out the objects whose shadows he had been used to seeing. What do you think he would say, if someone told him that what he had formerly seen was mean- ingless illusion, but now, being somewhat nearer to reality and turned towards more real objects, he was getting a truer view? Suppose further that he were shown the various objects being carried by and were made to say, in reply to questions, what each of them was. Would he not be perplexed and believe the objects now shown him to be not so real as what he formerly saw?

Yes, not nearly so real.

And if he were forced to look at the fire-light itself, would not his eyes ache, so that he would try to escape and turn back to the things which he could see dis- tinctly, convinced that they really were clearer than these other objects now being shown to him?

Yes.

And suppose someone were to drag him away forcibly up the steep and rugged ascent and not let him go until he had hauled him out into the sunlight, would he not suffer pain and vexation at such treatment, and, when he had come

---

*A modern Plato would compare his Cave to an underground cinema, where the audience watch the play of shadows thrown by the film passing before a light at their backs. The film itself is only an image of "real" things and events in the world outside the cinema. For the film Plato has to substitute the clumsier apparatus of a procession of artificial objects carried on their heads by persons who are merely part of the machinery, providing for the movement of the objects and the sounds whose echo the prisoners hear. The parapet prevents these persons' shadows from being cast on the wall of the Cave.—Tr.

out into the light, find his eyes so full of its radiance that he could not see a single one of the things that he was now told were real?

Certainly he would not see them all at once.

He would need, then, to grow accustomed before he could see things in that upper world. At first it would be easiest to make out shadows, and then the images of men and things reflected in water, and later on the things themselves. After that, it would be easier to watch the heavenly bodies and the sky itself by night, looking at the light of the moon and stars rather than the Sun and the Sun's light in the daytime.

Yes, surely.

Last of all, he would be able to look at the Sun and contemplate its nature, not as it appears when reflected in water or any alien medium, but as it is in itself in its own domain.

No doubt.

And now he would begin to draw the conclusion that it is the Sun that produces the seasons and the course of the year and controls everything in the visible world, and moreover is in a way the cause of all that he and his companions used to see.

Clearly he would come at last to that conclusion.

Then if he called to mind his fellow prisoners and what passed for wisdom in his former dwelling-place, he would surely think himself happy in the change and be sorry for them. They may have had a practice of honouring and commending one another, with prizes for the man who had the keenest eye for the passing shadows and the best memory for the order in which they followed or accompanied one another, so that he could make a good guess as to which was going to come next. Would our released prisoner be likely to covet those prizes or to envy the men exalted to honour and power in the Cave? Would he not feel like Homer's Achilles, that he would far sooner "be on earth as a hired servant in the house of a landless man" or endure anything rather than go back to his old beliefs and live in the old way?

Yes, he would prefer any fate to such a life.

Now imagine what would happen if he went down again to take his former seat in the Cave. Coming suddenly out of the sunlight, his eyes would be filled with darkness. He might be required once more to deliver his opinion on those shadows, in competition with the prisoners who had never been released, while his eyesight was still dim and unsteady; and it might take some time to become used to the darkness. They would laugh at him and say that he had gone up only to come back with his sight ruined; it was worth no one's while even to attempt the ascent. If they could lay hands on the man who was trying to set them free and lead them up, they would kill him.*

Yes, they would.

Every feature in this parable, my dear Glaucon, is meant to fit our earlier analysis. The prison dwelling corresponds to the region revealed to us through the sense of sight, and the fire-light within it to the power of the Sun. The ascent to see the things in the upper world you may take as standing for the upward journey

*An allusion to the fate of Socrates.—Tr.

of the soul into the region of the intelligible; then you will be in possession of what I surmise, since that is what you wish to be told. Heaven knows whether it is true; but this, at any rate, is how it appears to me. In the world of knowledge, the last thing to be perceived and only with great difficulty is the essential Form of Goodness. Once it is perceived, the conclusion must follow that, for all things, this is the cause of whatever is right and good; in the visible world it gives birth to light and to the lord of light, while it is itself sovereign in the intelligible world and the parent of intelligence and truth. Without having had a vision of this Form no one can act with wisdom, either in his own life or in matters of state.

So far as I can understand, I share your belief.

Then you may also agree that it is no wonder if those who have reached this height are reluctant to manage the affairs of men. Their souls long to spend all their time in that upper world—naturally enough, if here once more our parable holds true. Nor, again, is it at all strange that one who comes from the contemplation of divine things to the miseries of human life should appear awkward and ridiculous when, with eyes still dazed and not yet accustomed to the darkness, he is compelled, in a law court or elsewhere, to dispute about the shadows of justice or the images that cast those shadows, and to wrangle over the notions of what is right in the minds of men who have never beheld Justice itself.

It is not at all strange.

No, a sensible man will remember that the eyes may be confused in two ways—by a change from light to darkness or from darkness to light; and he will recognize that the same thing happens to the soul. When he sees it troubled and unable to discern anything clearly, instead of laughing thoughtlessly, he will ask whether, coming from a brighter existence, its unaccustomed vision is obscured by the darkness, in which case he will think its condition enviable and its life a happy one; or whether, emerging from the depths of ignorance, it is dazzled by excess of light. If so, he will rather feel sorry for it; or, if he were inclined to laugh, that would be less ridiculous than to laugh at the soul which has come down from the light.

That is a fair statement.

If this is true, then, we must conclude that education is not what it is said to be by some, who profess to put knowledge into a soul which does not possess it, as if they could put sight into blind eyes. On the contrary, our own account signifies that the soul of every man does possess the power of learning the truth and the organ to see it with; and that, just as one might have to turn the whole body round in order that the eye should see light instead of darkness, so the entire soul must be turned away from this changing world, until its eye can bear to contemplate reality and that supreme splendour which we have called the Good.

Study Questions

1. What is Glaucon's story of the ring of Gyges supposed to show? Do you agree or disagree with the point he is trying to make?

2. In your own words, describe Thrasymachus' views about justice and injustice. What in your view are both the weak points and the strong points in his views? How would a society that follows Thrasymachus' principles function?
3. What are Socrates's main reasons for thinking that the just person is better off than the unjust person? Should his views persuade Thrasymachus? Explain. Do you find his views persuasive? Why or why not?
4. What is the Allegory of the Cave supposed to represent. Is it a good description of the "human condition"? Analyze and assess the final statement about the nature of education.

Selected Bibliography

Annas, Julia. *An Introduction to Plato's Republic* (Oxford: Clarendon Press, 1981). Introductory book on the *Republic*.

———. *Platonic Ethics, Old and New* (Ithaca, N.Y.: Cornell University Press, 1999). Discussion of central themes in Plato's ethics.

Cornford, F. M. *Before and After Socrates* (New York/Cambridge: Cambridge University Press, 1993). Science and philosophy in classical Greek thought.

Irwin, Terence. *Plato's Ethics* (Oxford: Oxford University Press, 1982). The ethical views of Socrates and Plato.

Kraut, Richard, ed., *Plato's Republic: Critical Essays* (Lanham, Md.: Rowman & Littlefield Publishers, 1997). Anthology of recent essays.

Nettleship, R. L. *Lectures on the Republic of Plato* (New York: Macmillan, 1929). A respected study.

White, N. P. A. *A Companion to Plato's Republic* (Indianapolis: Hackett, 1979). A commentary on the *Republic*.

3

ARISTOTLE

—

Aristotle was born in 384 B.C., in the town of Stagira in Macedonia, where his father was physician in the royal court of Philip of Macedon. At the age of eighteen he went to Athens to enroll in Plato's Academy, where he remained until the master's death twenty years later. He then left Athens and, after spending several years in Asia Minor doing

> *The good of a human being is an activity of the soul in conformity with excellence or virtue, and if there are several virtues, in conformity with the best and most complete.*

scientific research, during which time he married the niece of a local king, he returned to Macedonia to become tutor to the heir to the throne (who later became Alexander the Great). Both strong personalities, Aristotle and Alexander soon clashed. After a short stay in Macedonia, Aristotle returned to Athens to found a school called the Lyceum, where he remained for twelve years, lecturing and writing. Meanwhile Alexander had ascended to the throne of Macedonia, had conquered most of the civilized world, and at the height of his power in 323 B.C. died suddenly, while returning from a triumphal expedition into India. The Athenians, seeing in Alexander's death an opportunity to throw off the Macedonian yoke, immediately rose in revolt. Aristotle, because of his earlier association with the conqueror, was naturally suspect. He was charged with impiety, but, instead of remaining to stand trial as Socrates had done, he fled the city with the remark that he did not wish to give the Athenians "a second chance of sinning against philosophy." He died in exile the following year.

Like Plato, Aristotle is one of the great figures in the history of thought. A perennial point of dispute among intellectual historians is the question of the extent of Plato's influence on his thinking. Some scholars have contended that the philosophies of Plato and Aristotle are diametrically opposed to each other. Adding to this view an appreciation of the historical influence of both, they have concluded that every subsequent philosopher in Western history is either a Platonist or an Aristotelian. Such a contrast seems overdrawn. Although differences between Plato and Aristotle undoubtedly exist, the two are much closer to each other, both in their own views and in their historical influence, than either is to the third great Greek thinker, the materialist Democritus.

Aristotle wrote two major treatises on ethics, the *Eudemian Ethics* and the *Nicomachean Ethics*. The *Nicomachean Ethics* is believed to be a revision of the earlier *Eudemian Ethics* that was written about 330 B.C. It thus represents Aristotle's mature thought. It takes its name from his son, who was probably responsible for editing it. The informal writing style is due to the fact that it consists of a detailed set of lecture notes. The *Nicomachean Ethics* develops an account of the human good, that which is the proper final end or overall objective of human action and of a good human life. Aristotle claims that the human good is *eudaimonia*—here translated as "happiness," but sometimes translated as "human flourishing." The claim that the good is happiness might seem a truism. But what is of greatest interest in Aristotle's ethics is his conception of happiness, which he defines as "an activity of the soul in conformity with excellence or virtue." For Aristotle, the human good is a life of activity in which the range of human excellences or virtues are fully realized under the guidance of reason. Because happiness consists in large part in the realization of various virtues, the details of Aristotle's conception of happiness come out in his discussion of the human virtues, to which much of the work is devoted.

The *Nicomachean Ethics* strongly influenced later Greek thought, in particular Stoicism and Epicureanism, as well as medieval thought. It is widely regarded as one of the great ethical works in the Western philosophical tradition, and continues to influence contemporary moral philosophy.

———

The Nicomachean Ethics

Book I

1. *The good as the aim of action*

Every art or applied science and every systematic investigation, and similarly every action and choice, seem to aim at some good; the good, therefore, has been well defined as that at which all things aim. But it is clear that there is a difference in the ends at which they aim: in some cases the activity is the end, in others the end is some product beyond the activity. In cases where the end lies beyond the action the product is naturally superior to the activity.

Since there are many activities, arts, and sciences, the number of ends is correspondingly large: of medicine the end is health, of shipbuilding a vessel, of strategy, victory, and of household management, wealth. In many instances several such pursuits are grouped together under a single capacity: the art of bridle-making, for example, and everything else pertaining to the equipment of a horse are grouped

From Aristotle, *The Nicomachean Ethics*, tr. Martin Ostwald. © Reprinted by permission of Pearson Education, Inc., Upper Saddle River, NJ.

together under horsemanship; horsemanship in turn, along with every other military action, is grouped together under strategy; and other pursuits are grouped together under other capacities. In all these cases the ends of the master sciences are preferable to the ends of the subordinate sciences, since the latter are pursued for the sake of the former. This is true whether the ends of the actions lie in the activities themselves or, as is the case in the disciplines just mentioned, in something beyond the activities.

2. *Politics as the master science of the good*

Now, if there exists an end in the realm of action which we desire for its own sake, an end which determines all our other desires; if, in other words, we do not make all our choices for the sake of something else—for in this way the process will go on infinitely so that our desire would be futile and pointless—then obviously this end will be the good, that is, the highest good. Will not the knowledge of this good, consequently, be very important to our lives? Would it not better equip us, like archers who have a target to aim at, to hit the proper mark? If so, we must try to comprehend in outline at least what this good is and to which branch of knowledge or to which capacity it belongs.

This good, one should think, belongs to the most sovereign and most comprehensive master science, and politics* clearly fits this description. For it determines which sciences ought to exist in states, what kind of sciences each group of citizens must learn, and what degree of proficiency each must attain. We observe further that the most honored capacities, such as strategy, household management, and oratory, are contained in politics. Since this science uses the rest of the sciences, and since, moreover, it legislates what people are to do and what they are not to do, its end seems to embrace the ends of the other sciences. Thus it follows that the end of politics is the good for man. For even if the good is the same for the individual and the state, the good of the state clearly is the greater and more perfect thing to attain and to safeguard. The attainment of the good for one man alone is, to be sure, a source of satisfaction; yet to secure it for a nation and for states is nobler and more divine. In short, these are the aims of our investigation, which is in a sense an investigation of social and political matters.

3. *The limitations of ethics and politics*

Our discussion will be adequate if it achieves clarity within the limits of the subject matter. For precision cannot be expected in the treatment of all subjects alike, any more than it can be expected in all manufactured articles. Problems of what is noble and just, which politics examines, present so much variety and irregularity that some people believe that they exist only by convention and not by nature. The

---

*Politikē is the science of the city state, the polis, and its members, not merely in our narrow "political" sense of the word but also in the sense that a civilized human existence is, according to Plato and Aristotle, only possible in the polis. Thus *politikē* involves not only the science of the state, "politics," but of our concept of "society" as well.—Tr.

problem of the good, too, presents a similar kind of irregularity, because in many cases good things bring harmful results. There are instances of men ruined by wealth, and others by courage. Therefore, in a discussion of such subjects, which has to start from a basis of this kind, we must be satisfied to indicate the truth with a rough and general sketch: when the subject and the basis of a discussion consist of matters that hold good only as a general rule, but not always, the conclusions reached must be of the same order. The various points that are made must be received in the same spirit. For a well schooled man is one who searches for that degree of precision in each kind of study which the nature of the subject at hand admits: it is obviously just as foolish to accept arguments of probability from a mathematician as to demand strict demonstrations from an orator.

Each man can judge competently the things he knows, and of these he is a good judge. Accordingly, a good judge in each particular field is one who has been trained in it, and a good judge in general, a man who has received an all-round schooling. For that reason, a young man is not equipped to be a student of politics; for he has no experience in the actions which life demands of him, and these actions form the basis and subject matter of the discussion. Moreover, since he follows his emotions, his study will be pointless and unprofitable, for the end of this kind of study is not knowledge but action. Whether he is young in years or immature in character makes no difference; for his deficiency is not a matter of time but of living and of pursuing all his interests under the influence of his emotions. Knowledge brings no benefit to this kind of person, just as it brings none to the morally weak. But those who regulate their desires and actions by a rational principle will greatly benefit from a knowledge of this subject. So much by way of a preface about the student, the limitations which have to be accepted, and the objective before us.

4. *Happiness is the good, but many views are held about it*

To resume the discussion: since all knowledge and every choice is directed toward some good, let us discuss what is in our view the aim of politics, i.e., the highest good attainable by action. As far as its name is concerned, most people would probably agree: for both the common run of people and cultivated men call it happiness, and understand by "being happy" the same as "living well" and "doing well." But when it comes to defining what happiness is, they disagree, and the account given by the common run differs from that of the philosophers. The former say it is some clear and obvious good, such as pleasure, wealth, or honor; some say it is one thing and others another, and often the very same person identifies it with different things at different times: when he is sick he thinks it is health, and when he is poor he says it is wealth; and when people are conscious of their own ignorance, they admire those who talk above their heads in accents of greatness. Some thinkers used to believe that there exists over and above these many goods another good, good in itself and by itself, which also is the cause of good in all these things. An examination of all the different opinions would perhaps be a little pointless, and it is sufficient to concentrate on those which are most in evidence or which seem to make some sort of sense.

Nor must we overlook the fact that arguments which proceed from funda-mental principles are different from arguments that lead up to them. Plato, too, rightly recognized this as a problem and used to ask whether the discussion was proceeding from or leading up to fundamental principles, just as in a race course there is a difference between running from the judges to the far end of the track and running back again. Now, we must start with the known. But this term has two connotations: "what is known to us" and "what is known" pure and simple. Therefore, we should start perhaps from what is known to us. For that reason, to be a competent student of what is right and just, and of politics generally, one must first have received a proper upbringing in moral conduct. The acceptance of a fact as a fact is the starting point, and if this is sufficiently clear, there will be no further need to ask why it is so. A man with this kind of background has or can easily acquire the foundations from which he must start. But if he neither has nor can acquire them, let him lend an ear to Hesiod's words:

> That man is all-best who himself works out
>   every problem. . . .
> That man, too, is admirable who follows one
>   who speaks well.
> He who cannot see the truth for himself, nor,
>   hearing it from others,
> store it away in his mind, that man
>   is utterly useless.*

5. *Various views on the highest good*

But to return to the point from which we digressed. It is not unreasonable that men should derive their concept of the good and of happiness from the lives which they lead. The common run of people and the most vulgar identify it with pleasure, and for that reason are satisfied with a life of enjoyment. For the most notable kinds of life are three: the life just mentioned, the political life, and the contemplative life.

The common run of people, as we saw, betray their utter slavishness in their preference for a life suitable to cattle; but their views seem plausible because many people in high places share the feelings of Sardanapallus.** Cultivated and active men, on the other hand, believe the good to be honor, for honor, one might say, is the end of the political life. But this is clearly too superficial an answer: for honor seems to depend on those who confer it rather than on him who receives it, whereas our guess is that the good is a man's own possession which cannot easily be taken away from him. Furthermore, men seem to pursue honor to assure them-selves of their own worth; at any rate, they seek to be honored by sensible men and

---

*Hesiod, *Works and Days* 293, 295–297, as translated by Richmond Lattimore in *Hesiod: The Works and Days; Theogony; The Shield of Herakles* (Ann Arbor: University of Michigan Press, 1959).—Tr.

**Sardanapallus is the Hellenized name of the Assyrian king Ashurbanipal (669–626 B.C.). Many stories about his sensual excesses were current in antiquity.—Tr.

by those who know them, and they want to be honored on the basis of their virtue or excellence.* Obviously, then, excellence, as far as they are concerned, is better than honor. One might perhaps even go so far as to consider excellence rather than honor as the end of political life. However, even excellence proves to be imperfect as an end: for a man might possibly possess it while asleep or while being inactive all his life, and while, in addition, undergoing the greatest suffering and misfortune. Nobody would call the life of such a man happy, except for the sake of maintaining an argument. But enough of this: the subject has been sufficiently treated in our publications addressed to a wider audience. In the third place there is the contemplative life, which we shall examine later on. As for the money-maker, his life is led under some kind of constraint: clearly, wealth is not the good which we are trying to find, for it is only useful, i.e., it is a means to something else. Hence one might rather regard the aforementioned objects as ends, since they are valued for their own sake. But even they prove not to be the good, though many words have been wasted to show that they are. Accordingly, we may dismiss them. . . .

7. *The good is final and self-sufficient; happiness is defined*

Let us return again to our investigation into the nature of the good which we are seeking. It is evidently something different in different actions and in each art: it is one thing in medicine, another in strategy, and another again in each of the other arts. What, then, is the good of each? Is it not that for the sake of which everything else is done? That means it is health in the case of medicine, victory in the case of strategy, a house in the case of building, a different thing in the case of different arts, and in all actions and choices it is the end. For it is for the sake of the end that all else is done. Thus, if there is some one end for all that we do, this would be the good attainable by action; if there are several ends, they will be the goods attainable by action.

Our argument has gradually progressed to the same point at which we were before and we must try to clarify it still further. Since there are evidently several ends, and since we choose some of these—e.g., wealth, flutes, and instruments generally—as a means to something else, it is obvious that not all ends are final. The highest good, on the other hand, must be something final. Thus, if there is only one final end, this will be the good we are seeking; if there are several, it will be the most final and perfect of them. We call that which is pursued as an end in itself more final than an end which is pursued for the sake of something else; and what is never chosen as a means to something else we call more final than that which is chosen both as an end in itself and as a means to something else. What is always chosen as an end in itself and never as a means to something else is called final in an unqualified sense. This description seems to apply to happiness above all

---

Aretē denotes the functional excellence of any person, animal, or thing—that quality which enables the possessor to perform his own particular function well. Thus the *aretai* (plural) of man in relation to other men are his qualities which enable him to function well in society. The translation "virtue" often seems too narrow, and accordingly "excellence" and "goodness," or a combination of these, will also be used.—Tr.

else: for we always choose happiness as an end in itself and never for the sake of something else. Honor, pleasure, intelligence, and all virtue we choose partly for themselves—for we would choose each of them even if no further advantage would accrue from them—but we also choose them partly for the sake of happiness, because we assume that it is through them that we will be happy. On the other hand, no one chooses happiness for the sake of honor, pleasure, and the like, nor as a means to anything at all.

We arrive at the same conclusion if we approach the question from the standpoint of self-sufficiency. For the final and perfect good seems to be self-sufficient. However, we define something as self-sufficient not by reference to the "self" alone. We do not mean a man who lives his life in isolation, but a man who also lives with parents, children, a wife, and friends and fellow citizens generally, since man is by nature a social and political being. But some limit must be set to these relationships; for if they are extended to include ancestors, descendants, and friends of friends, they will go on to infinity. However, this point must be reserved for investigation later. For the present we define as "self-sufficient" that which taken by itself makes life something desirable and deficient in nothing. It is happiness, in our opinion, which fits this description. Moreover, happiness is of all things the one most desirable, and it is not counted as one good thing among many others. But if it were counted as one among many others, it is obvious that the addition of even the least of the goods would make it more desirable; for the addition would produce an extra amount of good, and the greater amount of good is always more desirable than the lesser. We see then that happiness is something final and self-sufficient and the end of our actions.

To call happiness the highest good is perhaps a little trite, and a clearer account of what it is, is still required. Perhaps this is best done by first ascertaining the proper function of man. For just as the goodness and performance of a flute player, a sculptor, or any kind of expert, and generally of anyone who fulfills some function or performs some action, are thought to reside in his proper function, so the goodness and performance of man would seem to reside in whatever is his proper function. Is it then possible that while a carpenter and a shoemaker have their own proper functions and spheres of action, man as man has none, but was left by nature a good-for-nothing without a function? Should we not assume that just as the eye, the hand, the foot, and in general each part of the body clearly has its own proper function, so man too has some function over and above the functions of his parts? What can this function possibly be? Simply living? He shares that even with plants, but we are now looking for something peculiar to man. Accordingly, the life of nutrition and growth must be excluded. Next in line there is a life of sense perception. But this, too, man has in common with the horse, the ox, and every animal. There remains then an active life of the rational element. The rational element has two parts: one is rational in that it obeys the rule of reason, the other in that it possesses and conceives rational rules. Since the expression "life of the rational element" also can be used in two senses, we must make it clear that we mean a life determined by the activity, as opposed to the mere possession, of the rational element. For the activity, it seems, has a greater claim to be the function of man.

The proper function of man, then, consists in an activity of the soul in conformity with a rational principle or, at least, not without it. In speaking of the proper function of a given individual we mean that it is the same in kind as the function of an individual who sets high standards for himself: the proper function of a harpist, for example, is the same as the function of a harpist who has set high standards for himself. The same applies to any and every group of individuals: the full attainment of excellence must be added to the mere function. In other words, the function of the harpist is to play the harp; the function of the harpist who has high standards is to play it well. On these assumptions, if we take the proper function of man to be a certain kind of life, and if this kind of life is an activity of the soul and consists in actions performed in conjunction with the rational element, and if a man of high standards is he who performs these actions well and properly, and if a function is well performed when it is performed in accordance with the excellence appropriate to it; we reach the conclusion that the good of man is an activity of the soul in conformity with excellence or virtue, and if there are several virtues, in conformity with the best and most complete.

But we must add "in a complete life." For one swallow does not make a spring, nor does one sunny day; similarly, one day or a short time does not make a man blessed* and happy.

This will suffice as an outline of the good: for perhaps one ought to make a general sketch first and fill in the details afterwards. Once a good outline has been made, anyone, it seems, is capable of developing and completing it in detail, and time is a good inventor or collaborator in such an effort. Advances in the arts, too, have come about in this way, for anyone can fill in gaps. We must also bear in mind what has been said above, namely that one should not require precision in all pursuits alike, but in each field precision varies with the matter under discussion and should be required only to the extent to which it is appropriate to the investigation. A carpenter and a geometrician both want to find a right angle, but they do not want to find it in the same sense: the former wants to find it to the extent to which it is useful for his work, the latter, wanting to see truth, [tries to ascertain] what it is and what sort of thing it is. We must, likewise, approach other subjects in the same spirit, in order to prevent minor points from assuming a greater importance than the major tasks. Nor should we demand to know a causal explanation in all matters alike; in some instances, e.g., when dealing with fundamental principles, it is sufficient to point out convincingly that such-and-such is in fact the case. The fact here is the primary thing and the fundamental principle. Some fundamental principles can be apprehended by induction, others by sense perception, others again by some sort of habituation, and others by still other means. We must try to get at each of them in a way naturally appropriate to it, and must be scrupulous in defining it correctly, because it is of great importance for the subsequent course of the discussion. Surely, a good beginning is more than half the whole, and as it comes to light, it sheds light on many problems.

---

*The distinction Aristotle seems to observe between *makarios,* "blessed" or "supremely happy," and *eudaimōn,* "happy," is that the former describes happiness insofar as it is god-given, while the latter describes happiness as attained by man through his own efforts. —Tr.

8. *Popular views about happiness confirm our position*

We must examine the fundamental principle with which we are concerned, [happiness], not only on the basis of the logical conclusion we have reached and on the basis of the elements which make up its definition, but also on the basis of the views commonly expressed about it. For in a true statement, all the facts are in harmony; in a false statement, truth soon introduces a discordant note.

Good things are commonly divided into three classes: (1) external goods, (2) goods of the soul, and (3) goods of the body. Of these, we call the goods pertaining to the soul goods in the highest and fullest sense. But in speaking of "soul," we refer to our soul's actions and activities. Thus, our definition tallies with this opinion which has been current for a long time and to which philosophers subscribe. We are also right in defining the end as consisting of actions and activities; for in this way the end is included among the goods of the soul and not among external goods.

Also the view that a happy man lives well and fares well fits in with our definition: for we have all but defined happiness as a kind of good life and well-being.

Moreover, the characteristics which one looks for in happiness are all included in our definition. For some people think that happiness is virtue, others that it is practical wisdom, others that it is some kind of theoretical wisdom; others again believe it to be all or some of these accompanied by, or not devoid of, pleasure; and some people also include external prosperity in its definition. Some of these views are expressed by many people and have come down from antiquity, some by a few men of high prestige, and it is not reasonable to assume that both groups are altogether wrong; the presumption is rather that they are right in at least one or even in most respects.

Now, in our definition we are in agreement with those who describe happiness as virtue or as some particular virtue, for our term "activity in conformity with virtue" implies virtue. But it does doubtless make a considerable difference whether we think of the highest good as consisting in the possession or in the practice of virtue, viz., as being a characteristic or an activity. For a characteristic may exist without producing any good result, as for example, in a man who is asleep or incapacitated in some other respect. An activity, on the other hand, must produce a result: [an active person] will necessarily act and act well. Just as the crown at the Olympic Games is not awarded to the most beautiful and the strongest but to the participants in the contests—for it is among them that the victors are found—so the good and noble things in life are won by those who act rightly.

The life of men active in this sense is also pleasant in itself. For the sensation of pleasure belongs to the soul, and each man derives pleasure from what he is said to love: a lover of horses from horses, a lover of the theater from plays, and in the same way a lover of justice from just acts, and a lover of virtue in general from virtuous acts. In most men, pleasant acts conflict with one another because they are not pleasant by nature, but men who love what is noble derive pleasure from what is naturally pleasant. Actions which conform to virtue are naturally pleasant, and, as a result, such actions are not only pleasant for those who love the noble but also pleasant in themselves. The life of such men has no further need of pleasure as an added attraction, but it contains pleasure within itself. We may even go so far as to state that the man who does not enjoy performing noble actions is not a good man at all. Nobody would call a man just who does not enjoy acting justly, nor generous who does not enjoy generous actions, and so on. If this is true, actions performed in conformity with virtue are in themselves pleasant.

Of course it goes without saying that such actions are good as well as noble, and they are both in the highest degree, if the man of high moral standards displays any right judgment about them at all; and his judgment corresponds to our description. So we see that happiness is at once the best, noblest, and most pleasant thing, and these qualities are not separate, as the inscription at Delos makes out:

> The most just is most noble, but health is the best,
> and to win what one loves is pleasantest.

For the best activities encompass all these attributes, and it is in these, or in the best one of them, that we maintain happiness consists.

Still, happiness, as we have said, needs external goods as well. For it is impossible or at least not easy to perform noble actions if one lacks the wherewithal. Many actions can only be performed with the help of instruments, as it were: friends, wealth, and political power. And there are some external goods the absence of which spoils supreme happiness, e.g., good birth, good children, and beauty: for a man who is very ugly in appearance or ill-born or who lives all by himself and has no children cannot be classified as altogether happy; even less happy perhaps is a man whose children and friends are worthless, or one who has lost good children and friends through death. Thus, as we have said, happiness also requires well-being of this kind, and that is the reason why some classify good fortune with happiness, while others link it to virtue.

9. *How happiness is acquired*

This also explains why there is a problem whether happiness is acquired by learning, by discipline, or by some other kind of training, or whether we attain it by reason of some divine dispensation or even by chance. Now, if there is anything at all which comes to men as a gift from the gods, it is reasonable to suppose that happiness above all else is god-given; and of all things human it is the most likely to be god-given, inasmuch as it is the best. But although this subject is perhaps more appropriate to a different field of study, it is clear that happiness is one of the most divine things, even if it is not god-sent but attained through virtue and some kind of learning or training. For the prize and end of excellence and virtue is the best thing of all, and it is something divine and blessed. Moreover, if happiness depends on excellence, it will be shared by many people; for study and effort will make it accessible to anyone whose capacity for virtue is unimpaired. And if it is better that happiness is acquired in this way rather than by chance, it is reasonable to assume that this is the way in which it is acquired. For, in the realm of nature, things are naturally arranged in the best way possible—and the same is also true of the products of art and of any kind of causation, especially the highest. To leave the greatest and noblest of things to chance would hardly be right.

A solution of this question is also suggested by our earlier definition, according to which the good of man, happiness, is some kind of activity of the soul in conformity with virtue. All the other goods are either necessary prerequisites for happiness, or are by nature co-workers with it and useful instruments for attaining it. Our results also tally with what we said at the outset: for we stated that the end of politics is the best of ends; and the main concern of politics is to engender a certain character in the citizens and to make them good and disposed to perform noble actions.

We are right, then, when we call neither a horse nor an ox nor any other animal happy, for none of them is capable of participating in an activity of this kind. For the same reason, a child is not happy, either; for, because of his age, he cannot yet perform such actions. When we do call a child happy, we do so by reason of the hopes we have for his future. Happiness, as we have said, requires completeness in virtue as well as a complete lifetime. Many changes and all kinds of contingencies befall a man in the course of his life, and it is possible that the most prosperous man will encounter great misfortune in his old age, as the Trojan legends tell about Priam. When a man has met a fate such as his and has come to a wretched end, no one calls him happy. . . .

13. *The psychological foundations of the virtues*

Since happiness is a certain activity of the soul in conformity with perfect virtue, we must now examine what virtue or excellence is. For such an inquiry will perhaps better enable us to discover the nature of happiness. Moreover, the man who is truly concerned about politics seems to devote special attention to excellence, since it is his aim to make the citizens good and law-abiding. We have an example of this in the lawgivers of Crete and Sparta and in other great legislators. If an examination of virtue is part of politics, this question clearly fits into the pattern of our original plan.

There can be no doubt that the virtue which we have to study is human virtue. For the good which we have been seeking is a human good and the happiness a human happiness. By human virtue we do not mean the excellence of the body, but that of the soul, and we define happiness as an activity of the soul. If this is true, the student of politics must obviously have some knowledge of the workings of the soul, just as the man who is to heal eyes must know something about the whole body. In fact, knowledge is all the more important for the former, inasmuch as politics is better and more valuable than medicine, and cultivated physicians devote much time and trouble to gain knowledge about the body. Thus, the student of politics must study the soul, but he must do so with his own aim in view, and only to the extent that the objects of his inquiry demand: to go into it in greater detail would perhaps be more laborious than his purposes require.

Some things that are said about the soul in our less technical discussions are adequate enough to be used here, for instance, that the soul consists of two elements, one irrational and one rational. Whether these two elements are separate, like the parts of the body or any other divisible thing, or whether they are only logically separable though in reality indivisible, as convex and concave are in the circumference of a circle, is irrelevant for our present purposes.

Of the irrational element, again, one part seems to be common to all living things and vegetative in nature: I mean that part which is responsible for nurture and growth. We must assume that some such capacity of the soul exists in everything that takes nourishment, in the embryonic stage as well as when the organism is fully developed; for this makes more sense than to assume the existence of some different capacity at the latter stage. The excellence of this part of the soul is, therefore, shown to be common to all living things and is not exclusively human. This very part and this capacity seem to be most active in sleep. For in sleep the difference between a good man and a bad is least apparent—whence the saying that for half their lives the happy are no better off than the wretched. This is just what we would expect, for sleep is an inactivity of the soul in that it ceases to do things which cause it to be called good or bad. However, to a small extent some bodily movements do penetrate to the soul in sleep, and in this sense the dreams of honest men are better than those of average people. But enough of this subject: we may pass by the nutritive part, since it has no natural share in human excellence or virtue.

In addition to this, there seems to be another integral element of the soul which, though irrational, still does partake of reason in some way. In morally strong and morally weak men we praise the reason that guides them and the rational element of the soul, because it exhorts them to follow the right path and to do what is best. Yet we see in them also another natural strain different from the rational, which fights and resists the guidance of reason. The soul behaves in precisely the same manner as do the paralyzed limbs of the body. When we intend to move the limbs to the right, they turn to the left, and similarly, the impulses of morally weak persons turn in the direction opposite to that in which reason leads them. However, while the aberration of the body is visible, that of the soul is not. But perhaps we must accept it as a fact, nevertheless, that there is something in the soul besides the rational element, which opposes and reacts against it. In what way the two are distinct need not concern us here. But, as we have stated, it too seems to partake of reason; at any rate, in a morally strong man it accepts the leadership of reason, and is perhaps more obedient still in a self-controlled and courageous man, since in him everything is in harmony with the voice of reason.

Thus we see that the irrational element of the soul has two parts: the one is vegetative and has no share in reason at all, the other is the seat of the appetites and of desire in general and partakes of reason insofar as it complies with reason and accepts its leadership; it possesses reason in the sense that we say it is "reasonable" to accept the advice of a father and of friends, not in the sense that we have a "rational" understanding of mathematical propositions. That the irrational element can be persuaded by the rational is shown by the fact that admonition and all manner of rebuke and exhortation are possible. If it is correct to say that the appetitive part, too, has reason, it follows that the rational element of the soul has two subdivisions: the one possesses reason in the strict sense, contained within itself, and the other possesses reason in the sense that it listens to reason as one would listen to a father.

Virtue, too, is differentiated in line with this division of the soul. We call some virtues "intellectual" and others "moral": theoretical wisdom, understanding, and practical wisdom are intellectual virtues, generosity and self-control moral virtues. In speaking of a man's character, we do not describe him as wise or understanding, but as gentle or self-controlled; but we praise the wise man, too, for his characteristic, and praiseworthy characteristics are what we call virtues.

Book II

1. *Moral virtue as the result of habits*

Virtue, as we have seen, consists of two kinds, intellectual virtue and moral virtue. Intellectual virtue or excellence owes its origin and development chiefly to teaching, and for that reason requires experience and time. Moral virtue, on the other hand, is formed by habit, *ethos,* and its name, *ēthikē,* is therefore derived, by a slight variation, from *ethos.* This shows, too, that none of the moral virtues is implanted in us by nature, for nothing which exists by nature can be changed by habit. For example, it is impossible for a stone, which has a natural downward movement, to become habituated to moving upward, even if one should try ten thousand times to inculcate the habit by throwing it in the air; nor can fire be made to move downward, nor can the direction of any nature-given tendency be changed by habituation. Thus, the virtues are implanted in us neither by nature nor contrary to nature: we are by nature equipped with the ability to receive them, and habit brings this ability to completion and fulfillment.

Furthermore, of all the qualities with which we are endowed by nature, we are provided with the capacity first, and display the activity afterward. That this is true is shown by the senses: it is not by frequent seeing or frequent hearing that we acquired our senses, but on the contrary we first possess and then use them; we do not acquire them by use. The virtues, on the other hand, we acquire by first having put them into action, and the same is also true of the arts. For the things which we have to learn before we can do them we learn by doing: men become builders by building houses, and harpists by playing the harp. Similarly, we become just by the practice of just actions, self-controlled by exercising self-control, and courageous by performing acts of courage.

This is corroborated by what happens in states. Lawgivers make the citizens good by inculcating [good] habits in them, and this is the aim of every lawgiver; if he does not succeed in doing that, his legislation is a failure. It is in this that a good constitution differs from a bad one.

Moreover, the same causes and the same means that produce any excellence or virtue can also destroy it, and this is also true of every art. It is by playing the harp that men become both good and bad harpists, and correspondingly with builders and all the other craftsmen: a man who builds well will be a good builder, one who builds badly a bad one. For if this were not so, there would be no need for an instructor, but everybody would be born as a good or a bad craftsman. The same holds true of the virtues: in our transactions with other men it is by action that some become just and others unjust, and it is by acting in the face of danger and by developing the habit of feeling fear or confidence that some become brave men and others cowards. The same applies to the appetites and feelings of anger: by reacting in one way or in another to given circumstances some people become self controlled and gentle, and others self-indulgent and short-tempered. In a word, characteristics develop from corresponding activities. For that reason, we must see to it that our activities are of a certain kind, since any variations in them will be reflected in our characteristics. Hence it is no small matter whether one habit or another is inculcated in us from early childhood; on the contrary, it makes a considerable difference, or, rather, all the difference.

2. *Method in the practical sciences*

The purpose of the present study is not, as it is in other inquiries, the attainment of theoretical knowledge: we are not conducting this inquiry in order to know what virtue is, but in order to become good, else there would be no advantage in studying it. For that reason, it becomes necessary to examine the problem of actions, and to ask how they are to be performed. For, as we have said, the actions determine what kind of characteristics are developed.

That we must act according to right reason is generally conceded and may be assumed as the basis of our discussion. We shall speak about it later and discuss what right reason is and examine its relation to the other virtues. But let us first agree that any discussion on matters of action cannot be more than an outline and is bound to lack precision; for as we stated at the outset, one can demand of a discussion only what the subject matter permits, and there are no fixed data in matters concerning action and questions of what is beneficial, any more than there are in matters of health. And if this is true of our general discussion, our treatment of particular problems will be even less precise, since these do not come under the head of any art which can be transmitted by precept, but the agent must consider on each different occasion what the situation demands, just as in medicine and in navigation. But although such is the kind of discussion in which we are engaged, we must do our best.

First of all, it must be observed that the nature of moral qualities is such that they are destroyed by defect and by excess. We see the same thing happen in the case of strength and of health, to illustrate, as we must, the invisible by means of visible examples: excess as well as deficiency of physical exercise destroys our strength, and similarly, too much and too little food and drink destroys our health; the proportionate amount, however, produces, increases, and preserves it. The same applies to self-control, courage, and the other virtues: the man who shuns and fears everything and never stands his ground becomes a coward, whereas a man who knows no fear at all and goes to meet every danger becomes reckless. Similarly, a man who revels in every pleasure and abstains from none becomes self-indulgent, while he who avoids every pleasure like a boor becomes what might be called insensitive. Thus we see that self-control and courage are destroyed by excess and by deficiency and are preserved by the mean.

Not only are the same actions which are responsible for and instrumental in the origin and development of the virtues also the causes and means of their destruction, but they will also be manifested in the active exercise of the virtues. We can see the truth of this in the case of other more visible qualities, e.g., strength. Strength is produced by consuming plenty of food and by enduring much hard work, and it is the strong man who is best able to do these things. The same is also true of the virtues: by abstaining from pleasures we become self-controlled, and once we are self-controlled we are best able to abstain from pleasures. So also with courage: by becoming habituated to despise and to endure terrors we become courageous, and once we have become courageous we will best be able to endure terror.

3. *Pleasure and pain as the test of virtue*

An index to our characteristics is provided by the pleasure or pain which follows upon the tasks we have achieved. A man who abstains from bodily pleasures and enjoys doing so is self-controlled; if he finds abstinence troublesome, he is self-indulgent; a man who endures danger with joy, or at least without pain, is courageous; if he endures it with pain, he is a coward. For moral excellence is concerned with pleasure and pain; it is pleasure that makes us do base actions and pain that prevents is from doing noble actions. For that reason, as Plato says, men must be brought up from childhood to feel pleasure and pain at the proper things; for this is correct education.

Furthermore, since the virtues have to do with actions and emotions, and since pleasure and pain are a consequence of every emotion and of every action, it follows from this point of view, too, that virtue has to do with pleasure and pain. This is further indicated by the fact that punishment is inflicted by means of pain. For punishment is a kind of medical treatment and it is the nature of medical treatments to take effect through the introduction of the opposite of the disease. Again, as we said just now, every characteristic of the soul shows its true nature in its relation to and its concern with those factors which naturally make it better or worse. But it is through pleasures and pains that men are corrupted, i.e., through pursuing and avoiding pleasures and pains either of the wrong kind or at the wrong time or in the wrong manner, or by going wrong in some other definable respect. For that reason some people define the virtues as states of freedom from emotion and of quietude. However, they make the mistake of using these terms absolutely and without adding such qualifications as "in the right manner," "at the right or wrong time," and so forth. We may, therefore, assume as the basis of our discussion that virtue, being concerned with pleasure and pain in the way we have described, makes us act in the best way in matters involving pleasure and pain, and that vice does the opposite.

The following considerations may further illustrate that virtue is concerned with pleasure and pain. There are three factors that determine choice and three that determine avoidance: the noble, the beneficial, and the pleasurable, on the one hand, and on the other their opposites: the base, the harmful, and the painful.

Now a good man will go right and a bad man will go wrong when any of these, and especially when pleasure is involved. For pleasure is not only common to man and the animals, but also accompanies all objects of choice: in fact, the noble and the beneficial seem pleasant to us. Moreover, a love of pleasure has grown up with all of us from infancy. Therefore, this emotion has come to be ingrained in our lives and is difficult to erase. Even in our actions we use, to a greater or smaller extent, pleasure and pain as a criterion. For this reason, this entire study is necessarily concerned with pleasure and pain; for it is not unimportant for our actions whether we feel joy and pain in the right or the wrong way. Again, it is harder to fight against pleasure than against anger, as Heraclitus says; and both virtue and art are always concerned with what is harder, for success is better when it is hard to achieve. Thus, for this reason also, every study both of virtue and of politics must deal with pleasures and pains, for if a man has the right attitude to them, he will be good; if the wrong attitude, he will be bad.

We have now established that virtue or excellence is concerned with pleasures and pains; that the actions which produce it also develop it and, if differently performed, destroy it; and that it actualizes itself fully in those activities to which it owes its origin.

4. *Virtuous action and virtue*

However, the question may be raised what we mean by saying that men become just by performing just actions and self-controlled by practicing self-control. For if they perform just actions and exercise self-control, they are already just and self-controlled, in the same way as they are literate and musical if they write correctly and practice music.

But is this objection really valid, even as regards the arts? No, for it is possible for a man to write a piece correctly by chance or at the prompting of another: but he will be literate only if he produces a piece of writing in a literate way, and that means doing it in accordance with the skill of literate composition which he has in himself.

Moreover, the factors involved in the arts and in the virtues are not the same. In the arts, excellence lies in the result itself, so that it is sufficient if it is of a certain kind. But in the case of the virtues an act is not performed justly or with self-control if the act itself is of a certain kind, but only if in addition the agent has certain characteristics as he performs it: first of all, he must know what he is doing; secondly, he must choose to act the way he does, and he must choose it for its own sake; and in the third place, the act must spring from a firm and unchangeable character. With the exception of knowing what one is about, these considerations do not enter into the mastery of the arts; for the mastery of the virtues, however, knowledge is of little or no importance, whereas the other two conditions count not for a little but are all-decisive, since repeated acts of justice and self-control result in the possession of these virtues. In other words, acts are called just and self-controlled when they are the kind of acts which a just or self-controlled man would perform; but the just and self-controlled man is not he who performs these acts, but he who also performs them in the way just and self-controlled men do.

Thus our assertion that a man becomes just by performing just acts and self-controlled by performing acts of self-control is correct; without performing them, nobody could even be on the way to becoming good. Yet most men do not perform such acts, but by taking refuge in argument they think that they are engaged in philosophy and that they will become good in this way. In so doing, they act like sick men who listen attentively to what the doctor says, but fail to do any of the things he prescribes. That kind of philosophical activity will not bring health to the soul any more than this sort of treatment will produce a healthy body.

5. *Virtue defined: the genus*

The next point to consider is the definition of virtue or excellence. As there are three kinds of things found in the soul: (1) emotions, (2) capacities, and (3) characteristics, virtue must be one of these. By "emotions" I mean appetite, anger, fear, confidence, envy, joy, affection, hatred, longing, emulation, pity, and in general anything that is followed by pleasure or pain; by "capacities" I mean that by virtue of which we are said to be affected by these emotions, for example, the capacity which enables us to feel anger, pain, or pity; and by "characteristics" I mean the condition, either good or bad, in which we are, in relation to the emotions: for example, our condition in relation to anger is bad, if our anger is too violent or not violent enough, but if it is moderate, our condition is good; and similarly with our condition in relation to the other emotions.

Now the virtues and vices cannot be emotions, because we are not called good or bad on the basis of our emotions, but on the basis of our virtues and vices. Also, we are neither praised nor blamed for our emotions: a man does not receive praise for being frightened or angry, nor blame for being angry pure and simple, but for being angry in a certain way. Yet we are praised or blamed for our virtues and vices. Furthermore, no choice is involved when we experience anger or fear, while the virtues are some kind of choice or at least involve choice. Moreover, with regard to our emotions we are said to be "moved," but with regard to our virtues and vices we are not said to be "moved" but to be "disposed" in a certain way.

For the same reason, the virtues cannot be capacities, either, for we are neither called good or bad nor praised or blamed simply because we are capable of being affected. Further, our capacities have been given to us by nature, but we do not by nature develop into good or bad men. We have discussed this subject before. Thus, if the virtues are neither emotions nor capacities, the only remaining alternative is that they are characteristics. So much for the genus of virtue.

6. *Virtue defined: the differentia*

It is not sufficient, however, merely to define virtue in general terms as a characteristic: we must also specify what kind of characteristic it is. It must, then, be remarked that every virtue or excellence (1) renders good the thing itself of which it is the excellence, and (2) causes it to perform its function well. For example, the excellence of the eye makes both the eye and its function good, for good sight is due to the excellence of the eye. Likewise, the excellence of a horse makes it both good as a horse and good at running, at carrying its rider, and at facing the enemy. Now, if this is true of all things, the virtue or excellence of man, too, will be a characteristic which makes him a good man, and which causes him to perform his own function well. To some extent we have already stated how this will be true; the rest will become clear if we study what the nature of virtue is.

Of every continuous entity that is divisible into parts it is possible to take the larger, the smaller, or an equal part, and these parts may be larger, smaller, or equal either in relation to the entity itself, or in relation to us. The "equal" part is something median between excess and deficiency. By the median of an entity I understand a point equidistant from both extremes, and this point is one and the same for everybody. By the median relative to us I understand an amount neither too large nor too small, and this is neither one nor the same for everybody. To take an example: if ten is many and two is few, six is taken as the median in relation to the entity, for it exceeds and is exceeded by the same amount, and is thus the median in terms of arithmetical proportion. But the median relative to us cannot be determined in this manner: if ten pounds of food is much for a man to eat and two pounds little, it does not follow that the trainer will prescribe six pounds, for this may in turn be much or little for him to eat; it may be little for Milo* and much for someone who has just begun to take up athletics. The same applies to running and wrestling. Thus we see that an expert in any field avoids excess and deficiency, but seeks the median and chooses it—not the median of the object but the median relative to us.

If this, then, is the way in which every science perfects its work, by looking to the median and by bringing its work up to that point—and this is the reason why it is usually said of a successful piece of work that it is impossible to detract from it or to add to it, the implication being that excess and deficiency destroy success while the mean safeguards it (good craftsmen, we say, look toward this standard in the performance of their work)—and if virtue, like nature, is more precise and better than any art, we must conclude that virtue aims at the median. I am referring to moral virtue: for it is moral virtue that is concerned with emotions and actions, and it is in emotions and actions that excess, deficiency, and the median are found. Thus we can experience fear, confidence, desire, anger, pity, and generally any kind of pleasure and pain either too much or too little, and in either case not properly. But to experience all this at the right time, toward the right objects, toward the right people, for the right reason, and in the right manner—that is the median and the best course, the course that is a mark of virtue.

Similarly, excess, deficiency, and the median can also be found in actions. Now virtue is concerned with emotions and actions; and in emotions and actions excess and deficiency miss the mark, whereas the median is praised and constitutes success. But both praise and success are signs of virtue or excellence. Consequently, virtue is a mean in the sense that it aims at the median. This is corroborated by the fact that there are many ways of going wrong, but only one way which is right— for evil belongs to the indeterminate, as the Pythagoreans imagined, but good to

*Milo of Croton, said to have lived in the second half of the sixth century B.C. was a wrestler famous for his remarkable strength. —Tr.

the determinate. This, by the way, is also the reason why the one is easy and the other hard: it is easy to miss the target but hard to hit it. Here, then, is an additional proof that excess and deficiency characterize vice, while the mean characterizes virtue: for "bad men have many ways, good men but one."

We may thus conclude that virtue or excellence is a characteristic involving choice, and that it consists in observing the mean relative to us, a mean which is defined by a rational principle, such as a man of practical wisdom would use to determine it. It is the mean by reference to two vices: the one of excess and the other of deficiency. It is, moreover, a mean because some vices exceed and others fall short of what is required in emotion and in action, whereas virtue finds and chooses the median. Hence, in respect of its essence and the definition of its essential nature virtue is a mean, but in regard to goodness and excellence it is an extreme.

Not every action nor every emotion admits of a mean. There are some actions and emotions whose very names connote baseness, e.g., spite, shamelessness, envy; and among actions, adultery, theft, and murder. These and similar emotions and actions imply by their very names that they are bad; it is not their excess nor their deficiency which is called bad. It is, therefore, impossible ever to do right in performing them: to perform them is always to do wrong. In cases of this sort, let us say adultery, rightness and wrongness do not depend on committing it with the right woman at the right time and in the right manner, but the mere fact of committing such action at all is to do wrong. It would be just as absurd to suppose that there is a mean, an excess, and a deficiency in an unjust or a cowardly or a self-indulgent act. For if there were, we would have a mean of excess and a mean of deficiency, and an excess of excess and a deficiency of deficiency. Just as there cannot be an excess and a deficiency of self-control and courage—because the intermediate is, in a sense, an extreme—so there cannot be a mean, excess, and deficiency in their respective opposites: their opposites are wrong regardless of how they are performed; for, in general, there is no such thing as the mean of an excess or a deficiency, or the excess and deficiency of a mean.

7. Examples of the mean in particular virtues

However, this general statement is not enough; we must also show that it fits particular instances. For in a discussion of moral actions, although general statements have a wider range of application, statements on particular points have more truth in them: actions are concerned with particulars and our statements must harmonize with them. Let us now take particular virtues and vices from the following table.*

In feelings of fear and confidence courage is the mean. As for the excesses, there is no name that describes a man who exceeds in fearlessness—many virtues and vices have no name; but a man who exceeds in confidence is reckless, and a man who exceeds in fear and is deficient in confidence is cowardly.

---

*Aristotle evidently used a table here to illustrate graphically the various virtues and their opposite extremes. Probably the table mentioned here is the same as the "outline" given in *Eudemian Ethics* II. 3, 1220b38–1221a12, where the extremes and the mean are arranged in different parallel columns. —Tr.

In regard to pleasures and pains—not all of them and to a lesser degree in the case of pains—the mean is self-control and the excess self-indulgence. Men deficient in regard to pleasure are not often found, and there is therefore no name for them, but let us call them "insensitive."

In giving and taking money, the mean is generosity, the excess and deficiency are extravagance and stinginess. In these vices excess and deficiency work in opposite ways: an extravagant man exceeds in spending and is deficient in taking, while a stingy man exceeds in taking and is deficient in spending. For our present purposes, we may rest content with an outline and a summary, but we shall later define these qualities more precisely.

There are also some other dispositions in regard to money: magnificence is a mean (for there is a difference between a magnificent and a generous man in that the former operates on a large scale, the latter on a small); gaudiness and vulgarity are excesses, and niggardliness a deficiency. These vices differ from the vices opposed to generosity. But we shall postpone until later a discussion of the way in which they differ.

As regards honor and dishonor, the mean is high-mindedness, the excess is what we might call vanity, and the deficiency small-mindedness. The same relation which, as we said, exists between magnificence and generosity, the one being distinguished from the other in that it operates on a small scale, exists also between high-mindedness and another virtue: as the former deals with great, so the latter deals with small honors. For it is possible to desire honor as one should or more than one should or less than one should: a man who exceeds in his desires is called ambitious, a man who is deficient unambitious, but there is no name to describe the man in the middle. There are likewise no names for the corresponding dispositions except for the disposition of an ambitious man which is called ambition. As a result, the men who occupy the extremes lay claim to the middle position. We ourselves, in fact, sometimes call the middle person ambitious and sometimes unambitious; sometimes we praise an ambitious and at other times an unambitious man. The reason why we do that will be discussed in the sequel; for the present, let us discuss the rest of the virtues and vices along the lines we have indicated.

In regard to anger also there exists an excess, a deficiency, and a mean. Although there really are no names for them, we might call the mean gentleness, since we call a man who occupies the middle position gentle. Of the extremes, let the man who exceeds be called short-tempered and his vice a short temper, and the deficient man apathetic and his vice apathy.

There are, further, three other means which have a certain similarity with one another, but differ nonetheless one from the other. They are all concerned with human relations in speech and action, but they differ in that one of them is concerned with truth in speech and action and the other two with pleasantness: (a) pleasantness in amusement and (b) pleasantness in all our daily life. We must include these, too, in our discussion, in order to see more clearly that the mean is to be praised in all things and that the extremes are neither praiseworthy nor right, but worthy of blame. Here, too, most of the virtues and vices have no name, but for the sake of clarity and easier comprehension we must try to coin names for them, as we did in earlier instances.

To come to the point; in regard to truth, let us call the man in the middle position truthful and the mean truthfulness. Pretense in the form of exaggeration is boastfulness and its possessor boastful, while pretense in the form of understatement is self-depreciation and its possessor a self-depreciator.

Concerning pleasantness in amusement, the man in the middle position is witty and his disposition wittiness; the excess is called buffoonery and its possessor a buffoon; and the deficient man a kind of boor and the corresponding characteristic boorishness.

As far as the other kind of pleasantness is concerned, pleasantness in our daily life, a man who is as pleasant as he should be is friendly and the mean is friendliness. A man who exceeds is called obsequious if he has no particular purpose in being pleasant, but if he is acting for his own material advantage, he is a flatterer. And a man who is deficient and unpleasant in every respect is a quarrelsome and grouchy kind of person.

A mean can also be found in our emotional experiences and in our emotions. Thus, while a sense of shame is not a virtue, a bashful or modest man is praised. For even in these matters we speak of one kind of person as intermediate and of another as exceeding if he is terror-stricken and abashed at everything. On the other hand, a man who is deficient in shame or has none at all is called shameless, whereas the intermediate man is bashful or modest.

Righteous indignation is the mean between envy and spite, all of these being concerned with the pain and pleasure which we feel in regard to the fortunes of our neighbors. The righteously indignant man feels pain when someone prospers undeservedly; an envious man exceeds him in that he is pained when he sees anyone prosper; and a spiteful man is so deficient in feeling pain that he even rejoices (when someone suffers undeservedly).

But we shall have an opportunity to deal with these matters again elsewhere. After that, we shall discuss justice; since it has more than one meaning, we shall distinguish the two kinds of justice and show in what way each is a mean.

8. *The relation between the mean and its extremes*

There are, then, three kinds of disposition: two are vices (one marked by excess and one by deficiency), and one, virtue, the mean. Now, each of these dispositions is, in a sense, opposed to both the others: the extremes are opposites to the middle as well as to one another, and the middle is opposed to the extremes. Just as an equal amount is larger in relation to a smaller and smaller in relation to a larger amount, so, in the case both of emotions and of actions, the middle characteristics exceed in relation to the deficiencies and are deficient in relation to the excesses. For example, a brave man seems reckless in relation to a coward, but in relation to a reckless man he seems cowardly. Similarly, a self-controlled man seems self-indulgent in relation to an insensitive man and insensitive in relation to a self-indulgent man, and a generous man extravagant in relation to a stingy man and stingy in relation to an extravagant man. This is the reason why people at the extremes each push the man in the middle over to the other extreme: a coward calls a brave man reckless and a reckless man calls a brave man a coward, and similarly with the other qualities.

However, while these three dispositions are thus opposed to one another, the extremes are more opposed to one another than each is to the median; for they are further apart from one another than each is from the median, just as the large is further removed from the small and the small from the large than either one is from the equal. Moreover, there appears to be a certain similarity between some extremes and their median, e.g., recklessness resembles courage and extravagance generosity; but there is a very great dissimilarity between the extremes. But things that are furthest removed from one another are defined as opposites, and that means that the further things are removed from one another the more opposite they are.

In some cases it is the deficiency and in others the excess that is more opposed to the median. For example, it is not the excess, recklessness, which is more opposed to courage, but the deficiency, cowardice; while in the case of self-control it is not the defect, insensitivity, but the excess, self-indulgence which is more opposite. There are two causes for this. One arises from the nature of the thing itself: when one of the extremes is closer and more similar to the median, we do not treat it but rather the other extreme as the opposite of the median. For instance, since recklessness is believed to be more similar and closer to courage, and cowardice less similar, it is cowardice rather than recklessness which we treat as the opposite of courage. For what is further removed from the middle is regarded as being more opposite. So much for the first cause which arises from the thing itself. The second reason is found in ourselves: the more we are naturally attracted to anything, the more opposed to the median does this thing appear to be. For example, since we are naturally more attracted to pleasure we incline more easily to self-indulgence than to a disciplined kind of life. We describe as more opposed to the mean those things toward which our tendency is stronger; and for that reason the excess, self-indulgence, is more opposed to self-control than is its corresponding deficiency.

9. *How to attain the mean*

Our discussion has sufficiently established (1) that moral virtue is a mean and in what sense it is a mean; (2) that it is a mean between two vices, one of which is marked by excess and the other by deficiency; and (3) that it is a mean in the sense that it aims at the median in the emotions and in actions. That is why it is a hard task to be good; in every case it is a task to find the median: for instance, not everyone can find the middle of a circle, but only a man who has the proper knowledge. Similarly, anyone can get angry—that is easy—or can give away money or spend it; but to do all this to the right person, to the right extent, at the right time, for the right reason, and in the right way is no longer something easy that anyone can do. It is for this reason that good conduct is rare, praiseworthy, and noble.

The first concern of a man who aims at the median should, therefore, be to avoid the extreme which is more opposed to it, as Calypso advises: "Keep clear your ship of yonder spray and surf." For one of the two extremes is more in error than the other, and since it is extremely difficult to hit the mean, we must, as the saying has it, sail in the second best way and take the lesser evil; and we can best do that in the manner we have described.

Moreover, we must watch the errors which have the greatest attraction for us personally. For the natural inclination of one man differs from that of another, and we each come to recognize our own by observing the pleasure and pain produced in us [by the different extremes]. We must then draw ourselves away in the opposite direction, for by pulling away from error we shall reach the middle, as men do when they straighten warped timber. In every case we must be especially on our guard against pleasure and what is pleasant, for when it comes to pleasure we cannot act as unbiased judges. Our attitude toward pleasure should be the same as that of the Trojan elders was toward Helen, and we should repeat on every occasion the words they addressed to her. For if we dismiss pleasure as they dismissed her, we shall make fewer mistakes.

In summary, then, it is by acting in this way that we shall best be able to hit the median. But this is no doubt difficult, especially when particular cases are concerned. For it is not easy to determine in what manner, with what person, on what occasion, and for how long a time one ought to be angry. There are times when we praise those who are deficient in anger and call them gentle, and other times when we praise violently angry persons and call them manly. However, we do not blame a man for slightly deviating from the course of goodness, whether he strays toward excess or toward deficiency, but we do blame him if his deviation is great and cannot pass unnoticed. It is not easy to determine by a formula at what point and for how great a divergence a man deserves blame; but this difficulty is, after all, true of all objects of sense perception: determinations of this kind depend upon particular circumstances, and the decision rests with our [moral] sense.

This much, at any rate, is clear: that the median characteristic is in all fields the one that deserves praise, and that it is sometimes necessary to incline toward the excess and sometimes toward the deficiency. For it is in this way that we will most easily hit upon the median, which is the point of excellence.

Book VIII

1. *Why we need friendship*

Continuing in a sequence, the next subject which we shall have to discuss is friendship. For it is some sort of excellence or virtue, or involves virtue, and it is, moreover, most indispensable for life. No one would choose to live without friends, even if he had all other goods. Rich men and those who hold office and power are, above all others, regarded as requiring friends. For what good would their prosperity do them if it did not provide them with the opportunity for good works? And the best works done and those which deserve the highest praise are those that are done to one's friends. How could prosperity be safeguarded and preserved without friends? The greater it is the greater are the risks it brings with it. Also, in poverty and all other kinds of misfortune men believe that their only refuge consists in their friends. Friends help young men avoid error; to older people they give the care and help needed to supplement the failing powers of action which infirmity brings in its train; and to those in their prime they give the opportunity to perform noble actions. [This is what is meant when men quote Homer's verse:] "When two go together . . . ": friends enhance our ability to think and to act. Also, it seems that nature implants friendship in a parent for its offspring and in offspring for its parent, not only among men, but also among birds and most animals. [Not only members of the same family group but] also members of the same race feel it for one another, especially human beings, and that is why we praise men for being humanitarians or "lovers of their fellow men." Even when traveling abroad one can see how near and dear and friendly every man may be to another human being.

Friendship also seems to hold states together, and lawgivers apparently devote more attention to it than to justice. For concord seems to be something similar to friendship, and concord is what they most strive to attain, while they do their best to expel faction, the enemy of concord. When people are friends, they have no need of justice, but when they are just, they need friendship in addition. In fact, the just in the fullest sense is regarded as constituting an element of friendship. Friendship is noble as well as necessary: we praise those who love their friends and consider the possession of many friends a noble thing. And further, we believe of our friends that they are good men.

There are, however, several controversial points about friendship. Some people define it as a kind of likeness, and say that friends are those who are like us; hence, according to them, the proverb: "Like to like," "Birds of a feather flock together," and so forth. On the other side, there are those who say that when people are alike they quarrel with one another like potters. There are also more profound investigations into the matter along the lines of natural science: Euripides speaks of the parched earth as loving the rain while the majestic heaven, filled with rain, loves to fall upon the earth; Heraclitus says that opposites help one another, that different elements produce the most beautiful harmony, and that everything comes into being through strife; while Empedocles and others express the opposite view that like strives for like.

Let us leave aside problems which are an aspect of natural science—for they are not germane to our present field of study—and investigate those which pertain to man and are relevant to character and emotions. For example, can friendship develop in all men, or is it impossible for those who are wicked to be friends? Is there only one kind of friendship, or are there more than one? Those who think that there is only one kind on the ground that friendship admits of degrees rely on insufficient evidence: things different in kind also admit of degrees. But these matters have been discussed before.

2. *The three things worthy of affection*

The answers to these questions will perhaps become clear once we have ascertained what is the object worthy of affection. For, it seems, we do not feel affection for everything, but only for the lovable, and that means what is good, pleasant, or useful. However, since we regard a thing as useful when it serves as a means to some good or pleasure, we can say that as ends [only] the good and the pleasant are worthy of affection. Which good, then, is it that men love? Is it the good [in general] or is it what is good for them? For there is sometimes a discrepancy between these two, and a discrepancy also in the case of what is pleasant. Now it seems that each man loves what is good for him: in an unqualified sense it is the good which is worthy of affection, but for each individual it is what is good for him. Now, in fact, every man does not love what is really good for him, but what appears to him to be good. But that makes no difference [for our discussion]. It simply follows that what appears good will appear worthy of affection. . . .

3. *The three kinds of friendship*

These three motives differ from one another in kind, and so do the corresponding types of affection and friendship. In other words, there are three kinds of friendship, corresponding in number to the objects worthy of affection. In each of these, the affection can be reciprocated so that the partner is aware of it, and the partners' wish for each other's good in terms of the motive on which their affection is based. Now, when the motive of the affection is usefulness, the partners do not feel affection for one another *per se* but in terms of the good accruing to each from the other. The same is also true of those whose friendship is based on pleasure: we love witty people not for what they are, but for the pleasure they give us.

So we see that when the useful is the basis of affection, men love because of the good they get out of it, and when pleasure is the basis, for the pleasure they get out of it. In other words, the friend is loved not because he is a friend, but because he is useful or pleasant. Thus, these two kinds are friendship only incidentally, since the object of affection is not loved for being the kind of person he is, but for providing some good or pleasure. Consequently, such friendships are easily dissolved when the partners do not remain unchanged: the affection ceases as soon as one partner is no longer pleasant or useful to the other. Now, usefulness is not something permanent, but differs at different times. Accordingly, with the disappearance of the motive for being friends, the friendship, too, is dissolved, since the friendship owed its existence to these motives.

Friendships of this kind seem to occur most commonly among old people, because at that age men do not pursue the pleasant but the beneficial. They are also found among young men and those in their prime who are out for their own advantage. Such friends are not at all given to living in each other's company, for sometimes they do not even find each other pleasant. Therefore, they have no further need of this relationship, if they are not mutually beneficial. They find each other pleasant only to the extent that they have hopes of some good coming out of it. The traditional friendship between host and guest is also placed in this group.

Friendship of young people seems to be based on pleasure for their lives are guided by emotion, and they pursue most intensely what they find pleasant and what the moment brings. As they advance in years, different things come to be pleasant for them. Hence they become friends quickly and just as quickly cease to be friends. For as another thing becomes pleasant, the friendship, too, changes, and the pleasure of a young man changes quickly. Also, young people are prone to fall in love, since the greater part of falling in love is a matter of emotion and based on pleasure. That is why they form a friendship and give it up again so quickly that the change often takes place within the same day. But they do wish to be together all day and to live together, because it is in this way that they get what they want out of their friendship.

The perfect form of friendship is that between good men who are alike in excellence or virtue. For these friends wish alike for one another's good because they are good men, and they are good *per se,* [that is, their goodness is something intrinsic, not incidental]. Those who wish for their friends' good for their friends' sake are friends in the truest sense, since their attitude is determined by what their friends are and not by incidental considerations. Hence, their friendship lasts as long as they are good, [and that means it will last for a long time] since goodness or virtue is a thing that lasts. In addition, each partner is both good in the unqualified sense and good for his friend. For those who are good, i.e., good without qualification, are also beneficial to one another. In the same double sense, they are also pleasant to one another: for good men are pleasant both in an unqualified sense and to one another, since each finds pleasure in his own proper actions and in actions like them, and the actions of good men are identical with or similar to one another. That such a friendship is lasting stands to reason, because in it are combined all the qualities requisite for people to be friends. For, [as we have seen,] every friendship is based on some good pleasure—either in the unqualified sense or relative to the person who feels the affection—and implies some similarity [between the friends]. Now this kind of friendship has all the requisite qualities we have mentioned and has them *per se,* that is, as an essential part of the characters of the friends. For in this kind of friendship the partners are like one another, and the other objects worthy of affection—the unqualified good and the unqualified pleasant—are also found in it, and these are the highest objects worthy of affection. It is, therefore, in the friendship of good men that feelings of affection and friendship exist in their highest and best form.

Such friendships are of course rare, since such men are few. Moreover, time and familiarity are required. For, as the proverb has it, people cannot know each other until they have eaten the specified [measure of] salt together. One cannot extend friendship to or be a friend of another person until each partner has impressed the other that he is worthy of affection, and until each has won the other's confidence. Those who are quick to show the signs of friendship to one another are not really friends, though they wish to be; they are not true friends unless they are worthy of affection and know this to be so. The wish to be friends can come about quickly, but friendship cannot.

4. *Perfect friendship and imperfect friendship*

This, then, is perfect and complete friendship, both in terms of time and in all other respects, and each partner receives in all matters what he gives the other, in the same or in a similar form; that is what friends should be able to count on.

Friendship based on what is pleasant bears some resemblance to this kind, for good men are pleasant to one another. The same is also true of friendship based on the useful, for good men are useful to one another. Here, too, friendships are most durable when each one receives what he gives to the other, for example, pleasure, and not only that, he must also receive it from the same source, as happens, for example, in friendships between witty people, but not in the case of lover and beloved. For lover and beloved do not find pleasure in the same objects: the lover finds it in seeing his beloved, while the beloved receives it from the attention paid to him by his lover. But when the bloom of youth passes, the friendship sometimes passes, too: the lover does not find the sight pleasant [any more], and the beloved no longer receives the attentions of the lover. Still, many do remain friends if, through familiarity, they have come to love each other's characters, [discovering that] their characters are alike. But when it is the useful and not the pleasant that is exchanged in a love affair, the partners are less truly friends and their friendship is less durable. Those whose friendship is based on the useful dissolve it as soon as it ceases to be to their advantage, since they were friends not of one another but of what was profitable for them. . . .

5. *Friendship as a characteristic and as an activity*

As in the case of virtues, some men are called "good" because of a characteristic they have and others because of an activity in which they engage, so in the case of friendship there is a distinction [between the activity of friendship and the lasting characteristic]. When friends live together, they enjoy each other's presence and provide each other's good. When, however, they are asleep or separated geographically, they do not actively engage in their friendship, but they are still characterized by an attitude which could express itself in active friendship. For it is not friendship in the unqualified sense but only its activity that is interrupted by distance. But if the absence lasts for some time, it apparently also causes the friendship itself to be forgotten. Hence the saying: "Out of sight, out of mind." . . .

6. *Additional observations on the three kinds of friendship*

Friendship does not arise easily among the sour and the old, inasmuch as they are rather grouchy and find little joy in social relations. For a good temper and sociability are regarded as being most typical of and most conducive to friendship. That is why young men become friends quickly and old men do not: people do not become friends of those in whom they find no joy. (This also applies to the sour.) Such men do, however, display good will toward one another, since one may wish for another's good and be ready to meet his needs. But they are not really friends, because they do not spend their days together and do not find joy in one another, and these seem to be the chief marks of friendship.

To be friends with many people, in the sense of perfect friendship, is impossible, just as it is impossible to be in love with many people at the same time. For love is like an extreme, and an extreme tends to be unique. It does not easily happen that one man finds many people very pleasing at the same time, nor perhaps does it easily happen that there are many people who are good. Also, one must have some experience of the other person and have come to be familiar with him, and that is the hardest thing of all. But it is possible to please many people on the basis of usefulness and pleasantness, since many have these qualities, and the services they have to offer do not take a long time [to recognize].

Of these two kinds of friendship, the one that is based on what is pleasant bears a closer resemblance to [true] friendship, when both partners have the same to offer and when they find joy in one another or in the same objects. Friendships of young people are of this kind. There is a greater element of generosity in such friendships, whereas friendships based on usefulness are for hucksters. Also, those who are supremely happy have no need of useful people, but they do need pleasant ones: they do wish to live in the company of others, and, though they can bear what is painful for a short time, no one could endure it continually—in fact, no one could continually endure the Good itself if that were painful to him. It is for this reason that they seek friends who are pleasant. They should, however, look for friends who are good as well as pleasant, and not only good, but good for them; for in this way they will have everything that friends should have.

People in positions of power seem to keep their various friends in separate compartments. One group of friends is useful to them and another pleasant, but rarely do the same men belong in both groups. For these potentates do not seek friends who are both pleasant and virtuous nor friends who are useful for the attainment of noble objects. On the contrary, when their aim is to get something pleasant, they seek witty people, [and when they want what is useful, they seek] men who are clever at carrying out their orders, and these qualities are hardly ever found in the same person. Now, as we have stated, it is the good man who is pleasant and useful at the same time. But such a man does not become the friend of someone whose station is superior to his own, unless that person is also superior to him in virtue. Unless that is the case, his friendship will not be based on [proportionate] equality, since he will not be surpassed [by a virtue] proportionate [to the surpassing power]. But potentates of this sort are not often found.

In sum, the friendships we have so far discussed are based on equality; both partners receive and wish the same thing from and for one another, or they exchange one thing for another, for instance, pleasure for material advantage. That these kinds of friendship are inferior to and less lasting [than true friendship] has already been stated. Because of their resemblance and dissimilarity to the same thing, [namely, to true friendship,] they are regarded both as being and as not being friendship. They appear to be friendship in that they are like the friendship which is based on virtue or excellence: one of these friendships has what is pleasant and the other has what is useful, and both these elements are inherent in friendship based on virtue. But since friendship based on virtue is proof against slander and lasting, while these kinds—besides many other differences—change quickly, they do not appear to be friendships, because of their dissimilarity.

8. *Giving and receiving affection*

Most people, because of ambition, seem to wish to receive affection rather than to give it. That is why most men like flattery, for a flatterer is or pretends to be a friend in an inferior position, who pretends to give more affection than he receives. Receiving affection is regarded as closely related to being honored, and honor is, of course, the aim of most people. But, it seems, they do not choose honor for its own sake but only because it is incidental to something else. For most men enjoy being honored by those who occupy positions of power, because it raises their hopes. They think they will get anything they need from the powerful, and they enjoy the honor they get as a token of benefits to come. Those, on the other hand, who desire honor from good and knowing men aim at having their own opinion of themselves confirmed. They, therefore, enjoy [the honor they get] because [their belief in] their own goodness is reassured by the judgment of those who say that they are good. But [unlike honor], affection is enjoyed for its own sake. Thus, receiving affection would seem to be better than receiving honor, and friendship would seem to be desirable for its own sake.

Nevertheless, friendship appears to consist in giving rather than in receiving affection. This is shown by the fact that mothers enjoy giving affection. Some mothers give their children away to be brought up by others, and though they know them and feel affection for them, they do not seek to receive affection in return, if they cannot have it both ways. It seems to be sufficient for them to see their children prosper and to feel affection for them, even if the children do not render their mother her due, because they do not know her. Since, then, friendship consists in giving rather [than in receiving] affection, and since we praise those who love their friends, the giving of affection seems to constitute the proper virtue of friends, so that people who give affection to one another according to each other's merit are lasting friends and their friendship is a lasting friendship.

It is in this way that even unequals are most likely to be friends, since equality may thus be established between them [by a difference in the amount of affection given]. Friendship is equality and likeness, and especially the likeness of those who are similar in virtue. Because they are steadfast in themselves, they are also steadfast toward one another; they neither request nor render any service that is base. On the contrary, one might even say that they prevent base services; for what characterizes good men is that they neither go wrong themselves nor let their friends do so. Bad people, on the other hand, do not have the element of constancy, for they do not remain similar even to themselves. But they do become friends for a short time, when they find joy in one another's wickedness. Friends who are useful and pleasant to one another stay together for a longer time, for as long as they continue to provide each other with pleasures or material advantages.

It is chiefly from opposite partners that friendship based on usefulness seems to come into being, for example, from the combination of poor and rich, or ignorant and learned. For a man aims at getting something he lacks, and gives something else in return for it. We might also bring lover and beloved, beautiful and ugly, under this heading [of the union of opposites]. That is why lovers occasionally appear ridiculous, when they expect to receive as much affection as they give. If they are similarly lovable, they are equally entitled to expect affection, but if they have nothing lovable about them, this is a ridiculous expectation.

But perhaps opposites do not aim at each other as such but only incidentally, and perhaps their desire is really for what is median, since that is a good. The dry, for example, does not desire to become wet, but to arrive at a middle state, and similarly with the hot and with all other opposing principles. But let us dismiss these questions, as they belong to another subject, [namely, physics].

9. *Friendship and justice in the state*

As we stated initially, it seems that friendship and the just deal with the same objects and involve the same persons. For there seems to be a notion of what is just in every community, and friendship seems to be involved as well. Men address as friends their fellow travelers on a voyage, their fellow soldiers, and similarly also those who are associated with them in other kinds of community. Friendship is present to the extent that men share something in common, for that is also the extent to which they share a view of what is just. And the proverb "friends hold in common what they have" is correct, for friendship consists in community. Brothers and bosom companions hold everything in common, while all others only hold certain definite things in common—some more and others less, since some friendships are more intense than others. Questions of what is just also differ [with different forms of friendship]. What is just is not the same for parents with regard to their children and for brothers with regard to one another, nor is it the same for bosom companions as for fellow citizens, and similarly in the other kinds of friendship. There is of course a corresponding difference in what is unjust in each of these relationships: the gravity of an unjust act increases in proportion as the person to whom it is done is a closer friend. It is, for example, more shocking to defraud a bosom companion of money than a fellow citizen, to refuse help to a brother than to refuse it to a stranger, or to strike one's father than to strike any other person. It is natural that the element of justice increases with [the closeness of] the friendship, since friendship and what is just exist in the same relationship and are coextensive in range. . . .

Book IX

1. *How to measure what friends owe to one another*

Wherever friendships are dissimilar in kind, it is proportion which, as we have stated, establishes equality between the partners and preserves the friendship. In a friendship between fellow citizens, for example, a shoemaker receives an equivalent recompense in exchange for his shoes, and the same is true of a weaver and of the other craftsmen. Now, in these cases money has been devised as a common measure, and, consequently, money is the standard to which everything is related and by which everything is measured. In the friendship between lovers, on the other hand, the lover sometimes complains that his most passionate affection is not returned, though it may quite well be that there is nothing lovable about him, while frequently the complaint of the beloved is that the lover, who first promised everything, now fulfills none of his promises. . . .

When no agreement has been made regarding the service to be rendered, there is, as we said, no complaint against a person who gives freely for his partner's sake, since a friendship based on excellence is free from complaints: recompense must be made in terms of the giver's purpose or choice, for in a friend and in virtue it is the purpose that matters. This, it seems, is also the way it should be when [teacher and student] have studied philosophy together. For money is not the standard by which the worth [of a teacher] can be measured, and no honor could match what he has given. Still, it is perhaps sufficient to make what return we can, just as we do in the case of the gods and our parents. . . .

5. *Friendship and good will*

Good will looks like a friendly relationship, but friendship it is not. For we can have good will toward people we do not know and the fact that we have it may remain unnoticed, but there can be no friendship in such circumstances. That has already been stated. But good will is not even affection: it lacks intensity and desire, the qualities which [always] accompany affection. Further, affection involves familiarity, whereas good will can arise on the spur of the moment, as it does, for example, toward competitors in a contest: a spectator may come to have good will for a competitor and side with him without giving him any active assistance. For, as we said, the good will comes on the spur of the moment and the love is superficial.

So it seems that good will is the beginning of friendship, just as the pleasure we get from seeing a person is the beginning of falling in love. For no one falls in love who has not first derived pleasure from the looks of the beloved. But if someone finds joy in the looks of another, he is not in love with him for all that: [he is in love only] if he longs for the beloved when he is away and craves his presence. . . .

8. *Self-love*

A further problem is whether a person should love himself or someone else most of all. People decry those who love themselves most, and use the term "egoist" in a pejorative sense. Only a base man, it is thought, does everything for his own sake, and the more wicked he is the more selfishly he acts. He is, therefore, criticized, for example, for never doing anything unless he is made to do it. A good man, on the other hand, is regarded as acting on noble motives, and the better he is the nobler his motives are: he acts for his friend's sake and neglects his own affairs.

However, the facts are not in harmony with these arguments, and that is not surprising. It is said that we should love our best friend best, and the best friend is he who, when he wishes for someone's good, does so for that person's sake even if no one will ever know it. Now, a man has this sentiment primarily toward himself, and the same is true of all the other sentiments by which a friend is defined. . . .

Now those who use "egoist" as a term of opprobrium apply it to people who assign to themselves the larger share of material goods, honors, and bodily pleasures. For these are the objects which most people desire, and which they zealously pursue as being supremely good, and for this reason, too, they fight to get them. Those, therefore, who try to get more than their share of these things, gratify their appetites, their emotions in general, and the irrational part of their souls, and most people are of this kind. Hence, the [pejorative] use of the term is derived from the fact that the most common form of self-love is base, and those who are egoists in this sense are justly criticized. That most people usually apply the word "egoist" to persons who assign to themselves the large share of things of this sort, is quite clear. If a man were always to devote his attention above all else to acting justly himself, to acting with self-control, or to fulfilling whatever other demands virtue makes upon him, and if, in general, he were always to try to secure for himself what is noble, no one would call him an egoist and no one would find fault with him.

However, it would seem that such a person is actually a truer egoist or self-lover. At any rate, he assigns what is supremely noble and good to himself, he gratifies the most sovereign part of himself, and he obeys it in everything. Just as a state and every other organized system seems to be in the truest sense identical with the most sovereign element in it, so it is with man. Consequently, he is an egoist or self-lover in the truest sense who loves and gratifies the most sovereign element in him. Moreover, when we call a person "morally strong" or "morally weak," depending on whether or not his intelligence is the ruling element [within him], we imply that intelligence is the individual. And also, we regard a man as being an independent and voluntary agent in the truest sense when he has acted rationally. Thus it is clear that a man is—or is in the truest sense—the ruling element within him, and that a good man loves this more than anything else. Hence, it is he who is in the truest sense an egoist or self-lover. His self-love is different in kind from that of the egoist with whom people find fault: as different, in fact, as living by the guidance of reason is from living by the dictates of emotion, and as different as desiring what is noble is from desiring what seems to be advantageous. Those, then, whose active devotion to noble actions is outstanding win the recognition and praise of all; and if all men were to compete for what is noble and put all their efforts into the performance of the noblest actions, all the needs of the community will have been met, and each individual will have the greatest of goods, since that is what virtue is.

Therefore, a good man should be a self-lover, for he will himself profit by performing noble actions and will benefit his fellow men. But a wicked man should not love himself, since he will harm both himself and his neighbors in following his base emotions. What a wicked man does is not in harmony with what he ought to do, whereas a good man does what he ought to do. For intelligence always chooses what is best for itself, and a good man obeys his intelligence. . . .

9. *Friendship and happiness*

A further problem is whether or not a happy man will need friends. It is said that supremely happy and self-sufficient people do not need friends, since they already have the good things of life. Therefore, [it is argued,] since they are self-sufficient, they have no need of anything further; [we need] a friend, who is another self, only to provide what we are unable to provide by ourselves; hence the verse: "When fortune smiles, what need is there of friends?" However, it seems strange that we should assign all good things to a happy man without attributing friends to him, who are thought to be the greatest of external goods. Also, if the function of a friend is to do good rather than to be treated well, if the performance of good deeds is the mark of a good man and of excellence, and if it is nobler to do good to a friend than to a stranger, then a man of high moral standards will need people to whom he can do good. This raises the further question whether we need friends more in good or in bad fortune, and by raising it we imply that in misfortune a man needs someone who will do good to him, and in good fortune he will need someone to whom he may do good.

It is perhaps also strange to make a supremely happy man live his life in isolation. No one would choose to have all good things all by himself, for man is a social and political being and his natural condition is to live with others. Consequently, even a happy man needs society. . . .

10. *How many friends should we have?*

Ought we to make as many friends as possible? Or will the *mot juste* about hospitality, "not too many guests, nor yet none," also fit friendship in the sense that a person should neither be friendless nor have an excessive number of friends? The saying would seem to fit exactly those who become friends with a view to their [mutual] usefulness. To accommodate many people in return for what they have done to us is troublesome, and life is not long enough to do that. Accordingly, more friends than are sufficient for one's own life are superfluous and are an obstacle to the good life, so that there is no need of them. To give us pleasure a few friends are sufficient, just as it takes little to give food the right amount of sweetness.

But, as regards morally good men, should we have as many in number as possible as our friends? Or is there some limit to the number of friendly relations a person can have, just as there is a limit to the size of a city-state? Ten persons do not make a city-state, and when there are a hundred thousand, it is no longer a city-state. . . .

Those who have many friends and are on familiar terms with any chance acquaintance are thought to be friends to none, except in the sense in which there is friendship among fellow citizens. They are also called "obsequious." Now, in the kind of friendship that exists among fellow citizens, it is actually possible to be friends with many people without being obsequious and while remaining a truly good man. But to be a friend of many people is impossible, if the friendship is to be based on virtue or excellence and on the character of our friends. We must be content if we find even a few friends of this kind.

11. *Friendship in good and in bad fortune*

Is the need of friends greater in good fortune or in bad? Men seek them in both: in bad fortune they need their assistance, and in good fortune they need people with whom to live together and to whom they will be able to do good, since men wish to be beneficent. Accordingly, friends are more indispensable in bad fortune; and that is why the useful kind of friend is needed in such situations. But it is nobler to have friends in good fortune, and for that reason people look for good men [as their friends when they are well off], because it is more desirable to do good to them and to spend one's time with them. . . .

12. *Friends must live together*

What lovers love most is to see one another, and they prefer sight to all the other senses, because love exists and is generated by sight more than by any other sense. Is it, similarly, true of friends that the most desirable thing for them is to live together? [Apparently, yes,] for friendship is an association or community, and a person has the same attitude toward his friend as he has toward himself. Now, since a man's perception that he exists is desirable, his perception of his friend's existence is desirable, too. But only by living together can the perception of a friend's existence be activated, so that it stands to reason that friends aim at living together. And whatever his existence means to each partner individually or whatever is the purpose that makes his life desirable, he wishes to pursue it together with his friends. That is why some friends drink together or play dice together, while others go in for sports together and hunt together, or join in the study of philosophy: whatever each group of people loves most in life, in that activity they spend their days together. For since they wish to live together with their friends, they follow and share in those pursuits which, they think, constitute their life together. . . .

Book X

6. *Happiness and activity*

Now that we have completed our discussion of the virtues, and of the different kinds of friendship and pleasure, it remains to sketch an outline of happiness, since, as we assert, it is the end or goal of human [aspirations]. Our account will be more concise if we recapitulate what we have said so far.

We stated, then, that happiness is not a characteristic; [if it were,] a person who passes his whole life in sleep, vegetating like a plant, or someone who experiences the greatest misfortunes could possess it. If, then, such a conclusion is unacceptable, we must, in accordance with our earlier discussion, classify happiness as some sort of activity. Now, some activities are necessary and desirable only for the sake of something else, while others are desirable in themselves. Obviously, happiness must be classed as an activity desirable in itself and not for the sake of something else. For happiness lacks nothing and is self-sufficient. Activities desirable in themselves are those from which we seek to derive nothing beyond the actual exercise of the activity. Actions in conformity with virtue evidently constitute such activities; for to perform noble and good deeds is something desirable for its own sake.

Pleasant amusements, too, [are desirable for their own sake]. We do not choose them for the sake of something else, since they lead to harm rather than good when we become neglectful of our bodies and our property. But most of those who are considered happy find an escape in pastimes of this sort, and this is why people who are well versed in such pastimes find favor at the courts of tyrants; they make themselves pleasant by providing what the tyrants are after, and what they want is amusement. Accordingly, such amusements are regarded as being conducive to happiness, because men who are in positions of power devote their leisure to them. But perhaps such persons cannot be [regarded as] evidence. For virtue and intelligence, which are the sources of morally good activities, do not consist in wielding power. Also, if these men, who have never tasted pure and generous pleasure, find an escape in the pleasures of the body, this is no sufficient reason for thinking that such pleasures are in fact more desirable. For children, too, think that what they value is actually the best. It is, therefore, not surprising that as children apparently do not attach value to the same things as do adults, so bad men do not attach value to the same things as do good men. Accordingly, as we have stated repeatedly, what is valuable and pleasant to a morally good man actually is valuable and pleasant. Each individual considers that activity most desirable which corresponds to his own proper characteristic condition, and a morally good man, of course, so considers activity in conformity with virtue.

Consequently, happiness does not consist in amusement. In fact, it would be strange if our end were amusement, and if we were to labor and suffer hardships all our life long merely to amuse ourselves. For, one might say, we choose everything for the sake of something else—except happiness; for happiness is an end. Obviously, it is foolish and all too childish to exert serious efforts and toil for purposes of amusement. Anacharsis seems to be right when he advises to play in order to be serious; for amusement is a form of rest, and since we cannot work continuously we need rest. Thus rest is not an end, for we take it for the sake of [further] activity. The happy life is regarded as a life in conformity with virtue. It is a life which involves effort and is not spent in amusement. . . .

7. Happiness, intelligence, and the contemplative life

Now, if happiness is activity in conformity with virtue, it is to be expected that it should conform with the highest virtue, and that is the virtue of the best part of us. Whether this is intelligence or something else which, it is thought, by its very nature rules and guides us and which gives us our notions of what is noble and divine; whether it is itself divine or the most divine thing in us; it is the activity of this part [when operating] in conformity with the excellence or virtue proper to it that will be complete happiness. That it is an activity concerned with theoretical knowledge or contemplation has already been stated.

This would seem to be consistent with our earlier statements as well as the truth. For this activity is not only the highest—for intelligence is the highest possession we have in us, and the objects which are the concern of intelligence are the highest objects of knowledge—but also the most continuous: we are able to study continuously more easily than to perform any kind of action. Furthermore, we think of pleasure as a necessary ingredient in happiness. Now everyone agrees that of all the activities that conform with virtue activity in conformity with theoretical wisdom is the most pleasant. At any rate, it seems that [the pursuit of wisdom or] philosophy holds pleasures marvellous in purity and certainty, and it is not surprising that time spent in knowledge is more pleasant than time spent in research. Moreover, what is usually called "self-sufficiency" will be found in the highest degree in the activity which is concerned with theoretical knowledge. Like a just man and any other virtuous man, a wise man requires the necessities of life; once these have been adequately provided, a just man still needs people toward whom and in company with whom to act justly, and the same is true of a self-controlled man, a courageous man, and all the rest. But a wise man is able to study even by himself, and the wiser he is the more is he able to do it. Perhaps he could do it better if he had colleagues to work with him, but he still is the most self-sufficient of all. Again, study seems to be the only activity which is loved for its own sake. For while we derive a greater or a smaller advantage from practical pursuits beyond the action itself, from study we derive nothing beyond the activity of studying. Also, we regard happiness as depending on leisure; for our purpose in being busy is to have leisure, and we wage war in order to have peace. Now, the practical virtues are activated in political and military pursuits, but the actions involved in these pursuits seem to be unleisurely. This is completely true of military pursuits, since no one chooses to wage war or foments war for the sake of war; he would have to be utterly bloodthirsty if he were to make enemies of his friends simply in order to have battle and slaughter. But the activity of the statesman, too, has no leisure. It attempts to gain advantages beyond political action, advantages such as political power, prestige, or at least happiness for the statesman himself and his fellow citizens, and that is something other than political activity: after all, the very fact that we investigate politics shows that it is not the same [as happiness]. Therefore, if we take as established (1) that political and military actions surpass all other actions that conform with virtue in nobility and grandeur; (2) that they are unleisurely, aim at an end, and are not chosen for their own sake; (3) that the activity of our intelligence, inasmuch as it is an activity concerned with theoretical knowledge, is thought to be of greater value than the others, aims at no end beyond itself, and has a pleasure proper to itself—and pleasure increases activity; and (4) that the qualities of this activity evidently are self-sufficiency, leisure, as much freedom from fatigue as a human being can have, and whatever else falls to the lot of a supremely happy man; it follows that the activity of our intelligence constitutes the complete happiness of man, provided that it encompasses a complete span of life; for nothing connected with happiness must be incomplete.

However, such a life would be more than human. A man who would live it would do so not insofar as he is human, but because there is a divine element within him. This divine element is as far above our composite nature as its activity is above the active exercise of the other, [i.e., practical,] kind of virtue. So if it is true that intelligence is divine in comparison with man, then a life guided by intelligence is divine in comparison with human life. We must not follow those who advise us to have human thoughts, since we are [only] men, and mortal thoughts, as mortals should; on the contrary, we should try to become immortal as far as that is possible and do our utmost to live in accordance with what is highest in us. For though this is a small portion [of our nature] it far surpasses everything else in power and value. One might even regard it as each man's true self, since it is the controlling and better part. It would, therefore, be strange if a man chose not to live his own life but someone else's.

Moreover, what we stated before will apply here, too: what is by nature proper to each thing will be at once the best and the most pleasant for it. In other words, a life guided by intelligence is the best and most pleasant for man, inasmuch as intelligence, above all else, is man. Consequently, this kind of life is the happiest.

8. *The advantages of the contemplative life*

A life guided by the other kind of virtue, [the practical,] is happy in a secondary sense, since its active exercise is confined to man. It is in our dealings with one another that we perform just, courageous, and other virtuous acts, when we observe the proper kind of behavior toward each man in private transactions, in meeting his needs, in all manner of actions, and in our emotions, and all of these are, as we see, peculiarly human. Moreover, some moral acts seem to be determined by our bodily condition, and virtue or excellence of character seems in many ways closely related to the emotions. There is also a close mutual connection between practical wisdom and excellence of character, since the fundamental principles of practical wisdom are determined by the virtues of character, while practical wisdom determines the right standard for the moral virtues. The fact that these virtues are also bound up with the emotions indicates that they belong to our composite nature, and the virtues of our composite nature are human virtues; consequently, a life guided by these virtues and the happiness [that goes with it are likewise human]. The happiness of the intelligence, however, is quite separate [from that kind of happiness]. That is all we shall say about it here, for a more detailed treatment lies beyond the scope of our present task.

It also seems that such happiness has little need of external trimmings, or less need than moral virtue has. Even if we grant that both stand in equal need of the necessities of life, and even if the labors of a statesman are more concerned with the needs of our body and things of that sort—in that respect the difference between them may be small—yet, in what they need for the exercise of their activities, their difference will be great. A generous man will need money to perform generous acts, and a just man will need it to meet his obligations. For the mere wish to perform such acts is inscrutable, and even an unjust man can pretend that he wishes to act justly. And a courageous man will need strength if he is to accomplish an act that conforms with his virtue, and a man of self-control the possibility of indulgence. How else can he or any other virtuous man make manifest his excellence? Also, it is debatable whether the moral purpose or the action is the more decisive element in virtue, since virtue depends on both. It is clear of course that completeness depends on both. But many things are needed for the performance of actions, and the greater and nobler the actions the more is needed. But a man engaged in study has no need of any of these things, at least not for the active exercise of studying; in fact one might even go so far as to say that they are a hindrance to study. But insofar as he is human and lives in the society of his fellow men, he chooses to act as virtue demands, and accordingly, he will need externals for living as a human being.

A further indication that complete happiness consists in some kind of contemplative activity is this. We assume that the gods are in the highest degree blessed and happy. But what kind of actions are we to attribute to them? Acts of justice? Will they not look ridiculous making contracts with one another, returning deposits, and so forth? Perhaps acts of courage—withstanding terror and taking risks, because it is noble to do so? Or generous actions? But to whom will they give? It would be strange to think that they actually have currency or something of the sort. Acts of self-control? What would they be? Surely, it would be in poor taste to praise them for not having bad appetites. If we went through the whole list we would see that a concern with actions is petty and unworthy of the gods. Nevertheless, we all assume that the gods exist and, consequently, that they are active; for surely we do not assume them to be always asleep like Endymion. Now, if we take away action from a living being, to say nothing of production, what is left except contemplation? Therefore, the activity of the divinity which surpasses all others in bliss must be a contemplative activity, and the human activity which is most closely akin to it is, therefore, most conducive to happiness.

This is further shown by the fact that no other living being has a share in happiness, since they all are completely denied this kind of activity. The gods enjoy a life blessed in its entirety; men enjoy it to the extent that they attain something resembling the divine activity; but none of the other living beings can be happy, because they have no share at all in contemplation or study. So happiness is coextensive with study, and the greater the opportunity for studying, the greater the happiness, not as an incidental effect but as inherent in study; for study is in itself worthy of honor. Consequently, happiness is some kind of study or contemplation.

But we shall also need external well-being, since we are only human. Our nature is not self-sufficient for engaging in study: our body must be healthy and we must have food and generally be cared for. Nevertheless, if it is not possible for a man to be supremely happy without external goods, we must not think that his needs will be great and many in order to be happy; for self-sufficiency and moral action do not consist in an excess [of possessions]. It is possible to perform noble actions even without being ruler of land and sea; a man's actions can be guided by virtue also if his means are moderate. That this is so can be clearly seen in the fact that private individuals evidently do not act less honorably but even more honorably than powerful rulers. It is enough to have moderate means at one's disposal, for the life of a man whose activity is guided, by virtue will be happy. . . .

A man whose activity is guided by intelligence, who cultivates his intelligence and keeps it in the best condition, seems to be most beloved by the gods. For if the gods have any concern for human affairs—and they seem to have—it is to be expected that they rejoice in what is best and most akin to them, and that is our intelligence; it is also to be expected that they requite with good those who most love and honor intelligence, as being men who care for what is dear to the gods and who act rightly and nobly. That a wise man, more than any other, has all these qualities is perfectly clear. Consequently, he is the most beloved by the gods, and as such he is, presumably, also the happiest. Therefore, we have here a further indication that a wise man attains a higher degree of happiness than anyone. . . .

———

Study Questions

1. In defining happiness, Aristotle refers to "the proper function" of a human being. (I.7) What does he mean by our "proper function"? Is it plausible to think that human beings have a "function"?

2. What does Aristotle mean when he defines happiness as "an activity of the soul in conformity with excellence or virtue"? (I.7) Does this conception of happiness differ from contemporary beliefs and ideas? If so, how? Do you find it plausible?
3. What does Aristotle mean by a "virtue"? How does he think that virtues are acquired? Is his account of how a virtue is acquired plausible or implausible?
4. What is the difference between "moral virtue" and "intellectual virtue"? (II.1)
5. What does Aristotle mean when he says that moral excellence or virtue "has to do with pleasure and pain"? (II.3)
6. What does Aristotle have in mind when he says that virtue "consists in observing the mean relative to us . . . defined by a rational principle . . ."? (II.6) How is his doctrine of the mean illustrated in his examples? Do you accept his picture of the virtuous person? Why or why not?
7. Aristotle distinguishes three different kinds of friendship. What are they, and what are the main differences between them? (VIII.3–4) Does his classification of the different kinds of friendship fit your experience, and do you agree with his views about "perfect" or "true" friendship?
8. What does Aristotle mean by "true self-love"? (IX.8)

Selected Bibliography

All of the items listed are commentaries on Aristotle's ethics.

Broadie, S. *Ethics with Aristotle* (New York: Oxford University Press, 1993).

Cooper, J. M. *Reason and Human Good in Aristotle* (Cambridge: Harvard University Press, 1975), esp. Chap. 3.

Hardie, W. F. R. *Aristotle's Ethical Theory* (Oxford: Clarendon Press, 1968).

Kraut, R. *Aristotle on the Human Good* (Princeton: Princeton University Press, 1989).

Rorty, A. E., ed. *Essays on Aristotle's Ethics* (Berkeley: University of California Press, 1980).

Ross, W. D. *Aristotle* (London: Methuen, 1923), Chap. 7.

Sherman, Nancy, ed. *Aristotle's Ethics: Critical Essays* (Lanham, Md.: Rowman & Littlefield Publishers, 1999). Anthology of recent essays.

Urmson, J. O. *Aristotle's Ethics* (Oxford: Basil Blackwell, 1988).

Walsh, J. J., and H. L. Shapiro, eds. *Aristotle's Ethics* (Belmont: Wadsworth, 1967).

4

EPICURUS

Epicurus (c. 341–270 B.C.) was born on the island of Samos, off the coast of Asia Minor. While still a youth, he

> . . . we call pleasure the beginning and end of the blessed life.

moved to Athens, where he established a school of philosophy, the famous Garden of Epicurus. There he and his students lived, worked, and studied together in a quiet retreat secluded from the society that surrounded them. Epicurus derived his general philosophical theory, atomistic materialism, from the work of a great thinker of the fifth century, Democritus. According to this theory, the universe is composed of matter (in the form of atoms) in motion in empty space. All physical bodies, including human beings, are the result of combinations of these atoms. Because the soul, like everything else, is composed of atoms, death means its dissolution, so immortality is impossible. Since we have only this life to live, we should, Epicurus therefore argued, make it as pleasant as possible. Epicurus's theory, that pleasure is the only good in life, is known as *hedonism* (from the Greek word for pleasure). The hedonistic ideal, as Epicurus actually worked it out in practice, however, was quite unlike the style of life that we now label *epicurean*. For Epicurus's conception of the good life was mainly negative, stressing the avoidance of pain rather than the pursuit of pleasure. Just as he attempted to escape from the social and political turmoil of his times by retreating behind the walls of his garden, so he endeavored to escape the vicissitudes of life through a theory that, although based on pleasure, in practice became a doctrine of renunciation.

Epicurus was a *psychological* as well as an *ethical* hedonist. He believed not only that we *ought* always to act in such a way as to produce the greatest amount of pleasure (ethical hedonism), but also that we are so constituted psychologically that we inevitably *do* pursue pleasure in all our acts (psychological hedonism). Here a problem arises: If we necessarily seek pleasure in everything we do, what is added by saying that we *ought* to do so?

Epicurus was a prolific writer, but most of his writings have been lost to time. Of the few that remain, the letter to his follower Menoeceus gives the best statement of his views regarding the good life. The ethic of hedonism has had a long history through the ages. In the modern world it has received its most influential statement in the works of two British philosophers and social reformers of the nineteenth century, Jeremy Bentham and John Stuart Mill, whose form of the hedonistic doctrine has come to be known as *utilitarianism*.

———

Epicurus to Menoeceus

Let no one when young delay to study philosophy, nor when he is old grow weary of his study. For no one can come too early or too late to secure the health of his soul. And the man who says that the age of philosophy has either not yet come or has gone by is like the man who says that the age for happiness is not yet come to him, or has passed away. Wherefore both when young and old a man must study philosophy, that as he grows old he may be young in blessings through the grateful recollection of what has been, and that in youth he may be old as well, since he will know no fear of what is to come. We must then meditate on the things that make our happiness, seeing that when that is with us, we have all, but when it is absent, we do all to win it.

The things which I used unceasingly to commend to you, these do and practice, considering them to be the first principles of the good life. First of all, believe that god is a being immortal and blessed, even as the common idea of a god is engraved on men's minds, and do not assign to him anything alien to his immortality or ill-suited to his blessedness; but believe about him everything that can uphold his blessedness and immortality. For gods there are, since the knowledge of them is by clear vision. But they are not such as the many believe them to be: for indeed, they do not consistently represent them as they believe them to be. And the impious man is not he who denies the gods of the many, but he who attaches to the gods the beliefs of the many. For the statements of the many about the gods are not conceptions derived from sensation, but false suppositions, according to which the greatest misfortunes befall the wicked and the greatest blessings the good by the gift of the gods. For men being accustomed always to their own virtues welcome those like themselves, but regard all that is not of their nature as alien.

Become accustomed to the belief that death is nothing to us. For all good and evil consists in sensation, but death is deprivation of sensation. And, therefore, a right understanding that death is nothing to us makes the mortality of life enjoyable, not because it adds to it an infinite span of time, but because it takes away the craving for immortality. For there is nothing terrible in life for the man who has truly comprehended that there is nothing terrible in not living. So that the man speaks but idly who says that he fears death not because it will be painful when it comes, but because it is painful in anticipation. For that which gives no trouble when it comes is but an empty pain in anticipation. So death, the most terrifying of

Epicurus, "Epicurus to Menoeceus" in *The Extant Remains*, translated by C. Bailey. Reprinted by permission of the Oxford University Press.

ills, is nothing to us, since so long as we exist, death is not with us; but when death comes, then we do not exist. It does not then concern either the living or the dead, since for the former it is not, and the latter are no more.

But the many at one moment shun death as the greatest of evils, at another yearn for it as a respite from the evils in life. But the wise man neither seeks to escape life nor fears the cessation of life, for neither does life offend him nor does the absence of life seem to be any evil. And just as with food he does not seek simply the larger share and nothing else, but rather the most pleasant, so he seeks to enjoy not the longest period of time, but the most pleasant.

And he who counsels the young man to live well, but the old man to make a good end, is foolish, not merely because of the desirability of life, but also because it is the same training which teaches to live well and die well. Yet much worse still is the man who says it is good not to be born, but "once born make haste to pass the gates of Death." For if he says this from conviction, why does he not pass away out of life? For it is open to him to do so, if he had firmly made up his mind to this. But if he speaks in jest, his words are idle among men who cannot receive them.

We must then bear in mind that the future is neither ours, nor yet wholly not ours, so that we may not altogether expect it as sure to come, nor abandon hope of it, as if it will certainly not come.

We must consider that of desires some are natural, others vain, and of the natural some are necessary and others merely natural; and of the necessary some are necessary for happiness, others for the repose of the body, and others for very life. The right understanding of these facts enables us to refer all choice and avoidance to the health of the body and the soul's freedom from disturbance, since this is the aim of the life of blessedness. For it is to obtain this end that we always act, namely, to avoid pain and fear. And when this is once secured for us, all the tempest of the soul is dispersed, since the living creature has not to wander as though in search of something that is missing, and to look for some other thing by which he can fulfill the good of the soul and the good of the body. For it is then that we have need of pleasure, when we feel pain owing to the absence of pleasure; but when we do not feel pain, we no longer need pleasure. And for this cause we call pleasure the beginning and end of the blessed life. For we recognize pleasure as the first good innate in us, and from pleasure we begin every act of choice and avoidance, and to pleasure we return again, using the feeling as the standard by which we judge every good.

And since pleasure is the first good and natural to us, for this very reason we do not choose every pleasure, but sometimes we pass over many pleasures, when greater discomfort accrues to us as the result of them; and similarly we think many pains are better than pleasures, since a greater pleasure comes to us when we have endured pains for a long time. Every pleasure, then, because of its natural kinship to us is good, yet not every pleasure is to be chosen: even as every pain also is an evil, yet not all are always of a nature to be avoided. Yet by a scale of comparison and by the consideration of advantages and disadvantages we must form our judgment on all these matters. For the good on certain occasions we treat as bad, and conversely the bad as good.

And again independence of desire we think a great good—not that we may at all times enjoy but a few things, but that, if we do not possess many, we may enjoy the few in the genuine persuasion that those have the sweetest pleasure in luxury who least need it, and that all that is natural is easy to be obtained, but that which is superfluous is hard. And so plain savours bring us a pleasure equal to a luxurious diet, when all the pain due to want is removed; and bread and water produce the highest pleasure, when one who needs them puts them to his lips. To grow accustomed, therefore, to simple and not luxurious diet gives us health to the full, and makes a man alert for the needful employments of life, and when after long intervals we approach luxuries disposes us better towards them, and fits us to be fearless of fortune.

When, therefore, we maintain that pleasure is the end, we do not mean the pleasures of profligates and those that consist in sensuality, as is supposed by some who are either ignorant or disagree with us or do not understand, but freedom from pain in the body and from trouble in the mind. For it is not continuous drinkings and revellings, nor the satisfaction of lusts, nor the enjoyment of fish and other luxuries of the wealthy table, which produce a pleasant life, but sober reasoning, searching out the motives for all choice and avoidance, and banishing mere opinions, to which are due the greatest disturbance of the spirit.

Of all this the beginning and the greatest good is prudence. Wherefore prudence is a more precious thing even than philosophy: for from prudence are sprung all the other virtues, and it teaches us that it is not possible to live pleasantly without living prudently and honourably and justly, nor, again, to live a life of prudence, honour, and justice without living pleasantly. For the virtues are by nature bound up with the pleasant life, and the pleasant life is inseparable from them. For indeed who, think you, is a better man than he who holds reverent opinions concerning the gods, and is at all times free from fear of death, and has reasoned out the end ordained by nature? He understands that the limit of good things is easy to fulfil and easy to attain, whereas the course of ills is either short in time or slight in pain: he laughs at destiny, whom some have introduced as the mistress of all things. He thinks that with us lies the chief power in determining events, some of which happen by necessity and some by chance, and some are within our control; for while necessity cannot be called to account, he sees that chance is inconstant, but that which is in our control is subject to no master, and to it are naturally attached praise and blame. For indeed, it was better to follow the myths about the gods than to become a slave to the destiny of the natural philosophers: for the former suggests a hope of placating the gods by worship, whereas the latter involves a necessity which knows no placation. As to chance, he does not regard it as a god as most men do (for in a god's acts there is no disorder), nor as an uncertain cause of all things: for he does not believe that good and evil are given by chance to man for the framing of a blessed life, but that opportunities for great good and great evil are afforded by it. He therefore thinks it better to be unfortunate in reasonable action than to prosper in unreason. For it is better in a man's actions that what is well chosen should fail, rather than that what is ill chosen should be successful owing to chance.

Meditate therefore on these things and things akin to them night and day by yourself, and with a companion like to yourself, and never shall you be disturbed waking or asleep, but you shall live like a god among men. For a man who lives among immortal blessings is not like to a mortal being.

———

Study Questions

1. "Death," said Epicurus, "is nothing to us." How does he defend this view? Do you consider his argument persuasive?
2. If you agreed with Epicurus that pleasure is the only good, would you also agree with the lifestyle he recommends in his letter?
3. According to Epicurus, the most pleasant life is that of the philosopher. Why did he say this? Do you think he is right? Would you like to live in his "garden"?
4. Epicurus's predecessor, Democritus, committed suicide in his old age. Do you think such an action is rational? Morally acceptable? Can it be one and not the other?

Selected Bibliography

Annas, Julia. "Epicurus on Pleasure and Happiness," *Philosophical Topics* 15 (1987): 5–21. Account of Epicurus's eudaimonism.

Bailey, C. *The Greek Atomists and Epicurus* (Oxford: Clarendon Press, 1928), Part 2, Chap. 10. General commentary.

Epicurus. *The Extant Remains*, tr. C. Bailey (Oxford: Clarendon Press, 1926), Chaps. 1–5. Translation and commentary on Epicurus' extant writings.

Long, A. A. *Hellenistic Philosophy: Stoics, Epicureans and Sceptics*, 2nd edition (Berkeley: University of California Press, 1987). Contains a general introduction to Epicureanism.

Mitsis, P. *Epicurus' Ethical Theory: The Pleasures of Invulnerability* (Ithaca, N.Y.: Cornell University Press, 1988). An analysis of Epicurean ethics.

Rist, J. M. *Epicurus* (Cambridge: Cambridge University Press, 1972), Chap. 6. Commentary on Epicurus' ethics.

5

EPICTETUS

———

Stoic is a word that most of us probably have used but which few of us could really define. This fact is not necessarily to be deplored, however, because it gives evidence of the extent to which the Stoic view of life has permeated our intellectual tradition. The history of

> *Do not seek to have everything that happens happen as you wish, but wish for everything to happen as it actually does happen, and your life will be serene.*

Stoicism is long, going back to a Greek philosopher named Zeno who lived in the third century B.C. In the following century, as the result of an unusual reciprocal conquest—of Greece by Roman arms and of Rome by Greek ideas—Stoicism was taken to Rome, where it later developed into the leading philosophy of the city. It reached its greatest popularity in the early period of the Empire, during the first and second centuries A.D., when it included among its followers such prominent Romans as Seneca (4 B.C.–A.D. 65), the dramatist and political adviser of the notorious emperor Nero, and the great Roman emperor Marcus Aurelius (A.D. 121–A.D. 180).

Epictetus, the most influential of all the Stoic philosophers (with the possible exception of Marcus Aurelius), was born in Asia Minor about the middle of the first century A.D., the exact date being unknown. He was sold into slavery as a child and became a member of the household of one Epaphroditus, an officer in Nero's imperial guard. Because of his unusual intellectual abilities he was given an education. Later, after having been freed from slavery, he became a teacher of philosophy, first in Rome and then in Epirus, on the Greek mainland. He died early in the second century. Epictetus's interests in philosophy were limited almost exclusively to the field of ethics. His basic ethical teachings are summarized in *The Encheiridion,* or *Manual.* Judging from its style and content, this short treatise was intended to be an instruction booklet for young people who aspired to become Stoic philosophers. *The Encheiridion* was not actually written by Epictetus (who wrote nothing) but was edited from lecture notes taken by one of his students, a fact that helps to account for some of the oddities of its organization and argu-

Reprinted from Epictetus, *The Discourses,* Vol. II, translated by W. A. Oldfather, Cambridge, Mass.: Harvard University Press, by permissions of the publishers and The Loeb Classical Library.

ment. The Stoic philosophers made an incalculable contribution to civilization by their *cosmopolitanism,* the idea that no matter when or where we may live, we are all "citizens of one city."

As a philosophy of rigid austerity and self-denial, Stoicism has traditionally been contrasted with Epicureanism, the philosophy of pleasure. Epictetus himself rejected the pursuit of pleasure, advocating a way of life that he believed to be the opposite of that followed by the Epicureans. Nevertheless, one who compares *The Encheiridion* with Epicurus's *Letter to Menoeceus* cannot help but be struck by the fact that, although the theoretical assumptions of the two men diverge on several points, their ideals of human conduct are in many respects remarkably alike. Epictetus's moral philosophy can also be compared with another type of morality, which was beginning to spread across the Mediterranean during his lifetime— Christianity. Not only are several of the passages in *The Encheiridion* verbally similar to parts of the New Testament, but the nature of the treatise itself, as a series of practical precepts, resembles closely the teachings of Jesus as recorded in the Gospels. These similarities provide evidence for a view that has gained wide acceptance among historians and theologians, that the early Christian writers were influenced in their beliefs by Stoic philosophy.

———

The Encheiridion

1. Some things are under our control, while others are not under our control. Under our control are conception, choice, desire, aversion, and, in a word, everything that is our own doing; not under our control are our body, our property, reputation, office, and, in a word, everything that is not our own doing. Furthermore, the things under our control are by nature free, unhindered, and unimpeded; while the things not under our control are weak, servile, subject to hindrance, and not our own. Remember, therefore, that if what is naturally slavish you think to be free, and what is not your own to be your own, you will be hampered, will grieve, will be in turmoil, and will blame both gods and men; while if you think only what is your own to be your own, and what is not your own to be, as it really is, not your own, then no one will ever be able to exert compulsion upon you, no one will hinder you, you will blame no one, will find fault with no one, will do absolutely nothing against your will, you will have no personal enemy, no one will harm you, for neither is there any harm that can touch you.

With such high aims, therefore, remember that you must bestir yourself with no slight effort to lay hold of them, but you will have to give up some things entirely, and defer others for the time being. But if you wish for these things also, and at the same time for both office and wealth, it may be that you will not get even these latter, because you aim also at the former, and certainly you will fail to get the former, which alone bring freedom and happiness.

Make it, therefore, your study at the very outset to say to every harsh external impression, "You are an external impression and not at all what you appear to be." After that examine it and test it by these rules which you have, the first and most important of which is this: Whether the impression has to do with the things which are under our control, or with those which are not under our control; and, if it has to do with some one of the things not under our control, have ready to hand the answer, "It is nothing to me."

2. Remember that the promise of desire is the attainment of what you desire, that of aversion is not to fall into what is avoided, and that he who fails in his desire is unfortunate, while he who falls into what he would avoid experiences misfortune. If, then, you avoid only what is unnatural among those things which are under your control, you will fall into none of the things which you avoid; but if you try to avoid disease, or death, or poverty, you will experience misfortune. Withdraw, therefore, your aversion from all the matters that are not under our control, and transfer it to what is unnatural among those which are under our control. But for the time being remove utterly your desire; for if you desire some one of the things that are not under our control, you are bound to be unfortunate; and, at the same time, not one of the things that are under our control, which it would be excellent for you to desire, is within your grasp. But employ only choice and refusal, and these too but lightly, and with reservations, and without straining.

3. With everything which entertains you, is useful, or of which you are fond, remember to say to yourself, beginning with the very least things, "What is its nature?" If you are fond of a jug, say, "I am fond of a jug;" for when it is broken, you will not be disturbed. If you kiss your own child or wife, say to yourself that you are kissing a human being; for when it dies, you will not be disturbed.

4. When you are on the point of putting your hand to some undertaking, remind yourself what the nature of that undertaking is. If you are going out of the house to bathe, put before your mind what happens at a public bath—those who splash you with water, those who jostle against you, those who vilify you and rob you. And thus you will set about your undertaking more securely if at the outset you say to yourself, "I want to take a bath, and, at the same time, to keep my moral purpose in harmony with nature." And so do in every undertaking. For thus, if anything happens to hinder you in your bathing, you will be ready to say, "Oh, well, this was not the only thing that I wanted, but I wanted also to keep my moral purpose in harmony with nature; and I shall not so keep it if I am vexed at what is going on."

5. It is not the things themselves that disturb men, but their judgments about these things. For example, death is nothing dreadful, or else Socrates, too would have thought so, but the judgment that death is dreadful, *this* is the dreadful thing. When, therefore, we are hindered, or disturbed, or grieved, let us never blame anyone but ourselves, that means, our own judgments. It is the part of an uneducated person to blame others where he himself fares ill; to blame himself is the part of one whose education has begun; to blame neither another nor his own self is the part of one whose education is already complete.

6. Be not elated at any excellence which is not your own. If the horse in his elation were to say, "I am beautiful," it could be endured; but when you say in your elation, "I have a beautiful horse," rest assured that you are elated at some-

thing good which belongs to a horse. What, then, is your own? The use of external impressions. Therefore, when you are in harmony with nature in the use of external impressions, then be elated; for then it will be some good of your own at which you will be elated.

7. Just as on a voyage, when your ship has anchored, if you should go on shore to get fresh water, you may pick up a small shellfish or little bulb on the way, but you have to keep your attention fixed on the ship, and turn about frequently for fear lest the captain should call; and if he calls, you must give up all these things, if you would escape being thrown on board all tied up like the sheep. So it is also in life: If there be given you, instead of a little bulb and a small shellfish, a little wife and child, there will be no objection to that; only, if the captain calls, give up all these things and run to the ship, without even turning around to look back. And if you are an old man, never even get very far away from the ship, for fear that when he calls you may be missing.

8. Do not seek to have everything that happens happen as you wish, but wish for everything to happen as it actually does happen, and your life will be serene.

9. Disease is an impediment to the body, but not to the moral purpose, unless that consents. Lameness is an impediment to the leg, but not to the moral purpose. And say this to yourself at each thing that befalls you; for you will find the thing to be an impediment to something else, but not to yourself.

10. In the case of everything that befalls you, remember to turn to yourself and see what faculty you have to deal with it. If you see a handsome lad or woman, you will find continence the faculty to employ here; if hard labour is laid upon you, you will find endurance; if reviling, you will find patience to bear evil. And if you habituate yourself in this fashion, your external impressions will not run away with you.

11. Never say about anything, "I have lost it," but only "I have given it back." Is your child dead? It has been given back. Is your wife dead? She has been given back. "I have had my farm taken away." Very well, this too has been given back. "Yet it was a rascal who took it away." But what concern is it of yours by whose instrumentality the Giver called for its return? So long as He gives it to you, take care of it as of a thing that is not your own, as travelers treat their inn.

12. If you wish to make progress, dismiss all reasoning of this sort: "If I neglect my affairs, I shall have nothing to live on." "If I do not punish my slave-boy, he will turn out bad." For it is better to die of hunger, but in a state of freedom from grief and fear, than to live in plenty, but troubled in mind. And it is better for your slave-boy to be bad than for you to be unhappy. Begin, therefore, with the little things. Your paltry oil gets spilled, your miserable wine stolen; say to yourself; "This is the price paid for a calm spirit, this the price for peace of mind." Nothing is got without a price. And when you call your slave-boy, bear in mind that it is possible he may not heed you, and again, that even if he does heed, he may not do what you want done. But he is not in so happy a condition that your peace of mind depends upon him.

13. If you wish to make progress, then be content to appear senseless and foolish in externals, do not make it your wish to give the appearance of knowing anything; and if some people think you to be an important personage, distrust yourself. For be assured that it is no easy matter to keep your moral purpose in a

state of conformity with nature, and, at the same time, to keep externals; but the man who devotes his attention to one of these two things must inevitably neglect the other.

14. If you make it your will that your children and your wife and your friends should live forever, you are silly; for you are making it your will that things not under your control should be under your control, and that what is not your own should be your own. In the same way, too, if you make it your will that your slave-boy be free from faults, you are a fool; for you are making it your will that vice be not vice, but something else. If, however, it is your will not to fail in what you desire, this is in your power. Wherefore, exercise yourself in that which is in your power. Each man's master is the person who has the authority over what the man wishes or does not wish, so as to secure it, or take it away. Whoever, therefore, wants to be free, let him neither wish for anything, nor avoid anything, that is under the control of others; or else he is necessarily a slave.

15. Remember that you ought to behave in life as you would at a banquet. As something is being passed around it comes to you; stretch out your hand and take a portion of it politely. It passes on; do not detain it. Or it has not come to you yet; do not project your desire to meet it, but wait until it comes in front of you. So act toward children, so toward a wife, so toward office, so toward wealth; and then some day you will be worthy of the banquets of the gods. But if you do not take these things even when they are set before you, but despise them, then you will not only share the banquet of the gods, but share also their rule. For it was by so doing that Diogenes and Heracleitus, and men like them, were deservedly divine and deservedly so called.

16. When you see someone weeping in sorrow, either because a child has gone on a journey, or because he has lost his property, beware that you be not carried away by the impression that the man is in the midst of external ills, but straightway keep before you this thought: "It is not what has happened that distresses this man (for it does not distress another), but his judgment about it." Do not, however, hesitate to sympathize with him so far as words go, and, if occasion offers, even to groan with him: but be careful not to groan also in the centre of your being.

17. Remember that you are an actor in a play, the character of which is determined by the Playwright; if He wishes the play to be short, it is short; if long, it is long; if He wishes you to play the part of a beggar, remember to act even this rôle adroitly; and so if your rôle be that of a cripple, an official, or a layman. For this is your business, to play admirably the rôle assigned you; but the selection of that rôle is Another's.

18. When a raven croaks inauspiciously, let not the external impression carry you away, but straightway draw a distinction in your mind, and say, "None of these portents are for me, but either for my paltry body, or my paltry estate, or my paltry opinion, or my children, or my wife. But for me every portent is favourable, if I so wish; for whatever be the outcome, it is within my power to derive benefit from it."

19. You can be invincible if you never enter a contest in which victory is not under your control. Beware lest, when you see some person preferred to you in honour, or possessing great power, or otherwise enjoying high repute, you are ever carried away by the external impression, and deem him happy. For if the true nature of the good is one of the things that are under our control, there is no place for either envy or jealousy; and you yourself will not wish to be a praetor, or a senator, or a consul, but a free man. Now there is but one way that leads to this, and that is to despise the things that are not under our control.

20. Bear in mind that it is not the man who reviles or strikes you that insults you, but it is your judgment that these men are insulting you. Therefore, when someone irritates you, be assured that it is your own opinion which has irritated you. And so make it your first endeavor not to be carried away by the external impression; for if once you gain time and delay, you will more easily become master of yourself.

21. Keep before your eyes day by day death and exile, and everything that seems terrible, but most of all death; and then you will never have any abject thought, nor will you yearn for anything beyond measure.

22. If you yearn for philosophy, prepare at once to be met with ridicule, to have many people jeer at you, and say, "Here he is again, turned philosopher all of a sudden," and "Where do you suppose he got that high brow?" But do you not put on a high brow, and do you so hold fast to the things which to you seem best, as a man who has been assigned by God to this post; and remember that if you abide by the same principles, those who formerly used to laugh at you will later come to admire you, but if you are worsted by them, you will get the laugh on yourself twice.

23. If it should ever happen to you that you turn to externals with a view to pleasing someone, rest assured that you have lost your plan of life. Be content, therefore, in everything to *be* a philosopher, and if you wish also to be taken for one, show to yourself that you are one, and you will be able to accomplish it.

24. Let not these reflections oppress you: "I shall live without honour, and be nobody anywhere." For, if lack of honour is an evil, you cannot be in evil through the instrumentality of some other person, any more than you can be in shame. It is not your business, is it, to get office, or to be invited to a dinner-party? Certainly not. How, then, can this be any longer a lack of honour? And how is it that you will be "nobody anywhere," when you ought to be somebody only in those things which are under your control, wherein you are privileged to be a man of the very greatest honour? But your friends will be without assistance? What do you mean by being "without assistance"? They will not have paltry coin from you, and you will not make them Roman citizens. Well, who told you that these are some of the matters under our control, and not rather things which others do? And who is able to give another what he does not himself have? "Get money, then," says some friend, "in order that we too may have it." If I can get money and at the same time keep myself self-respecting, and faithful, and high-minded, show me the way and I will get it. But if you require me to lose the good things that belong to me, in order that you may acquire the things that are not good, you can see for yourselves how unfair and inconsiderate you are. And which do you really prefer? Money, or a faithful and self-respecting friend? Help me, therefore, rather to this end, and do not require me to do those things which will make me lose these qualities.

"But my country," says he, "so far as lies in me, will be without assistance." Again I ask, what kind of assistance do you mean? It will not have loggias or baths of your providing. And what does that signify? For neither does it have shoes provided by the blacksmith, nor has it arms provided by the cobbler; but it is sufficient if each man fulfill his own proper function. And if you secured for it another faithful and self-respecting citizen, would you not be doing it any good? "Yes." Very well, and then you also would not be useless to it. "What place, then, shall I have in the State?" says he. Whatever place you *can* have, and at the same time maintain the man of fidelity and self-respect that is in you. But if, through your desire to help the State, you lose these qualities, of what good would you become to it, when in the end you turned out to be shameless and unfaithful?

25. Has someone been honoured above you at a dinner-party, or in salutation, or in being called in to give advice? Now if these matters are good, you ought to be happy that he got them; but if evil, be not distressed because you did not get them; and bear in mind that, if you do not act the same way that others do, with a view to getting things which are not under our control, you cannot be considered worthy to receive an equal share with others. Why, how is it possible for a person who does not haunt some man's door, to have equal shares with the man who does? For the man who does not do escort duty, with the man who does? For the man who does not praise, with the man who does? You will be unjust, therefore, and insatiable, if, while refusing to pay the price for which such things are bought, you want to obtain them for nothing. Well, what is the price for heads of lettuce? An obol, perhaps. If then, somebody gives up his obol and gets his heads of lettuce, while you do not give your obol, and do not get them, do not imagine that you are worse off than the man who gets his lettuce. For as he has his heads of lettuce, so you have your obol which you have not given away.

Now it is the same way also in life. You have not been invited to somebody's dinner-party? Of course not; for you didn't give the host the price at which he sells his dinner. He sells it for praise; he sells it for personal attention. Give him the price, then, for which it is sold, if it is to your interest. But if you wish both not to give up the one and yet to get the other, you are insatiable and a simpleton. Have you, then, nothing in place of the dinner? Indeed you have; you have not had to praise the man you did not want to praise; you have not had to put up with the insolence of his doorkeepers.

26. What the will of nature is may be learned from a consideration of the points in which we do not differ from one another. For example, when some other person's slave-boy breaks his drinking-cup, you are instantly ready to say, "That's one of the things which happen." Rest assured, then, that when your own drinking-cup gets broken, you ought to behave in the same way that you do when the other man's cup is broken. Apply now the same principle to the matters of greater importance. Some other person's child or wife has died; no one but would say, "Such is the fate of man." Yet when a man's own child dies, immediately the cry is, "Alas! Woe is me!" But we ought to remember how we feel when we hear of the same misfortune befalling others.

27. Just as a mark is not set up in order to be missed, so neither does the nature of evil arise in the universe.

28. If someone handed over your body to any person who met you, you would be vexed; but that you hand over your mind to any person that comes along, so that, if he reviles you, it is disturbed and troubled—are you not ashamed of that?

29. In each separate thing that you do, consider the matters which come first and those which follow after, and only then approach the thing itself. Otherwise, at the start you will come to it enthusiastically, because you have never reflected upon any of the subsequent steps, but later on, when some difficulties appear, you will give up disgracefully. Do you wish to win an Olympic victory? So do I, by the gods! for it is a fine thing. But consider the matters which come before that, and that which follow after, and only when you have done that, put your hand to the task. You have to submit to discipline, follow a strict diet, give up sweet cakes, train under compulsion, at a fixed hour, in heat or in cold; you must not drink cold water, nor wine just whenever you feel like it; you must have turned yourself over to your trainer precisely as you would to a physician. Then when the contest comes on, you have to "dig in" beside your opponent, and sometimes dislocate your wrist, sprain your ankle, swallow quantities of sand, sometimes take a scourging, and along with all that get beaten. After you have considered all these points, go on into the games, if you still wish to do so; otherwise, you will be turning back like children. Sometimes they play wrestlers, again gladiators, again they blow trumpets, and then act a play. So you too are now an athlete, now a gladiator, then a rhetorician, then a philosopher, yet with your whole soul nothing; but like an ape you imitate whatever you see, and one thing after another strikes your fancy. For you have never gone out after anything with circumspection, nor after you had examined it all over, but you act at haphazardly and half-heartedly.

In the same way, when some people have seen a philosopher and have heard someone speaking like Euphrates (though, indeed, who can speak like him?), they wish to be philosophers themselves. Man, consider first the nature of the business, and then learn your own natural ability, if you are able to bear it. Do you wish to be a contender in the pentathlon, or a wrestler? Look to your arms, your thighs, see what your loins are like. For one man has a natural talent for one thing, another for another. Do you suppose that you can eat in the same fashion, drink in the same fashion, give way to impulse and to irritation, just as you do now? You must keep vigils, work hard, abandon your own people, be despised by a paltry slave, be laughed to scorn by those who meet you, in everything get the worst of it, in honour, in office, in court, in every paltry affair. Look these drawbacks over carefully, if you are willing at the price of these things to secure tranquility, freedom, and calm. Otherwise, do not approach philosophy; don't act like a child— now a philosopher, later on a tax-gatherer, then a rhetorician, then a procurator of Caesar. These things do not go together. You must be one person, either good or bad; you must labour to improve either your own governing principle or externals; you must work hard either on the inner man, or on things outside; that is, play either the role of a philosopher or else that of a layman.

30. Our duties are in general measured by our social relationships. He is a father. One is called upon to take care of him, to give way to him in all things, to submit when he reviles or strikes you. "But he is a bad father." Did nature, then, bring you into relationship with a *good* father? No, but simply with a father. "My brother does me wrong." Very well, then, maintain the relation that you have toward him; and do not consider what he is doing, but what you will have to do, if your moral purpose is to be in harmony with nature. For no one will harm you without your consent; you will have been harmed only when you think you are harmed. In this way, therefore, you will discover what duty to expect of your neighbour, your citizen, your commanding officer, if you acquire the habit of looking at your social relations with them.

31. In piety towards the gods, I would have you know, the chief element is this, to have right opinions about them—as existing and as administering the universe well and justly—and to have set yourself to obey them and to submit to everything that happens, and to follow it voluntarily, in the belief that it is being fulfilled by the highest intelligence. For if you act in this way, you will never blame the gods, nor find fault with them for neglecting you. But this result cannot be secured in any other way than by withdrawing your idea of the good and the evil from the things which are not under our control, and placing it in those which are under our control, and in those alone. Because, if you think any of those former things to be good or evil, then, when you fail to get what you want and fall into what you do not want, it is altogether inevitable that you will blame and hate those who are responsible for these results. For this is the nature of every living creature, to flee from and to turn aside from the things that appear harmful, and all that produces them, and to pursue after and to admire the things that are helpful, and all that produces them. Therefore, it is impossible for a man who thinks that he is being hurt to take pleasure in that which he thinks is hurting him, just as it is also impossible for him to take pleasure in the hurt itself. Hence it follows that even a father is reviled by a son when he does not give his child some share in the things that seem to be good; and this it was which made Polyneices and Eteocles enemies of one another, the thought that the royal power was a good thing. That is why the farmer reviles the gods, and so also the sailor, and the merchant, and those who lost their wives and their children. For where a man's interest lies, there is also his piety. Wherefore, whoever is careful to exercise desire and aversion as he should is at the same time careful also about piety. But it is always appropriate to make libations, and sacrifices, and to give of the first fruits after the manner of our fathers, and to do all this with purity, and not in a slovenly or careless fashion, nor, indeed, in a niggardly way, nor yet beyond our means.

32. When you have recourse to divination, remember that you do not know what the issue is going to be, but that you have come in order to find this out from the diviner; yet if you are indeed a philosopher, you know, when you arrive, what the nature of it is. For if it is one of the things which is not under our control, it is altogether necessary that what is going to take place is neither good nor evil. Do not, therefore, bring to the diviner desire or aversion, and do not approach him with trembling, but having first made up your mind that every issue is indifferent and nothing to you, but that, whatever it may be, it will be possible for you to turn it to good use, and that no one will prevent this. Go, then, with confidence to the gods as to counsellors; and after that, when some counsel has been given you, remember whom you have taken as counsellors, and whom you will be disregarding if you disobey. But go to divination as Socrates thought that men should go, that is, in cases where the whole inquiry has reference to the outcome, and where neither from reason nor from any other technical art are means vouchsafed for discovering the matter in question. Hence, when it is your duty to share the danger of a friend or of your country, do not ask the diviner whether you ought to share that danger.

For if the diviner forewarns you that the omens of sacrifice have been unfavourable, it is clear that death is portended, or the injury of some member of your body, or exile; yet reason requires that even at this risk you are to stand by your friend, and share the danger with your country. Wherefore, give heed to the greater diviner, the Pythian Apollo, who cast out of his temple the man who had not helped his friend when he was being murdered.

33. Lay down yourself, at the outset, a certain stamp and type of character for yourself, which you are to maintain whether you are by yourself or are meeting with people. And be silent for the most part, or else make only the most necessary remarks, and express these in few words. But [speak] rarely, and when occasion requires you to talk, indeed, but about no ordinary topics. Do not talk about gladiators, or horse races, or athletes, or things to eat or drink—topics that arise on all occasions; but above all, do not talk about people, either blaming, or praising, or comparing them. If, then, you can, by your own conversation bring over that of your companions to what is seemly. But if you happen to be left alone in the presence of aliens, keep silence.

Do not laugh much, nor at many things, nor boisterously.

Refuse, if you can, to take an oath at all, but if that is impossible, refuse as far as circumstances allow.

Avoid entertainments given by outsiders and by persons ignorant of philosophy; but if an appropriate occasion arises for you to attend, be on the alert to avoid lapsing into the behavior of such laymen. For you may rest assured, that, if a man's companion be dirty, the person who keeps close company with him must of necessity get a share of his dirt, even though he himself happens to be clean.

In things that pertain to the body take only as much as your bare need requires; I mean such things as food, drink, clothing, shelter, and household slaves; but cut down on everything which is for outward show or luxury.

In your sex-life preserve purity, as far as you can, before marriage, and, if you indulge, take only those privileges which are lawful. However, do not make yourself offensive, or censorious, to those who do indulge, and do not make frequent mention of the fact that you do not yourself indulge.

If someone brings you word that So-and-so is speaking ill of you, do not defend yourself against what has been said, but answer, "Yes, indeed, for he did not know the rest of the faults that attach to me; if he had, these would not have been the only ones he mentioned."

It is not necessary, for the most part, to go to the public shows. If, however, a suitable occasion ever arises, show that your principal concern is for none other than yourself, which means, wish only for that to happen which does happen, and for him only to win who does win; for so you will suffer no hindrance. But refrain utterly from shouting, or laughter at anyone, or great excitement. And after you have left, do not talk a great deal about what took place, except insofar as it contributes to your own improvement; for such behavior indicates that the spectacle has aroused your admiration.

Do not go rashly or readily to people's public readings, but when you do go, maintain your own dignity and gravity, and at the same time be careful not to make yourself disagreeable.

When you are about to meet somebody, in particular when it is one of those men who are held in very high esteem, propose to yourself the question, "What would Socrates or Zeno have done under these circumstances?" and then you will not be at a loss to make proper use of the occasion. When you go to see one of those men who have great power, propose to yourself the thought that you will not find him at home, that you will be shut out, that the door will be slammed in your face, that he will pay no attention to you. And if, despite all this, it is your duty to go, go and take what comes, and never say to yourself, "It was not worth all the trouble." For this is characteristic of the layman, that is, a man who is vexed at externals.

In your conversation avoid making mention at great length and excessively of your own deeds or dangers, because it is not as pleasant for others to hear about your adventures, as it is for you to call to mind your own dangers.

Avoid also raising a laugh, for this is a kind of behavior that slips easily into vulgarity, and at the same time is calculated to lessen the respect which your neighbours have of you. It is dangerous also to lapse into foul language. When, therefore, anything of the sort occurs, if the occasion be suitable, go even so far as to reprove the person who has made such a lapse; if, however, the occasion does not arise, at all events show by keeping silence, and blushing, and frowning, that you are displeased by what has been said.

34. When you get an external impression of some pleasure, guard yourself, as with impressions in general, against being carried away by it; nay, let the matter wait upon *your* leisure, and give yourself a little delay. Next think of the two periods of time, first, that in which you will enjoy your pleasure, and second, that in which, after the enjoyment is over, you will later repent and revile your own self; and set over against these two periods of time how much joy and self-satisfaction you will get if you refrain. However, if you feel that a suitable occasion has arisen to do the deed, be careful not to allow its enticement, and sweetness, and attractiveness to overcome you; but set over against all this the thought, how much better is the consciousness of having won a victory over it.

35. When you do a thing which you have made up your mind ought to be done, never try not to be seen doing it, even though most people are likely to think unfavourably about it. If, however, what you are doing is not right, avoid the deed itself altogether; but if it is right, why fear those who are going to rebuke you wrongly?

36. Just as the propositions, "It is day," and "It is night," are full of meaning when separated, but meaningless if united; so also, granted that for you to take the larger share at a dinner is good for your body, still, it is bad for the maintenance of the proper kind of social feeling. When, therefore, you are eating with another person, remember to regard, not merely the value for your body of what lies before you, but also to maintain your respect for your host.

37. If you undertake a rôle which is beyond your powers, you both disgrace yourself in that one, and at the same time neglect the rôle which you might have filled with success.

38. Just as you are careful, in walking about, not to step on a nail or to sprain your ankle, so be careful also not to hurt your governing principle. And if we observe this rule in every action, we shall be more secure in setting about it.

39. Each man's body is a measure for his property, just as the foot is a measure for his shoe. If, then, you abide by this principle, you will maintain the proper measure, but if you go beyond it, you cannot help but fall headlong over a precipice, as it were, in the end. So also in the case of your shoe; if once you go beyond the foot, you get first a gilded shoe, then a purple one, then an embroidered one. For once you go beyond the measure, there is no limit.

40. Immediately after they are fourteen, women are called "ladies" by men. And so when they see that they have nothing else but only to be the bedfellows of men, they begin to beautify themselves, and put all their hopes in that. It is worthwhile for us to take pains, therefore, to make them understand that they are honoured for nothing else but only for appearing modest and self-respecting.

41. It is a mark of an ungifted man to spend a great deal of time in what concerns his body, as in much exercise, much eating, much drinking, much evacuating of the bowels, much copulating. But these things are to be done in passing; and let your whole attention be devoted to the mind.

42. When someone treats you ill or speaks ill of you, remember that he acts or speaks thus because he thinks it is incumbent upon him. That being the case, it is impossible for him to follow what appears good to you, but what appears good to himself; whence it follows, that, if he gets a wrong view of things, the man that suffers is the man that has been deceived. For if a person thinks a true composite judgment to be false, the composite judgment does not suffer, but the person who has been deceived. If, therefore, you start from this point of view, you will be gentle with the man who reviles you. For you should say on each occasion, "He thought that way about it."

43. Everything has two handles, by one of which it ought to be carried and by the other not. If your brother wrongs you, do not lay hold of the matter by the handle of the wrong that he is doing, because this is the handle by which the matter ought not to be carried; but rather by the other handle—that he is your brother, that you were brought up together, and then you will be laying hold of the matter by the handle by which it ought to be carried.

44. The following statements constitute a *non sequitur:* "I am richer than you are, therefore I am superior to you"; or, "I am more eloquent than you are, therefore I am superior to you." But the following conclusions are better: "I am richer than you are, therefore my property is superior to yours"; or, "I am more eloquent than you are, therefore my elocution is superior to yours." But *you* are neither property nor elocution.

45. Somebody is hasty about bathing; do not say that he bathes badly, but that he is hasty about bathing. Somebody drinks a good deal of wine; do not say that he drinks badly, but that he drinks a good deal. For until you have decided what judgment prompts him, how do you know that what he is doing is bad? And thus the final result will not be that you receive convincing sense-impressions of some things, but give your assent to others.

46. On no occasion call yourself a philosopher, and do not, for the most part, talk among laymen about your philosophic principles, but do what follows from your principles. For example, at a banquet do not say how people ought to eat, but eat as a man ought. For remember how Socrates had so completely eliminated the thought of ostentation, that people came to him when they wanted him to introduce them to philosophers, and he used to bring them along. So well did he submit to being overlooked. And if talk about some philosophic principle arises among laymen, keep silence for the most part, for there is great danger that you will spew up immediately what you have not digested. So when a man tells you that you know nothing, and you, like Socrates, are not hurt, then rest assured that you are making a beginning with the business you have undertaken. For sheep, too, do not bring their fodder to the shepherds and show how much they have eaten, but they digest their food within them, and on the outside produce wool and milk. And so do you, therefore, make no display to the laymen of your philosophical principles, but let them see the results which come from these principles when digested.

47. When you have become adjusted to simple living in regard to your bodily wants, do not preen yourself about the accomplishment; and so likewise, if you are a water-drinker, do not on every occasion say that you are a water-drinker. And if ever you want to train to develop physical endurance, do it by yourself and not for outsiders to behold; do not throw your arms around statues, but on occasion, when you are very thirsty, take cold water into your mouth, and then spit it out, without telling anybody.

48. This is the position and character of a layman: He never looks for either help or harm from himself, but only from externals. This is the position and character of the philosopher: He looks for all his help or harm from himself.

Signs of one who is making progress are: He censures no one, praises no one, blames no one, finds fault with no one, says nothing about himself as though he were somebody or knew something. When he is hampered or prevented, he blames himself. And if anyone compliments him, he smiles to himself at the person complimenting; while if anyone censures him, he makes no defense. He goes about like an invalid, being careful not to disturb, before it has grown firm, any part which is getting well. He has put away from himself his every desire, and has transferred his aversion to those things only, of what is under our control, which are contrary to nature. He exercises no pronounced choice in regard to anything. If he gives the appearance of being foolish or ignorant, he does not care. In a word, he keeps guard against himself as though he were his own enemy lying in wait.

49. When a person gives himself airs because he can understand and interpret the books of Chrysippus,* say to yourself, "If Chrysippus had not written obscurely, this man would have nothing about which to give himself airs."

But what is it I want? To learn nature and to follow her. I seek, therefore, someone to interpret her; and having heard that Chrysippus does so, I go to him. But I do not understand what he has written; I seek, therefore, the person who interprets Chrysippus. And down to this point there is nothing to justify pride. But when I find the interpreter, what remains is to put his precepts into practice; this is the only thing to be proud about. If, however, I admire the mere act of interpretation, what have I done but turned into a grammarian instead of a philosopher? The only difference, indeed, is that I interpret Chrysippus instead of Homer. Far from being proud, therefore, when somebody says to me, "Read me Chrysippus," I blush rather, when I am unable to show him such deeds as match and harmonize with his words.

*A Greek Stoic philosopher (c. 279–206 B.C.)—Ed.

50. Whatever principles are set before you, stand fast by these like laws, feeling that it would be impiety for you to transgress them. But pay no attention to what somebody says about you, for this is, at length, not under your control.

51. How long will you still wait to think yourself worthy of the best things, and in nothing to transgress against the distinctions set up by the reason? You have received the philosophical principles which you ought to accept, and you have accepted them. What sort of a teacher, then, do you still wait for, that you should put off reforming yourself until he arrives? You are no longer a lad, but already a full-grown man. If you are now neglectful and easy-going, and always making one delay after another, and fixing first one day and then another, after which you will pay attention to yourself, then without realizing it you will make no progress, but, living and dying, will continue to be a layman throughout. Make up your mind, therefore, before it is too late, that the fitting thing for you to do is to live as a mature man who is making progress, and let everything which seems to you to be best be for you a law that must not be transgressed. And if you meet anything that is laborious, or sweet, or held in high repute, or in no repute, remember that *now* is the contest, and here before you are the Olympic games, and that it is impossible to delay any longer, and that it depends on a single day and a single action, whether progress is lost or saved. This is the way Socrates became what he was, by paying attention to nothing but his reason in everything that he encountered. And even if you are not yet a Socrates, still you ought to live as one who wishes to be a Socrates.

52. The first and most necessary division in philosophy is that which has to do with the application of the principles, as, for example, Do not lie. The second deals with the demonstrations, as, for example, How comes it that we ought not to lie? The third confirms and discriminates between these processes, as, for example, How does it come that this is a proof? For what is a proof, what is logical consequence, what contradiction, what truth, what falsehood? Therefore, the third division is necessary because of the second, and the second because of the first; while the most necessary of all, and the one in which we ought to rest, is the first. But we do the opposite; for we spend our time in the third division, and all our zeal is devoted to it, while we utterly neglect the first. Wherefore, we lie, indeed, but are ready with the arguments which prove that one ought not to lie.

53. Upon every occasion we ought to have the following thoughts at our command:

> Lead thou me on, O Zeus, and Destiny.
> To that goal long ago to me assigned.
> I'll follow and not falter; if my will
> Prove weak and craven, still I'll follow on.

> "Who so has rightly with necessity complied,
> We count him wise, and skilled in things divine."

> "Well, O Crito, if so it is pleasing to the gods, so let it be."
> "Anytus and Meletus can kill me, but they cannot hurt me."

Study Questions

1. For Epictetus, the distinction between what is under our control and what is not under our control is fundamental. What sorts of things does he think are under our control? What sorts of things are not? How does this distinction figure in his prescriptions for achieving happiness?
2. Analyze the claims made in Section 5. Do you agree or disagree with what he says there? Why?
3. Should you respond as Epictetus recommends to the death of a loved one? (See, e.g., Sections 3 and 11.) Could you?
4. What is Epictetus saying in Section 17? Do you agree or disagree?
5. According to Epictetus, how should we behave in society? How does your public behavior compare with this ideal?
6. What is your overall assessment of Epictetus's ethical outlook?

Selected Bibliography

Aurelius, Marcus. *The Meditations.* (Available in many editions.) Thoughts of a famous Stoic, mainly about ethics.

Hicks, R. D. *Stoic and Epicurean* (New York: Russell and Russell, 1962), Chaps. 3 and 4. A commentary on Stoic ethics.

Long, A. A. *Hellenistic Philosophy: Stoics, Epicureans and Sceptics,* 2nd edition (Berkeley: University of California Press, 1987). Contains a general introduction to Stoicism.

Rist, J. M., ed. *The Stoics* (Berkeley: University of California Press, 1978), Essays 11 and 12. Discussion of aspects of Stoic ethics.

6

ST. AUGUSTINE

St. Augustine (354–430) is one of the greatest of all the Christian theologians. Born near Carthage in North Africa of a pagan father and a Christian mother, he was attracted as a youth first to the Manichean religion, a variation of

> *God then remains, in following after whom we live well, and in reaching whom we live both well and happily.*

Zoroastrianism that had spread through the Roman Empire, and later to the mysticism of the Neo-Platonists, whose influence is discernible throughout his writings. After being educated both in Carthage and Rome, he took a position in Milan as a professor of rhetoric. There he came under the influence of St. Ambrose, bishop of Milan, who succeeded in leading him into the Christian fold. After his conversion, Augustine devoted the remainder of his life to the strengthening of the church, especially in North Africa. In 395 he was appointed bishop of Hippo (near Carthage), a post he retained until his death. In spite of his heavy clerical duties, he wrote voluminously, particularly on philosophy and theology. His importance as a theologian rests mainly on his careful and systematic development of the doctrine of original sin, which had first been formulated by the apostle Paul. In its Augustinian rendition this doctrine, with later additions by John Calvin, has remained the foundation of almost all subsequent Christian theology.

In the two selections that follow, although St. Augustine is directly concerned with ethical questions, it is apparent that his religious beliefs are shaping his thought. In the first he inquires, in the fashion of Aristotle, after the chief or highest good of human life, which we ordinarily call happiness. He rejects the body as the basis of this good, arguing instead that it must be an attribute of the soul. Then, through a series of steps, he reaches the conclusion that this good is virtue, which the soul attains through seeking and following God. In the second selection, he confronts a question with which Christian philosophers have struggled ever since he raised it: If God created the universe and everything in it and God is both omnipotent and perfect, why does evil exist? Many answers have been given to this question; that of St. Augustine is one of the most ingenious. Is it also convincing?

Of the Morals of
the Catholic Church

Happiness is in the enjoyment of man's chief good.
Two conditions of the chief good: 1st, Nothing is better than it;
2nd, it cannot be lost against the will.

How then, according to reason, ought man to live? We all certainly desire to live happily; and there is no human being but assents to this statement almost before it is made. But the title happy cannot, in my opinion, belong either to him who has not what he loves, whatever it may be, or to him who has what he loves if it is hurtful, or to him who does not love what he has, although it is good in perfection. For one who seeks what he cannot obtain suffers torture, and one who has got what is not desirable is cheated, and one who does not seek for what is worth seeking for is diseased. Now in all these cases the mind cannot but be unhappy, and happiness and unhappiness cannot reside at the same time in one man; so in none of these cases can the man be happy. I find, then, a fourth case, where the happy life exists—when that which is man's chief good is both loved and possessed. For what do we call enjoyment but having at hand the object of love? And no one can be happy who does not enjoy what is man's chief good, nor is there any one who enjoys this who is not happy. We must then have at hand our chief good, if we think of living happily.

We must now inquire what is man's chief good, which of course cannot be anything inferior to man himself. For whoever follows after what is inferior to himself, becomes himself inferior. But every man is bound to follow what is best. Wherefore man's chief good is not inferior to man. Is it then something similar to man himself? It must be so, if there is nothing above man which he is capable of enjoying. But if we find something which is both superior to man, and can be possessed by the man who loves it, who can doubt that in seeking for happiness man should endeavour to reach that which is more excellent than the being who makes the endeavour? For if happiness consists in the enjoyment of a good than which there is nothing better, which we call the chief good, how can a man be properly called happy who has not yet attained his chief good? or how can that be the chief good beyond which something better remains for us to arrive at? Such, then, being the chief good, it must be something which cannot be lost against the will. For no one can feel confident regarding a good which he knows can be taken from him, although he wishes to keep and cherish it. But if a man feels no confidence regarding the good which he enjoys, how can he be happy while in such fear of losing it?

From *The Works of Aurelius Augustine*, edited by M. Dods, Vol. IX (Edinburgh: T & T Clark, 1892).

Man—what?

Let us then see what is better than man. This must necessarily be hard to find, unless we first ask and examine what man is. I am not now called upon to give a definition of man. The question here seems to me to be—since almost all agree, or at least, which is enough, those I have now to do with are of the same opinion with me, that we are made up of soul and body—What is man? Is he both of these? or is he the body only, or the soul only? For although the things are two, soul and body, and although neither without the other could be called man (for the body would not be man without the soul, nor again would the soul be man if there were not a body animated by it), still it is possible that one of these may be held to be man, and may be called so. What then do we call man? Is he soul and body, as in a double harness, or like a centaur? Or do we mean the body only, as being in the service of the soul which rules it, as the word lamp denotes not the light and the case together, but only the case, though on account of the light? Or do we mean only the mind, and that on account of the body which it rules, as horseman means not the man and the horse, but the man only, and that as employed in ruling the horse? This dispute is not easy to settle; or, if the proof is plain, the statement requires time. This is an expenditure of time and strength which we need not incur. For whether the name man belongs to both, or only to the soul, the chief good of man is not the chief good of the body; but what is the chief good either of both soul and body, or of the soul only, that is man's chief good.

Man's chief good is not the chief good of the body only, but the chief good of the soul.

Now if we ask what is the chief good of the body, reason obliges us to admit that it is that by means of which the body comes to be in its best state. But of all the things which invigorate the body, there is nothing better or greater than the soul. The chief good of the body, then, is not bodily pleasure, not absence of pain, not strength, not beauty, not swiftness, or whatever else is usually reckoned among the goods of the body, but simply the soul. For all the things mentioned the soul supplies to the body by its presence, and, what is above them all, life. Hence I conclude that the soul is not the chief good of man, whether we give the name of man to soul and body together, or to the soul alone. For as, according to reason, the chief good of the body is that which is better than the body, and from which the body receives vigour and life, so whether the soul itself is man, or soul and body both, we must discover whether there is anything which goes before the soul itself, in following which the soul comes to the perfection of good of which it is capable in its own kind. If such a thing can be found, all uncertainty must be at an end, and we must pronounce this to be really and truly the chief good of man.

If, again, the body is man, it must be admitted that the soul is the chief good of man. But clearly, when we treat of morals—when we inquire what manner of life must be held in order to obtain happiness—it is not the body to which the precepts are addressed, it is not bodily discipline which we discuss. In short, the observance of good customs belongs to that part of us which inquires and learns, which are the prerogatives of the soul; so, when we speak of attaining to virtue, the question does not regard the body. But if it follows, as it does, that the body which is ruled over by a soul possessed of virtue is ruled both better and more honourably, and is in its greatest perfection in consequence of the perfection of the soul which rightfully governs it, that which gives perfection to the soul will be man's chief good, though we call the body man. For if my coachman, in obedience to me, feeds and drives the horses he has charge of in the most satisfactory manner, himself enjoying the more of my bounty in proportion to his good conduct, can any one deny that the good condition of the horses, as well as that of the coachman, is due to me? So the question seems to me to be not whether soul and body is man, or the soul only, or body only, but what gives perfection to the soul; for when this is obtained, a man cannot but be either perfect, or at least much better than in the absence of this one thing.

Virtue gives perfection to the soul; the soul obtains virtue by following God; following God is the happy life.

No one will question that virtue gives perfection to the soul. But it is a very proper subject of inquiry whether this virtue can exist by itself or only in the soul. Here again arises a profound discussion, needing lengthy treatment but perhaps my summary will serve the purpose. God will, I trust, assist me, so that, notwithstanding our feebleness, we may give instruction on these great matters briefly as well as intelligibly. In either case, whether virtue can exist by itself without the soul, or can exist only in the soul, undoubtedly in the pursuit of virtue the soul follows after something, and this must be either the soul itself, or virtue, or something else. But if the soul follows after itself in the pursuit of virtue, it follows after a foolish thing; for before obtaining virtue it is foolish. Now the height of a follower's desire is to reach that which he follows after. So the soul must either not wish to reach what it follows after, which is utterly absurd and unreasonable, or, in following after itself while foolish, it reaches the folly which it flees from. But if it follows after virtue in the desire to reach it, how can it follow what does not exist? or how can it desire to reach what it already possesses? Either, therefore, virtue exists beyond the soul, or if we are not allowed to give the name of virtue except to the habit and disposition of the wise soul, which can exist only in the soul, we must allow that the soul follows after something else in order that virtue may be produced in itself; for neither by following after nothing, nor by following after folly, can the soul, according to my reasoning, attain to wisdom.

This something else, then, by following after which the soul becomes possessed of virtue and wisdom, is either a wise man or God. But we have said already that it must be something that we cannot lose against our will. No one can think it necessary to ask whether a wise man, supposing we are content to follow after him, can be taken from us in spite of our unwillingness or our persistence. God then remains, in following after whom we live well, and in reaching whom we live both well and happily.

The Enchiridion

The supremely good Creator made all things good.

By the Trinity, thus supremely and equally and unchangeably good, all things were created; and these are not supremely and equally and unchangeably good, but yet they are good, even taken separately. Taken as a whole, however, they are very good, because their *ensemble* constitutes the universe in all its wonderful order and beauty.

What is called evil in the universe is but the absence of good.

And in the universe, even that which is called evil, when it is regulated and put in its own place, only enhances our admiration of the good; for we enjoy and value the good more when we compare it with the evil. For the Almighty God, who, as even the heathen acknowledge, has supreme power over all things, being Himself supremely good, would never permit the existence of anything evil among His works, if He were not so omnipotent and good that He can bring good even out of evil. For what is that which we call evil but the absence of good? In the bodies of animals, disease and wounds mean nothing but the absence of health; for when a cure is effected, that does not mean that the evils which were present—namely, the diseases and wounds—go away from the body and dwell elsewhere: they altogether cease to exist; for the wound or disease is not a substance, but a defect in the fleshly substance—the flesh itself being a substance, and therefore something good, of which those evils—that is, privations of the good which we call health—are accidents. Just in the same way, what are called vices in the soul are nothing but privations of natural good. And when they are cured, they are not transferred elsewhere: when they cease to exist in the healthy soul, they cannot exist anywhere else.

All beings were made good, but not being made perfectly good, are liable to corruption.

All things that exist, therefore, seeing that the Creator of them all is supremely good, are themselves good. But because they are not, like their Creator, supremely and unchangeably good, their good may be diminished and increased. But for good to be diminished is an evil, although, however much it may be diminished, it is necessary, if the being is to continue, that some good should remain to constitute the being. For however small or of whatever kind the being may be, the good which makes it a being cannot be destroyed without destroying the being itself. An uncorrupted nature is justly held in esteem. But if, still further, it be incorruptible, it is undoubtedly considered of still higher value. When it is corrupted, however, its corruption is an evil, because it is deprived of some sort of good. For if it be deprived of no good, it receives no injury; but it does receive injury, therefore it is deprived of good. Therefore, so long as a being is in process of corruption, there is in it some good of which it is being deprived; and if a part of the being should remain which cannot be corrupted, this will certainly be an incorruptible being, and accordingly the process of corruption will result in the manifestation of this great good. But if it does not cease to be corrupted, neither can it cease to possess good of which corruption may deprive it. But if it should be thoroughly and completely consumed by corruption, there will then be no good left, because there will be no being. Wherefore corruption can consume the good only by consuming the being. Every being, therefore, is a good; a great good, if it cannot be corrupted; a little good, if it can; but in any case, only the foolish or ignorant will deny that it is a good. And if it be wholly consumed by corruption, then the corruption itself must cease to exist, as there is no being left in which it can dwell.

Study Questions

1. Augustine writes that happiness cannot be ascribed "either to him who has not what he loves, whatever it may be, or to him who has what he loves if it is hurtful, or to him who does not love what he has, although it is good in perfection." Explain what he means here. Do you agree or disagree?
2. According to Augustine, what should we seek in order to attain the highest good in this life? How does he defend his view?
3. What is Augustine's account of the existence of evil? Explain. What are both the strong and weak points of his view?
4. Augustine states "All things that exist . . . are themselves good." How does he support this conclusion? Can you think of counter-examples to this view? How might Augustine deal with them?

Selected Bibliography

Bourke, Vernon, ed. *The Essential Augustine* (Cambridge, Mass.: Hackett Publishing, 1978). A collection of Augustine's most important writings.

Brown, Peter. *Augustine of Hippo* (Berkeley: University of California Press, 1977). An excellent biography.

Deane, H. A. *The Political and Social Ideas of St. Augustine* (New York: Columbia University Press, 1963), esp. Chap. 3.

Evans, G. R. *Augustine on Evil* (New York/Cambridge: Cambridge University Press, 1982). Discussion of Augustine on the problem of evil.

Gilson, E. *The Christian Philosophy of St. Augustine* (New York: Random House, 1960), Introduction and Part 2.

Kirwan, Christopher. *Augustine* (London: Routledge, 1989). General study.

Rist, John M. *Augustine: Ancient Thought Baptized* (New York/Cambridge: Cambridge University Press, 1994). General study.

7

ST. THOMAS AQUINAS

——

St. Augustine and St. Thomas Aquinas, the two most important theologian-philosophers of medieval Christianity, lived eight hundred years apart, but more than mere

> *. . . man's ultimate happiness consists solely in the contemplation of God. . . .*

time separates them. The former was one of the last significant intellectual figures of the classical era, the latter one of the precursors of modern times. Between them lay more than a half-millennium of cultural stagnation in Europe—the Dark Ages. However, during those long centuries of European somnolence (a result of the decline of Roman influence and power in the West), the Near East was enjoying a Golden Age. Islam had absorbed the learning of the ancients and found in it the stimulus for significant cultural progress. When the Muslims extended their power across northern Africa into Spain, they made contact with western Europeans who through them became reacquainted with the cultural heritage of Greece and Rome. Western Europe awakened from its long sleep, with a flowering of culture that began to bud in the eleventh century, was in bloom in the twelfth, and reached full fruition in the thirteenth—the high Middle Ages.

Thomas Aquinas (c. 1225–1274), the most important intellectual figure of high medieval civilization, was born in Italy of a noble family. He received his first education at the famous Abbey of Monte Cassino, going on from there to the University of Naples. In 1243 he joined the Dominican monastic order, much to the displeasure of his parents, who had higher aspirations for him. In an attempt to frustrate his plans, they called him home and tried to persuade him to abandon the habit of a monk. When he refused, they imprisoned him in the family castle, where he remained for two years until his mother relented, passing him a rope by which he let himself out a window and down the castle wall. Escaping, he rejoined the Dominicans and set out for Cologne, to study under the greatest teacher of the day, Albertus Magnus. From there he went to the University of Paris, which remained his academic headquarters for most of his career. A highly successful teacher, Thomas attracted so many students to his lectures that it was difficult to find a hall large enough to seat them. But more important, he was a writer. In the short space of about 20 years, he completed 17 volumes of works on philosophy and theology. It is said that he could dictate simultaneously to four secretaries, each on a different subject.

Thomas was one of the greatest intellectual synthesizers in Western thought. The task he set for himself was to combine the philosophy of Aristotle, which had been brought back into Europe through the agency of the Muslims, with the theology of the Christian church. The fact that these two ingredients are so disparate is a measure of his accomplishment. Although questions have been raised about the logical coherence of the Thomistic synthesis, it must be acknowledged that his writings form the philosophical basis for much of subsequent Catholic theology. His appeal to both the Christian tradition and the thought of Aristotle, apparent throughout his writings, can clearly be seen in the two selections on ethics that follow, taken from his most important works, the *Summa Contra Gentiles* and *Summa Theologica*.

In reading the selections from the *Summa Theologica*, note that each of the Articles addresses an issue that falls under the topic of the Question. The Articles follow the rules of academic disputation of Aquinas's day. He begins by stating objections to the position that he will eventually defend. He then states what he takes to be the correct position, sometimes backing this view by citing the views of a recognized authority (such as Augustine or Aristotle). He develops and explains his view further by giving his replies to the initial objections.

Thomas died before reaching the age of fifty, while en route from Naples (where he had been teaching) to the Council of Lyons, which had been called to promote a Crusade. After his death he was accused of heresy by members of the church hierarchy. But he was absolved of the accusations and later canonized.

———

Summa Contra Gentiles

Third Book

I. Foreword

We have shown in the preceding books that there is one First Being, possessing the full perfection of all being, whom we call God, and who of the abundance of His perfection, bestows being on all that exists, so that He is proved to be not only the first of beings, but also the beginning of all. Moreover, He bestows being on others, not through natural necessity, but according to the decree of His will, as we have shown above. Hence it follows that He is the Lord of the things made by Him: since we dominate over those things that are subject to our will. And this is a perfect dominion that He exercises over things made by Him, forasmuch as in their making He needs neither the help of an extrinsic agent, nor matter as the foundation of His work: since He is the universal efficient cause of all being.

Now everything that is produced through the will of an agent is directed to an end by that agent: because the good and the end are the proper object of the

St. Thomas Aquinas, *Summa Contra Gentiles*. New York: Benziger, 1928. (Translated by the English Dominican Fathers.) Reprinted by permission of Benziger.

will, wherefore whatever proceeds from a will must needs be directed to an end. And each thing attains its end by its own action, which action needs to be directed by him who endowed things with principles whereby they act.

Consequently God, who in Himself is perfect in every way, and by His power endows all things with being, must needs be the Ruler of all, Himself ruled by none: nor is anything to be excepted from His ruling, as neither is there anything that does not owe its being to Him. Therefore as He is perfect in being and causing, so is He perfect in ruling.

The effect of this ruling is seen to differ in different things, according to the difference of natures. For some things are so produced by God that, being intelligent, they bear a resemblance to Him and reflect His image: wherefore not only are they directed, but they direct themselves to their appointed end by their own actions. And if in thus directing themselves they be subject to the divine ruling, they are admitted by that divine ruling to the attainment of their last end; but are excluded therefrom if they direct themselves otherwise.

II. That Every Agent Acts for an End

Accordingly, we must first show that every agent, by its action, intends an end.

For in those things which clearly act for an end, we declare the end to be that towards which the movement of the agent tends: for when this is reached, the end is said to be reached, and to fail in this is to fail in the end intended; as may be seen in the physician who aims at health, and in a man who runs towards an appointed goal. Nor does it matter, as to this, whether that which tends to an end be cognitive or not: for just as the target is the end of the archer, so is it the end of the arrow's flight. Now the movement of every agent tends to something determinate: since it is not from any force that any action proceeds, but heating proceeds from heat, and cooling from cold; wherefore actions are differentiated by their active principles. Action sometimes terminates in something made, for instance building terminates in a house, healing ends in health: while sometimes it does not so terminate, for instance, understanding and sensation. And if action terminate in something made, the movement of the agent tends by that action towards that thing made: while if it does not terminate in something made, the movement of the agent tends to the action itself. It follows, therefore, that every agent intends an end while acting, which end is sometimes the action itself, sometimes a thing made by the action.

Again. In all things that act for an end, that is said to be the last end, beyond which the agent seeks nothing further: thus the physician's action goes as far as health, and this being attained, his efforts cease. But in the action of every agent, a point can be reached beyond which the agent does not desire to go; else actions would tend to infinity, which is impossible, for since *it is not possible to pass through an infinite medium*, the agent would never begin to act, because nothing moves towards what it cannot reach. Therefore every agent acts for an end.

Moreover, if the actions of an agent proceed to infinity, these actions must need result either in something made, or not. If the result is something made, the being of that thing made will follow after an infinity of actions. But that which presupposes an infinity of things, cannot possibly be, since *an infinite medium cannot be passed through.* Now impossibility of being argues impossibility of becoming: and that which cannot become, it is impossible to make. Therefore it is impossible for an agent to begin to make a thing for the making of which an infinity of actions is presupposed. If, however, the result of such actions be not something made, the order of these actions must be either according to the order of active forces, (for instance if a man feels that he may imagine, and imagine that he may understand, and understand that he may will): or according to the order of objects, (for instance I consider the body that I may consider the soul, which I consider in order to consider a separate substance, which again I consider so that I may consider God). Now it is not possible to proceed to infinity, either in active forces, as neither is this possible in the forms of things, as proved in 2 *Metaph.,* since the form is the principle of activity: or in objects, as neither is this possible in beings, since there is one first being, as we have proved above. Therefore it is not possible for agents to proceed to infinity: and consequently there must be something, which being attained, the efforts of the agent cease. Therefore every agent acts for an end.

Further, in things that act for an end, whatsoever comes between the first agent and the last end, is an end in respect to what precedes, and an active principle in respect of what follows. Hence, if the effort of the agent does not tend to something determinate, and if its action, as stated, proceeds to infinity, the active principles must need proceed to infinity: which is impossible, as we have shown above. Therefore the effort of the agent must of necessity tend to something determinate.

Again. Every agent acts either by nature or by intelligence. Now there can be no doubt that those which act by intelligence act for an end; since they act with an intellectual preconception of what they attain by their action, and act through such preconception, for this is to act by intelligence. Now just as in the preconceiving intellect there exists the entire likeness of the effect that is attained by the action of the intellectual being, so in the natural agent there pre-exists the similitude of the natural effect, by virtue of which similitude its action is determined to the appointed effect: for fire begets fire, and an olive produces an olive. Wherefore even as that which acts by intelligence tends by its action to a definite end, so also does that which acts by nature. Therefore every agent acts for an end.

Moreover, fault is not found save in those things which are for an end: for we do not find fault with one who fails in that to which he is not appointed; thus we find fault with a physician if he fail to heal, but not with a builder or a grammarian. But we find fault in things done according to art, as when a grammarian fails to speak correctly; and in things that are ruled by nature, as in the case of monstrosities. Therefore every agent, whether according to nature, or according to art, or acting of set purpose, acts for an end.

Again. Were an agent not to act for a definite effect, all effects would be indifferent to it. Now that which is indifferent to many effects does not produce one rather than another: wherefore from that which is indifferent to either of two effects, no effect results, unless it be determined by something to one of them. Hence, it would be impossible for it to act. Therefore every agent tends to some definite effect, which is called its end.

There are, however, certain actions which would seem not to be for an end, such as playful and contemplative actions, and those which are done without attention, such as scratching one's beard, and the like: whence some might be led to think that there is an agent that acts not for an end. But we must observe that contemplative actions are not for another end, but are themselves an end. Playful actions are sometimes an end, when one plays for the mere pleasure of play; and sometimes they are for an end, as when we play that afterwards we may study better. Actions done without attention do not proceed from the intellect, but from some sudden act of the imagination, or some natural principle: thus a disordered humour produces an itching sensation and is the cause of a man scratching his beard, which he does without his mind attending to it. Such actions do tend to an end, although outside the order of the intellect. Hereby is excluded the error of certain natural philosophers of old, who maintained that all things happen by natural necessity, thus utterly banishing the final cause from things.

III. That Every Agent Acts for a Good

Hence, we must go on to prove that every agent acts for a good.

For that every agent acts for an end clearly follows from the fact that every agent tends to something definite. Now that to which an agent tends definitely must need be befitting to that agent: since the latter would not tend to it save on account of some fittingness thereto. But that which is befitting to a thing is good for it. Therefore every agent acts for a good.

Further, the end is that wherein the appetite of the agent or mover is at rest, as also the appetite of that which is moved. Now it is the very notion of good to be the term of appetite, since *good is the object of every appetite*. Therefore all action and movement is for a good.

Again. All action and movement would seem to be directed in some way to being: either for the preservation of being in the species or in the individual; or for the acquisition of being. Now this itself, being to wit, is a good: and for this reason all things desire being. Therefore all action and movement is for a good.

Furthermore, all action and movement is for some perfection. For if the action itself be the end, it is clearly a second perfection of the agent. And if the action consists in the transformation of external matter, clearly the mover intends to induce some perfection into the thing moved: towards which perfection the movable tends, if the movement be natural. Now when we say a thing is perfect, we mean that it is good. Therefore every action and movement is for a good.

Also, every agent acts according as it is actual. Now by acting it tends to something similar to itself. Therefore it tends to an act. But an act has the ratio of good: since evil is not found save in a potentiality lacking act. Therefore every action is for a good.

Moreover, the intellectual agent acts for an end, as determining on its end: whereas the natural agent, though it acts for an end, as proved above, does not determine on its end, since it knows not the ratio of end, but is moved to the end determined for it by another. Now an intellectual agent does not determine the end for itself except under the aspect of good; for the intelligible object does not move except it be considered as a good, which is the object of the will. Therefore also the natural agent is not moved, nor does it act for an end, except insofar as this end is a good: since the end is determined for the natural agent by an appetite. Therefore every agent acts for a good.

Again. To shun evil and to seek good are in the same ratio: even as movement from below and upward movement are in the same ratio. Now we observe that all things shun evil: for intellectual agents shun a thing for the reason that they apprehend it as an evil: and all natural agents, in proportion to their strength, resist corruption which is the evil of everything. Therefore all things act for a good.

XVII. That All Things Are Directed to One End, Which Is God

From the foregoing it is clear that all things are directed to one good as their last end.

For if nothing tends to something as its end, except insofar as this is good, it follows that good, as such, is an end. Consequently, that which is the supreme good is supremely the end of all. Now there is but one Supreme good, namely God, as we have shown in the First Book. Therefore all things are directed to the Supreme good, namely God, as their end.

Again. *That which is supreme in any genus, is the cause of everything in that genus:* thus fire which is supremely hot is the cause of heat in other bodies. Therefore the Supreme good, namely God, is the cause of goodness in all things good. Therefore He is the cause of every end being an end: since whatever is an end, is such, insofar as it is good. Now *the cause of a thing being such, is yet more so.* Therefore God is supremely the end of all things.

Further. In every series of causes, the first cause is more a cause than the second cause: since the second cause is not a cause save through the first. Therefore that which is the first cause in the series of final causes must needs be more the final cause of each thing, than the proximate final cause. Now God is the first cause in the series of final causes: for He is supreme in the order of good things. Therefore He is the end of each thing more even than any proximate end.

Moreover, in all mutually subordinate ends the last must need be the end of each preceding end: thus if a potion be mixed to be given to a sick man; and is given to him that he may be purged and he be purged that he may be lowered, and lowered that he may be healed, it follows that health is the end of the lowering, and of the purging, and of those that precede. Now all things are subordinate in various degrees of goodness to the one supreme good, that is the cause of all goodness: and so, since good has the aspect of an end, all things are subordinate to God as preceding ends under the last end. Therefore God must be the end of all.

Furthermore, the particular good is directed to the common good as its end: for the being of the part is on account of the whole: wherefore *the good of the nation is more godlike than the good of one man.* Now the supreme good, namely God, is the common good, since the good of all things depends on him: and the good whereby each thing is good, is the particular good of that thing, and of those that depend thereon. Therefore all things are directed to one good, God to wit, as their end.

Again. Order among ends is consequent to the order among agents: for just as the supreme agent moves all second agents, so must all the ends of second agents be directed to the end of the supreme agent: since whatever the supreme agent does, it does for its own end. Now the supreme agent is the active principle of the actions of all inferior agents, by moving all to their actions, and consequently to their ends. Hence, it follows that all the ends of second agents are directed by the first agent to its proper end. Now the first agent in all things is God, as we proved in the Second Book. And His will has no other end but His own goodness, which is Himself, as we showed in the First Book. Therefore all things whether they were made by Him immediately, or by means of secondary causes, are directed to God as their end. But this applies to all things: for as we proved in the Second Book, there can be nothing that has not its being from Him. Therefore all things are directed to God as their end.

Moreover, the last end of every maker, as such, is himself: for what we make we use for our own sake: and if at any time a man make a thing for the sake of something else, it is referred to his own good, whether his use, his pleasure, or his virtue. Now God is the cause of all things being made; of some immediately, of others by means of other causes, as we have explained above. Therefore He is the end of all things.

And again. The end holds the highest place among causes, and it is from it that all other causes derive their actual causality: since the agent acts not except for the end, as was proved. And it is due to the agent that the matter is brought to the actuality of the form: wherefore the matter is made actually the matter, and the form is made the form, of this particular thing, through the agent's action, and consequently through the end. The later end also, is the cause of the preceding end being intended as an end: for a thing is not moved towards a proximate end, except for the sake of the last end. Therefore the last end is the first cause of all. Now it must need befit the First Being, namely God, to be the first cause of all, as we proved above. Therefore God is the last end of all.

Hence it is written: *The Lord hath made all things for himself*: and *I am Alpha and Omega, the first and the last.*

XXX. That Man's Happiness Does Not Consist in Wealth

Hence, it is evident that neither is wealth man's supreme good. For wealth is not sought except for the sake of something else: because of itself it brings us no good, but only when we use it, whether for the support of the body, or for some similar purpose. Now the supreme good is sought for its own, and not for another's sake. Therefore wealth is not man's supreme good.

Again, man's supreme good cannot consist in the possession or preservation of things whose chief advantage for man consists in their being spent. Now the chief advantage of wealth is in its being spent; for this is its use. Therefore the possession of wealth cannot be man's supreme good.

Moreover, acts of virtue deserve praise according as they lead to happiness. Now acts of liberality and magnificence which are concerned with money, are deserving of praise, on account of money being spent, rather than on account of its being kept: and it is from this that these virtues derive their names. Therefore man's happiness does not consist in the possession of wealth.

Besides, man's supreme good must consist in obtaining something better than man. But man is better than wealth: since it is something directed to man's use. Therefore not in wealth does man's supreme good consist.

Further, man's supreme good is not subject to chance. For things that happen by chance, escape the forethought of reason: whereas man has to attain his own end by means of his reason. But chance occupies the greater place in the attaining of wealth. Therefore human happiness consists not in wealth.

Moreover, this is evident from the fact that wealth is lost unwillingly. Also because wealth can come into the possession of evil persons, who, of necessity, must lack the sovereign good. Again, because wealth is unstable. Other similar reasons can be gathered from the arguments given above.

XXXI. That Happiness Consists Not in Worldly Power

In like manner neither can worldly power be man's supreme happiness: since in the achievement thereof chance can effect much. Again it is unstable; and is not subject to man's will; and is often obtained by evil men. These are incompatible with the supreme good, as already stated.

Again, man is said to be good especially according as he approaches the supreme good. But in respect to his having power, he is not said to be either good or evil: since not everyone who can do good deeds is good, nor is a person evil because he can do evil deeds. Therefore the supreme good does not consist in being powerful.

Besides, every power implies reference to something else. But the supreme good is not referred to anything further. Therefore power is not man's supreme good.

Moreover, man's supreme good cannot be a thing that one can use both well and ill: for the better things are *those that we cannot abuse*. But one can use one's power both well and ill: for *rational powers can be directed to contrary objects*. Therefore human power is not man's supreme good.

Further, if any power be man's supreme good, it must be most perfect. Now human power is most imperfect: for it is based on human will and opinion, which are full of inconsistencies. Also the greater a power is reputed to be, the greater number of people does it depend on: which again conduces to its weakness, since what depends on many, is in many ways destructible. Therefore man's supreme good does not consist in worldly power. Consequently man's happiness consists in no external good: for all external goods, which are known as *goods of chance*, are contained under those we have mentioned.

XXXII. That Happiness Consists Not in Goods of the Body

Like arguments avail to prove that man's supreme good does not consist in goods of the body, such as health, beauty, and strength. For they are common to good and evil: and are unstable: and are not subject to the will.

Besides. The soul is better than the body, which neither lives, nor possesses these goods, without the soul. Wherefore the soul's good, such as understanding and the like, is better than the body's good. Therefore the body's good is not man's supreme good.

Again. These goods are common to man and other animals: whereas happiness is a good proper to man. Therefore man's happiness does not consist in the things mentioned.

Moreover. Many animals surpass man in goods of the body: for some are fleeter than he, some more sturdy, and so on. Accordingly, if man's supreme good consisted in these things, man would not excel all animals: which is clearly untrue. Therefore human happiness does not consist in goods of the body.

XXXIII. That Human Happiness Is Not Seated in the Senses

By the same arguments it is evident that neither does man's supreme good consist in goods of his sensitive faculty. For these goods again, are common to man and other animals.

Again. Intellect is superior to sense. Therefore the intellect's good is better than the sense's. Consequently man's supreme good is not seated in the senses.

Besides. The greatest sensual pleasures are those of the table and of sex, wherein the supreme good must needs be, if seated in the senses. But it does not consist in them. Therefore man's supreme good is not in the senses.

Moreover. The senses are appreciated for their utility and for knowledge. Now the entire utility of the senses is referred to the goods of the body. Again, sensitive knowledge is directed to intellective: wherefore animals devoid of intelligence take no pleasure in sensation except in reference to some bodily utility, insofar as by sensitive knowledge they obtain food or sexual intercourse. Therefore man's supreme good which is happiness is not seated in the sensitive faculty.

——

XXXVII. That Man's Ultimate Happiness Consists in Contemplating God

Accordingly if man's ultimate happiness consists not in external things, which are called goods of chance; nor in goods of the body; nor in goods of the soul, as regards the sensitive faculty; nor as regards the intellective faculty, in the practice of moral virtue; nor as regards intellectual virtue in those which are concerned about action, namely art and prudence; it remains for us to conclude that man's ultimate happiness consists in the contemplation of the truth.

For this operation alone is proper to man, and none of the other animals communicates with him therein.

Again. This is not directed to anything further as its end: since the contemplation of the truth is sought for its own sake.

Again. By this operation man is united to things above him, by becoming like them: because of all human actions, this alone is both in God and in separate substances. Also, by this operation man comes into contact with those higher beings, through knowing them in any way whatever.

Besides, man is more self-sufficing for this operation, seeing that he stands in little need of the help of external things in order to perform it.

Further. All other human operations seem to be directed to this as their end. Because perfect contemplation requires that the body should be disencumbered, and to this effect are directed all the products of art that are necessary for life. Moreover, it requires freedom from the disturbance caused by the passions, which is achieved by means of the moral virtues and prudence; and freedom from external disturbance, to which all the regulations of the civil life are directed. So that, if we consider the matter rightly, we shall see that all human occupations are brought into the service of those who contemplate the truth. Now, it is not possible that man's ultimate happiness consists in contemplation based on the understanding of first principles: for this is most imperfect, as being universal and containing potential knowledge of things. Moreover, it is the beginning and not the end of human study, and comes to us from nature, and not through the study of the truth. Nor does it consist in contemplation based on the sciences that have the lowest things for their object: since happiness must consist in an operation of the intellect in relation to the highest objects of intelligence. It follows then that man's ultimate happiness consists in wisdom, based on the consideration of divine things. It is therefore evidence by way of induction that man's ultimate happiness consists solely in the contemplation of God, which conclusion was proved above by arguments.

XLVIII. That Man's Ultimate Happiness Is Not in This Life

Seeing then that man's ultimate happiness does not consist in that knowledge of God whereby he is known by all or many in a vague kind of opinion, nor again in that knowledge of God whereby he is known in science through demonstration; nor in that knowledge whereby he is known through faith, as we have proved above: and seeing that it is not possible in this life to arrive at a higher knowledge of God in His essence, or at least so that we understand other separate substances, and thus know God through that which is nearest to Him, so to say, as we have proved; and since we must place our ultimate happiness in some kind of knowledge of God, as we have shown; it is impossible for man's happiness to be in this life.

Again. Man's last end is the term of his natural appetite, so that when he has obtained it, he desires nothing more: because if he still has a movement towards something, he has not yet reached an end wherein to be at rest. Now, this cannot happen in this life: since the more man understands, the more is the desire to understand increased in him—this being natural to man—unless perhaps someone there be who understands all things: and in this life this never did nor can happen to anyone who was a mere man; seeing that in this life we are unable to know separate substances which in themselves are most intelligible, as we have proved. Therefore man's ultimate happiness cannot possibly be in this life.

Besides. Whatever is in motion towards an end, has a natural desire to be established and at rest therein: hence a body does not move away from the place towards which it has a natural movement, except by a violent movement which is contrary to that appetite. Now happiness is the last end which man desires naturally. Therefore it is his natural desire to be established in happiness. Consequently unless together with happiness he acquires a state of immobility, he is not yet happy, since his natural desire is not yet at rest. When therefore a man acquires happiness, he also acquires stability and rest; so that all agree in conceiving stability as a necessary condition of happiness: hence the Philosopher [Aristotle] says: *We do not look upon the happy man as a kind of chameleon.* Now, in this life there is no sure stability; since, however happy a man may be, sickness and misfortune may come upon him, so that he is hindered in the operation, whatever it be, in which his happiness consists. Therefore man's ultimate happiness cannot be in this life.

Moreover. It would seem unfitting and unreasonable for a thing to take a long time in becoming, and to have but a short time in being: for it would follow that for a longer duration of time nature would be deprived of its end; hence we see that animals which live but a short time, are perfected in a short time. But, if happiness consists in a perfect operation according to perfect virtue, whether intellectual or moral, it cannot possibly come to man except after a long time. This is most evidence in speculative matters, wherein man's ultimate happiness consists, as we have proved: for hardly is man able to arrive at perfection in the speculations of science, even though he reach the last stage of life: and then in the majority of cases, but a short space of life remains to him. Therefore man's ultimate happiness cannot be in this life.

Further. All admit that happiness is a perfect good: else it would not bring rest to the appetite. Now perfect good is that which is wholly free from any admixture of evil: just as that which is perfectly white is that which is entirely free from any admixture of black. But man cannot be wholly free from evils in this state of life; not only from evils of the body, such as hunger, thirst, heat, cold, and the like, but also from evils of the soul. For no one is there who at times is not disturbed by inordinate passions; who sometimes does not go beyond the mean, wherein virtue consists, either in excess or in deficiency; who is not deceived in some thing or another; or at least ignores what he would wish to know, or feels doubtful about an opinion of which he would like to be certain. Therefore no man is happy in this life.

Again. Man naturally shuns death, and is sad about it: not only shunning it now when he feels its presence, but also when he thinks about it. But man, in this life, cannot obtain not to die. Therefore it is not possible for man to be happy in this life.

Besides. Ultimate happiness consists not in a habit but in an operation: since habits are for the sake of actions. But in this life it is impossible to perform any action continuously. Therefore man cannot be entirely happy in this life.

Further. The more a thing is desired and loved, the more does its loss bring sorrow and pain. Now happiness is most desired and loved. Therefore its loss brings the greatest sorrow. But if there be ultimate happiness in this life, it will certainly be lost, at least by death. Nor is it certain that it will last till death: since it is possible for every man in this life to encounter sickness, whereby he is wholly hindered from the operation of virtue; such as madness and the like which hinder the use of reason. Such happiness, therefore, always has sorrow naturally connected with it: and consequently it will not be perfect happiness.

But someone might say that, since happiness is a good of the intellectual nature, perfect and true happiness is for those in whom the intellectual nature is perfect, namely in separate substances: and that it is imperfect in man, by way of a kind of participation because he can arrive at a full understanding of the truth only by a sort of movement of inquiry; and fails entirely to understand things that are by nature most intelligible, as we have proved. Wherefore neither is happiness, in its perfect form, possible to man: yet he has a certain participation thereof, even in this life. This seems to have been Aristotle's opinion about happiness. Wherefore inquiring whether misfortunes destroy happiness, he shows that happiness seems especially to consist in deeds of virtue, which seem to be most stable in this life, and concludes that those who in this life attain to this perfection, are happy *as men,* as though not attaining to happiness simply, but in a human way.

We must now show that this explanation does not avoid the foregoing arguments. For although man is below the separate substances in the natural order, he is above irrational creatures: wherefore he attains his ultimate end in a more perfect way than they. Now these attain their last end so perfectly that they seek nothing further: thus a heavy body rests when it is in its own proper place; and when an animal enjoys sensible pleasure, its natural desire is at rest. Much more therefore when man has obtained his last end, must his natural desire be at rest. But this cannot happen in this life. Therefore in this life man does not obtain happiness considered as his proper end, as we have proved. Therefore he must obtain it after this life.

Summa Theologica

Question 91
Of the Various Kinds of Law

First Article

Whether There Is an Eternal Law?
We proceed thus to the First Article:—

Objection 1. It would seem that there is no eternal law. Because every law is imposed on someone. But there was not someone from eternity on whom a law could be imposed: since God alone was from eternity. Therefore no law is eternal.

Obj. 2. Further, promulgation is essential to law. But promulgation could not be from eternity: because there was no one to whom it could be promulgated from eternity. Therefore no law can be eternal.

Obj. 3. Further, a law implies order to an end. But nothing ordained to an end is eternal for the last end alone is eternal. Therefore no law is eternal.

On the contrary, Augustine says: *That Law which is the Supreme Reason cannot be understood to be otherwise than unchangeable and eternal.*

St. Thomas Aquinas, *Summa Theologica.* New York: Benziger, 1947. (Translated by the English Dominican Fathers.) Reprinted by permission of Benziger.

I answer that, As stated above, a law is nothing else but a dictate of practical reason emanating from the ruler who governs a perfect community. Now it is evident, granted that the world is ruled by Divine Providence, as was stated in the First Part, that the whole community of the universe is governed by Divine Reason. Wherefore the very Idea of the government of things in God the Ruler of the universe has the nature of a law. And since the Divine Reason's conception of things is not subject to time but is eternal, according to Prov. viii. 23, therefore it is that this kind of law must be called eternal.

Reply Obj. 1. Those things that are not in themselves, exist with God, inasmuch as they are foreknown and preordained by Him, according to Rom. iv. 17: *Who calls those things that are not, as those that are.* Accordingly, the eternal concept of the Divine law bears the character of an eternal law, insofar as it is ordained by God to the government of things foreknown by Him.

Reply Obj. 2. Promulgation is made by word of mouth or in writing; and in both ways the eternal law is promulgated: because both the Divine Word and the writing of the Book of Life are eternal. But the promulgation cannot be from eternity on the part of the creature that hears or reads.

Reply Obj. 3. The law implies order to the end actively, insofar as it directs certain things to the end; but not passively—that is to say, the law itself is not ordained to the end—except accidentally, in a governor whose end is extrinsic to him, and to which end his law must needs be ordained. But the end of the Divine government is God Himself, and His law is not distinct from Himself. Wherefore the eternal law is not ordained to another end.

Second Article

Whether There Is in Us a Natural Law?
We proceed thus to the Second Article:—

Objection 1. It would seem that there is no natural law in us. Because man is governed sufficiently by the eternal law: for Augustine says that *the eternal law is that by which it is right that all things should be most orderly.* But nature does not abound in superfluities as neither does she fail in necessaries. Therefore no law is natural to man.

Obj. 2. Further, by the law man is directed, in his acts, to the end, as stated above. But the directing of human acts to their end is not a function of nature, as is the case in irrational creatures, which act for an end solely by their natural appetite; whereas man acts for an end by his reason and will. Therefore no law is natural to man.

Obj. 3. Further, the more a man is free, the less is he under the law. But man is freer than all the animals, on account of his free-will, with which he is endowed above all other animals. Since therefore other animals are not subject to a natural law, neither is man subject to a natural law.

On the contrary, A gloss on Rom. iii, 14: *When the Gentiles, who have not the law, do by nature those things that are of the law,* comments as follows: *Although they have no written law, yet they have the natural law, whereby each one knows, and is conscious of, what is good and what is evil.*

I answer that, As stated above, law being a rule and measure, can be in a person in two ways: in one way, as in him that rules and measures; in another way, as in that which is ruled and measured, since a thing is ruled and measured, insofar as it partakes of the rule or measure. Wherefore, since all things subject to Divine providence are ruled and measured by the eternal law, as was stated above; it is evident that all things partake somewhat of the eternal law, insofar as, namely, from its being imprinted on them, they derive their respective inclinations to their proper acts and ends. Now among all others, the rational creature is subject to Divine providence in the most excellent way, insofar as it partakes of a share of providence, by being provident both for itself and for others. Wherefore it has a share of the Eternal Reason, whereby it has a natural inclination to its proper act and end: and this participation of the eternal law in the rational creature is called the natural law. Hence the Psalmist after saying: *Offer up the sacrifice of justice,* as though someone asked what the works of justice are, adds: *Many say, Who showeth us good things?* in answer to which question he says: *The light of Thy countenance, O Lord, is signed upon us;* thus implying that the light of natural reason, whereby we discern what is good and what is evil, which is the function of the natural law, is nothing else than an imprint on us of the Divine light. It is therefore evident that the natural law is nothing else than the rational creature's participation of the eternal law.

Reply Obj. 1. This argument would hold, if the natural law were something different from the eternal law: whereas it is nothing but a participation thereof, as stated above.

Reply Obj. 2. Every act of reason and will in us is based on that which is according to nature, as stated above: for every act of reasoning is based on principles that are known naturally, and every act of appetite in respect of the means is derived from the natural appetite in respect of the last end. Accordingly, the first direction of our acts to their end must needs be in virtue of the natural law.

Reply Obj. 3. Even irrational animals partake in their own way of the Eternal Reason, just as the rational creature does. But because the rational creature partakes thereof in an intellectual and rational manner, therefore the participation of the eternal law in the rational creature is properly called a law, since a law is something pertaining to reason, as stated above. Irrational creatures, however, do not partake thereof in a rational manner, wherefore there is no participation of the eternal law in them, except by way of similitude.

Question 94
Of the Natural Law

———

Second Article

Whether the Natural Law Contains Several Precepts, or One Only?
We proceed thus to the Second Article:—

Objection 1. It would seem that the natural law contains, not several precepts, but one only. For law is a kind of precept, as stated above. If, therefore, there were many precepts of the natural law, it would follow that there are also many natural laws.

Obj. 2. Further, the natural law is consequent to human nature. But human nature, as a whole, is one; though, as to its parts, it is manifold. Therefore, either there is but one precept of the law of nature, on account of the unity of nature as a whole; or there are many, by reason of the number of parts of human nature. The result would be that even things relating to the inclination of the concupiscible faculty belong to the natural law.

Obj. 3. Further, law is something pertaining to reason, as stated above. Now reason is but one in man. Therefore there is only one precept of the natural law.

On the contrary, The precepts of the natural law in man stand in relation to practical matters, as the first principles to matters of demonstration. But there are several first indemonstrable principles. Therefore there are also several precepts of the natural law.

I answer that, As stated above, the precepts of the natural law are to the practical reason, what the first principles of demonstrations are to the speculative reason; because both are self-evident principles. Now a thing is said to be self-evident in two ways: first, in itself; secondly, in relation to us. Any proposition is said to be self-evident in itself, if its predicate is contained in the notion of the subject: although to one who knows not the definition of the subject, it happens that such a proposition is not self-evident. For instance, this proposition, *Man is a rational being,* is, in its very nature, self-evident, since who says *man, says a rational being:* and yet to one who knows not what a man is, this proposition is not self-evident. Hence it is that, as Boethius says, certain axioms or propositions are universally self-evident to all; and such are those propositions whose terms are known to all, as, *Every whole is greater than its part,* and, *Things equal to one and the same are equal to one another.* But some propositions are self-evident only to the wise, who understand the meaning of the terms of such propositions: thus to one who understands that an angel is not a body, it is self-evident that an angel is not circumscriptively in a place: but this is not evident to the unlearned, for they cannot grasp it.

Now a certain order is to be found in those things that are apprehended universally. For that which, before aught else, falls under apprehension, is *being,* the notion of which is included in all things whatsoever a man apprehends. Wherefore the first indemonstrable principle is that *the same thing cannot be affirmed and denied at the same time,* which is based on the notion of *being* and *not-being:* and on this principle all others are based, as is stated in *Metaph.* iv, text. 9. Now as *being* is the first thing that falls under the apprehension simply, so *good* is the first thing that falls under the apprehension of the practical reason, which is directed to action: since every agent acts for an end under the aspect of good. Consequently the first principle in the practical reason is one founded in the notion of good, viz., that *good is that which all things seek after.* Hence this is the first precept of law, that *good is to be done and pursued, and evil is to be avoided.* All other precepts of the natural law are based upon this: so that whatever the practical reason naturally apprehends as man's good (or evil) belongs to precepts of the natural law as something to be done or avoided.

Since, however, good has the nature of an end, and evil, the nature of a contrary, hence it is that all those things to which man has a natural inclination, are naturally apprehended by reason as being good, and consequently as objects of pursuit, and their contraries as evil, and objects of avoidance. Wherefore according to the order of natural inclinations, is the order of the precepts of the natural law. Because in man there is first of all an inclination to good in accordance with the nature which he has in common with all substances: inasmuch as every substance seeks the preservation of its own being, according to its nature: and by reason of this inclination, whatever is a means of preserving human life, and of warding off its obstacles, belongs to the natural law. Secondly, there is in man an inclination to things that pertain to him more specially, according to that nature which he has in common with other animals: and in virtue of this inclination, those things are said to belong to the natural law, which nature has taught to all animals, such as sexual intercourse, education of offspring, and so forth. Thirdly, there is in man an inclination to good, according to the nature of his reason, which nature is proper to him: thus man has a natural inclination to know the truth about God, and to live in society: and in this respect, whatever pertains to this inclination belongs to the natural law; for instance, to shun ignorance, to avoid offending those among whom one has to live, and other such things regarding the above inclination.

Reply Obj. 1. All these precepts of the law of nature have the character of one natural law, inasmuch as they flow from one first precept.

Reply Obj. 2. All the inclinations of any parts whatsoever of human nature, *e.g.,* of the concupiscible and irascible parts, insofar as they are ruled by reason, belong to the natural law, and are reduced to one first precept, as stated above: so that the precepts of the natural law are many in themselves, but are based on one common foundation.

Reply Obj. 3. Although reason is one in itself, yet it directs all things regarding man; so that whatever can be ruled by reason, is contained under the law of reason.

Third Article

Whether All Acts of Virtue Are Prescribed by the Natural Law?
We proceed thus to the Third Article:—

Objection 1. It would seem that not all acts of virtue are prescribed by the natural law. Because, as stated above it is essential to a law that it be ordained to the common good. But some acts of virtue are ordained to the private good of the individual, as is evident especially in regards to acts of temperance. Therefore not all acts of virtue are the subject of natural law.

Obj. 2. Further, every sin is opposed to some virtuous act. If therefore all acts of virtue are prescribed by the natural law, it seems to follow that all sins are against nature: whereas this applies to certain special sins.

Obj. 3. Further, those things which are according to nature are common to all. But acts of virtue are not common to all: since a thing is virtuous in one, and vicious in another. Therefore not all acts of virtue are prescribed by the natural law.

On the contrary, Damascene* says that *virtues are natural.* Therefore virtuous acts also are a subject to the natural law.

*A Greek theologian of the eighth century.—Ed.

I answer that, We may speak of virtuous acts in two ways: first, under the aspect of virtuous; secondly, as such and such acts considered in their proper species. If then we speak of acts of virtue, considered as virtuous, thus all virtuous acts belong to the natural law. For it has been stated that to the natural law belongs everything to which a man is inclined according to his nature. Now each thing is inclined naturally to an operation that is suitable to it according to its form: thus fire is inclined to give heat. Wherefore, since the rational soul is the proper form of man, there is in every man a natural inclination to act according to reason: and this is to act according to virtue. Consequently, considered thus, all acts of virtue are prescribed by the natural law: since each one's reason naturally dictates to him to act virtuously. But if we speak of virtuous acts, considered in themselves, i.e., in their proper species, thus not all virtuous acts are prescribed by the natural law: for many things are done virtuously, to which nature does not incline at first; but which, through the inquiry of reason, have been found by men to be conducive to well-living.

Reply Obj. 1. Temperance is about the natural concupiscences of food, drink, and sexual matters, which are indeed ordained to the natural common good, just as other matters of law are ordained to the moral common good.

Reply Obj. 2. By human nature we may mean either that which is proper to man—and in this sense all sins, as being against reason, are also against nature, as Damascene states: or we may mean that nature which is common to man and other animals; and in this sense, certain special sins are said to be against nature; thus contrary to sexual intercourse, which is natural to all animals, is unisexual lust, which has received the special name of the unnatural crime.

Reply Obj. 3. This argument considers acts in themselves. For it is owing to the various conditions of men, that certain acts are virtuous for some, as being proportionate and becoming to them, while they are vicious for others, as being out of proportion to them.

Fourth Article

Whether the Natural Law Is the Same in All Men?
We proceed thus to the Fourth Article:—

Objection 1. It would seem that the natural law is not the same in all. For it is stated in the Decretals that *the natural law is that which is contained in the Law and the Gospel.* But this is not common to all men; because, as it is written, *all do not obey the gospel.* Therefore the natural law is not the same in all men.

Obj. 2. Further, *Things which are according to the law are said to be just,* as stated in *Ethic.* v. But it is stated in the same book that nothing is so universally just as not to be subject to change in regard to some men. Therefore even the natural law is not the same in all men.

Obj. 3. Further, as stated above, to the natural law belongs everything to which a man is inclined according to his nature. Now different men are naturally inclined to different things; some to the desire of pleasures, others to the desire of honors, and other men to other things. Therefore there is not one natural law for all.

On the contrary, Isidore says: *The natural law is common to all nations.*

I answer that, As stated above, to the natural law belongs those things to which a man is inclined naturally: and among these it is proper to man to be inclined to act according to reason. Now the process of reason is from the common to the proper, as stated in *Phys. i.* The speculative reason, however, is differently situated in this matter, from the practical reason. For, since the speculative reason is busied chiefly with necessary things, which cannot be otherwise than they are, its proper conclusions, like the universal principles, contain the truth without fail. The practical reason, on the other hand, is busied with contingent matters, about which human actions are concerned: and consequently, although there is necessity in the general principles, the more we descend to matters of detail, the more frequently we encounter defects. Accordingly then in speculative matters truth is the same in all men, both as to principles and as to conclusions: although the truth is not known to all as regards the conclusions, but only as regards the principles which are called common notions. But in matters of action, truth or practical rectitude is not the same for all, as to matters of detail, but only as to the general principles: and where there is the same rectitude in matters of detail, it is not equally known to all.

It is therefore evident that, as regards the general principles whether of speculative or of practical reason, truth or rectitude is the same for all, and is equally known by all. As to the proper conclusions of the speculative reason, the truth is the same for all, but is not equally known to all: thus it is true for all that the three angles of a triangle are together equal to two right angles, although it is not known to all. But as to the proper conclusions of the practical reason, neither is the truth or rectitude the same for all, nor, where it is the same, is it equally known by all. Thus it is right and true for all to act according to reason: and from this principle it follows as a proper conclusion, that goods entrusted to another should be restored to their owner. Now this is true for the majority of cases: but it may happen in a particular case that it would be injurious, and therefore unreasonable, to restore goods held in trust; for instance if they are claimed for the purpose of fighting against one's country. And this principle will be found to fail the more, according as we descend further into detail, *e.g.,* if one were to say that goods held in trust should be restored with such and such a guarantee, or in such and such a way; because the greater number of conditions added, the greater the number of ways in which the principle may fail, so that it be not right to restore or not to restore.

Consequently we must say that the natural law, as to general principles, is the same for all, both as to rectitude and as to knowledge. But as to certain matters of detail, which are conclusions, as it were, of those general principles, it is the same for all in the majority of cases, both as to rectitude and as to knowledge; and yet in some few cases it may fail, both as to rectitude, by reason of certain obstacles (just as natures subject to generation and corruption fail in some few cases on account of some obstacle), and as to knowledge, since in some the reason is perverted by passion, or evil habit, or an evil disposition of nature; thus formerly, theft, although it is expressly contrary to the natural law, was not considered wrong among the Germans, as Julius Caesar relates.

Reply Obj. 1. The meaning of the sentence quoted is not that whatever is contained in the Law and the Gospel belongs to the natural law, since they contain many things that are above nature; but that whatever belongs to the natural law is fully contained in them. Wherefore Gratian, after saying that *the natural law is what is contained in the Law and the Gospel,* adds at once, by way of example, *by which everyone is commanded to do to others as he would be done by.*

Reply Obj. 2. The saying of the Philosopher is to be understood of things that are naturally just, not as general principles, but as conclusions drawn from them, having rectitude in the majority of cases, but failing in a few.

Reply Obj. 3. As, in man, reason rules and commands the other powers, so all the natural inclinations belonging to the other powers must need be directed according to reason. Wherefore it is universally right for all men, that all their inclinations should be directed according to reason.

Study Questions

1. Aquinas claims that every agent acts for a good. How does he support this claim? Can you think of counter-examples to this view? How might Aquinas deal with them?
2. What does our ultimate happiness consist in, according to Aquinas? How does he arrive at this conclusion? What do you find plausible and what implausible in his arguments?
3. What does Aquinas mean by natural law? How is it related to eternal law? Must natural law stem from God, as Aquinas says? If not, what might be its source?
4. How does Aquinas answer the question whether natural law is the same for all men? (In thinking about this question, take note of his distinction between general principles and conclusions drawn from them about matters of detail, and the distinction between what is true and what is known or believed.) Is his answer persuasive?

Selected Bibliography

Baumgarth, William P. and Regan, Richard J., *Saint Thomas Aquinas on Law Morality and Politics* (Cambridge, Mass.: Hackett Publishing, 1988). A collection of Aquinas' writings on conscience, natural law, justice, and other moral issues.

Finnis, John. *Aquinas: Moral, Political and Legal Theory* (Oxford: Oxford University Press, 1998). A general and comprehensive study.

Flew, A., ed. *Aquinas* (Garden City, N.Y.: Doubleday, 1969), Part 2. Collection of essays.

Gilson, E. *The Christian Philosophy of St. Thomas Aquinas,* trans. L. K. Shook (Notre Dame: University of Notre Dame Press, 1994), Part 3. Thomistic ethics analyzed by an eminent contemporary Catholic scholar.

Kretzmann, Normann, and Stump, Eleanor, eds. *The Cambridge Companion to Aquinas* (New York: Cambridge University Press, 1993). Recent essays on Aquinas.

McInery, Ralph. *Ethics Thomistica* (Washington, D.C.: Catholic University of America Press, 1997). A general study.

PART
TWO

THE MODERN WORLD

It is generally agreed that the early modern period represents an important break with the medieval epoch. The 15th and 16th centuries saw important changes in social, political, and religious life, and in intellectual culture, that profoundly altered the character of western civilization. These changes brought the medieval epoch to an end and laid the foundations of modern society. No precise date can be given to the beginning of the modern period, and it is difficult to isolate all of the events that led to these changes. But several developments are worth mentioning here, all of which had an impact on the character of moral and political thought in the modern period. One is the religious upheaval in 16th century northern Europe now called the Reformation. By successfully challenging the authority of the Catholic church, Martin Luther and John Calvin, along with other Protestant reformers, broke the undisputed religious sway of the most powerful institution of medieval society. The Reformation fragmented the religious unity of the medieval period and ushered in a period of religious pluralism, and with it conflict between proponents of different Christian denominations. Another is the development of modern science in the 16th and 17th centuries, which led to a fundamentally different picture of the universe and a different approach to explaining events in the natural world. A third is the development of the modern state, in which political power is highly centralized. The first modern states to emerge were ruled by absolute monarchs. However, as time went on, their power was either limited or transferred to parliaments and national assemblies by constitutional arrangements, often as a result of protracted political struggle.

As we move into the modern period, we find important changes in the understanding of ethics and the overall orientation of moral philosophy, one of which we shall focus on here. Although broad generalizations are necessarily inexact, in the ancient and medieval periods the fundamental question of moral philosophy concerned the nature of the highest good or true happiness. This good was understood as a good for the individual—the ultimate end that individuals would ideally choose for themselves under the direction of reason. The virtues—such as courage, self-control, generosity, justice and practical wisdom—are states of character that embody norms of conduct, and they can lead to restraints and control of one's desires and to concern for others and for the needs of society. But ultimately they are seen as either means to or components of the good for the individual. The virtues are among the goods that are part of true individual happiness. In Aquinas we see a different element in addition because the virtues are understood to rest on natural law, or divine law. Natural law is a source of commands or prescriptions that obligate us. Human beings ought to perform the virtuous actions prescribed by natural law simply because they are commanded by God, regardless of whether they see a connection with their own individual good. But Aquinas's conception of the universe does not permit any ultimate conflict between following the natural law and an individual's good, or between the good of one individual and that of another, because natural law directs all individuals to their natural ends. By following the natural law, individuals achieve their true good.

In contrast to the ancient and medieval periods, the early modern understanding of morality gives a central place to the notions of right conduct and of duty or obligation. Morality is seen as imposing demands or requirements on individuals that can limit or restrict their pursuit of their own good. Moreover, the demands of right conduct and considerations of an individual's good can come apart in ways that they could not in the ancient and medieval periods. The authority of the principles of right conduct is independent of an individual's good, in that the reasons to fulfill our duties and obligations do not refer to our own good. And there is the possibility of conflict, whether apparent or real, between our duties and obligations and our own happiness. Under certain circumstances, it seems, morality can require that we refrain from certain actions, or give up certain aims that we would very much like to pursue.

The shift in emphasis from the good for the individual to the principles of right conduct alters the problems that concern moral philosophers in the modern period. There is general agreement about what is right and wrong—agreement about what we might think of as the core of a common sense morality that includes duties of honesty, keeping promises and agreements, justice, beneficence and concern for the welfare of others, gratitude to benefactors, and so on. The concern of these philosophers is not to determine what our duties are, but rather to determine what these duties are based on and how they can bind us. The need to explain the basis of obligation is particularly pressing in view of the ways in which morality can constrain the pursuit of personal interests and the apparent possibility of conflict between duty and happiness. If I can have a duty to refrain from an action that would contribute to my own happiness, or to give up some aim that would provide me with great personal satisfaction, what reason do I have to do my duty? How can duty be binding in such a situation? The claims of duty and obligation need some kind of explanation. One thing that we find in this period is that different theorists develop alternative conceptions of the source of our duties and of how they obligate us. Often the differences in their moral theories reflect divergent views about human nature and human motivation, or about reason and rationality. Although again we need to be careful about making sweeping generalizations, disagreements among the great philosophers of this period are by and large not about the content of morality. Rather they are differences about the basis of moral obligation, often rooted in differing underlying conceptions of human nature and rationality.

Two other important trends also need to be noted. Many of the theorists of this period—though certainly not all—were religious believers. Even so, they seek a basis for morality that is independent of religion and church authority. Undoubtedly there are many explanations for this fact. One is that because of religious pluralism and the conflict that it engendered, there is a need for an account of the basis of morality that does not tie it to any particular religious order or source of religious authority. Another is a growing confidence in the capacity of individuals to think for themselves and to resolve basic questions of good conduct on their own without deference to established authorities. The second trend is that theorists of this period seek a conception of morality that is consistent with the new science. As emerging modern science comes up with increasingly more powerful explanations of natural phenomena, there is a need for a conception of morality that fits into the resulting picture of the world.

The selections included in this part can, of course, encompass only a sampling of the diverse accounts of moral thought put forward in the 17th through the 19th centuries. The aim has been to choose core sections of some of the works that have been historically most important and have exerted greatest influence on later thought. Many of these works have had a continuing impact and have provided the starting point or inspiration for various contemporary moral theorists. Taken together, they present a range of views that will challenge and stimulate the reader who wishes to inquire into the nature of morality. Each is likely to resonate with certain features of one's own moral outlook. Indeed, it may be that each contains some element of the truth.

Although these readings represent only a small selection from modern moral thought, their diversity will be apparent. Thomas Hobbes (1588–1679) tries to ground morality on rational self-interest by arguing that ordinary moral precepts should be understood as conventions that are needed for peaceful and productive social cooperation, in the absence of which no one can expect to lead a satisfactory life. Morality is thus a set of rules that it is in our collective self-interest to adopt. Although moral rules require us to limit our natural freedom, and thus restrict the pursuit of self-interest, the ultimate reason to view them as binding is that it is in our interest to do so. Somewhat paradoxically perhaps, each self-interested individual can expect to do better in the long run if he or she accepts binding limits on the pursuit of his or her private interests and agrees to adhere to certain rules regardless of the effect on their immediate interests—assuming, that is, that others accept such limits as well. Butler, Hume, and Kant, as well as Bentham and Mill, all in different ways reject Hobbes's egoistic starting point. Joseph Butler (1692–1752) thinks that judicious observation of human motives reveals many desires that are not self-interested—compassion, to name just one. Moreover, we are moral agents in virtue of possessing conscience, which he regards as an autonomous source of motivation that is independent of self-love, and that gives us a direct concern for acting rightly and avoiding wrong. Butler tries to explain the authority of moral obligation by arguing that conscience plays a special role in what he calls the "constitution of human nature," so that in acting virtuously we follow our nature.

David Hume (1711–1776) had little use for religion, and his philosophical temperament led him by a different route to a deep skepticism about the power of reason. But that is not to say that he was a moral skeptic. Rather, he views morality as an entirely naturalistic phenomenon, and he seeks an explanation of the moral judgments that we make and the virtues and vices that we recognize, in certain sentiments and feelings that are part of human psychology. The feature of human psychology that Hume identifies as the basis of moral judgment is the capacity to feel the pleasures and pains of others, which he calls sympathy. For Hume, both the content of morality—what we judge to be virtue and vice—and our motivation to act virtuously are tied, in different ways, to the operation of sympathy.

There are marked contrasts between Hume's approach to morality and Immanuel Kant's (1724–1804). Whereas Hume tries to base morality in human psychology, Kant adamantly denies that true moral principles can be derived from "special characteristics of human nature." For Kant, the special authority of moral requirements can be justified only by showing that moral principles represent requirements of reason. Kant's project is to articulate the fundamental principle that he believes underlies ordinary moral thought—a principle that he calls the Categorical Imperative—and to show that it is a requirement of reason that is entirely independent of desire and self-interest.

Butler and Kant both believe that morality has a basis in reason, and that moral principles pick out certain ways of acting as good in themselves, where the goodness of such actions lies in the underlying principle from which the action is performed, not in its goal or consequences. In Kant's case, it is not that the consequences of an action do not matter at all. Rather what gives the action its moral value is the character of its underlying principle, and whether that principle can be universally adopted or shows proper respect for the value of persons. Because Butler and Kant locate rightness in the nature of an action or its underlying principle, rather than in its consequences, they are generally regarded as "deontologists." Jeremy Bentham (1748–1832) and John Stuart Mill (1806–1873) represent a different tradition in the modern period known as "consequentialism." Specifically, they accept a form of consequentialism known as "utilitarianism." Bentham and Mill are philosophical descendents of Hume in that sympathy and a tendency to identify with the interests of society figure in their explanation of both the content of morality and the motivation to right conduct. They also explicitly develop a tendency that one sees emerging in Hume's view. Both hold that the rightness of an action lies in its tendency to promote general happiness, in other words, its contribution to the balance of happiness over unhappiness in all of the people affected by an action. They are consequentialists because they believe that the rightness of an action is determined by its consequences, or by the good that it brings about in the world. What makes them utilitarians is that general happiness is the measure of good consequences.

Karl Marx (1818–1883) and Friedrich Nietzsche (1844–1900) offer different perspectives on moral thought. Both evince a deep-seated skepticism toward what we have referred to as ordinary moral thought. Marx was not a moral theorist but a political economist and critic of modern capitalism, whose work was directed at revolutionary social change. His skepticism about morality comes from regarding what he terms "bourgeois morality" and appeals to the "rights of man" as ideological tools whose social function is to maintain the power of the propertied class. Still, it is difficult to avoid the conclusion that his egalitarianism and his concern for the well-being and flourishing of the oppressed classes have a deep moral basis.

Marx's political outlook appears to share certain elements with Kant's princi[] that rational agents are to be treated as ends in themselves and never merely as means. He also shares Mill's view that the principle of utility is fully satisfied only when people at all social levels have the opportunity to develop and to enjoy the exercise of their higher faculties. Nietzsche offers a skeptical account of the origin of moral distinctions. Modern common-sense morality does not represent principles with a basis in reason, or the operation of a healthy moral sense with a natural basis in human psychology. Morality—or better, a morality—is a set of value distinctions created by one social group to validate its own traits, in contrast to the traits of other social groups from which it distinguishes itself. The dominant morality of the modern era, which stresses equal worth or equal concern for all, is a set of valuations developed by the weak and faceless masses as a form of self-protection and self-validation. Nietzsche's view seems to be that we would be better off without the system of modern morality and that it should not survive a clear unmasking of its origins. His views certainly present a challenge to the other views in this section that is worth reflecting on.*

*Readers wishing further historical background on the moral philosophy of the early modern period are urged to consult J. B. Schneewind, *Moral Philosophy from Montaigne to Kant: An Anthology* (New York/Cambridge: Cambridge University Press, 1990), Introduction to Volume I; Stephen Darwall, *The British Moralists and the Internal 'Ought': 1640–1740* (New York/Cambridge: Cambridge University Press, 1995), pp. 1–23; and John Rawls, *Lectures on the History of Moral Philosophy* (Cambridge: Harvard University Press, 2000), pp. 1–20. I have drawn on all of these sources in this introductory note.

8

THOMAS HOBBES

———

Thomas Hobbes is most famous as a political philosopher, his *Leviathan* being a classic in the history of political theory. But this work contains much more, includ-

> *. . . of the voluntary acts of every man, the object is some good to himself.*

ing metaphysics, theology, psychology, and ethics. Hobbes is a major figure in the social contract tradition who viewed both political institutions, such as law and government, and social rules, such as ordinary moral precepts, as products of human agreements and convention. Hobbes analyzes the basis of political authority and political obligation by considering the "state of nature"—a condition in which there are no political or legal structures in place to maintain social order. Hobbes argues that the state of nature—he calls it "the natural condition" of humankind—would be a condition of perpetual insecurity and mutual distrust that makes productive social cooperation impossible, a "war of every man against every man." He thought that the dangers of the state of nature were sufficient to justify the establishment of an absolute sovereign. Hobbes did not think that the state of nature actually existed prior to the formation of governments, but he did think that we run the risk of falling into the insecurity of the state of nature if our existing political and social order were to collapse. Unfortunately, his observations have been borne out by events in many regions of the modern world that have been ravaged by civil war and anarchy.

Hobbes is generally regarded as both a psychological egoist and an ethical egoist. His major contribution to moral theory was to argue that morality can be grounded on self-interest. Previous thinkers had viewed morality as a set of eternal truths about right conduct, grounded in reason or in the nature of things. Beginning from his views about the state of nature, Hobbes argues that moral rules are conventions that serve our collective self-interest. Because effective moral rules are needed for security and for productive social cooperation, it is in each person's rational self-interest to support commonly agreed on moral rules, as well as social mechanisms for their enforcement. Moral rules are in this sense "theorems concerning what conduceth to the conservation and defense" of individuals in society. Hobbes's view that morality must be grounded on self-interest remains influential today.

Historians generally agree that Hobbes's dark views about human nature, as well as his advocacy of absolutism as a solution to human political problems, was in large part a result of his experiences during the period of the Puritan Revolution in England, in which he witnessed the corrosive effects on both individual character and national institutions of protracted civil war. Whatever the causes of Hobbes's views may have been, the effects of their publication were noteworthy. On every hand he was denounced—as immoral, irreligious, and inhuman. For the next hundred years almost every English moral philosopher felt he had to preface his own views with a refutation of the errors of Hobbes. Most of these writers have long since been retired into oblivion, but the *Leviathan* is a work that we continue to read and to study.

Hobbes was born in 1588. It is said that his birth occurred prematurely, as a result of his mother's fright at the approach of the Spanish Armada to the English coastline. As he later remarked, "Fear and I, like twins, were born together." Personally he belied his own description of man, for he was, on the whole, gentle, well-mannered, and considerate. During his long life he met many of the leading intellectuals of the age, including Francis Bacon, Gassendi, and Galileo. At one time during the Puritan Revolution he acted as tutor to Prince Charles (later Charles II), who had fled from England to Paris after the execution of his father. Hobbes died in 1679, at the ripe old age of ninety-one. Today a plaque can be seen on the house in Tewkesbury, England, where he was born.

———

Leviathan

Of the Interior Beginnings of Voluntary Motions Commonly Called the Passions and the Speeches by Which They Are Expressed

There be in animals, two sorts of *motions* peculiar to them: one called *vital;* begun in generation, and continued without interruption through their whole life; such as are the *course* of the *blood*, the *pulse*, the *breathing*, the *concoction, nutrition, excretion*, etc. to which motions there need no help of imagination: the other is *animal motion*, otherwise called *voluntary motion:* as to *go*, to *speak*, to *move* any of our limbs, in such manner as is first fancied in our minds. That sense is motion in the organs and interior parts of man's body, caused by the action of the things we see, hear, etc.; and that fancy is but the relics of the same motion, remaining after sense, has been already said in the first and second chapters. And because *going, speaking*, and the like voluntary motions, depend always upon a precedent thought of *whither, which way*, and *what;* it is evident, that the imagination is the first internal beginning of all voluntary motion. And although unstudied men do not conceive any motion at all to be there, where the thing moved is invisible; or the space it is moved in is, for the shortness of it, insensible; yet that doth not hinder, but that such motions are. For let a space be never so little, that which is moved over a greater space,

First published in 1651. The spelling has been modernized.

whereof that little one is part, must first be moved over that. These small beginnings of motion, within the body of man, before they appear in walking, speaking, striking, and other visible actions, are commonly called ENDEAVOR.

This endeavour, when it is toward something which causes it, is called AP-PETITE, or DESIRE; the latter, being the general name; and the other oftentimes restrained to signify the desire for food, namely *hunger* and *thirst*. And when the endeavour is fromward something, it is generally called AVERSION. These words, *appetite* and *aversion*, we have from the Latins; and they both of them signify the motions, one of approaching, the other of retiring. . . .

That which men desire, they are also said to LOVE: and to HATE those things for which they have aversion. So that desire and love are the same thing; save that by desire, we always signify the absence of the object; by love, most commonly the presence of the same. So also by aversion, we signify the absence; and by hate, the presence of the object.

Of appetites and aversions, some are born with men; as appetite of food, appetite of excretion, and exoneration, which may also and more properly be called aversions, from somewhat they feel in their bodies; and some other appetites, not many. The rest, which are appetites of particular things, proceed from experience, and trial of their effects upon themselves or other men. For of things we know not at all, or believe not to be, we can have no further desire, than to taste and try. But aversion we have for things, not only which we know have hurt us, but also that we do not know whether they will hurt us, or not.

Those things which we neither desire, nor hate, we are said to *contemn;* CON-TEMPT being nothing else but an immobility, or contumacy of the heart, in resisting the action of certain things; and proceeding from that the heart is already moved otherwise, by other more potent objects; or from want of experience of them.

And because the constitution of a man's body is in continual mutation, it is impossible that all the same things should always cause in him the same appetites, and aversions: much less can all men consent, in the desire of almost any one and the same object.

But whatsoever is the object of any man's appetite or desire, that is it which he for his part calleth *good:* and the object of his hate and aversion, *evil;* and of his contempt, *vile* and *inconsiderable.* For these words of good, evil, and contemptible, are ever used with relation to the person that useth them: there being nothing simply and absolutely so; nor any common rule of good and evil, to be taken from the nature of the objects themselves; but from the person of the man, where there is no commonwealth; or, in a commonwealth, from the person that representeth it; or from an arbitrator or judge, whom men disagreeing shall by consent set up, and make his sentence the rule thereof. . . .

Of Power, Worth, Dignity, Honour, and Worthiness

The power *of a man,* to take it universally, is his present means, to obtain some future apparent good, and is either *original* or *instrumental.*

Natural power, is the eminence of the faculties of body, or mind: as extraordinary strength, form, prudence, arts, eloquence, liberality, nobility. *Instrumental* are those powers, which acquired by these, or by fortune, are means and instruments to acquire more: as riches, reputation, friends, and the secret working of God, which men call good luck. For the nature of power, is in this point, like to fame, increasing as it proceeds; or like the motion of heavy bodies, which the further they go, make still the more haste.

The greatest of human powers, is that which is compounded of the powers of most men, united by consent, in one person, natural, or civil, that has the use of all their powers depending on his will; such as is the power of a commonwealth: or depending on the wills of each particular; such as is the power of a faction or of divers factions leagued. Therefore to have servants, is power; to have friends, is power: for they are strengths united.

Also riches joined with liberality, is power; because it procureth friends, and servants: without liberality, not so; because in this case they defend not; but expose men to envy, as a prey.

Reputation of power, is power; because it draweth with it the adherence of those that need protection.

So is reputation of love of a man's country called popularity, for the same reason.

Also, what quality soever maketh a man beloved, or feared of many; or the reputation of such quality, is power; because it is a means to have the assistance, and service of many.

Good success is power; because it maketh reputation of wisdom, or good fortune; which makes men either fear him, or rely on him.

Affability of men already in power, is increase of power; because it gaineth love.

Reputation of prudence in the conduct of peace or war, is power; because to prudent men, we commit the government of ourselves, more willingly than to others.

Nobility is power, not in all places, but only in those commonwealths, where it has privileges: for in such privileges, consisteth their power.

Eloquence is power, because it is seeming prudence.

Form is power; because being a promise of good, it recommendeth men to the favour of women and strangers.

The sciences are small power; because not eminent; and therefore, not acknowledged in any man; nor are at all, but in a few, and in them, but of a few things. For science is of that nature, as none can understand it to be, but such as in a good measure have attained it.

Arts of public use, as fortification, making of engines, and other instruments of war; because they confer to defence, and victory, are power: and though the true mother of them be science, namely the mathematics; yet, because they are brought into the light, by the hand of the artificer, they be esteemed, the midwife passing with the vulgar for the mother, as his issue.

The *value*, or WORTH of a man, is as of all other things, his price; that is to say, so much as would be given for the use of his power: and therefore is not absolute; but a thing dependent on the need and judgment of another. An able conductor of soldiers is of great price in time of war present, or imminent; but in peace not so. A learned and uncorrupt judge, is much worth in time of peace; but not so much in war. And as in other things, so in men, not the seller, but the buyer determines the price. For let a man, as most men do, rate themselves at the highest value they can; yet their true value is no more than it is esteemed by others.

The manifestation of the value we set on one another, is that which is commonly called honouring, and dishonouring. To value a man at a high rate, is to *honour* him; at a low rate, is to *dishonour* him. But high, and low, in this case, is to be understood by comparison to the rate that each man setteth on himself.

The public worth of a man, which is the value set on him by the commonwealth, is that which men commonly call DIGNITY. And this value of him by the commonwealth, is understood, by offices of command, judicature, public employment; or by names and titles, introduced for distinction of such value. . . .

Of the Difference of Manners

By manners, I mean not here, decency of behaviour; as how one should salute another, or how a man should wash his mouth, or pick his teeth before company, and such other points of the *small morals;* but those qualities of mankind that concern their living together in peace and unity. To which end we are to consider that the felicity of this life, consisteth not in the repose of a mind satisfied. For there is no such *finis ultimus,* utmost aim, nor *summum bonum,* greatest good, as is spoken of in the books of the old moral philosophers. Nor can a man any more live, whose desires are at an end, than he, whose senses and imaginations are at a stand. Felicity is a continual progress of the desire, from one object to another; the attaining of the former, being still but the way to the latter. The cause whereof is, that the object of man's desire, is not to enjoy once only, and for one instant of time; but to assure forever, the way of his future desire. And therefore the voluntary actions, and inclinations of all men, tend, not only to the procuring, but also to the assuring of a contented life; and differ only in the way: which ariseth partly from the diversity of passions, in divers men; and partly from the difference of the knowledge, or opinion each one has of the causes, which produce the effect desired.

So that in the first place, I put for a general inclination of all mankind, a perpetual and restless desire of power after power, that ceaseth only in death. And the cause of this, is not always that a man hopes for a more intensive delight, than he has already attained to; or that he cannot be content with a moderate power: but because he cannot assure the power and means to live well, which he hath present, without the acquisition of more. And from hence it is, that kings, whose power is greatest, turn their endeavours to the assuring it at home by laws, or abroad by wars. . . .

Of the Natural Condition of Mankind as Concerning Their Felicity and Misery

Nature hath made men so equal, in the faculties of the body, and mind; as that though there be found one man sometimes manifestly stronger in body, or of quicker mind than another, but when all is reckoned together, the difference between man and man, is not so considerable, as that one man can thereupon claim to himself any benefit, to which another may not pretend, as well as he. For as to the strength of body, the weakest has strength enough to kill the strongest, either by secret machination, or by confederacy with others, that are in the same danger with himself.

And as to the faculties of the mind, setting aside the arts grounded upon words, and especially that skill of proceeding upon general, and infallible rules, called science; which very few have, and but in few things; as being not a native faculty, born with us; nor attained, as prudence, while we look after somewhat else, I find yet a greater equality amongst men, than that of strength. For prudence, is but experience; which equal time, equally bestows on all men, in those things they equally apply themselves unto. That which may perhaps make such equality incredible, is but a vain conceit of one's own wisdom, which almost all men think they have in a greater degree, than the vulgar; that is, than all men but themselves, and a few others, whom by fame, or for concurring with themselves, they approve. For such is the nature of men, that howsoever they may acknowledge many others to be more witty, or more eloquent, or more learned; yet they will hardly believe there be many so wise as themselves; for they see their own wit at hand, and other men's at a distance. For this proveth rather that men are in that point equal, than unequal. For there is not ordinarily a greater sign of the equal distribution of any thing, than that every man is contented with his share.

From this equality of ability, ariseth equality of hope in the attaining of our ends. And therefore if any two men desire the same thing, which nevertheless they cannot both enjoy, they become enemies; and in the way to their end, which is principally their own conservation, and sometimes their delectation only, endeavour to destroy, or subdue one another. And from hence it comes to pass, that where an invader hath no more to fear, than another man's single power; if one plant, sow, build, or possess a convenient seat, others may probably be expected to come prepared with forces united, to dispossess, and deprive him, not only of the fruit of his labour, but also of his life or liberty. And the invader again is in the like danger of another.

And from this diffidence of another, there is no way for any man to secure himself, so reasonable, as anticipation; that is, by force, or wiles, to master the persons of all men he can, so long, till he see no other power great enough to endanger him: and this is no more than his own conservation requireth, and is generally allowed. Also because there be some, that taking pleasure in contemplating their own power in the acts of conquest, which they pursue farther than their security requires; if others, that otherwise would be glad to be at ease within modest bounds, should not by invasion increase their power, they would not be able, long time, by standing only on their defence, to subsist. And by consequence, such augmentation of dominion over men being necessary to a man's conservation, it ought to be allowed him.

Again, men have no pleasure, but on the contrary a great deal of grief, in keeping company, where there is no power able to over-awe them all. For every man looketh that his companion should value him, at the same rate he sets upon himself: and upon all signs of contempt, or undervaluing, naturally endeavours, as far as he dares, (which amongst them that have no common power to keep them in quiet, is far enough to make them destroy each other), to extort a greater value from his contemners, by damage; and from others, by the example.

So that in the nature of man, we find three principal causes of quarrel. First, competition; secondly, diffidence; thirdly, glory.

The first, maketh men invade for gain; the second, for safety; and the third, for reputation. The first use violence, to make themselves masters of other men's persons, wives, children, and cattle; the second, to defend them; the third, for trifles, as a word, a smile, a different opinion, and any other sign of undervalue, either direct in their persons, or by reflection in their kindred, their friends, their nation, their profession, or their name.

Hereby it is manifest, that during the time men live without a common power to keep them all in awe, they are in that condition which is called war; and such a war, as is of every man, against every man. For WAR, consisteth not in battle only, or the act of fighting; but in a tract of time, wherein the will to contend by battle is sufficiently known: and therefore the notion of *time,* is to be considered in the nature of war; as it is in the nature of weather. For as the nature of foul weather, lieth not in a shower or two of rain; but in an inclination thereto of many days together: so the nature of war, consisteth not in actual fighting; but in the known disposition thereto, during all the time there is no assurance to the contrary. All other time is PEACE.

Whatsoever therefore is consequent to a time of war, where every man is enemy to every man; the same is consequent to the time, wherein men live without other security, than what their own strength, and their own invention shall furnish them withal. In such condition, there is no place for industry; because the fruit thereof is uncertain: and consequently no culture of the earth; no navigation, nor use of the commodities that may be imported by sea; no commodious building; no instruments of moving, and removing, such things as require much force; no knowledge of the face of the earth; no account of time; no arts; no letters, no society; and which is worst of all, continual fear, and danger of violent death; and the life of man, solitary, poor, nasty, brutish, and short.

It may seem strange to some man, that has not well weighed these things; that nature should thus dissociate, and render men apt to invade, and destroy one another: and he may therefore, not trusting to this inference, made from the passions, desire perhaps to have the same confirmed by experience. Let him therefore consider with himself, when taking a journey, he arms himself, and seeks to go well accompanied; when going to sleep, he locks his doors; when even in his house he locks his chests; and this when he knows there be laws, and public officers, armed, to revenge all injuries shall be done him; what opinion he has of his fellow-subjects, when he rides armed; of his fellow citizens, when he locks his doors; and of his children, and servants, when he locks his chests. Does he not there as much accuse mankind by his actions, as I do by my words? But neither of us accuse man's nature in it. The desires, and other passions of man, are in themselves no sin. No more are the actions, that proceed from those passions, till they know a law that forbids them: which till laws be made they cannot know: nor can any law be made, till they have agreed upon the person that shall make it.

It may peradventure be thought, there was never such a time, nor condition of war as this; and I believe it was never generally so, over all the world: but there are many places, where they live so now. For the savage people in many places of America, except the government of small families, the concord whereof dependeth on natural lust, have no government at all; and live at this day in that brutish manner, as I said before. Howsoever it may be perceived what manner of life there would be, where there were no common power to fear, by the manner of life, which men that have formerly lived under a peaceful government, use to degenerate into, in a civil war.

But though there had never been any time, wherein particular men were in a condition of war one against another; yet in all times, kings, and persons of sovereign authority, because of their independency, are in continual jealousies, and in the state and posture of gladiators; having their weapons pointing, and their eyes fixed on one another; that is, their forts, garrisons, and guns upon the frontiers of their kingdoms; and continual spies upon their neighbours; which is a posture of war. But because they uphold thereby, the industry of their subjects; there does not follow from it, that misery, which accompanies the liberty of particular men.

To this war of every man, against every man, this also is consequent; that nothing can be unjust. The notions of right and wrong, justice and injustice have there no place. Where there is no common power, there is no law: where no law, no injustice. Force, and fraud, are in war the two cardinal virtues. Justice, and injustice are none of the faculties neither of the body, nor mind. If they were, they might be in a man that were alone in the world, as well as his senses, and passions. They are qualities, that relate to men in society, not in solitude. It is consequent also to the same condition, that there be no propriety, no dominion, no *mine* and *thine* distinct; but only that to be every man's, that he can get; and for so long, as he can keep it. And thus much for the ill condition, which man by mere nature is actually placed in; though with a possibility to come out of it, consisting partly in the passions, partly in his reason.

The passions that incline men to peace, are fear of death; desire of such things as are necessary to commodious living; and a hope by their industry to obtain them. And reason suggesteth convenient articles of peace, upon which men may be drawn to agreement. These articles, are they, which otherwise are called the Laws of Nature: whereof I shall speak more particularly, in the two following chapters.

Of the First and Second Natural Laws and of Contracts

The right of nature, which writers commonly call *jus naturale,* is the liberty each man hath, to use his own power, as he will himself, for the preservation of his own nature; that is to say, of his own life; and consequently, of doing any thing, which in his own judgment, and reason, he shall conceive to be the aptest means thereunto.

By liberty, is understood, according to the proper signification of the word, the absence of external impediments: which impediments, may oft take away part of a man's power to do what he would; but cannot hinder him from using the power left him, according to his judgment, and reason shall dictate to him.

A law of nature, *lex naturalis,* is a precept or general rule, found out by reason, by which a man is forbidden to do that, which is destructive of his life, or taketh away the means of preserving the same; and to omit that, by which he thinketh it may be best preserved. For though they that speak of this subject used to confound *jus,* and *lex, right* and *law:* yet they ought to be distinguished; because RIGHT, consisteth in liberty to do, or to forbear; whereas LAW, determineth, and bindeth to one of them: so that law, and right, differ as much, as obligation, and liberty, which in one and the same matter are inconsistent.

And because the condition of man, as hath been declared in the precedent chapters, is a condition of war of every one against every one: in which case every one is governed by his own reason; and there is nothing he can make use of, that may not be a help unto him, in preserving his life against his enemies; it followeth, that in such a condition, every man has a right to every thing; even to one another's body. And therefore, as long as this natural right of every man to every thing endureth, there can be no security to any man, how strong or wise soever he be, of living out the time, which nature ordinarily alloweth men to live. And consequently it is a precept, or general rule of reason, *that every man, ought to endeavour peace, as far as he has hope of obtaining it; and when he cannot obtain it, that he may seek, and use, all helps, and advantages of war.* The first branch of which rule, containeth the first, and fundamental law of nature; which is, *to seek peace, and follow it.* The second, the sum of the right of nature; which is, *by all means we can, to defend ourselves.*

From this fundamental law of nature by which men are commanded to endeavour peace, is derived this second law; *that a man be willing, when others are so too, as far-forth, as for peace, and defence of himself he shall think it necessary, to lay down this right to all things; and be contented with so much liberty against other men, as he would allow other men against himself.* For as long as every man holdeth this right, of doing any thing he liketh; so long are all men in the condition of war. But if other men will not lay down their right, as well as he; then there is no reason for any one, to divest himself of his: for that were to expose himself to prey, which no man is bound to, rather than to dispose himself to peace. This is that law of the Gospel; *whatsoever you require that others should do to you, that do ye to them.* And that law of all men, *quod tibi fieri non vis, alteri ne feceris.*

To *lay down* a man's *right* to any thing, is to *divest* himself of the *liberty* of hindering another of the benefit of his own right to the same. For he that renounceth, or passeth away his right, giveth not to any other man a right which he had not before; because there is nothing to which every man had not right by nature: but only standeth out of his way, that he may enjoy his own original right, without hindrance from him; not without hindrance from another. So that the effect which redoundeth to one man, by another man's defect of right, is but so much diminution of impediments to the use of his own right original.

Right is laid aside, either by simply renouncing it; or by transferring it to another. By *simply* RENOUNCING; when he cares not to whom the benefit thereof redoundeth. By TRANSFERRING; when he intendeth the benefit thereof to some certain person, or persons. And when a man hath in either manner abandoned, or granted away his right; then is he said to be OBLIGED, or BOUND, not to hinder those, to whom such right is granted, or abandoned, from the benefit of it: and that he *ought*, and it is his DUTY, not to make void that voluntary act of his own: and that such hindrance is INJUSTICE, and INJURY, as being *sine jure;* the right being before renounced, or transferred. So that *injury*, or *injustice*, in the controversies of the world, is somewhat like to that, which in the disputations of scholars is called *absurdity*. For as it is there called an absurdity, to contradict what one maintained in the beginning: so in the world, it is called injustice, and injury, voluntarily to undo that, which from the beginning he had voluntarily done. The way by which a man either simply renounceth, or transferreth his right, is a declaration, or signification, by some voluntary and sufficient sign, or signs, that he doth so renounce, or transfer; or hath so renounced, or transferred the same, to him that accepteth it. And these signs are either words only, or actions only; or, as it happeneth most often, both words, and actions. And the same are the BONDS, by which men are bound, and obliged: bonds, that have their strength, not from their own nature, for nothing is more easily broken than a man's word, but from fear of some evil consequence upon the rupture.

Whensoever a man transferreth his right, or renounceth it; it is either in consideration of some right reciprocally transferred to himself; or for some other good he hopeth for thereby. For it is a voluntary act: and of the voluntary acts of every man, the object is some *good to himself*. And therefore there be some rights, which no man can be understood by any words, or other signs, to have abandoned, or transferred. As first a man cannot lay down the right of resisting them, that assault him by force, to take away his life; because he cannot be understood to aim thereby, at any good to himself. The same may be said of wounds, and chains, and imprisonment; both because there is no benefit consequent to such patience; as there is to the patience of suffering another to be wounded, or imprisoned: as also because a man cannot tell, when he seeth men proceed against him by violence, whether they intend his death or not. And lastly the motive, and end for which this renouncing, and transferring of right is introduced, is nothing else but the security of a man's person, in his life, and in the means of so preserving life, as not to be weary of it. And therefore if a man by words, or other signs, seem to despoil himself of the end, for which those signs were intended; he is not to be understood as if he meant it, or that it was his will; but that he was ignorant of how such words and actions were to be interpreted.

The mutual transferring of right, is that which men call CONTRACT.

There is difference, between transferring of right to the thing; and transferring, or tradition, that is, delivery of the thing itself. For the thing may be delivered together with the translation of the right; as in buying and selling with ready money; or exchange of goods, or lands: and it may be delivered some time after.

Again, one of the contractors, may deliver the thing contracted for on his part, and leave the other to perform his part at some determinate time after, and in the mean time be trusted; and then the contract on his part, is called PACT, or COVENANT: Or both parts may contract now, to perform hereafter: in which cases, he that is to perform in time to come, being trusted, his performance is called keeping of promise, or faith; and the failing of performance (if it be voluntary) violation of faith. . . .

If a covenant be made, wherein neither of the parties perform presently, but trust one another; in the condition of mere nature, (which is a condition of war of every man against every man,) upon any reasonable suspicion, it is void: But if there be a common power set over them both, with right and force sufficient to compel performance; it is not void. For he that performeth first, has no assurance the other will perform after; because the bonds of words are too weak to bridle men's ambition, avarice, anger, and other passions, without the fear of some coercive power; which in the condition of mere nature, where all men are equal, and judges of the justness of their own fears, cannot possibly be supposed. And therefore he which performeth first, does but betray himself to his enemy; contrary to the right (he can never abandon) of defending his life, and means of living.

But in a civil estate, where there is a power set up to constrain those that would otherwise violate their faith, that fear is no more reasonable; and for that cause, he which by the covenant is to perform first, is obliged so to do.

The cause of fear, which maketh such a covenant invalid, must be always something arising after the covenant made; as some new fact, or other sign of the will not to perform: else it cannot make the covenant void. For that which could not hinder a man from promising, ought not to be admitted as a hindrance of performing. . . .

Of Other Laws of Nature

From that law of nature, by which we are obliged to transfer to another, such rights, as being retained, hinder the peace of mankind, there followeth a third; which is this, *That men perform their covenants made*: without which, covenants are in vain, and but empty words; and the right of all men to all things remaining, we are still in the condition of war.

And in this law of nature, consisteth the fountain and original of JUSTICE. For where no covenant hath preceded, there hath no right been transferred, and every man has right to every thing; and consequently, no action can be unjust. But when a covenant is made, then to break it is unjust: And the definition of injustice, is no other than *the not performance of covenant*. And whatsoever is not unjust, is *just*.

But because covenants of mutual trust, where there is a fear of not performance on either part, (as hath been said in the former chapter,) are invalid; though the original of justice be the making of covenants; yet injustice actually there can be none, till the cause of such fear be taken away; which while men are in the natural condition of war, cannot be done. Therefore before the names of just, and unjust can have place, there must be some coercive power, to compel men equally to the performance of their covenants, by the terror of some punishment, greater than the benefit they expect by the breach of their covenant; and to make good that propriety, which by mutual contract men acquire, in recompense of the universal right they abandon: and such power there is none before the erection of a common wealth. And this is also to be gathered out of the ordinary definition of justice in the schools: For they say, that *justice is the constant will of giving to every man his own*. And therefore where there is no own, that is, no propriety, there is no injustice; and where there is no coercive power erected, that is, where there is no common wealth, there is no propriety; all men having right to all things: Therefore where there is no common wealth, there nothing is unjust. So that the nature of justice, consisteth in keeping of valid covenants: but the validity of covenants begins not but with the constitution of a civil power, sufficient to compel men to keep them: And then it is also that propriety begins.

The fool hath said in his heart, there is no such thing as justice; and sometimes also with his tongue; seriously alleging, that every man's conservation, and contentment, being committed to his own care, there could be no reason, why every man might not do what he thought conduced thereunto: and therefore also to make, or not make; keep, or not keep covenants, was not against reason, when it conduced to one's benefit. He does not therein deny, that there be covenants; and that they are sometimes broken, sometimes kept; and that such breach of them may be called injustice, and the observance of them justice: but he questioneth, whether injustice, taking away the fear of God, (for the same fool hath said in his heart there is no God,) may not sometimes stand with that reason, which dictateth to every man his own good; and particularly then, when it conduceth to such a benefit, as shall put a man in a condition, to neglect not only the dispraise, and revilings, but also the power of other men. The kingdom of God is gotten by violence: but what if it could be gotten by unjust violence? were it against reason so to get it, when it is impossible to receive hurt by it? and if it be not against reason, it is not against justice: or else justice is not to be approved for good. From such reasoning as this, successful wickedness hath obtained the name of virtue: and some that in all other things have disallowed the violation of faith; yet have allowed it, when it is for the getting of a kingdom. And the heathen that believed, that *Saturn* was deposed by his own son *Jupiter,* believed nevertheless the same *Jupiter* to be the avenger of injustice: Somewhat like to a piece of law in *Coke's* Commentaries on *Litleton;* where he says, If the right heir of the Crown be attainted of treason; yet the Crown shall descend to him, and *eo instante* the atteinder be void: From which instances a man will be very prone to infer; that when the heir apparent of a kingdom, shall kill him that is in possession, though his father; you may call it injustice, or by what other name you will; yet it can never be against reason, seeing all the voluntary actions of men tend to the benefit of themselves; and those actions are most reasonable, that conduce most to their ends. This specious reasoning is nevertheless false.

For the question is not of promises mutual, where there is no security of performance on either side; as when there is no civil power erected over the parties promising; for such promises are no covenants: But either where one of the parties has performed already; or where there is a power to make him perform; there is the question whether it be against reason, that is, against the benefit of the other to perform, or not. And I say it is not against reason. For the manifestation whereof, we are to consider; first, that when a man doth a thing, which notwithstanding any thing can be foreseen, and reckoned on, tendeth to his own destruction, howsoever some accident which he could not expect, arriving, may turn it to his benefit; yet such events do not make it reasonably or wisely done. Secondly, that in a condition of war, wherein every man to every man, for want of a common power to keep them all in awe, is an enemy, there is no man can hope by his own strength, or wit, to defend himself from destruction, without the help of confederates; where every one expects the same defense by the confederation, that any one else does: and therefore he which declares he thinks it reason to deceive those that help him, can in reason expect no other means of safety, than what can be had from his own single power. He therefore that breaketh his covenant, and consequently declareth that he thinks he may with reason do so, cannot be received into any society, that unite themselves for peace and defense, but by the error of them that receive him; nor when he is received, be retained in it, without seeing the danger of their error; which errors a man cannot reasonably reckon upon as the means of his security: and therefore if he be left, or cast out of society, he perisheth; and if he live in society, it is by the errors of other men, which he could not foresee, nor reckon upon; and consequently against the reason of his preservation; and so, as all men that contribute not to his destruction, forbear him only out of ignorance of what is good for themselves. . . .

These are the laws of nature, dictating peace, for a means of the conservation of men in multitudes; and which only concern the doctrine of civil society. There be other things tending to the destruction of particular men; as drunkenness, and all other parts of intemperance; which may therefore also be reckoned amongst those things which the law of nature hath forbidden; but are not necessary to be mentioned, nor are pertinent enough to this place.

And though this may seem too subtle a deduction of the laws of nature, to be taken notice of by all men; whereof the most part are too busy in getting food, and the rest too negligent to understand; yet to leave all men inexcusable, they have been contracted into one easy sum, intelligible, even to the meanest capacity; and that is, *Do not that to another, which thou wouldest not have done to thy self*; which showeth him, that he has no more to do in learning the laws of nature, but, when weighing the actions of other men with his own, they seem too heavy, to put them into the other part of the balance, and his own into their place, that his own passions, and self-love, may add nothing to the weight; and then there is none of these laws of nature that will not appear unto him very reasonable.

The laws of nature oblige *in foro interno*; that is to say, they bind to a desire they should take place: but *in foro externo*; that is, to the putting them in act, not always. For he that should be modest, and tractable, and perform all he promises, in such time, and place, where no man else should do so, should but make himself a prey to others, and procure his own certain ruin, contrary to the ground of all laws of nature, which tend to nature's preservation. And again, he that having sufficient security, that others shall observe the same laws towards him, observes them not himself, seeketh not peace, but war; and consequently the destruction of his nature by violence.

And whatsoever laws bind *in foro interno,* may be broken, not only by a fact contrary to the law, but also by a fact according to it, in case a man think it contrary. For though his action in this case, be according to the law; yet his purpose was against the law; which where the obligation is *in foro interno,* is a breach.

The laws of nature are immutable and eternal; for injustice, ingratitude, arrogance, pride, iniquity, acception of persons, and the rest, can never be made lawful. For it can never be that war shall preserve life, and peace destroy it.

The same laws, because they oblige only to a desire, and endeavor, I mean an unfeigned and constant endeavor, are easy to be observed. For in that they require nothing but endeavor; he that endeavoreth their performance, fulfilleth them; and he that fulfilleth the law, is just.

And the science of them, is the true and only moral philosophy. For moral philosophy is nothing else but the science of what is *good* and *evil,* in the conversation, and society of mankind. *Good,* and *evil,* are names that signify our appetites, and aversions; which in different tempers, customs, and doctrines of men, are different: And diverse men, differ not only in their judgement, on the senses of what is pleasant, and unpleasant to the taste, smell, hearing, touch, and sight; but also of what is conformable, or disagreeable to reason, in the actions of common life. Nay, the same man, in diverse times, differs from himself; and one time praiseth, that is calleth good, what another time he dispraiseth, and calleth evil: From whence arise disputes, controversies, and at last war. And therefore so long a man is in the condition of mere nature (which is a condition of war,) as private appetite is the measure of good, and evil: And consequently all men agree on this, that peace is good, and therefore also the way, or means of peace, which (as I have showed before) are *justice, gratitude, modesty, equity, mercy,* and the rest of the laws of nature, are good; that is to say, *moral virtues;* and their contrary vices, evil. Now the science of virtue and vice is moral philosophy; and therefore the true doctrine of the laws of nature, is the true moral philosophy. But the writers of moral philosophy, though they acknowledge the same virtues and vices; yet not seeing wherein consisted their goodness; nor that they come to be praised, as the means of peaceable, sociable, and comfortable living; place them in a mediocrity of passions: as if not the cause, but the degree of daring, made fortitude; or not the cause, but the quantity of a gift, made liberality.

These dictates of reason, men use to call by the name of laws, but improperly: for they are but conclusions, or theorems concerning what conduceth to the conservation and defense of themselves; whereas law properly is the word of him, that by right hath command over others. But yet if we consider the same theorems, as delivered in the word of God, that by right commandeth all things; then are they properly called laws.

—

Study Questions

1. How does Hobbes explain the meaning of the concepts good and evil? Will there be any universal truths about good and evil according to his view? Do you agree or disagree with his explanation of these concepts? Why?
2. One of Hobbes's best known and most notorious claims is that the "natural condition" of humankind, or state of nature, is a condition of war—the war of all against all—in which life is "solitary, poor, nasty, brutish and short." How does Hobbes arrive at this claim? What conclusions should we draw if he is right?
3. Why does Hobbes think that in the state of nature "the notions of right and wrong, justice and injustice there have no place"?

4. What does Hobbes mean by the "right of nature"? What does he mean by a "law of nature"? Does Hobbes's theory allow for "inalienable rights"? Explain.
5. "Of the voluntary acts of every man, the object is some good to himself." Do you agree with this statement? If so, what are its implications for ethics?
6. Why does Hobbes think that in the state of nature, covenants are void upon any reasonable suspicion? How does this contribute to the instability of the state of nature?
7. Hobbes addresses "the fool" who says in his heart that there is no such thing as justice. What exactly does "the fool" say? What is Hobbes's reply to "the fool"? Is his reply successful—in other words, is this person really a "fool" as Hobbes implies?
8. Do you agree with Hobbes's view that the "laws of nature" (i.e., precepts of common morality) are nothing more than conclusions about what is conducive to self-defense and peace in social life?

Selected Bibliography

Gauthier, D. P. *The Logic of Leviathan* (Oxford: Clarendon Press, 1969), Chaps. 1 and 2. A critical exposition of Hobbes's ethics.

Hampton, Jean. *Hobbes and the Social Contract Tradition* (New York/Cambridge: Cambridge University Press, 1986). A study of Hobbes's social contract theory

Kavka, G. *Hobbesian Moral and Political Theory* (Princeton: Princeton University Press, 1986). A study of Hobbes's moral and political thought.

Lloyd, Sharon. *Ideals as Interests in Hobbes's Leviathan: The Power of Mind over Matter* (New York/Cambridge: Cambridge University Press, 1992). A study of Hobbes's social and political views.

Oakeshott, M. *Hobbes on Civil Association* (Berkeley: University of California Press, 1975). An interpretation of Hobbes's ethical views.

Raphael, D. D. *Hobbes: Morals and Politics* (London: Allen & Unwin, 1977), Chaps. 4 and 5. A summary and analysis of Hobbes's views.

9

JOSEPH BUTLER

——

By profession Joseph Butler was a clergyman. Born into a Presbyterian family in Berkshire in southern England, Butler (1692–1752) was brought up on the stern doctrines of Calvinism and trained to enter the ministry. As he grew older, he be-

> *Had it strength, as it has right; had it power, as it has manifest authority, [conscience] would absolutely govern the world.*

came increasingly critical of Calvinistic theology until finally, to the great disappointment of his father, he embraced the Anglican communion and was ordained into the clergy of the established church. After holding various posts in the church, he was offered the Archbishopric of Canterbury, an honor he declined. In 1750, just before his death, he became bishop of Durham. In addition to his reputation as a moral philosopher, Butler is known as the author of *The Analogy of Religion,* a closely reasoned defense of orthodox Christianity against the deists.

The most complete statement of Butler's moral theory appears in a series of sermons that he preached at the Rolls Chapel in London while he was still a young man. Although he developed his views in sermons, his approach to morality is not primarily theological, but is based on careful and critical observation of the actual beliefs and practices of humankind. Much of the strength of his arguments stems from his perceptive insight into human psychology. One of Butler's aims is to defend the view that virtue consists in following our nature, whereas vice is a deviation from our nature—in a word, that our nature is "adapted to virtue." To do so, he develops a complex and insightful conception of human nature that takes into account not just the various natural desires and propensities by which we are moved—the components of our nature, as it were—but their relationships to each other. The proper relationships of the components of our nature to each other he terms the "constitution of human nature." Human beings are moved by a variety of natural desires, affections, and interests that are directed at particular objects. Some are concerned with one's private good—for example, desires for various pleasures and comforts, for wealth, honor, power, and so on. Other motives, such as kindness, compassion, love, concern for friends, gratitude, and a sense of fairness, are oriented toward the good of others or the good of society. In addition, Butler distinguishes two higher-order interests that are also components of our nature—self-love and conscience. Self-love is a concern with our long-term self-interest and assesses particular motives in relation to this interest. Conscience is an authoritative faculty that reflects on all our particular motives and either approves or disapproves of them as right or wrong. Self-love and conscience are distinguished not by their *strength*—for they are not always the strongest motives in us—but by their superior *authority,* and this gives them their role in human nature. Conscience in particular occupies a special place in the constitution of human nature because its role is to pass final judgment on the acceptability of all our particular motives and actions. Because an accurate understanding of our nature must take into account the authority of conscience, Butler can argue that our nature is adapted to virtue. In acting virtuously, we follow our nature because we follow the authority of conscience.

Relying on his distinction between desires for particular objects and self-love as a higher-order interest, Butler also developed an acute critique of psychological egoism—the view seen, for example, in Hobbes, that human beings are moved exclusively by self-interest. Judicious observation tells us that many of the desires by which we are moved are directed at objects outside the self. Examples might include kindness, benevolence, gratitude, curiosity, the desire for knowledge, and so on. Moreover, self-love cannot be the only human motive, because it is essentially a concern for the satisfaction of our particular interests over time. If we did not have particular desires and interests for ends outside the self, self-love would have nothing to do. Butler thus believed that psychological egoism overlooks important distinctions among the variety of human motives. In order to arrive at the truth in any matter, particularly in moral philosophy, it is essential not to identify with each other things that are really different. As he put the point, simply but effectively, "Everything is what it is, and not another thing."

Sermons

Preface

. . . There are two ways in which the subject of morals may be treated. One begins from inquiring into the abstract relations of things; the other, from a matter of fact, namely, what the particular nature of man is, its several parts, their economy or constitution; from whence it proceeds to determine what course of life it is, which is correspondent to this whole nature. In the former method the conclusion is expressed thus, that vice is contrary to the nature and reasons of things; in the latter, that it is a violation or breaking in upon our own nature. Thus they both lead us to the same thing, our obligations to the practice of virtue; and thus they exceedingly strengthen and enforce each other. The first seems the most direct formal proof, and in some respects the least liable to cavil and dispute: The latter is in a peculiar man-

New edition, London, 1839. Omissions from the Preface include general introductory remarks not directly relevant to Butler's argument. First published in 1726.

ner adapted to satisfy a fair mind, and is more easily applicable to the several particular relations and circumstances in life.

The following discourses proceed chiefly in this latter method. The three first wholly. They were intended to explain what is meant by the nature of man, when it is said that virtue consists in following, and vice in deviating from it; and, by explaining, to show that the assertion is true. . . .

Whoever thinks it worthwhile to consider this matter thoroughly, should begin with stating to himself exactly the idea of a system, economy, or constitution, or any particular nature, or any particular thing; and he will, I suppose, find, that it is a one or a whole, made up of several parts; but yet that the several parts, even considered as a whole, do not complete the idea, unless in the notion of a whole, you include the relations and respects which those parts have to each other. Every work, both of nature and of art, is a system: And as every particular thing, both natural and artificial, is for some use or purpose out of and beyond itself, one may add to what has been already brought into the idea of a system, its conduciveness to this one or more ends. Let us instance in a watch: Suppose the several parts of it taken to pieces, and placed apart from each other: Let a man have ever so exact a notion of these several parts, unless he considers the respect and relations which they have to each other, he will not have any thing like the idea of a watch. Suppose these several parts brought together and any how united: Neither will he yet, be the union ever so close, have an idea which will bear any resemblance to that of a watch. But let him view those several parts put together, or consider them as to be put together, in the manner of a watch; let him form a notion of the relations which those several parts have to each other—all conducive, in their respective ways, to this purpose, showing the hour of the day; and then he has the idea of a watch. Thus it is with regard to the inward frame of man. Appetites, passions, affections, and the principle of affection, considered merely as the several parts of our inward nature, do not at all give us an idea of the system or constitution of this nature: because the constitution is formed by somewhat not yet taken into consideration, namely, by the relations which these several parts have to each other; the chief of which is the authority of reflection or conscience. It is from considering the relations which the several appetites and passions in the inward frame have to each other, and, above all, the supremacy of reflection or conscience, that we get the idea of the system or constitution of human nature. And from the idea itself it will as fully appear, that this our nature, *i.e.* constitution, is adapted to virtue, as from the idea of a watch it appears, that its nature, *i.e.* constitution or system, is adapted to measure time. What in fact or event commonly happens, is nothing to this question. Every work of art is apt to be out of order; but this is so far from being according to its system, that let the disorder increase, and it will totally destroy it. This is merely by way of explanation, what an economy, system, or constitution is. And thus far the cases are perfectly parallel. If we go further, there is indeed a difference, nothing to the present purpose, and too important a one ever to be omitted. A machine is inanimate and passive: But we are agents. Our constitution is put in our power; we are charged with it, and therefore are accountable for any disorder or violation of it.

Thus nothing can possibly be more contrary to nature than vice; meaning by nature not only the *several parts* of our internal frame, but also the *constitution* of it. Poverty and disgrace, tortures and death, are not so contrary to it. Misery and injustice are indeed equally contrary to some different parts of our nature taken singly; but injustice is moreover contrary to the whole constitution of the nature. . . .

Though I am persuaded the force of this conviction is felt by almost every one, yet since, considered as an argument and put in words, it appears somewhat abstruse, and since the connexion of it is broken in the three first sermons, it may not be amiss to give the reader the whole argument here in one view.

Mankind has various instincts and principles of action, as brute creatures have; some leading most directly and immediately to the good of the community, and some most directly to private good.

Man has several which brutes have not; particularly reflection or conscience, an approbation of some principles or actions, and disapprobation of others.

Brutes obey their instincts or principles of action, according to certain rules; suppose the constitution of their body, and the objects around them.

The generality of mankind also obey their instincts and principles, all of them; those propensions we call good, as well as the bad, according to the same rules— namely, the constitution of their body, and the external circumstances which they are in. (Therefore it is not a true representation of mankind, to affirm that they are wholly governed by self-love, the love of power and sensual appetites: since, as on the one hand, they are often actuated by these, without any regard to right or wrong; so on the other, it is manifest fact, that the same persons, the generality, are frequently influenced by friendship, compassion, gratitude, and even a general abhorrence of what is base, and liking of what is fair and just, takes its turn amongst the other motives of action. This is the partial inadequate notion of human nature treated in the first discourse: and it is by this nature, if one may speak so, that the world is in fact influenced, and kept in that tolerable order in which it is.)

Brutes, in acting according to the rules before mentioned, their bodily constitution and circumstances, act suitably to their whole nature. It is however to be distinctly noted, that the reason why we affirm this, is not merely that brutes in fact act so; for this alone, however universal, does not at all determine whether such course of action be correspondent to their whole nature. But the reason of the assertion is, that as, in acting thus, they plainly act conformably to somewhat in their nature so, from all observations we are able to make upon them, there does not appear the least ground to imagine them to have any thing else in their nature, which requires a different rule or course of action.

Mankind also, in acting thus, would act suitably to their whole nature, if no more were to be said of man's nature than what has been now said; if that, as it is a true, were also a complete, adequate account of our nature.

But that is not a complete account of man's nature. Somewhat further must be brought in to give us an adequate notion of it—namely, that one of those principles of action, conscience, or reflection, compared with the rest, as they all stand together in the nature of man, plainly bears upon it marks of authority over all the rest, and claims the absolute direction of them all, to allow or forbid their gratification; a disapprobation of reflection being in itself a principle manifestly superior to a mere propension. And the conclusion is, that to allow no more to this superior principle or part of our nature, than to other parts; to let it govern and guide only occasionally in common with the rest, as its turn happened to come, from the temper and circumstances one happens to be in; this is not to act conformably to the constitution of man. Neither can any human creature be said to act conformably to his constitution of nature, unless he allows to that superior principle the absolute authority which is due to it. And this conclusion is abundantly confirmed from hence, that one may determine what course of action the economy of man's nature requires, without so much as knowing in what degrees of *strength* the several principles prevail, or which of them have actually the greatest influence.

The practical reason of insisting so much upon this natural authority of the principle of reflection or conscience is that it seems in a great measure overlooked by many, who are by no means the worst sort of men. It is thought sufficient to abstain from gross wickedness, and to be humane and kind to such as happen to come in their way. Whereas, in reality, the very constitution of our nature requires that we bring our whole conduct before this superior faculty; wait its determination; enforce upon ourselves its authority; and make it the business of our lives, as it is absolutely the whole business of a moral agent, to conform ourselves to it. This is the true meaning of that ancient precept, *Reverence thyself.* . . .

There is a strange affectation in many people of explaining away all particular affections, and representing the whole of life as nothing but one continued exercise of self-love. Hence arises that surprising confusion and perplexity in the Epicureans of old, Hobbes, the author of *Reflections, Sentences, et Maximes Morales,* and this whole set of writers; the confusion of calling actions interested, which are done in contradiction to the most manifest known interest, merely for the gratification of a present passion. Now, all this confusion might easily be avoided, by stating to ourselves wherein the idea of self-love in general consists, as distinguished from all particular movements towards particular external objects; the appetites of sense, resentment, compassion, curiosity, ambition, and the rest. When this is done, if the words *selfish* and *interested* cannot be parted with, but must be applied to everything; yet, to avoid such total confusion of all language, let the distinction be made by epithets; and the first may be called cool, or settled selfishness, and the other passionate, or sensual selfishness. But the most natural way of speaking plainly is, to call the first only, self-love, and the actions proceeding from it, interested; and to say of the latter, that they are not love to ourselves, but movements towards somewhat external—honour, power, the harm or good of another: And that the pursuit of these external objects, so far as it proceeds from these movements, (for it may proceed from self-love,) is not otherwise interested, than as every action of every creature must, from the nature of the thing, be; for no one can act but from a desire, or choice, or preference of his own.

Self-love and any particular passion may be joined together; and from this complication, it becomes impossible, in numberless instances, to determine precisely how far an action, perhaps even of one's own, has for its principle general self-love, or some particular passion. But this need create no confusion in the ideas themselves of self-love and particular passions. We distinctly discern what one is, and what the other are; though we may be uncertain how far one or the other influences us. And though, from this uncertainty, it cannot but be, that there will be different opinions concerning mankind, as more or less governed by interest; and some will ascribe actions to self-love, which others will ascribe to particular passions; yet it is absurd to say, that mankind are wholly actuated by either; since it is manifest that both have their influence. For as, on the one hand, men form a general notion of interest, some placing it in one thing, and some in another, and have a considerable regard to it throughout the course of their life, which is owing to self-love; so, on the other hand, they are often set on work by the particular passions themselves, and a considerable part of life is spent in the actual gratification of them; *i.e.* is employed, not by self-love, but by the passions.

Besides, the very idea of an interested pursuit, necessarily presupposes particular passions or appetites; since the very idea of interest, or happiness, consists in this, that an appetite, or affection, enjoys its object. It is not because we love ourselves that we find delight in such and such objects, but because we have particular affections towards them. Take away these affections, and you leave self-love absolutely nothing at all to employ itself about; no end, or object, for it to pursue, excepting only that of avoiding pain. Indeed, the Epicureans, who maintained that absence of pain was the highest happiness, might, consistently with themselves, deny all affection, and, if they had so pleased, every sensual appetite too: But the very idea of interest, or happiness, other than absence of pain, implies particular appetites or passions; these being necessary to constitute that interest or happiness.

The observation, that benevolence is no more disinterested than any of the common particular passions, seems in itself worth being taken notice of; but is insisted upon to obviate that scorn, which one sees rising upon the faces of people, who are said to know the world, when mention is made of a disinterested, generous, or public-spirited action. The truth of that observation might be made to appear in a more formal manner of proof: For, whoever will consider all the possible respects and relations which any particular affection can have to self-love and private interest, will, I think, see demonstrably, that benevolence is not in any respect more at variance with self-love, than any other particular affection whatever, but that it is, in every respect, at least as friendly to it.

If the observation be true, it follows, that self-love and benevolence, virtue and interest, are not to be opposed, but only to be distinguished from each other; in the same way as virtue and any other particular affection, love of arts, suppose, are to be distinguished. Every thing is what it is, and not another thing. The goodness, or badness of actions, does not arise from hence, that the epithet, interested, or disinterested, may be applied to them, any more than that any other indifferent epithet, suppose inquisitive or jealous, may, or may not, be applied to them; not from their being attended with present or future pleasure or pain, but from their being what they are; namely, what becomes such creatures as we are, what the state of the case requires, or the contrary. Or, in other words, we may judge and determine that an action is morally good or evil, before we so much as consider, whether it be interested or disinterested. This consideration no more comes in to determine, whether an action be virtuous, than to determine whether it be resentful. Self-love, in its degree, is as just and morally good as any affection whatever. Benevolence towards particular persons may be to a degree of weakness, and so be blameable. And disinterestedness is so far from being in itself commendable, that the utmost possible depravity, which we can in imagination conceive, is that of disinterested cruelty.

Neither does there appear any reason to wish self-love were weaker in the generality of the world than it is. The influence which it has, seems plainly owing to its being constant and habitual, which it cannot but be, and not to the degree or strength of it. Every caprice of the imagination, every curiosity of the understanding, every affection of the heart, is perpetually showing its weakness, by prevailing over it. Men daily, hourly, sacrifice the greatest known interest to fancy, inquisitiveness, love or hatred, any vagrant inclination. The thing to be lamented is, not that men have so great regard to their own good or interest in the present world, for they have not enough; but that they have so little to the good of others. And this seems plainly owing to their being so much engaged in the gratification of particular passions unfriendly to benevolence, and which happen to be most prevalent in them, much more than to self-love. As a proof of this may be observed, that there is no character more void of friendship, gratitude, natural affection, love to their country, common justice, or more equally and uniformly hard-hearted, than the *abandoned* in, what is called, the way of pleasure—hard-hearted and totally without feeling in behalf of others; except when they cannot escape the sight of distress, and so are interrupted by it in their pleasures. And yet it is ridiculous to call such an abandoned course of pleasure interested, when the person engaged in it knows beforehand, and goes on under the feeling and apprehension, that it will be as ruinous to himself, as to those who depend upon him.

Upon the whole, if the generality of mankind were to cultivate within themselves the principle of self-love; if they were to accustom themselves often to set down and consider, what was the greatest happiness they were capable of attaining for themselves in this life; and if self-love were so strong and prevalent, as that they would uniformly pursue this their supposed chief temporal good, without being diverted from it by any particular passion, it would manifestly prevent numberless follies and vices. This was in a great measure the *Epicurean* system of philosophy. . . .

Sermon II

Upon Human Nature (Romans ii, 14)

> For when the Gentiles, which have not the law, do by nature the things contained in the law, these having not the law, are a law unto themselves.

As speculative truth admits of different kinds of proof, so likewise moral obligations may be shown by different methods. If the real nature of any creature leads him, and is adapted to such and such purposes only, or more than to any other, this is a reason to believe the Author of that nature intended it for those purposes. Thus there is no doubt the eye was intended for us to see with. And the more complex any constitution is, and the greater variety of parts there are which thus tend to some one end, the stronger is the proof that such end was designed. However, when the inward frame of man is considered as any guide in morals, the utmost caution must be used that none make peculiarities in their own temper, or any thing which is the effect of particular customs, though observable in several, the standard of what is common to the species; and, above all, that the highest principle be not forgot or excluded, that to which belongs the adjustment and correction of all other inward movements and affections: which principle will of course have some influence, but which, being in nature supreme, as shall now be shown, ought to preside over and govern all the rest. The difficulty of rightly observing the two former cautions, the appearance there is of some small diversity amongst mankind with respect to this faculty, with respect to their natural sense of moral good and evil; and the attention necessary to survey with any exactness what passes within, have occasioned that it is not so much agreed what is the standard of the internal nature of man, as of his external form. Neither is this last exactly settled. Yet we understand one another when we speak of the shape of a human body; so likewise we do when we speak of the heart and inward principles, how far soever the standard is from being exact or precisely fixed. There is, therefore, ground for an attempt of showing men to themselves, of showing them what course of life and behaviour their real nature points out, and would lead them to. Now, obligations of virtue shown, and motives to the practice of it enforced, from a review of the nature of man, are to be considered as an appeal to each particular person's heart and natural conscience; as the external senses are appealed to for the proof of things cognizable by them. Since, then, our inward feelings, and the perceptions we received from our external senses, are equally real; to argue from the former to life and conduct, is as little liable to exception, as to argue from the latter, to absolute speculative truth. A man can as little doubt whether his eyes were given him to see with, as he can doubt of the truth of the science of *optics,* deduced from ocular experiments. And allowing the inward feeling, shame; a man can as little doubt whether it was given him to prevent his doing shameful actions, as he can doubt whether his eyes were given him to guide his steps. And as to these inward feelings themselves; that they are real—that man has in his nature passions and affections, can no more be questioned, than that he has external senses. Neither can the former be wholly mistaken, though to a certain degree liable to greater mistakes than the latter.

There can be no doubt but that several propensions or instincts, several principles in the heart of man, carry him to society, and to contribute to the happiness of it, in a sense and a manner in which no inward principle leads him to evil. These principles, propensions, or instincts, which lead him to do good, are approved of by a certain faculty within, quite distinct from these propensions themselves. All this hath been fully made out in the foregoing discourse.

But it may be said, "What is all this, though true, to the purpose of virtue and religion? These require, not only that we do good to others when we are led this way, by benevolence or reflection happening to be stronger than other principles, passions, or appetites; but likewise, that the *whole* character be formed upon thoughts and reflection; that *every* action be directed by some determinate rule, some other rule than the strength and prevalency of any principle or passion. What sign is there in our nature (for the inquiry is only about what is to be collected from thence) that this was intended by its Author? Or how does so various and fickle a temper as that of man appear adapted thereto? It may indeed be absurd and unnatural for men to act without any reflection; nay, without regard to that particular kind of reflection which you call conscience; because this does belong to our nature. For, as there never was a man but who approved one place, prospect, building, before another; so it does not appear that there ever was a man who would not have approved an action of humanity rather than of cruelty; interest and passion being quite out of the case. But interest and passion do come in, and are often too strong for, and prevail over reflection and conscience. Now, as brutes have various instincts, by which they are carried on to the end the Author of their nature intended them for; is not man in the same condition, with this difference only, that to his instincts (*i.e.,* appetites and passions) is added the principle of reflection or conscience? And as brutes act agreeably to their nature, in following that principle or particular instinct which for the present is strongest in them; does not man likewise act agreeably to his nature, or obey the law of his creation, by following that principle, be it passion or conscience, which for the present happens to be strongest in him? Thus, different men are by their particular nature hurried on to pursue honour, or riches, or pleasure; there are also persons whose temper leads them in an uncommon degree to kindness, compassion, doing good to their fellow-creatures; as there are others who are given to suspend their judgment, to weigh and consider things, and to act upon thought and reflection. Let every one then quietly follow his nature; as passion, reflection, appetite, the several parts of it, happen to be the strongest; but let not the man of virtue take upon him to blame the ambitious, the covetous, the dissolute; since these, equally with him, obey and follow their nature. Thus, as in some cases, we follow our nature in doing the works *contained in the law,* so in other cases we follow nature in doing contrary."

Now, all this licentious talk entirely goes upon a supposition, that men follow their nature in the same sense, in violating the known rules of justice and honesty for the sake of a present gratification, as they do in following those rules when they have no temptation to the contrary. And if this were true, that could not be so which St. Paul asserts, that men are "by nature a law to themselves." If by following nature were meant only acting as we please, it would indeed be ridiculous to speak of nature as any guide in morals: nay, the very mention of deviating from nature would be absurd; and the mention of following it, when spoken by way of distinction, would absolutely have no meaning. For, did ever any one act otherwise than as he pleased? And yet the ancients speak of deviating from nature, as vice; and of following nature so much as a distinction, that, according to them, the perfection of virtue consists therein. So that language itself should teach people another sense to the words *following nature,* than barely acting as we please. Let it however be observed, though the words *human nature* are to be explained, yet the real question of this discourse is not concerning the meaning of words, any otherwise than as the explanation of them may be needful to make out and explain the assertion, *that every man is naturally a law to himself, that every one may find within himself the rule of right, and obligations to follow it.* This St. Paul affirms in the words of the text, and this the foregoing objection really denies, by seeming to allow it. And the objection will be fully answered, and the text before us explained, by observing, that *nature* is considered in different views, and the word is used in different senses; and by showing in what view it is considered, and in what sense the word is used, when intended to express and signify that which is the guide of life, that by which men are a law to themselves. I say, the explanation of the terms will be sufficient, because from thence it will appear, that in some senses of the word, *nature* cannot be, but that in another sense, it manifestly is a law to us.

I. By nature is often meant no more than some principle in man, without re-gard either to the kind or degree of it. Thus, the passion of anger, and the affec-tion of parents to their children, would be called equally *natural*. And as the same person hath often contrary principles, which at the same time draw contrary ways, he may by the same action both follow and contradict his nature in this sense of the word; he may follow one passion, and contradict another.

II. *Nature* is frequently spoken of as consisting in those passions which are strongest, and most influence the actions; which being vicious ones, mankind is in this sense naturally vicious, or vicious by nature. Thus St. Paul says of the Gentiles, *who were dead in trespasses and sins, and walked according to the spirit of disobedi-ence*, that *they were by nature the children of wrath*. They could be no otherwise children of wrath by nature, than they were vicious by nature.

Here then are two different senses of the word *nature*, in neither of which men can at all be said to be a law to themselves. They are mentioned only to be excluded; to prevent their being confounded, as the latter is in the objection, with another sense of it, which is now to be inquired after and explained.

III. The apostle asserts, that the Gentiles *do by nature the things contained in the law*. Nature is indeed here put by way of distinction from revelation, but yet it is not a mere negative. He intends to express more than that by which they *did not*, that by which they *did* the works of the law; namely, by nature. It is plain the meaning of the word is not the same in this passage as in the former, where it is spoken of as evil; for in the latter it is spoken of as good; as that by which they acted, or might have acted virtuously. What that is in man by which he is *naturally a law to himself*, is explained in the following words: *which shows the work of the law written in their hearts, their consciences also bearing witness, and their thoughts the meanwhile accusing or else excusing one another*. If there be a distinction to be made between the *works written in their hearts*, and the *witnesses of conscience;* by the former must be meant, the natural disposition to kindness and compassion, to do what is of good report, to which this apostle often refers; that part of the nature of man, treated of in the foregoing discourse, which, with very little reflection and of course, leads him to society, and by means of which he naturally acts a just and good part in it, unless other passions or interest lead him astray. Yet since other passions, and regards to private interest, which lead us (though indirectly, yet they lead us) astray, are themselves in a degree equally nat-ural, and often most prevalent; and since we have no method of seeing the par-ticular degrees in which one or the other is placed in us by nature, it is plain the former, considered merely as natural, good and right as they are, can no more be a law to us than the latter. But there is a superior principle of reflection or con-science in every man, which distinguishes between the internal principles of his heart, as well as his external actions; which passes judgment upon himself and them; pronounces determinately some actions to be in themselves just, right, good; others to be in themselves evil, wrong, unjust; which, without being consulted, without being advised with, magisterially exerts itself, and approves or condemns him, the doer of them, accordingly; and which, if not forcibly stopped, naturally and always of course goes on to anticipate a higher and more effectual sentence, which shall hereafter second and affirm its own. But this part of the office of conscience is beyond my present design explicitly to consider. It is by this faculty natural to man, that he is a moral agent, that he is a law to himself: by this faculty, I say, not to be considered merely as a principle in his heart, which is to have some influence as well as others; but considered as a faculty, in kind and in nature, supreme over all others, and which bears its own authority of being so.

This *prerogative*, this *natural supremacy*, of the faculty which surveys, approves, or disapproves the several affections of our mind, and actions of our lives, being that by which men *are a law to themselves*, their conformity, or disobedience to which law of our nature renders their actions, in the highest and most proper sense, natural or unnatural; it is fit it be further explained to you: and I hope it will be so, if you will attend to the following reflections.

Man may act according to that principle or inclination which for the present happens to be strongest, and yet act in a way disproportionate to, and violate his real proper nature. Suppose a brute creature, by any bait to be allured into a snare, by which he is destroyed; he plainly followed the bent of his nature, leading him to gratify his appetite: there is an entire correspondence between his whole nature and such an action: such action therefore is natural. But suppose a man, foreseeing the same danger of certain ruin, should rush into it for the sake of a present gratification: he in this instance would follow his strongest desire, as did the brute creature, but there would be as manifest a disproportion between the nature of man and such an action, as between the meanest work of art and the skill of the greatest master in that art; which disproportion arises, not from considering the action singly in *itself*, or in its *consequences*, but from *comparison* of it with the nature of the agent. And since such an action is utterly disproportionate to the nature of man, it is in the strictest and most proper sense unnatural; this word expressing that disproportion. Therefore, instead of the words *disproportionate to his nature*, the word *unnatural* may now be put; this being more familiar to us: but let it be observed, that it stands for the same thing precisely.

Now, what is it which renders such a rash action unnatural? Is it that he went against the principle of reasonable and cool self-love, considered *merely* as a part of his nature? No: for if he had acted the contrary way, he would equally have gone against a principle, or part of his nature, namely, passion or appetite. But to deny a present appetite, from foresight that the gratification of it would end in immediate ruin or extreme misery, is by no means an unnatural action: whereas to contradict or go against cool self-love for the sake of such gratification, is so in the instance before us. Such an action then being unnatural, and its being so not arising from a man's going against a principle or desire barely, nor in going against that principle or desire which happens for the present to be strongest; it necessarily follows, that there must be some other difference or distinction to be made between these two principles, passion and cool self-love, than what I have yet taken notice of. And this difference, not being a difference in strength or degree, I call a difference in *nature* and in *kind*. And since, in the instance still before us, if passion prevails over self-love, the consequent action is unnatural; but if self-love prevails over passion, the action is natural; it is manifest, that self-love is in human nature a superior principle to passion. This may be contradicted without violating that nature, but the former cannot. So that, if we will act conformably to the economy of man's nature reasonable self-love must govern. Thus, without particular consideration of conscience, we may have a clear conception of the *superior nature* of one inward principle to another; and see that there really is this natural superiority, quite distinct from degrees of strength and prevalency.

Let us now take a view of the nature of man, as consisting partly of various appetites, passions, affections, and partly of the principle of reflection or conscience; leaving quite out all consideration of the different degrees of strength, in which either of them prevail; and it will further appear, that there is this natural superiority of one inward principle to another, or that it is even part of the idea of reflection or conscience.

Passion or appetite implies a direct simple tendency towards such and such objects, without distinction of the means by which they are to be obtained. Consequently, it will often happen there will be a desire of particular objects, in cases where they cannot be obtained without manifest injury to others. Reflection, or conscience, comes in, and disapproves the pursuit of them in these circumstances; but the desire remains. Which is to be obeyed, appetite or reflection? Cannot this question be answered from the economy and constitution of human nature merely, without saying which is strongest? or need this all come into consideration? Would not the question be *intelligibly* and fully answered by saying, that the principle of reflection or conscience being compared with the various appetites, passions, and affections in men, the former is manifestly superior and chief, without regard to strength? And how often soever the latter happens to prevail, it is mere *usurpation*. The former remains in nature and in kind its superior: and every instance of such prevalence of the latter, is an instance of breaking in upon, and violation of the constitution of man.

All this is no more than the distinction which everybody is acquainted with, between *mere power* and *authority;* only, instead of being intended to express the difference between what is possible, and what is lawful in civil government, here it has been shown applicable to the several principles in the mind of man. Thus, that principle by which we survey, and either approve or disapprove our own heart, temper, and actions, is not only to be considered as what is in its turn to have some influence; which may be said of every passion, of the lowest appetites; but likewise as being superior; as from its very nature manifestly claiming superiority over all others; insomuch that you cannot form a notion of this faculty, conscience, without taking in judgment, direction, superintendency. This is a constituent part of the idea, that is, of the faculty itself: and to preside and govern, from the very economy and constitution of man, belongs to it. Had it strength, as it has right; had it power, as it has manifest authority, it would absolutely govern the world.

This gives us a further view of the nature of man; shows us what course of life we were made for; not only that our real nature leads us to be influenced in some degree by reflection and conscience, but likewise in what degree we are to be influenced by it, if we will fall in with, and act agreeably to the constitution of our nature: that this faculty was placed within to be our proper governor; to direct and regulate all under principles, passions, and motives of action. This is its right and office; thus sacred is its authority. And how often soever men violate and rebelliously refuse to submit to it, for supposed interest which they cannot otherwise obtain, or for the sake of passion which they cannot otherwise gratify; this makes no alteration as to the *natural right* and *office* of conscience. . . .

Sermon III

The natural supremacy of reflection or conscience being thus established; we may from it form a distinct notion of what is meant by *human nature,* when virtue is said to consist in following it, and vice in deviating from it.

As the idea of a civil constitution implies in it united strength, various subordinations, under one direction, that of the supreme authority; the different strength of each particular member of the society not coming into the idea: whereas, if you leave out the subordination, the union, and the one direction, you destroy and lose it; so reason, several appetites, passions, and affections, prevailing in different degrees of strength, is not *that* idea or notion of *human nature;* but *that nature* consists in these several principles considered as having a natural respect to each other, in the several passions being naturally subordinate to the one superior principle of reflection or conscience. Every bias, instinct, propension within, is a real part of our nature but not the whole: add to these the superior faculty, whose office it is to adjust, manage, and preside over them, and take in this its natural superiority, and you complete the idea of human nature. And as in civil government the constitution is broken in upon and violated, by power and strength prevailing over authority; so the constitutional man is broken in upon and violated by the lower faculties or principles within prevailing over that, which is in its nature supreme over them all. Thus, when it is said by ancient writers, that tortures and death are not so contrary to human nature as injustice; by this, to be sure, is not meant, that the aversion to the former in mankind is less strong and prevalent than their aversion to the latter; but that the former is only contrary to our nature, considered in a partial view, and which takes in only the lowest part of it, that which we have in common with the brutes; whereas the latter is contrary to our nature, considered in a higher sense, as a system and constitution, contrary to the whole economy of man.*

---

*Every man, in his physical nature, is one individual single agent. He has likewise properties and principles, each of which may be considered separately, and without regard to the respects which they have to each other. Neither of these are the nature we are taking a view of. But it is the inward frame of man, considered as a *system or constitution;* whose several parts are united, not by a physical principle of individuation, but by the respects they have to each other, the chief of which is the subjection which the appetites, passions, and particular affections have to the one supreme principle of reflection or conscience. The system, or constitution, is formed by, and consists in these respects and this subjection. Thus, the body is a *system or constitution;* so is a tree; so is every machine. Consider all the several parts of a tree; but add these respects, and this gives you the idea. The body may be impaired by sickness, a tree may decay, a machine may be out of order, and yet the system and constitution of them not totally dissolved. There is plainly somewhat which answers to all this in the moral constitution of man. Whoever

And from all these things put together, nothing can be more evident, than that, exclusive of revelation, man cannot be considered as a creature left by his Maker to act at random, and live at large up to the extent of his natural power, as passion, humour, wilfulness, happen to carry him; which is the condition brute creatures are in; but that, *from his make, constitution, or nature, he is, in the strictest and most proper sense, a law to himself.* He hath the rule of right within: what is wanting is only that he honestly attend to it.

The inquiries which have been made by men of leisure after some general rule, the conformity to, or disagreement from, which should denominate our actions good or evil, are in many respects of great service. Yet, let any plain, honest man, before he engages in any course of action, ask himself, is this I am going about right, or is it wrong? Is it good, or is it evil? I do not in the least doubt but that this question would be answered agreeably to truth and virtue, by almost any fair man in almost any circumstance. Neither do there appear any cases which look like exceptions to this; but those of superstition and of partiality to ourselves. Superstition may, perhaps, be somewhat of an exception; but partiality to ourselves is not; this being itself dishonesty. For a man to judge that to be the equitable, the moderate, the right part for him to act, which he would see to be hard, unjust, oppressive in another: this is plain vice, and can proceed only from great unfairness of mind.

But, allowing that mankind hath the rule of right within himself, yet it may be asked, "What obligations are we under to attend and follow it?" I answer: it has been proved, that man by his nature is a law to himself, without the particular distinct consideration of the positive sanctions of that law; the rewards and punishments which we feel, and those which, from the light of reason, we have ground to believe are annexed to it. The question then carries its own answer along with it. Your obligation to obey this law, is its being the law of your nature. That your conscience approves of and attests to such a course of action, is itself alone an obligation. Conscience does not only offer itself to show us the way we should walk in, but it likewise carries its own authority with it, that it is our natural guide, the guide assigned us by the Author of our nature: it therefore belongs to our condition of being; it is our duty to walk in that path, and follow this guide, without looking about to see whether we may not possibly forsake them with impunity.

However, let us hear what is to be said against obeying this law of our nature. And the sum is no more than this: "Why should we be concerned about any thing

will consider his own nature will see, that the several appetites, passions, and particular affections, have different respects among themselves. They are restraints upon, and are in proportion to, each other. The proportion is just and perfect, when all those under principles are perfectly coincident with conscience, so far as their nature permits, and, in all cases, under its absolute and entire direction. The least excess or defect, the least alteration of the due proportions amongst themselves, or of their coincidence with conscience, though not proceeding into action, is some degree of disorder in the moral constitution. But perfection, though plainly intelligible and supposable, was never attained by any man. If the higher principle of reflection maintains its place, and, as much as it can, corrects that disorder, and hinders it from breaking out into action, that is all that can be expected in such a creature as man. And though the appetites and passions have not their exact due proportion to each other; though they often strive for mastery with judgment or reflection; yet, since the superiority of this principle to all others is the chief respect which forms the constitution, so far as this superiority is maintained, the character, the man, is good, worthy, virtuous.

out of, and beyond ourselves? If we do find within ourselves regards to others, and restraints of we know not how many different kinds; yet these being embarrassments, and hindering us from going the nearest way to our own good, why should we not endeavour to suppress and get over them?"

Thus, people go on with words, which, when applied to human nature, and the condition in which it is placed in this world, have really no meaning. For does not all this kind of talk go upon supposition, that our happiness in this world consists in somewhat quite distinct from regards to others, and that it is the privilege of vice to be without restraint or confinement? Whereas, on the contrary, the enjoyments, in a manner all the common enjoyments of life, even the pleasures of vice, depend upon these regards of one kind or another to our fellow-creatures. Throw off all regards to others, and we should be quite indifferent to infamy and to honour: there could be no such thing at all as ambition, and scarce any such thing as covetousness; for we should likewise be equally indifferent to the disgrace of poverty, the several neglects and kinds of contempt which accompany this state; and to the reputation of riches, the regard and respect they usually procure. Neither is restraint by any means peculiar to one course of life; but our very nature, exclusive of conscience, and our condition, lay us under an absolute necessity of it. We cannot gain any end whatever without being confined to the proper means, which is often the most painful and uneasy confinement. And, in numberless instances, a present appetite cannot be gratified without such apparent and immediate ruin and misery, that the most dissolute man in the world chooses to forego the pleasure, rather than endure the pain.

Is the meaning, then, to indulge those regards to our fellow-creatures, and submit to those restraints, which, upon the whole, are attended with more satisfaction than uneasiness, and get over only those which bring more uneasiness and inconvenience than satisfaction? "Doubtless this was our meaning." You have changed sides, then. Keep to this: be consistent with yourselves; and you and the men of virtue are, in general, perfectly agreed. But let us take care, and avoid mistakes. Let it not be taken for granted, that the temper of envy, rage, resentment, yields greater delight than meekness, forgiveness, compassion and goodwill: especially when it is acknowledged, that rage, envy, resentment, are in themselves mere misery; and the satisfaction arising from the indulgence of them is little more than relief from that misery; whereas the temper of compassion and benevolence is itself delightful; and the indulgence of it, by doing good, affords new positive delight and enjoyment. Let it not be taken for granted, that the satisfaction arising from the reputation of riches and power, however obtained, and from the respect paid to them, is greater than the satisfaction arising from the reputation of justice, honesty, charity, and the esteem which is universally acknowledged to be their due. And if it be doubtful which of these satisfactions is the greatest, as there are persons who think neither of them very considerable, yet there can be no doubt concerning ambition and covetousness, virtue and a good mind, considered in themselves, and as leading to different courses of life; there can, I say, be no doubt, which temper and which course is attended with most peace and tranquility of mind; which, with most perplexity, vexation and inconvenience. And both the virtues and vices which have been now mentioned, do in a manner equally imply in them regards of one kind or another to our fellow-creatures. And with respect to restraint and confinement: whoever will consider the restraints from fear and shame, the dissimulation, mean arts of concealment, servile compliances, one or other of which belong to almost every course of vice, will soon be convinced, that the man of virtue is by no means upon a disadvantage in this respect. How many instances are there in which men feel, and own, and cry aloud under the chains of vice with which they are enthralled, and which yet they will not shake off? How many instances, in which persons manifestly go through more pain and self-denial to gratify a vicious passion, than would have been necessary to the conquest of it? To this is to be added, that when virtue is become habitual, when the temper of it is acquired, what was before confinement ceases to be so, by becoming choice and delight. Whatever restraint and guard upon ourselves may be needful to unlearn any unnatural distortion or odd gesture; yet, in all propriety of speech, natural be- haviour must be the most easy and unrestrained. It is manifest, that in the com- mon course of life there is seldom any inconsistency between our duty and what is called interest: it is much seldomer that there is an inconsistency between duty and what is really our present interest: meaning by interest, happiness and satisfaction. Self-love, then, though confined to the interest of the present world, does in gen- eral perfectly coincide with virtue, and leads us to one and the same course of life. But, whatever exceptions there are to this, which are much fewer than they are commonly thought, all shall be set right at the final distribution of things. It is a manifest absurdity to suppose evil prevailing finally over good, under the conduct and administration of a perfect mind.

The whole argument which I have been now insisting upon, may be thus summed up and given you in one view. The nature of man is adapted to some course of action or other. Upon comparing some actions with this nature, they ap- pear suitable and correspondent to it: from comparison of other actions with the same nature, there arises to our view some unsuitableness or disproportion. The correspondence of actions to the nature of the agent, renders them natural; their disproportion to it, unnatural. That an action is correspondent to the nature of the agent, does not arise from its being agreeable to the principle which happens to be the strongest; for it may be so, and yet be quite disproportionate to the nature of the agent. The correspondence, therefore, or disproportion, arises from somewhat else. This can be nothing but a difference in nature and kind (altogether distinct from strength) between the inward principles. Some, then, are in nature and kind superior to others. And the correspondence arises from the action being con- formable to the higher principle; and the unsuitableness, from its being contrary to it. Reasonable self-love and conscience are the chief or superior principles in the nature of man: because an action may be suitable to this nature, though all other principles be violated; but becomes unsuitable, if either of those are. Conscience and self-love, if we understand our true happiness, always lead us the same way. Duty and interest are perfectly coincident; for the most part in this world, but en- tirely, and in every instance, if we take in the future, and the whole; this being im- plied in the notion of a good and perfect administration of things. Thus, they who have been so wise in their generation, as to regard only their own supposed inter- est, at the expense and to the injury of others, shall at last find, that he who has given up all the advantages of the present world, rather than violate his conscience and the relations of life, has infinitely better provided for himself, and secured his own interest and happiness.

———

Study Questions

1. Butler develops his idea of the "constitution of human nature" by comparing human nature to a watch. What is his point in this comparison? Is it an important point? Why?
2. Butler makes a basic distinction between the strength or power of a motive and its authority. What is he getting at here? How does this distinction figure in his view? Is the distinction plausible?
3. What does Butler mean by saying that vice is contrary to human nature? What are some of the objections that he must answer in order to argue this point? Is he right?
4. Not only does Butler deny that all human action is self-interested, he argues that many people are not self-interested enough. Why does he say this? Does his point apply to you?
5. What does Butler mean by "conscience"? Where do the dictates of conscience come from? Are the dictates of one's conscience ever wrong? Should everyone always act as his or her conscience dictates?
6. "Conscience and self-love, if we understand our true happiness, always lead us the same way." Why does Butler say this? Is his claim plausible?

Selected Bibliography

Broad, C. D. *Five Types of Ethical Theory* (London: Routledge, 1930), Chap. 3. An exposition of Butler's views.

Butler, Joseph. *Five Sermons*, ed. Stephen Darwall (Indianapolis: Hackett Publishing, 1983). A collection of five of Butler's fifteen sermons.

Hudson, W. H. *Ethical Intuitionism* (London: Macmillan, 1967), Chaps. 6 and 10. A brief exposition and critique of Butler and ethical intuitionism.

Penelhum, T. *Butler* (London: Routledge & Kegan Paul, 1985), Part 1. A survey of Butler's ethics.

Price, R. *A Review of the Principal Questions in Morals* (New York: Oxford University Press, 1975). A similar view by a contemporary of Butler.

Rorty, Amélie O. "Butler on Benevolence and Conscience," *Philosophy* 53 (1978): 171–184. A discussion of Butler's views on conscience.

Sturgeon, Nicholas L. "Nature and Conscience in Butler's Ethics," *The Philosophical Review* 85 (1976): 316–356. A discussion of Butler's views on conscience.

10

DAVID HUME

——

David Hume's *Treatise of Human Nature* is one of the most important philosophical books written in the English language. In

> *Reason is, and ought only to be the slave of the passions. . . .*

this book Hume raises searching questions about the nature and scope of human knowledge and develops a thoroughgoing skepticism about the power of reason. He directs his skeptical conclusions both at scientific knowledge and at morality: just as the relation between cause and effect cannot be established by reason, neither can the difference between good and evil. Denying that knowledge and morality have a rational basis, Hume instead searches for their origins in features of human psychology.

Hume's 17th and 18th century predecessors by and large regarded virtue and vice, moral right and wrong, as objective facts about conduct discovered by reason. Hume mounts a many pronged attack against such rationalism in ethics. Reason by itself cannot motivate us to act. All human motivation is instead based on desire and feeling. Because moral judgments do have motivating power, they cannot be based on reason, but must be based on desire and feeling. The feeling to which Hume assigns a foundational role in morality is sympathy, by which he means our natural psychological capacity for sympathetic identification with the well-being of others. Moral properties are not facts that are discovered by reason, but rather are features of conduct and character to which we are led to respond by feelings of approval and disapproval that are ultimately based on sympathy. Moral right and wrong, virtue and vice, are just the tendencies of certain kinds of actions and traits of character to evoke sentiments of approval and disapproval in us. But the strength of feelings of sympathy varies from one person to another. If moral judgments are based in sympathy, doesn't that mean that judgments of virtue and vice, right and wrong will vary from one person to another and will be entirely subjective? No, responds Hume. We have a social need for shared judgments about virtue and vice. Accordingly, it is understood that moral judgments are based on the feelings that we have when we take up a "general point of view" that involves focusing on the people affected by an action while setting aside our personal relationship to them. Thus, Hume's view in the end is that moral judgments are based on the "esteem of a judicious spectator"—the feelings of approval or disapproval that we experience when we reflect from a common point of view on the people affected by an action or trait of character.

David Hume was born in Edinburgh in 1711, into a good but far from wealthy Scottish family. He was forced to earn his own living and, in securing a livelihood, he had many unusual adventures. For a time he served as companion to a mad nobleman. A little later he became secretary to the general in charge of a military expedition to Canada which missed its objective and instead made an abortive attack on the coast of France. After that he was appointed as a librarian in Edinburgh but was soon discharged for stocking the shelves with obscene books. Late in his life he served as secretary in the British embassy in Paris. There he was immensely popular, being lionized by the intellectual and social elite of France. In spite of all these occupations Hume wrote voluminously, first on philosophical subjects—he completed his monumental *Treatise of Human Nature* at the astonishing age of twenty-six—and later, after switching from philosophy to history, a multivolumed *History of England*. He died in 1776, at the age of sixty-five. Just before his death he heard about the American Declaration of Independence, of which he heartily approved. His tomb, in Edinburgh, stands near a statue of Abraham Lincoln erected as a memorial to local citizens who fought as volunteers in the Civil War.

—

A Treatise of Human Nature

Of the Influencing Motives of the Will

Nothing is more usual in philosophy, and even in common life, than to talk of the combat of passion and reason, to give the preference to reason, and to assert that men are only so far virtuous as they conform themselves to its dictates. Every rational creature, it is said, is obliged to regulate his actions by reason; and if any other motive or principle challenge the direction of his conduct, he ought to oppose it, till it be entirely subdued, or at least brought to a conformity with that superior principle. On this method of thinking the greatest part of moral philosophy, ancient and modern, seems to be founded; nor is there an ampler field, as well for metaphysical arguments, as popular declamations, than this supposed pre-eminence of reason above passion. The eternity, invariableness, and divine origin of the former have been displayed to the best advantage: The blindness, inconstancy, and deceitfulness of the latter have been as strongly insisted on. In order to show the fallacy of all this philosophy, I shall endeavor to prove *first,* that reason alone can never be a motive to any action of the will; and *secondly,* that it can never oppose passion in the direction of the will.

The understanding exerts itself after two different ways, as it judges from demonstration or probability; as it regards the abstract relations of our ideas, or those relations of objects, of which experience only gives us information. I believe

First published in 1738. The spelling has been modernized.

it scarce will be asserted, that the first species of reasoning alone is ever the cause of any action. As its proper province is the world of ideas, and as the will always places us in that of realities, demonstration and volition seem, upon that account, to be totally removed, from each other. Mathematics, indeed, are useful in all mechanical operations, and arithmetic in almost every art and profession: But it is not of themselves they have any influence. Mechanics are the art of regulating the motions of bodies *to some designed end or purpose;* and the reason why we employ arithmetic in fixing the proportions of numbers is only that we may discover the proportions of their influence and operation. A merchant is desirous of knowing the sum total of his accounts with any person: Why? but that he may learn what sum will have the same *effects* in paying his debt, and going to market, as all the particular articles taken together. Abstract or demonstrative reasoning, therefore, never influences any of our actions, but only as it directs our judgment concerning causes and effects; which leads us to the second operation of the understanding.

It is obvious, that when we have the prospect of pain or pleasure from any object, we feel a consequent emotion of aversion or propensity, and are carried to avoid or embrace what will give us this uneasiness or satisfaction. It is also obvious, that this emotion rests not here, but making us cast our view on every side, comprehends whatever objects are connected with its original one by the relation of cause and effect. Here then reasoning takes place to discover this relation; and according as our reasoning varies, our actions receive a subsequent variation. But it is evident in this case, that the impulse arises not from reason, but is only directed by it. It is from the prospect of pain or pleasure that the aversion or propensity arises towards any object: And these emotions extend themselves to the causes and effects of that object, as they are pointed out to us by reason and experience. It can never in the least concern us to know, that such objects are causes, and such others effects, if both the causes and effects be indifferent to us. Where the objects themselves do not affect us, their connection can never give them any influence; and it is plain, that as reason is nothing but the discovery of this connection, it cannot be by its means that the objects are able to affect us.

Since reason alone can never produce any action, or give rise to volition, I infer, that the same faculty is as incapable of preventing volition, or of disputing the preference with any passion or emotion. This consequence is necessary. It is impossible reason could have the latter effect of preventing volition, but by giving an impulse in a contrary direction to our passion; and that impulse, had it operated alone, would have been able to produce volition. Nothing can oppose or retard the impulse of passion, but a contrary impulse; and if this contrary impulse ever arises from reason, that latter faculty must have an original influence on the will, and must be able to cause, as well as hinder any act of volition. But if reason has no original influence, it is impossible it can withstand any principle, which has such an efficacy, or ever keep the mind in suspense a moment. Thus it appears, that the principle, which opposes our passion, cannot be the same with reason, and is only called so in an improper sense. We speak not strictly and philosophically when we talk of the combat of passion and reason. Reason is, and ought only to be the slave of the passions, and can never pretend to any other office than to serve and obey them. As this opinion may appear somewhat extraordinary, it may not be improper to confirm it by some other considerations.

A passion is an original existence, or, if you will, modification of existence, and contains not any representative quality, which renders it a copy of any other existence or modification. When I am angry, I am actually possessed with the passion, and in that emotion have no more a reference to any other object, than when I am thirsty, or sick, or more than five foot high. It is impossible, therefore, that this passion can be opposed by, or be contradictory to truth and reason; since this contradiction consists in the disagreement of ideas, considered as copies, with those objects, which they represent.

What may at first occur on this head, is, that as nothing can be contrary to truth or reason, except what has a reference to it, and as the judgments of our understanding only have this reference, it must follow, that passions can be contrary to reason only so far as they are accompanied with some judgment or opinion. According to this principle, which is so obvious and natural, it is only in two senses, that any affection can be called unreasonable. First, when a passion, such as hope or fear, grief or joy, despair or security, is founded on the supposition of the existence of objects, which really do not exist. Secondly, when in exerting any passion in action, we choose means insufficient for the designed end, and deceive ourselves in our judgment of causes and effects. Where a passion is neither founded on false suppositions, nor chooses means insufficient for the end, the understanding can neither justify nor condemn it. It is not contrary to reason to prefer the destruction of the whole world to the scratching of my finger. It is not contrary to reason for me to choose my total ruin, to prevent the least uneasiness of an *Indian* or person wholly unknown to me. It is as little contrary to reason to prefer even my own acknowledged lesser good to my greater, and have a more ardent affection for the former than the latter. A trivial good may, from certain circumstances, produce a desire superior to what arises from the greatest and most valuable enjoyment; nor is there any thing more extraordinary in this, than in mechanics to see one pound weight raise up a hundred by the advantage of its situation. In short, a passion must be accompanied with some false judgment, in order to its being unreasonable; and even then it is not the passion, properly speaking, which is unreasonable, but the judgment.

The consequences are evident. Since a passion can never, in any sense, be called unreasonable, but when founded on a false supposition, or when it chooses means insufficient for the designed end, it is impossible, that reason and passion can ever oppose each other, or dispute for the government of the will and actions. The moment we perceive the falsehood of any supposition, or the insufficiency of any means our passions yield to our reason without any opposition. I may desire any fruit as of an excellent relish; but whenever you convince me of my mistake, my longing ceases. I may will the performance of certain actions as means of obtaining any desired good; but as my willing of these actions is only secondary, and founded on the supposition, that they are causes of the proposed effect; as soon as I discover the falsehood of that supposition, they must become indifferent to me.

It is natural for one, that does not examine objects with a strict philosophic eye, to imagine, that those actions of the mind are entirely the same, which produce not a different sensation, and are not immediately distinguishable to the feeling and perception. Reason, for instance, exerts itself without producing any sensible emotion; and except in the more sublime disquisitions of philosophy, or in the frivolous subtleties of the schools, scarce ever conveys any pleasure or uneasiness. Hence it proceeds, that every action of the mind, which operates with the same calmness and tranquillity, is confounded with reason by all those who judge of things from the first view and appearance. Now it is certain, there are certain calm desires and tendencies, which, though they be real passions, produce little emotion in the mind, and are more known by their effects than by the immediate feeling or sensation. These desires are of two kinds; either certain instincts originally implanted in our natures, such as benevolence and resentment, the love of life, and kindness to children; or the general appetite to good, and aversion to evil, considered merely as such. When any of these passions are calm, and cause no disorder in the soul, they are very readily taken for the determinations of reason, and are supposed to proceed from the same faculty, with that which judges of truth and falsehood. Their nature and principles have been supposed the same, because their sensations are not evidently different.

Beside these calm passions, which often determine the will, there are certain violent emotions of the same kind, which have likewise a great influence on that faculty. When I receive any injury from another, I often feel a violent passion of resentment, which makes me desire his evil and punishment, independent of all considerations of pleasure and advantage to myself. When I am immediately threatened with any grievous ill, my fears, apprehensions, and aversions rise to a great height, and produce a sensible emotion.

The common error of metaphysicians has lain in ascribing the direction of the will entirely to one of these principles, and supposing the other to have no influence. Men often act knowingly against their interest: For which reason the view of the greatest possible good does not always influence them. Men often counter-act a violent passion in prosecution of their interests and designs: It is not therefore the present uneasiness alone, which determines them. In general we may observe, that both these principles operate on the will; and where they are contrary, that either of them prevails, according to the *general* character or *present* disposition of the person. What we call strength of mind, implies the prevalence of the calm passions above the violent; though we may easily observe, there is no man so constantly possessed of this virtue, as never on any occasion to yield to the solicitations of passion and desire. From these variations of temper proceeds the great difficulty of deciding concerning the actions and resolutions of men, where there is any contrariety of motives and passions.

Moral Distinctions Not Derived from Reason

It has been observed that nothing is ever present to the mind but its perceptions; and that all the actions of seeing, hearing, judging, loving, hating, and thinking, fall under this denomination. The mind can never exert itself in any action, which we may not comprehend under the term of *perception;* and consequently that term is no less applicable to those judgments, by which we distinguish moral good and evil, than to every other operation of the mind. To approve of one character, to condemn another, are only so many different perceptions.

Now as perceptions resolve themselves into two kinds, viz., *impressions* and *ideas*, this distinction gives rise to a question, with which we shall open up our present enquiry concerning morals, *Whether it is by means of our* ideas *or* impressions *we distinguish between vice and virtue, and pronounce an action blameable or praiseworthy?* This will immediately cut off all loose discourses and declamations, and reduce us to something precise and exact on the present subject.

Those who affirm that virtue is nothing but a conformity to reason, that there are eternal fitnesses and unfitnesses of things, which are the same to every rational being that considers them; that the immutable measures of right and wrong impose an obligation, not only on human creatures, but also on the Deity himself: All these systems concur in the opinion, that morality, like truth, is discerned merely by ideas, and by their juxtaposition and comparison. In order, therefore, to judge of these systems, we need only consider, whether it be possible, from reason alone, to distinguish between moral good and evil, or whether there must concur some other principles to enable us to make that distinction.

If morality had naturally no influence on human passions and actions, it were in vain to take such pains to inculcate it; and nothing would be more fruitless than that multitude of rules and precepts, with which all moralists abound. Philosophy is commonly divided into *speculative* and *practical;* and as morality is always comprehended under the latter division, it is supposed to influence our passions and actions, and to go beyond the calm and indolent judgments of the understanding. And this is confirmed by common experience, which informs us, that men are often governed by their duties, and are deterred from some actions by the opinion of injustice, and impelled to others by that of obligation.

Since morals, therefore, have an influence on the actions and affections, it follows, that they cannot be derived from reason; and that because reason alone, as we have already proved, can never have any such influence. Morals excite passions, and produce or prevent actions. Reason of itself is utterly impotent in this particular. The rules of morality, therefore, are not conclusions of our reason.

No one, I believe, will deny the justness of this inference; nor is there any other means of evading it, than by denying that principle, on which it is founded. As long as it is allowed, that reason has no influence on our passions and actions, it is in vain to pretend that morality is discovered only by a deduction of reason. An active principle can never be founded on an inactive; and if reason be inactive in itself, it must remain so in all its shapes and appearances, whether it exerts itself in natural or moral subjects, whether it considers the powers of external bodies, or the actions of rational beings.

It would be tedious to repeat all the arguments, by which I have proved, that reason is perfectly inert, and can never either prevent or produce any action or affection. It will be easy to recollect what has been said upon that subject. I shall only recall on this occasion one of these arguments, which I shall endeavour to render still more conclusive, and more applicable to the present subject.

Reason is the discovery of truth or falsehood. Truth or falsehood consists in an agreement or disagreement either to the *real* relations of ideas, or to *real* existence and matter of fact. Whatever, therefore, is not susceptible of this agreement or disagreement, is incapable of being true or false, and can never be an object of

our reason. Now it is evident our passions, volitions, and actions, are not susceptible of any such agreement or disagreement; being original facts and realities, complete in themselves, and implying no reference to other passions, volitions, and actions. It is impossible, therefore, they can be pronounced either true or false, and
be either contrary or conformable to reason.

This argument is of double advantage to our present purpose. For it proves
directly, that actions do not derive their merit from a conformity to reason, nor
their blame from a contrariety to it; and it proves the same truth more *indirectly,*
by showing us, that as reason can never immediately prevent or produce any action by contradicting or approving of it, it cannot be the source of moral good and
evil, which are found to have that influence. Actions may be laudable or blameable;
but they cannot be reasonable or unreasonable: Laudable or blameable, therefore,
are not the same with reasonable or unreasonable. The merit and demerit of actions frequently contradict, and sometimes control our natural propensities. But
reason has no such influence. Moral distinctions, therefore, are not the offspring
of reason. Reason is wholly inactive, and can never be the source of so active a
principle as conscience, or a sense of morals. . . .

Thus upon the whole, it is impossible that the distinction between moral good
and evil can be made by reason; since that distinction has an influence upon our
actions, of which reason alone is incapable. Reason and judgment may, indeed, be
the mediate cause of an action, by prompting, or by directing a passion: But it is
not pretended, that a judgment of this kind, either in its truth or falsehood, is attended with virtue or vice. And as to the judgments, which are caused by our judgments, they can still less bestow those moral qualities on the actions, which are
their causes. . . .

Nor does this reasoning only prove, that morality consists not in any relations,
that are the objects of science; but if examined, will prove with equal certainty, that
it consists not in any *matter of fact,* which can be discovered by the understanding.
This is the *second* part of our argument; and if it can be made evident, we may conclude, that morality is not an object of reason. But can there be any difficulty in
proving, that vice and virtue are not matters of fact, whose existence we can infer
by reason? Take any action allowed to be vicious: Wilful murder, for instance.
Examine it in all lights, and see if you can find that matter of fact, or real existence,
which you call *vice.* In whichever way you take it, you find only certain passions,
motives, volitions, and thoughts. There is no other matter of fact in the case. The
vice entirely escapes you, as long as you consider the object. You never can find it,
till you turn your reflection into your own breast, and find a sentiment of disapprobation, which arises in you, towards this action. Here is a matter of fact; but it
is the object of feeling, not of reason. It lies in yourself, not in the object. So that
when you pronounce any action or character to be vicious, you mean nothing, but
that from the constitution of your nature you have a feeling or sentiment of blame
from the contemplation of it. Vice and virtue, therefore, may be compared to
sounds, colours, heat and cold, which, according to modern philosophy, are not
qualities in objects, but perceptions in the mind: And this discovery in morals like
that other in physics, is to be regarded as a considerable advancement of the speculative sciences; though like that too, it has little or no influence on practice.

Nothing can be more real, or concern us more, than our own sentiments of pleasure and uneasiness; and if these be favourable to virtue, and unfavourable to vice, no more can be requisite to the regulation of our conduct and behaviour.

I cannot forbear adding to these reasonings an observation, which may, perhaps, be found of some importance. In every system of morality, which I have hitherto met with, I have always remarked that the author proceeds for some time in the ordinary way of reasoning, and establishes the being of a God, or makes observations concerning human affairs; when of a sudden I am surprised to find, that instead of the usual copulations of propositions, *is,* and *is not,* I meet with no proposition that is not connected with an *ought,* or *ought not.* This change is imperceptible; but is, however, of the last consequence. For as this *ought,* or *ought not,* expresses some new relation or affirmation, it is necessary that it should be observed and explained; and at the same time that a reason should be given, for what seems altogether inconceivable, how this new relation can be a deduction from others, which are entirely different from it. But as authors do not commonly use this precaution, I shall presume to recommend it to the readers; and am persuaded, that this small attention would subvert all the vulgar systems of morality, and let us see, that the distinction of vice and virtue is not founded merely on the relations of objects, nor is perceived by reason.

Moral Distinctions Derived from a Moral Sense

Thus the course of the argument leads us to conclude, that since vice and virtue are not discoverable merely by reason, or the comparison of ideas, it must be by means of some impression or sentiment they occasion, that we are able to mark the difference between them. Our decisions concerning moral rectitude and depravity are evidently perceptions; and as all perceptions are either impressions or ideas, the exclusion of the one is a convincing argument for the other. Morality, therefore, is more properly felt than judged of; though this feeling or sentiment is commonly so soft and gentle, that we are apt to confound it with an idea, according to our common custom of taking all things for the same, which have any near resemblance to each other.

The next question: Of what nature are these impressions, and after what manner do they operate upon us? Here we cannot remain long in suspense, but must pronounce the impression arising from virtue, to be agreeable, and that proceeding from vice to be uneasy. Every moment's experience must convince us of this. There is no spectacle so fair and beautiful as a noble and generous action; nor any which gives us more abhorrence than one that is cruel and treacherous. No enjoyment equals the satisfaction we receive from the company of those we love and esteem; as the greatest of all punishments is to be obliged to pass our lives with those we hate or condemn. A very play or romance may afford us instances of this pleasure, which virtue conveys to us, and pain, which arises from vice.

Now since the distinguishing impressions, by which moral good or evil is known, are nothing but *particular* pains or pleasures; it follows, that in all enquiries concerning these moral distinctions, it will be sufficient to shew the principles, which make us feel a satisfaction or uneasiness from the survey of any character, in order to satisfy us why the character is laudable or blameable. An action, or sentiment, or character is virtuous or vicious; why? because its view causes a pleasure or uneasiness of a particular kind. In giving a reason, therefore, for the pleasure or uneasiness, we sufficiently explain the vice or virtue. To have the sense of virtue, is nothing but to *feel* a satisfaction of a particular kind from the contemplation of a character. The very *feeling* constitutes our praise or admiration. We go no farther; nor do we inquire into the cause of the satisfaction. We do not infer a character to be virtuous, because it pleases: But in feeling that it pleases after such a particular manner, we in effect feel that it is virtuous. The case is the same as in our judgments concerning all kinds of beauty, and tastes, and sensations. Our approbation is implied in the immediate pleasure they convey to us.

Of the Origin of the Natural Virtues and Vices

. . . We have already observed, that moral distinctions depend entirely on certain peculiar sentiments of pain and pleasure, and that whatever mental quality in ourselves or others gives us a satisfaction, by the survey or reflection, is of course virtuous; as every thing of this nature, that gives uneasiness, is vicious. Now since every quality in ourselves or others, which gives pleasure, always causes pride or love; as every one, that produces uneasiness, excites humility or hatred: It follows, that these two particulars are to be considered as equivalent, with regard to our mental qualities, *virtue* and the power of producing love or pride, vice and the power of producing humility or hatred. In every case, therefore, we must judge of the one by the other; and may pronounce any quality of the mind virtuous, which causes love or pride; and any one vicious, which causes hatred or humility.

If any *action* be either virtuous or vicious, it is only as a sign of some quality or character. It must depend upon durable principles of the mind, which extend over the whole conduct, and enter into the personal character. Actions themselves, not proceeding from any constant principle, have no influence on love or hatred, pride or humility; and consequently are never considered in morality.

This reflection is self-evident, and deserves to be attended to, as being of the utmost importance in the present subject. We are never to consider any single action in our enquiries concerning the origin of morals; but only the quality or character from which the action proceeded. These alone are *durable* enough to affect our sentiments concerning the person. Actions are, indeed, better indications of a character than words, or even wishes and sentiments; but it is only so far as they are such indications, that they are attended with love or hatred, praise or blame.

To discover the true origin of morals, and of that love or hatred, which arises from mental qualities, we must take the matter pretty deep, and compare some principles, which have been already examined and explained.

We may begin with considering anew the nature and force of *sympathy*. The minds of all men are similar in their feelings and operations; nor can any one be actuated by any affection, of which all others are not, in some degree, susceptible. As in strings equally wound up, the motion of one communicates itself to the rest;

so all the affections readily pass from one person to another, and beget correspondent movements in every human creature. When I see the *effects* of passion in the voice and gesture of any person, my mind immediately passes from these effects to their causes, and forms such a lively idea of the passion, as is presently converted into the passion itself. In like manner, when I perceive the *causes of* any emotion, my mind is conveyed to the effects, and is actuated with a like emotion. Were I present at any of the more terrible operations of surgery, it is certain, that even before it begun, the preparation of the instruments, the laying of the bandages in order, the heating of the irons, with all the signs of anxiety and concern in the patient and assistants, would have a great effect upon my mind, and excite the strongest sentiments of pity and terror. No passion of another discovers itself immediately to the mind. We are only sensible of its causes or effects. From *these* we infer the passion: And consequently *these* give rise to our sympathy.

Our sense of beauty depends very much on this principle; and where any object has a tendency to produce pleasure in its possessor, it is always regarded as beautiful; as every object, that has a tendency to produce pain, is disagreeable and deformed. Thus the conveniency of a house, the fertility of a field, the strength of a horse, the capacity, security, and swift-sailing of a vessel, form the principal beauty of these several objects. Here the object, which is denominated beautiful, pleases only by its tendency to produce a certain effect. That effect is the pleasure or advantage of some other person. Now the pleasure of a stranger, for whom we have no friendship, pleases us only by sympathy. To this principle, therefore, is owing the beauty, which we find in every thing that is useful. How considerable a part this is of beauty will easily appear upon reflection. Wherever an object has a tendency to produce pleasure in the possessor, or in other words, is the proper *cause* of pleasure, it is sure to please the spectator, by a delicate sympathy with the possessor. Most of the works of art are esteemed beautiful, in proportion to their fitness for the use of man, and even many of the productions of nature derive their beauty from that source. Handsome and beautiful, on most occasions, is not an absolute but a relative quality, and pleases us by nothing but its tendency to produce an end that is agreeable.

The same principle produces, in many instances, our sentiments of morals, as well as those of beauty. No virtue is more esteemed than justice, and no vice more detested than injustice; nor are there any qualities, which go farther to the fixing the character, either as amiable or odious. Now justice is a moral virtue, merely because it has that tendency to the good of mankind; and, indeed, is nothing but an artificial invention to that purpose. The same may be said of allegiance, of the laws of nations, of modesty, and of good-manners. All these are mere human contrivances for the interest of society. And since there is a very strong sentiment of morals, which in all nations, and all ages, has attended them, we must allow, that the reflecting on the tendency of characters and mental qualities, is sufficient to give us the sentiments of approbation and blame. Now as the means to an end can only be agreeable, where the end is agreeable; and as the good of society, where our own interest is not concerned, or that of our friends, pleases only by sympathy: It follows, that sympathy is the source of the esteem, which we pay to all the artificial virtues.

Thus it appears, *that* sympathy is a very powerful principle in human nature, *that* it has a great influence on our taste of beauty, and *that* it produces our sentiment of morals in all the artificial virtues. From thence we may presume, that it also gives rise to many of the other virtues; and that qualities acquire our approbation, because of their tendency to the good of mankind. This presumption must become a certainty, when we find that most of those qualities, which we *naturally* approve of, have actually that tendency, and render a man a proper member of society: While the qualities, which we *naturally* disapprove of, have a contrary tendency, and render any intercourse with the person dangerous or disagreeable. For having found, that such tendencies have force enough to produce the strongest sentiment of morals, we can never reasonably, in these cases, look for any other cause of approbation or blame; it being an inviolable maxim in philosophy, that where any particular cause is sufficient for an effect, we ought to rest satisfied with it, and ought not to multiply causes without necessity. We have happily attained experiments in the artificial virtues, where the tendency of qualities to the good of society, is the sole cause of our approbation, without any suspicion of the concurrence of another principle. From thence we learn the force of that principle. And where that principle may take place, and the quality approved of is really beneficial to society, a true philosopher will never require any other principle to account for the strongest approbation and esteem.

That many of the natural virtues have this tendency to the good of society, no one can doubt of. Meekness, beneficence, charity, generosity, clemency, moderation, equity bear the greatest figure among the moral qualities, and are commonly denominated the *social* virtues, to mark their tendency to the good of society. This goes so far, that some philosophers have represented all moral distinctions as the effect of artifice and education, when skillful politicians endeavoured to restrain the turbulent passions of men, and make them operate to the public good, by the notions of honour and shame. This system, however, is not consistent with experience. For, *first,* there are other virtues and vices beside those which have this tendency to the public advantage and loss. *Secondly,* had not men a natural sentiment of approbation and blame, it could never be excited by politicians; nor would the words *laudable* and *praise-worthy, blameable* and *odious* be any more intelligible, than if they were a language perfectly known to us, as we have already observed. But though this system be erroneous, it may teach us, that moral distinctions arise, in a great measure, from the tendency of qualities and characters to the interests of society, and that it is our concern for that interest, which makes us approve or disapprove of them. Now we have no such extensive concern for society but from sympathy; and consequently it is that principle, which takes us so far out of ourselves, as to give us the same pleasure or uneasiness in the characters of others, as if they had a tendency to our own advantage or loss.

The only difference between the natural virtues and justice lies in this, that the good, which results from the former, arises from every single act, and is the object of some natural passion: Whereas a single act of justice, considered in itself, may often be contrary to the public good; and it is only the concurrence of mankind, in a general scheme or system of action, which is advantageous. When I relieve persons in distress, my natural humanity is my motive; and so far as my succour extends, so far have I promoted the happiness of my fellow creatures. But if we examine all the questions, that come before any tribunal of justice, we shall find, that, considering each case apart, it would as often be an instance of humanity to decide contrary to the laws of justice as conformable them. Judges take from a poor man to give to a rich; they bestow on the dissolute the labour of the industrious; and put into the hands of the vicious the means of harming both themselves and others. The whole scheme, however, of law and justice is advantageous to the society; and it was with a view to this advantage, that men, by their voluntary conventions, established it. After it is once established by these conventions, it is *naturally* attended with a strong sentiment of morals; which can proceed from nothing but our sympathy with the interests of society. We need no other explication of that esteem, which attends such of the natural virtues, as have a tendency to the public good. . . .

Before I proceed farther, I must observe two remarkable circumstances in this affair, which may seem objections to the present system. The first may be thus explained. When any quality, or character, has a tendency to the good of mankind, we are pleased with it, and approve of it; because it presents the lively idea of pleasure; which idea affects us by sympathy, and is itself a kind of pleasure. But as this sympathy is very variable, it may be thought, that our sentiments of morals must admit of all the same variations. We sympathize more with persons contiguous to us, than with persons remote from us: With our acquaintance, than with strangers: With our countrymen, than with foreigners. But notwithstanding this variation of our sympathy, we give the same approbation to the same moral qualities in *China* as in *England*. They appear equally virtuous, and recommend themselves equally to the esteem of a judicious spectator. The sympathy varies without a variation in our esteem. Our esteem, therefore, proceeds not from sympathy.

To this I answer: The approbation of moral qualities most certainly is not derived from reason, or any comparison of ideas; but proceeds entirely from a moral taste, and from certain sentiments of pleasure or disgust, which arise upon the contemplation and view of particular qualities or characters. Now it is evident, that those sentiments, whenever they are derived, must vary according to the distance or contiguity of the objects; nor can I feel the same lively pleasure from the virtues of a person, who lived in *Greece* two thousand years ago, that I feel from the virtues of a familiar friend and acquaintance. Yet I do not say, that I esteem the one more than the other: And therefore, if the variation of the sentiment, without a variation of the esteem, be an objection, it must have equal force against every other system, as against that of sympathy. But to consider the matter aright, it has no force at all; and it is the easiest matter in the world to account for it. Our situation, with regard both to persons and things, is in continual fluctuation; and a man, that lies at a distance from us, may, in a little time, become a familiar acquaintance. Besides, every particular man has a peculiar position with regard to others; and it is impossible we could ever converse together on any reasonable terms, were each of us to consider characters and persons, only as they appear from his peculiar point of view. In order, therefore, to prevent those continual *contradictions,* and arrive at a more *stable* judgment of things, we fix on some *steady* and *general* points of view; and always, in our thoughts, place ourselves in them, whatever may be our present situation. In like manner, external beauty is determined merely by pleasure; and it is evident, a beautiful countenance cannot give so much pleasure, when seen at the distance of twenty paces, as when it is brought nearer us. We say not, however, that it appears to us less beautiful: Because we know what effect it will have in such a position, and by that reflection we correct its momentary appearance.

In general, all sentiments of blame or praise are variable, according to our situation of nearness or remoteness, with regard to the person blamed or praised, and according to the present disposition of our mind. But these variations we regard not in our general decision, but still apply the terms expressive of our liking or dislike, in the same manner, as if we remained in one point of view. Experience soon teaches us this method of correcting our sentiments, or at least, of correcting our language, where the sentiments are more stubborn and inalterable. Our servant, if diligent and faithful, may excite stronger sentiments of love and kindness than Marcus Brutus, as represented in history; but we say not upon that account, that the former character is more laudable than the latter. We know, that were we to approach equally near to that renowned patriot, he would command a much higher degree of affection and admiration. Such corrections are common with regard to all the senses; and indeed it would be impossible we could ever make use of language, or communicate our sentiments to one another, did we not correct the momentary appearances of things, and overlook our present situation.

It is therefore from the influence of characters and qualities, upon those who have an intercourse with any person, that we blame or praise him. We consider not whether the persons, affected by the qualities, be our acquaintance or strangers, countrymen or foreigners. Nay, we overlook our own interest in those general judgments; and blame not a man for opposing us in any of our pretensions, when his own interest is particularly concerned. We make allowance for a certain degree of selfishness in men; because we know it to be inseparable from human nature, and inherent in our frame and constitution. By this reflection we correct those sentiments of blame, which so naturally arise upon any opposition.

But however the general principle of our blame or praise may be corrected by those other principles, it is certain, they are not altogether efficacious, nor do our passions often correspond entirely to the present theory. It is seldom men heartily love what lies at a distance from them, and what no way redounds to their particular benefit; as it is no less rare to meet with persons, who can pardon another any opposition he makes to their interest, however justifiable that opposition may be by the general rules of morality. Here we are contented with saying, that reason requires such an impartial conduct, but that it is seldom we can bring ourselves to it, and that our passions do not readily follow the determination of our judgment. This language will be easily understood, if we consider what we formerly said concerning that reason, which is able to oppose our passion; and which we have found to be nothing but a general calm determination of the passions, founded on some distant view or reflection. When we form our judgments of persons, merely from the tendency of their characters to our own benefit, or to that of our friends, we find so many contradictions to our sentiments in society and conversation, and such an uncertainty from the incessant changes of our situation, that we seek some other standard of merit and demerit, which may not admit of so great variation. Being thus loosened from our first station, we cannot afterwards fix ourselves so commodiously by any means as by a sympathy with those, who have any commerce with the person we consider. This is far from being as lively as when our own interest is concerned, or that of our particular friends; nor has it such an influence on our love and hatred: But being equally conformable to our calm and general principles, it is said to have an equal authority over our reason, and to command our judgment and opinion. We blame equally a bad action, which we read of in history, with one performed in our neighbourhood the other day: The meaning of which is, that we know from reflection, that the former action would excite as strong sentiments of disapprobation as the latter, were it placed in the same position. . .

Thus, to take a general review of the present hypothesis: Every quality of the mind is denominated virtuous, which gives pleasure by the mere survey; as every quality, which produces pain, is called vicious. This pleasure and this pain may arise from four different sources. For we reap a pleasure from the view of a character, which is naturally fitted to be useful to others, or to the person himself, or which is agreeable to others, or to the person himself. One may, perhaps, be surprised, that amidst all these interests and pleasures, we should forget our own, which touch us so nearly on every other occasion. But we shall easily satisfy ourselves on this head, when we consider, that every particular person's pleasure and interest being different, it is impossible men could ever agree in their sentiments and judgments, unless they chose some common point of view, from which they might survey their object, and which might cause it to appear the same to all of them. Now in judging of characters, the only interest or pleasures which appears the same to every spectator, is that of the person himself, whose character is examined; or that of persons, who have a connection with him. And though such interests and pleasures touch us more faintly than our own, yet being more constant and universal, they counter-balance the latter even in practice, and are alone admitted in speculation as the standard of virtue and morality. They alone produce that particular feeling or sentiment, on which moral distinctions depend. . . . .

———

Study Questions

1. Hume claims that "It is not contrary to reason to prefer the destruction of the whole world to the scratching of my little finger . . . it is as little contrary to reason to prefer even my own acknowledged lesser good to my greater, and have a more ardent affection for the former than the latter." What is Hume getting at here? Do you agree or disagree with these claims about reason and rationality? Imagine someone who has these preferences: Is that person irrational?

2. Hume removes morality from the province of reason by limiting the scope of our rational powers. What are his main arguments for thinking that morality is not derived from reason? Do you think that reason is as limited as Hume claims?

3. Hume argues that when we consider a wrongful action such as murder, there is no property of the action itself that we can identify with its being wrong. All we find are certain feelings of disapproval evoked by the action. Do you agree or disagree? If you disagree, how would you argue against Hume?
4. Do you agree with Hume that sympathy plays a central role in judgments of right and wrong? Is sympathy always a reliable guide to assessing right and wrong? Explain.
5. Toward the end of the selection, Hume argues that when we make moral judgments, we need to correct for differences and variations in our feelings by taking up a general or impartial point of view. Is this feature of his theory consistent with his denial that moral distinctions are derived from reason?

Selected Bibliography

Ayer, A. J. *Hume: Past Masters* (New York: Hill & Wang, 1980). A brief overview of Hume's philosophy

Baier, Annette. *A Progress of the Sentiments: Reflections on Hume's Treatise* (Cambridge: Harvard University Press, 1991). A general study of Hume's philosophy.

Broad, C. D. *Five Types of Ethical Theory* (London: Routledge, 1930), Chap. 4. An exposition of Hume's ethical views.

Flew, A. *David Hume* (Oxford: Basil Blackwell, 1986), Chaps. 9–10. A brief analysis of Hume's moral philosophy.

Hume, D. *An Enquiry Concerning the Principles of Morals.* (Available in many editions.) Hume's later work on ethics.

Mackie, J. L. *Hume's Moral Theory* (London: Routledge & Kegan Paul, 1980). A summary of Hume's ethics.

Norton, David Fate, ed. *The Cambridge Companion to Hume* (New York/Cambridge: Cambridge University Press, 1993). A collection of recent essays on aspects of Hume's philosophy.

Penelhum, T. *Hume* (London: Macmillan, 1975), Chap. 7. A psychological interpretation of Hume's ethics.

Rawls, John. *Lectures on the History of Moral Philosophy* (Cambridge: Harvard University Press, 2000), Part I. An interpretation of Hume's moral philosophy by a leading contemporary philosopher.

Stroud, B. *Hume* (London: Routledge & Kegan Paul, 1977), Chaps. 7–9. An interpretation of Hume's ethics.

11

IMMANUEL KAN

———

1724-
1804

Kant's *Foundations of the Meta-physics of Morals* (sometimes translated as the *Groundwork of the Metaphysics of Morals*) is one of the most important works in western moral philosophy. In the preface to this work Kant states that his aim is

> *Act only on that maxim through which you can at the same time will that it should become a universal law.*

the "search for and establishment of the supreme principle of morality." He sets out to state and to justify the basic principle that underlies ordinary moral thought and to defend the view that moral requirements are requirements of reason. Kant thinks that one of the central notions of ordinary morality is that we are subject to duties that apply with "necessity" and "universality"; he often expresses this by saying that duties represent "practical laws." Their necessity is the fact that duties override other kinds of reasons. If I am morally bound to tell the truth in some situation, then I must tell the truth—whether I want to or not, and whether it serves my interests or not. Universality means that duties apply to us simply by virtue of the fact that we are rational agents and result from the application of universally valid principles. Kant thinks that if moral requirements truly apply with necessity and universality, they cannot be based in features of human nature or human psychology, as Hume thought. Rather, they must have an *a priori* basis in reason. As Kant says, a duty represents a requirement or practical law for us because it holds "for the will of every rational being."

Kant's views about morality lead him to a more complex—and not uncontroversial—view of human motivation. In constrast to Hume and other theorists in the British empiricist tradition, Kant thinks that we have the capacity to be motivated by reason alone. For example, the conscientious moral agent with a "good will" does the right thing simply because it is right. Even if we rarely do so, we can perform an action simply because it is our duty. If duties are requirements of reason, then the agent who acts from duty is motivated to act by his or her grasp of a principle of conduct that is based in reason—that is, motivated by reason alone.

Despite the difficulties of the *Foundations of the Metaphysics of Morals*, it is based on a set of ideas with powerful intuitive appeal. The Second Section states different versions of the basic principle of morality—what Kant calls "the Categorical Imperative"—that he thinks are at root equivalent. The first version, known as the "Formula of Universal Law," reads, "Act only on that maxim through which you can same time will that it should become a universal law." Although many ideas are put into this formula, it requires, among other things, that we should act from universally valid principles that are sufficient to justify our actions to anyone. To assess the acceptability of an action, we should ask whether it is rational to will that everyone adopt the principle from which we propose to act. (Note that the issue is not just how I would like it if everyone adopted the principle; rather, it is whether I can rationally and without inconsistency will the universal adoption of the principle.) The second, often referred to as the "Formula of Humanity," states, "Act in such a way that you always treat humanity, whether in your own person or in the person of another, always as an end, and never as a means only." By "humanity" Kant means the capacity for rational choice that is distinctive of persons. The Formula of Humanity expresses the idea that persons, as rational agents, have an equal and incomparable worth that must always be respected; the incomparable value, or inherent dignity, of persons sets limits on how we may act. One way to connect these formulas is as follows: one shows respect for the persons affected by one's actions when one acts from universally valid principles that can be cited to justify one's actions.

Immanuel Kant was born in 1724 in Königsberg, a university town on the Baltic Sea in East Prussia. He is a major figure in the history of philosophy. His greatest and most difficult work, the *Critique of Pure Reason* (1781, revised in 1787), is a classic in epistemology and metaphysics that was tremendously influential in later philosophy. Besides the *Foundations of the Metaphysics of Morals* (1785), his other major works in moral philosophy include the *Critique of Practical Reason* (1788) and *The Metaphysics of Morals* (1797). Kant's personal life was almost without incident. Following the completion of his education, he worked for several years as a private tutor. He then became a lecturer, and later a professor at the University of Königsberg, where he was greatly admired as a teacher. Kant died in 1804, in his eightieth year, never having traveled more than 40 miles from the city of his birth.

Foundations of the Metaphysics of Morals

First Section

Transition from the Common Rational Knowledge of Morals to the Philosophical

Nothing in the world—indeed nothing even beyond the world—can possibly be conceived which could be called good without qualification except a *good will*. Intelligence, wit, judgment, and the other talents of the mind, however they may

From *Foundations of the Metaphysics of Morals*, 2nd ed., by Immanuel Kant (trans. by L. W. Beck), © Reprinted by permission of Pearson Education, Inc., Upper Saddle River, NJ.

be named, or courage, resoluteness, and perseverance as qualities of temperament are doubtless in many respects good and desirable. But they can become extremely bad and harmful if the will, which is to make use of these gifts of nature and which in its special constitution is called character, is not good. It is the same with the gifts of fortune. Power, riches, honor, and even health, general well-being, and the contentment with one's condition which is called happiness make for pride and even arrogance, if there is not a good will to correct their influence on the mind and on its principles of action, so as to make it universally conformable to its end. It need hardly be mentioned that the sight of a being adorned with no feature of a pure and good will yet enjoying uninterrupted prosperity can never give pleasure to a rational impartial observer. Thus the good will seems to constitute the indispensable condition even of worthiness to be happy.

Some qualities seem to be conducive to this good will and can facilitate its action, but, in spite of that, they have no intrinsic unconditional worth. They rather presuppose a good will, which limits the high esteem which one otherwise rightly has for them and prevents their being held to be absolutely good. Moderation in emotions and passions, self-control, and calm deliberation not only are good in many respects but even seem to constitute a part of the inner worth of the person. But however unconditionally they were esteemed by the ancients, they are far from being good without qualification. For, without the principles of a good will, they can become extremely bad, and the coolness of a villain makes him not only far more dangerous but also more directly abominable in our eyes than he would have seemed without it.

The good will is not good because of what it effects or accomplishes or because of its adequacy to achieve some proposed end; it is good only because of its willing, i.e., it is good of itself. And, regarded for itself, it is to be esteemed incomparably higher than anything which could be brought about by it in favor of any inclination or even of the sum total of all inclinations. Even if it should happen that, by a particularly unfortunate fate or by the niggardly provision of a stepmotherly nature, this will should be wholly lacking in power to accomplish its purpose, and if even the greatest effort should not avail it to achieve anything of its end, and if there remained only the good will (not as a mere wish but as the summoning of all the means in our power), it would sparkle like a jewel in its own right, as something that had its full worth in itself. Usefulness or fruitlessness can neither diminish nor augment this worth. Its usefulness would be only its setting, as it were, so as to enable us to handle it more conveniently in commerce or to attract the attention of those who are not yet connoisseurs, but not to recommend it to those who are experts or to determine its worth.

But there is something so strange in this idea of the absolute worth of the will alone, in which no account is taken of any use, that, notwithstanding the agreement even of common sense, the suspicion must arise that perhaps only high-flown fancy is its hidden basis, and that we may have misunderstood the purpose of nature in its appointment of reason as the ruler of our will. We shall therefore examine this idea from this point of view.

In the natural constitution of an organized being, i.e., one suitably adapted to life, we assume as an axiom that no organ will be found for any purpose which is not the fittest and best adapted to that purpose. Now if its preservation, welfare—in a word, its happiness—were the real end of nature in a being having reason and will, then nature would have hit upon a very poor arrangement in appointing the reason of the creature to be the executor of this purpose. For all the actions which the creature has to perform with this intention, and the entire rule of its conduct, would be dictated much more exactly by instinct, and that end would be far more certainly attained by instinct than it ever could be by reason. And if, over and above this, reason should have been granted to the favored creature, it would have served only to let it contemplate the happy constitution of its nature, to admire it, to rejoice in it, and to be grateful for it to its beneficent cause. But reason would not have been given in order that the being should subject its faculty of desire to that weak and elusive guidance and to meddle with the purpose of nature. In a word, nature would have taken care that reason did not break forth into practical use nor have the presumption, with its weak insight, to think out for itself the plan of happiness and the means of attaining it. Nature would have taken over not only the choice of ends but also that of the means and with wise foresight would have intrusted both to instinct alone.

And, in fact, we find that the more a cultivated reason deliberately devotes itself to the enjoyment of life and happiness, the more the man falls short of true contentment. From this fact there arises in many persons, if only they are candid enough to admit it, a certain degree of misology, hatred of reason. This is particularly the case with those who are most experienced in its use. After counting all the advantages which they draw—I will not say from the invention of the arts of common luxury—from the sciences (which in the end seemed to them to be also a luxury of the understanding), they nevertheless find that they have actually brought more trouble on their shoulders instead of gaining in happiness; they finally envy, rather than despise, the common run of men who are better guided by mere natural instinct and who do not permit their reason much influence on their conduct. And we must at least admit that a morose attitude or ingratitude to the goodness with which the world is governed is by no means always found among those who temper or refute the boasting eulogies which are given of the advantages of happiness and contentment with which reason is supposed to supply us. Rather their judgment is based on the idea of another and far more worthy purpose of their existence for which, instead of happiness, their reason is properly intended, this purpose, therefore, being the supreme condition to which the private purposes of men must for the most part defer.

Reason is not, however, competent to guide the will safely with regard to its objects and the satisfaction of all our needs (which it in part multiplies), and to this end an innate instinct would have led with far more certainty. But reason is given to us as a practical faculty, i.e., one which is meant to have an influence on the will. As nature has elsewhere distributed capacities suitable to the functions they are to perform, reason's proper function must be to produce a will good in itself and not one good merely as a means, for to the former reason is absolutely essential. This will must indeed not be the sole and complete good but the highest good and the condition of all others, even of the desire for happiness. In this case it is entirely compatible with the wisdom of nature that the cultivation of reason, which is required for the former unconditional purpose, at least in this life restricts in many ways—indeed can reduce to less than nothing—the achievement of the latter conditional purpose, happiness. For one perceives that nature here does not proceed unsuitably to its purpose, because reason, which recognizes its highest practical vocation in the establishment of a good will, is capable only of a contentment of its own kind, i.e., one that springs from the attainment of a purpose, which in turn is determined by reason, even though this injures the ends of inclination.

We have, then, to develop the concept of a will which is to be esteemed as good of itself without regard to anything else. It dwells already in the natural sound understanding and does not need so much to be taught as only to be brought to light. In the estimation of the entire worth of our actions it always takes first place and is the condition of everything else. In order to show this, we shall take the concept of duty. It contains that of a good will, though with certain subjective restrictions and hindrances; but these are far from concealing it and making it unrecognizable, for they rather bring it out by contrast and make it shine forth all the brighter.

I here omit all actions which are recognized as opposed to duty, even though they may be useful in one respect or another, for with these the question does not arise at all as to whether they may be done *from* duty, since they conflict with it. I also pass over the actions which are really in accordance with duty and to which one has no direct inclination, rather doing them because impelled to do so by another inclination. For it is easily decided whether an action in accord with duty is done from duty, or for some selfish purpose. It is far more difficult to note this difference when the action is in accordance with duty and, in addition, the subject has a direct inclination to do it. For example, it is in fact in accordance with duty that a dealer should not overcharge an inexperienced customer, and wherever there is much business the prudent merchant does not do so, having a fixed price for everyone, so that a child may buy of him as cheaply as any other. Thus the customer is honestly served. But this is far from sufficient to justify the belief that the merchant has behaved in this way from duty and principles of honesty. His own advantage required this behavior; but it cannot be assumed that over and above that he had a direct inclination to the purchaser and that, out of love, as it were, he gave none an advantage in price over another. Therefore the action was done neither from duty nor from direct inclination but only for a selfish purpose.

On the other hand, it is a duty to preserve one's life, and moreover, everyone has a direct inclination to do so. But, for that reason, the often anxious care which most men take of it has no intrinsic worth, and the maxim of doing so has no moral import. They preserve their lives according to duty, but not from duty. But if adversities and hopeless sorrow completely take away the relish for life; if an unfortunate man, strong in soul, is indignant rather than despondent or dejected over his fate and wishes for death, and yet preserves his life without loving it and from neither inclination nor fear but from duty—then his maxim has a moral import.

To be kind where one can is duty, and there are, moreover, many persons so sympathetically constituted that without any motive of vanity or selfishness they find an inner satisfaction in spreading joy and rejoice in the contentment of others which they have made possible. But I say that, however dutiful and amiable it may be, that kind of action has no true moral worth. It is on a level with [actions done from] other inclinations, such as the inclination to honor, which, if fortunately directed to what in fact accords with duty and is generally useful and thus honorable, deserve praise and encouragement but no esteem. For the maxim lacks the moral import of an action done not from inclination but from duty. But assume that the mind of that friend to mankind was clouded by a sorrow of his own which extinguished all sympathy with the lot of others and that he still had the power to benefit others in distress, but that their need left him untouched because he was preoccupied with his own need. And now suppose him to tear himself, unsolicited by inclination, out of his dead insensibility and to do this action only from duty and without any inclination—then for the first time his action has genuine moral worth. Furthermore, if nature has put little sympathy in the heart of a man, and if he, though an honest man, is by temperament cold and indifferent to the sufferings of others perhaps because he is provided with special gifts of patience and fortitude, and expects or even requires that others should have the same—and such a man would certainly not be the meanest product of nature—would not he find in himself a source from which to give himself a far higher worth than he could have got by having a good-natured temperament? This is unquestionably true even though nature did not make him philanthropic, for it is just here that the worth of the character is brought out, which is morally and incomparably the highest of all: he is beneficent not from inclination but from duty.

To secure one's own happiness is at least indirectly a duty, for discontent with one's condition under pressure from many cares and amid unsatisfied wants could easily become a great temptation to transgress duties. But, without any view to duty, all men have the strongest and deepest inclination to happiness, because in this idea all inclinations are summed up. But the precept of happiness is often so formulated that it definitely thwarts some inclinations, and men can make no definite and certain concept of the sum of satisfaction of all inclinations, which goes under the name of happiness. It is not to be wondered at, therefore, that a single inclination, definite as to what it promises and as to the time at which it can be satisfied, can outweigh a fluctuating idea, and that, for example, a man with the gout can choose to enjoy what he likes and to suffer what he may, because according to his calculations at least on this occasion he has not sacrificed the enjoyment of the present moment to a perhaps groundless expectation of a happiness supposed to lie in health. But, even in this case, if the universal inclination to happiness did not determine his will, and if health were not at least for him a necessary factor in these calculations, there yet would remain, as in all the other cases, a law that he ought to promote his happiness, not from inclination but from duty. Only from this law would his conduct have true moral worth.

It is in this way, undoubtedly, that we should understand those passages of Scripture which command us to love our neighbor and even our enemy, for love as an inclination cannot be commanded. But beneficence from duty, also when no inclination impels it and even when it is opposed by a natural and unconquerable aversion, is practical love, not pathological love; it resides in the will and not in the propensities of feeling, in principles of action and not in tender sympathy; and it alone can be commanded.

[Thus the first proposition of morality is that to have moral worth an action must be done from duty.] The second proposition is: An action done from duty does not have its moral worth in the purpose which is to be achieved through it but in the maxim by which it is determined. Its moral value, therefore, does not depend on the reality of the object of the action but merely on the principle of volition by which the action is done without any regard to the objects of the faculty of desire. From the preceding discussion it is clear that the purposes we may have for our actions and their effects as ends and incentives of the will cannot give the actions any unconditional and moral worth. Wherein, then, can this worth lie, if it is not in the will in relation to its hoped-for effect? It can lie nowhere else than in the principle of the will irrespective of the ends which can be realized by such action. For the will stands, as it were, at the crossroads halfway between its a priori principle which is formal and its a posteriori incentive which is material. Since it must be determined by something, if it is done from duty, it must be determined by the formal principle of volition as such, since every material principle has been withdrawn from it.

The third principle, as a consequence of the two preceding, I would express as follows: Duty is the necessity of an action done from respect for the law. I can certainly have an inclination to the object as an effect of the proposed action, but I can never have respect for it precisely because it is a mere effect and not an activity of a will. Similarly, I can have no respect for any inclination whatsoever, whether my own or that of another; in the former case I can at most approve of it and in the latter I can even love it, i.e., see it as favorable to my own advantage. But that which is connected with my will merely as ground and not as consequence, that which does not serve my inclination but overpowers it or at least excludes it from being considered in making a choice—in a word, the law itself—can be an object of respect and thus a command. Now as an act from duty wholly excludes the influence of inclination and therewith every object of the will, nothing remains which can determine the will objectively except the law and subjectively except pure respect for this practical law. This subjective element is the maxim* that I should follow such a law even if it thwarts all my inclinations.

Thus the moral worth of an action does not lie in the effect which is expected from it or in any principle of action which has to borrow its motive from this expected effect. For all these effects (agreeableness of condition, indeed, even the promotion of the happiness of others) could be brought about through other causes and would not require the will of a rational being, while the highest and unconditional good can be found only in such a will. Therefore, the pre-eminent good can consist only in the conception of the law in itself (which can be present only in a rational being) so far as this conception and not the hoped-for effect is the determining ground of the will. This pre-eminent good, which we call moral, is already present in the person who acts according to this conception, and we do not have to expect it first in the result.**

---

*A maxim is the subjective principle of volition. The objective principle (i.e., that which would serve all rational beings also subjectively as a practical principle if reason had full power over the faculty of desire) is the practical law.

**It might be objected that I seek to take refuge in an obscure feeling behind the word "respect," instead of clearly resolving the question with a concept of reason. But though respect is a feeling, it is not one received through any [outer] influence but is self-wrought by a rational concept; thus it differs specifically from all feelings of the former kind which may be referred to inclination or fear. What I recognize directly as a law for myself I recognize with respect, which means merely the consciousness of the submission of my will to a law without the intervention of other influences on my mind. The direct determination of the will by the law and the consciousness of this determination is respect; thus respect can be regarded as the effect of the law on the subject and not as the cause of the law. Respect is properly the conception of a worth which thwarts my self-love. Thus it is regarded as an object neither of inclination

But what kind of a law can that be, the conception of which must determine the will without reference to the expected result? Under this condition alone the will can be called absolutely good without qualification. Since I have robbed the will of all impulses which could come to it from obedience to any law, nothing remains to serve as a principle of the will except universal conformity of its action to law as such. That is, I should never act in such a way that I could not will that my maxim should be a universal law. Mere conformity to law as such (without assuming any particular law applicable to certain actions) serves as the principle of the will, and it must serve as such a principle if duty is not to be a vain delusion and chimerical concept. The common reason of mankind in its practical judgments is in perfect agreement with this and has this principle constantly in view.

Let the question, for example, be: May I, when in distress, make a promise with the intention not to keep it? I easily distinguish the two meanings which the question can have, viz., whether it is prudent to make a false promise, or whether it conforms to my duty. Undoubtedly the former can often be the case, though I do see clearly that it is not sufficient merely to escape from the present difficulty by this expedient, but that I must consider whether inconveniences much greater than the present one may not later spring from this lie. Even with all my supposed cunning, the consequences cannot be so easily foreseen. Loss of credit might be far more disadvantageous than the misfortune I now seek to avoid, and it is hard to tell whether it might not be more prudent to act according to a universal maxim and to make it a habit not to promise anything without intending to fulfill it. But it is soon clear to me that such a maxim is based only on an apprehensive concern with consequences.

To be truthful from duty, however, is an entirely different thing from being truthful out of fear of disadvantageous consequences, for in the former case the concept of the action itself contains a law for me, while in the latter I must first look about to see what results for me may be connected with it. For to deviate from the principle of duty is certainly bad, but to be unfaithful to my maxim of prudence can sometimes be very advantageous to me, though it is certainly safer to abide by it. The shortest but most infallible way to find the answer to the question as to whether a deceitful promise is consistent with duty is to ask myself: Would I be content that my maxim (of extricating myself from difficulty by a false promise) should hold as a universal law for myself as well as for others? And could I say to myself that everyone may make a false promise when he is in a difficulty from which he otherwise cannot escape? I immediately see that I could will the lie but not a universal law to lie. For with such a law there would be no promises at all inasmuch as it would be futile to make a pretense of my intention in regard to future actions to those who would not believe this pretense or—if they overhastily

nor of fear, though it has something analogous to both. The only object of respect is the law, and indeed only the law which we impose on ourselves and yet recognize as necessary in itself. As a law we are subject to it without consulting self-love; as imposed on us by ourselves, it is a consequence of our will. In the former respect it is analogous to fear and in the latter to inclination. All respect for a person is only respect for the law (of righteousness, etc.) of which the person provides an example. Because we see the improvement of our talents as a duty, we think of a person of talents as the example of a law, as it were (the law that we should by practice become like him in his talents), and that constitutes our respect. All so-called moral interest consists solely in respect for the law.

did so—who would pay me back in my own coin. Thus my maxim would necessarily destroy itself as soon as it was made a universal law.

I do not, therefore, need any penetrating acuteness in order to discern what I have to do in order that my volition may be morally good. Inexperienced in the course of the world, incapable of being prepared for all its contingencies, I only ask myself: Can I will that my maxim become a universal law? If not, it must be rejected, not because of any disadvantage accruing to myself or even to others, but because it cannot enter as a principle into a possible universal legislation, and reason extorts from me an immediate respect for such legislation. I do not as yet discern on what it is grounded (a question the philosopher may investigate), but I at least understand that it is an estimation of the worth which far outweighs all the worth of whatever is recommended by the inclinations, and that the necessity of my actions from pure respect for the practical law constitutes duty. To duty every other motive must give place, because duty is the condition of a will good in itself, whose worth transcends everything. . . .

Innocence is indeed a glorious thing, but, on the other hand, it is very sad that it cannot well maintain itself, being easily led astray. For this reason, even wisdom—which consists more in acting than in knowing—needs science, not so as to learn from it but to secure admission and permanence to its precepts. Man feels in himself a powerful counterpoise against all commands of duty which reason presents to him as so deserving of respect; this counterpoise is his needs and inclinations, the complete satisfaction of which he sums up under the name of happiness. Now reason issues inexorable commands without promising anything to the inclinations. It disregards, as it were, and holds in contempt those claims which are so impetuous and yet so plausible, and which will not allow themselves to be abolished by any command. From this a natural dialectic arises, i.e., a propensity to argue against the stern laws of duty and their validity, or at least to place their purity and strictness in doubt and, where possible, to make them more accordant with our wishes and inclinations. This is equivalent to corrupting them in their very foundations and destroying their dignity—a thing which even common practical reason cannot ultimately call good. . . .

Second Section

Transition from the Popular Moral
Philosophy to the Metaphysics of Morals

. . . In this study we do not advance merely from the common moral judgment (which here is very worthy of respect) to the philosophical, as this has already been done, but we advance by natural stages from a popular philosophy (which goes no further than it can grope by means of examples) to metaphysics (which is not held back by anything empirical and which, as it must measure out the entire scope of rational knowledge of this kind, reaches even Ideas, where examples fail us). In order to make this advance, we must follow and clearly present the practical faculty of reason from its universal rules of determination to the point where the concept of duty arises from it.

Everything in nature works according to laws. Only a rational being has the capacity of acting according to the conception of laws, i.e., according to principles. This capacity is will. Since reason is required for the derivation of actions from laws, will is nothing else than practical reason. If reason infallibly determines the will, the actions which such a being recognizes as objectively necessary are also subjectively necessary. That is, the will is a faculty of choosing only that which reason, independently of inclination, recognizes as practically necessary, i.e., as good. But if reason of itself does not sufficiently determine the will, and if the will is subjugated to subjective conditions (certain incentives) which do not always agree with objective conditions; in a word, if the will is not of itself in complete accord with reason (the actual case of men), then the actions which are recognized as objectively necessary are subjectively contingent, and the determination of such a will according to objective laws is constraint. That is, the relation of objective laws to a will which is not completely good is conceived as the determination of the will of a rational being by principles of reason to which this will is not by nature necessarily obedient.

The conception of an objective principle, so far as it constrains a will, is a command (of reason), and the formula of this command is called an *imperative.*

All imperatives are expressed by an "ought" and thereby indicate the relation of an objective law of reason to a will which is not in its subjective constitution necessarily determined by this law. This relation is that of constraint. Imperatives say that it would be good to do or to refrain from doing something, but they say it to a will which does not always do something simply because it is presented to it as a good thing to do. Practical good is what determines the will by means of the conception of reason and hence not by subjective causes but, rather, objectively, i.e., on grounds which are valid for every rational being as such. It is distinguished from the pleasant, as that which has an influence on the will only by means of a sensation from merely subjective causes, which hold only for the senses of this or that person and not as a principle of reason which holds for everyone.*

A perfectly good will, therefore, would be equally subject to objective laws (of the good), but it could not be conceived as constrained by them to act in accord with them, because, according to its own subjective constitution, it can be determined to act only through the conception of the good. Thus no imperatives hold for the divine will or, more generally, for a holy will. The "ought" is here out of place, for the volition of itself is necessarily in unison with the law. Therefore im-

*The dependence of the faculty of desire on sensations is called inclination, and inclination always indicates a need. The dependence of a contingently determinable will on principles of reason, however, is called interest. An interest is present only in a dependent will which is not of itself always in accord with reason; in the divine will we cannot conceive of an interest. But the human will can take an interest in something without thereby acting from interest. The former means the practical interest in the action; the latter, the pathological interest in the object of the action. The former indicates only the dependence of the will on principles of reason in themselves, while the latter indicates dependence on the principles of reason for the purpose of inclination, since reason gives only the practical rule by which the needs of inclination are to be aided. In the former case the action interests me, and in the latter the object of the action (so far as it is pleasant for me) interests me. In the first section we have seen that, in the case of an action done from duty, no regard must be given to the interest in the object, but merely in the action itself and its principle in reason (i.e., the law).

peratives are only formulas expressing the relation of objective laws of volition in general to the subjective imperfection of the will of this or that rational being, e.g., the human will.

All imperatives command either hypothetically or categorically. The former present the practical necessity of a possible action as means to achieving something else which one desires (or which one may possibly desire). The categorical imperative would be one which presented an action as of itself objectively necessary, without regard to any other end.

Since every practical law presents a possible action as good and thus as necessary for a subject practically determinable by reason, all imperatives are formulas of the determination of action which is necessary by the principle of a will which is in any way good. If the action is good only as a means to something else, the imperative is hypothetical; but if it is thought of as good in itself, and hence as necessary in a will which of itself conforms to reason as the principle of this will, the imperative is categorical.

The imperative thus says what action possible to me would be good, and it presents the practical rule in relation to a will which does not forthwith perform an action simply because it is good, in part because the subject does not always know that the action is good and in part (when it does know it) because his maxims can still be opposed to the objective principles of practical reason.

The hypothetical imperative, therefore, says only that the action is good to some purpose, possible or actual. In the former case it is a problematical, in the latter an assertorical, practical principle. The categorical imperative, which declares the action to be of itself objectively necessary without making any reference to a purpose, i.e., without having any other end, holds an apodictical (practical) principle.

We can think of that which is possible through the mere powers of some rational being as a possible purpose of any will. As a consequence, the principles of action, insofar as they are thought of as necessary to attain a possible purpose which can be achieved by them, are in reality infinitely numerous. All sciences have some practical part which consists of problems of some end which is possible for us and of imperatives as to how it can be reached. These can therefore generally be called imperatives of skill. Whether the end is reasonable and good is not in question at all, for the question is only of what must be done in order to attain it. The precepts to be followed by a physician in order to cure his patient and by a poisoner in order to bring about certain death are of equal value insofar as each does that which will perfectly accomplish his purpose. Since in early youth we do not know what ends may occur to us in the course of life, parents seek to let their children learn a great many things and provide for skill in the use of means to all sorts of arbitrary ends, among which they cannot determine whether any one of them may later become an actual purpose of their pupil, though it is possible that he may someday have it as his actual purpose. And this anxiety is so great that they commonly neglect to form and correct their judgment on the worth of things which they may make their ends.

There is one end, however, which we may presuppose as actual in all rational beings so far as imperatives apply to them, i.e., so far as they are dependent beings; there is one purpose not only which they *can* have but which we can presuppose that they all *do* have by necessity of nature. This purpose is happiness. The hypothetical imperative which represents the practical necessity of action as means to the promotion of happiness is an assertorical imperative. We may not expound it as merely necessary to an uncertain and a merely possible purpose, but as necessary to a purpose which we can a priori and with assurance assume for everyone because it belongs to his essence. Skill in the choice of means to one's own highest welfare can be called prudence* in the narrowest sense. Thus the imperative which refers to the choice of means to one's own happiness, i.e., the precept of prudence, is still only hypothetical; the action is not absolutely commanded but commanded only as a means to another end.

Finally, there is one imperative which directly commands a certain conduct without making its condition some purpose to be reached by it. This imperative is categorical. It concerns not the material of the action and its intended result but the form and the principle from which it results. What is essentially good in it consists in the intention, the result being what it may. This imperative may be called the imperative of morality.

Volition according to these three principles is plainly distinguished by dissimilarity in the constraint to which they subject the will. In order to clarify this dissimilarity, I believe that they are most suitably named if one says that they are either rules of skill, counsels of prudence, or commands (laws) of morality, respectively. For law alone implies the concept of an unconditional and objective and hence universally valid necessity, and commands are laws which must be obeyed, even against inclination. Counsels do indeed involve necessity, but a necessity that can hold only under a subjectively contingent condition, i.e., whether this or that man counts this or that as part of his happiness; but the categorical imperative, on the other hand, is restricted by no condition. As absolutely, though practically, necessary it can be called a command in the strict sense. We could also call the first imperative technical (belonging to art), the second pragmatic** (belonging to welfare), and the third moral (belonging to free conduct as such, i.e., to morals).

The question now arises: How are all these imperatives possible? This question does not require an answer as to how the action which the imperative commands can be performed but merely as to how the constraint of the will, which the imperative expresses in the problem, can be conceived. How an imperative of skill is possible requires no particular discussion. Whoever wills the end, so far as reason has decisive influence on his action, wills also the indispensably necessary means to

---

*The word "prudence" may be taken in two senses, and it may bear the name of prudence with reference to things of the world and private prudence. The former sense means the skill of a man in having an influence on others so as to use them for his own purposes. The latter is the ability to unite all these purposes to his own lasting advantage. The worth of the first is finally reduced to the latter, and of one who is prudent in the former sense but not in the latter we might better say that he is clever and cunning yet, on the whole, imprudent.

**It seems to me that the proper meaning of the word "pragmatic" could be most accurately defined in this way. For sanctions which properly flow not from the law of states as necessary statutes but from provision for the general welfare are called pragmatic. A history is pragmatically composed when it teaches prudence, i.e., instructs the world how it could provide for its interest better than, or at least as well as, has been done in the past.

it that lie in his power. This proposition, in what concerns the will, is analytical; for, in willing an object as my effect, my causality as an acting subject, i.e., the use of the means, is already thought, and the imperative derives the concept of necessary actions to this end from the concept of willing this end. Synthetical propositions undoubtedly are necessary in determining the means to a proposed end, but they do not concern the ground, the act of the will, but only the way to make the object real. Mathematics teaches, by synthetical propositions only, that in order to bisect a line according to an infallible principle, I must make two intersecting arcs from each of its extremities; but if I know the proposed result can be obtained only by such an action, then it is an analytical proposition that, if I fully will the effect, I must also will the action necessary to produce it. For it is one and the same thing to conceive of something as an effect which is in a certain way possible through me and to conceive of myself as acting in this way.

If it were only easy to give a definite concept of happiness, the imperatives of prudence would completely correspond to those of skill and would be likewise analytical. For it could be said in this case as well as in the former that whoever wills the end wills also (necessarily according to reason) the only means to it which are in his power. But it is a misfortune that the concept of happiness is such an indefinite concept that, although each person wishes to attain it, he can never definitely and self-consistently state what it is he really wishes and wills. The reason for this is that all elements which belong to the concept of happiness are empirical, i.e., they must be taken from experience, while for the idea of happiness an absolute whole, a maximum, of well-being is needed in my present and in every future condition. Now it is impossible even for a most clear-sighted and omnipotent but finite being to form here a definite concept of that which he really wills. If he wills riches, how much anxiety, envy, and intrigues might he not thereby draw upon his shoulders! If he wills much knowledge and vision, perhaps it might become only an eye that much sharper to show him as more dreadful the evils which are now hidden from him and which are yet unavoidable or to burden his desires—which already sufficiently engage him—with even more needs! If he wills a long life, who guarantees that it will not be long misery? If he wills at least health, how often has not the discomfort of the body restrained him from excesses into which perfect health would have led him? In short, he is not capable, on any principle and with complete certainty, of ascertaining what would make him truly happy; omniscience would be needed for this. He cannot, therefore, act according to definite principles so as to be happy, but only according to empirical counsels, e.g., those of diet, economy, courtesy, restraint, etc., which are shown by experience best to promote welfare on the average. Hence the imperatives of prudence cannot, in the strict sense, command, i.e., present actions objectively as practically necessary; thus they are to be taken as counsels (*consilia*) rather than as commands (*praecepta*) of reason, and the task of determining infallibly and universally what action will promote the happiness of a rational being is completely unsolvable. There can be no imperative which would, in the strict sense, command us to do what makes for happiness, because happiness is an ideal not of reason but of imagination, depending only on empirical grounds which one would expect in vain to determine an action through which the totality of consequences—which is in fact infinite—could be achieved. Assuming that the means to happiness could be infallibly stated, this imperative of prudence would be an analytical proposition, for it differs from the imperative of skill only in that its end is given while in the latter case it is merely possible. Since both, however, only command the means to that which one presupposes, the imperative which commands the willing of the means to him who wills the end are both analytical. There is, consequently, no difficulty in seeing the possibility of such an imperative.

To see how the imperative of morality is possible is then, without doubt, the only question needing an answer. It is not hypothetical, and thus the objectively conceived necessity cannot be supported by any presupposition, as was the case with the hypothetical imperatives. But it must not be overlooked that it cannot be shown by any example (i.e., it cannot be empirically shown) whether or not there is such an imperative; it is rather to be suspected that all imperatives which appear to be categorical be yet hypothetical, but in a hidden way. For instance, when it is said, "Thou shalt not make a false promise," we assume that the necessity of this avoidance is not a mere counsel for the sake of escaping of some other evil, so that it would read, "Thou shalt not make a false promise so that, if it comes to light, thou ruinest thy credit"; we assume rather that an action of this kind must be regarded as of itself bad and that the imperative of the prohibition is categorical. But we cannot show with certainty by any example that the will is here determined by the law alone without any other incentives, even though this appears to be the case. For it is always possible that secret fear of disgrace, and perhaps also obscure apprehension of other dangers, may have had an influence on the will. Who can prove by experience the nonexistence of a cause when experience shows us only that we do not perceive the cause? But in such a case the so-called moral imperative, which as such appears to be categorical and unconditional, would be actually only a pragmatic precept which makes us attentive to our own advantage and teaches us to consider it.

Thus we shall have to investigate purely a priori the possibility of a categorical imperative, for we do not have the advantage that experience would give us the reality of this imperative, so that the [demonstration of its] possibility would be necessary only for its explanation and not for its establishment. In the meantime, this much may at least be seen: the categorical imperative alone can be taken as a practical *law*, while all the others may be called principles of the will but not laws. This is because what is necessary merely for the attainment of an arbitrary purpose can be regarded as itself contingent, and we get rid of the precept once we give up the purpose, whereas the unconditional command leaves the will no freedom to choose the opposite. Thus it alone implies the necessity which we require of a law.

Secondly, in the case of the categorical imperative or law of morality, the cause of difficulty in discerning its possibility is very weighty. This imperative is an a priori synthetical practical proposition,* and, since to discern the possibility of propo-

---

*I connect a priori the will, without a presupposed condition resulting from an inclination, with the action (though I do so only objectively, i.e., under the idea of a reason which would have complete power over all subjective motives). This is, therefore, a practical proposition which does not analytically derive the willing of an action from some other volition already presupposed (for we do not have such a perfect will); it rather connects it directly with the concept of the will of a rational being as something which is not contained within it.

sitions of this sort is so difficult in theoretical knowledge, it may well be gathered that it will be no less difficult in the practical.

In attacking this problem, we will first inquire whether the mere concept of a categorical imperative does not also furnish the formula containing the proposition which alone can be a categorical imperative. For even when we know the formula of the imperative, to learn how such an absolute law is possible will require difficult and special labors which we shall postpone to the last section.

If I think of a hypothetical imperative as such, I do not know what it will contain until the condition is stated [under which it is an imperative]. But if I think of a categorical imperative, I know immediately what it contains. For since the imperative contains besides the law only the necessity of the maxim* of acting in accordance with this law, while the law contains no condition to which it is restricted, there is nothing remaining in it except the universality of law as such to which the maxim of the action should conform; and in effect this conformity alone is represented as necessary by the imperative.

There is, therefore, only one categorical imperative. It is: Act only according to that maxim by which you can at the same time will that it should become a universal law.

Now if all imperatives of duty can be derived from this one imperative as a principle, we can at least show what we understand by the concept of duty and what it means, even though it remains undecided whether that which is called duty is an empty concept or not.

The universality of law according to which effects are produced constitutes what is properly called nature in the most general sense (as to form), i.e., the existence of things so far as it is determined by universal laws. [By analogy], then, the universal imperative of duty can be expressed as follows: Act as though the maxim of your action were by your will to become a universal law of nature.

We shall now enumerate some duties, adopting the usual division of them into duties to ourselves and to others and into perfect and imperfect duties.**

1. A man who is reduced to despair by a series of evils feels a weariness with life but is still in possession of his reason sufficiently to ask whether it would not be contrary to his duty to himself to take his own life. Now he asks whether the maxim of his action could become a universal law of nature. His maxim, however, is: For love of myself, I make it my principle to shorten my life when by a longer

*A maxim is the subjective principle of acting and must be distinguished from the objective principle, i.e., the practical law. The former contains the practical rule which reason determines according to the conditions of the subject (often its ignorance or inclinations) and is thus the principle according to which the subject acts. The law, on the other hand, is the objective principle valid for every rational being, and the principle by which it ought to act, i.e., an imperative.
**It must be noted here that I reserve the division of duties for a future *Metaphysics of Morals* and that the division here stands as only an arbitrary one (chosen in order to arrange my examples). For the rest, by a perfect duty I here understand a duty which permits no exception in the interest of inclination; thus I have not merely outer but also inner perfect duties. This runs contrary to the usage adopted in the schools, but I am not disposed to defend it here because it is all one to my purpose whether this is conceded or not.

duration it threatens more evil than satisfaction. But it is questionable whether this principle of self-love could become a universal law of nature. One immediately sees a contradiction in a system of nature, whose law would be to destroy life by the feeling whose special office is to impel the improvement of life. In this case it would not exist as nature; hence that maxim cannot obtain as a law of nature, and thus it wholly contradicts the supreme principle of all duty.

2. Another man finds himself forced by need to borrow money. He well knows that he will not be able to repay it, but he also sees that nothing will be loaned him if he does not firmly promise to repay it at a certain time. He desires to make such a promise, but he has enough conscience to ask himself whether it is not improper and opposed to duty to relieve his distress in such a way. Now, assuming he does decide to do so, the maxim of his action would be as follows: When I believe myself to be in need of money, I will borrow money and promise to repay it, although I know I shall never do so. Now this principle of self-love or of his own benefit may very well be compatible with his whole future welfare, but the question is whether it is right. He changes the pretension of self-love into a universal law and then puts the question: How would it be if my maxim became a universal law? He immediately sees that it could never hold as a universal law of nature and be consistent with itself; rather it must necessarily contradict itself. For the universality of a law which says that anyone who believes himself to be in need could promise what he pleased with the intention of not fulfilling it would make the promise itself and the end to be accomplished by it impossible; no one would believe what was promised to him but would only laugh at any such assertion as vain pretense.

3. A third finds in himself a talent which could, by means of some cultivation, make him in many respects a useful man. But he finds himself in comfortable circumstances and prefers indulgence in pleasure to troubling himself with broadening and improving his fortunate natural gifts. Now, however, let him ask whether his maxim of neglecting his gifts, besides agreeing with his propensity to idle amusement, agrees also with what is called duty. He sees that a system of nature could indeed exist in accordance with such a law, even though man (like the inhabitants of the South Sea Islands) should let his talents rust and resolve to devote his life merely to idleness, indulgence, and propagation—in a word, to pleasure. But he cannot possibly will that this should become a universal law of nature or that it should be implanted in us by a natural instinct. For, as a rational being, he necessarily wills that all his faculties should be developed, inasmuch as they are given to him for all sorts of possible purposes.

4. A fourth man, for whom things are going well, sees that others (whom he could help) have to struggle with great hardships, and he asks, "What concern of mine is it? Let each one be as happy as heaven wills, or as he can make himself; I will not take anything from him or even envy him; but to his welfare or to his assistance in time of need I have no desire to contribute." If such a way of thinking were a universal law of nature, certainly the human race could exist, and without doubt even better than in a state where everyone talks of sympathy and good will or even exerts himself occasionally to practice them while, on the other hand, he cheats when he can and betrays or otherwise violates the rights of man. Now although it is possible that a universal law of nature according to that maxim could exist, it is nevertheless impossible to will that such a principle should hold every-where as a law of nature. For a will which resolved this would conflict with itself, since instances can often arise in which he would need the love and sympathy of others, and in which he would have robbed himself, by such a law of nature springing from his own will, of all hope of the aid he desires.

The foregoing are a few of the many actual duties, or at least of duties we hold to be real, whose derivation from the one stated principle is clear. We must be able to will that a maxim of our action become a universal law; this is the canon of the moral estimation of our action generally. Some actions are of such a nature that their maxim cannot even be thought as a universal law of nature without contra-diction, far from it being possible that one could will that it should be such. In others this internal impossibility is not found, though it is still impossible to will that their maxim should be raised to the universality of a law of nature, because such a will would contradict itself. We easily see that the former maxim conflicts with the stricter or narrower (imprescriptable) duty, the latter with broader (meri-torious) duty. Thus all duties, so far as the kind of obligation (not the object of their action) is concerned, have been completely exhibited by these examples in their dependence on the one principle.

When we observe ourselves in any transgression of a duty, we find that we do not actually will that our maxim should become a universal law. That is impossible for us; rather, the contrary of this maxim should remain as a law generally, and we only take the liberty of making an exception to it for ourselves or for the sake of our inclination, and for this one occasion. Consequently, if we weighed everything from one and the same standpoint, namely, reason, we would come upon a contradiction in our own will, viz., that a certain principle is objectively necessary as a universal law and yet subjectively does not hold universally but rather admits exceptions. However, since we regard our action at one time from the point of view of a will wholly conformable to reason and then from that of a will affected by inclinations, there is actually no contradiction, but rather an opposition of inclination to the pre-cept of reason (*antagonismus*). In this the universality of the principle (*universalitas*) is changed into mere generality (*generalitas*), whereby the practical principle of rea-son meets the maxim halfway. Although this cannot be justified in our own impartial judgment, it does show that we actually acknowledge the validity of the categorical imperative and allow ourselves (with all respect to it) only a few exceptions which seem to us to be unimportant and forced upon us.

We have thus at least established that if duty is a concept which is to have sig-nificance and actual legislation for our actions, it can be expressed only in categor-ical imperatives and not at all in hypothetical ones. For every application of it we have also clearly exhibited the content of the categorical imperative which must contain the principle of all duty (if there is such). This is itself very much. But we are not yet advanced far enough to prove a priori that that kind of imperative really exists, that there is a practical law which of itself commands absolutely and without any incentives, and that obedience to this law is duty.

With a view to attaining this, it is extremely important to remember that we must not let ourselves think that the reality of this principle can be derived

from the particular constitution of human nature. For duty is practical unconditional necessity of action; it must, therefore, hold for all rational beings (to
which alone an imperative can apply), and only for that reason can it be a law
for all human wills. Whatever is derived from the particular natural situation of
man as such, or from certain feelings and propensities, or even from a particular tendency of the human reason which might not hold necessarily for the will
of every rational being (if such a tendency is possible), can give a maxim valid
for us but not a law; that is, it can give a subjective principle by which we may
act but not an objective principle by which we would be directed to act even if
all our propensity, inclination, and natural tendency were opposed to it. This
is so far the case that the sublimity and intrinsic worth of the command is the
better shown in a duty the fewer subjective causes there are for it and the more
they are against it; the latter do not weaken the constraint of the law or diminish its validity. . . .

The question then is: Is it a necessary law for all rational beings that they should
always judge their actions by such maxims that they themselves could will to serve as
universal laws? If it is such a law, it must be connected (wholly a priori) with the concept of the will of a rational being as such. But in order to discover this connection, we must, however, reluctantly, take a step into metaphysics, although into a region of it different from speculative philosophy, i.e., the metaphysics of morals. In a
practical philosophy it is not a question of assuming grounds for what happens but
of assuming laws of what ought to happen even though it may never happen, that is
to say, objective, practical laws. Hence in practical philosophy we need not inquire
into the reasons why something pleases or displeases, how the pleasure of mere feeling differs from taste, and whether this is distinct from a general satisfaction of reason. Nor need we ask on what the feeling of pleasure or displeasure rests, how desires and inclinations arise, and how, finally, maxims arise from desires and
inclination under the co-operation of reason. For all these matters belong to an empirical psychology, which would be the second part of physics, if we consider it as
philosophy of nature so far as it rests on empirical laws. But here it is a question of
objectively practical laws and thus of the relation of a will to itself so far as it determines itself only by reason; for everything which has a relation to the empirical au-
tomatically falls away, because if reason of itself alone determines conduct, it must
necessarily do so a priori. The possibility of reason's thus determining conduct must
now be investigated.

The will is thought of as a faculty of determining itself to action in accordance
with the conception of certain laws. Such a faculty can be found only in rational
beings. That which serves the will as the objective ground of its self-determination
is an end, and, if it is given by reason alone, it must hold alike for all rational beings. On the other hand, that which contains the ground of the possibility of the
action, whose result is an end, is called the means. The subjective ground of desire
is the incentive, while the objective ground of volition is the motive. Thus arises
the distinction between subjective ends, which rest on incentives, and objective
ends, which depend on motives valid for every rational being. Practical principles
are formal when they disregard all subjective ends; they are material when they

have subjective ends, and thus certain incentives, as their basis. The ends which a rational being arbitrarily proposes to himself as consequences of his action are material ends and are without exception only relative, for only their relation to a particularly constituted faculty of desire in the subject gives them their worth. And this worth cannot, therefore, afford any universal principles for all rational beings or valid and necessary principles for every volition. That is, they cannot give rise to any practical laws. All these relative ends, therefore, are grounds for hypothetical imperatives only.

But suppose that there were something the existence of which in itself had absolute worth, something which, as an end in itself, could be a ground of definite laws. In it and only in it could lie the ground of a possible categorical imperative, i.e., of a practical law.

Now, I say, man and, in general, every rational being exists as an end in himself and not merely as a means to be arbitrarily used by this or that will. In all his actions, whether they are directed to himself or to other rational beings, he must always be regarded at the same time as an end. All objects of inclinations have only a conditional worth, for if the inclinations and the needs founded on them did not exist, their object would be without worth. The inclinations themselves as the sources of needs, however, are so lacking in absolute worth that the universal wish of every rational being must be indeed to free himself completely from them. Therefore, the worth of any objects to be obtained by our actions is at all times conditional. Beings whose existence does not depend on our will but on nature, if they are not rational beings, have only a relative worth as means and are therefore called "things"; on the other hand, rational beings are designated "persons," because their nature indicates that they are ends in themselves, i.e., things which may not be used merely as means. Such a being is thus an object of respect and, so far, restricts all [arbitrary] choice. Such beings are not merely subjective ends whose existence as a result of our action has a worth for us but are objective ends, i.e., beings whose existence in itself is an end. Such an end is one for which no other end can be substituted, to which these beings should serve merely as means. For, without them, nothing of absolute worth could be found, and if all worth is conditional and thus contingent, no supreme practical principle for reason could be found anywhere.

Thus if there is to be a supreme practical principle and a categorical imperative for the human will, it must be one that forms an objective principle of the will from the conception of that which is necessarily an end for everyone because it is an end in itself. Hence this objective principle can serve as a universal practical law. The ground of this principle is: rational nature exists as an end in itself. Man necessarily thinks of his own existence in this way; thus far it is a subjective principle of human actions. Also every other rational being thinks of his existence by means of the same rational ground which holds also for myself;* thus it is at the same time an objective principle from which, as a supreme practical ground, it must be possible to derive all laws of the

---

*Here I present this proposition as a postulate, but in the last section grounds for it will be found.

will. The practical imperative, therefore, is the following: Act so that you treat humanity, whether in your own person or in that of another, always as an end and never as a means only. Let us now see whether this can be achieved.

To return to our previous examples:

First, according to the concept of necessary duty to one's self, he who contemplates suicide will ask himself whether his action can be consistent with the idea of humanity as an end in itself. If, in order to escape from burdensome circumstances, he destroys himself, he uses a person merely as a means to maintain a tolerable condition up to the end of life. Man, however, is not a thing, and thus not something to be used merely as a means; he must always be regarded in all his actions as an end in himself. Therefore, I cannot dispose of man in my own person so as to mutilate, corrupt, or kill him. (It belongs to ethics proper to define more accurately this basic principle so as to avoid all misunderstanding, e.g., as to the amputation of limbs in order to preserve myself, or to exposing my life to danger in order to save it; I must, therefore, omit them here.)

Second, as concerns necessary or obligatory duties to others, he who intends a deceitful promise to others sees immediately that he intends to use another man merely as a means, without the latter containing the end in himself at the same time. For he whom I want to use for my own purposes by means of such a promise cannot possibly assent to my mode of acting against him and cannot contain the end of this action in himself. This conflict against the principle of other men is even clearer if we cite examples of attacks on their freedom and property. For then it is clear that he who transgresses the rights of men intends to make use of the persons of others merely as a means, without considering that, as rational beings, they must always be esteemed at the same time as ends, i.e., only as beings who must be able to contain in themselves the end of the very same action.*

Third, with regard to contingent (meritorious) duty to one's self, it is not sufficient that the action not conflict with humanity in our person as an end in itself; it must also harmonize with it. Now in humanity there are capacities for greater perfection which belong to the end of nature with respect to humanity in our own person; to neglect these might perhaps be consistent with the preservation of humanity as an end in itself but not with the furtherance of that end.

Fourth, with regard to meritorious duty to others, the natural end which all men have is their own happiness. Humanity might indeed exist if no one contributed to the happiness of others, provided he did not intentionally detract from it; but this harmony with humanity as an end in itself is only negative rather than positive if everyone does not also endeavor, so far as he can, to further the ends of others. For the ends of any person, who is an end in himself, must as far as possible also be my end, if that conception of an end in itself is to have its full effect on me.

---

*Let it not be thought that the banal "*quod tibi non vis fieri, etc.*" could here serve as guide or principle, for it is only derived from the principle and is restricted by various limitations. It cannot be a universal law, because it contains the ground neither of duties to one's self nor of the benevolent duties to others (for many a man would gladly consent that others should not benefit him, provided only that he might be excused from showing benevolence to them). Nor does it contain the ground of obligatory duties to another, for the criminal would argue on this ground against the judge who sentences him. And so on.

This principle of humanity and of every rational creature as an end in itself is the supreme limiting condition on freedom of the actions of each man. It is not borrowed from experience, first, because of its universality, since it applies to all rational beings generally, and experience does not suffice to determine anything about them; and, secondly, because in experience humanity is not thought of (subjectively) as the end of men, i.e., as an object which we of ourselves really make our end. Rather it is thought of as the objective end which should constitute the supreme limiting condition of all subjective ends, whatever they may be. Thus this principle must arise from pure reason. Objectively the ground of all practical legislation lies (according to the first principle) in the rule and in the form of universality, which makes it capable of being a law (at most a natural law); subjectively, it lies in the end. But the subject of all ends is every rational being as an end in itself (by the second principle); from this there follows the third practical principle of the will as the supreme condition of its harmony with universal practical reason, viz., the idea of the will of every rational being as making universal law.

By this principle all maxims are rejected which are not consistent with the universal lawgiving of will. The will is thus not only subject to the law but subject in such a way that it must be regarded also as legislative and only for this reason as being subject to the law (of which it can regard itself as the author).

In the foregoing mode of conception, in which imperatives are conceived universally either as conformity to law by actions—a conformity which is similar to a natural order—or as the prerogative of rational beings as such, the imperatives exclude from their legislative authority all admixture of any interest as an incentive. They do so because they were conceived as categorical. They were only assumed to be categorical, however, because we had to make such an assumption if we wished to explain the concept of duty. But that there were practical propositions which commanded categorically could not here be proved independently, just as little as it can be proved anywhere in this section. One thing, however, might have been done: to indicate in the imperative itself, by some determination which it contained, that in volition from duty the renunciation of all interest is the specific mark of the categorical imperative, distinguishing it from the hypothetical. And this is now being done in the third formulation of the principle, i.e., in the idea of the will of every rational being as a will giving universal law. A will which stands under laws can be bound to this law by an interest. But if we think of a will giving universal laws, we find that a supreme legislating will cannot possibly depend on any interest, for such a dependent will would itself need still another law which would restrict the interest of its self-love to the condition that [the maxims of this will] should be valid as universal law.

Thus the principle of every human will as a will giving universal laws in all its maxims is very well adapted to being a categorical imperative, provided it is otherwise correct. Because of the idea of universal lawgiving, it is based on no interest, and, thus of all possible imperatives, it alone can be unconditional. Or, better, converting the proposition: if there is a categorical imperative (a law for the will of every rational being), it can only command that everything be done from the maxim of its will as one which could have as its object only itself considered as giving universal laws. For only in this case are the practical principle and the imperative which the will obeys unconditional, because the will can have no interest as its foundation.

If we now look back upon all previous attempts which have ever been undertaken to discover the principle of morality, it is not to be wondered at that they all had to fail. Man was seen to be bound to laws by his duty, but it was not seen that he is subject only to his own, yet universal, legislation, and that he is only bound to act in accordance with his own will, which is, however, designed by nature to be a will giving universal laws. For if one thought of him as subject only to a law (whatever it may be), this necessarily implied some interest as a stimulus or compulsion to obedience because the law did not arise from his will. Rather, his will was constrained by something else according to a law to act in a certain way. By this strictly necessary consequence, however, all the labor of finding a supreme ground for duty was irrevocably lost, and one never arrived at duty but only at the necessity of action from a certain interest. This might be his own interest or that of another, but in either case the imperative always had to be conditional and could not at all serve as a moral command. This principle I will call the principle of *autonomy* of the will in contrast to all other principles which I accordingly count under *heteronomy*.

The concept of each rational being as a being that must regard itself as giving universal law through all the maxims of its will, so that it may judge itself and its actions from this standpoint leads to a very fruitful concept, namely, that of a *realm of ends*.

By "realm" I understand the systematic union of different rational beings through common laws. Because laws determine ends with regard to their universal validity, if we abstract from the personal difference of rational beings and thus from all content of their private ends, we can think of a whole of all ends in systematic connection, a whole of rational beings as ends in themselves as well as of the particular ends which each may set for himself. This is a realm of ends, which is possible on the aforesaid principles. For all rational beings stand under the law that each of them should treat himself and all others never merely as means but in every case also as an end in himself. Thus there arises a systematic union of rational beings through common objective laws. This is a realm which may be called a realm of ends (certainly only an ideal), because what these laws have in view is just the relation of these beings to each other as ends and means.

A rational being belongs to the realm of ends as a member when he gives universal laws in it while also himself subject to these laws. He belongs to it as sovereign when he, as legislating, is subject to the will of no other. The rational being must regard himself always as legislative in a realm of ends possible through the freedom of the will, whether he belongs to it as member or as sovereign. He cannot maintain the latter position merely through the maxims of his will but only when he is a completely independent being without need and with power adequate to his will.

Morality, therefore, consists in the relation of every action to that legislation through which alone a realm of ends is possible. This legislation, however, must be found in every rational being. It must be able to arise from his will, whose principle then is to do no action according to any maxim which would be inconsistent with its being a universal law and thus to act only so that the will through its maxims could regard itself at the same time as universally lawgiving. If now the maxims do not by their nature already necessarily conform to this objective principle of rational beings as universally lawgiving, the necessity of acting according to that principle is called practical constraint, i.e., duty. Duty pertains not to the sovereign in the realm of ends, but rather to each member, and to each in the same degree.

The practical necessity of acting according to this principle, i.e., duty, does not rest at all on feelings, impulses, and inclinations; it rests merely on the relation of rational beings to one another, in which the will of a rational being must always be regarded as legislative, for otherwise it could not be thought of as an end in itself. Reason, therefore, relates every maxim of the will as giving universal laws to every other will and also to every action toward itself; it does so not for the sake of any other practical motive or future advantage but rather from the idea of the dignity of a rational being, which obeys no law except that which he himself also gives.

In the realm of ends, everything has either a *price* or a *dignity*. Whatever has a price can be replaced by something else as its equivalent; on the other hand, whatever is above all price, and therefore admits of no equivalent, has a dignity.

That which is related to general human inclinations and needs has a market price. That which, without presupposing any need, accords with a certain taste, i.e., with pleasure in the mere purposeless play of our faculties, has an *affective price*. But that which constitutes the condition under which alone something can be an end in itself does not have mere relative worth, i.e., a price, but an intrinsic worth, i.e., dignity.

Now morality is the condition under which alone a rational being can be an end in itself, because only through it is it possible to be a legislative member in the realm of ends. Thus morality and humanity, so far as it is capable of morality, alone have dignity. Skill and diligence in work have a market value; wit, lively imagination, and humor have an affective price; but fidelity in promises and benevolence on principle (not from instinct) have intrinsic worth. Nature and likewise art contain nothing which could replace their lack, for their worth consists not in effects which flow from them, nor in advantage and utility which they procure; it consists only in intentions, i.e., maxims of the will, which are ready to reveal themselves in this manner through actions even though success does not favor them. These actions need no recommendation from any subjective disposition or taste in order that they may be looked upon with immediate favor and satisfaction, nor do they have need of any immediate propensity or feeling directed to them. They exhibit the will which performs them as the object of an immediate respect, since nothing but reason is required in order to impose them on the will. The will is not to be cajoled into them, for this, in the case of duties, would be a contradiction. This esteem lets the worth of such a turn of mind be recognized as dignity and puts it infinitely beyond any price, with which it cannot in the least be brought into competition or comparison without, as it were, violating its holiness.

And what is it that justifies the morally good disposition or virtue in making such lofty claims? It is nothing less than the participation it affords the rational being in giving universal laws. He is thus fitted to be a member in a possible realm of ends to which his own nature already destined him. For, as an end in himself, he is destined to be legislative in the realm of ends, free from all laws of nature and obedient only to those which he himself gives. Accordingly, his maxims can belong to a universal legislation to which he is at the same time also subject. A thing has no worth other than that determined for it by the law. The legislation which determines all worth must therefore have a dignity, i.e., unconditional and incomparable worth. For the esteem, which a rational being must have for it, only the word "respect" supplies a suitable expression. Autonomy is thus the basis of the dignity of both human nature and every rational nature.

Study Questions

1. In the opening three paragraphs, Kant begins with some remarkable pronouncements about the absolute value of a good will. What does he mean here? Are the claims that he makes commonly accepted beliefs? Does it matter if they are not?

2. Kant draws a distinction between a helpful action performed out of natural sympathy and a helpful action performed out of a sense of duty, and says that only the second has "true moral worth." Many people think that Kant makes a fundamental error here. Why does Kant make this claim, and how might one try to support it? What differences do you see between Kant's views on this point and, say, Aristotle's or Hume's? Is Kant's claim defensible? Explain.

3. What is the distinction between hypothetical imperatives and categorical imperatives? Try to give some examples of each. Kant thinks that moral duties and requirements, as we ordinarily understand them, must be expressed as categorical imperatives and not hypothetical imperatives? Is he right about this?

4. Kant argues that the maxim of making a deceitful promise in order to get money and the maxim of never contributing to the welfare of others who are in need cannot rationally be willed as universal laws. What are his reasons for thinking this? Do his arguments succeed? Consider both objections to his arguments and ways in which these objections might be addressed.

5. According to Kant, what is involved in respecting humanity or rational nature as an end in itself and never as a means only? Is it really possible to satisfy Kant's principle in our interactions with others? Explain.

6. Does Kant's view ever permit us to lie?

7. Given the emphasis on respect for rational agents, is Kant's theory able to give proper moral standing to animals and nature? What about children, who are not yet rational agents? Explain.

8. Contrast Kant's view of the role of reason and feeling in morality with the view of Hume. Which view is closest to the truth?

Selected Bibliography

Guyer, Paul. *Kant's Groundwork of the Metaphysics of Morals: Critical Essays* (Lanham, Md.: Rowman & Littlefield Publishers, 1998). An anthology of recent essays.

Herman, Barbara. *The Practice of Moral Judgment* (Cambridge: Harvard University Press, 1993). Essays on Kant's ethics by a leading contemporary interpreter.

Hill, T. E., Jr. *Dignity and Practical Reason* (Ithaca: Cornell University Press, 1992). Essays on Kant's ethics by a leading contemporary interpreter.

Kant, Immanuel, *Critique of Practical Reason,* tr. Mary J. Gregor (New York/Cambridge: Cambridge University Press, 1997).

―――. *Lectures on Ethics,* tr. and ed. Peter Heath and J. B. Schneewind (New York/Cambridge: Cambridge University Press, 1997).

―――. *The Metaphysics of Morals,* tr. Mary J. Gregor (New York/Cambridge: Cambridge University Press, 1996)

Korsgaard, Christine. *Creating the Kingdom of Ends* (New York/Cambridge: Cambridge University Press, 1996), Chaps. 1–7. Essays on Kant's ethics by a leading contemporary interpreter.

Nell (O'Neill), Onora. *Acting on Principle: An Essay on Kantian Ethics* (New York: Columbia University Press, 1975). An influential study of the categorical imperative.

O'Neill, Onora. *Constructions of Reason* (New York/Cambridge: Cambridge University Press, 1989), esp. Chaps. 5–7. Essays on Kant's ethics by a leading contemporary interpreter.

Paton, H. J. *The Categorical Imperative* (Philadelphia: University of Pennsylvania Press, 1971). A well-respected older study.

Rawls, John. *Lectures on the History of Moral Philosophy* (Cambridge: Harvard University Press, 2000), Part II. An interpretation of Kant's moral philosophy by a leading contemporary philosopher.

Wood, Allen. *Kant's Ethical Thought* (New York/Cambridge: Cambridge University Press, 1999), Part I. A general study of Kant's ethics by a leading Kant scholar.

12

JEREMY BENTHAM

—

Jeremy Bentham(1748–1832) was one of the founders of the movement in moral philosophy known as utilitarianism. The "utility" of an action is its tendency to contribute to or increase the happiness of the individuals that it affects. "Individual utility" refers to the contribution of an action to the happiness of an individual. "General utility" or "overall utility" refers to the contribution of an action to the

> ... *the principle of utility ...* *approves or disapproves of every* *action whatsoever, according to* *the tendency which it appears to* *have to augment or diminish the* *happiness of the party whose in-* *terest is in question ...*

overall happiness of *all* of the individuals affected; it is ascertained by balancing the total happiness that an action would produce in all of the individuals that it affects against the total unhappiness it would produce. The principle of utility in its simplest form, known as "act utilitarianism," holds that the right action is that which, of all the actions open to an agent, has the highest general utility. Utilitarianism is a "consequentialist" theory because it holds that the moral value of an action is entirely a function of its consequences. Thus utilitarians hold that the right action is the action that has the best overall consequences, or does the most overall good, as measured in terms of general utility.

Bentham was both a psychological hedonist and an ethical hedonist. That is, he thought that all human action is motivated by the desire for pleasure. He also thought that pleasure is the sole good, and that other things are good only as a means to pleasure. His theory is a form of hedonistic utilitarianism because he defined utility in terms of pleasure. One important feature of Bentham's hedonism is his belief that all pleasures are qualitatively on a par and are of equal value, the only difference among them being that of quantity. Because of this view he concluded that, if two experiences contained equal amounts of pleasure, then, no matter what other differences there might be between the experiences, neither in itself is better or worse than the other. As he put the point in a famous quotation, "Quantity of pleasure being equal, pushpin is as good as poetry." On this point, John Stuart Mill, his hedonistic utilitarian follower, refused to follow him.

For Bentham, utilitarianism provided a theoretical basis for social reform, and he thought that any act or institution of government must be justified by the principle of utility. Although a distinguished philosopher, Bentham was more interested in practical than in purely theoretical issues. Indeed he devoted most of his long life to social reform. A leader in a group called the Philosophical Radicals, out of which the British Liberal Party later developed, he undertook the task of modernizing Britain's political and social institutions. In this endeavor, he was extraordinarily successful. The greatest of his many triumphs came with the passage of the Reform Bill of 1832, which transformed British politics by wresting control of Parliament from the landed aristocracy, putting it in the hands of the urban bourgeoisie.

—

An Introduction to the Principles of Morals and Legislation

Chapter I

Of the Principle of Utility

I. Nature has placed mankind under the governance of two sovereign masters, *pain* and *pleasure*. It is for them alone to point out what we ought to do, as well as to determine what we shall do. On the one hand the standard of right and wrong, on the other the chain of causes and effects, are fastened to their throne. They govern us in all we do, in all we say, in all we think: every effort we can make to throw off our subjection, will serve but to demonstrate and confirm it. In words a man may pretend to abjure their empire: but in reality he will remain subject to it all the while. The *principle of utility** recognizes this subjection, and assumes it for the foundation of that system, the object of which is to rear the fabric of felicity by

*Note by the author, July 1822.

To this denomination has of late been added, or substituted, the *greatest happiness or greatest felicity* principle: this for shortness, instead of saying at length *that principle* which states the greatest happiness of all those whose interest is in question, as being the right and proper, and only right and proper and universally desirable, end of human action: of human action in every situation, and in particular in that of a functionary or set of functionaries exercising the powers of Government. The word *utility* does not so clearly point to the ideas of *pleasure* and *pain* as the words *happiness* and *felicity* do: nor does it lead us to the consideration of the *number,* of the interests affected; to the *number,* as being the circumstance, which contributes, in the largest proportion, to the formation of the standard here in question; the *standard of right and wrong,* by which alone the propriety of human conduct, in every situation can with propriety be tried. This want of a sufficiently manifest connexion between the ideas of *happiness* and *pleasure* on the one hand, and the idea of *utility* on the other, I have every now and then found operating, and with but too much efficiency, as a bar to the acceptance, that might otherwise have been given, to this principle.

New edition, Oxford, 1823. Some of the author's footnotes have been omitted. First published in 1789.

the hands of reason and of law. Systems which attempt to question it, deal in sounds instead of sense, in caprice instead of reason, in darkness instead of light.

But enough of metaphor and declamation: it is not by such means that moral science is to be improved.

II. The principle of utility is the foundation of the present work: it will be proper therefore at the outset to give an explicit and determinate account of what is meant by it. By the principle of utility is meant that principle which approves or disapproves of every action whatsoever, according to the tendency which it appears to have to augment or diminish the happiness of the party whose interest is in question: or, what is the same thing in other words, to promote or to oppose that happiness. I say of every action whatsoever, and therefore not only of every action of a private individual, but of every measure of government.

III. By utility is meant that property in any object, whereby it tends to pro-duce benefit, advantage, pleasure, good, or happiness, (all this in the present case comes to the same thing) or (what comes again to the same thing) to prevent the happening of mischief, pain, evil, or unhappiness to the party whose interest is considered: if that party be the community in general, then the happiness of the community: if a particular individual, then the happiness of that individual.

IV. The interest of the community is one of the most general expressions that can occur in the phraseology of morals: no wonder that the meaning of it is often lost. When it has a meaning, it is this: the community is a fictitious *body,* composed of the individual persons who are considered as constituting as it were its *members.* The interest of the community then is, what?—the sum of the interests of the several members who compose it.

V. It is in vain to talk of the interest of the community, without understanding what is the interest of the individual.* A thing is said to promote the interest, or to be *for* the interest, of an individual, when it tends to add to the sum total of his plea-sures: or, what comes to the same thing, to diminish the sum total of his pains.

VI. An action then may be said to be conformable to the principle of utility, or, for shortness sake, to utility, (meaning with respect to the community at large) when the tendency it has to augment the happiness of the community is greater than any it has to diminish it.

VII. A measure of government (which is but a particular kind of action, per-formed by a particular person or persons) may be said to be conformable to or dic-tated by the principle of utility, when in like manner the tendency which it has to aug-ment the happiness of the community is greater than any which it has to diminish it.

VIII. When an action, or in particular a measure of government, is supposed by a man to be conformable to the principle of utility, it may be convenient, for the purposes of discourse, to imagine a kind of law or dictate, called a law or dic-tate of utility: and to speak of the action in question, as being conformable to such law or dictate.

IX. A man may be said to be a partisan of the principle of utility, when the ap-probation or disapprobation he annexes to any action, or to any measure, is deter-

---

*Interest is one of those words, which not having any superior *genus,* cannot in the ordinary way be defined.

mined by and proportioned to the tendency which he conceives it to have to aug-ment or to diminish the happiness of the community: or in other words, to its con-formity or unconformity to the laws or dictates of utility.

X. Of an action that is conformable to the principle of utility one may always say either that it is one that ought to be done, or at least that it is not one that ought not to be done. One may say also, that it is right it should be done; at least that it is not wrong it should be done: that it is a right action; at least that it is not a wrong action. When thus interpreted, the words *ought,* and *right* and *wrong,* and others of that stamp, have a meaning: when otherwise, they have none.

XI. Has the rectitude of this principle been ever formally contested? It should seem that it had, by those who have not known what they have been meaning. Is it susceptible of any direct proof? it should seem not: for that which is used to prove every thing else, cannot itself be proved: a chain of proofs must have their com-mencement somewhere. To give such proof is as impossible as it is needless.

XII. Not that there is or ever has been that human creature breathing, however stupid or perverse, who has not on many, perhaps on most occasions of his life, deferred to it. By the natural constitution of the human frame, on most occasions of their lives men in general embrace this principle, without thinking of it: if not for the ordering of their own actions, yet for the trying of their own actions, as well as those of other men. There have been, at the same time, not many, perhaps, even of the most intelligent, who have been disposed to embrace it purely and without reserve. There are even few who have not taken some occasion or other to quarrel with it, either on account of their not understanding always how to apply it, or on account of some prejudice or other which they were afraid to examine into, or could not bear to part with. For such is the stuff that man is made of: in principle and in practice, in a right track and in a wrong one, the rarest of all human qualities is consistency.

XIII. When a man attempts to combat the principle of utility, it is with rea-sons drawn, without his being aware of it, from that very principle itself. His argu-ments, if they prove any thing, prove not that the principle is *wrong,* but that, ac-cording to the applications he supposes to be made of it, it is *misapplied.* Is it possible for a man to move the earth? Yes; but he must first find out another earth to stand upon.

XIV. To disprove the propriety of it by arguments is impossible; but, from the causes that have been mentioned, or from some confused or partial view of it, a man may happen to be disposed not to relish it. Where this is the case, if he thinks the settling of his opinions on such a subject worth the trouble, let him take the following steps, and at length, perhaps, he may come to reconcile himself to it.

1. Let him settle with himself, whether he would wish to discard this princi-ple altogether; if so, let him consider what it is that all his reasonings (in matters of politics especially) can amount to?
2. If he would, let him settle with himself, whether he would judge and act without any principle, or whether there is any other he would judge and act by?

3. If there be, let him examine and satisfy himself whether the principle he thinks he has found is really any separate intelligible principle; or whether it be not a mere principle in words, a kind of phrase, which at bottom expresses neither more nor less than the mere averment of his own unfounded sentiments; that is, what in another person he might be apt to call caprice?

4. If he is inclined to think that his own approbation or disapprobation, annexed to the idea of an act, without any regard to its consequences, is a sufficient foundation for him to judge and act upon, let him ask himself whether his sentiment is to be a standard of right and wrong, with respect to every other man, or whether every man's sentiment has the same privilege of being a standard to itself?

5. In the first case, let him ask himself whether his principle is not despotical, and hostile to all the rest of the human race?

6. In the second case, whether it is not anarchical, and whether at this rate there are not as many different standards of right and wrong as there are men? and whether even to the same man, the same thing, which is right today, may not (without the least change in its nature) be wrong tomorrow? and whether the same thing is not right and wrong in the same place at the same time? and in either case, whether all argument is not at an end? and whether, when two men have said, "I like this," and "I don't like it," they can (upon such a principle) have anything more to say?

7. If he should have said to himself, No: for that the sentiment which he proposes as a standard must be grounded on reflection, let him say on what particulars the reflection is to turn? If on particulars having relation to the utility of the act, then let him say whether this is not deserting his own principle, and borrowing assistance from that very one in opposition to which he sets it up: or if not on those particulars, on what other particulars?

8. If he should be for compounding the matter, and adopting his own principle in part, and the principle of utility in part, let him say how far he will adopt it?

9. When he has settled with himself where he will stop, then let him ask himself how he justifies to himself the adopting it so far? and why he will not adopt it any farther?

10. Admitting any other principle than the principle of utility to be a right principle, a principle that it is right for a man to pursue; admitting (what is not true) that the word *right* can have a meaning without reference to utility, let him say whether there is any such thing as a *motive* that a man can have to pursue the dictates of it: if there is, let him say what that motive is, and how it is to be distinguished from those which enforce the dictates of utility: if not, then lastly let him say what it is this other principle can be good for?* . . .

---

*In Chapter II, which is omitted here, Bentham criticizes theories opposed to his own—Ed.

Chapter IV

Value of a Lot of Pleasure or Pain, How to Be Measured

I. Pleasures then, and the avoidance of pains, are the *ends* which the legislator has in view: it behooves him therefore to understand their *value*. Pleasures and pains are the *instruments* he has to work with: it behooves him therefore to understand their force, which is again, in other words, their value.

II. To a person considered *by himself,* the value of a pleasure or pain considered *by itself,* will be greater or less, according to the four following circumstances:*

1. Its *intensity.*
2. Its *duration.*
3. Its *certainty* or *uncertainty.*
4. Its *propinquity* or *remoteness.*

III. These are the circumstances which are to be considered in estimating a pleasure or a pain considered each of them by itself. But when the value of any pleasure or pain is considered for the purpose of estimating the tendency of any *act* by which it is produced, there are two other circumstances to be taken into account; these are

5. Its *fecundity,* or the chance it has of being followed by sensations of the *same* kind: that is, pleasures, if it be a pleasure: pains, if it be a pain.
6. Its *purity,* or the chance it has of *not* being followed by sensations of the *opposite* kind: that is, pains, if it be a pleasure: pleasures, if it be a pain.

These two last, however, are in strictness scarcely to be deemed properties of the pleasure or the pain itself; they are not, therefore, in strictness to be taken into the account of the value of that pleasure or that pain. They are in strictness to be deemed properties only of the act, or other event, by which such pleasure or pain has been produced; and accordingly are only to be taken into the account of the tendency of such act or such event.

IV. To a *number* of persons, with reference to each of whom the value of a pleasure or a pain is considered, it will be greater or less, according to seven circumstances: to wit, the six preceding ones; viz.

---

*These circumstances have since been denominated *elements* or *dimensions* of *value* in a pleasure or a pain.

Not long after the publication of the first edition, the following memoriter verses were framed, in the view of lodging more effectually, in the memory, these points, on which the whole fabric of morals and legislation may be seen to rest.

> *Intense, long, certain, speedy, fruitful, pure—*
> Such marks in *pleasures* and in *pains* endure.
> Such pleasures seek, if *private* be thy end:
> If it be *public,* wide let them *extend.*
> Such *pains* avoid, whichever be thy view:
> If pains *must* come, let them *extend* to few.

1. Its *intensity.*
2. Its *duration.*
3. Its *certainty* or *uncertainty.*
4. Its *propinquity* or *remoteness.*
5. Its *fecundity.*
6. Its *purity.*

And one other; to wit:

7. Its *extent;* that is, the number of persons to whom it *extends;* or (in other words) who are affected by it.

V. To take an exact account then of the general tendency of any act, by which the interests of a community are affected, proceed as follows. Begin with any one person of those whose interests seem most immediately to be affected by it: and take an account

1. Of the value of each distinguishable *pleasure* which appears to be produced by it in the *first* instance.
2. Of the value of each *pain* which appears to be produced by it in the *first* instance.
3. Of the value of each pleasure which appears to be produced by it *after* the first. This constitutes the *fecundity* of the first *pleasure* and the *impurity* of the first *pain.*
4. Of the value of each *pain* which appears to be produced by it after the first. This constitutes the *fecundity* of the first *pain,* and the *impurity* of the first *pleasure.*
5. Sum up all the values of all the *pleasures* on the one side, and those of all the *pains* on the other. The balance, if it be on the side of pleasure, will give the *good* tendency of the act upon the whole, with respect to the interests of that *individual* person; if on the side of pain, the *bad* tendency of it upon the whole.
6. Take an account of the *number* of persons whose interests appear to be concerned; and repeat the above process with respect to each. *Sum up* the numbers expressive of the degrees of *good* tendency which the act has, with respect to each individual, in regard to whom the tendency of it is *good* upon the whole: . . . do this again with respect to each individual, in regard to whom the tendency of it is *bad* upon the whole. Take the *balance;* which, if on the side of *pleasure,* will give the general *good tendency* of the act, with respect to the total number or community of individuals concerned; if on the side of pain, the general *evil tendency,* with respect to the same community.

VI. It is not to be expected that this process should be strictly pursued previously to every moral judgment, or to every legislative or judicial operation. It may, however, be always kept in view: and as near as the process actually pursued on these occasions approaches to it, so near will such process approach to the character of an exact one.

VII. The same process is alike applicable to pleasure and pain, in whatever shape they appear: and by whatever denomination they are distinguished: to pleasure, whether it be called *good* (which is properly the cause or instrument of pleasure) or *profit* (which is distant pleasure, or the cause or instrument of distant pleasure,) or *convenience*, or *advantage, benefit, emolument, happiness*, and so forth: to pain, whether it be called *evil*, (which corresponds to *good*) or *mischief*, or *inconvenience*, or *disadvantage*, or *loss*, or *unhappiness*, and so forth.

VIII. Nor is this a novel and unwarranted, any more than it is a useless theory. In all this there is nothing but what the practice of mankind, wheresoever they have a clear view of their own interest, is perfectly conformable to. An article of property, an estate in land, for instance, is valuable, on what account? On account of the pleasures of all kinds which it enables a man to produce, and what comes to the same thing the pains of all kinds which it enables him to avert. But the value of such an article of property is universally understood to rise or fall according to the length or shortness of the time which a man has in it: the certainty or uncertainty of its coming into possession: and the nearness or remoteness of the time at which, if at all, it is to come into possession. As to the *intensity* of the pleasures which a man may derive from it, this is never thought of, because it depends upon the use which each particular person may come to make of it; which cannot be estimated till the particular pleasures he may come to derive from it, or the particular pains he may come to exclude by means of it, are brought to view. For the same reason, neither does he think of the *fecundity* or *purity* of those pleasures.

Chapter X

Of Motives

2. *No motives either constantly good or constantly bad*

IX. In all this chain of motives, the principal or original link seems to be the last internal motive in prospect: it is to this that all the other motives in prospect owe their materiality: and the immediately acting motive its existence. This motive in prospect, we see is always some pleasure, or some pain; some pleasure, which the act in question is expected to be a means of continuing or producing: some pain which it is expected to be a means of discontinuing or preventing. A motive is substantially nothing more than pleasure or pain, operating in a certain manner.

X. Now, pleasure is in *itself* a good: nay, even setting aside immunity from pain, the only good: pain is in itself an evil; and, indeed, without exception, the only evil; or else the words good and evil have no meaning. And this is alike true of every sort of pain, and of every sort of pleasure. It follows, therefore, immediately and incontestably, that *there is no such thing as any sort of motive that is in itself a bad one.*

XI. It is common, however, to speak of actions as proceeding from *good* or *bad* motives: in which case the motives meant are such as are internal. The expression is far from being an accurate one; and as it is apt to occur in the consideration of almost every kind of offence, it will be requisite to settle the precise meaning of it, and observe how far it quadrates with the truth of things.

XII. With respect to goodness and badness, as it is with everything else that is not itself either pain or pleasure, so is it with motives. If they are good or bad, it is only on account of their effects: good, on account of their tendency to produce pleasure, or avert pain: bad, on account of their tendency to produce pain, or avert pleasure. Now the case is, that from one and the same motive, and from every kind of motive, may proceed actions that are good, others that are bad, and others that are indifferent.

Study Questions

1. Where in the reading do we see evidence of Bentham's psychological hedonism? Is his psychological hedonism convincing as an account of human motivation?
2. What does Bentham mean by the "principle of utility"?
3. Bentham developed a "hedonistic calculus" (described in Chapter IV of the selection) aimed at guiding practical decision-making. How is it supposed to work? Is it feasible as a method of making moral decisions?
4. Bentham wrote:"Quality of pleasure being equal, pushpin is as good as poetry." Do you agree or disagree? Why?
5. "[T]here is no such thing as any sort of motive that is in itself a bad one." Why does Bentham say this? Do you agree?
6. What is your overall assessment of utilitarianism, as presented by Bentham? What are both its strengths and weaknesses as a guide to moral decision-making?

Selected Bibliography

Dinwiddy, John. *Bentham* (Oxford: Oxford University Press, 1989). A short introduction to Bentham's moral and political theories.

Harrison, R. *Bentham* (London: Routledge & Kegan Paul, 1983), Chaps. V–VII. The applications of Bentham's ethics.

Moore, G. E. *Ethics* (Oxford: Oxford University Press, 1912), Chaps. 1 and 2. An analytic exposition of utilitarianism.

Plamenatz, J. *The English Utilitarians* (Oxford: Blackwell, 1966), Chap. 4. A critical exposition of Bentham's views.

Sidgwick, H. *The Methods of Ethics* (Indianapolis: Hackett Publishing, 1981). A classic work by a leading 19th century defender of utilitarianism.

Stephen, L. *The English Utilitarians* (London: Duckworth, 1900), Vol I, Chaps. 5 and 6. A lengthy exposition of Bentham's views.

13

KARL MARX

———

Although Karl Marx wrote very little directly on the subject of ethics, he is included in this book for two reasons. First, his writings on history, economics, and politics offer a perspective on the nature of society that embodies a con-

> *The* devaluation *of the human world increases in direct relation with the* increase in value *of the world of things.*

ception of justice highly critical of the practices of modern civilization. Second, his writings, although sometimes in distorted interpretations, have provided the intellectual foundations for social experiments on a vast scale in the twentieth century, which have had profound effects on the lives of billions of people since his day.

The selection that follows is taken from one of Marx's earliest works, a series of four manuscripts he wrote in Paris in 1844. These manuscripts were never completed and exist only in fragmentary form; neither were they published during his lifetime but only many years after his death. Although several of the major themes that Marx would develop in his later writings appear in the selection in an embryonic state, none is developed in detail. In particular, the manuscripts contain no mention of his solution to the economic, political, and ethical problems of his society; namely, the emergence, following a revolution by the proletariat (workers), of an ideal classless society. Rather, Marx's main concern in the selection is to describe the kind of life lived by workers in the industrial world of his time under the capitalistic system. The key concept in his analysis is the notion of *alienation* or estrangement. Marx sees the modern industrial worker as being almost totally alienated and, as a result, as living a life that can only be charitably described as human. This deplorable condition, furthermore, is no fault of the worker but the inevitable result of the entire social structure generated and maintained by bourgeois capitalism.

Karl Marx was born in Trier, in the German Moselle Valley, in 1818. While a student of philosophy at the University of Berlin, he was greatly influenced by the works of the great German idealist, G. W. F. Hegel. He soon abandoned Hegelian idealism, however, to become a political agitator and revolutionary. Expelled from several European countries for his "subversive" activities, he finally settled in London in 1849, where he lived the rest of his life and wrote his monumental work *Capital*.

Marx died in 1883. His tomb, in a cemetery in Southgate, London, is a place of pilgrimage for Marxists today. His funeral eulogy was delivered by his close friend and long-time collaborator, Friedrich Engels, who said of him:

> Marx was the best hated and most calumniated man of his time. Governments, both absolutist and republican, deported him from their territories. Bourgeois, whether conservative or ultra-democratic, vied with one another in heaping slanders upon him. All this he brushed aside as though it were cobweb, ignoring it, answering only when extreme necessity compelled him. And he died beloved, revered, and mourned by millions of revolutionary fellow-workers—from the mines of Siberia to California, in all parts of Europe and America—and I make bold to say that though he may have had many opponents, he had hardly one personal enemy.

———

Economic and Philosophical Manuscripts

First Manuscript

We have begun from the presuppositions of political economy.* We have accepted its terminology and its laws. We presupposed private property, the separation of labor, capital and land, as also of wages, profit and rent, the division of labor, competition, the concept of exchange value, etc. From political economy itself, in its own words, we have shown that the worker sinks to the level of a commodity, and to a most miserable commodity; that the misery of the worker increases with the power and volume of his production; that the necessary result of competition is the accumulation of capital in a few hands, and thus a restoration of monopoly in a more terrible form; and finally that the distinction between capitalist and landlord, and between agricultural laborer and industrial worker, must disappear and the whole of society divide into the two classes of property *owners* and propertyless *workers*.

———

Thus we have now to grasp the real connection between this whole system of alienation—private property, acquisitiveness, the separation of labor, capital and land, exchange and competition, value and the devaluation of man, monopoly and competition—and the system of *money*.

Let us not begin our explanation, as does the economist, from a legendary primordial condition. Such a primordial condition does not explain anything; it

---

*Marx is referring here to the writings of the "classical" economists of his time.—Ed.

From Karl Marx, *Economic and Philosophical Manuscripts*, tr. T. B. Bottomore, in E. Fromm, *Marx's Concept of Man* (New York: Frederick Ungar Publishing Co., 1961). Reprinted by permission of T. B. Bottomore.

merely removes the question into a gray and nebulous distance. It asserts as a fact or event what it should deduce, namely, the necessary relation between two things; for example, between the division of labor and exchange. In the same way theology explains the origin of evil by the fall of man; that is, it asserts as a historical fact what it should explain.

We shall begin from a *contemporary* economic fact. The worker becomes poorer the more wealth he produces and the more his production increases in power and extent. The worker becomes an ever cheaper commodity the more goods he creates. The *devaluation* of the human world increases in direct relation with the *increase in value* of the world of things. Labor does not only create goods; it also produces itself and the worker as a *commodity,* and indeed in the same proportion as it produces goods.

This fact simply implies that the object produced by labor, its product, now stands opposed to it as an *alien being,* as a *power independent* of the producer. The product of labor is labor which has been embodied in an object and turned into a physical thing; this product is an *objectification* of labor. The performance of work is at the same time its objectification. The performance of work appears in the sphere of political economy as a *vitiation* of the worker, objectification as a *loss* and as *servitude to the object,* and appropriation as *alienation.*

So much does the performance of work appear as vitiation that the worker is vitiated to the point of starvation. So much does objectification appear as loss of the object that the worker is deprived of the most essential things not only of life but also of work. Labor itself becomes an object which he can acquire only by the greatest effort and with unpredictable interruptions. So much does the appropriation of the object appear as alienation that the more objects the worker produces the fewer he can possess and the more he falls under the domination of his product, of capital.

All these consequences follow from the fact that the worker is related to the *product of his labor* as to an *alien* object. For it is clear on this presupposition that the more the worker expends himself in work the more powerful becomes the world of objects which he creates in face of himself, the poorer he becomes in his inner life, and the less he belongs to himself. It is just the same as in religion. The more of himself man attributes to God the less he has left in himself. The worker puts his life into the object, and his life then belongs no longer to himself but to the object. The greater his activity, therefore, the less he possesses. What is embodied in the product of his labor is no longer his own. The greater this product is, therefore, the more he is diminished. The *alienation* of the worker in his product means not only that his labor becomes an object, assumes an *external* existence, but that it exists independently, *outside himself,* and alien to him, and that it stands opposed to him as an autonomous power. The life which he has given to the object sets itself against him as an alien and hostile force.

Let us now examine more closely the phenomenon of *objectification,* the worker's production and the *alienation* and *loss* of the object it produces, which is involved in it. The worker can create nothing without *nature,* without the *sensuous external world.* The latter is the material in which his labor is realized, in which it is active, out of which and through which it produces things.

But just as nature affords the *means of existence* of labor in the sense that labor cannot *live* without objects upon which it can be exercised, so also it provides the *means of existence* in a narrower sense; namely the means of physical existence for the *worker* himself. Thus, the more the worker *appropriates* the external world of sensuous nature by his labor the more he deprives himself of *means of existence*, in two respects; first, that the sensuous external world becomes progressively less an object belonging to his labor or a means of existence of his labor, and secondly, that it becomes progressively less a means of existence in the direct sense, a means for the physical subsistence of the worker.

In both respects, therefore, the worker becomes a slave of the object; first, in that he receives an *object of work*, i.e., receives *work*, and secondly that he receives *means of subsistence*. Thus the object enables him to exist, first as a *worker* and secondly, as a *physical subject*. The culmination of this enslavement is that he can only maintain himself as a *physical subject* so far as he is a *worker*, and that it is only as a *physical subject* that he is a worker.

(The alienation of the worker in his object is expressed as follows in the laws of political economy: the more the worker produces the less he has to consume; the more value he creates the more worthless he becomes; the more refined his product the more crude and misshapen the worker; the more civilized the product the more barbarous the worker; the more powerful the work the more feeble the worker; the more the work manifests intelligence the more the worker declines in intelligence and becomes a slave of nature.)

Political economy conceals the alienation in the nature of labor insofar as it does not examine the direct relationship between the worker (work) and production. Labor certainly produces marvels for the rich but it produces privation for the worker. It produces palaces, but hovels for the worker. It produces beauty, but deformity for the worker. It replaces labor by machinery, but it casts some of the workers back into a barbarous kind of work and turns the others into machines. It produces intelligence, but also stupidity and cretinism for the workers.

The direct relationship of labor to its products is the relationship of the worker to the objects of his production. The relationship of property owners to the objects of production and to production itself is merely a *consequence* of this first relationship and confirms it. We shall consider this second aspect later.

Thus when we ask what is the important relationship of labor, we are concerned with the relationship of the *worker* to production.

So far we have considered the alienation of the worker only from one aspect; namely *his relationship with the products of his labor.* However, alienation appears not only in the result, but also in the *process* of *production,* within *productive activity* itself. How could the worker stand in an alien relationship to the product of his activity if he did not alienate himself in the act of production itself? The product is indeed only the *résumé* of activity, of production. Consequently, if the product of labor is alienation, production itself must be active alienation—the alienation of activity and the activity of alienation. The alienation of the object of labor merely summarizes the alienation in the work activity itself.

What constitutes the alienation of labor? First, that the work is *external* to the worker, that it is not part of his nature; and that, consequently, he does not fulfill himself in his work but denies himself, has a feeling of misery rather than well-being, does not develop freely his mental and physical energies but is physically exhausted and mentally debased. The worker therefore feels himself at home only during his leisure time, whereas at work he feels homeless. His work is not voluntary but imposed, *forced labor.* It is not the satisfaction of a need, but only *a means* for satisfying other needs. Its alien character is clearly shown by the fact that as soon as there is no physical or other compulsion it is avoided like the plague. External labor, labor in which man alienates himself, is a labor of self- sacrifice, of mortification. Finally, the external character of work for the worker is shown by the fact that it is not his own work but work for someone else, that in work he does not belong to himself but to another person.

Just as in religion the spontaneous activity of human fantasy, of the human brain and heart, reacts independently as an alien activity of gods or devils upon the individual, so the activity of the worker is not his own spontaneous activity. It is another's activity and a loss of his own spontaneity.

We arrive at the result that man (the worker) feels himself to be freely active only in his animal functions—eating, drinking, and procreating, or at most also in his dwelling and in personal adornment—while in his human functions he *is* reduced to an animal. The animal becomes human and the human becomes animal.

Eating, drinking and procreating are of course also genuine human functions. But abstractly considered, apart from the environment of other human activities, and turned into final and sole ends, they are animal functions.

We have now considered the act of alienation of practical human activity, labor, from two aspects: (1) the relationship of the worker to the *product of labor* as an alien object which dominates him. This relationship is at the same time the relationship to the sensuous external world, to natural objects, as an alien and hostile world; (2) the relationship of labor to the *act of production* within *labor.* This is the relationship of the worker to his own activity as something alien and not belonging to him, activity as suffering (passivity), strength as powerlessness, creation as emasculation, the *personal* physical and mental energy of the worker, his personal life (for what is life but activity?) as an activity which is directed against himself, independent of him and not belonging to him. This is *self-alienation* as against the above-mentioned alienation of the *thing.*

We have now to infer a third characteristic of *alienated labor* from the two we have considered.

Man is a species-being* not only in the sense that he makes the community (his own as well as those of other things) his object both practically and theoretically, but also (and this is simply another expression for the same thing) in the sense that he treats himself as the present, living species, as a *universal* and consequently free being.

Species-life, for man as for animals, has its physical basis in the fact that man (like animals) lives from inorganic nature, and since man is more universal than an

---

*The term "species-being" is taken from [Ludwig] Feuerbach's *Das Wesen des Christentums* (*The Essence of Christianity*). Feuerbach [German philosopher (1804–1872)] used the notion in making a distinction between consciousness in man and in animals. Man is conscious not merely of himself as an individual but of the human species or "human essence."—*Tr. Note*

animal so the range of inorganic nature from which he lives is more universal. Plants, animals, minerals, air, light, etc. constitute, from the theoretical aspect, a part of human consciousness as objects of natural science and art; they are man's spiritual inorganic nature, his intellectual means of life, which he must first prepare for enjoyment and perpetuation. So also, from the practical aspect they form a part of human life and activity. In practice man lives only from these natural products, whether in the form of food, heating, clothing, housing, etc. The universality of man appears in practice in the universality which makes the whole of nature into his inorganic body: (1) as a direct means of life; and equally (2) as the material object and instrument of his life activity. Nature is the *inorganic body* of man; that is to say, nature excluding the human body itself. To say that man *lives* from nature means that nature is his *body* with which he must remain in a continuous interchange in order not to die. The statement that the physical and mental life of man, and nature, are interdependent means simply that nature is interdependent with itself, for man is a part of nature.

Since alienated labor: (1) alienates nature from man; and (2) alienates man from himself, from his own active function, his life activity; so it alienates him from the species. It makes *species-life* into a means of individual life. In the first place it alienates species-life and individual life, and secondly, it turns the latter, as an abstraction, into the purpose of the former, also in its abstract and alienated form.

For labor, *life activity, productive life,* now appear to man only as *means* for the satisfaction of a need, the need to maintain his physical existence. Productive life is, however, species-life. It is life creating life. In the type of life activity resides the whole character of a species, its species-character; and free, conscious activity is the species-character of human beings. Life itself appears only as a *means of life*.

The animal is one with its life activity. It does not distinguish the activity from itself. It is *its activity*. But man makes his life activity itself an object of his will and consciousness. He has a conscious life activity. It is not a determination with which he is completely identified. Conscious life activity distinguishes man from the life activity of animals. Only for this reason is he a species-being. Or rather, he is only a self-conscious being, i.e., his own life is an object for him, because he is a species-being. Only for this reason is his activity free activity. Alienated labor reverses the relationship, in that man because he is a self-conscious being makes his life activity, his *being*, only a means for his *existence*.

The practical construction of an *objective world*, the *manipulation* of inorganic nature, is the confirmation of man as a conscious species-being, i.e., a being who treats the species as his own being or himself as a species-being. Of course, animals also produce. They construct nests, dwellings, as in the case of bees, beavers, ants, etc. But they only produce what is strictly necessary for themselves or their young. They produce only in a single direction, while man produces universally. They produce only under the compulsion of direct physical need, while man produces when he is free from physical need and only truly produces in freedom from such need. Animals produce only themselves, while man reproduces the whole of nature. The products of animal production belong directly to their physical bodies, while man is free in face of his product. Animals construct only in accordance with the standards and needs of the species to which they belong, while man knows how to produce in accordance with the standards of every species and knows how to apply the appropriate standard to the object. Thus man constructs also in accordance with the laws of beauty.

It is just in his work upon the objective world that man really proves himself as a *species-being*. This production is his active species life. By means of it nature appears as *his* work and his reality. The object of labor is, therefore, the *objectification of man's species life:* for he no longer reproduces himself merely intellectually, as in consciousness, but actively and in a real sense, and he sees his own reflection in a world which he has constructed. While, therefore, alienated labor takes away the object of production from man, it also takes away his *species life,* his real objectivity as a species-being, and changes his advantage over animals into a disadvantage insofar as his inorganic body, nature, is taken from him.

Just as alienated labor transforms free and self-directed activity into a means, so it transforms the species life of man into a means of physical existence.

Consciousness, which man has from his species, is transformed through alienation so that species life becomes only a means for him.

(3) Thus alienated labor turns the *species life of man,* and also nature as his mental species-property, into an *alien* being and into a *means* for his *individual existence.* It alienates from man his own body, external nature, his mental life and his *human* life.

(4) A direct consequence of the alienation of man from the product of his labor, from his life activity and from his species life is that *man is alienated* from other *men.* When man confronts himself he also confronts *other* men. What is true of man's relationship to his work, to the product of his work and to himself, is also true of his relationship to other men, to their labor and to the objects of their labor.

In general, the statement that man is alienated from his species life means that each man is alienated from others, and that each of the others is likewise alienated from human life.

Human alienation, and above all the relation of man to himself, is first realized and expressed in the relationship between each man and other men. Thus in the relationship of alienated labor every man regards other men according to the standards and relationships in which he finds himself placed as a worker.

We begin with an economic fact, the alienation of the worker and his production. We have expressed this fact in conceptual terms as *alienated labor,* and in analyzing the concept we have merely analyzed an economic fact.

Let us now examine further how this concept of alienated labor must express and reveal itself in reality. If the product of labor is alien to me and confronts me as an alien power, to whom does it belong? If my own activity does not belong to me but is an alien, forced activity, to whom does it belong? To a being *other* than myself. And who is this being? The *gods*? It is apparent in the earliest stages of advanced production, e.g., temple building, etc. in Egypt, India, Mexico, and in the service rendered to gods, that the product belonged to the gods. But the gods alone were never the lords of labor. And no more was *nature*. What a contradiction it would be if the more man subjugates nature by his labor, and the more the marvels of the gods are rendered superfluous by the marvels of industry, he should abstain from his joy in producing and his enjoyment of the product for love of these powers.

The *alien* being to whom labor and the product of labor belong, to whose service labor is devoted, and to whose enjoyment the product of labor goes, can only be *man* himself. If the product of labor does not belong to the worker, but confronts him as an alien power, this can only be because it belongs to *a man other than the worker*. If his activity is a torment to him, it must be a source of enjoyment and pleasure to another. Not the gods, nor nature, but only man himself can be this alien power over men.

Consider the earlier statement that the relation of man to himself is first realized, objectified, through his relation to other men. If therefore he is related to the product of his labor, his objectified labor, as to an *alien* hostile, powerful and independent object, he is related in such a way that another alien, hostile, powerful and independent man is the lord of this object. If he is related to his own activity as to unfree activity, then he is related to it as activity in the service, and under the domination, coercion and yoke, of another man.

Every self-alienation of man, from himself and from nature, appears in the relation which he postulates between other men and himself and nature. Thus religious self-alienation is necessarily exemplified in the relation between laity and priest, or, since it is here a question of the spiritual world, between the laity and a mediator. In the real world of practice this self-alienation can only be expressed in the real, practical relation of man to his fellow-men. The medium through which alienation occurs is itself a *practical* one. Through alienated labor, therefore, man not only produces his relation to the object and to the process of production as to alien and hostile men; he also produces the relation of other men to his production and his product, and the relation between himself and other men. Just as he creates his own production as a vitiation, a punishment, and his own product as a loss, as a product which does not belong to him, so he creates the domination of the nonproducer over production and its product. As he alienates his own activity, so he bestows upon the stranger an activity which is not his own.

———

Thus, through alienated labor the worker creates the relation of another man, who does not work and is outside the work process, to this labor. The relation of the worker to work also produces the relation of the capitalist (or whatever one likes to call the lord of labor) to work. *Private property* is therefore the product, the necessary result, of *alienated labor*, of the external relation of the worker to nature and to himself.

Private property is thus derived from the analysis of the concept of *alienated labor;* that is, alienated man, alienated labor, alienated life, and estranged man.

———

Third Manuscript

Private property has made us so stupid and partial that an object is only *ours* when we have it, when it exists for us as capital or when it is directly eaten, drunk, worn, inhabited, etc., in short, *utilized* in some way; although private property itself only conceives these various forms of possession as *means of life*, and the life for which they serve as means is the *life of private property*—labor and creation of capital.

Thus *all* the physical and intellectual senses have been replaced by the simple alienation of *all* these senses; the sense of *having*. The human being had to be reduced to this absolute poverty in order to be able to give birth to all his inner wealth.

The supersession of private property is therefore the complete *emancipation* of all the human qualities and senses. It is this emancipation because these qualities and senses have become *human*, from the subjective as well as the objective point of view. The eye has become a *human* eye when its *object* has become a *human*, social object, created by man and destined for him. The senses have therefore become directly theoreticians in practice. They relate themselves to the thing for the sake of the thing, but the thing itself is an *objective human* relation to itself and to man, and vice versa. Need and enjoyment have thus lost their *egoistic* character, and nature has lost its mere *utility* by the fact that its utilization has become *human* utilization.

Similarly, the senses and minds of other men have become my *own* appropriation. Thus besides these direct organs, *social* organs are constituted, in the form of society; for example, activity in direct association with others has become an organ for the manifestation of life and a mode of appropriation of *human* life.

It is evident that the human eye appreciates things in a different way from the crude, non-human eye, the human *ear* differently from the crude ear. As we have seen, it is only when the object becomes a *human* object, or objective *humanity*, that man does not become lost in it. This is only possible when the object becomes a *social* object, and when he himself becomes a social being and society becomes a being for him in this object.

On the one hand, it is only when objective reality everywhere becomes for man in society the reality of human faculties, human reality, and thus the reality of his own faculties, that all *objects* become for him the *objectification of himself.* The objects then confirm and realize his individuality; they are *his own* objects, i.e., man himself becomes the object. *The manner in which* these objects become his own depends upon the *nature of the object* and the nature of the corresponding faculty; for it is precisely the *determinate character* of this relation which constitutes the specific *real* mode of affirmation. The object is not the same for the *eye* as for the *ear*, for the ear as for the eye. The *distinctive character* of each faculty is precisely its *characteristic* essence and thus also the characteristic mode of its objectification, of its *objectively real*, living *being*. It is therefore not only in thought, but through *all* the senses that man is affirmed in the objective world.

Let us next consider the subjective aspect. Man's musical sense is only awakened by music. The most beautiful music has no meaning for the nonmusical ear, is not an object for it, because my object can only be the confirmation of one of my own faculties. It can only be so for me insofar as my faculty exists for itself as a subjective capacity, because the meaning of an object for me extends only as far as the sense extends (only makes sense for an appropriate sense). For this reason, the *senses* of social man are *different* from those of non-social man. It is only through the objectively deployed wealth of the human being that the wealth of subjective *human* sensibility (a musical ear, an eye which is sensitive to the beauty of form, in short, senses which are capable of human satisfaction and which confirm themselves as human faculties) is cultivated or created. For it is not only the five senses, but also the so-called spiritual senses, the practical senses (desiring, loving, etc.), in brief, human sensibility and the human character of the senses, which can only come into being through the existence of *its* object, through humanized nature. The cultivation of the five senses is the work of all previous history. Sense which is subservient to crude needs has only a restricted meaning. For a starving man the human form of food does not exist, but only its abstract character as food. It could just as well exist in the most crude form, and it is impossible to say in what way this feeding-activity would differ from that of animals. The needy man, burdened with cares, has no appreciation of the most beautiful spectacle. The dealer in minerals sees only their commercial value, not their beauty or their particular characteristics; he has no mineralogical sense. Thus, the objectification of the human essence, both theoretically and practically, is necessary in order to *humanize* man's *senses*, and also to create the *human senses* corresponding to all the wealth of human and natural being.

Just as society at its beginnings finds, through the development of *private property* with its wealth and poverty (both intellectual and material), the materials necessary for this *cultural development,* so the fully constituted society produces man in all the plenitude of his being, the wealthy man endowed with all the senses, as an enduring reality. It is only in a social context that subjectivism and objectivism, spiritualism and materialism, activity and passivity, cease to be antinomies and thus cease to exist as such antinomies. The resolution of the *theoretical* contradictions is possible *only* through *practical* means, only through the practical energy of man. Their resolution is not by any means, therefore, only a problem of knowledge, but is a *real* problem of life which philosophy was unable to solve precisely because it saw there a purely theoretical problem.

Study Questions

1. What are the main ways in which, according to Marx, modern workers become alienated? Whom else besides workers does contemporary society alienate? What are the chief causes of such alienation? Is all alienation bad?
2. Marx thinks that chronic unemployment is an essential feature of modern industrial capitalism? Do you think that he is right about this?
3. What connections (if any) do you see between Marx's analysis of alienated labor and Kant's principle of treating humanity as an end and never as a means only?

4. What is Marx's analysis of private property? Do you think that private property should be eliminated? If not, why not?

5. Marx wrote well over a hundred years ago. Do you think that his analysis of the condition of the worker and the relationship between capital and labor is relevant to today's industrial world? Can you find examples of the kind of alienation that Marx describes in today's world?

Selected Bibliography

Buchanan, Allen. *Marx and Justice* (Totowa, N.J.: Rowman & Littlefield, 1982). A discussion of Marx's views abut justice in relation to recent liberalism.

Marx, K. and Engels, F. *Manifesto of the Communist Party* (San Francisco: China Books and Periodicals, 1965). The famous revolutionary document, written jointly by Marx and Engels.

McLellan, D. *Karl Marx* (New York: Viking Press, 1975). A short survey of Marx's life, thought, and reputation.

Miller, Richard. *Analyzing Marx: Morality, Power and History* (Princeton, N.J.: Princeton University Press, 1984). A general study.

Nielsen, K. and Patten, S. C., eds. *Marx and Morality* (Guelph, Ontario: Canadian Association for Publishing Philosophy, 1981). Essays on Marx's views on morality.

Ollman, B. *Alienation: Marx's Conception of Man in Capitalist Society*, 2nd ed. (New York/Cambridge: Cambridge University Press, 1976). A detailed analysis of Marx's conception of human nature and alienation.

Peffer, R. G. *Marxism, Morality and Social Justice* (Princeton, N.J.: Princeton University Press, 1990). A study of Marx on morality.

Wood, Allen. *Marx.* (London: Routledge, 1981). A general study of Marx's philosophical views.

14

JOHN STUART MILL

John Stuart Mill (1806–1873), was educated at home by his father, James Mill, a prominent economist and member of the Philosophical Radicals, and Jeremy Bentham. These two tutors, in fact, used young Mill as a kind of guinea pig

> *It is better to be a human being dissatisfied than a pig satisfied; better to be Socrates dissatisfied than a fool satisfied.*

on whom they could try out some of their novel pedagogical theories. Whether because of or in spite of his unusual education, Mill turned out to be a very apt pupil and an extraordinarily precocious child. He began the study of Greek at the age of three and was reading the *History* of Herodotus in the original before he was eight. From the age of twelve on he devoted his most serious attention to philosophy, starting with Aristotle's logic and continuing with the study of political theory. Before he was twenty he suffered a nervous breakdown.

The influence of Bentham and James Mill is clearly apparent in John Stuart Mill's career. Throughout his life he devoted himself to programs for social reform, carrying on the tradition of the Philosophical Radicals. Like Bentham, John Stuart Mill found a theoretical justification for his political views and practices in the theory of utilitarianism. Mill did much to popularize utilitarianism and to extend the theory to new areas of social concern. He became an eloquent spokesman for the cause of individual freedom with his essay *On Liberty*—a classic defense of a robust set of individual civil liberties that is developed within a utilitarian framework. Likewise, his essay *The Subjection of Women*, written with his wife Harriet Taylor, is a powerful and insightful defense of the social and political equality of women.

Mill's *Utilitarianism* is a classic statement of utilitarian moral theory that was written for a general audience. Mill begins the second chapter of this work with an affirmation of ethical hedonism that seems close to Bentham, but important differences soon emerge. Bentham claimed that all pleasures are qualitatively on a par (" . . . pushpin is as good as poetry"). Mill, on the contrary, maintained that there are qualitative differences among pleasures and developed a distinction between "higher" and "lower" pleasures. His distinction appears to rest on the psychological thesis that human beings have a preference for complex activities that exercise the higher faculties of intellect, imagination, judgment, choice, responsibility, and so on, over activities that offer only the pleasures of sensation; moreover, assuming that certain basic needs are satisfied and that we enjoy adequate levels of sensory contentment, we seek further opportunities to exercise our "higher" faculties, even though these activities may be accompanied by a certain amount of discontentment. Much of *Utilitarianism* is devoted to answering criticisms leveled at the theory by Mill's contemporaries, and his defense of the theory anticipates and addresses many objections that would be raised by later generations of theorists.

Utilitarianism

Chapter II

What Utilitarianism Is

. . . The creed which accepts as the foundation of morals, Utility, or the Greatest Happiness Principle, holds that actions are right in proportion as they tend to promote happiness, wrong as they tend to produce the reverse of happiness. By happiness is intended pleasure, and the absence of pain; by unhappiness, pain and the privation of pleasure. To give a clear view of the moral standard set up by the theory, much more requires to be said; in particular, what things it includes in the ideas of pain and pleasure; and to what extent this is left an open question. But these supplementary explanations do not affect the theory of life on which this theory of morality is grounded—namely, that pleasure, and freedom from pain, are the only things desirable as ends; and that all desirable things (which are as numerous in the utilitarian as in any other scheme) are desirable either for the pleasure inherent in themselves, or as means of the promotion of pleasure and the prevention of pain.

Now, such a theory of life excites in many minds, and among them in some of the most estimable in feeling and purpose, inveterate dislike. To suppose that life has (as they express it) no higher end than pleasure—no better and nobler object of desire and pursuit—they designate as utterly mean and grovelling; as a doctrine worthy only of swine, to whom the followers of Epicurus were, at a very early period, contemptuously likened; and modern holders of the doctrine are occasionally made the subject of equally polite comparisons by its German, French, and English assailants.

When thus attacked, the Epicureans have always answered, that it is not they, but their accusers, who represent human nature in a degrading light; since the accusation supposes human beings to be capable of no pleasures except those of which swine are capable. If this supposition were true, the charge could not be gainsaid, but would then be no longer an imputation: for if the sources of pleasure were precisely the same to human beings and to swine, the rule of life which is

Thirteenth edition, London, 1897. First published in 1861.

good enough for the one would be good enough for the other. The comparison of the Epicurean life to that of beasts is felt as degrading, precisely because a beast's pleasures do not satisfy a human being's conceptions of happiness. Human beings have faculties more elevated than the animal appetites, and when once made conscious of them, do not regard anything as happiness which does not include their gratification. I do not, indeed, consider the Epicureans to have been by any means faultless in drawing out their scheme of consequences from the utilitarian principle. To do this in any sufficient manner, many Stoic, as well as Christian elements require to be included. But there is no known Epicurean theory of life which does not assign to the pleasures of the intellect, of the feelings and imagination, and of the moral sentiments, a much higher value as pleasures than to those of mere sensation. It must be admitted, however, that utilitarian writers in general have placed the superiority of mental over bodily pleasures chiefly in the greater permanency, safety, uncostliness, &c., of the former—that is, in their circumstantial advantages rather than in their intrinsic nature. And on all these points utilitarians have fully proved their case; but they might have taken the other, and, as it may be called, higher ground, with entire consistency. It is quite compatible with the principle of utility to recognize the fact, that some *kinds* of pleasure are more desirable and more valuable than others. It would be absurd that while, in estimating all other things, quality is considered as well as quantity, the estimation of pleasures should be supposed to depend on quantity alone.

If I am asked, what I mean by difference of quality in pleasures, or what makes one pleasure more valuable than another, merely as a pleasure, except its being greater in amount, there is but one possible answer. Of two pleasures, if there be one to which all or almost all who have experience of both give a decided preference, irrespective of any feeling of moral obligation to prefer it, that is the more desirable pleasure. If one of the two is, by those who are competently acquainted with both, placed so far above the other that they prefer it, even though knowing it to be attended with a greater amount of discontent, and would not resign it for any quantity of the pleasure which their nature is capable of, we are justified in ascribing to the preferred enjoyment a superiority in quality, so far outweighing quantity as to render it, in comparison, of small account.

Now it is an unquestionable fact that those who are equally acquainted with, and equally capable of appreciating and enjoying, both, do give a most marked preference to the manner of existence which employs their higher faculties. Few human creatures would consent to be changed into any of the lower animals, for a promise of the fullest allowance of a beast's pleasures; no intelligent human being would consent to be a fool, no instructed person would be an ignoramus, no person of feeling and conscience would be selfish and base, even though they should be persuaded that the fool, the dunce, or the rascal is better satisfied with his lot than they are with theirs. They would not resign what they possess more than he, for the most complete satisfaction of all the desires which they have in common with him. If they ever fancy they would, it is only in cases of unhappiness so extreme, that to escape from it they would exchange their lot for almost any other, however undesirable in their own eyes. A being of higher faculties requires more to make him happy, is capable probably of more acute suffering, and is certainly accessible to it at more points, than one of an inferior type; but in spite of these liabilities, he can never really wish to sink into what he feels to be a lower grade of existence. We may give what explanation we please of this unwillingness; we may attribute it to pride, a name which is given indiscriminately to some of the most and to some of the least estimable feelings of which mankind is capable; we may refer it to the love of liberty and personal independence, an appeal to which was with the Stoics one of the most effective means for the inculcation of it; to the love of power, or to the love of excitement, both of which do really enter into and contribute to it: but its most appropriate appellation is a sense of dignity, which all human beings possess in one form or another, and in some, though by no means in exact, proportion to their higher faculties, and which is so essential a part of the happiness of those in whom it is strong, that nothing which conflicts with it could be, otherwise than momentarily, an object of desire to them. Whoever supposes that this preference takes place at a sacrifice of happiness—that the superior being, in anything like equal circumstances, is not happier than the inferior—confounds the two very different ideas, of happiness, and content. It is indisputable that the being whose capacities of enjoyment are low, has the greatest chance of having them fully satisfied; and a highly endowed being will always feel that any happiness which he can look for, as the world is constituted, is imperfect. But he can learn to bear its imperfections, if they are at all bearable; and they will not make him envy the being who is indeed unconscious of the imperfections, but only because he feels not at all the good which those imperfections qualify. It is better to be a human being dissatisfied than a pig satisfied; better to be Socrates dissatisfied than a fool satisfied. And if the fool, or the pig, is of a different opinion, it is because they only know their own side of the question. The other party to the comparison knows both sides.

It may be objected, that many who are capable of the higher pleasures, occasionally, under the influence of temptation, postpone them to the lower. But this is quite compatible with a full appreciation of the intrinsic superiority of the higher. Men often, from infirmity of character, make their election for the nearer good, though they know it to be less valuable; and this no less when the choice is between two bodily pleasures, than when it is between bodily and mental. They pursue sensual indulgences to the injury of health, though perfectly aware that health is the greater good. It may be further objected, that many who begin with youthful enthusiasm for everything noble, as they advance in years sink into indolence and selfishness. But I do not believe that those who undergo this very common change, voluntarily choose the lower description of pleasures in preference to the higher. I believe that before they devote themselves exclusively to the one, they have already become incapable of the other. Capacity for the nobler feelings is in most natures a very tender plant, easily killed, not only by hostile influences, but by mere want of sustenance; and in the majority of young persons it speedily dies away if the occupations to which their position in life has devoted them, and the society into which it has thrown them, are not favourable to keeping that higher capacity in exercise. Men lose their high aspirations as they lose their intellectual tastes, because they have not time or opportunity for indulging them; and they addict themselves to inferior pleasures, not because they deliberately prefer them, but because they are either the only ones to which they have access, or the only ones which they are any longer capable of enjoying. It may be questioned whether any-one who has remained equally susceptible to both classes of pleasures, ever knowingly and calmly preferred the lower; though many, in all ages, have broken down in an ineffectual attempt to combine both.

From this verdict of the only competent judges, I apprehend there can be no appeal. On a question which is the best worth having of two pleasures or which of two modes of existence is the most grateful to the feelings, apart from its moral at-tributes and from its consequences, the judgment of those who are qualified by knowledge of both, or, if they differ, that of the majority among them, must be admitted as final. And there needs be the less hesitation to accept this judgment respecting the quality of pleasures, since there is no other tribunal to be referred to even on the question of quantity. What means are there of determining which is the acutest of two pains, or the intensest of two pleasurable sensations, except the general suffrage of those who are familiar with both? Neither pains nor pleasures are homogeneous, and pain is always heterogeneous with pleasure. What is there to decide whether a particular pleasure is worth purchasing at the cost of a partic-ular pain, except the feelings and judgment of the experienced? When, therefore, those feelings and judgment declare the pleasures derived from the higher faculties to be preferable *in kind*, apart from the question of intensity, to those of which the animal nature, disjoined from the higher faculties, is susceptible, they are entitled on this subject to the same regard.

I have dwelt on this point, as being a necessary part of a perfectly just concep-tion of Utility or Happiness, considered as the directive rule of human conduct. But it is by no means an indispensable condition to the acceptance of the utilitar-ian standard; for that standard is not the agent's own greatest happiness, but the greatest amount of happiness altogether; and if it may possibly be doubted whether a noble character is always the happier for its nobleness, there can be no doubt that it makes other people happier, and that the world in general is im-mensely a gainer by it. Utilitarianism, therefore, could only attain its end by the general cultivation of nobleness of others, and his own, so far as happiness is con-cerned, were a sheer deduction from the benefit. But the bare enunciation of such an absurdity as this last, renders refutation superfluous.

According to the Greatest Happiness Principle, as above explained, the ultimate end, with reference to and for the sake of which all other things are desirable (whether we are considering our own good or that of other people), is an existence exempt as far as possible from pain, and as rich as possible in enjoyments, both in point of quantity and quality; the test of quality, and the rule for measuring it against quantity, being the preference felt by those who, in their opportunities of experience, to which must be added their habits of self-consciousness and self-ob-servation, are best furnished with the means of comparison. This, being, according to the utilitarian opinion, the end of human action, is necessarily also the standard of morality; which may accordingly be defined, the rules and precepts for human con-duct, by the observance of which an existence such as has been described might be, to the greatest extent possible, secured to all mankind; and not to them only, but, so far as the nature of things admits, to the whole sentient creation.

Against this doctrine, however, rises another class of objectors, who say that happiness, in any form, cannot be the rational purpose of human life and action; because, in the first place, it is unattainable: and they contemptuously ask, What right hast thou to be happy? a question which Mr. Carlyle clenches by the addition, What right, a short time ago, hadst thou even *to be?* Next, they say, that men can do *without* happiness; that all noble human beings have felt this, and could not have become noble but by learning the lesson of *Entsagen,* or renunciation; which lesson, thoroughly learnt and submitted to, they affirm to be the beginning and necessary condition of all virtue.

The first of these objections would go to the root of the matter were it well founded; for if no happiness is to be had at all by human beings, the attainment of it cannot be the end of morality, or of any rational conduct. Though, even in that case, something might still be said for the utilitarian theory; since utility includes not solely the pursuit of happiness, but the prevention or mitigation of unhappiness; and if the former aim be chimerical, there will be all the greater scope and more imperative need for the latter, so long at least as mankind think fit to live, and do not take refuge in the simultaneous act of suicide recommended under certain conditions by Novalis.* When, however, it is thus positively asserted to be impossible that human life should be happy, the assertion, if not something like a verbal quibble, is at least an exaggeration. If by happiness be meant a continuity of highly pleasurable excitement, it is evident enough that this is impossible. A state of exalted pleasure lasts only moments, or in some cases, and with some intermissions, hours or days, and is the occasional brilliant flash of enjoyment, not its permanent and steady flame. Of this the philosophers who have taught that happiness is the end of life were as fully aware as those who taunt them. The happiness which they meant was not a life of rapture; but moments of such, in an existence made up of few and transitory pains, many and various pleasures, with a decided predominance of the active over the passive, and having as the foundation of the whole, not to expect more from life than it is capable of bestowing. A life thus composed, to those who have been fortunate enough to obtain it, has always appeared worthy of the name of happiness. And such an existence is even now the lot of many, during some considerable portion of their lives. The present wretched education, and wretched social arrangements, are the only real hindrance to its being attainable by almost all.

The objectors perhaps may doubt whether human beings, if taught to consider happiness as the end of life, would be satisfied with such a moderate share of it. But great numbers of mankind have been satisfied with much less. The main constituents of a satisfied life appear to be two, either of which by itself is often found sufficient for the purpose: tranquillity, and excitement. With much tranquillity, many find that they can be content with very little pleasure: with much excitement, many can reconcile themselves to a considerable quantity of pain. There is assuredly no inherent impossibility in enabling even the mass of mankind to unite both; since the two are so far from being incompatible that they are in natural alliance, the prolongation of either being a preparation for, and exciting a wish for, the other. It is only those

*Eighteenth-century German romantic poet.—Ed.

in whom indolence amounts to a vice, that do not desire excitement after an interval of repose; it is only those in whom the need of excitement is a disease, that feel the tranquillity which follows excitement dull and insipid, instead of pleasurable in direct proportion to the excitement which preceded it. When people who are tolerably fortunate in their outward lot do not find in life sufficient enjoyment to make it valuable to them, the cause generally is, caring for nobody but themselves. To those who have neither public nor private affections, the excitements of life are much curtailed, and in any case dwindle in value as the time approaches when all selfish interests must be terminated by death: while those who leave after them objects of personal affection, and especially those who have also cultivated a fellow-feeling with the collective interests of mankind, retain as lively an interest in life on the eve of death as in the vigour of youth and health. Next to selfishness, the principal cause which makes life unsatisfactory, is want of mental cultivation. A cultivated mind—I do not mean that of a philosopher, but any mind to which the fountains of knowledge have been opened, and which has been taught, in any tolerable degree, to exercise its faculties—finds sources of inexhaustible interest in all that surrounds it; in the objects of nature, the achievements of art, the imaginations of poetry, the incidents of history, the ways of mankind past and present, and their prospects in the future. It is possible, indeed, to become indifferent to all this, and that too without having exhausted a thousandth part of it; but only when one has had from the beginning no moral or human interest in these things and has sought in them only the gratification of curiosity.

Now there is absolutely no reason in the nature of things why an amount of mental culture sufficient to give an intelligent interest in these objects of contemplation, should not be the inheritance of every one born in a civilised country. As little is there an inherent necessity that any human being should be a selfish egotist, devoid of every feeling or care but those which centre in his own miserable individuality. Something far superior to this is sufficiently common even now, to give ample earnest of what the human species may be made. Genuine private affections, and a sincere interest in the public good, are possible, though in unequal degrees, to every rightly brought up human being. In a world in which there is so much to interest, so much to enjoy, and so much also to correct and improve, everyone who has this moderate amount of moral and intellectual requisites is capable of an existence which may be called enviable, and unless such a person, through bad laws, or subjection to the will of others, is denied the liberty to use the sources of happiness within his reach, he will not fail to find this enviable existence, if he escape the positive evils of life, the great sources of physical and mental suffering—such as indigence, disease, and the unkindness, worthlessness, or premature loss of objects of affection. The main stress of the problem lies, therefore, in the contest with these calamities, from which it is a rare good fortune entirely to escape; which, as things now are cannot be obviated, and often cannot be in any material degree mitigated. Yet no one whose opinion deserves a moment's consideration can doubt that most of the great positive evils of the world are in themselves removable, and will, if human affairs continue to improve, be in the end reduced within narrow limits. Poverty, in any sense implying suffering, may be completely extinguished by the wisdom of society, combined with the good sense and providence of individuals. Even that most intractable of enemies, disease, may be indefinitely reduced in dimensions by good physical and moral education, and proper control of noxious influences; while the progress of science holds out a promise for the future of still more direct conquests over this detestable foe. And every advance in that direction relieves us from some, not only of the chances which cut short our own lives, but, what concerns us still more, which deprive us of those in whom our happiness is wrapt up. As for vicissitudes of fortune, and other disappointments connected with worldly circumstances, these are principally the effect either of gross imprudence, of ill-regulated desires, or of bad or imperfect social institutions. All the grand sources, in short, of human suffering are in a great degree, many of them almost entirely, conquerable by human care and effort; and though their removal is grievously slow—though a long succession of generations will perish in the breach before the conquest is completed, and this world becomes all that, if will and knowledge were not wanting, it might easily be made—yet every mind sufficiently intelligent and generous to bear a part, however small and inconspicuous, in the endeavour, will draw a noble enjoyment from the contest itself, which he would not for any bribe in the form of selfish indulgence consent to be without.

And this leads to the true estimation of what is said by the objectors concerning the possibility and the obligation, of learning to do without happiness. Unquestionably it is possible to do without happiness; it is done involuntarily by nineteen-twentieths of mankind, even in those parts of our present world which are least deep in barbarism; and it often has to be done voluntarily by the hero or the martyr, for the sake of something which he prizes more than his individual happiness. But this something, what is it, unless the happiness of others, or some of the requisites of happiness? It is noble to be capable of resigning entirely one's own portion of happiness, or chances of it: but, after all, this self-sacrifice must be for some end; it is not its own end; and if we are told that its end is not happiness, but virtue, which is better than happiness, I ask, would the sacrifice be made if the hero or martyr did not believe that it would earn for others immunity from similar sacrifices? Would it be made, if he thought that his renunciation of happiness for himself would produce no fruit for any of his fellow creatures, but to make their lot like his, and place them also in the condition of persons who have renounced happiness? All honour to those who can abnegate for themselves the personal enjoyment of life, when by such renunciation they contribute worthily to increase the amount of happiness in the world; but he who does it, or professes to do it, for any other purpose, is no more deserving of admiration than the ascetic mounted on his pillar. He may be an inspiriting proof of what men *can* do, but assuredly not an example of what they *should*.

Though it is only in a very imperfect state of the world's arrangements that anyone can best serve the happiness of others by the absolute sacrifice of his own, yet so long as the world is in that imperfect state, I fully acknowledge that the readiness to make such a sacrifice is the highest virtue which can be found in man. I will add, that in this condition of the world, paradoxical as the assertion may be, the conscious ability to do without happiness gives the best prospect of realizing such happiness as is attainable. For nothing except that consciousness can raise a person above the chances of life, by making him feel that, let fate and fortune do their worst, they have not power to subdue him: which, once felt, frees him from excess of anxiety concerning the evils of life, and enables him, like many a Stoic in the worst times of the Roman Empire, to cultivate in tranquillity the sources of satisfaction accessible to him, without concerning himself about the uncertainty of their duration, any more than about their inevitable end.

Meanwhile, let utilitarians never cease to claim the morality of self-devotion as a possession which belongs by as good a right to them, as either to the Stoic or to the Transcendentalist. The utilitarian morality does recognize in human beings the power of sacrificing their own greatest good for the good of others. It only refuses to admit that the sacrifice is itself a good. A sacrifice which does not increase, or tend to increase, the sum total of happiness, it considers as wasted. The only self-renunciation which it applauds, is devotion to the happiness, or to some of the means of happiness, of others; either mankind collectively, or of individuals within the limits imposed by the collective interests of mankind.

I must again repeat, what the assailants of utilitarianism seldom have the justice to acknowledge, that the happiness which forms the utilitarian standard of what is right in conduct, is not the agent's own happiness, but that of all concerned. As between his own happiness and that of others, utilitarianism requires him to be as strictly impartial as a disinterested and benevolent spectator. In the golden rule of Jesus of Nazareth, we read the complete spirit of the ethics of utility. To do as one would be done by, and to love one's neighbour as oneself constitute the ideal perfection of utilitarian morality. As the means of making the nearest approach to this ideal, utility would enjoin, first, that laws and social arrangements should place the happiness, or (as speaking practically it may be called) the interest, of every individual, as nearly as possible in harmony with the interest of the whole; and secondly, that education and opinion, which have so vast a power over human character, should so use that power as to establish in the mind of every individual an indissoluble association between his own happiness and the good of the whole; especially between his own happiness and the practice of such modes of conduct, negative and positive, as regard for the universal happiness prescribes: so that not only he may be unable to conceive the possibility of happiness to himself, consistently with conduct opposed to the general good, but also that a direct impulse to promote the general good may be in every individual one of the habitual motives of action, and the sentiments connected therewith may fill a large and prominent place in every human being's sentient existence. If the impugners of the utilitarian morality represented it to their own minds in this its true character, I know not what recommendation possessed by any other morality they could possibly affirm to be wanting to it: what more beautiful or more exalted developments of human nature any other ethical system can be supposed to foster, or what springs of action, not accessible to the utilitarian, such systems rely on for giving effect to their mandates.

The objectors to utilitarianism cannot always be charged with representing it in a discreditable light. On the contrary, those among them who entertain anything like a just idea of its disinterested character, sometimes find fault with its standard as being too high for humanity. They say it is exacting too much to require that people shall always act from the inducement of promoting the general interests of society. But this is to mistake the very meaning of a standard of morals, and to confound the rule of action with the motive of it. It is the business of ethics to tell us what are our duties, or by what test we may know them; but no system of ethics requires that the sole motive of all we do shall be a feeling of duty; on the contrary, ninety-nine hundredths of all our actions are done from other motives, and rightly so done, if the rule of duty does not condemn them. It is the more unjust to utilitarianism that this particular misapprehension should be made a ground of objection to it, inasmuch as utilitarian moralists have gone beyond almost all others in affirming that the motive has nothing to do with the morality of the action, though much with the worth of the agent. He who saves a fellow creature from drowning does what is morally right, whether his motive be duty, or the hope of being paid for his trouble: he who betrays the friend that trusts him, is guilty of a crime, even if his object be to serve another friend to whom he is under greater obligations.* But to speak only of actions done from the motive of duty, and in direct obedience to principle: it is a misapprehension of the utilitarian mode of thought, to conceive it as implying that people should fix their minds upon so wide a generality as the world, or society at large. The great majority of good actions are intended, not for the benefit of the world, but for that of individuals, of which the good of the world is made up; and the thoughts of the most virtuous man need not on these occasions travel beyond the particular persons concerned, except so far as is necessary to assure himself that in benefiting them he is not violating the rights—that is, the legitimate and authorized expectations—of any one else. The multiplication of happiness is, according to the utilitarian ethics, the object of virtue: the occasions on which any person (except one in a thousand) has it in his power to do this on an extended scale, in other words, to be a public benefactor, are but exceptional; and on these occasions alone is he called on to consider public utility; in every other case, private utility, the interest or happiness of some

---

*An opponent, whose intellectual and moral fairness it is a pleasure to acknowledge (the Rev. J. Llewelyn Davies), has objected to this passage, saying, "Surely the rightness or wrongness of saving a man from drowning does depend very much upon the motive with which it is done. Suppose that a tyrant, when his enemy jumped into the sea to escape from him, saved him from drowning simply in order that he might inflict upon him more exquisite tortures, would it tend to clearness to speak of that rescue as a morally right action?" Or suppose again, according to one of the stock illustrations of ethical inquiries, that a man betrayed a trust received from a friend, because the discharge of it would fatally injure that friend himself or some one belonging to him, would utilitarianism compel one to call the betrayal 'a crime' as much as if it had been done from the meanest motive?"

I submit, that he who saves another from drowning in order to kill him by torture afterwards, does not differ only in motive from him who does the same thing from duty or benevolence; the act itself is different. The rescue of the man is, in the case supposed, only the necessary first step of an act far more atrocious than leaving him to drown would have been. Had Mr. Davies said, "The rightness or wrongness of saving a man from drowning does depend very much"—not upon the motive, but— "upon the *intention*," no utilitarian would have differed from him. Mr. Davies, by an oversight too common not to be quite venial, has in this case confounded the very different ideas of Motive and Intention. There is no point which utilitarian thinkers (and Bentham pre-eminently) have taken more pains to illustrate than this. The morality of the action depends entirely upon the intention—that is, upon what the agent *wills to do*. But the motive, that is, the feeling which makes him will so to do, when it makes no difference in the act, makes none in the morality: though it makes a great difference in our moral estimation of the agent, especially if it indicates a good or a bad habitual *disposition*—a bent of character from which useful, or from which hurtful actions are likely to arise.

few persons, is all he has to attend to. Those alone the influence of whose actions extends to society in general, need concern themselves habitually about so large an object. In the case of abstinences indeed—of things which people forbear to do, from moral considerations, though the consequences in the particular case might be beneficial—it would be unworthy of an intelligent agent not to be consciously aware that the action is of a class which, if practised generally, would be generally injurious, and that this is the ground of the obligation to abstain from it. The amount of regard for the public interest implied in this recognition, is no greater than is demanded by every system of morals; for they all enjoin to abstain from whatever is manifestly pernicious to society.

The same considerations dispose of another reproach against the doctrine of utility, founded on a still grosser misconception of the purpose of a standard of morality, and of the very meaning of the words right and wrong. It is often affirmed that utilitarianism renders men cold and unsympathizing; that it chills their moral feelings towards individuals; that it makes them regard only the dry and hard consideration of the consequences of actions not taking into their moral estimate the qualities from which those actions emanate. If the assertion means that they do not allow their judgment respecting the rightness or wrongness of an action to be influenced by their opinion of the qualities of the person who does it, this is a complaint not against utilitarianism, but against any standard of morality at all; for certainly no known ethical standard decides an action to be good or bad because it is done by a good or a bad man, still less because done by an amiable, a brave, or a benevolent man, or the contrary. These considerations are relevant, not to the estimation of actions, but of persons; and there is nothing in the utilitarian theory inconsistent with the fact that there are other things which interest us in persons besides the rightness and wrongness of their actions. The Stoics, indeed, with the paradoxical misuse of language which was part of their system, and by which they strove to raise themselves above all concern about anything but virtue, were fond of saying that he who has that has everything; that he, and only he, is rich, is beautiful, is a king. But no claim of this description is made for the virtuous man by the utilitarian doctrine. Utilitarians are quite aware that there are other desirable possessions and qualities besides virtue, and are perfectly willing to allow to all of them full worth. They are also aware that a right action does not necessarily indicate a virtuous character, and that actions which are blameable often proceed from qualities entitled to praise. When this is apparent in any particular case, it modifies their estimation, not certainly of the act, but of the agent. I grant that they are, notwithstanding, of opinion, that in the long run the best proof of a good character is good actions; and resolutely refuse to consider any mental disposition as good, of which the predominant tendency is to produce bad conduct. This makes them unpopular with many people; but it is an unpopularity which they must share with every one who regards the distinction between right and wrong in a serious light; and the reproach is not one which a conscientious utilitarian need to be anxious to repel.

If no more be meant by the objection than that many utilitarians look on the morality of actions, as measured by the utilitarian standard, with too exclusive a regard, and do not lay sufficient stress upon the other beauties of character which go towards making a human being loveable or admirable, this may be admitted. Utilitarians who have cultivated their moral feelings, but not their sympathies nor their artistic perceptions, do fall into this mistake; and so do all other moralists under the same conditions. What can be said in excuse for other moralists is equally available for them, namely, that if there is to be any error, it is better that it should be on that side. As a matter of fact, we may affirm that among utilitarians as among adherents of other systems, there is every imaginable degree of rigidity and of laxity in the application of their standard: some are even puritanically rigorous, while others are as indulgent as can possibly be desired by sinner or by sentimentalist. But on the whole, a doctrine which brings prominently forward the interest that mankind has in the repression and prevention of conduct which violates the moral law is likely to be inferior to no other in turning the sanctions of opinion against such violations. It is true, the question, What does violate the moral law? is one on which those who recognize different standards of morality are likely now and then to differ. But difference of opinion on moral questions was not first introduced into the world by utilitarianism, while that doctrine does supply, if not always an easy, at all events a tangible and intelligible mode of deciding such differences.

It may not be superfluous to notice a few more of the common misapprehensions of utilitarian ethics, even those which are so obvious and gross that it might appear impossible for any person of candour and intelligence to fall into them: since persons, even of considerable mental endowments, often give themselves so little trouble to understand the bearings of any opinion against which they entertain a prejudice, and men are in general so little conscious of this voluntary ignorance as a defect, that the vulgarest misunderstandings of ethical doctrines are continually met with in the deliberate writings of persons of the greatest pretensions both to high principle and to philosophy. We not uncommonly hear the doctrine of utility inveighed against as a *godless* doctrine. If it be necessary to say anything at all against so mere an assumption, we may say that the question depends upon what idea we have formed of the moral character of the Deity. If it be a true belief that God desires, above all things, the happiness of his creatures, and that this was his purpose in their creation, utility is not only not a godless doctrine, but more profoundly religious than any other. If it be meant that utilitarianism does not recognize the revealed will of God as the supreme law of morals, I answer, that an utilitarian who believes in the perfect goodness and wisdom of God, necessarily believes that whatever God has thought fit to reveal on the subject of morals, must fulfil the requirements of utility in a supreme degree. But others besides utilitarians have been of opinion that the Christian revelation was intended, and is fitted, to inform the hearts and minds of mankind with a spirit which should enable them to find for themselves what is right, and incline them to do it when found, rather than to tell them, except in a very general way, what it is: and that we need a doctrine of ethics, carefully followed out, to *interpret* to us the will of God. Whether this opinion is correct or not, it is superfluous here to discuss; since whatever aid religion, either natural or revealed, can afford to ethical investigation, is as open to the utilitarian moralist as to any other. He can use it as the testimony of God to the usefulness or hurtfulness of any given course of action, by as good a right as others can use it for the indication of a transcendental law, having no connection with usefulness or with happiness.

Again, Utility is often summarily stigmatized as an immoral doctrine by giving it the name of Expediency, and taking advantage of the popular use of that term to contrast it with Principle. But the Expedient, in the sense in which it is opposed to the Right, generally means that which is expedient for the particular interest of the agent himself; as when a minister sacrifices the interests of his country to keep himself in place. When it means anything better than this, it means that which is expedient for some immediate object, some temporary purpose, but which violates a rule whose observance is expedient in a much higher degree. The Expedient, in this sense, instead of being the same thing with the useful, is a branch of the hurtful. Thus, it would often be expedient, for the purpose of getting over some momentary embarrassment, or attaining some object immediately useful to ourselves or others, to tell a lie. But inasmuch as the cultivation in ourselves of a sensitive feeling on the subject of veracity, is one of the most useful, and the enfeeblement of that feeling one of the most hurtful, things to which our conduct can be instrumental; and inasmuch as any, even unintentional, deviation from truth, does that much towards weakening the trustworthiness of human assertion, which is not only the principal support of all present social well-being, but the insufficiency of which does more than any one thing that can be named to keep back civilization, virtue, everything on which human happiness on the largest scale depends; we feel that the violation, for a present advantage, of a rule of such transcendent expediency, is not expedient, and that he who, for the sake of convenience to himself or to some other individual, does what depends on him to deprive mankind of the good, and inflict upon them the evil, involved in the greater or less reliance which they can place in each other's word, acts the part of one of their worst enemies. Yet that even this rule, sacred as it is, admits of possible exceptions, is acknowledged by all moralists; the chief of which is when the withholding of some fact (as of information from a male-factor, or of bad news from a person dangerously ill) would preserve some one (especially a person other than oneself) from great and unmerited evil, and when the withholding can only be effected by denial. But in order that the exception may not extend itself beyond the need, and may have the least possible effect in weakening reliance on veracity, it ought to be recognized, and, if possible, its limits defined; and if the principle of utility is good for anything, it must be good for weighing these conflicting utilities against one another, and marking out the region within which one or the other preponderates.

Again, defenders of utility often find themselves called upon to reply to such objections as this—that there is not time, previous to action, for calculating and weighing the effects of any line of conduct on the general happiness. This is exactly as if anyone were to say that it is impossible to guide our conduct by Christianity, because there is not time, on every occasion on which anything has to be done, to read through the Old and New Testaments. The answer to the objection is, that there has been ample time, namely, the whole past duration of the human species. During all that time mankind has been learning by experience the tendencies of actions; on which experience all the prudence, as well as all the morality of life, is dependent. People talk as if the commencement of this course of experience had hitherto been put off, and as if, at the moment when some man feels tempted to meddle with the property or life of another, he had to begin considering for the first time whether murder and theft are injurious to human happiness. Even then I do not think that he would find the question very puzzling; but, at all events, the matter is now done to his hand. It is truly a whimsical supposition, that if mankind was agreed in considering utility to be the test of morality, it would remain without any agreement as to what *is* useful, and would take no measures for having its notions on the subject taught to the young, and enforced by law and opinion. There is no difficulty in proving any ethical standard whatever to work ill, if we suppose universal idiocy to be conjoined with it, but on any hypothesis short of that, mankind must by this time have acquired positive beliefs as to the effects of some actions on its happiness; and the beliefs which have thus come down are the rules of morality for the multitude, and for the philosopher until he has succeeded in finding better. That philosophers might easily do this, even now, on many subjects; that the received code of ethics is by no means of divine right; and that mankind has still much to learn as to the effects of actions on the general happiness, I admit, or rather, earnestly maintain. The corollaries from the principle of utility, like the precepts of every practical art, admit of indefinite improvement, and, in a progressive state of the human mind, their improvement is perpetually going on. But to consider the rules of morality as improvable, is one thing; to pass over the intermediate generalisations entirely, and endeavour to test each individual action directly by the first principle, is another. It is a strange notion that the acknowledgment of a first principle is inconsistent with the admission of secondary ones. To inform a traveller respecting the place of his ultimate destination, is not to forbid the use of landmarks and direction-posts on the way. The proposition that happiness is the end and aim of morality, does not mean that no road ought to be laid down to that goal, or that persons going thither should not be advised to take one direction rather than another. Men really ought to leave off talking a kind of nonsense on this subject, which they would neither talk nor listen to on other matters of practical concernment. Nobody argues that the art of navigation is not founded on astronomy, because sailors cannot wait to calculate the *Nautical Almanack*. Being rational creatures, they go to sea with it ready calculated; and all rational creatures go out upon the sea of life with their minds made up on the common questions of right and wrong, as well as on many of the far more difficult questions of wise and foolish. And this, as long as foresight is a human quality, it is to be presumed they will continue to do. Whatever we adopt as the fundamental principle of morality, we require subordinate principles to apply it by: the impossibility of doing without them, being common to all systems, can afford no argument against any one in particular: but gravely to argue as if no such secondary principles could be had, and as if mankind had remained till now, and always must remain, without drawing any general conclusions from the experience of human life, is as high a pitch, I think, as absurdity has ever reached in philosophical controversy.

The remainder of the stock arguments against utilitarianism mostly consists in laying to its charge the common infirmities of human nature, and the general difficulties which embarrass conscientious persons in shaping their course through life. We are told that an utilitarian will be apt to make his own particular case an exception to moral rules, and when under temptation, will see an utility in the breach of a rule greater than he will see in its observance. But is utility the only creed which is able to furnish us with excuses for evil doing, and means of cheating our own conscience? They are afforded in abundance by all doctrines which recognize as a fact in morals the existence of conflicting considerations; which all doctrines do, that have been believed by sane persons. It is not the fault of any creed, but of the complicated nature of human affairs, that rules of conduct cannot be so framed as to require no exceptions, and that hardly any kind of action can safely be laid down as either always obligatory or always condemnable. There is no ethical creed which does not temper the rigidity of its laws, by giving a certain latitude, under the moral responsibility of the agent, for accommodation to peculiarities of circumstances; and under every creed, at the opening thus made, self-deception and dishonest casuistry get in. There exists no moral system under which there do not arise unequivocal cases of conflicting obligation. These are the real difficulties, the knotty points both in the theory of ethics, and in the conscientious guidance of personal conduct. They are overcome practically with greater or with less success according to the intellect and virtue of the individual; but it can hardly be pretended that anyone will be the less qualified for dealing with them, from possessing an ultimate standard to which conflicting rights and duties can be referred. If utility is the ultimate source of moral obligations, utility may be invoked to decide between them when their demands are incompatible. Though the application of the standard may be difficult, it is better than none at all: while in other systems, the moral laws all claiming independent authority, there is no common umpire entitled to interfere between them; their claims to precedence one over another rest on little better than sophistry, and unless determined, as they generally are, by the unacknowledged influence of considerations of utility, afford a free scope for the action of personal desires and partialities. We must remember that only in these cases of conflict between secondary principles is it requisite that first principles should be appealed to. There is no case of moral obligation in which some secondary principle is not involved; and if only one, there can seldom be any real doubt which one it is, in the mind of any person by whom the principle itself is recognized.

———

Chapter V

On the Connection Between Justice and Utility

In all ages of speculation one of the strongest obstacles to the reception of the doctrine that utility or happiness is the criterion of right and wrong has been drawn from the idea of justice. The powerful sentiment and apparently clear perception which that word recalls with a rapidity and certainty resembling an instinct have seemed to the majority of thinkers to point to an inherent quality in things; to show that the just must have an existence in nature as something absolute, generically distinct from every variety of the expedient and, in idea, opposed to it, though (as is commonly acknowledged) never, in the long run, disjoined from it in fact.

In the case of this, as of our other moral sentiments, there is no necessary connection between the question of its origin and that of its binding force. That a feeling is bestowed on us by nature does not necessarily legitimate all its promptings. The feeling of justice might be a peculiar instinct, and might yet require, like our other instincts, to be controlled and enlightened by a higher reason. If we have intellectual instincts leading us to judge in a particular way, as well as animal instincts that prompt us to act in a particular way, there is no necessity that the former should be more infallible in their sphere than the latter in theirs; it may as well happen that wrong judgments are occasionally suggested by those, as wrong actions by these. But though it is one thing to believe that we have natural feelings of justice, and another to acknowledge them as an ultimate criterion of conduct, these two opinions are very closely connected in point of fact. Mankind are always predisposed to believe that any subjective feeling, not otherwise accounted for, is a revelation of some objective reality. Our present object is to determine whether the reality to which the feeling of justice corresponds is one which needs any such special revelation, whether the justice or injustice of an action is a thing intrinsically peculiar and distinct from all its other qualities or only a combination of certain of those qualities presented under a peculiar aspect. . . .

To throw light upon this question, it is necessary to attempt to ascertain what is the distinguishing character of justice, or of injustice; what is the quality, or whether there is any quality, attributed in common to all modes of conduct designated as unjust (for justice, like many other moral attributes, is best defined by its opposite), and distinguishing them from such modes of conduct as are disapproved, but without having that particular epithet of disapprobation applied to them. If in everything which men are accustomed to characterize as just or unjust some one common attribute or collection of attributes is always present, we may judge whether this particular attribute or combination of attributes would be capable of gathering round it a sentiment of that peculiar character arid intensity by virtue of the general laws of our emotional constitution, or whether the sentiment is inexplicable and requires to be regarded as a special provision of nature. If we find the former to be the case, we shall, in resolving this question, have resolved also the main problem; if the latter, we shall have to seek for some other mode of investigating it.

To find the common attributes of a variety of objects, it is necessary to begin by surveying the objects themselves in the concrete. Let us therefore advert successively to the various modes of action and arrangements of human affairs which are classed, by universal or widely spread opinion, as just or as unjust. The things well known to excite the sentiments associated with those names are of a very multifarious character. I shall pass them rapidly in review, without studying any particular arrangement.

In the first place, it is mostly considered unjust to deprive anyone of his personal liberty, his property, or any other thing which belongs to him by law. Here, therefore, is one instance of the application of the terms "just" and "unjust" in a perfectly definite sense, namely, that it is just to respect, unjust to violate, the legal rights of anyone. But this judgment admits of several exceptions, arising from the other forms in which the notions of justice and injustice present themselves. For example, the person who suffers the deprivation may (as the phrase is) have *forfeited* the rights which he is so deprived of—a case to which we shall return presently. But also—

Secondly, the legal rights of which he is deprived may be rights which *ought* not to have belonged to him; in other words, the law which confers on him these rights may be a bad law. When it is so or when (which is the same thing for our purpose) it is supposed to be so, opinions will differ as to the justice or injustice of infringing it. Some maintain that no law, however bad, ought to be disobeyed by an individual citizen; that his opposition to it, if shown at all, should only be shown in endeavoring to get it altered by competent authority. This opinion (which condemns many of the most illustrious benefactors of mankind, and would often protect pernicious institutions against the only weapons which, in the state of things existing at the time, have any chance of succeeding against them) is defended by those who hold it on grounds of expediency, principally on that of the importance to the common interest of mankind, of maintaining inviolate the sentiment of submission to law. Other persons, again, hold the directly contrary opinion that any law, judged to be bad, may blamelessly be disobeyed, even though it be not judged to be unjust but only inexpedient, while others would confine the license of disobedience to the case of unjust laws; but, again, some say that all laws which are inexpedient are unjust, since every law imposes some restriction on the natural liberty of mankind, which restriction is an injustice unless legitimated by tending to their good. Among these diversities of opinion it seems to be universally admitted that there may be unjust laws, and that law, consequently, is not the ultimate criterion of justice, but may give to one person a benefit, or impose on another an evil, which justice condemns. When, however, a law is thought to be unjust, it seems always to be regarded as being so in the same way in which a breach of law is unjust, namely, by infringing somebody's right, which, as it cannot in this case be a legal right, receives a different appellation and is called a moral right. We may say, therefore, that a second case of injustice consists in taking or withholding from any person that to which he has a *moral right*.

Thirdly, it is universally considered just that each person should obtain that (whether good or evil) which he *deserves*, and unjust that he should obtain a good or be made to undergo an evil which he does not deserve. This is, perhaps, the clearest and most emphatic form in which the idea of justice is conceived by the general mind. As it involves the notion of desert, the question arises what constitutes desert? Speaking in a general way, a person is understood to deserve good if he does right, evil if he does wrong; and in a more particular sense, to deserve good from those to whom he does or has done good, and evil from those to whom he does or has done evil. The precept of returning good for evil has never been regarded as a case of the fulfillment of justice, but as one in which the claims of justice are waived, in obedience to other considerations.

Fourthly, it is confessedly unjust to *break faith* with anyone: to violate an engagement, either express or implied, or disappoint expectations raised by our own conduct, at least if we have raised those expectations knowingly and voluntarily. Like the other obligations of justice already spoken of, this one is not regarded as absolute, but as capable of being overruled by a stronger obligation of justice on the other side, or by such conduct on the part of the person concerned as is deemed to absolve us from our obligation to him and to constitute a *forfeiture* of the benefit which he has been led to expect.

Fifthly, it is, by universal admission, inconsistent with justice to be *partial*—to show favor or preference to one person over another in matters to which favor and preference do not properly apply. Impartiality, however, does not seem to be regarded as a duty in itself, but rather as instrumental to some other duty; for it is admitted that favor and preference are not always censurable, and, indeed, the cases in which they are condemned are rather the exception than the rule. A person would be more likely to be blamed than applauded for giving his family or friends no superiority in good offices over strangers when he could do so without violating any other duty; and no one thinks it unjust to seek one person in preference to another as a friend, connection, or companion. Impartiality where rights are concerned is of course obligatory, but this is involved in the more general obligation of giving to everyone his right. A tribunal, for example, must be impartial because it is bound to award, without regard to any other consideration, a disputed object to the one of two parties who has the right to it. There are other cases in which impartiality means being solely influenced by desert, as with those who, in the capacity of judges, preceptors, or parents, administer reward and punishment as such. There are cases, again, in which it means being solely influenced by consideration for the public interest, as in making a selection among candidates for a government employment. Impartiality, in short, as an obligation of justice, may be said to mean being exclusively influenced by the considerations which it is supposed ought to influence the particular case in hand, and resisting solicitation of any motives which prompt to conduct different from what those considerations would dictate.

Nearly allied to the idea of impartiality is that of *equality*, which often enters as a component part both into the conception of justice and into the practice of it, and, in the eyes of many persons, constitutes its essence. But in this, still more than in any other case, the notion of justice varies in different persons, and always conforms in its variations to their notion of utility. Each person maintains that equality is the dictate of justice, except where he thinks that expediency requires inequality. The justice of giving equal protection to the rights of all is maintained by those who support the most outrageous inequality in the rights themselves. Even in slave countries it is theoretically admitted that the rights of the slave, such as they are, ought to be as sacred as those of the master, and that a tribunal which fails to enforce them with equal strictness is wanting in justice; while, at the same time, institutions which leave to the slave scarcely any rights to enforce are not deemed unjust because they are not deemed inexpedient. Those who think that utility requires distinctions of rank do not consider it unjust that riches and social privileges should be unequally dispensed; but those who think this inequality inexpedient think it unjust also. Whoever thinks that government is necessary sees no injustice in as much inequality as is constituted by giving to the magistrate powers not granted to other people. Even among those who hold leveling doctrines, there are differences of opinion about expediency. Some communists consider it unjust that the produce of the labor of the community should be shared on any other principle than that of exact equality; others think it just that those should receive most whose wants are greatest; while others hold that those who work harder, or who produce more, or whose services are more valuable to the community, may justly claim a larger quota in the division of the produce. And the sense of natural justice may he plausibly appealed to in behalf of every one of these opinions. . . .

. . . [T]he character is still to be sought which distinguishes justice from other branches of morality. Now it is known that ethical writers divide moral duties into two classes, denoted by the ill-chosen expressions, duties of perfect and of imperfect obligation; the latter being those in which, though the act is obligatory, the particular occasions of performing it are left to our choice, as in the case of charity or beneficence, which we are indeed bound to practice but not toward any definite person, nor at any prescribed time. In the more precise language of philosophic jurists, duties of perfect obligation are those duties in virtue of which a correlative right resides in some person or persons; duties of imperfect obligation are those moral obligations which do not give birth to any right. I think it will be found that this distinction exactly coincides with that which exists between justice and the other obligations of morality. In our survey of the various popular acceptations of justice, the term appeared generally to involve the idea of a personal right—a claim on the part of one or more individuals, like that which the law gives when it confers a proprietary or other legal right. Whether the injustice consists in depriving a person of a possession, or in breaking faith with him, or in treating him worse than he deserves, or worse than other people who have no greater claims—in each case the supposition implies two things: a wrong done, and some assignable person who is wronged. Injustice may also be done by treating a person better than others; but the wrong in this case is to his competitors, who are also assignable persons. It seems to me that this feature in the case—a right in some person, correlative to the moral obligation—constitutes the specific difference between justice and generosity or beneficence. Justice implies something which it is not only right to do, and wrong not to do, but which some individual person can claim from us as his moral right. No one has a moral right to our generosity or beneficence because we are not morally to practice those virtues toward any given individual. . . .

Having thus endeavored to determine the distinctive elements which enter into the composition of the idea of justice, we are ready to enter on the inquiry whether the feeling which accompanies the idea is attached to it by a special dispensation of nature, or whether it could have grown up, by any known laws, out of the idea itself; and, in particular, whether it can have originated in considerations of general expediency.

I conceive that the sentiment itself does not arise from anything which would commonly or correctly be termed an idea of expediency, but that, though the sentiment does not, whatever is moral in it does.

We have seen that the two essential ingredients in the sentiment of justice are the desire to punish a person who has done harm and the knowledge or belief that there is some definite individual or individuals to whom harm has been done.

Now it appears to me that the desire to punish a person who has done harm to some individual is a spontaneous outgrowth from two sentiments, both in the highest degree natural and which either are or resemble instincts: the impulse of self-defense and the feeling of sympathy.

It is natural to resent and to repel or retaliate any harm done or attempted against ourselves or against those with whom we sympathize. The origin of this sentiment it is not necessary here to discuss. Whether it be an instinct or a result of intelligence, it is, we know, common to all animal nature; for every animal tries to hurt those who have hurt, or who it thinks are about to hurt, itself or its young. Human beings, on this point, only differ from other animals in two particulars. First, in being capable of sympathizing, not solely with their offspring, or, like some of the more noble animals, with some superior animal who is kind to them, but with all human, and even with all sentient, beings; secondly, in having a more developed intelligence, which gives a wider range to the whole of their sentiments, whether self-regarding or sympathetic. By virtue of his superior intelligence, even apart from his superior range of sympathy, a human being is capable of apprehending a community of interest between himself and the human society of which he forms a part, such that any conduct which threatens the security of the society generally is threatening to his own, and calls forth his instinct (if instinct it be) of self-defense. The same superiority of intelligence, joined to the power of sympathizing with human beings generally, enables him to attach himself to the collective idea of his tribe, his country, or mankind in such a manner that any act hurtful to them raises his instinct of sympathy and urges him to resistance.

The sentiment of justice, in that one of its elements which consists of the desire to punish, is thus, I conceive, the natural feeling of retaliation or vengeance, rendered by intellect and sympathy applicable to those injuries, that is, to those hurts, which wound us through, or in common with, society at large. This sentiment, in itself, has nothing moral in it; what is moral is the exclusive subordination of it to the social sympathies, so as to wait on and obey their call. For the natural feeling would make us resent indiscriminately whatever anyone does that is disagreeable to us; but, when moralized by the social feeling, it only acts in the directions conformable to the general good: just persons resenting a hurt to society, though not otherwise a hurt to themselves, and not resenting a hurt to themselves, however painful, unless it be of the kind which society has a common interest with them in the repression of. . . .

To recapitulate: the idea of justice supposes two things—a rule of conduct and a sentiment which sanctions the rule. The first must be supposed common to all mankind and intended for their good. The other (the sentiment) is a desire that punishment may be suffered by those who infringe the rule. There is involved, in addition, the conception of some definite person who suffers by the infringement, whose rights (to use the expression appropriated to the case) are violated by it. And the sentiment of justice appears to me to be the animal desire to repel or retaliate a hurt or damage to oneself or to those with whom one sympathizes, widened so as to include all persons, by the human capacity of enlarged sympathy and the human conception of intelligent self-interest. From the latter elements the feeling derives its morality; from the former, its peculiar impressiveness and energy of self-assertion.

I have, throughout, treated the idea of a *right* residing in the injured person and violated by the injury, not as a separate element in the composition of the idea and sentiment, but as one of the forms in which the other two elements clothe themselves. These elements are a hurt to some assignable person or persons, on the one hand, and a demand for punishment, on the other. An examination of our own minds, I think, will show that these two things include all that we mean when we speak of violation of a right. When we call anything a person's right, we mean that he has a valid claim on society to protect him in the possession of it, either by the force of law or by that of education and opinion. If he has what we consider a sufficient claim, on whatever account, to have something guaranteed to him by society, we say that he has a right to it. If we desire to prove that anything does not belong to him by right, we think this done as soon as it is admitted that society ought not to take measure for securing it to him, but should leave him to chance or to his own exertions. Thus a person is said to have a right to what he can earn in fair professional competition, because society ought not to allow any other person to hinder him from endeavoring to earn in that manner as much as he can. But he has not a right to three hundred a year, though he may happen to be earning it; because society is not called on to provide that he shall earn that sum. On the contrary, if he owns ten thousand pounds three-percent stock, he *has* a right to three hundred a year because society has come under an obligation to provide him with an income of that amount.

To have a right, then, is, I conceive, to have something which society ought to defend me in the possession of. If the objector goes on to ask why it ought, I can give him no other reason than general utility. If that expression does not seem to convey a sufficient feeling of the strength of the obligation, nor to account for the peculiar energy of the feeling, it is because there goes to the composition of the sentiment, not a rational only but also an animal element—the thirst for retaliation; and this thirst derives its intensity, as well as its moral justification, from the extraordinarily important and impressive kind of utility which is concerned. The interest involved is that of security, to everyone's feelings the most vital of all interests. All other earthly benefits are needed by one person, not needed by another; and many of them can, if necessary, be cheerfully foregone or replaced by something else; but security no human being can possibly do without; on it we depend for all our immunity from evil and for the whole value of all and every good, beyond the passing moment, since nothing but the gratification of the instant could be of any worth to us if we could be deprived of everything the next instant by whoever was momentarily stronger than ourselves. Now this most indispensable of all necessaries, after physical nutriment, cannot be had unless the machinery for providing it is kept unintermittedly in active play. Our notion, therefore, of the claim we have on our fellow creatures to join in making safe for us the very groundwork of our existence gathers feelings around it so much more intense than those concerned in any of the more common cases of utility that the difference in degree (as is often the case in psychology) becomes a real difference in kind. The claim assumes that character of absoluteness, that apparent infinity and incommensurability with all other considerations which constitute the distinction between the feeling of right and wrong and that of ordinary expediency and inexpediency. The feelings concerned are so powerful, and we count so positively on finding a responsive feeling in others (all being alike interested) that *ought* and *should* grow into *must,* and recognized indispensability becomes a moral necessity, analogous to physical, and often not inferior to it in binding force. . . .

. . . While I dispute the pretensions of any theory which sets up an imaginary standard of justice not grounded on utility, I account the justice which is grounded on utility to be the chief part, and incomparably the most sacred and binding part, of all morality. Justice is a name for certain classes of moral rules which concern the essentials of human well-being more nearly, and are therefore of more absolute obligation, than any other rules for the guidance of life; and the notion which we have found to be of the essence of the idea of justice—that of a right residing in an individual—implies and testifies to this more binding obligation.

The moral rules which forbid mankind to hurt one another (in which we must never forget to include a wrongful interference with each other's freedom) are more vital to human well-being than any maxims, however important, which only point out the best mode of managing some department of human affairs. They have also the peculiarity that they are the main element in determining the whole of the social feelings of mankind. It is their observance which alone preserves peace among human beings; if obedience to them were not the rule, and disobedience the exception, everyone would see in everyone else an enemy against whom he must be perpetually guarding himself. What is hardly less important, these are the precepts which mankind have the strongest and the most direct inducements for impressing upon one another. By merely giving to each other prudential instruction or exhortation, they may gain, or think they gain, nothing; in inculcating on each other the duty of positive beneficence, they have an unmistakable interest, but far less in degree; a person may possibly not need the benefits of others, but he always needs that they should not do him hurt. Thus the moralities which protect every individual from being harmed by others, either directly or by being hindered in his freedom of pursuing his own good, are at once those which he himself has most at heart and those which he has the strongest interest in publishing and enforcing by word and deed. It is by a person's observance of these that his fitness to exist as one of the fellowship of human beings is tested and decided; for on that depends his being a nuisance or not to those with whom he is in contact. Now it is these moralities primarily which compose the obligations of justice. The most marked cases of injustice, and those which give the tone to the feeling of repugnance which characterizes the sentiment, are acts of wrongful aggression or wrongful exercise of power over someone; the next are those which consist in wrongfully withholding from him something which is his due—in both cases inflicting on him a positive hurt, either in the form of direct suffering or of the privation of some good which he had reasonable ground, either of a physical or of a social kind, for counting upon.

The same powerful motives which command the observance of these primary moralities enjoin the punishment of those who violate them; and as the impulses of self-defense, of defense of others, and of vengeance are all called forth against such persons, retribution, or evil for evil, becomes closely connected with the sentiment of justice, and is universally included in the idea. Good for good is also one of the dictates of justice; and this, though its social utility is evident, and though it carries with it a natural human feeling, has not at first sight that obvious connection with hurt or injury which, existing in the most elementary cases of just and unjust, is the source of the characteristic intensity of the sentiment. But the connection, though less obvious, is not less real. He who accepts benefits and denies a return of them when needed inflicts a real hurt by disappointing one of the most natural and reasonable of expectations, and one which he must at least tacitly have encouraged, otherwise the benefits would seldom have been conferred. The important rank, among human evils and wrongs, of the disappointment of expectation is shown in the fact that it constitutes the principal criminality of two such highly immoral acts as a breach of friendship and a breach of promise. Few hurts which human beings can sustain are greater, and none wound more, than when that on which they habitually and with full assurance relied fails them in the hour of need; and few wrongs are greater than this mere withholding of good; none excite more resentment, either in the person suffering or in a sympathizing spectator. The principle, therefore, of giving to each what they deserve, that is, good for good as well as evil for evil, is not only included within the idea of justice as we have defined it, but is a proper object of that intensity of sentiment which places the just human estimation above the simply expedient.

Most of the maxims of justice current in the world, and commonly appealed to in its transactions, are simply instrumental to carrying into effect the principles of justice which we have now spoken of. That a person is only responsible for what he has done voluntarily, or could voluntarily have avoided, that it is unjust to condemn any person unheard; that the punishment ought to be proportioned to the offense, and the like, are maxims intended to prevent the just principle of evil for evil from being perverted to the infliction of evil without that justification. The greater part of these common maxims have come into use from the practice of courts of justice, which have been naturally led to a more complete recognition and elaboration than was likely to suggest itself to others, of the rules necessary to enable them to fulfill their double function—of inflicting punishment when due, and of awarding to each person his right.

That first of judicial virtues, impartiality, is an obligation of justice, partly for the reason last mentioned, as being a necessary condition of the fulfillment of other obligations of justice. But this is not the only source of the exalted rank, among human obligations, of those maxims of equality and impartiality, which, both in popular estimation and in that of the most enlightened, are included among the precepts of justice. In one point of view, they may be considered as corollaries from the principles already laid down. If it is a duty to do to each according to his deserts, returning good for good, as well as repressing evil by evil, it necessarily follows that we should treat all equally well (when no higher duty forbids) who have deserved equally well of us, and that society should treat all equally well who have deserved equally well of it, that is, who have deserved equally well absolutely. This is the highest abstract standard of social and distributive justice, toward which all institutions and the efforts of all virtuous citizens should be made in the utmost possible degree to converge. But this great moral duty rests upon a still deeper foundation, being a direct emanation from the first principle of morals, and not a mere logical corollary from secondary or derivative doctrines. It is involved in the very meaning of utility, or the greatest happiness principle. That principle is a mere form of words without rational signification unless one person's happiness, supposed equal in degree (with the proper allowance made for kind), is counted for exactly as much as another's. Those conditions being supplied, Bentham's dictum "everybody to count for one, nobody for more than one," might be written under the principle of utility as an explanatory commentary. The equal claim of everybody to happiness, in the estimation of the moralist and of the legislator, involves an equal claim to all the means of happiness except in so far as the inevitable conditions of human life and the general interest in which that of every individual is included set limits to the maxim; and those limits ought to be strictly construed. As every other maxim of justice, so this is by no means applied or held applicable universally; on the contrary, as I have already remarked, it bends to every person's ideas of social expediency. But in whatever case it is deemed applicable at all, it is held to be the dictate of justice. All persons are deemed to have a *right* to equality of treatment, except when some recognized social expediency requires the reverse. And hence all social inequalities which have ceased to be considered expedient assume the character, not of simple inexpediency, but of injustice, and appear so tyrannical that people are apt to wonder how they ever could have been tolerated—forgetful that they themselves, perhaps, tolerate other inequalities under an equally mistaken notion of expediency, the correction of which would make that which they approve seem quite as monstrous as what they have at last learned to condemn. The entire history of social improvement has been a series of transitions by which one custom or institution after another, from being a supposed primary necessity of social existence, has passed into the rank of a universally stigmatized injustice and tyranny. So it has been with the distinctions of slaves and freemen, nobles and serfs, patricians and plebeians; and so it will be, and in part already is, with the aristocracies of color, race, and sex.

It appears from what has been said that justice is a name for certain moral requirements which, regarded collectively, stand higher in the scale of social utility, and are therefore of more paramount obligation, than any others, though particular cases may occur in which some other social duty is so important as to overrule any one of the general maxims of justice. Thus, to save a life, it may not only be allowable, but a duty, to steal or take by force the necessary food or medicine, or to kidnap and compel to officiate the only qualified medical practitioner. In such cases, as we do not call anything justice which is not a virtue, we usually say, not that justice must give way to some other moral principle, but that what is just in ordinary cases is, by reason of that other principle, not just in the particular case. By this useful accommodation of language, the character of indefeasibility attributed to justice is kept up, and we are saved from the necessity of maintaining that there can be laudable injustice.

The considerations which have now been adduced resolve, I conceive, the only real difficulty in the utilitarian theory of morals. It has always been evident that all cases of justice are also cases of expediency; the difference is in the peculiar sentiment which attaches to the former, as contradistinguished from the latter. If this characteristic sentiment has been sufficiently accounted for; if there is no necessity to assume for it any peculiarity of origin; if it is simply the natural feeling of resentment, moralized by being made co-extensive with the demands of social good; and if this feeling not only does but ought to exist in all the classes of cases to which the idea of justice corresponds—that idea no longer presents itself as a stumbling block to the utilitarian ethics. Justice remains the appropriate name for certain social utilities which are vastly more important, and therefore more absolute and imperative, than any others are as a class (though not more so than others may be in particular cases); and which, therefore, ought to be, as well as naturally are, guarded by a sentiment, not only different in degree, but also in kind; distinguished from the milder feeling which attaches to the mere idea of promoting human pleasure or convenience at once by the more definite nature of its commands and by the sterner character of its sanctions.

Study Questions

1. Mill thinks that it is important to take into account the quality of a pleasure as well as the quantity, and this leads to his well-known distinction between the "higher" and "lower" pleasures. How does he draw this distinction? What determines whether a pleasure is higher or lower? How does this distinction distinguish his theory from Bentham's? Is this a plausible or important distinction?
2. Mill writes that "as between his own happiness and that of others, utilitarianism requires [one] to be as strictly impartial as a disinterested and benevolent spectator." What does he have in mind here? What are your reactions to this feature of the theory?
3. In answering the objection that the principle of utility is "too high for humanity," Mill is led to distinguish the "rule of action" from the "motive" of an action. What does this distinction amount to and how does it respond to the objection? Are motives important for a utilitarian?
4. Mill writes that "a right action does not necessarily indicate a virtuous character, and that actions which are blamable often proceed from qualities entitled to praise." How can that be?
5. What is Mill's account of why lying is wrong? What are the main differences between Mill's treatment of this issue and Kant's? Whose theory do you find more plausible on this issue?
6. Mill thinks that there is an important difference between justice and the kind of duty associated with generosity or beneficence. What is the difference?
7. Toward the end of the selection, Mill develops a utilitarian account of justice. What are the main features of his account? Is his account able to explain the importance that we attach to the idea of justice and to the priority that we give to claims of justice?
8. A standard objection to utilitarianism is that it must permit the violation of what we ordinarily think of as certain individual rights when that will promote greater general happiness. Does Mill's theory provide a satisfactory response to this objection?

Selected Bibliography

Berger, F. R. *Happiness, Justice and Freedom* (Berkeley: University of California Press, 1984), Part I. A review of Mill's ethics.
Crisp, Roger. *Mill on Utilitarianism* (London/New York: Routledge, 1997). A study of Mill's *Utilitarianism*.

Donner, Wendy. *The Liberal Self: John Stuart Mill's Moral and Political Philosophy* (Ithaca: Cornell University Press, 1991). Emphasizes importance of personal development in Mill's philosophy.

Lyons, David. *Rights, Welfare and Mill's Moral Theory* (Oxford: Oxford University Press, 1994). A general study of Mill's moral and political views.

———, ed. *Mill's Utilitarianism: Critical Essays* (Lanham, Md.: Rowman & Littlefield Publishers, 1997). An anthology of recent essays.

Mill, John Stuart, *On Liberty* (available in many editions). Mill's classic defense of individual civil liberties.

———. *The Subjection of Women* (available in many editions). Mill's defense of the equality of women.

Plamenatz, J. *The English Utilitarians* (Oxford: Blackwell, 1966), Chap. 8. A critical exposition of Mill's ethical views.

Ryan, A. *J.S. Mill* (London: Routledge & Kegan Paul, 1974), Chap. 4. A critical exposition of Mill's ethical views.

Skorupski, J. *John Stuart Mill* (London: Routledge, 1989), Chap. 9. A critical exposition of Mill's ethics.

15

FRIEDRICH NIETZSCHE

———

Friedrich Nietzsche (1844–1900) is both an influential and a highly controversial figure in the history of modern thought. His principal works on the subject of morality are *The Genealogy of Morals* and *Beyond Good and Evil.* Nietzsche is primarily a critic of modern morality, and he carries out his critique through a "genealogical method" that consists of an analysis, to some extent speculative, of the origin of moral terms. Historically, moral thought in the west has been influ-

> *Every elevation of the type "man," has hitherto been the work of an aristocratic society—and so will it always be—a society believing in a long scale of gradations of rank and differences of worth among human beings, and requiring slavery in some form or other.*

enced by the Judeo-Christian religious traditions and has found expression in the rise of modern democratic thought. Modern moral thought is egalitarian, both affirming the equal worth of all and expressing a concern for the well-being of all. However, Nietzsche believes that once we inquire into the origins of moral distinctions, they are not what they seem on the surface. He draws a distinction between "master-morality" and "slave-morality." Each is a set of distinctions invented by one social group, or kind of individual, for the purpose of conferring value on its own qualities and traits, in contradistinction to others. The master-morality of good and bad reflects the perspective of the noble, the powerful, the ruling class. Slave-morality is primarily a reaction by the masses to the evaluations contained in master-morality, and is based on fear and envy of the noble class. In Nietzsche's view, modern egalitarian morality is the slave-morality. Likewise, he thought that two of the dominant institutions of western society, democracy and Christianity, are expressions of slave-morality—democracy because it advocates the equality of all citizens, and Christianity because of its concern for the meek and those who suffer.

For Nietzsche, moralities are created through human beings as an act of self-assertion, and accepted moralities reflect existing relations of power. His critical attitude toward the accepted morality of his time seems based on what he regards as its leveling tendencies, because of which it is a barrier to the development of truly splendid human beings. Nietzsche at first glance appears to be an amoralist. To some extent that label is accurate, if "morality" is identified with the morality of good and evil that he rejects. But in a letter to a friend he spoke of himself as having "a more severe morality than anybody." The explanation of such apparent inconsistency is that, although he rejected the accepted morality of his own time, he had high moral standards of his own.

Although he was born in Germany, Nietzsche was contemptuous of German culture. Most of his adult life was spent outside his native land, first in Switzerland, where he was professor of classical philology at the University of Basel, and after his health broke down, in retirement in Italy, where he did most of his writing. Although Nietzsche was not widely read in his own lifetime, his work became very influential in the 20th century, and he is now regarded as a major figure in western thought.

———

Beyond Good and Evil

What Is Noble?

· **257.** Every elevation of the type "man," has hitherto been the work of an aristocratic society—and so will it always be—a society believing in a long scale of gradations of rank and differences of worth among human beings, and requiring slavery in some form or other. Without the *pathos of distance,* such as grows out of the incarnated difference of classes, out of the constant out-looking and down-looking of the ruling caste on subordinates and instruments, and out of their equally constant practice of obeying and commanding, of keeping down and keeping at a distance—that other more mysterious pathos could never have arisen, the longing for an ever new widening of distance within the soul itself, the formation of ever higher, rarer, further, more extended, more comprehensive states, in short, just the elevation of the type "man," the continued "self-surmounting of man," to use a moral formula in a supermoral sense. To be sure, one must not resign oneself to any humanitarian illusions about the history of the origin of an aristocratic society (that is to say, of the preliminary condition for the elevation of the type "man"): the truth is hard. Let us acknowledge unprejudicedly how every higher civilisation hitherto has *originated!* Men with a still natural nature, barbarians in every terrible sense of the word, men of prey, still in possession of unbroken strength of will and desire for power, threw themselves upon weaker, more moral, more peaceful races (perhaps trading or cattle-rearing

From Friedrich Nietzsche, *Beyond Good and Evil,* translated by Helen Zimmern, Vol. 12 of *The Complete Works of Friedrich Nietzsche,* General editor, Oscar Levy [1909–1911] (New York: Russell & Russell, 1964; London: George Allen & Unwin, Ltd.). Reprinted by permission of George Allen & Unwin, Ltd.

communities), or upon old mellow civilisations in which the final vital force was flickering out in brilliant fireworks of wit and depravity. At the commencement, the noble caste was always the barbarian caste: their superiority did not consist first of all in their physical, but in their psychical power—they were more *complete* men (which at every point also implies the same as "more complete beasts").

258. Corruption—as the indication that anarchy threatens to break out among the instincts, and that the foundation of the emotions, called "life," is convulsed—is something radically different according to the organisation in which it manifests itself. When, for instance, an aristocracy like that of France at the beginning of the Revolution, flung away its privileges with sublime disgust and sacrificed itself to an excess of its moral sentiments, it was corruption: it was really only the closing act of the corruption which had existed for centuries, by virtue of which that aristocracy had abdicated step by step its lordly prerogatives and lowered itself to a *function* of royalty (in the end even to its decoration and parade-dress). The essential thing, however, in a good and healthy aristocracy is that it should *not* regard itself as a function either of the kingship or the commonwealth, but as the *significance* and highest justification thereof—that it should therefore accept with a good conscience the sacrifice of a legion of individuals, who, *for its sake,* must be suppressed and reduced to imperfect men, to slaves and instruments. Its fundamental belief must be precisely that society is *not* allowed to exist for its own sake, but only as a foundation and scaffolding, by means of which a select class of beings may be able to elevate themselves to their higher duties, and in general to a higher *existence:* like those sun-seeking climbing plants in Java—they are called *Sipo Matador*—which encircle an oak so long and so often with their arms, until at last, high above it, but supported by it, they can unfold their tops in the open light, and exhibit their happiness.

259. To refrain mutually from injury, from violence, from exploitation, and put one's will on a par with that of others: this may result in a certain rough sense in good conduct among individuals when the necessary conditions are given (namely, the actual similarity of the individuals in amount of force and degree of worth, and their co-relation within one organisation). As soon, however, as one wished to take this principle more generally, and if possible even as *the fundamental principle of society,* it would immediately disclose what it really is—namely, a Will to the *denial* of life, a principle of dissolution and decay. Here one must think profoundly to the very basis and resist all sentimental weakness: life itself is *essentially* appropriation, injury, conquest of the strange and weak, suppression, severity, obtrusion of peculiar forms, incorporation, and at the least, putting it mildest, exploitation; but why should one forever use precisely these words on which for ages a disparaging purpose has been stamped? Even the organisation within which, as was previously supposed, the individuals treat each other as equal—it takes place in every healthy aristocracy—must itself, if it be a living and not a dying organisation, do all that towards other bodies, which the individuals within it refrain from doing to each other: it will have to be the incarnated Will to Power, it will endeavour to grow, to gain ground, attract to itself and acquire ascendency—not owing to any morality or immorality, but because it *lives,* and because life *is* precisely Will to Power. On no point, however, is the ordinary consciousness of Europeans more unwilling to be corrected than on this matter; people now rave everywhere, even under the guise of science, about coming conditions of society in which "the exploiting character" is to be absent: that sounds to my ears as if they promised to invent a mode of life which should refrain from all organic functions. "Exploitation" does not belong to a depraved, or imperfect and primitive society: it belongs to the *nature* of the living being as a primary organic function; it is a consequence of the intrinsic Will to Power, which is precisely the Will to Life. Granting that as a theory this is a novelty—as a reality it is the *fundamental fact* of all history: let us be so far honest towards ourselves!

260. In a tour through the many finer and coarser moralities which have hitherto prevailed or still prevail on the earth, I found certain traits recurring regularly together, and connected with one another, until finally two primary types revealed themselves to me, and a radical distinction was brought to light. There is *master-morality* and *slave-morality*—I would at once add, however, that in all higher and mixed civilisations, there are also attempts at the reconciliation of the two moralities; but one finds still oftener the confusion and mutual misunderstanding of them, indeed, sometimes their close juxtaposition—even in the same man, within one soul. The distinctions of moral values have either originated in a ruling caste, pleasantly conscious of being different from the ruled—or among the ruled class, the slaves and dependents of all sorts. In the first case, when it is the rulers who determine the conception "good," it is the exalted, proud disposition which is regarded as the distinguishing feature, and that which determines the order of rank. The noble type of man separates from himself the beings in whom the opposite of this exalted, proud disposition displays itself: he despises them. Let it at once be noted that in this first kind of morality the antithesis "good" and "bad" means practically the same as "noble" and "despicable"—the antithesis "good" and "*evil*" is of a different origin. The cowardly, the timid, the insignificant, and those thinking merely of narrow utility are despised; moreover, also, the distrustful, with their constrained glances, the self-abasing, the dog-like kind of men who let themselves be abused, the mendicant flatterers, and above all the liars: it is a fundamental belief of all aristocrats that the common people are untruthful. "We truthful ones"—the nobility in ancient Greece called themselves. It is obvious that everywhere the designations of moral value were at first applied to *men,* and were only derivatively and at a later period applied to *actions;* it is a gross mistake, therefore, when historians of morals start with questions like, "Why have sympathetic actions been praised?" The noble type of man regards *himself* as a determiner of values; he does not require to be approved of; he passes the judgment: "What is injurious to me is injurious in itself"; he knows that it is he himself only who confers honour on things; he is a *creator of values.* He honours whatever he recognizes in himself: such morality is self-glorification. In the foreground there is the feeling of plenitude, of power, which seeks to overflow, the happiness of high tension, the consciousness of a wealth which would fain give and bestow: the noble man also helps the unfortunate, but not—or scarcely—out of pity, but rather from an impulse generated by the superabundance of power. The noble man honours in himself the powerful one, him also who has power over himself, who knows how to speak and how to keep silence, who takes pleasure in subjecting himself to severity and hardness, and has reverence for all that is severe and hard. "Wotan placed a hard heart in my breast," says an old Scandinavian Saga: it is thus rightly expressed from the soul of a proud Viking. Such a type of man is even proud of *not* being made for sympathy; the hero of the Saga, therefore, adds warningly: "He who has not a hard heart when young, will never have one." The noble and brave who think thus are the furthest removed from the morality which sees precisely in sympathy, or in acting for the good of others, or in *désintéressement,* the characteristic of the moral; faith in one-self, pride in oneself, radical enmity and irony toward "selflessness," belong as def-initely to noble morality, as do a careless scorn and precaution in presence of sym-pathy and the "warm heart." It is the powerful who *know* how to honour, it is their art, their domain for invention. The profound reverence for age and for tra-dition—all law rests on this double reverence—the belief and prejudice in favour of ancestors and unfavourable to newcomers, is typical in the morality of the pow-erful; and if, reversely, men of "modern ideas" believe almost instinctively in "progress" and the "future," and are more and more lacking in respect for old age, the ignoble origin of these "ideas" has complacently betrayed itself thereby. A morality of the ruling class, however, is more especially foreign and irritating to present-day taste in the sternness of its principle that one has duties only to one's equals; that one may act towards beings of a lower rank, towards all that is foreign, just as seems good to one, or "as the heart desires," and in any case "beyond good and evil": it is here that sympathy and similar sentiments can have a place. The ability and obligation to exercise prolonged gratitude and prolonged revenge—both only within the circle of equals—artfulness in retaliation, *raffinement* of the idea in friendship, a certain necessity to have enemies (as outlets for the emotions of envy, quarrelsomeness, arrogance—in fact, in order to be a good *friend*): all these are typical characteristics of the noble morality, which, as has been pointed out, is not the morality of "modern ideas," and is therefore at present difficult to realise, and also to unearth and disclose.—It is otherwise with the second type of morality, *slave-morality.* Supposing that the abused, the oppressed, the suffering, the unemancipated, the weary, and those uncertain of themselves, should moralise, what will be the common element in their moral estimates? Probably a pessimistic suspicion with regard to the entire situation of man will find expression, perhaps a condemnation of man, together with his situation. The slave has an unfavourable eye for the virtues of the powerful; he has a scepticism and distrust, a *refinement* of distrust of everything "good" that is there honoured—he would fain persuade himself that the very happiness there is not genuine. On the other hand, *those* qual-ities which serve to alleviate the existence of sufferers are brought into prominence and flooded with light; it is here that sympathy, the kind, helping hand, the warm heart, patience, diligence, humility, and friendliness attain to honour; for here these are the most useful qualities, and almost the only means of supporting the burden of existence. Slave-morality is essentially the morality of utility. Here is the seat of the origin of the famous antithesis "good" and *"evil":* power and danger-ousness are assumed to reside in the evil, a certain dreadfulness, subtlety, and strength, which do not admit of being despised. According to slave-morality, therefore, the "evil" man arouses fear; according to master-morality, it is precisely the "good" man who arouses fear and seeks to arouse it, while the bad man is re-garded as the despicable being. The contrast attains its maximum when, in accor-dance with the logical consequences of slave-morality, a shade of depreciation—it may be slight and well-intentioned—at last attaches itself even to the "good" man of this morality; because, according to the servile mode of thought, the good man must in any case be the *safe* man: he is good-natured, easily deceived, perhaps a little stupid, *un bonhomme*. Everywhere that slave-morality gains the ascendency, language shows a tendency to approximate the significations of the words "good" and "stupid." A last fundamental difference: the desire for *freedom*, the instinct for happiness and the refinements of the feeling of liberty belong as necessarily to slave-morals and morality, as artifice and enthusiasm in reverence and devotion are the regular symptoms of an aristocratic mode of thinking and estimating. Hence we can understand without further detail why love *as a passion*—it is our European specialty—must absolutely be of noble origin; as is well known, its invention is due to the Provençal poet-cavaliers, those brilliant ingenious men of the *"gai saber,"* to whom Europe owes so much, and almost owes itself.

261. Vanity is one of the things which is perhaps most difficult for a noble man to understand: he will be tempted to deny it, where another kind of man thinks he sees it self-evidently. The problem for him is to represent to his mind beings who seek to arouse a good opinion of themselves which they themselves do not possess—and consequently also do not "deserve,"—and who yet *believe* in this good opinion afterwards. This seems to him on the one hand such bad taste and so self-disrespectful, and on the other hand so grotesquely unreasonable, that he would like to consider vanity an exception, and is doubtful about it in most cases when it is spoken of. He will say, for instance, "I may be mistaken about my value, and on the other hand may nevertheless demand that my value should be acknowledged by others precisely as I rate it: that, however, is not vanity (but self-conceit, or, in most cases, that which is called 'humility,' and also 'modesty')." Or he will even say, "For many reasons I can delight in the good opinion of others, perhaps because I love and honour them, and rejoice in all their joys, perhaps also because their good opinion endorses and strengthens my belief in my own good opinion, perhaps because the good opinion of others, even in cases where I do not share it, is useful to me, or gives promise of usefulness: all this, however, is not vanity." The man of noble character must first bring it home forcibly to his mind, especially with the aid of history, that, from time immemorial, in all social strata in any way dependent, the ordinary man *was* only that which he *passed for*—not being at all accustomed to fix values, he did not assign even to himself any other value than that which his master assigned to him (it is the peculiar *right of masters* to create values). It may be looked upon as the result of an extraordinary atavism, that the ordinary man, even at present, is still always *waiting* for an opinion about himself, and then instinctively submitting himself to it; yet by no means only to a "good" opinion, but also to a bad and unjust one (think, for instance, of the greater part of the self-appreciations and self-depreciations which believing women learn from their confessors, and which in general the believing Christian learns from his Church). In fact, conformably to the slow rise of the democratic social order (and its cause, the blending of the blood of masters and slaves), the originally noble and rare impulse of the masters to assign a value to themselves and to "think well" of themselves, will now be more and more encouraged and extended; but it has at all times an older, ampler, and more radically ingrained propensity opposed to it—and in the phenomenon of "vanity" this older propensity over-masters the younger. The vain person rejoices over *every* good opinion which he hears about himself (quite apart from the point of view of its usefulness, and equally regardless of its truth or falsehood), just as he suffers from every bad opinion: for he subjects himself to both, he *feels* himself subjected to both, by that oldest instinct of subjection which breaks forth in him. It is "the slave" in the vain man's blood, the remains of the slave's craftiness—and how much of the "slave" is still left in woman, for instance!—which seeks to *seduce* to good opinions of itself; it is the slave, too, who immediately afterwards falls prostrate himself before these opinions, as though he had not called them forth. And to repeat it again: vanity is an atavism.

262. A *species* originates, and a type becomes established and strong in the long struggle with essentially constant *unfavourable* conditions. On the other hand, it is known by the experience of breeders that species which receive superabundant nourishment, and in general a surplus of protection and care, immediately tend in the most marked way to develop variations, and are fertile in prodigies and monstrosities (also in monstrous vices). Now look at an aristocratic commonwealth, say an ancient Greek *polis,* or Venice, as a voluntary or involuntary contrivance for the purpose of *rearing* human beings; there are these men beside one another, thrown upon their own resources, who want to make their species prevail, chiefly because they *must* prevail, or else run the terrible danger of being exterminated. The favour, the superabundance, the protection are there lacking under which variations are fostered; the species needs itself as species, as something which, precisely by virtue of its hardness, its uniformity, and simplicity of structure, can in general prevail and make itself permanent in constant struggle with its neighbours, or with rebellious or rebellion-threatening vassals. The most varied experience teaches it what are the qualities to which it principally owes the fact that it still exists, in spite of all Gods and men, and has hitherto been victorious: these qualities it calls virtues, and these virtues alone it develops to maturity. It does so with severity, indeed it desires severity; every aristocratic morality is intolerant in the education of youth, in the control of women, in the marriage customs, in the relations of old and young, in the penal laws (which have an eye only for the degenerating): it counts intolerance itself among the virtues, under the name of "justice." A type with few, but very marked features, a species of severe, warlike, wisely silent, reserved and reticent men (and as such, with the most delicate sensibility for the charm and *nuances* of society) is thus established, unaffected by the vicissitudes of generations; the constant struggle with uniform *unfavourable* conditions is, as already remarked, the cause of a type becoming stable and hard. Finally, however, a happy state of things results, the enormous tension is relaxed; there are perhaps no more enemies among the neighbouring peoples, and the means of life, even of the enjoyment of life, are present in superabundance. With one stroke the bond and constraint of the old discipline severs: it is no longer regarded as necessary, as a condition of existence—if it would continue, it can only do so as a form of *luxury,* as an archaising *taste.* Variations, whether they be deviations (into the higher, finer, and rarer), or deteriorations and monstrosities, appear suddenly on the scene in the greatest exuberance and splendour; the individual dares to be individual and detach himself. At this turning-point of history there manifest themselves, side by side, and often mixed and entangled together, a magnificent, manifold, virgin-forest-like up-growth and up-striving, a kind of *tropical tempo* in the rivalry of growth, and an extraordinary decay and self-destruction, owing to the savagely opposing and seemingly exploding egoisms, which strive with one another "for sun and light," and

can no longer assign any limit, restraint, or forbearance for themselves by means of the hitherto existing morality. It was this morality itself which piled up the strength so enormously, which bent the bow in so threatening a manner: it is now "out of date," it is getting "out of date." The dangerous and disquieting point has been reached when the greater, more manifold, more comprehensive life *is lived beyond* the old morality; the "individual" stands out, and is obliged to have recourse to his own law-giving, his own arts and artifices for self-preservation, self-elevation, and self-deliverance. Nothing but new "Whys," nothing but new "Hows," no common formulas any longer, misunderstanding and disregard in league with each other, decay, deterioration, and the loftiest desires frightfully entangled, the genius of the race overflowing from all the cornucopias of good and bad, a portentous simultaneousness of Spring and Autumn, full of new charms and mysteries peculiar to the fresh, still unexhausted, still unwearied corruption. Danger is again present, the mother of morality, great danger; this time shifted into the individual, into the neighbour and friend, into the street, into their own child, into their own heart, into all the most personal and secret recesses of their desires and volitions. What will the moral philosophers who appear at this time have to preach? They discover, these sharp onlookers and loafers, that the end is quickly approaching, that everything around them decays and produces decay, that nothing will endure until the day after tomorrow, except one species of man, the incurably *mediocre*. The mediocre alone have a prospect of continuing and propagating themselves—they will be the men of the future, the sole survivors; "be like them! become mediocre!" is now the only morality which has still a significance, which still obtains a hearing. But it is difficult to preach this morality of mediocrity! It can never avow what it is and what it desires! It has to talk of moderation and dignity and duty and brotherly love—it will have difficulty *in concealing its irony!*

263. There is an *instinct for rank,* which more than anything else is already the sign of a *high rank;* there is a *delight* in the *nuances* of reverence which leads one to infer noble origin and habits. The refinement, goodness, and loftiness of a soul are put to a perilous test when something passes by that is of the highest rank, but is not yet protected by the awe of authority from obtrusive touches and incivilities: something that goes its way like a living touchstone, undistinguished, undiscovered, and tentative, perhaps voluntarily veiled and disguised. He whose task and practice it is to investigate souls, will avail himself of many varieties of this very art to determine the ultimate value of a soul, the unalterable, innate order of rank to which it belongs: he will test it by its *instinct for reverence.* *Differérence engendre haine:* the vulgarity of many a nature spurts up suddenly like dirty water, when any holy vessel, any jewel from closed shrines, any book bearing the marks of great destiny, is brought before it; while on the other hand, there is an involuntary silence, a hesitation of the eye, a cessation of all gestures, by which it is indicated that a soul *feels* the nearness of what is worthiest of respect. The way in which, on the whole, the reverence for the *Bible* has hitherto been maintained in Europe, is perhaps the best example of discipline and refinement of manners which Europe owes to Christianity: books of such profoundness and supreme significance require for their protection an external tyranny of authority, in order to acquire the *period* of thousands of years which is necessary to exhaust and unriddle them. Much has been achieved when the sentiment has been at last instilled into the masses (the shallow-pates and the boobies of every kind) that they are not allowed to touch everything, that there are holy experiences before which they must take off their shoes and keep away the unclean hand—it is almost their highest advance towards humanity. On the contrary, in the so-called cultured classes, the believers in "modern ideas," nothing is perhaps so repulsive as their lack of shame, the easy insolence of eye and hand with which they touch, taste, and finger everything; and it is possible that even yet there is more *relative* nobility of taste, and more tact for reverence among the people, among the lower classes of the people, especially among peasants, than among the newspaper-reading *demimonde* of intellect, the cultured class.

264. It cannot be effaced from a man's soul what his ancestors have preferably and most constantly done: whether they were perhaps diligent economisers attached to a desk and a cash-box, modest and citizen-like in their desires, modest also in their virtues; or whether they were accustomed to commanding from morning till night, fond of rude pleasures and probably of still ruder duties and responsibilities; or whether, finally, at one time or another, they have sacrificed old privileges of birth and possession, in order to live wholly for their faith—for their "God,"—as men of an inexorable and sensitive conscience, which blushes at every compromise. It is quite impossible for a man *not* to have the qualities and predilections of his parents and ancestors in his constitution, whatever appearances may suggest to the contrary. This is the problem of race. Granted that one knows something of the parents, it is admissible to draw a conclusion about the child: any kind of offensive incontinence, any kind of sordid envy, or of clumsy self-vaunting—the three things which together have constituted the genuine plebeian type in all times—such must pass over to the child, as surely as bad blood; and with the help of the best education and culture one will only succeed in *deceiving* with regard to such heredity. And what else does education and culture try to do nowadays! In our very democratic, or rather, very plebeian age, "education" and "culture" *must* be essentially the art of deceiving—deceiving with regard to origin, with regard to the inherited plebeianism in body and soul. An educator who nowadays preached truthfulness above everything else, and called out constantly to his pupils: "Be true! Be natural! Show yourselves as you are!"—even such a virtuous and sincere ass would learn in a short time to have recourse to the *furca* of Horace, *naturam expellere:* with what results? "Plebeianism" *usque recurret.*

265. At the risk of displeasing innocent ears, I submit that egoism belongs to the essence of a noble soul; I mean the unalterable belief that to a being such as "we," other beings must naturally be in subjection, and have to sacrifice themselves. The noble soul accepts the fact of his egoism without question, and also without consciousness of harshness, constraint, or arbitrariness therein, but rather as something that may have its basis in the primary law of things: if he sought a designation for it he would say: "It is justice itself." He acknowledges under certain circumstances, which made him hesitate at first, that there are other equally privileged ones; as soon as he has settled this question of rank, he moves among those equals and equally privileged ones with the same assurance, as regards modesty and delicate respect, which he enjoys in intercourse with himself—in accordance with an innate heavenly mechanism which all the stars understand. It is an *additional* instance of his egoism, this artfulness and self-limitation in intercourse with his equals—every star is a similar egoist;

he honours *himself* in them, and in the rights which he concedes to them, he has no doubt that the exchange of honours and rights, as the *essence* of all intercourse, belongs also to the natural condition of things. The noble soul gives as he takes, prompted by the passionate and sensitive instinct of requital, which is at the root of his nature. The notion of "favour" has, *inter pares,* neither significance nor good repute; there may be a sublime way of letting gifts as it were light upon one from above, and of drinking them thirstily like dewdrops; but for those arts and displays the noble soul has no aptitude. His egoism hinders him here: in general, he looks "aloft" unwillingly—he looks either *forward,* horizontally and deliberately, or downwards—*he knows that he is on a height.*

———

Study Questions

1. Nietzsche distinguishes two dichotomies, "good" versus "bad," and "good" versus "evil." How does he think that these two dichotomies originate? What are the values associated with each of these dichotomies? How plausible is Nietzsche's account of their origin?
2. What do you think Nietzsche means by the title of his book?
3. Nietzsche presents a critique of the "morality of modern ideas" (or "the morality of utility") by calling it "slave-morality." What is his critique? If Nietzsche's account of the origin of "modern morality" is correct, what should our response be?
4. What is Nietzsche's attitude toward democracy? Christianity? What is your response to his views?
5. Using Nietzsche's descriptions, how would you classify yourself—as one of the "masters"? One of the "slaves"? Neither? Why?
6. What is Nietzsche's own positive ethical outlook in this essay?

Selected Bibliography

Ansell-Pearson, Keith. *Nietzsche contra Rousseau: A Study of Nietzsche's Moral and Political Thought* (New York/Cambridge: Cambridge University Press, 1991). A study of Nietzsche's moral and political thought.

Berkowitz, P. *Nietzsche: Ethics of an Immoralist* (Cambridge, Mass.: Harvard University Press, 1995). A commentary on some of Nietzsche's main writings.

Danto, A. *Nietzsche as Philosopher* (New York: Macmillan, 1965), esp. Chap. 5. A critical exposition of Nietzsche's views.

Magnus, Bernd and Higgins, Kathleen M. *The Cambridge Companion to Nietzsche* (New York/Cambridge: Cambridge University Press, 1996). An anthology of essays on Nietzsche's philosophy.

Nehemas, Alexander. *Nietzsche: Life as Literature* (Cambridge, Mass.: Harvard University Press, 1985). An important study.

Schacht, Richard. *Nietzsche* (London: Routledge and Kegan Paul, 1983). A general study of Nietzsche's philosophy.

———, ed. *Nietzsche, Genealogy, Morality* (Berkeley, University of California Press, 1994). A collection of recent essays.

PART
THREE

—

THE CONTEMPORARY ERA

Moral philosophy is currently one of the most active areas of contemporary philosophy. One reason for its vitality is that, although it approaches value questions at a level of abstraction that removes them a step from ordinary life, moral philosophy addresses issues of ongoing practical concern. The issues include questions about the nature of right action, the requirements of justice, the virtues that make a life good, whether there are universally valid moral principles, the basis of moral obligation and the source of moral motivation, and the weight of moral concerns relative to nonmoral reasons and the role of moral concerns in giving value and meaning to life. All are questions that arise in a natural way when we reflect about how to act and interact with others, and about how to live.

For much of the 20th century, moral philosophers were more concerned with meta-ethics than with normative ethics. Normative ethics is concerned with identifying and arguing for substantive principles and values by which to assess conduct, the ends of action, states of character, social structures, public policy, and so on. Utilitarianism, Kantianism and other deontological theories, and theories of the virtues are all examples of normative ethical theories. Likewise, applied ethical theories that address contemporary social issues, such as the morality of abortion, physician-assisted suicide, capital punishment, affirmative action, or the justification of war, fall under normative ethics. Meta-ethics, by contrast, is concerned with such issues as the nature and status of moral discourse, the distinction between factual claims and value claims, the meaning of moral terms such as "right" and "good," and the ways in which moral claims are justified. Philosophers who pursue meta-ethical questions tend to abstract from the normative content of moral claims, without committing themselves to any specific normative view. That said, in many areas it is difficult to maintain a sharp separation between meta-ethical and normative questions, and a philosopher's meta-ethical views may lead to a particular normative view, and vice versa. The work of G. E. Moore at the beginning of the 20th century was instrumental in shifting the focus of moral philosophy in the English-speaking world towards meta-ethical questions. The selection from Moore presented here asks whether the value term "good" can be defined in terms of or reduced to purely descriptive and psychological terms, such as "is the object of desire." Moore denies that it can and adopts a position, sometimes called "non-naturalism," according to which moral and evaluative language (such as "good," "right," and so on) cannot be defined in naturalistic terms; it contains an ineliminable normative dimension that cannot be captured in naturalistic or purely descriptive language.

Although meta-ethical questions remain important, there has been a shift in emphasis in the last several decades back towards normative ethics and related issues in the foundations of ethics. This change is often traced to the appearance in 1971 of John Rawls's *A Theory of Justice*. Since the 19th century, utilitarianism in different forms had been the reigning (though of course not the only) normative theory in the English-speaking world. Rawls's book presented a systematic theory of social justice that took its inspiration from Kant and the social contract tradition. It provided an alternative to utilitarianism, and moreover addressed important social questions. As a result, Rawls's work rekindled a number of debates in normative ethics and led to renewed attention to Kantian approaches to ethics. It elicited replies and critical responses from utilitarians, as well as from many other quarters, and in addition led many philosophers to pursue Kantian approaches to moral theory. A great deal of moral theory from the last three decades shows the influence of Rawls in one way or another, either by developing views in opposition to his or by building on or trying to extend his insights.

Whatever the explanation for this shift towards normative ethics, it is now a flourishing enterprise. Part III of this anthology concentrates on normative theories and tries to provide representative selections from some of the leading writers and major trends in normative ethics and related issues in the foundations of ethics.

One basic distinction among normative moral theories is the distinction between teleological or consequentialist theories and deontological or nonconsequentialist theories—although, as we shall see in a moment, this classification is far from exhaustive. Consequentialist theories assess the rightness of an action in terms of its overall consequences, or its tendency to promote a certain overall end (or *telos*). Somewhat more precisely, a consequentialist theory begins by developing a theory of the good. It then defines right action as that action available to an agent that produces the most overall good. Such theories are concerned with the promotion or maximization of "aggregate" good: to assess the rightness of an action, one must take into account all the expected good and bad consequences, estimate the overall amount of good produced, and compare that amount to the total good that would be produced by the alternatives. An example of consequentialism is utilitarianism, which defines the good as utility—understood variously as the balance of pleasure over pain, satisfaction of human preferences, or happiness—and then defines the right as that which maximizes overall utility.

Deontological theories are nonconsequentialist because they do not define what is right in terms of what maximizes overall good. Although they do not ignore the consequences of action, they claim that certain ways of acting are right or wrong in themselves, independently of their consequences or of the ends that they promote. Deontological theories hold that there are principles of right conduct that apply immediately to our actions, requiring or prohibiting certain actions in certain circumstances without reference to any further end beyond the action. One role of deontological principles is to function as constraints on the ends or goals that we may permissibly adopt, or to restrict the means that we may take to our permissible ends. Kant's moral theory is deontological because it understands acting rightly as conformity to principle—acting from principles that can be willed as universal law for all rational agents, or from principles that respect humanity as an end-in-itself. Actions and ends that cannot be universalized, or that fail to respect humanity as an end, are impermissible and have no value. This is a feature of Kant's doctrine of the absolute value of the good will: The good will is the condition of the goodness of anything else, in that nothing can have value unless it is consistent with the requirements of a good will (a will that acts from moral principle so understood).

Deontological theories are represented in the selections from W. D. Ross, John Rawls, T. M. Scanlon, and Thomas Nagel. W. D. Ross was an important proponent of the deontological approach to ethics in the first half of the 20th century. He rejected the utilitarian view that actions are made right simply by the goodness of their consequences, arguing instead that certain kinds of action are *prima facie* right or wrong simply because of the kinds of acts they are. For example, we should keep a promise simply because we have made it, or show gratitude towards a benefactor simply because of the service that we have received; an act of injuring others is wrong in itself. John Rawls's theory of social justice is a deontological theory that draws on certain aspects of Kant. Rawls's theory of "justice as fairness" holds that the most reasonable principles of justice for a modern democratic society are those that would result from a hypothetical choice that is fair to all citizens. Principles of justice are those that free and equal persons would choose for themselves to regulate the basic structure of their society. They are the basis of fundamental individual rights that may not be overridden for reasons of overall social welfare. T. M. Scanlon outlines a natural extension of Rawls's theory of social justice into a general moral theory that he calls "contractualism." Contractualism is a philosophical account of the nature of right and wrong that ties these notions to reasonable agreement among individuals. It holds that an act is wrong if it would be disallowed by principles that no one could reasonably reject. For Scanlon, to be reasonable is to be moved by a desire to find generally acceptable principles that people can cite to justify their actions to each other. Thomas Nagel addresses a problem that can arise for deontological views. As Ross pointed out, deontology acknowledges that an action can be right even if some alternative has better overall consequences. But some theorists have asked, how can it be rational not to choose the better overall outcome? Nagel offers an explanation that defends the reality of deontological constraints.

Throughout its history, utilitarianism has had both passionate expositors and critics. G. E. Moore and R. M. Hare represent utilitarianism in this section. Moore supports a utilitarian approach by arguing that ethics must be concerned with what produces the most overall good, and he develops an analysis of the structure of utilitarian reasoning. Important criticisms of utilitarianism have been articulated by Ross, in response to Moore, and later by Rawls. One common criticism is that utilitarianism has implications that are highly counterintuitive and at odds with common sense—for example, that utilitarianism must permit the sacrifice of the few, or the violation of common sense moral rules, if that will promote greater overall utility. (Rawls offers an influential diagnosis of this problem.) R. M. Hare has been a prominent defender of utilitarianism in recent decades. Hare lays out the general theoretical basis for utilitarianism. He then argues that a distinction exists between two levels of moral thinking, what he calls "critical thinking" and "intuitive thinking"—elements of which can be found in Mill's *Utilitarianism*. Hare argues that proper use of this distinction can defend utilitarianism against the common objections.

Recent decades have seen the emergence of an alternative to standard deontological and consequentialist approaches to normative ethics, which is known as "virtue theory" or "virtue ethics." A number of philosophers, inspired by classical Greek philosophers—in particular Aristotle—and by Aquinas, have argued that contemporary moral theory has ignored important regions of ethical thought and that greater attention to the subject of the virtues is needed to remedy this defect. Despite their differences, deontological and consequentialist theories both develop theories of right action in which the notions of duty and obligation figure centrally. Virtue theorists, however, focus on character, the good or worthy life, and the role of the virtues therein. As is sometimes said, the basic question for virtue theory is not "How should I act?", but "How should I live?" or "What kind of person should I be?" Philippa Foot is one writer who has directed the attention of contemporary philosophers to the virtues, and her essay develops several theses about the concept of a virtue. The essay by Rosalind Hursthouse takes up the issue of whether virtue theory, given its emphasis on agents rather than actions, can indeed provide guidance about action, which it must if it is to be a real and viable alternative to deontology and consequentialism.

Another important recent trend is the emergence of feminist ethics. Like virtue theorists, some feminist philosophers have voiced the concern that mainstream moral theory, due to its emphasis on general and impersonal principles, has overlooked significant dimensions of moral thought. They have thought that the leading moral theories have not been fully representative of the perspective and concerns of women, and that they fail to detect some of the barriers to the full social equality of women. Annette Baier develops a critique of the primacy assigned to justice and impersonal principles by contemporary Kantian theories, and explores the shortcomings of a moral theory that relies exclusively on such notions. Martha Nussbaum analyzes some of the main objections that feminists have directed at contemporary liberal theories and shows how they can be addressed.

Alongside the controversies between the leading normative theories, contemporary moral philosophers have continued to grapple with what one might call "foundational" questions. One such issue that has been very important in the contemporary era is that of moral relativism—the claim that there are no universal moral principles. This issue figures in selections by Bernard Williams and Gilbert Harman. Williams points out a fallacy in certain very simple forms of moral relativism. Harman develops a version of moral relativism that avoids this fallacy and attempts to pinpoint the assumptions that divide relativists from absolutists, though without trying to resolve the controversy. Another cluster of issues concerns the basis of moral obligation: Where do moral obligations get their hold on us, or their normative force? What is the connection between morality and rational self-interest? What is the source of moral motivation, and the importance that we assign to moral requirements? The selection by Williams ("The Amoralist") raises some of these questions in stark form by depicting a figure who is completely indifferent to moral concerns. Can such a person be given a reason to be moral? What does such a figure show us about the reasons we have for being moral? David Gauthier develops a modern Hobbesian account of the basis of moral obligation, arguing that we have reasons of long-term self-interest to accept and to comply with moral constraints. Moreover, according to Gauthier morality can have rational force for us only if it can be based in this way on self-interest. T. M. Scanlon and Christine Korsgaard develop Kantian approaches to these foundational questions that reject the Hobbesian tenet that reasons must be based in self-interest. Scanlon's contractualism identifies the desire to be able to justify our actions to others as the basis of moral motivation and of the importance that we accord moral considerations. Korsgaard locates the basis of moral obligation in the capacity to give laws to oneself that is part of being a reflective, rational agent. Finally, Jean-Paul Sartre's existentialism bases all values on a radical form of human freedom. There is no fixed human nature that can ground values; rather, as individuals we are responsible for creating ourselves and our values through the choices that we make in life.

In any survey of the questions that have occupied moral philosophers, as well as the divergent answers that have been proposed to these questions, one is struck by how rich and fertile this area of human inquiry is. It is nearly impossible to predict where moral philosophy will take us in the 21st century. But if the developments of the 20th century are any indication of what is to come, we have much to look forward to.

16

G. E. MOORE

—

G. E. Moore's *Principia Ethica* was one of the most influential books in moral philosophy during the first half of the 20th century. Moore strove for precision and

> *If I am asked "What is good?" my answer is that good is good, and that is the end of the matter.*

rigor, believing that many problems of traditional moral theory rested on errors that could have been avoided had the writers been more careful. In particular, through painstaking analysis he tried to avoid what he considered the most egregious error of writing about ethical theory—identifying concepts and things that are in fact different from each other. It is significant that his title page quotes as a motto Bishop Butler's famous statement: "Everything is what it is, and not another thing."

One reason for the importance of *Principia Ethica* is that it shifted the focus of moral philosophy for much of the 20th century. Moore's main interest was not with questions such as "What is the greatest good in life?" or "How ought one to act?" Although he discussed such issues, he was more concerned with the quite different question, "What is the meaning of 'good'?" Ethical theory, for him, was not so much the elaboration of a theory of the good life or of moral conduct as it was the attempt to understand the meaning of the basic concepts of moral thought. The study of the meaning of ethical terms and related issues is known as "meta-ethics," in contrast with "normative ethics," which is concerned with substantive questions such as the nature of the good, the basic principles of right action, or the human virtues. Following Moore's lead, most moral philosophy in the Anglo-American tradition in the half century following the publication of *Principa Ethica* was concerned with problems of meta-ethics, and meta-ethical questions remain important today.

In this vein, Moore argues that "good" refers to a simple and indefinable quality, and argues that it is a mistake to identify goodness with any other property or complex of properties. In particular, it is a mistake to identify goodness with any natural property, such as being pleasurable or being the object of desire. He supports his claims with the so-called "open question argument." Suppose that someone claims that "good" means "is the object of desire," or identifies the property of goodness with that of being the object of desire. We can still ask, "But is the object of desire good?" But if this question is meaningful, then these properties are not the same. More generally, for any natural property, X, that is purportedly identical with goodness, it is still an open question as to whether X is good. But if this question is significant, goodness cannot be identified with that property.

Despite Moore's focus on meta-ethical questions, he did not neglect traditional ethical issues. He developed a substantive view about the good, and made a major contribution to utilitarian theory. He agreed with Bentham and Mill that the rightness of our acts is determined by the goodness of their consequences, but denied that the pleasure and pain produced by actions are the only consequences to be taken into account. In other words, he accepted the basic framework of utilitarianism but rejected a hedonistic account of the good. His reason for this rejection was his conviction that life contains many intrinsic goods other than pleasure. To distinguish Moore's view from the hedonistic utilitarianism of Bentham and Mill, it has been called *ideal utilitarianism*.

Most of G. E. Moore's life (1873–1958) was spent at Cambridge University. He entered Trinity College as a student in 1892 and, except between 1904 and 1911, he remained at the university until he retired as a professor of philosophy in 1939. During World War II he spent several years in the United States, lecturing at various colleges and universities. He was awarded the Order of Merit, the highest honor the British government can bestow on one of its citizens.

Principia Ethica

Preface

It appears to me that in Ethics, as in all other philosophical studies, the difficulties and disagreements, of which its history is full, are mainly due to a very simple cause: namely to the attempt to answer questions, without first discovering precisely *what* question it is which you desire to answer. I do not know how far this source of error would be done away, if philosophers would *try* to discover what question they were asking, before they set about to answer it; for the work of analysis and distinction is often very difficult: we may often fail to make the necessary discovery, even though we make a definite attempt to do so. But I am inclined to think that in many cases a resolute attempt would be sufficient to ensure success; so that, if only this attempt were made, many of the most glaring difficulties and disagreements in philosophy would disappear. At all events, philosophers seem, in general, not to make the attempt; and, whether in consequence of this omission or not, they are constantly endeavouring to prove that "Yes" or "No" will answer questions, to which *neither* answer is correct, owing to the fact that what they have before their minds is not one question, but several, to some of which the true answer is "No," to others "Yes."

From G. E. Moore, *Principia Ethica* (Cambridge University Press). Reprinted by permission of Cambridge University Press, New York.

I have tried in this book to distinguish clearly two kinds of questions, which moral philosophers have always professed to answer, but which, as I have tried to shew, they have almost always confused both with one another and with other questions. These two questions may be expressed, the first in the form: What kind of things ought to exist for their own sakes? the second in the form: What kind of actions ought we to perform? I have tried to show exactly what it is that we ask about a thing, when we ask whether it ought to exist for its own sake, is good in itself or has intrinsic value; and exactly what it is that we ask about an action, when we ask whether we ought to do it, whether it is a right action or a duty.

But from a clear insight into the nature of these two questions, there appears to me to follow a second most important result: namely, what is the nature of the evidence, by which alone any ethical proposition can be proved or disproved, confirmed or rendered doubtful. Once we recognize the exact meaning of the two questions, I think it also becomes plain exactly what kind of reasons are relevant as arguments for or against any particular answer to them. It becomes plain that, for answers to the *first* question, no relevant evidence whatever can be adduced: from no other truth, except themselves alone, can it be inferred that they are either true or false. We can guard against error only by taking care, that, when we try to answer a question of this kind, we have before our minds that question only, and not some other or others; but that there is great danger of such errors of confusion I have tried to show, and also what are the chief precautions by the use of which we may guard against them. As for the *second* question, it becomes equally plain, that any answer to it *is* capable of proof or disproof—that, indeed, so many different considerations are relevant to its truth or falsehood, as to make the attainment of probability very difficult, and the attainment of certainty impossible. Nevertheless, the kind of evidence, which is both necessary and alone relevant to such proof and disproof, is capable of exact definition. Such evidence must contain propositions of two kinds and of two kinds only: it must consist, in the first place, of truths with regard to the results of the action in question—of *causal* truths—but it must *also* contain ethical truths of our first or self-evident class. Many truths of both kinds are necessary to the proof that any action ought to be done; and any other kind of evidence is wholly irrelevant. . . .

One main object of this book may, then, be expressed by slightly changing one of Kant's famous titles. I have endeavoured to write "Prolegomena to any future Ethics that can possibly pretend to be scientific." In other words, I have endeavoured to discover what are the fundamental principles of ethical reasoning; and the establishment of these principles, rather than of any conclusions which may be attained by their use, may be regarded as my main object. I have, however, also attempted . . . to present some conclusions, with regard to the proper answer of the question "What is good in itself?" which are very different from any which have commonly been advocated by philosophers. I have tried to define the classes within which all great goods and evils fall; and I have maintained that very many different things are good and evil in themselves, and that neither class of things possesses any other property which is both common to all its members and peculiar to them. . . .

Chapter 1

The Subject-Matter of Ethics

1. It is very easy to point out some among our everyday judgments, with the truth of which Ethics is undoubtedly concerned. Whenever we say, "So and so is a good man," or "That fellow is a villain"; whenever we ask, "What ought I to do?" or "Is it wrong for me to do like this?"; whenever we hazard such remarks as "Temperance is a virtue and drunkenness a vice"—it is undoubtedly the business of Ethics to discuss such questions and such statements; to argue what is the true answer when we ask what it is right to do, and to give reasons for thinking that our statements about the character of persons or the morality of actions are true or false. In the vast majority of cases, where we make statements involving any of the terms "virtue," "vice," "duty," "right," "ought," "good," "bad," we are making ethical judgments; and if we wish to discuss their truth, we shall be discussing a point of Ethics.

So much as this is not disputed; but it falls very short of defining the province of Ethics. That province may indeed be defined as the whole truth about that which is at the same time common to all such judgments and peculiar to them. But we have still to ask the question: What is it that is thus common and peculiar? And this is a question to which very different answers have been given by ethical philosophers of acknowledged reputation, and none of them, perhaps, completely satisfactory.

2. If we take such examples as those given above, we shall not be far wrong in saying that they are all of them concerned with the question of "conduct"—with the question, what, in the conduct of us, human beings, is good, and what is bad, what is right, and what is wrong. For when we say that a man is good, we commonly mean that he acts rightly; when we say that drunkenness is a vice, we commonly mean that to get drunk is a wrong or wicked action. And this discussion of human conduct is, in fact, that with which the name "Ethics" is most intimately associated. It is so associated by derivation; and conduct is undoubtedly by far the commonest and most generally interesting object of ethical judgments.

Accordingly, we find that many ethical philosophers are disposed to accept as an adequate definition of "Ethics" the statement that it deals with the question what is good or bad in human conduct. They hold that its enquiries are properly confined to "conduct" or "practice"; they hold that the name "practical philosophy" covers all the matter with which it has to do. Now, without discussing the proper meaning of the word (for verbal questions are properly left to the writers of dictionaries and other persons interested in literature; philosophy, as we shall see, has no concern with them), I may say that I intend to use "Ethics" to cover more than this—a usage, for which there is, I think, quite sufficient authority. I am using it to cover an enquiry for which, at all events, there is no other word: the general enquiry into what is good.

Ethics is undoubtedly concerned with the question what good conduct is; but, being concerned with this, it obviously does not start at the beginning, unless it is prepared to tell us what is good as well as what is conduct. For "good conduct" is a complex notion: all conduct is not good; for some is certainly bad and some may be indifferent. And on the other hand, other things, beside conduct, may be good; and if they are so, then, "good" denotes some property, that is common to them and conduct; and if we examine good conduct alone of all good things, then we shall be in danger of mistaking for this property, some property which is not shared by those other things: and thus we shall have made a mistake about Ethics even in this limited sense; for we shall not know what good conduct really is. This is a mistake which many writers have actually made, from limiting their enquiry to conduct. And hence I shall try to avoid it by considering first what is good in general; hoping, that if we can arrive at any certainty about this, it will be much easier to settle the question of good conduct: for we all know pretty well what "conduct" is. This, then, is our first question: What is good? and What is bad? and to the discussion of this question (or these questions) I give the name of Ethics, since that science must, at all events, include it.

3. But this is a question which may have many meanings. If, for example, each of us were to say, "I am doing good now" or "I had a good dinner yesterday," these statements would each of them be some sort of answer to our question, although perhaps a false one. So, too, when A asks B what school he ought to send his son to, B's answer will certainly be an ethical judgment. And similarly all distribution of praise or blame to any personage or thing that has existed, now exists, or will exist, does give some answer to the question "What is good?" In all such cases some particular thing is judged to be good or bad: the question "What?" is answered by "This." But this is not the sense in which a scientific Ethics asks the question. Not one, of all the many million answers of this kind, which must be true, can form a part of an ethical system; although that science must contain reasons and principles sufficient for deciding on the truth of all of them. There are far too many persons, things, and events in the world, past, present, or to come, for a discussion of their individual merits to be embraced in any science. Ethics, therefore, does not deal at all with facts of this nature, facts that are unique, individual, absolutely particular; facts with which such studies as history, geography, astronomy, are compelled, in part at least, to deal. And, for this reason, it is not the business of the ethical philosopher to give personal advice or exhortation. . . .

5. But our question, "What is good?" may have still another meaning. We may, in the third place, mean to ask, not what thing or things are good, but how "good" is to be defined. This is an enquiry which belongs only to Ethics, not to Casuistry; and this is the enquiry which will occupy us first.

It is an enquiry to which most special attention should be directed; since this question, how "good" is to be defined, is the most fundamental question in all Ethics. That which is meant by "good" is, in fact, except its converse "bad," the *only* simple object of thought which is peculiar to Ethics. Its definition is, therefore, the most essential point in the definition of Ethics; and moreover a mistake with regard to it entails a far larger number of erroneous ethical judgments than any other. Unless this first question be fully understood, and its true answer clearly recognized, the rest of Ethics is as good as useless from the point of view of systematic knowledge. True ethical judgments, of the two kinds last dealt with, may indeed be made by those who do not know the answer to this question as well as by those who do; and it goes without saying that the two classes of people may lead equally good lives. But it is extremely unlikely that the *most general* ethical judgments will be equally valid, in the absence of a true answer to this question: I shall presently try to shew that the gravest errors have been largely due to beliefs in a false answer. And, in any case, it is impossible that, till the answer to this question be known, anyone should know *what is the evidence* for any ethical judgment whatsoever. But the main object of Ethics, as a systematic science, is to give correct *reasons* for thinking that this or that is good; and, unless this question be answered, such reasons cannot be given. Even, therefore, apart from the fact that a false answer leads to false conclusions, the present enquiry is a most necessary and important part of the science of Ethics.

6. What, then, is good? How is good to be defined? Now, it may be thought that this is a verbal question. A definition does indeed often mean the expressing of one word's meaning in other words. But this is not the sort of definition I am asking for. Such a definition can never be of ultimate importance in any study except lexicography. If I wanted that kind of definition, I should have to consider in the first place how people generally used the word "good"; but my business is not with its proper usage, as established by custom. I should, indeed, be foolish, if I tried to use it for something which it did not usually denote: if, for instance, I were to announce that, whenever I used the word "good," I must be understood to be thinking of that object which is usually denoted by the word "table." I shall, therefore, use the word in the sense in which I think it is ordinarily used; but at the same time I am not anxious to discuss whether I am right in thinking that it is so used. My business is solely with that object or idea, which I hold, rightly or wrongly, that the word is generally used to stand for. What I want to discover is the nature of that object or idea, and about this I am extremely anxious to arrive at an agreement.

But, if we understand the question in this sense, my answer to it may seem a very disappointing one. If I am asked "What is good?" my answer is that good is good, and that is the end of the matter. Or if I am asked "How is good to be defined?" my answer is that it cannot be defined, and that is all I have to say about it. But disappointing as these answers may appear, they are of the very last importance. To readers who are familiar with philosophic terminology, I can express their importance by saying that they amount to this: That propositions about the good are all of them synthetic and never analytic; and that is plainly no trivial matter. And the same thing may be expressed more popularly, by saying that, if I am right, then nobody can foist upon us such an axiom as that "Pleasure is the only good" or that "The good is the desired" on the pretence that this is "the very meaning of the word."

7. Let us, then, consider this position. My point is that "good" is a simple notion, just as "yellow" is a simple notion; that, just as you cannot, by any manner of means, explain to anyone who does not already know it, what yellow is, so you cannot explain what good is. Definitions of the kind that I was asking for, definitions which describe the real nature of the object or notion denoted by a word, and which do not merely tell us what the word is used to mean, are only possible when the object or notion in question is something complex. You can give a definition of a horse, because a horse has many different properties and qualities, all of

which you can enumerate. But when you have enumerated them all, when you have reduced a horse to his simplest terms, then you can no longer define those terms. They are simply something which you think of or perceive, and to anyone who cannot think of or perceive them, you can never, by any definition, make their nature known. It may perhaps be objected to this that we are able to describe to others, objects which they have never seen or thought of. We can, for instance, make a man understand what a chimaera is, although he has never heard of one or seen one. You can tell him that it is an animal with a lioness's head and body, with a goat's head growing from the middle of its back, and with a snake in place of a tail. But here the object which you are describing is a complex object; it is entirely composed of parts, with which we are all perfectly familiar—a snake, a goat, a lioness; and we know, too, the manner in which those parts are to be put together, because we know what is meant by the middle of a lioness's back, and where her tail is wont to grow. And so it is with all objects, not previously known, which we are able to define: they are all complex; all composed of parts, which may themselves, in the first instance, be capable of similar definition, but which must in the end be reducible to simplest parts, which can no longer be defined. But yellow and good, we say, are not complex: they are notions of that simple kind, out of which definitions are composed and with which the power of further defining ceases.

8. When we say, as Webster says, "The definition of horse is 'a hoofed quadruped of the genus Equus,'" we may, in fact, mean three different things. (1) We may mean merely: "When I say 'horse,' you are to understand that I am talking about a hoofed quadruped of the genus Equus." This might be called the arbitrary verbal definition: and I do not mean that good is indefinable in that sense. (2) We may mean, as Webster ought to mean: "When most English people say 'horse,' they mean a hoofed quadruped of the genus Equus." This may be called the verbal definition proper, and I do not say that good is indefinable in this sense either; for it is certainly possible to discover how people use a word: otherwise, we could never have known that "good" may be translated by "gut" in German and by "bon" in French. But (3) we may, when we define horse, mean something much more important. We may mean that a certain object, which we all of us know, is composed in a certain manner: that it has four legs, a head, a heart, a liver, etc., etc., all of them arranged in definite relations to one another. It is in this sense that I deny good to be definable. I say that it is not composed of any parts, which we can substitute for it in our minds when we are thinking of it. We might think just as clearly and correctly about a horse, if we thought of all its parts and their arrangement instead of thinking of the whole: we could, I say, think how a horse differed from a donkey just as well, just as truly, in this way, as now we do, only not so easily; but there is nothing whatsoever which we could so substitute for good; and that is what I mean, when I say that good is indefinable.

9. But I am afraid I have still not removed the chief difficulty, which may prevent acceptance of the proposition that good is indefinable. I do not mean to say that *the* good, that which is good, is thus indefinable; if I did think so, I should not be writing on Ethics, for my main object is to help towards discovering that definition. It is just because I think there will be less risk of error in our search for a definition of "the good," that I am now insisting that *good* is indefinable. I must try to explain the difference between these two. I suppose it may be granted that "good" is an adjective. Well "the good," "that which is good," must therefore be the substantive to which the adjective "good" will apply: it must be the whole of that to which the adjective will apply, and the adjective must *always* truly apply to it. But if it is that to which the adjective will apply, it must be something different from that adjective itself; and the whole of that something different, whatever it is, will be our definition of *the* good. Now it may be that this something will have other adjectives, beside "good," that will apply to it. It may be full of pleasure, for example; it may be intelligent: and if these two adjectives are really part of its definition, then it will certainly be true, that pleasure and intelligence are good. And many people appear to think that, if we say, "Pleasure and intelligence are good," or if we say, "Only pleasure and intelligence are good," we are defining "good." Well, I cannot deny that propositions of this nature may sometimes be called definitions; I do not know well enough how the word is generally used to decide upon this point. I only wish it to be understood that that is not what I mean when I say there is no possible definition of good, and that I shall not mean this if I use the word again. I do most fully believe that some true proposition of the form "Intelligence is good and intelligence alone is good" can be found; if none could be found, our definition of *the* good would be impossible. As it is, I believe *the* good to be definable; and yet I still say that good itself is indefinable.

10. "Good," then, if we mean by it that quality which we assert to belong to a thing, when we say that the thing is good, is incapable of any definition, in the most important sense of that word. The most important sense of "definition" is that in which a definition states what are the parts which invariably compose a certain whole; and in this sense "good" has no definition because it is simple and has no parts. It is one of those innumerable objects of thought which are themselves incapable of definition, because they are the ultimate terms by reference to which whatever *is* capable of definition must be defined. That there must be an indefinite number of such terms is obvious, on reflection; since we cannot define anything except by an analysis, which, when carried as far as it will go, refers us to something, which is simply different from anything else, and which by that ultimate difference explains the peculiarity of the whole which we are defining: for every whole contains some parts which are common to other wholes also. There is, therefore, no intrinsic difficulty in the contention that "good" denotes a simple and indefinable quality. There are many other instances of such qualities.

Consider yellow, for example. We may try to define it, by describing its physical equivalent; we may state what kind of light-vibrations must stimulate the normal eye, in order that we may perceive it. But a moment's reflection is sufficient to show that those light-vibrations are not themselves what we mean by yellow. *They* are not what we perceive. Indeed we should never have been able to discover their existence, unless we had first been struck by the patent difference of quality between the different colours. The most we can be entitled to say of those vibrations is that they are what corresponds in space to the yellow which we actually perceive.

Yet a mistake of this simple kind has commonly been made about "good." It may be true that all things which are good are *also* something else, just as it is true that all things which are yellow produce a certain kind of vibration in the light.

288 G. E. M O O R E
And it is a fact, that Ethics aims at discovering what are those other properties belonging to all things which are good. But far too many philosophers have thought that when they named those other properties they were actually defining good; that these properties, in fact, were simply not "other," but absolutely and entirely the same with goodness. This view I propose to call the "naturalistic fallacy" and of it I shall now endeavour to dispose.

11. Let us consider what it is such philosophers say. And first it is to be noticed that they do not agree among themselves. They not only say that they are right as to what good is, but they endeavour to prove that other people who say that it is something else, are wrong. One, for instance, will affirm that good is pleasure, another, perhaps, that good is that which is desired; and each of these will argue eagerly to prove that the other is wrong. But how is that possible? One of them says that good is nothing but the object of desire, and at the same time tries to prove that it is not pleasure. But from his first assertion, that good just means the object of desire, one of the two things must follow as regards his proof:

(1) He may be trying to prove that the object of desire is not pleasure. But, if this be all, where is his Ethics? The position he is maintaining is merely a psychological one. Desire is something which occurs in our minds, and pleasure is something else which so occurs; and our would-be ethical philosopher is merely holding that the latter is not the object of the former. But what has that to do with the question in dispute? His opponent held the ethical proposition that pleasure was the good, and although he should prove a million times over the psychological proposition that pleasure is not the object of desire, he is no nearer proving his opponent to be wrong. . . . Well, that is one alternative which any naturalistic Ethics has to face; if good is *defined* as something else, it is then impossible either to prove that any other definition is wrong or even to deny such definition.

(2) The other alternative will scarcely be more welcome. It is that the discussion is after all a verbal one. When A says, "Good means pleasant" and B says, "Good means desired," they may merely wish to assert that most people have used the word for what is pleasant and for what is desired respectively. And this is quite an interesting subject for discussion: only it is not a whit more an ethical discussion than the last was. Nor do I think that any exponent of naturalistic Ethics would be willing to allow that this was all he meant. They are all so anxious to persuade us that what they call the good is what we really ought to do. "Do, pray, act so, because the word 'good' is generally used to denote actions of this nature": such, on this view, would be the substance of their teaching. And insofar as they tell us how we ought to act, their teaching is truly ethical, as they mean it to be. But how perfectly absurd is the reason they would give for it! "You are to do this, because most people use a certain word to denote conduct such as this." "You are to say the thing which is not, because most people call it lying." That is an argument just as good!—My dear sirs, what we want to know from you as ethical teachers, is not how people use a word; it is not even what kind of actions they approve, which the use of this word "good" may certainly imply: what we want to know is simply what *is* good. We may indeed agree that what most people do think good is actually so; we shall at all events be glad to know their opinions: but when we say their opinions about what *is* good, we do mean what we say; we do not care

whether they call that thing which they mean "horse" or "table" or "chair," "gut" or "bon" or ἀγαθός; we want to know what it is that they so call. When they say, "Pleasure is good," we cannot believe that they merely mean "Pleasure is pleasure" and nothing more than that. . . .

13. In fact, if it is not the case that "good" denotes something simple and indefinable, only two alternatives are possible: either it is a complex, a given whole, about the correct analysis of which there may be disagreement; or else it means nothing at all, and there is no subject as Ethics. In general, however, ethical philosophers have attempted to define good, without recognizing what such an attempt must mean. They actually use arguments which involve one or both of the absurdities considered in §11. We are, therefore, justified in concluding that the attempt to define good is chiefly due to want of clearness as to the possible nature of definition. There are, in fact, only two serious alternatives to be considered, in order to establish the conclusion that "good" does denote a simple and indefinable notion. It might possibly denote a complex, as "horse" does; or it might have no meaning at all. Neither of these possibilities has, however, been clearly conceived and seriously maintained, as such, by those who presume to define good; and both may be dismissed by a simple appeal to facts.

(1) The hypothesis that disagreement about the meaning of good is disagreement with regard to the correct analysis of a given whole, may be most plainly seen to be incorrect by consideration of the fact that, whatever definition be offered, it may be always asked, with significance, of the complex so defined, whether it is itself good. To take, for instance, one of the more plausible, because one of the more complicated, of such proposed definitions, it may easily be thought, at first sight, that to be good may mean to be that which we desire to desire. Thus if we apply this definition to a particular instance and say, "When we think A is good, we are thinking that A is one of the things which we desire to desire," our proposition may seem quite plausible. But, if we carry the investigation further, and ask ourselves, "Is it good to desire to desire A?" it is apparent, on a little reflection, that this question is itself as intelligible, as the original question "Is A good?"— that we are, in fact, now asking for exactly the same information about the desire to desire A, for which we formerly asked with regard to A itself. But it is also apparent that the meaning of this second question cannot be correctly analysed into "Is the desire to desire A one of the things which we desire to desire?": we have not before our minds anything so complicated as the question "Do we desire to desire to desire A?" Moreover, anyone can easily convince himself by inspection that the predicate of this preposition—"good"—is positively different from the notion of "desiring to desire," which enters into its subject: "That we should desire to desire A is good" is *not* merely equivalent to "That A should be good is good." It may indeed be true that what we desire to desire is always also good; perhaps, even the converse may be true: but it is very doubtful whether this is the case, and the mere fact that we understand very well what is meant by doubting it, shews clearly that we have two different notions before our minds.

(2) And the same consideration is sufficient to dismiss the hypothesis that "good" has no meaning whatsoever. It is very natural to make the mistake of supposing that what is universally true is of such a nature that its negation would be

self-contradictory: the importance which has been assigned to analytic propositions in the history of philosophy shews how easy such a mistake is. And thus it is very easy to conclude that what seems to be a universal ethical principle is in fact an identical proposition; that, if, for example, whatever is called "good" seems to be pleasant, the proposition "Pleasure is the good" does not assert a connection between two different notions, but involves only one, that of pleasure, which is easily recognized as a distinct entity. But whoever will attentively consider with himself what is actually before his mind when he asks the question "Is pleasure (or whatever it may be) after all good?" can easily satisfy himself that he is not merely wondering whether pleasure is pleasant. And if he will try this experiment with each suggested definition in succession, he may become expert enough to recognize that in every case he has before his mind a unique object, with regard to the connection of which with any other object, a distinct question may be asked. Everyone does in fact understand the question "Is this good?" When he thinks of it, his state of mind is different from what it would be, were he asked "Is this pleasant, or desired, or approved?" It has a distinct meaning for him, even though he may not recognize in what respect it is distinct. Whenever he thinks of "intrinsic value," or "intrinsic worth," or says that a thing "ought to exist," he has before his mind the unique object—the unique property of things—which I mean by "good." Everybody is constantly aware of this notion, although he may never become aware at all that it is different from other notions of which he is also aware. But, for correct ethical reasoning, it is extremely important that he should become aware of this fact; and, as soon as the nature of the problem is clearly understood, there should be little difficulty in advancing so far in analysis.

15. Our first conclusion as to the subject matter of Ethics is, then, that there is a simple, indefinable, unanalysable object of thought by reference to which it must be defined. By what name we call this unique object is a matter of indifference, so long as we clearly recognize what it is and that it does differ from other objects. The words which are commonly taken as signs of ethical judgments all do refer to it; and they are expressions of ethical judgments solely because they do so refer. But they may refer to it in two different ways, which it is very important to distinguish, if we are to have a complete definition of the range of ethical judgments. Before I proceeded to argue that there was such an indefinable notion involved in ethical notions, I stated (Section 4) that it was necessary for Ethics to enumerate all true universal judgments, asserting that such and such a thing was good, whenever it occurred. But, although all such judgments do refer to that unique notion which I have called "good," they do not refer to it in the same way. They may either assert that this unique property does always attach to the thing in question, or else they may assert only that the thing in question is a *cause or necessary condition* for the existence of other things to which this unique property does attach. The nature of these two species of universal ethical judgments is extremely different. . . .

17. There are, then, judgments which state that certain kinds of things have good effects; and such judgments, for the reasons just given, have the important characteristics (1) that they are unlikely to be true, if they state that the kind of thing in question *always* has good effects, and (2) that, even if they only state that it *generally* has good effects, many of them will only be true in certain periods of the world's history. On the other hand there are judgments which state that certain kinds of things are themselves good; and these differ from the last in that, if true at all, they are all of them universally true. It is, therefore, extremely important to distinguish these two kinds of possible judgments. Both may be expressed in the same language; in both cases we commonly say "Such and such a thing is good." But in the one case "good" will mean "good as a means," *i.e.* merely that the thing is a means to good—will have good effects: in the other case it will mean "good as end"—we shall be judging that the thing itself has the property which, in the first case, we asserted only to belong to its effects. It is plain that these are very different assertions to make about the thing; it is plain that either or both of them may be made, both truly or falsely, about all manner of things; and it is certain that unless we are clear as to which of the two things we mean to assert, we shall have a very poor chance of deciding rightly whether our assertion is true or false. It is precisely this clearness as to the meaning of the question asked which has hitherto been almost entirely lacking in ethical speculation. Ethics has always been predominantly concerned with the investigation of a limited class of actions. With regard to these we may ask *both* how far they are good in themselves *and* how far they have a general tendency to produce good results. And the arguments brought forward in ethical discussion have always been of both classes—both such as would prove the conduct in question to be good in itself and such as would prove it to be good as a means. But that these are the only questions which any ethical discussion can have to settle, and that to settle the one is *not* the same thing as to settle the other—these two fundamental facts have in general escaped the notice of ethical philosophers. Ethical questions are commonly asked in an ambiguous form. It is asked "What is a man's duty under these circumstances?" or "Is it right to act this way?" or "What ought we to aim at securing?" But all these questions are capable of further analysis; a correct answer to any of them involves both judgments of what is good in itself and causal judgments. This is implied even by those who maintain that we have a direct and immediate judgment of absolute rights and duties. Such a judgment can only mean that the course of action in question is the best thing to do; that, by acting so, every good that *can* be secured will have been secured. . . . In asserting that the action is *the* best thing to do, we assert that it together with its consequences presents a greater sum of intrinsic value than any possible alternative. And this condition may be realized by any of the three cases: — *(a)* If the action itself has greater intrinsic value than any alternative, whereas both its consequences and those of the alternatives are absolutely devoid either of intrinsic merit or intrinsic demerit; or *(b)* if, though its consequences are intrinsically bad, the balance of intrinsic value is greater than would be produced by any alternative; or *(c)* if, its consequences being intrinsically good, the degree of value belonging to them and it conjointly is greater than that of any alternative series. In short, to assert that a certain line of conduct is, at a given time, absolutely right or obligatory, is obviously to assert that more good or less evil will exist in the world, if it be adopted than if anything else be done instead. But this implies a judgment as to the value both of its own consequences and of those of any possible alternative. And that an action will have such and such consequences involves a number of causal judgments . . .

Study Questions

1. Moore claims that ethics is "the general inquiry into what is good." What does he mean by this? Do you agree or disagree with this view about the subject matter of ethics?
2. Moore claims that "good" refers to a simple and indefinable quality. Why does he say this? Does it mean that "good" is unknowable? Why does he think that this point is so important?
3. Moore says that good is indefinable, but says that *the* good is definable. What is the difference?
4. Moore develops what is generally called the "open question" argument against any naturalistic definition of good. (See Section 13.) What does this argument mean and why is it important?
5. What is the naturalistic fallacy? Give some examples of it? Is it really a fallacy?
6. Do you agree with Moore's claim that ethics is only concerned with what is good in itself and with what is good as a means, or in other words has a tendency to produce good results?

Selected Bibliography

Baldwin, T. *G. E. Moore* (London: Routledge, 1990), Chaps. 3 and 4. Moore's critical and constructive ethics.
Frankena, W. K. "The Naturalistic Fallacy," *Mind*, 48 (1939), 446–477. A critical analysis of Moore's argument against naturalism.
Moore, G. E. *Ethics* (Oxford: Oxford University Press, 1912, 1958).
———. "Is Goodness a Quality?" in *Philosophical Papers* (London: Allen & Unwin, 1959).
Regan, Tom. *Bloomsbury's Prophet: G.E. Moore and the Development of His Moral Philosophy* (Philadelphia: Temple University Press, 1986). A general study of Moore's moral theory.
Schilpp, P. (ed.). *The Philosophy of G.E. Moore* (New York: Tudor, 1952), Essays 1–6 and pp. 535–627. Several essays on Moore's ethics and Moore's replies.
Warnock, M. *Ethics Since 1900* (Oxford/New York: Oxford University Press, 1960), Chap. 2. A critical summary of Moore's ethics.

17

W. D. ROSS

From the time of Jeremy Bentham in the 18th century up to G. E.

> *. . . a promise is a promise. . . .*

Moore in the early 20th century, British moral theory was dominated by teleological (or consequentialist) theories, in particular by the utilitarian tradition. Basing the rightness or wrongness of an action on its consequences is perhaps given its most unequivocal statement in G. E. Moore's comment: "'Right' does and can mean nothing but 'cause of a good result.'" The deontological approach to ethics, which emphasizes duty and holds that the rightness or wrongness of an action is not determined by its consequences, had lain largely dormant for 150 years. But it was far from dead. Its revival began with an article published in 1912 by H. A. Prichard and bearing the arresting title "Does Moral Philosophy Rest on a Mistake?" Answering his question in the affirmative, Prichard argued for the unpopular thesis that the entire teleological way of viewing human conduct involved a basic error.

Because of its iconoclasm the article received little attention and its deontological thesis might have died in being reborn had not Prichard taken his message to his students at Oxford University. There he got the response that he had failed to generate among the established university philosophers. The most influential of his students turned out to be W. D. Ross, who took up Prichard's cause in two important books, *The Right and the Good* (1930) and *Foundations of Ethics* (1939). In Ross's view, utilitarianism in all of its forms is an inadequate ethical theory because it is not consonant with the moral convictions on which ordinary people, without benefit of philosophy, act. Although he acknowledges that we accept as one of our duties the obligation to promote the best possible consequences, he denies that all of our duties can be subsumed under this one. On the contrary, he urges, we often find ourselves in situations in which we believe it to be our duty to do a certain act even though we are convinced that we could promote better consequences by doing some other act instead. In such a situation it is our duty to go ahead and do the act we believe we ought to do, in spite of the consequences. We should do this act because we recognize, by direct intuition, that it is our duty.

Ross (1877–1971), besides being an eminent moral philosopher, was editor of the Oxford translation of the works of Aristotle. In addition, he served in important administrative posts as Provost of Oriel College, Oxford, and also Vice-Chancellor (the equivalent of a university president in the United States) of Oxford University. He was awarded a knighthood by the British government.

———

The Right and the Good

What Makes Right Acts Right?

The real point at issue between hedonism and utilitarianism on the one hand and their opponents on the other is not whether "right" means "productive of so and so"; for it cannot with any plausibility be maintained that it does. The point at issue is that to which we now pass, viz., whether there is any general character which makes right acts right, and if so, what it is. Among the main historical attempts to state a single characteristic of all right actions which is the foundation of their rightness are those made by egoism and utilitarianism. But I do not propose to discuss these, not because the subject is unimportant, but because it has been dealt with so often and so well already, and because there has come to be so much agreement among moral philosophers that neither of these theories is satisfactory. A much more attractive theory has been put forward by Professor Moore: that what makes actions right is that they are productive of more *good* than could have been produced by any other action open to the agent.

This theory is in fact the culmination of all the attempts to base rightness on productivity of some sort of result. The first form this attempt takes is the attempt to base rightness on conduciveness to the advantage or pleasure of the agent. This theory comes to grief over the fact, which stares us in the face, that a great part of duty consists in an observance of the rights and a furtherance of the interests of others, whatever the cost to ourselves may be. Plato and others may be right in holding that a regard for the rights of others never in the long run involves a loss of happiness for the agent, that "the just life profits a man." But this, even if true, is irrelevant to the rightness of the act. As soon as a man does an action *because* he thinks he will promote his own interests thereby, he is acting not from a sense of its rightness but from self-interest.

To the egoistic theory hedonistic utilitarianism supplies a much-needed amendment. It points out correctly that the fact that a certain pleasure will be enjoyed by the agent is no reason why he *ought* to bring it into being rather than an equal or greater pleasure to be enjoyed by another, though, human nature being what it is, it makes it not unlikely that he *will* try to bring it into being. But hedonistic utilitarianism in its turn needs a correction. On reflection it seems clear that pleasure is not the only thing in life that we think good in itself, that, for instance, we think the possession of a good character, or an intelligent understanding of the world, as good or

From W. D. Ross, *The Right and the Good*. Reprinted by permission of the Oxford University Press.

better. A great advance is made by the substitution of "productive of the greatest good" for "productive of the greatest pleasure."

Not only is this theory more attractive than hedonistic utilitarianism, but its logical relation to that theory is such that the latter could not be true unless *it* were true, while it might be true though hedonistic utilitarianism were not. It is in fact one of the logical bases of hedonistic utilitarianism. For the view that what produces the maximum pleasure is right has for its bases the views (1) that what produces the maximum good is right, and (2) that pleasure is the only thing good in itself. If they were not assuming that what produces a maximum *good* is right, the utilitarians' attempt to show that pleasure is the only good in itself, which is in fact the point they take most pains to establish, would have been quite irrelevant to their attempt to prove that only what produces the maximum *pleasure* is right. If, therefore, it can be shown that productivity of the maximum good is not what makes all right actions right, we shall *a fortiori* have refuted hedonistic utilitarianism.

When a plain man fulfills a promise because he thinks he ought to do so, it seems clear that he does so with no thought of its total consequences, still less with any opinion that these are likely to be the best possible. He thinks in fact much more of the past than of the future. What makes him think it right to act in a certain way is the fact that he has promised to do so—that and, usually, nothing more. That his act will produce the best possible consequences is not his reason for calling it right. What lends colour to the theory we are examining, then, is not the actions (which form probably a great majority of our actions) in which some such reflection as "I have promised" is the only reason we give ourselves for thinking a certain action right, but the exceptional cases in which the consequences of fulfilling a promise (for instance) would be so disastrous to others that we judge it right not to do so. It must of course be admitted that such cases exist. If I have promised to meet a friend at a particular time for some trivial purpose, I should certainly think myself justified in breaking my engagement if by doing so I could prevent a serious accident or bring relief to the victims of one. And the supporters of the view we are examining hold that my thinking so is due to my thinking that I shall bring more good into existence by the one action than by the other. A different account may, however, be given of the matter, an account which will, I believe, show itself to be the true one. It may be said that besides the duty of fulfilling promises I have and recognize a duty of relieving distress,* and that when I think it right to do the latter at the cost of not doing the former, it is not because I think I shall produce more good thereby but because I think it the duty which is in the circumstances more of a duty. This account surely corresponds much more closely with what we really think in such a situation. If, so far as I can see, I could bring equal amounts of good into being by fulfilling my promise and by helping someone to whom I had made no promise, I should not hesitate to regard the former as my duty. Yet on the view that what is right is right because it is productive of the most good I should not so regard it.

There are two theories, each in its way simple, that offer a solution of such cases of conscience. One is the view of Kant, that there are certain duties of perfect

---

*These are not strictly speaking duties, but things that tend to be our duty, or *prima facie* duties.

obligation, such as those of fulfilling promises, of paying debts, of telling the truth, which admit of no exception whatever in favour of duties of imperfect obligation, such as that of relieving distress. The other is the view of, for instance, Professor Moore and Dr. Rashdall,* that there is only the duty of producing good, and that all "conflicts of duties" should be resolved by asking "by which action will most good be produced?" But it is more important that our theory fit the facts than that it be simple, and the account we have given above corresponds (it seems to me) better than either of the simpler theories with what we really think, viz., that normally promise-keeping, for example, should come before benevolence, but that when and only when the good to be produced by the benevolent act is very great and the promise comparatively trivial, the act of benevolence becomes our duty.

In fact the theory of "ideal utilitarianism," if I may for brevity refer so to the theory of Professor Moore, seems to simplify unduly our relations to our fellows. It says, in effect, that the only morally significant relation in which my neighbours stand to me is that of being possible beneficiaries by my action.** They do stand in this relation to me, and this relation is morally significant. But they may also stand to me in the relation of promisee to promiser, of creditor to debtor, of wife to husband, of child to parent, of friend to friend, of fellow countryman to fellow countryman, and the like; and each of these relations is the foundation of a *prima facie* duty, which is more or less incumbent on me according to the circumstances of the case. When I am in a situation, as perhaps I always am, in which more than one of these *prima facie* duties is incumbent on me, what I have to do is to study the situation as fully as I can until I form the considered opinion (it is never more) that in the circumstances one of them is more incumbent than any other; then I am bound to think that to do this *prima facie* duty is my duty *sans phrase* in the situation.

I suggest "*prima facie* duty" or "conditional duty" as a brief way of referring to the characteristic (quite distinct from that of being a duty proper) which an act has, in virtue of being of a certain kind (e.g., the keeping of a promise), of being an act which would be a duty proper if it were not at the same time of another kind which is morally significant. Whether an act is a duty proper or actual duty depends on *all* the morally significant kinds it is an instance of. The phrase "*prima facie* duty" must be apologized for, since (1) it suggests that what we are speaking of is a certain kind of duty, whereas it is in fact not a duty, but something related in a special way to duty. Strictly speaking, we want not a phrase in which duty is qualified by an adjective, but a separate noun. (2) "*Prima*" facie suggests that one is speaking only of an appearance which a moral situation presents at first sight, and which may turn out to be illusory; whereas what I am speaking of is an objective fact involved in the nature of the situation, or more strictly in an element of its nature, though not, as duty proper does, arising from its *whole* nature. I can, however, think of no term which fully meets the case. "Claim" has been suggested by Professor Prichard. The word "claim" has the advantage of being quite a familiar

---

*English philosopher (1858–1924)—Ed.

**Some will think it, apart from other considerations, a sufficient refutation of this view to point out that I also stand in that relation to myself, so that for this view the distinction of oneself from others is morally insignificant.

one in this connexion, and it seems to cover much of the ground. It would be quite natural to say, "a person to whom I have made a promise has a claim on me," and also, "a person whose distress I could relieve (at the cost of breaking the promise) has a claim on me." But (1) while "claim" is appropriate from *their* point of view, we want a word to express the corresponding fact from the agent's point of view—the fact of his being subject to claims that can be made against him; and ordinary language provides us with no such correlative to "claim." And (2) (what is more important) "claim" seems inevitably to suggest two persons, one of whom might make a claim on the other; and while this covers the ground of social duty, it is inappropriate in the case of that important part of duty which is the duty of cultivating a certain kind of character in oneself. It would be artificial, I think, and at any rate metaphorical, to say that one's character has a claim on oneself.

There is nothing arbitrary about these *prima facie* duties. Each rests on a definite circumstance which cannot seriously be held to be without moral significance. Of *prima facie* duties I suggest, without claiming completeness or finality for it, the following division.*

(1) Some duties rest on previous acts of my own. These duties seem to include two kinds, (a) those resting on a promise or what may fairly be called an implicit promise, such as the implicit undertaking not to tell lies which seems to be implied in the act of entering into conversation (at any rate by civilized men), or of writing books that purport to be history and not fiction. These may be called the duties of fidelity. (b) Those resting on a previous wrongful act. These may be called the duties of reparation. (2) Some rest on previous acts of other men, i.e., services done by them to me. These may be loosely described as the duties of gratitude. (3) Some rest on the fact or possibility of a distribution of pleasure or happiness (or of the means thereto) which is not in accordance with the merit of the persons concerned; in such cases there arises a duty to upset or prevent such a distribution. These are the duties of justice. (4) Some rest on the mere fact that there are other beings in the world whose condition we can make better in respect of virtue, or of intelligence, or of pleasure. These are the duties of beneficence. (5) Some rest on the fact that we can improve our own condition in respect of virtue or of intelligence. These are the duties of self-improvement. (6) I think that we should distinguish from (4) the duties that may be summed up under the title of "not injuring others." No doubt to injure others is incidentally to fail to do them good; but it seems to me clear that non-maleficence is apprehended as a duty distinct from that of beneficence, and as a duty of a more stringent character. It will be noticed that this alone among the types of duty has been stated in a negative way. An attempt

*I should make it plain at this stage that I am assuming the correctness of some of our main convictions as to *prima facie* duties, or, more strictly, am claiming that we *know* them to be true. To me it seems as self-evident as anything could be, that to make a promise, for instance, is to create a moral claim on us in someone else. Many readers will perhaps say that they do *not* know this to be true. If so, I certainly cannot prove it to them; I can only ask them to reflect again, in the hope that they will ultimately agree that they also know it to be true. The main moral convictions of the plain man seem to me to be, not opinions which it is for philosophy to prove or disprove, but knowledge from the start; and in my own case I seem to find little difficulty in distinguishing these essential convictions from other moral convictions which I also have, which are merely fallible opinions based on an imperfect study of the working for good or evil of certain institutions or types of action.

might no doubt be made to state this duty, like the others, in a positive way. It might be said that it is really the duty to prevent ourselves from acting either from an inclination to harm others or from an inclination to seek our own pleasure, in doing which we should incidentally harm them. But on reflection it seems clear that the primary duty here is the duty not to harm others, this being a duty whether or not we have an inclination that if followed would lead to our harming them; and that when we have such an inclination the primary duty not to harm others gives rise to a consequential duty to resist the inclination. The recognition of this duty of non-maleficence is the first step on the way to the recognition of the duty of beneficence; and that accounts for the prominence of the commands "thou shalt not kill," "thou shalt not commit adultery," "thou shalt not steal," "thou shalt not bear false witness," in so early a code as the Decalogue. But even when we have come to recognize the duty of beneficence, it appears to me that the duty of non-maleficence is recognized as a distinct one, and as *prima facie* more binding. We should not in general consider it justifiable to kill one person in order to keep another alive, or to steal from one in order to give alms to another.

The essential defect of the "ideal utilitarian" theory is that it ignores, or at least does not do full justice to, the highly personal character of duty. If the only duty is to produce the maximum of good, the question who is to have the good— whether it is myself, or my benefactor, or a person to whom I have made a promise to confer that good on him, or a mere fellow man to whom I stand in no such special relation—should make no difference to my having a duty to produce that good. But we are all in fact sure that it makes a vast difference.

One or two other comments must be made on this provisional list of the divisions of duty.

1. The nomenclature is not strictly correct. For by "fidelity" or "gratitude" we mean, strictly, certain states of motivation; and, as I have urged, it is not our duty to have certain motives, but to do certain acts. By "fidelity," for instance, is meant, strictly, the disposition to fulfill promises and implicit promises *because we have made them.* We have no general word to cover the actual fulfillment of promises and implicit promises *irrespective of motive;* and I use "fidelity," loosely but perhaps conveniently, to fill this gap. So, too, I use "gratitude" for the returning of services, irrespective of motive. The term "justice" is not so much confined, in ordinary usage, to a certain state of motivation, for we should often talk of a man as acting justly even when we did not think his motive was the wish to do what was just simply for the sake of doing so. Less apology is therefore needed for our use of "justice" in this sense. And I have used the word "beneficence" rather than "benevolence," in order to emphasize the fact that it is our duty to do certain things, and not to do them from certain motives.

2. If the objection be made, that this catalogue of the main types of duty is an unsystematic one resting on no logical principle, it may be replied, first, that it makes no claim to being ultimate. It is a *prima facie* classification of the duties which reflection on our moral convictions seems actually to reveal. And if these convictions are, as I would claim that they are, of the nature of knowledge, and if I have not misstated them, the list will be a list of authentic conditional duties, correct as far as it goes though not necessarily complete. The list of *goods* put forward by the rival theory is reached by exactly the same method—the only sound one in the circumstances—viz. that of direct reflection on what we really think. Loyalty to the facts is worth more than a symmetrical architectonic or a hastily reached simplicity. If further reflection discovers a perfect logical basis for this or for a better classification, so much the better.

3. It may, again, be objected that our theory that there are these various and often conflicting types of *prima facie* duty leaves us with no principle upon which to discern what is our actual duty in particular circumstances. But this objection is not one which the rival theory is in a position to bring forward. For when we have to choose between the production of two heterogeneous goods, say, knowledge and pleasure, the "ideal utilitarian" theory can only fall back on an opinion, for which no logical basis can be offered, that one of the goods is the greater; and this is no better than a similar opinion that one of two duties is the more urgent. And again, when we consider the infinite variety of the effects of our actions in the way of pleasure, it must surely be admitted that the claim which *hedonism* sometimes makes, that it offers a readily applicable criterion of right conduct, is quite illusory.

I am unwilling, however, to content myself with an *argumentum ad hominem*, and I would contend that in principle there is no reason to anticipate that every act that is our duty is so for one and the same reason. Why should two sets of circumstances, or one set of circumstances, *not* possess different characteristics, any one of which makes a certain act our *prima facie* duty? When I ask what it is that makes me in certain cases sure that I have a *prima facie* duty to do so and so, I find that it lies in the fact that I have made a promise; when I ask the same question in another case, I find the answer lies in the fact that I have done a wrong. And if on reflection I find (as I think I do) that neither of these reasons is reducible to the other, I must not on any *a priori* ground assume that such a reduction is possible.

An attempt may be made to arrange in a more systematic way the main types of duty which we have indicated. In the first place it seems self-evident that if there are things that are intrinsically good, it is *prima facie* a duty to bring them into existence rather than not to do so, and to bring as much of them into existence as possible. It will be argued in our fifth chapter that there are three main things that are intrinsically good—virtue, knowledge, and, with certain limitations, pleasure. And since a given virtuous disposition, for instance, is equally good whether it is realized in myself or in another, it seems to be my duty to bring it into existence whether in myself or in another. So too with a given piece of knowledge.

The case of pleasure is difficult; for while we clearly recognize a duty to produce pleasure for others, it is by no means so clear that we recognize a duty to produce pleasure for ourselves. This appears to arise from the following facts. The thought of an act as our duty is one that presupposes a certain amount of reflection about the act; and for that reason does not normally arise in connexion with acts towards which we are already impelled by another strong impulse. So far, the cause of our not thinking of the promotion of our own pleasure as a duty is analogous to the cause which usually prevents a highly sympathetic person from thinking of the promotion of the pleasure of others as a duty. He is impelled so strongly by direct interest in the well-being of others towards promoting their pleasure that he does not stop to ask whether it is his duty to promote it; and we are all impelled so strongly towards a promotion of our own pleasure that we do not stop to ask whether it is a duty or not. But there is a further reason why even when we stop to think about the matter it does not usually present itself as a duty: viz., that, since the performance of most of our duties involves the giving up of some pleasure that we desire, the doing of duty and the getting of pleasure for ourselves come by a natural association of ideas to be thought of as incompatible things. This association of ideas is in the main salutary in its operation, since it puts a check on what but for it would be much too strong, the tendency to pursue one's own pleasure without thought of other considerations. Yet if pleasure is good, it seems in the long run clear that it is right to get it for ourselves as well as to produce it for others, when this does not involve the failure to discharge some more stringent *prima facie* duty. The question is a very difficult one, but it seems that this conclusion can be denied only on one or other of three grounds: (1) that pleasure is not *prima facie* good (i.e., good when it is neither the actualization of a bad disposition nor underserved), (2) that there is no *prima facie* duty to produce as much that is good as we can, or (3) that though there is a *prima facie* duty to produce other things that are good, there is no *prima facie* duty to produce pleasure which will be enjoyed by ourselves. I give reasons later for not accepting the first contention. The second hardly admits of argument but seems to me plainly false. The third seems plausible only if we hold that an act that is pleasant or brings pleasure to ourselves must for that reason not be a duty; and this would lead to paradoxical consequences, such as that if a man enjoys giving pleasure to others or working for their moral improvement, it cannot be his duty to do so. Yet it seems to be a very stubborn fact, that in our ordinary consciousness we are not aware of a duty to get pleasure for ourselves; and by way of partial explanation of this I may add that though, as I think, one's own pleasure is a good and there is a duty to produce it, it is only if we *think* of our own pleasure not as simply our own pleasure, but as an objective good, something that an impartial spectator would approve, that we can think of the getting it as a duty; and we do not habitually think of it in this way.

If these contentions are right, what we have called the duty of beneficence and the duty of self-improvement rest on the same ground. No different principles of duty are involved in the two cases. If we feel a special responsibility for improving our own character rather than that of others, it is not because a special principle is involved, but because we are aware that the one is more under our control than the other. It was on this ground that Kant expressed the practical law of duty in the form "seek to make yourself good and other people happy." He was so persuaded of the internality of virtue that he regarded any attempt by one person to produce virtue in another as bound to produce, at most, only a counterfeit of virtue, the doing of externally right acts not from the true principle of virtuous action but out of regard to another person. It must be admitted that one man cannot compel another to be virtuous; compulsory virtue would just not be virtue. But experience clearly shows that Kant overshoots the mark when he contends that one man cannot do anything to *promote* virtue in another, to bring such influences to bear upon him that his own response to them is more likely to be virtuous than his response to other influences would have been. And our duty to do this is not different in kind from our duty to improve our own characters.

It is equally clear, and clear at an earlier stage of moral development, that if there are things that are bad in themselves, we ought, *prima facie,* not to bring them upon others; and on this fact rests the duty of non-maleficence.

The duty of justice is particularly complicated, and the word is used to cover things which are really very different—things such as the payment of debts, the reparation of injuries done by oneself to another, and the bringing about of a distribution of happiness between other people in proportion to merit. I use the word to denote only the last of these three. In the fifth chapter I shall try to show that besides the three (comparatively) simple goods, virtue, knowledge, and pleasure, there is a more complex good, not reducible to these, consisting in the proportionment of happiness to virtue. The bringing of this about is a duty which we owe to all men alike, though it may be reinforced by special responsibilities that we have undertaken to particular men. This, therefore, with beneficence and self-improvement, comes under the general principle that we should produce as much good as possible, though the good here involved is different in kind from any other.

But besides this general obligation, there are special obligations. These may arise, in the first place incidentally, from acts which were not essentially meant to create such an obligation, but which nevertheless create it. From the nature of the case such acts may be of two kinds—the infliction of injuries on others, and the acceptance of benefits from them. It seems clear that these put us under a special obligation to other men, and that only these acts can do so incidentally. From these arise the twin duties of reparation and gratitude.

And finally there are special obligations arising from acts the very intention of which, when they were done, was to put us under such an obligation. The name for such acts is "promises"; the name is wide enough if we are willing to include under it implicit promises, i.e., modes of behaviour in which without explicit verbal promises we intentionally create an expectation that we can be counted on to behave in a certain way in the interest of another person.

These seem to be, in principle, all the ways in which *prima facie* duties arise. In actual experience they are compounded together in highly complex ways. Thus, for example, the duty of obeying the laws of one's country arises partly (as Socrates contends in the *Crito*) from the duty of gratitude for the benefits one has received from it; partly from the implicit promise to obey which seems to be involved in permanent residence in a country whose laws we know we are *expected* to obey, and still more clearly involved when we ourselves invoke the protection of its laws (this is the truth underlying the doctrine of the social contract); and partly (if we are fortunate in our country) from the fact that its laws are potent instruments for the general good.

Or again, the sense of a general obligation to bring about (so far as we can) a just apportionment of happiness to merit is often greatly reinforced by the fact that many of the existing injustices are due to a social and economic system which we have, not indeed created, but taken part in and assented to; the duty of justice is then reinforced by the duty of reparation.

It is necessary to say something by way of clearing up the relation between *prima facie* duties and the actual or absolute duty to do one particular act in particular circumstances. If, as almost all moralists except Kant are agreed, and as most plain men think, it is sometimes right to tell a lie or to break a promise, it must be maintained that there is a difference between *prima facie* duty and actual or absolute duty. When we think ourselves justified in breaking, and indeed morally obliged to break, a promise in order to relieve some one's distress, we do not for a moment cease to recognize a *prima facie* duty to keep our promise, and this leads us to feel, not indeed shame or repentance, but certainly compunction, for behaving as we do; we recognize, further, that it is our duty to make up somehow to the promisee for the breaking of the promise. We have to distinguish from the characteristic of being our duty that of tending to be our duty. Any act that we do contains various elements in virtue of which it falls under various categories. In virtue of being the breaking of a promise, for instance, it tends to be wrong; in virtue of being an instance of relieving distress it tends to be right. Tendency to be one's duty may be called a parti-resultant attribute, i.e., one which belongs to an act in virtue of some one component in its nature. *Being* one's duty is a toti-resultant attribute, one which belongs to an act in virtue of its whole nature and of nothing less than this. This distinction between parti-resultant and toti-resultant attributes is one which we shall meet in another context also.

Another instance of the same distinction may be found in the operation of natural laws. *Qua* subject to the force of gravitation towards some other body, each body tends to move in a particular direction with a particular velocity; but its actual movement depends on *all* the forces to which it is subject. It is only by recognizing this distinction that we can preserve the absoluteness of laws of nature, and only by recognizing a corresponding distinction that we can preserve the absoluteness of the general principles of morality. But an important difference between the two cases must be pointed out. When we say that in virtue of gravitation a body tends to move in a certain way, we are referring to a causal influence actually exercised on it by another body or other bodies. When we say that in virtue of being deliberately untrue a certain remark tends to be wrong, we are referring to no causal relation, to no relation that involves succession in time, but to such a relation as connects the various attributes of a mathematical figure. And if the word "tendency" is thought to suggest too much a causal relation, it is better to talk of certain types of act as being *prima facie* right or wrong (or of different persons as having different and possibly conflicting claims upon us), than of their tending to be right or wrong.

Something should be said of the relation between our apprehension of the *prima facie* rightness of certain types of acts and our mental attitude towards particular acts. It is proper to use the word "apprehension" in the former case and not in the latter. That an act, *qua* fulfilling a promise, or *qua* effecting a just distribution of good, or *qua* returning services rendered, or *qua* promoting the good of others, or *qua* promoting the virtue or insight of the agent, is *prima facie* right, is self-evident; not in the sense that it is evident from the beginning of our lives, or as soon as we attend to the proposition for the first time, but in the sense that when we have reached sufficient mental maturity and have given sufficient attention to the proposition it is evident without any need of proof, or of evidence beyond itself. It is self-evident just as a mathematical axiom, or the validity of a form of inference, is evident. The moral order expressed in these propositions is just as much part of the fundamental nature of the universe (and, we may add, of any possible universe in which there were moral agents at all) as is the spatial or numerical structure expressed in the axioms of geometry or arithmetic. In our confidence that these propositions are true there is involved the same trust in our reason that is involved in our confidence in mathematics; and we should have no justification for trusting in the latter sphere and distrusting it in the former. In both cases we are dealing with propositions that cannot be proved, but that just as certainly need no proof.

Some of these general principles of *prima facie* duty may appear to be open to criticism. It may be thought, for example, that the principle of returning good for good is a falling off from the Christian principle, generally and rightly recognized as expressing the highest morality, of returning good for evil. To this it may be replied that I do not suggest that there is a principle commanding us to return good for good and forbidding us to return good for evil, and that I do suggest that there is a positive duty to seek the good of all men. What I maintain is that an act in which good is returned for good is recognized as *specially* binding on us just because it is of that character, and that *ceteris paribus* any one would think it his duty to help his benefactors rather than his enemies, if he could not do both; just as it is generally recognized that *ceteris paribus* we should pay our debts rather than give our money in charity, when we cannot do both. A benefactor is not only a man, calling for our effort on his behalf on that ground, but also our benefactor, calling for our *special* effort on *that* ground.

Our judgements about our actual duty in concrete situations have none of the certainty that attaches to our recognition of the general principles of duty. A statement is certain, i.e., is an expression of knowledge, only in one or other of two cases: when it is either self-evident, or a valid conclusion from self-evident premises. And our judgements about our particular duties have neither of these characters. (1) They are not self-evident. Where a possible act is seen to have two characteristics, in virtue of one of which it is *prima facie* right, and in virtue of the other *prima facie* wrong, we are (I think) well aware that we are not certain whether we ought or ought not to do it; that whether we do it or not, we are taking a moral risk. We come in the long run, after consideration, to think one duty more pressing than the other, but we do not feel certain that it is so. And though we do not always recognize that a possible act has two such characteristics, and though there *may* be cases in which it has not, we are never certain that any particular possible act has not, and therefore never certain that it is right, nor certain that it is wrong. For, to go no further in the analysis, it is enough to point out that any particular act will in all probability in the course of time contribute to the bringing about of good or of evil for many human beings, and thus have a *prima facie* rightness or wrongness of which we know nothing. (2) Again, our judgements about our particular duties are not logical conclusions from self-evident premises. The only possible premises would be the general principles stating their *prima facie* rightness or wrongness *qua* having the different characteristics they do have; and even if we could (as we cannot) apprehend the extent to which an act will tend on the one hand, for example, to bring about advantages for our benefactors, and on the other hand to bring about disadvantages for fellow men who are not our benefactors, there is no principle by which we can draw the conclusion that it is on the whole right or on the whole wrong. In this respect the judgement as to the rightness of a particular act is just like the judgement as to the beauty of a particular natural object or work of art. A poem is, for instance, in respect of certain qualities beautiful and in respect of certain others not beautiful; and our judgement as to the degree of beauty it possesses on the whole is never reached by logical reasoning from the apprehension of its particular beauties or particular defects. Both in this and in the moral case we have more or less probable opinions which are not logically justified conclusions from the general principles that are recognized as self-evident.

There is therefore much truth in the description of the right act as a fortunate act. If we cannot be certain that it is right, it is our good fortune if the act we do is the right act. This consideration does not, however, make the doing of our duty a mere matter of chance. There is a parallel here between the doing of duty and the doing of what will be to our personal advantage. We never *know* what act will in the long run be to our advantage. Yet it is certain that we are more likely in general to secure our advantage if we estimate to the best of our ability the probable tendencies of our actions in this respect, than if we act on caprice. And similarly we are more likely to do our duty if we reflect to the best of our ability on the *prima facie* rightness or wrongness of various possible acts in virtue of the characteristics we perceive them to have, than if we act without reflection. With this greater likelihood we must be content.

Many people would be inclined to say that the right act for me is not that whose general nature I have been describing, viz., that which if I were omniscient, I should see to be my duty, but that which on all the evidence available to me I should think to be my duty. But suppose that from the state of partial knowledge in which I think act A to be my duty, I could pass to a state of perfect knowledge in which I saw act B to be my duty, should I not say, "Act B was the right act for me to do"? I should no doubt add, "Though I am not to be blamed for doing act A." But in adding this, am I not passing from the question "what is right" to the question "what is morally good"? At the same time I am not making the *full* passage from the one notion to the other; for in order that the act should be morally good, or an act I am not to be blamed for doing, it must not merely be the act which it is reasonable for me to think my duty; it must also be done for that reason, or from some other morally good motive. Thus the conception of the right act as the act which it is reasonable for me to think my duty is an unsatisfactory compromise between the true notion of the right act and the notion of the morally good action.

The general principles of duty are obviously not self-evident from the beginning of our lives. How do they come to be so? The answer is, that they come to be self-evident to us just as mathematical axioms do. We find by experience that this couple of matches and that couple make four matches, that this couple of balls on a wire and that couple make four balls; and by reflection on these and similar discoveries we come to see that it is of the nature of two and two to make four. In a precisely similar way, we see the *prima facie* rightness of an act which would be the fulfillment of a particular promise, and of another which would be the fulfillment of another promise, and when we have reached sufficient maturity to think in general terms, we apprehend *prima facie* rightness to belong to the nature of any ful-fillment of promise. What comes first in time is the apprehension of the self-evi-dent *prima facie* rightness of an individual act of a particular type. From this we come by reflection to apprehend the self-evident general principle of *prima facie* duty. From this, too, perhaps along with the apprehension of the self-evident *prima facie* rightness of the same act in virtue of its having another characteristic as well, and perhaps in spite of the apprehension of its *prima facie* wrongness in virtue of its having some third characteristic, we come to believe something not self-evident at all, but an object of probable opinion, viz., that this particular act is (not *prima facie* but) actually right.

In this respect there is an important difference between rightness and mathe-matical properties. A triangle which is isosceles necessarily has two of its angles equal, whatever other characteristics the triangle may have—whatever, for in-stance, be its area, or the size of its third angle. The equality of the two angles is a parti-resultant attribute. And the same is true of all mathematical attributes. It is true, I may add, of *prima facie* rightness. But no act is ever, in virtue of falling under some general description, necessarily actually right; its rightness depends on its whole nature* and not on any element in it. The reason is that no mathematical object (no figure, for instance, or angle) ever has two characteristics that tend to give opposite resultant characteristics, while moral acts often (as every one knows) and indeed always (as on reflection we must admit) have different characteristics that tend to make them at the same time *prima facie* right and *prima facie* wrong; there is probably no act, for instance, which does good to anyone without doing harm to someone else, and *vice versa*.

Supposing it is agreed, as I think on reflection it must, that no one *means* by "right" just "productive of the best possible consequences," or "optimific," the at-tributes "right" and "optimific" might stand in either of two kinds of relation to each other. (1) They might be so related that we could apprehend *a priori*, either immediately or deductively, that any act that is optimific is right and any act that is right is optimific, as we can apprehend that any triangle that is equilateral is equiangular and *vice versa*. Professor Moore's view is, I think, that the coexten-siveness of "right" and "optimific" is apprehended immediately. He rejects the possibility of any proof of it. Or (2) the two attributes might be such that the question whether they are invariably connected had to be answered by means of an inductive inquiry. Now at first sight it might seem as if the constant connexion of the two attributes could be immediately apprehended. It might seem absurd to suggest that it could be right for anyone to do an act which would produce conse-quences less good than those which would be produced by some other act in his power. Yet a little thought will convince us that this is not absurd. The type of case in which it is easiest to see that this is so is, perhaps, that in which one has made a

---

*To avoid complicating unduly the statement of the general view I am putting forward, I have here rather overstated it. Any act is the origination of a great variety of things many of which make no dif-ference to its rightness or wrongness. But there are always many elements in its nature (i.e., in what it is the origination of) that make a difference to its rightness or wrongness, and no element in its nature can be dismissed without consideration as indifferent.

promise. In such a case we all think that *prima facie* it is our duty to fulfill the promise irrespective of the precise goodness of the total consequences. And though we do not think it is necessarily our actual or absolute duty to do so, we are far from thinking that any, even the slightest, gain in the value of the total consequences will necessarily justify us in doing something else instead. Suppose, to simplify the case by abstraction, that the fulfillment of a promise to A would produce 1,000 units of good* for him, but that by doing some other act I could produce 1,001 units of good for B, to whom I have made no promise, the other consequences of the two acts being of equal value; should we really think it self-evident that it was our duty to do the second act and not the first? I think not. We should, I fancy, hold that only a much greater disparity of value between the total consequences would justify us in failing to discharge our *prima facie* duty to A. After all, a promise is a promise, and is not to be treated so lightly as the theory we are examining would imply. What, exactly, a promise is, is not so easy to determine, but we are surely agreed that it constitutes a serious moral limitation to our freedom of action. To produce the 1,001 units of good for B rather than fulfill our promise to A would be to take, not perhaps our duty as philanthropists too seriously, but certainly our duty as makers of promises too lightly.

Or consider another phase of the same problem. If I have promised to confer on A a particular benefit containing 1,000 units of good, is it self-evident that if by doing some different act I could produce 1,001 units of good for A himself (the other consequences of the two acts being supposed equal in value), would it be right for me to do so? Again, I think not. Apart from my general *prima facie* duty to do A what good I can, I have another *prima facie* duty to do him the particular service I have promised to do him, and this is not to be set aside in consequence of a disparity of good of the order of 1,001 to 1,000, though a much greater disparity might justify me in so doing.

Or again, suppose that A is a very good and B a very bad man, should I then, even when I have made no promise, think it self-evidently right to produce 1,001 units of good for B rather than 1,000 for A? Surely not. I should be sensible of a *prima facie* duty of justice, i.e., of producing a distribution of goods in proportion to merit, which is not outweighed by such a slight disparity in the total goods to be produced.

Such instances—and they might easily be added to—make it clear that there is no self-evident connexion between the attributes "right" and "optimific." The theory we are examining has a certain attractiveness when applied to our decision that a particular act is our duty (though I have tried to show that it does not agree with our actual moral judgements even here). But it is not even plausible when applied to our recognition of *prima facie* duty. For if it were self-evident that the right coincides with the optimific, it should be self-evident that what is *prima facie* right is *prima facie* optimific. But whereas we are certain that keeping a promise is *prima facie* right, we are not certain that it is *prima facie* optimific (though we are

---

*I am assuming that good is objectively quantitative, but not that we can accurately assign an exact quantitative measure to it. Since it is of a definite amount, we can make the *supposition* that its amount is so-and-so, though we cannot with any confidence *assert* that it is.

perhaps certain that it is *prima facie* bonific). Our certainty that it is *prima facie* right depends not on its consequences but on its being the fulfillment of a promise. The theory we are examining involves too much difference between the evident ground of our conviction about *prima facie* duty and the alleged ground of our conviction about actual duty.

The coextensiveness of the right and the optimific is, then, not self-evident. And I can see no way of proving it deductively; nor, so far as I know, has anyone tried to do so. There remains the question whether it can be established inductively. Such an inquiry, to be conclusive, would have to be very thorough and extensive. We should have to take a large variety of acts which we, to the best of our ability, judge to be right. We should have to trace as far as possible their consequences, not only for the persons directly affected but also for those indirectly affected, and to these no limit can be set. To make our inquiry thoroughly conclusive, we should have to do what we cannot do, viz., trace these consequences into an unending future. And even to make it reasonably conclusive, we should have to trace them far into the future. It is clear that the most we could possibly say is that a large variety of typical acts that are judged right appear, so far as we can trace their consequences, to produce more good than any other acts possible to the agents in the circumstances. And such a result falls far short of proving the constant connexion of the two attributes. But it is surely clear that no inductive inquiry justifying even this result has ever been carried through. The advocates of utilitarian systems have been so much persuaded either of the identity or of the self-evident connexion of the attributes "right" and "optimific" (or "felicific") that they have not attempted even such an inductive inquiry as is possible. And in view of the enormous complexity of the task and the inevitable inconclusiveness of the result, it is worth no one's while to make the attempt. What, after all, would be gained by it? If, as I have tried to show, for an act to be right and to be optimific are not the same thing, and an act's being optimific is not even the ground of its being right, then if we could ask ourselves (though the question is really unmeaning) which we ought to do, right acts because they are right or optimific acts because they are optimific, our answer must be the former. If they are optimific as well as right, that is interesting but not morally important; we still ought to do them (which is only another way of saying that they *are* the right acts), and the question whether they are optimific has no importance for moral theory.

There is one direction in which a fairly serious attempt has been made to show the connexion of the attributes "right" and "optimific." One of the most evident facts of our moral consciousness is the sense which we have of the sanctity of promises, a sense which does not, on the face of it, involve the thought that one will be bringing more good into existence by fulfilling the promise than by breaking it. It is plain, I think, that in our normal thought we consider that the fact that we have made a promise is in itself sufficient to create a duty of keeping it, the sense of duty resting on remembrance of the past promise and not on thoughts of the future consequences of its fulfillment. Utilitarianism tries to show that this is not so, that the sanctity of promises rests on the good consequences of the fulfillment of them and the bad consequences of their non-fulfillment. It does so in this way: it points out that when you break a promise, you not only fail to confer a certain advantage on your promisee but you diminish his confidence, and indirectly the confidence of others, in the fulfillment of promise. You thus strike a blow at one of the devices that have been found most useful in the relations between man and man—the device on which, for example, the whole system of commercial credit rests—and you tend to bring about a state of things wherein each man, being entirely unable to rely on the keeping of promises by others, will have to do everything for himself, to the enormous impoverishment of human well-being.

To put the matter otherwise, utilitarians say that when a promise ought to be kept it is because the total good to be produced by keeping it is greater than the total good to be produced by breaking it, the former including as its main element the maintenance and strengthening of general mutual confidence, and the latter being greatly diminished by a weakening of this confidence. They say, in fact, that the case I put some pages back never arises—the case in which by fulfilling a promise I shall bring into being 1,000 units of good for my promisee, and by breaking it 1,001 units of good for some one else, the other effects of the two acts being of equal value. The other effects, they say, never are of equal value. By keeping my promise I am helping to strengthen the system of mutual confidence; by breaking it I am helping to weaken this; so that really the first act produces $1,000 + x$ units of good, and the second $1,001 - y$ units, and the difference between $+ x$ and $- y$ is enough to outweigh the slight superiority in the *immediate* effect of the second act. In answer to this it may be pointed out that there must be *some* amount of good that exceeds the difference between $+ x$ and $- y$ (i.e., exceeds $x + y$); say, $x + y + z$. Let us suppose the *immediate* good effects of the second act to be assessed not at 1,001 but at $1,000 + x + y + z$. Then its *net* good effects are $1,000 + x + z$, i.e., greater than those of the fulfillment of the promise; and the utilitarian is bound to say forthwith that the promise should be broken. Now, we may ask whether that is really the way we think about promises? Do we really think that the production of the slightest balance of good, no matter who will enjoy it, by the breach of a promise frees us from the obligation to keep our promise? We need not doubt that a system by which promises are made and kept is one that has great advantages for the general well-being. But that is not the whole truth. To make a promise is not merely to adapt an ingenious device for promoting the general well-being; it is to put oneself in a new relation to one person in particular, a relation which creates a specifically new *prima facie* duty to him, not reducible to the duty of promoting the general well-being of society. By all means let us try to foresee the net good effects of keeping one's promise and the net good effects of breaking it, but even if we assess the first at $1,000 + x$ and the second at $1,000 + x + z$, the question still remains whether it is not our duty to fulfill the promise. It may be suspected, too, that the effect of a single keeping or breaking of a promise in strengthening or weakening the fabric of mutual confidence is greatly exaggerated by the theory we are examining. And if we suppose two men dying together alone, do we think that the duty of one to fulfill before he dies a promise he has made to the other would be extinguished by the fact that neither act would have any effect on the general confidence? Anyone who holds this may be suspected of not having reflected on what a promise is.

I conclude that the attributes "right" and "optimific" are not identical, and that we do not know either by intuition, by deduction, or by induction that they coincide in their application, still less that the latter is the foundation of the former. It must be added, however, that if we are ever under no special obligation such as that of fidelity to a promisee or of gratitude to a benefactor, we ought to do what will produce most good; and that even when we are under a special obligation the tendency of acts to promote general good is one of the main factors in determining whether they are right.

———

Study Questions

1. What are Ross's main objections to Moore's "ideal utilitarianism"? Does he reject it completely, that is, does Ross retain any elements of Moore's utilitarianism?
2. What does Ross mean by a *prima facie* duty? What is the difference between a *prima facie* duty and an actual duty?
3. How, according to Ross, do we come to know the principles of *prima facie* duty? Do you find his account plausible?
4. Ross claims that "a promise is a promise," and the simple fact that one has made a promise is normally sufficient reason to keep it? Do you agree with Ross about the "sanctity" of the duty to keep one's promises? Why should one keep one's promises?
5. Imagine yourself in a situation like the one that Ross describes at the end of the selection (end of the second to last paragraph) in which you make a promise to a dying person. No one else knows that you have made this promise. Should you keep it? Does it matter if you don't? Explain.
6. Ross thinks that an act can be right even if some other action that one can perform has better consequences overall or produces more overall good. Give some examples to illustrate what Ross has in mind. Is this view of Ross's plausible? Do you agree with his view that the fact that an action produces greater overall good than the alternatives need not make it right?

Selected Bibliography

Pritchard, H. A. *Moral Obligation* (Oxford: Oxford University Press, 1949, 1968), especially Chaps. 1 ("Does Morality Rest on a Mistake?") and 2 ("Moral Obligation").
Ross, W. D. *The Right and the Good* (Oxford: Oxford University Press, 1930. Reprinted by Hackett Publishing, 1988).
———. *The Foundations of Ethics* (Oxford: Oxford University Press, 1939).

18

JEAN-PAUL SARTRE

——

Existentialism is easy to define. The problem comes later, when trying to understand what the definition means. In the essay that follows, Sartre defines existentialism, simply but not without obscurity, | *. . . to say that we invent values means nothing else but this: life has no meaning* a priori. *. . . it is up to you to give it a meaning.*

as the view that for human beings "existence precedes essence." Once this dictum is interpreted, it acquires intense practical significance. Sartre's contention is that there is no fixed human essence, or fixed human nature, that provides a set of objective values that can guide our actions and give meaning to our lives. Rather we are thrown into the world, and as individuals we are both free and confronted with the challenge of choosing our own values and what we are to be. What each of us becomes depends on our own decisions and actions. As we live our lives, we both create ourselves and create a set of values. Sartre's existentialism is a philosophy of radical freedom and radical responsibility. His view of individual human self-creativity has a number of ethical implications, some of which he discusses in this selection.

Although existentialism is an intellectual movement of the 20th century, it had its origins in the 19th, particularly with such writers as Søren Kierkegaard and Friedrich Nietzsche. As Sartre points out, it has taken two divergent paths, one Christian and the other atheistic (which he himself represents). Much existentialist writing, including the bulk of Sartre's own work, has been in the form of literary pieces (plays, novels, short stories) rather than philosophical treatises.

Jean-Paul Sartre was born in 1905, in Paris. After completing his education in France and teaching for several years, he went to Berlin where he studied German philosophy, laying the groundwork for the version of existentialism that he would later develop. During World War II he was active in the French Resistance movement against the German armies of occupation. Following the war, he became the acknowledged leader of the French intellectual *avant garde,* whose unofficial headquarters were the sidewalk cafes on the Parisian Left Bank (of the Seine River). In recognition of his many novels and plays, Sartre was awarded the Nobel prize for literature in 1964, an honor he refused to accept. He died in 1980.

Existentialism

[Existentialism] is the least scandalous, the most austere of doctrines. It is intended strictly for specialists and philosophers. Yet it can be defined easily. What complicates matters is that there are two kinds of existentialists; first, those who are Christian, among whom I would include Jaspers and Gabriel Marcel, both Catholic; and on the other hand the atheistic existentialists among whom I class Heidegger,* and the French existentialists and myself. What they have in common is that they think that existence precedes essence, or, if you prefer, that subjectivity must be the starting point.

Just what does that mean? Let us consider some object that is manufactured, for example, a book or a paper-cutter: here is an object which has been made by an artisan whose inspiration came from a concept. He referred to the concept of what a paper-cutter is and likewise to a known method of production, which is part of the concept, something which is, by and large, a routine. Thus, the paper-cutter is at once an object produced in a certain way and, on the other hand, one having a specific use; and one cannot postulate a man who produces a paper-cutter but does not know what it is used for. Therefore, let us say that, for the paper-cutter, essence—that is, the ensemble of both the production routines and the properties which enable it to be both produced and defined—precedes existence. Thus, the presence of the paper-cutter or book in front of me is determined. Therefore, we have here a technical view of the world whereby it can be said that production precedes existence.

When we conceive God as the Creator, He is generally thought of as a superior sort of artisan. Whatever doctrine we may be considering, whether one like that of Descartes or that of Leibniz,** we always grant that will more or less follows understanding or, at the very least, accompanies it, and that when God creates He knows exactly what He is creating. Thus, the concept of man in the mind of God is comparable to the concept of a paper-cutter in the mind of the manufacturer, and, following certain techniques and conception, God produces man, just as the artisan, following a definition and a technique, makes a paper-cutter. Thus, the individual man is the realization of a certain concept in the divine intelligence. . . .

Atheistic existentialism, which I represent, . . . states that if God does not exist, there is at least one being in whom existence precedes essence, a being who exists before he can be defined by any concept, and that this being is man, or as Heidegger says, human reality. What is meant here by saying that existence precedes essence? It

*Karl Jaspers, German philosopher (1883–1969); Gabriel Marcel, French philosopher (1889–1973); Martin Heidegger, German philosopher (1889–1976)—Ed.
**René Descartes, French philosopher (1596–1650); G. W. Leibniz, German philosopher (1646–1716)—Ed.

From Jean-Paul Sartre, "The Humanism of Existentialism," *Essays in Existentialism,* ed. Wade Baskin, tr. B. Frechtman (Secaucus, NJ: The Citadel Press, 1972), Copyright © The Philosophical Library. Reprinted with permission of The Philosophical Library, New York.

means that, first of all, man exists, turns up, appears on the scene, and, only afterwards, defines himself. If man, as the existentialist conceives him, is indefinable, it is because at first he is nothing. Only afterward will he be something, and he himself will have made what he will be. Thus, there is no human nature, since there is no God to conceive it. Not only is man what he conceives himself to be, but he is also only what he wills himself to be after this thrust toward existence.

Man is nothing else but what he makes of himself. Such is the first principle of existentialism. It is also what is called subjectivity, the name we are labeled with when charges are brought against us. But what do we mean by this, if not that man has a greater dignity than a stone or table? For we mean that man first exists, that is, that man first of all is the being who hurls himself toward a future and who is conscious of imagining himself as being in the future. Man is at the start a plan which is aware of itself, rather than a patch of moss, a piece of garbage, or a cauliflower; nothing exists prior to this plan; there is nothing in heaven; man will be what he will have planned to be. Not what he will want to be. Because by the word "will" we generally mean a conscious decision, which is subsequent to what we have already made of ourselves. I may want to belong to a political party, write a book, get married; but all that is only a manifestation of an earlier, more spontaneous choice that is called "will." But if existence really does precede essence, man is responsible for what he is. Thus, existentialism's first move is to make every man aware of what he is and to make the full responsibility of his existence rest on him. And when we say that a man is responsible for himself, we do not only mean that he is responsible for his own individuality, but that he is responsible for all men.

The word subjectivism has two meanings, and our opponents play on the two. Subjectivism means, on the one hand, that an individual chooses and makes himself; and, on the other, that it is impossible for man to transcend human subjectivity. The second of these is the essential meaning of existentialism. When we say that man chooses his own self, we mean that every one of us does likewise; but we also mean by that that in making this choice he also chooses all men. In fact, in creating the man that we want to be, there is not a single one of our acts which does not at the same time create an image of man as we think he ought to be. To choose to be this or that is to affirm at the same time the value of what we choose, because we can never choose evil. We always choose the good, and nothing can be good for us without being good for all. . . .

The existentialists say at once that man is anguish. What that means is this: the man who involves himself and who realizes that he is not only the person he chooses to be, but also a lawmaker who is, at the same time, choosing all mankind as well as himself, cannot help escape the feeling of his total and deep responsibility. Of course, there are many people who are not anxious; but we claim that they are hiding their anxiety, that they are fleeing from it. Certainly, many people believe that when they do something, they themselves are the only ones involved, and when someone says to them, "What if everyone acted that way?" they shrug their shoulders and answer, "Everyone doesn't act that way." But really, one should always ask himself, "What would happen if everybody looked at things that way?" There is no escaping this disturbing thought except by a kind of double-dealing. A man who lies and makes excuses for himself by saying, "Not everybody does that," is someone with an uneasy conscience, because the act of lying implies that a universal value is conferred upon the lie. . . .

There is no question here of the kind of anguish which would lead to quietism, to inaction. It is a matter of a simple sort of anguish that anybody who has had responsibilities is familiar with. For example, when a military officer takes the responsibility for an attack and sends a certain number of men to death, he chooses to do so, and in the main he alone makes the choice. Doubtless, orders come from above, but they are too broad; he interprets them, and on this interpretation depend the lives of ten or fourteen or twenty men. In making a decision he can not help having a certain anguish. All leaders know this anguish. That doesn't keep them from acting; on the contrary, it is the very condition of their action. For it implies that they envisage a number of possibilities, and when they choose one, they realize that it has value only because it is chosen. We shall see that this kind of anguish, which is the kind that existentialism describes, is explained, in addition, by a direct responsibility to the other men whom it involves. It is not a curtain separating us from action, but is part of action itself.

When we speak of forlornness, a term Heidegger was fond of, we mean only that God does not exist and that we have to face all the consequences of this. The existentialist is strongly opposed to a certain kind of secular ethics which would like to abolish God with the least possible expense. About 1880, some French teachers tried to set up a secular ethics which went something like this: God is a useless and costly hypothesis; we are discarding it; but, meanwhile, in order for there to be an ethics, a society, a civilization, it is essential that certain values be taken seriously and that they be considered as having an *a priori* existence. It must be obligatory, *a priori*, to be honest, not to lie, not to beat your wife, to have children, etc., etc. So we're going to try a little device which will make it possible to show that values exist all the same, inscribed in a heaven of ideas, though otherwise God does not exist. In other words—and this, I believe, is the tendency of everything called reformism in France—nothing will be changed if God does not exist. We shall find ourselves with the same norms of honesty, progress, and humanism, and we shall have made of God an outdated hypothesis which will peacefully die off by itself.

The existentialist, on the contrary, thinks it very distressing that God does not exist, because all possibility of finding values in a heaven of ideas disappears along with Him; there can no longer be an *a priori* Good, since there is no infinite and perfect consciousness to think it. Nowhere is it written that the Good exists, that we must be honest, that we must not lie; because the fact is we are on a plane where there are only men. Dostoievsky said, "If God didn't exist, everything would be possible." That is the very starting point of existentialism. Indeed, everything is permissible if God does not exist, and as a result man is forlorn, because neither within him nor without does he find anything to cling to. He can't start making excuses for himself.

If existence really does precede essence, there is no explaining things away by reference to a fixed and given human nature. In other words, there is no determinism, man is free, man is freedom. On the other hand, if God does not exist, we find no values or commands to turn to which legitimize our conduct. So, in the bright realm of values, we have no excuse behind us, nor justification before us. We are alone, with no excuses.

That is the idea I shall try to convey when I say that man is condemned to be free. Condemned, because he did not create himself, yet, in other respects is free; because, once thrown into the world, he is responsible for everything he does. . . .

To give you an example which will enable you to understand forlornness better, I shall cite the case of one of my students who came to see me under the following circumstances: his father was on bad terms with his mother, and, moreover, was inclined to be a collaborationist; his older brother had been killed in the German offensive of 1940, and the young man, with somewhat immature but generous feelings, wanted to avenge him. His mother lived alone with him, very much upset by the half-treason of her husband and the death of her older son; the boy was her only consolation.

The boy was faced with the choice of leaving for England and joining the Free French Forces—that is, leaving his mother behind—or remaining with his mother and helping her to carry on. He was fully aware that the woman lived only for him and that his going-off—and perhaps his death—would plunge her into despair. He was also aware that every act that he did for his mother's sake was a sure thing, in the sense that it was helping her to carry on, whereas every effort he made toward going off and fighting was an uncertain move which might run aground and prove completely useless; for example, on his way to England he might, while passing through Spain, be detained indefinitely in a Spanish camp; he might reach England or Algiers and be stuck in an office at a desk job. As a result, he was faced with two very different kinds of action: one, concrete, immediate, but concerning only one individual; the other concerned an incomparably vaster group, a national collectivity, but for that very reason was dubious, and might be interrupted en route. And, at the same time, he was wavering between two kinds of ethics. On the one hand, an ethics of sympathy, of personal devotion; on the other, a broader ethics, but one whose efficacy was more dubious. He had to choose between the two.

Who could help him choose? Christian doctrine? No. Christian doctrine says, "Be charitable, love your neighbor, take the more rugged path, etc., etc." But which is the more rugged path? Whom should he love as a brother? The fighting man or his mother? Which does the greater good, the vague act of fighting in a group, or the concrete one of helping a particular human being to go on living? Who can decide *a priori*? Nobody. No book of ethics can tell him. The Kantian ethics says, "Never treat any person as a means, but as an end." Very well, if I stay with mother, I'll treat her as an end and not as a means; but by virtue of this very fact, I'm running the risk of treating the people around me who are fighting as means; and, conversely, if I go to join those who are fighting, I'll be treating them as an end, and, by doing that, I run the risk of treating my mother as a means.

If values are vague, and if they are always too broad for the concrete and specific case that we are considering, the only thing left for us is to trust our instincts. That's what this young man tried to do; and when I saw him, he said, "In the end, feeling is what counts. I ought to choose whichever pushes me in one direction. If I feel that I love my mother enough to sacrifice everything else for her—my desire for vengeance, for action, for adventure—then I'll stay with her. If, on the contrary, I feel that my love for my mother isn't enough, I'll leave."

But how is the value of a feeling determined? What gives his feeling for his mother value? Precisely the fact that he remained with her. I may say that I like so-and-so well enough to sacrifice a certain amount of money for him, but I may say so only if I've done it. I may say "I love my mother well enough to remain with her" if I have remained with her. The only way to determine the value of this affection is, precisely, to perform an act which confirms and defines it. But, since I require this affection to justify my act, I find myself caught in a vicious circle.

On the other hand, Gide has well said that a mock feeling and a true feeling are almost indistinguishable; to decide that I love my mother and will remain with her, or to remain with her by putting on an act, amount somewhat to the same thing. In other words, the feeling is formed by the acts one performs; so, I can not refer to it in order to act upon it. Which means that I can neither seek within myself the true condition which will impel me to act, nor apply to a system of ethics for concepts which will permit me to act. You will say, "At least, he did go to a teacher for advice." But if you seek advice from a priest, for example, you have chosen this priest; you already knew, more or less, just about what advice he was going to give you. In other words, choosing your adviser is involving yourself. The proof of this is that if you are a Christian, you will say, "Consult a priest." But some priests are collaborating, some are just marking time, some are resisting. Which to choose? If the young man chooses a priest who is resisting or collaborating, he has already decided on the kind of advice he's going to get. Therefore, in coming to see me he knew the answer I was going to give him, and I had only one answer to give: "You're free, choose, that is, invent." No general ethics can show you what is to be done; there are no omens in the world. The Catholics will reply, "But there are." Granted—but, in any case, I myself choose the meaning they have. . . .

The doctrine I am presenting is the very opposite of quietism, since it declares, "There is no reality except in action." Moreover, it goes further, since it adds, "Man is nothing else than his plan; he exists only to the extent that he fulfills himself; he is therefore nothing else than the ensemble of his acts, nothing else than his life."

According to this, we can understand why our doctrine horrifies certain people. Because often the only way they can bear their wretchedness is to think, "Circumstances have been against me. What I've been and done doesn't show my true worth. To be sure, I've had no great love, no great friendship, but that's because I haven't met a man or woman who was worthy. The books I've written haven't been very good because I haven't had the proper leisure. I haven't had children to devote myself to because I didn't find a man with whom I could have spent my life. So there remains within me, unused and quite viable, a host of propensities, inclinations, possibilities, that one wouldn't guess from the mere series of things I've done."

Now, for the existentialist there is really no love other than one which manifests itself in a person's being in love. There is no genius other than one which is expressed in works of art; the genius of Proust is the sum of Proust's works; the genius of Racine is his series of tragedies. Outside of that, there is nothing. Why say that Racine could have written another tragedy, when he didn't write it? A man is involved in life, leaves his impress on it, and outside of that there is nothing. To be sure, this may seem a harsh thought to someone whose life hasn't been a success. But, on the other hand, it prompts people to understand that reality alone is what counts, that dreams, expectations, and hopes warrant no more than to define a man as a disappointed dream, as miscarried hopes, as vain expectations. In other words, to define him negatively and not positively. However, when we say, "You are nothing else than your life," that does not imply that the artist will be judged solely on the basis of his works of art; a thousand other things will contribute toward summing him up. What we mean is that a man is nothing else than a series of undertakings, that he is the sum, the organization, the ensemble of the relationships which make up these undertakings.

When all is said and done, what we are accused of, at bottom, is not our pessimism, but an optimistic toughness. If people throw up to us our works of fiction in which we write about people who are soft, weak, cowardly, and sometimes even downright bad, it's not because these people are soft, weak, cowardly, or bad; because if we were to say, as Zola did, that they are that way because of heredity, the workings of environment, society, because of biological or psychological determinism, people would be reassured. They would say, "Well, that's what we're like, no one can do anything about it." But when the existentialist writes about a coward, he says that this coward is responsible for his cowardice. He's not like that because he has a cowardly heart or lung or brain; he's not like that on account of his physiological make-up; but he's like that because he has made himself a coward by his acts. There's no such thing as a cowardly constitution; there are nervous constitutions; there is poor blood, as the common people say, or there are strong constitutions. But the man whose blood is poor is not a coward on that account, for what makes cowardice is the act of renouncing or yielding. A constitution is not an act; the coward is defined on the basis of the acts he performs. People feel, in a vague sort of way, that this coward we're talking about is guilty of being a coward, and the thought frightens them. What people would like is that a coward or a hero be born that way. . . .

This does not entirely settle the objection to subjectivism. In fact, the objection still takes several forms. First, there is the following: we are told, "So you're able to do anything, no matter what!" This is expressed in various ways. First we are accused of anarchy; then they say, "You're unable to pass judgment on others, because there's no reason to prefer one configuration to another"; finally they tell us, "Everything is arbitrary in this choosing of yours. You take something from one pocket and pretend you're putting it into the other."

These three objections aren't very serious. Take the first objection. "You're able to do anything, no matter what" is not to the point. In one sense choice is possible, but what is not possible is not to choose. I can always choose, but I ought to know that if I do not choose, I am still choosing. Though this may seem purely formal, it is highly important for keeping fantasy and caprice within bounds. If it is true that in facing a situation, for example, one in which, as a person capable of having sexual relations, of having children, I am obliged to choose an attitude, and if I in any way assume responsibility for a choice which, in involving myself, also involves all mankind, this has nothing to do with caprice, even if no *a priori* value determines my choice. . . .

In the second place, it is said that we are unable to pass judgment on others. In a way this is true, and in another way, false. It is true in this sense, that, whenever a man sanely and sincerely involves himself and chooses his configuration, it is impossible for him to prefer another configuration, regardless of what his own may be in other respects. It is true in this sense, that we do not believe in progress. Progress is betterment. Man is always the same. The situation confronting him varies. Choice always remains a choice in a situation. The problem has not changed since the time one could choose between those for and those against slavery, for example, at the time of the Civil War, and the present time, when one can side with the Maquis Resistance Party, or with the Communists.

But, nevertheless, one can still pass judgment, for, as I have said, one makes a choice in relationship to others. First, one can judge (and this is perhaps not a judgment of value, but a logical judgment) that certain choices are based on error and others on truth. If we have defined man's situation as a free choice, with no excuses and no recourse, every man who takes refuge behind the excuse of his passions, every man who sets up a determinism, is a dishonest man.

The objection may be raised, "But why mayn't he choose himself dishonestly?" I reply that I am not obliged to pass moral judgment on him, but that I do define his dishonesty as an error. One can not help considering the truth of the matter. Dishonesty is obviously a falsehood because it belies the complete freedom of involvement. On the same grounds, I maintain that there is also dishonesty if I choose to state that certain values exist prior to me; it is self-contradictory for me to want them and at the same time state that they are imposed on me. Suppose someone says to me, "What if I want to be dishonest?" I'll answer, "There's no reason for you not to be, but I'm saying that that's what you are, and that the strictly coherent attitude is that of honesty."

Besides, I can bring moral judgment to bear. When I declare that freedom in every concrete circumstance can have no other aim than to want itself, if man has once become aware that in his forlornness he imposes values, he can no longer want but one thing, and that is freedom, as the basis of all values. That doesn't mean that he wants it in the abstract. It means simply that the ultimate meaning of the acts of honest men is the quest for freedom as such. A man who belongs to a communist or revolutionary union wants concrete goals; these goals imply an abstract desire for freedom; but this freedom is wanted in something concrete. We want freedom for freedom's sake and in every particular circumstance. And in wanting freedom we discover that it depends entirely on the freedom of others, and that the freedom of others depends on ours. Of course, freedom as the definition of man does not depend on others, but as soon as there is involvement, I am obliged to want others to have freedom at the same time that I want my own freedom. I can take freedom as my goal only if I take that of others as a goal as well. Consequently, when, in all honesty, I've recognized that man is a being in whom existence precedes essence, that he is a free being who, in various circumstances, can want only his freedom, I have at the same time recognized that I can want only the freedom of others.

Therefore, in the name of this will for freedom, which freedom itself implies, I may pass judgment on those who seek to hide from themselves the complete arbitrariness and the complete freedom of their existence. . . .

The third objection is the following: "You take something from one pocket and put it into the other. That is, fundamentally, values aren't serious, since you choose them." My answer to this is that I'm quite vexed that that's the way it is; but if I've discarded God the Father, there has to be someone to invent values. You've got to take things as they are. Moreover, to say that we invent values means nothing else but this: life has no meaning a priori. Before you come alive, life is nothing; it's up to you to give it a meaning, and value is nothing else but the meaning that you choose. In that way, you see, there is a possibility of creating a human community. . . .

But there is another meaning of humanism. Fundamentally it is this: man is constantly outside of himself; in projecting himself, in losing himself outside of himself, he makes for man's existing; and, on the other hand, it is by pursuing transcendent goals that he is able to exist; man, being this state of passing-beyond, and seizing upon things only as they bear upon this passing-beyond, is at the heart, at the center of this passing-beyond. There is no universe other than a human universe, the universe of human subjectivity. This connection between transcendency, as a constituent element of man—not in the sense that God is transcendent, but in the sense of passing beyond—and subjectivity, in the sense that man is not closed in on himself but is always present in a human universe, is what we call existentialist humanism. Humanism, because we remind man that there is no lawmaker other than himself, and that in his forlornness he will decide by himself; because we point out that man will fulfill himself as man, not in turning toward himself, but in seeking outside of himself a goal which is just this liberation, just this particular fulfillment. . . .

Study Questions

1. In the beginning of the selection, Sartre refers to a paper-cutter as an example of something in which "essence precedes existence." What does it mean to say that the essence of a paper-cutter precedes its existence? What would it mean to say of human beings that their essence precedes their existence? What does it mean, in contrast, to say of human beings that "existence precedes essence"?
2. Sartre says that each person is responsible for his or her own life, but that in choosing for oneself, one chooses for all human beings and creates an image of human beings as we think they ought to be. "We always choose the good, and nothing can be good for us without being good for all." Is this claim plausible? What sorts of constraints does he impose on free choices by making this claim?
3. Sartre writes that "man is condemned to be free." What does he mean by this? Is it true?
4. According to Sartre, "If God does not exist, we find no values or commands to turn to which legitimize our conduct." Could there be another source of such values and commands? If so, what?
5. Sartre gives the example of a young man who must choose between joining the Resistance (the "Free French Forces") and staying with his mother. How

should the young man decide what to do? What does Sartre think that this kind of choice shows us?

6. Do you accept Sartre's judgment that you alone are responsible for what you are? If not, who else bears responsibility?

7. How does Sartre respond to the objection that he is unable to pass judgment on others? (See p. 317.) In your view, does Sartre's theory leave room for moral judgment, as he claims?

Selected Bibliography

Anderson, Thomas C. *Sartre's Two Ethics: From Authenticity to Integral Humanity* (Chicago: Open Court, 1993).

Barnes, Hazel E. *An Existentialist Ethics* (New York: Vintage, 1967).

Bell, Linda A. *Sartre's Ethics of Authenticity* (Tuscaloosa: The University of Alabama Press, 1989).

Catalano, J. S. *Good Faith and Other Essays: Perspectives on a Sartrean Ethics* (Lanham, MD: Rowman & Littlefield, 1996).

Danto, Arthur. *Jean-Paul Sartre* (New York: Viking Press, 1975), esp. Chap. 5.

de Beauvoir, Simone. *The Ethics of Ambiguity*, tr. Bernard Frechtman (New York: Citadel, 1964).

Dobson, A. *Jean-Paul Sartre and the Politics of Reason* (Cambridge/New York: Cambridge University Press, 1993).

Flynn, Thomas R. *Sartre and Marxist Existentialism: The Test Case of Collective Responsibility* (Chicago: The University of Chicago Press, 1984).

Jeanson, Francis. *Sartre and the Problem of Morality* (Bloomington: Indiana University Press, 1947, 1980).

Murdoch, Iris. *Sartre: Romantic Rationalist* (New Haven, CT: Yale University Press, 1959).

19

BERNARD WILLIAMS

—

The next set of selections, by Bernard Williams, takes up two issues that many have thought pose a threat to morality and raise questions of moral skepticism. One is the figure of the "amoralist" and the other is the question of moral relativism. An amoralist would be a person who is completely indifferent to and unmoved by moral considerations. The amoralist may understand what others are talking

> *. . . having sympathetic concern for others . . . is the only way "into morality. . . ."*
>
> *. . . it cannot be a consequence of the nature of morality itself that no society ought ever to interfere with another. . . .*

about when they engage in moral discourse and may realize that others are moved by moral claims, but he or she does not acknowledge their force. A question for moral philosophy is whether such a person can be given a reason to care about morality. If not, does that mean that we—assuming here that we do recognize the force of moral considerations—do not really have any reason to care about morality? Trying to imagine a complete amoralist is an interesting thought experiment because it leads us to think about the different elements that go into the moral point of view, as well as to consider how deeply rooted in our psychology they are—at least in most people.

Moral relativism is the view that there are no universally valid moral principles or moral requirements—principles or requirements that apply to everyone. Rather, different people are subject to different moral requirements depending on the principles or conventions that their societies accept. Accordingly, an action might be morally permissible for a member of one society, but wrong for a member of another. Moral relativism is not just the factual claim (sometimes called "descriptive relativism") that societies have differed in their beliefs about right and wrong or have accepted different moral principles and values. The defender of universally valid moral principles recognizes this fact and might reply that many societies have accepted values and practices that were wrong. For example, slavery was accepted by parts of our country in the 18th and 19th centuries. But most people hold that slavery violates basic human rights, and that it was wrong—then as now—whether or not people at the time believed it to be wrong. In other words, the fact that the

320

values and practices of societies differ does not mean that there are no principles that all societies ought to accept. The moral relativist must go beyond the descriptive claim to hold that there are no universal moral principles that everyone ought to accept, and that the moral demands to which people are subject are relative to the principles and conventions accepted by their society.

Williams raises the question of whether accepting moral relativism should lead to tolerance. It is a tricky issue, and harder to resolve than one might think.

Bernard Williams is one of the most important and original contemporary moral philosophers, and has written on a wide range of topics in moral philosophy and moral psychology. His books include *Moral Luck* (1981) and *Ethics and the Limits of Philosophy* (1985). He has taught at Cambridge University, where he was Provost of King's College. He is a professor at Oxford University and at the University of California, Berkeley.

—

The Amoralist

"Why should I do anything?" Two of the many ways of taking that question are these: as an expression of despair or hopelessness, when it means something like Give me a reason for doing anything; everything is meaningless"; and as sounding a more defiant note, against morality, when it means something like "Why is there anything that I *should, ought to,* do?"

Even though we can paraphrase the question in the first spirit as "Give me a reason . . . ," it is very unclear that we can in fact give the man who asks it a reason—that, starting from so far down, we could argue him into caring about something. We might indeed "give him a reason" in the sense of finding something that he is prepared to care about, but that is not inducing him to care by reasoning, and it is very doubtful whether there could be any such thing. What he needs is help, or hope, not reasonings. Of course it is true that if he stays alive he will be doing *something,* than something else, and thus in some absolutely minimal sense he has some sort of reason, some minimal preference, for doing those things rather than other things. But to point this out gets us hardly anywhere; he does those things just mechanically, perhaps, to keep going, and they mean nothing to him. Again, if he sees his state as a reason for suicide, then that would be to make a real decision; as a way out of making any decisions, suicide comes inevitably one decision too late (as Camus points out in *Le Mythe de Sisyphe*). But it would be no victory for us or for him if it turned out there was after all just one decision that he was prepared to acknowledge, that one.

I do not see how it could be regarded as a defeat for reason or rationality that it had no power against this man's state; his state is rather a defeat for humanity. But the man who asks the question in the second spirit has been regarded by many moralists as providing a real challenge to moral reasoning. He, after all, acknowledges some reasons for doing things; he is, moreover, like most of us some of the time. If morality can be got off the ground rationally, then we ought to be able to get it off the ground in an argument against him; while, in his pure form—in which we can call him the *amoralist*—he may not be actually persuaded, it might seem a comfort to morality if there were reasons which, if he were rational, would persuade him.

We might ask first what motivations he does have. He is indifferent to moral considerations, but there are things that he cares about, and he has some real preferences and aims. They might be, presumably, pleasure or power; or they might be something much odder, such as some passion for collecting things. Now these ends in themselves do not exclude some acknowledgement of morality; what do we have to leave out to represent him as paying no such acknowledgement? Presumably such things as his caring about other people's interests, having any inclination to tell the truth or keep promises if it does not suit him to do so, being disposed to reject courses of action on the ground that they are unfair or dishonourable or selfish. These are some of the substantial materials of morality. We should perhaps also leave out a more formal aspect of morality, namely any disposition on his part to stand back and have the thought that if it is "all right" him to act in these ways, it must be "all right" for others to act similarly against him. For if he is prepared to take this stance, we might be able to take a step towards saying that he was not a man without a morality, but a man with a peculiar one.

However, we need a distinction here. In one way, it is possible for a man to think it "all right" for everyone to behave self-interestedly, without his having got into any distinctively moral territory of thought at all: if, roughly, "it's all right" means "I am not going to moralize about it." He will be in some moral territory if "all right" means something like "permitted," for that would carry implications such as "people ought not to interfere with other people's pursuit of their own interests," and that is not a thought which, as an amoralist, he can have. Similarly, if he objects (as he no doubt will) to other people treating him as he treats them, this will be perfectly consistent so long as his objecting consists just in such things as his not liking it and fighting back. What he cannot consistently do is resent it or disapprove of it, for these are attitudes within the moral system. It may be difficult to discover whether he has given this hostage to moral argument or not, since he will no doubt have discovered that insincere expressions of resentment and moral hurt serve to discourage some of the more squeamish in his environment from hostile action.

This illustrates, as do many of his activities, the obvious fact that this man is a parasite on the moral system, and he and his satisfactions could not exist as they do unless others operated differently. For, in general, there can be no society without some moral rules, and he needs society; also he takes more particular advantage of moral institutions like promising and of moral dispositions of people around him. He cannot deny, as a fact, his parasitic position; but he is very resistant to suggestions of its relevance. For if we try saying "How would it be for you if everyone behaved like that?" he will reply, "Well, if they did, not good, I suppose—though in fact I might do better in the resulting chaos than some of the others. But the fact is, most of them are not going to do so; and if they do ever get round to it, I shall be dead by then." The appeal to the consequences of an *imagined* universalization is an essentially moral argument, and he is, consistently, not impressed by it.

In maintaining this stance, there are several things he must, in consistency, avoid. One—as we noticed before, in effect—is any tendency to say that the more or less moral majority have *no right* to dislike him, reject him, or treat him as an enemy, if indeed they are inclined to do so (his power, or charm, or dishonesty may be such that they do not). No thoughts about justification, at least of that sort, are appropriate to him. Again, he must resist, if consistent, a more insidious tendency to think of himself as being in character really rather splendid—in particular, as being by comparison with the craven multitude notably courageous. For in entertaining such thoughts, he will run a constant danger of getting outside the world of his own desires and tastes into the region in which certain dispositions are regarded as excellent for human beings to have, or good to have in society, or such things; and while such thoughts need not lead directly to moral considerations, they give a substantial footing to them, since they immediately invite questions about what is so good about those dispositions, and it will be difficult for him to pursue those questions very far without thinking in terms of the *general* interests and needs of his fellow human beings, which would land him once more back in the world of moral thought from which he is excluding himself.

The temptation to think of himself as courageous is a particularly dangerous one, since it is itself very nearly a moral notion and draws with it a whole chain of distinctively moral reflections. This man's application of the notion will also have a presupposition which is false: namely, that the more moral citizens would be amoral if they could get away with it, or if they were not too frightened, or if they were not passively conditioned by society—if, in general, they did not suffer from inhibitions. It is the idea that they are afraid that gives him the idea of his own courage. But these presuppositions are absurd. If he means that if as an individual one could be sure of getting away with it, one would break any moral rule (the idea behind the model of Gyges' ring of invisibility in Plato's *Republic*), it is just false of many agents, and there is reason why: the more basic moral rules and conceptions are strongly internalized in upbringing, at a level from which they do not merely evaporate with the departure of policemen or censorious neighbours. This is part of what it is for them to be moral rules, as opposed to *merely* legal requirements or matters of social convention. The effects of moral education can actually be to make people *want* to act, quite often, in a non-self-interested way, and it often succeeds in making it at least quite difficult, for internal reasons, to behave appallingly.

But this, he will say, is just social conditioning; remove that, and you will find no moral motivations.—We can reject the rhetoric of the word "conditioning"; even if there were a true theory, which there is not, which could explain all moral and similar education in terms of behaviourist learning theory, it would itself have to explain the very evident differences between successful and intelligent upbringing, which produces insight, and the production of conditioned reflexes. Then let us say instead that all moral motivation is the product of social influences, teaching, culture, etc. It is no doubt true. But virtually everything else about a man is such a product, including his language, his methods of thought, his tastes, and even his emotions, including most of the dispositions that the amoralist sets store by.—But, he may say, suppose we grant that anything complex, even my desires, are influenced by culture and environment, and in many cases produced by these; nevertheless there are *basic* impulses, of a self-interested kind, which are at the bottom of it all: these constitute what men are *really* like.

If "basic" means "genetically primitive," he may possibly be right: it is a matter of psychological theory. But even if true in this sense, it is once more irrelevant (to his argument, not to questions about how to bring up children); if there is such a thing as what men are *really* like, it is not identical with what very small children are like, since very small children have no language, again, nor many other things which men really have. If the test of what men are *really* like is made, rather, of how men may behave in conditions of great stress, deprivation, or scarcity (the test that Hobbes, in his picture of the state of nature, imposed), one can only ask again, why should that be the test? Apart from the unclarity of its outcome, why is the test even appropriate? Conditions of great stress and deprivation are not the conditions for observing the typical behaviour of any animal nor for observing other characteristics of human beings. If someone says that if you want to see what men are *really* like, see them after they have been three weeks in a lifeboat, it is unclear why that is any better a maxim with regard to their motivations than it is with regard to their physical condition.

If there is such a thing as what men are *really* like, it may be that (in these sorts of respects, at least) it is not so different from what they are *actually* like; that is, creatures in whose lives moral considerations play an important, formative, but often insecure role.

The amoralist, then, would probably be advised to avoid most forms of self-congratulatory comparison of himself with the rest of society. The rest may, of course, have some tendency to admire him, or those may who are at such a distance that he does not tread directly on their interests and affections. He should not be too encouraged by this, however, since it is probably wish-fulfilment (which does not mean that they would be like him if they could, since a wish is different from a frustrated desire). Nor will they admire him, still less like him, if he is not recognizably human. And this raises the question, whether we have left him enough to be that.

Does he care for anybody? Is there anybody whose sufferings or distress would affect him? If we say "no" to this, it looks as though we have produced a psychopath. If he is a psychopath, the idea of arguing him into morality is surely idiotic, but the fact that it is idiotic has equally no tendency to undermine the basis of morality or of rationality. The activity of justifying morality must surely get any point it has from the existence of an alternative—there being something to justify it *against*. The amoralist seemed important because he seemed to provide an alternative; his life, after all, seemed to have its attractions. The psychopath is, in a certain way, important to moral thought; but his importance lies in the fact that he appals us, and we must seek some deeper understanding of how and why he appals us. His importance does not lie in his having an appeal as an alternative form of life.

The amoralist we loosely sketched before did seem to have possibly more appeal than this; one might picture him as having some affections, occasionally caring for what happens to somebody else. Some stereotype from a gangster movie might come to mind, of the ruthless and rather glamorous figure who cares about his mother, his child, even his mistress. He is still recognizably amoral, in the sense that no general considerations weigh with him, and he is extremely short on fairness and similar considerations. Although he acts for other people from time to time, it all depends on how he happens to feel. With this man, of course, in actual fact arguments of moral philosophy are not going to work; for one thing, he always has something he would rather do than listen to them. This is not the point (though it is more of a point than some discussions of moral argument would lead one to suppose). The point is rather that he provides a model in terms of which we may glimpse what morality needs in order to get off the ground, even though it is unlikely in practice to get off the ground in a conversation with him.

He gives us, I think, almost enough. For he has the notion of doing something *for* somebody, because that person needs something. He operates with this notion in fact only when he is so inclined; but it is not itself the notion of his being so inclined. Even if he helps these people because he wants to, or because he likes them, and for no other reason (not that, so far as these particular actions are concerned, he needs to improve on those excellent reasons), what he wants to do is *to help them in their need,* and the thought he has when he likes someone and acts in this way is "they need help," not the thought "I like them and they need help." This is a vital point: this man is capable of thinking in terms of others' interests, and his failure to be a moral agent lies (partly) in the fact that he is only intermittently and capriciously disposed to do so. But there is no bottomless gulf between this state and the basic dispositions of morality. There are people who need help who are not people who at the moment he happens to want to help, or likes; and there are other people who like and want to help other particular people in need. To get him to consider their situation seems rather an extension of his imagination and his understanding, than a discontinuous step onto something quite different, the "moral plane." And if we could get him to consider their situation, in the sense of thinking about it and imagining it, he might conceivably start to show some consideration for it: we extend his sympathies. And if we can get him to extend his sympathies to less immediate persons who need help, we might be able to do it for less immediate persons whose interests have been violated, and so get him to have some primitive grasp on notions of fairness. If we can get him all this way, then, while he has no doubt an extremely shaky hold on moral considerations, he has some hold on them; at any rate, he is not the amoralist we started with.

This model is not meant to sketch the outline of a construction of the whole of morality from the possibility of sympathy and the extensions of sympathy: that would be impossible. (Even Hume, who perhaps came nearest to it, did not attempt that. His system, among the many interesting and valuable things that it contains, has a distinction between the "natural" and the "artificial" virtues which is relevant to this point.) The model is meant to suggest just one thing: that if we grant a man with even a minimal concern for others, then we do not have to ascribe to him any fundamentally new kind of thought or experience to include him in the world of morality, but only what is recognizably an extension of what he already has. He is not very far into it, and it is an extensive territory: as we saw in drawing up the amoralist, you have to travel quite a long way to get out of it. But the man with the extended sympathies, the ability to think about the needs of people beyond his own immediate involvement, is recognizably in it.

It does not follow from this that having sympathetic concern for others is a necessary condition of being in the world of morality, that the way sketched is the *only* way "into morality." It does not follow from what has so far been said; but it is true. . . .

———

Relativism

Let us at this stage of the argument about subjectivism take a brief rest and look round a special view or assemblage of views which has been built on the site of moral disagreements between societies. This is *relativism*, the anthropologist's heresy, possibly the most absurd view to have been advanced even in moral philosophy. In its vulgar and unregenerate form (which I shall consider, since it is both the most distinctive and the most influential form) it consists of three propositions: that "right" means (can only be coherently understood as meaning) "right for a given society"; that "right for a given society" is to be understood in a functionalist sense; and that (therefore) it is wrong for people in one society to condemn, interfere with, etc., the values of another society. A view with a long history, it was popular with some liberal colonialists, notably British administrators in places (such as West Africa) in which white men held no land. In that historical role, it may have had, like some other muddled doctrines, a beneficent influence, though modern African nationalism may well deplore its tribalist and conservative implications.

Whatever its results, the view is clearly inconsistent, since it makes a claim in its third proposition, about what is right and wrong in one's dealings with other societies, which uses a *nonrelative* sense of "right" not allowed for in the first proposition. The claim that human sacrifice, for instance, was "right for" the Ashanti comes to be taken as saying that human sacrifice was right among the Ashanti, and this in turn as saying that human sacrifice among the Ashanti was right; i.e., we had no business to interfere with it. But this last is certainly not the sort of claim allowed by the theory. The most the theory can allow is the claim that it was right for (i.e., functionally valuable for) our society not to interfere with Ashanti society, and, first, this is certainly not all that was meant, and, second, is very dubiously true.

Apart from its logically unhappy attachment of a nonrelative morality of toleration or noninterference to a view of morality as relative, the theory suffers in its functionalist aspects from some notorious weaknesses of functionalism in general, notably difficulties that surround the identification of "a society." If "society" is regarded as a cultural unit, identified in part through its values, then many of the functionalist propositions will cease to be empirical propositions and become bare tautologies: it is tediously a necessary condition of the survival of a group-with-certain-values that the group should retain those values. At the other extreme, the survival of a society could be understood as the survival of certain persons and their having descendants, in which case many functionalist propositions about the necessity of cultural survival will be false. When in Great Britain some Welsh nationalists speak of the survival of the Welsh language as a condition of the survival of Welsh society, they manage sometimes to convey an impression that it is a condition of the survival of Welsh people, as though the forgetting of Welsh were literally lethal.

In between these two extremes is the genuinely interesting territory, a province of informative social science, where there is room for such claims as that a given practice or belief is integrally connected with much more of a society's fabric than may appear on the surface, that it is not an excrescence, so that discouragement or modification of this may lead to much larger social change than might have been expected; or, again, that a certain set of values or institutions may be such that if they are lost, or seriously changed, the people in the society, while they may physically survive, will do so only in a deracinated and hopeless condition. Such propositions, if established, would of course be of first importance in deciding what to do; but they cannot take over the work of deciding what to do.

Here, and throughout the questions of conflict of values between societies, we need (and rarely get) some mildly realistic picture of what decisions might be being made by whom, of situations to which the considerations might be practically relevant. Of various paradigms that come to mind, one is that of conflict, such as the confrontation of other societies with Nazi Germany. Another is that of control, where (to eliminate further complications of the most obvious case, colonialism) one might take such a case as that of the relations of the central government of Ghana to residual elements of traditional Ashanti society. In neither case would functionalist propositions in themselves provide any answers at all. Still less will they where a major issue is whether a given group should be realistically or desirably regarded as "a society" in a relevant sense, or whether its values and its future are to be integrally related to those of a larger group—as with the case of blacks in the United States.

The central confusion of relativism is to try to conjure out of the fact that societies have differing attitudes and values an *a priori* nonrelative principle to determine the attitude of one society to another; this is impossible. If we are going to say that there are ultimate moral disagreements between societies, we must include, in the matters they can disagree about, their attitudes to other moral outlooks. It is also true, however, that there are inherent features of morality that tend to make it difficult to regard a morality as applying only to a group. The element of universalization which is present in any morality, but which applies under tribal morality perhaps only to members of the tribe, progressively comes to range over persons as such. Less formally, it is essential (as was remarked earlier) to morality and its role in any society that certain sorts of reactions and motivations should be strongly internalized, and these cannot merely evaporate because one is confronted with human beings in another society. Just as *de gustibus non disputandum* is not a maxim which applies to morality, neither is "when in Rome do as the Romans do," which is at best a principle of etiquette.

Nor is it just a case of doing as the Romans do, but of putting up with it. Here it would be a platitude to point out that of course someone who gains wider experience of the world may rightly come to regard some moral reaction of his to unfamiliar conduct as parochial and will seek to modify or discount it. There are many important distinctions to be made here between the kinds of thoughts appropriate to such a process in different cases: sometimes he may cease to regard a certain issue as a moral matter at all, sometimes he may come to see that what abroad looked the same as something he would have deplored at home was actually, in morally relevant respects, a very different thing. (Perhaps—though one can scarcely believe it—there were some missionaries or others who saw the men in a polygamous society in the light of seedy bigamists at home.) But it would be a particular moral view, and one both psychologically and morally implausible, to insist that these adaptive reactions were the only correct ones, that confronted with practices which are found and felt as inhuman, for instance, there is an *a priori* demand of acceptance. In the fascinating book by Bernal de Diaz, who went with Cortez to Mexico, there is an account of what they all felt when they came upon the sacrificial temples. This morally unpretentious collection of bravos was genuinely horrified by the Aztec practices. It would surely be absurd to regard this reaction as merely parochial or self-righteous. It rather indicated something which their conduct did not always indicate, that they regarded the Indians as men rather than as wild animals.

It is fair to press this sort of case, and in general the cases of actual confrontation. "Every society has its own standards" may be, even if confused, a sometimes useful maxim of social study; as a maxim of social study it is also painless. But what, after all, is one supposed to do if confronted with a human sacrifice?—not a real question for many of us, perhaps, but a real question for Cortez. It wasn't their business," it may be said; "they had no right to be there anyway." Perhaps—though this, once more, is necessarily a nonrelative moral judgement itself. But even if they had no right to be there, it is a matter for real moral argument what would *follow* from that. For if a burglar comes across the owner of the house trying to murder somebody, is he morally obliged not to interfere because he is trespassing?

None of this is to deny the obvious facts that many have interfered with other societies when they should not have done; have interfered without understanding; and have interfered often with a brutality greater than that of anything they were trying to stop. I am saying only that it cannot be a consequence of the nature of morality itself that no society ought ever to interfere with another, or that individuals from one society confronted with the practices of another ought, if rational, to react with acceptance. To draw these consequences is the characteristic (and inconsistent) step of vulgar relativism.

———

Study Questions

1. Are there, or can there be, people who are complete amoralists? Do you know any people who fit this description? If you are not such a person, would you be one if you could? Why or why not?

2. Why can't the amoralist consistently resent it if other people show no concern for his needs or interests? Similarly, why can't the amoralist think well of himself or herself in comparison with others?
3. Can one give the amoralist a reason to care about morality? If not, does that mean that there is really no reason for anyone to care about morality? Explain.
4. What is the "fallacy of vulgar relativism"? Why is it a fallacy?
5. Assume for a moment that you are a moral relativist, and that you are faced with a society or a group that accepts certain practices that you or your society condemns. (To make it vivid, imagine that the other group or society practices human sacrifice, or something comparable.) How should you respond to their practices, given that you are a relativist? Can you consistently pass judgment on what they do? Why or why not?

Selected Bibliography

Harman, Gilbert. *The Nature of Morality: An Introduction to Ethics* (New York: Oxford University Press, 1977), Chap. 12, "Egoism."

Nagel, Thomas, *What Does it All Mean?* (Oxford/New York: Oxford University Press, 1987), Chap. 7, "Right and Wrong."

Williams, Bernard. *Ethics and the Limits of Philosophy* (Cambridge, MA: Harvard University Press, 1985) Williams' most important book on ethics.

————, *Moral Luck* (Cambridge/New York: Cambridge University Press, 1981), esp. Chaps. 1, 2, and 8. A collection of Williams's essays.

————, *Morality* (Cambridge/New York: Cambridge University Press, 1972, 1993). An introductory treatment from which these selections are taken.

Further reading on the topic of moral relativism is listed after the selection by Gilbert Harman, "Is There a Single True Morality?"

20

John Rawls

During much of the 20th century, the dominant concern of moral philosophers was with meta-ethical questions about the meaning of ethical terms rather than substantive normative questions about the principles of right con-

> *Each person possesses an inviolability founded on justice that even the welfare of society as a whole cannot override.*

duct, justice, and the nature of the human good. Against the background of the pressing moral questions raised by the social and political turmoil of the 1960s, the concerns of moral philosophers seemed remote and in danger of becoming irrelevant. This situation changed dramatically in 1971 when John Rawls published his monumental work *A Theory of Justice*. Rawls's book is a systematic treatment of social justice that addresses fundamental questions of political philosophy such as the basic rights and freedoms of individuals, equal opportunity, and distributive justice or the fair distribution of social and economic advantage. *A Theory of Justice* revitalized moral philosophy and led to a renewed interest in substantive moral questions, and at the same time set the terms of debate in contemporary political philosophy. It is now widely recognized as a classic in political philosophy that rivals the great works of Hobbes, Locke, Rousseau, Kant, Mill, and Marx.

Rawls's theory of justice revives the social contract tradition, which had been superseded by the utilitarian tradition in the 19th century, and in doing so develops an alternative to utilitarianism in moral and political philosophy. Whereas the classical social contract theorists—Hobbes, Locke, Rousseau, and Kant—used the idea of a social contract to develop a theory of legitimate government, Rawls uses the idea of a fair agreement between free and equal persons to derive the fundamental principles of a just society. He calls his theory "Justice as Fairness." This phrase refers to two different parts of the theory. First, it refers to his two principles, which he states as follows:

P1: Each person has an equal right to a fully adequate scheme of equal basic liberties that is compatible with the same scheme of liberties for all.

P2: Social and economic inequalities are to satisfy two conditions: they are (a) to be attached to positions open to all under conditions of fair equal opportunity; and (b) are to be to the greatest benefit of the least advantaged members of society.

The first principle is a principle of equal liberty, and the second governs permissible social inequalities. The idea behind the second part of P2, called "the difference principle," is that inequalities are fair when the least well off, whoever they are, are better off than they would be under alternative social arrangements.

"Justice as Fairness" also refers to Rawls's modified social contract argument in support of his principles. He justifies his principles by arguing that they are the principles of justice that would be the result of a hypothetical rational choice among free and equal persons that is fair to all. This choice situation he calls "the original position," and one of its striking features is the stipulation that the parties choose under a "veil of ignorance." That is, they are deprived of all particular information about themselves and their social position in order to guarantee that they choose under fair conditions. If the choice is made under fair conditions, then any principles chosen will be fair, and a society that satisfies these principles treats its citizens fairly. Rawls's use of the idea of a hypothetical rational choice or agreement to derive normative principles has been highly influential in recent moral philosophy.

John Rawls was born in Baltimore in 1921 and died at his home in Lexington, Massachusetts, in 2002. He received both his B.A. and his Ph.D. from Princeton University. After teaching at Princeton, Cornell, and MIT, he joined Harvard's faculty in 1962. His other major works include *Political Liberalism* (1993, 1996), *The Law of Peoples* (1999), and *Justice as Fairness: A Restatement* (2001). He was made University Professor at Harvard in 1979, and in 1999 received the National Humanities Medal. In 1999 the Royal Swedish Academy of Sciences awarded him the Rolf Schock Prize, which is the equivalent of a Nobel Prize.

———

A Theory of Justice

1. The Role of Justice

Justice is the first virtue of social institutions, as truth is of systems of thought. A theory however elegant and economical must be rejected or revised if it is untrue; likewise laws and institutions no matter how efficient and well-arranged must be reformed or abolished if they are unjust. Each person possesses an inviolability founded on justice that even the welfare of society as a whole cannot override. For this reason justice denies that the loss of freedom for some is made right by a greater good shared by others. It does not allow that the sacrifices imposed on a few are outweighed by the larger sum of advantages enjoyed by many. Therefore in a just society the liberties of equal citizenship are taken as settled; the rights secured by justice are not subject to political bargaining or to the calculus of social interests. The only thing that permits us to acquiesce in an erroneous theory is the lack of a better one; analogously, an injustice is tolerable only when it is necessary to avoid an even greater injustice. Being first virtues of human activities, truth and justice are uncompromising.

These propositions seem to express our intuitive conviction of the primacy of justice. No doubt they are expressed too strongly. In any event I wish to inquire whether these contentions or others similar to them are sound, and if so how they can be accounted for. To this end it is necessary to work out a theory of justice in the light of which these assertions can be interpreted and assessed. I shall begin by considering the role of the principles of justice. Let us assume, to fix ideas, that a society is a more or less self-sufficient association of persons who in their relations to one another recognize certain rules of conduct as binding and who for the most part act in accordance with them. Suppose further that these rules specify a system of cooperation designed to advance the good of those taking part in it. Then, although a society is a cooperative venture for mutual advantage, it is typically marked by a conflict as well as by an identity of interests. There is an identity of interests since social cooperation makes possible a better life for all than any would have if each were to live solely by his own efforts. There is a conflict of interests since persons are not indifferent as to how the greater benefits produced by their collaboration are distributed, for in order to pursue their ends they each prefer a larger to a lesser share. A set of principles is required for choosing among the various social arrangements which determine this division of advantages and for underwriting an agreement on the proper distributive shares. These principles are the principles of social justice: they provide a way of assigning rights and duties in the basic institutions of society and they define the appropriate distribution of the benefits and burdens of social cooperation.

Now let us say that a society is well-ordered when it is not only designed to advance the good of its members but when it is also effectively regulated by a public conception of justice. That is, it is a society in which (1) everyone accepts and knows that the others accept the same principles of justice, and (2) the basic social institutions generally satisfy and are generally known to satisfy these principles. In this case while men may put forth excessive demands on one another, they nevertheless acknowledge a common point of view from which their claims may be adjudicated. If men's inclination to self-interest makes their vigilance against one another necessary, their public sense of justice makes their secure association together possible. Among individuals with disparate aims and purposes a shared conception of justice establishes the bonds of civic friendship; the general desire for justice limits the pursuit of other ends. One may think of a public conception of justice as constituting the fundamental charter of a well-ordered human association.

Existing societies are of course seldom well-ordered in this sense, for what is just and unjust is usually in dispute. Men disagree about which principles should define the basic terms of their association. Yet we may still say, despite this disagreement, that they each have a conception of justice. That is, they understand the need for, and they are prepared to affirm, a characteristic set of principles for assigning basic rights and duties and for determining what they take to be the proper distribution of the benefits and burdens of social cooperation. Thus it seems natural to think of the concept of justice as distinct from the various conceptions of justice and as being specified by the role which these different sets of principles, these different conceptions, have in common.* Those who hold different conceptions of justice can, then, still agree that institutions are just when no arbitrary distinctions are made between persons in the assigning of basic rights and duties and when the rules determine a proper balance between competing claims to the advantages of social life. . . .

2. The Subject of Justice

Many different kinds of things are said to be just and unjust: not only laws, institutions, and social systems, but also particular actions of many kinds, including decisions, judgments, and imputations. We also call the attitudes and dispositions of persons, and persons themselves, just and unjust. Our topic, however, is that of social justice. For us the primary subject of justice is the basic structure of society, or more exactly, the way in which the major social institutions distribute fundamental rights and duties and determine the division of advantages from social cooperation. By major institutions I understand the political constitution and the principal economic and social arrangements. Thus the legal protection of freedom of thought and liberty of conscience, competitive markets, private property in the means of production, and the monogamous family are examples of major social institutions. Taken together as one scheme, the major institutions define men's rights and duties and influence their life prospects, what they can expect to be and how well they can hope to do. The basic structure is the primary subject of justice because its effects are so profound and present from the start. The intuitive notion here is that this structure contains various social positions and that men born into different positions have different expectations of life determined, in part, by the political system as well as by economic and social circumstances. In this way the institutions of society favor certain starting places over others. These are especially deep inequalities. Not only are they pervasive, but they affect men's initial chances in life: yet they cannot possibly be justified by an appeal to the notions of merit or desert. It is these inequalities, presumably inevitable in the basic structure of any society, to which the principles of social justice must in the first instance apply. These principles, then, regulate the choice of a political constitution and the main elements of the economic and social system. The justice of a social scheme depends essentially on how fundamental rights and duties are assigned and on the economic opportunities and social conditions in the various sectors of society.

The scope of our inquiry is limited in two ways. First of all, I am concerned with a special case of the problem of justice. I shall not consider the justice of institutions and social practices generally, nor except in passing the justice of the law of nations and of relations between states. Therefore, if one supposes that the concept of justice applies whenever there is an allotment of something rationally regarded as advantageous or disadvantageous, then we are interested in only one

*Here I follow H. L. A. Hart, *The Concept of Law* (Oxford, The Clarendon Press, 1961), pp. 155–159.

instance of its application. There is no reason to suppose ahead of time that the principles satisfactory for the basic structure hold for all cases. These principles may not work for the rules and practices of private associations or for those of less comprehensive social groups. They may be irrelevant for the various informal conventions and customs of everyday life; they may not elucidate the justice, or perhaps better, the fairness of voluntary cooperative arrangements or procedures for making contractual agreements. The conditions for the law of nations may require different principles arrived at in a somewhat different way. I shall be satisfied if it is possible to formulate a reasonable conception of justice for the basic structure of society conceived for the time being as a closed system isolated from other societies. The significance of this special case is obvious and needs no explanation. It is natural to conjecture that once we have a sound theory for this case, the remaining problems of justice will prove more tractable in the light of it. With suitable modifications such a theory should provide the key for some of these other questions.

The other limitation on our discussion is that for the most part I examine the principles of justice that would regulate a well-ordered society. Everyone is presumed to act justly and to do his part in upholding just institutions. Though justice may be, as Hume remarked, the cautious, jealous virtue, we can still ask what a perfectly just society would be like.*

3. The Main Idea of the Theory of Justice

My aim is to present a conception of justice which generalizes and carries to a higher level of abstraction the familiar theory of the social contract as found, say, in Locke, Rousseau, and Kant.** In order to do this we are not to think of the original contract as one to enter a particular society or to set up a particular form of government. Rather, the guiding idea is that the principles of justice for the basic structure of society are the object of the original agreement They are the principles that free and rational persons concerned to further their own interests would accept in an initial position of equality as defining the fundamental terms of their association. These principles are to regulate all further agreements; they specify the kinds of social cooperation that can be entered into and the forms of government that can be established. This way of regarding the principles of justice I shall call justice as fairness.

Thus we are to imagine that those who engage in social cooperation choose together, in one joint act, the principles which are to assign basic rights and duties and to determine the division of social benefits. Men are to decide in advance how

* *An Enquiry Concerning the Principles of Morals*, sec. III, pt. I, par. 3, ed. L. A. Selby-Bigge, 2nd edition (Oxford, 1902), p. 184.

**As the text suggests, I shall regard Locke's *Second Treatise of Government*, Rousseau's *The Social Contract*, and Kant's ethical works beginning with *The Foundations of the Metaphysics of Morals* as definitive of the contract tradition. For all of its greatness, Hobbes's *Leviathan* raises special problems. A general historical survey is provided by J. W. Gough, *The Social Contract*, 2nd ed. (Oxford, The Clarendon Press, 1957), and Otto Gietke, *Natural Law and the Theory of Society*, trans. with an introduction by Ernest Barker (Cambridge, The University Press, 1934). A presentation of the contract view as primarily an ethical theory is to be found in G. R. Grice, *The Grounds of Moral Judgment* (Cambridge, The University Press. 1967). . . .

they are to regulate their claims against one another and what is to be the foundation charter of their society. Just as each person must decide by rational reflection what constitutes his good, that is, the system of ends which it is rational for him to pursue, so a group of persons must decide once and for all what is to count among them as just and unjust. The choice which rational men would make in this hypothetical situation of equal liberty, assuming for the present that this choice problem has a solution, determines the principles of justice.

In justice as fairness the original position of equality corresponds to the state of nature in the traditional theory of the social contract. This original position is not, of course, thought of as an actual historical state of affairs, much less as a primitive condition of culture. It is understood as a purely hypothetical situation characterized so as to lead to a certain conception of justice.* Among the essential features of this situation is that no one knows his place in society, his class position or social status, nor does any one know his fortune in the distribution of natural assets and abilities, his intelligence, strength, and the like. I shall even assume that the parties do not know their conceptions of the good or their special psychological propensities. The principles of justice are chosen behind a veil of ignorance. This ensures that no one is advantaged or disadvantaged in the choice of principles by the outcome of natural chance or the contingency of social circumstances. Since all are similarly situated and no one is able to design principles to favor his particular condition, the principles of justice are the result of a fair agreement or bargain. For given the circumstances of the original position, the symmetry of everyone's relations to each other, this initial situation is fair between individuals as moral persons, that is, as rational beings with their own ends and capable, I shall assume, of a sense of justice. The original position is, one might say, the appropriate initial status quo, and thus the fundamental agreements reached in it are fair. This explains the propriety of the name "justice as fairness": it conveys the idea that the principles of justice are agreed to in an initial situation that is fair. The name does not mean that the concepts of justice and fairness are the same, any more than the phrase "poetry as metaphor" means that the concepts of poetry and metaphor are the same.

Justice as fairness begins, as I have said, with one of the most general of all choices which persons might make together, namely, with the choice of the first principles of a conception of justice which is to regulate all subsequent criticism and reform of institutions. Then, having chosen a conception of justice, we can suppose that they are to choose a constitution and a legislature to enact laws, and so on, all in accordance with the principles of justice initially agreed upon. Our social situation is just if it is such that by this sequence of hypothetical agreements we would have contracted into the general system of rules which defines it. Moreover, assuming that the original position does determine a set of principles (that is, that a particular conception of justice would be chosen), it will then be

---

*Kant is clear that the original agreement is hypothetical. See *The Metaphysics of Morals*, pt. I (*Rechtslehre*), especially §§47, 52; and pt. II of the essay "Concerning the Common Saying: This May Be True in Theory but It Does Not Apply in Practice," in *Kant's Political Writings*, ed. Hans Reiss and trans. by H. B. Nisbet (Cambridge, The University Press, 1970), pp. 73–87. See Georges Vlachos, *La Pensée politique de Kant* (Paris, Presses Universitaires de France, 1962), pp. 326–335; and J. G. Murphy, *Kant: The Philosophy of Right* (London, Macmillan, 1970), pp. 109–112, 133–136, for a further discussion.

true that whenever social institutions satisfy these principles those engaged in them can say to one another that they are cooperating on terms to which they would agree if they were free and equal persons whose relations with respect to one another were fair. They could all view their arrangements as meeting the stipulations which they would acknowledge in an initial situation that embodies widely accepted and reasonable constraints on the choice of principles. The general recognition of this fact would provide the basis for a public acceptance of the corresponding principles of justice. No society can, of course, be a scheme of cooperation which men enter voluntarily in a literal sense; each person finds himself placed at birth in some particular position in some particular society, and the nature of this position materially affects his life prospects. Yet a society satisfying the principles of justice as fairness comes as close as a society can to being a voluntary scheme, for it meets the principles which free and equal persons would assent to under circumstances that are fair. In this sense its members are autonomous and the obligations they recognize self-imposed.

One feature of justice as fairness is to think of the parties in the initial situation as rational and mutually disinterested. This does not mean that the parties are egoists, that is, individuals with only certain kinds of interests, say in wealth, prestige, and domination. But they are conceived as not taking an interest in one another's interests. They are to presume that even their spiritual aims may be opposed, in the way that the aims of those of different religions may be opposed. Moreover, the concept of rationality must be interpreted as far as possible in the narrow sense, standard in economic theory, of taking the most effective means to given ends. I shall modify this concept to some extent, as explained later . . . but one must try to avoid introducing into it any controversial ethical elements. The initial situation must be characterized by stipulations that are widely accepted.

In working out the conception of justice as fairness one main task clearly is to determine which principles of justice would be chosen in the original position. To do this we must describe this situation in some detail and formulate with care the problem of choice which it presents. These matters I shall take up in the immediately succeeding chapters. It may be observed, however, that once the principles of justice are thought of as arising from an original agreement in a situation of equality, it is an open question whether the principle of utility would be acknowledged. Offhand it hardly seems likely that persons who view themselves as equals, entitled to press their claims upon one another, would agree to a principle which may require lesser life prospects for some simply for the sake of a greater sum of advantages enjoyed by others. Since each desires to protect his interests, his capacity to advance his conception of the good, no one has a reason to acquiesce in an enduring loss for himself in order to bring about a greater net balance of satisfaction. In the absence of strong and lasting benevolent impulses, a rational man would not accept a basic structure merely because it maximized the algebraic sum of advantages irrespective of its permanent effects on his own basic rights and interests. Thus it seems that the principle of utility is incompatible with the conception of social cooperation among equals for mutual advantage. It appears to be inconsistent with the idea of reciprocity implicit in the notion of a well-ordered society. Or, at any rate, so I shall argue.

I shall maintain instead that the persons in the initial situation would choose two rather different principles: the first requires equality in the assignment of basic rights and duties, while the second holds that social and economic inequalities, for example inequalities of wealth and authority, are just only if they result in compensating benefits for everyone, and in particular for the least advantaged members of society. These principles rule out justifying institutions on the grounds that the hardships of some are offset by a greater good in the aggregate. It may be expedient but it is not just that some should have less in order that others may prosper. But there is no injustice in the greater benefits earned by a few provided that the situation of persons not so fortunate is thereby improved. The intuitive idea is that since everyone's well-being depends upon a scheme of cooperation without which no one could have a satisfactory life, the division of advantages should be such as to draw forth the willing cooperation of everyone taking part in it, including those less well situated. The two principles mentioned seem to be a fair basis on which those better endowed, or more fortunate in their social position, neither of which we can be said to deserve, could expect the willing cooperation of others when some workable scheme is a necessary condition of the welfare of all.* Once we decide to look for a conception of justice that prevents the use of the accidents of natural endowment and the contingencies of social circumstance as counters in a quest for political and economic advantage, we are led to these principles. They express the result of leaving aside those aspects of the social world that seem arbitrary from a moral point of view.

The problem of the choice of principles, however, is extremely difficult. I do not expect the answer I shall suggest to be convincing to everyone. It is, therefore, worth noting from the outset that justice as fairness, like other contract views, consists of two parts: (1) an interpretation of the initial situation and of the problem of choice posed there, and (2) a set of principles which, it is argued, would be agreed to. One may accept the first part of the theory (or some variant thereof), but not the other, and conversely. The concept of the initial contractual situation may seem reasonable although the particular principles proposed are rejected. To be sure, I want to maintain that the most appropriate conception of this situation does lead to principles of justice contrary to utilitarianism and perfectionism, and therefore that the contract doctrine provides an alternative to these views. Still, one may dispute this contention even though one grants that the contractarian method is a useful way of studying ethical theories and of setting forth their underlying assumptions. . . .

4. The Original Position and Justification

I have said that the original position is the appropriate initial status quo which insures that the fundamental agreements reached in it are fair. This fact yields the name "justice as fairness." It is clear, then, that I want to say that one conception of justice is more reasonable than another, or justifiable with respect to it, if rational persons in the initial situation would choose its principles over those of the

---

*For the formulation of this intuitive idea I am indebted to Allan Gibbard.

other for the role of justice. Conceptions of justice are to be ranked by their acceptability to persons so circumstanced. Understood in this way the question of justification is settled by working out a problem of deliberation: we have to ascertain which principles it would be rational to adopt given the contractual situation. This connects the theory of justice with the theory of rational choice.

If this view of the problem of justification is to succeed, we must, of course, describe in some detail the nature of this choice problem. A problem of rational decision has a definite answer only if we know the beliefs and interests of the parties, their relations with respect to one another, the alternatives between which they are to choose, the procedure whereby they make up their minds, and so on. As the circumstances are presented in different ways, correspondingly different principles are accepted. The concept of the original position, as I shall refer to it, is that of the most philosophically favored interpretation of this initial choice situation for the purposes of a theory of justice.

But how are we to decide what is the most favored interpretation? I assume, for one thing, that there is a broad measure of agreement that principles of justice should be chosen under certain conditions. To justify a particular description of the initial situation one shows that it incorporates these commonly shared presumptions. One argues from widely accepted but weak premises to more specific conclusions. Each of the presumptions should by itself be natural and plausible; some of them may seem innocuous or even trivial. The aim of the contract approach is to establish that taken together they impose significant bounds on acceptable principles of justice. The ideal outcome would be that these conditions determine a unique set of principles; but I shall be satisfied if they suffice to rank the main traditional conceptions of social justice.

One should not be misled, then, by the somewhat unusual conditions which characterize the original position. The idea here is simply to make vivid to ourselves the restrictions that it seems reasonable to impose on arguments for principles of justice, and therefore on these principles themselves. Thus it seems reasonable and generally acceptable that no one should be advantaged or disadvantaged by natural fortune or social circumstances in the choice of principles. It also seems widely agreed that it should be impossible to tailor principles to the circumstances of one's own case. We should insure further that particular inclinations and aspirations, and persons' conceptions of their good do not affect the principles adopted. The aim is to rule out those principles that it would be rational to propose for acceptance, however little the chance of success, only if one knew certain things that are irrelevant from the standpoint of justice. For example, if a man knew that he was wealthy, he might find it rational to advance the principle that various taxes for welfare measures be counted unjust; if he knew that he was poor, he would most likely propose the contrary principle. To represent the desired restrictions one imagines a situation in which everyone is deprived of this sort of information. One excludes the knowledge of those contingencies which sets men at odds and allows them to be guided by their prejudices. In this manner the veil of ignorance is arrived at in a natural way. This concept should cause no difficulty if we keep in mind the constraints on arguments that it is meant to express. At any time we can enter the original position, so to speak, simply by following a certain procedure, namely, by arguing for principles of justice in accordance with these restrictions.

It seems reasonable to suppose that the parties in the original position are equal. That is, all have the same rights in the procedure for choosing principles; each can make proposals, submit reasons for their acceptance, and so on. Obviously the purpose of these conditions is to represent equality between human beings as moral persons, as creatures having a conception of their good and capable of a sense of justice. The basis of equality is taken to be similarity in these two respects. Systems of ends are not ranked in value; and each man is presumed to have the requisite ability to understand and to act upon whatever principles are adopted. Together with the veil of ignorance, these conditions define the principles of justice as those which rational persons concerned to advance their interests would consent to as equals when none are known to be advantaged or disadvantaged by social and natural contingencies.

There is, however, another side to justifying a particular description of the original position. This is to see if the principles which would be chosen match our considered convictions of justice or extend them in an acceptable way. We can note whether applying these principles would lead us to make the same judgments about the basic structure of society which we now make intuitively and in which we have the greatest confidence; or whether, in cases where our present judgments are in doubt and given with hesitation, these principles offer a resolution which we can affirm on reflection. There are questions which we feel sure must be answered in a certain way. For example, we are confident that religious intolerance and racial discrimination are unjust. We think that we have examined these things with care and have reached what we believe is an impartial judgment not likely to be distorted by an excessive attention to our own interests. These convictions are provisional fixed points which we presume any conception of justice must fit. But we have much less assurance as to what is the correct distribution of wealth and authority. Here we may be looking for a way to remove our doubts. We can check an interpretation of the initial situation, then, by the capacity of its principles to accommodate our firmest convictions and to provide guidance where guidance is needed.

In searching for the most favored description of this situation we work from both ends. We begin by describing it so that it represents generally shared and preferably weak conditions. We then see if these conditions are strong enough to yield a significant set of principles. If not, we look for further premises equally reasonable. But if so, and these principles match our considered convictions of justice, then so far well and good. But presumably there will be discrepancies. In this case we have a choice. We can either modify the account of the initial situation or we can revise our existing judgments, for even the judgments we take provisionally as fixed points are liable to revision. By going back and forth, sometimes altering the conditions of the contractual circumstances, at others withdrawing our judgments and conforming them to principle, I assume that eventually we shall find a description of the initial situation that both expresses reasonable conditions and yields principles which match our considered judgments duly pruned and adjusted. This state of affairs I refer to as reflective equilibrium.* It is an equilibrium because at

---

*The process of mutual adjustment of principles and considered judgments is not peculiar to moral philosophy. See Nelson Goodman, *Fact, Fiction, and Forecast* (Cambridge, Mass., Harvard University Press, 1955), pp. 65–68, for parallel remarks concerning the justification of the principles of deductive and inductive inference.

last our principles and judgments coincide; and it is reflective since we know to what principles our judgments conform and the premises of their derivation. At the moment everything is in order. But this equilibrium is not necessarily stable. It is liable to be upset by further examination of the conditions which should be imposed on the contractual situation and by particular cases which may lead us to revise our judgments. Yet for the time being we have done what we can to render coherent and to justify our convictions of social justice. We have reached a conception of the original position.

I shall not, of course, actually work through this process. Still, we may think of the interpretation of the original position that I shall present as the result of such a hypothetical course of reflection. It represents the attempt to accommodate within one scheme both reasonable philosophical conditions on principles as well as our considered judgments of justice. In arriving at the favored interpretation of the initial situation there is no point at which an appeal is made to self-evidence in the traditional sense either of general conceptions or particular convictions. I do not claim for the principles of justice proposed that they are necessary truths or derivable from such truths. A conception of justice cannot be deduced from self-evident premises or conditions on principles; instead, its justification is a matter of the mutual support of many considerations, of everything fitting together into one coherent view.

A final comment. We shall want to say that certain principles of justice are justified because they would be agreed to in an initial situation of equality. I have emphasized that this original position is purely hypothetical. It is natural to ask why, if this agreement is never actually entered into, we should take any interest in these principles, moral or otherwise. The answer is that the conditions embodied in the description of the original position are ones that we do in fact accept. Or if we do not, then perhaps we can be persuaded to do so by philosophical reflection. Each aspect of the contractual situation can be given supporting grounds. Thus what we shall do is to collect together into one conception a number of conditions on principles that we are ready upon due consideration to recognize as reasonable. These constraints express what we are prepared to regard as limits on fair terms of social cooperation. One way to look at the idea of the original position, therefore, is to see it as an expository device which sums up the meaning of these conditions and helps us to extract their consequences. On the other hand, this conception is also an intuitive notion that suggests its own elaboration, so that led on by it we are drawn to define more clearly the standpoint from which we can best interpret moral relationships. We need a conception that enables us to envision our objective from afar: the intuitive notion of the original position is to do this for us.

5. Classical Utilitarianism

There are many forms of utilitarianism, and the development of the theory has continued in recent years. I shall not survey these forms here, nor take account of the numerous refinements found in contemporary discussions. My aim is to work out a theory of justice that represents an alternative to utilitarian thought generally and so to all of these different versions of it. I believe that the contrast between the contract view and utilitarianism remains essentially the same in all these cases. Therefore I shall compare justice as fairness with familiar variants of intuitionism, perfectionism, and utilitarianism in order to bring out the underlying differences in the simplest way. With this end in mind, the kind of utilitarianism I shall describe here is the strict classical doctrine which receives perhaps its clearest and most accessible formulation in Sidgwick. The main idea is that society is rightly ordered, and therefore just, when its major institutions are arranged so as to achieve the greatest net balance of satisfaction summed over all the individuals belonging to it.

We may note first that there is, indeed, a way of thinking of society which makes it easy to suppose that the most rational conception of justice is utilitarian. For consider: each man in realizing his own interests is certainly free to balance his own losses against his own gains. We may impose a sacrifice on ourselves now for the sake of a greater advantage later. A person quite properly acts, at least when others are not affected, to achieve his own greatest good, to advance his rational ends as far as possible. Now why should not a society act on precisely the same principle applied to the group and therefore regard that which is rational for one man as right for an association of men? Just as the well-being of a person is constructed from the series of satisfactions that are experienced at different moments in the course of his life, so in very much the same way the well-being of society is to be constructed from the fulfillment of the systems of desires of the many individuals who belong to it. Since the principle for an individual is to advance as far as possible his own welfare, his own system of desires, the principle for society is to advance as far as possible the welfare of the group, to realize to the greatest extent the comprehensive system of desire arrived at from the desires of its members. Just as an individual balances present and future gains against present and future losses, so a society may balance satisfactions and dissatisfactions between different individuals. And so by these reflections one reaches the principle of utility in a natural way: a society is properly arranged when its institutions maximize the net balance of satisfaction. The principle of choice for an association of men is interpreted as an extension of the principle of choice for one man. Social justice is the principle of rational prudence applied to an aggregative conception of the welfare of the group. . . .

This idea is made all the more attractive by a further consideration. The two main concepts of ethics are those of the right and the good; the concept of a morally worthy person is, I believe, derived from them. The structure of an ethical theory is, then, largely determined by how it defines and connects these two basic notions. Now it seems that the simplest way of relating them is taken by teleological theories: the good is defined independently from the right, and then the right is defined as that which maximizes the good.* More precisely, those institutions and acts are right which of the available alternatives produce the most good, or at least as much good as any of the other institutions and acts open as real possibilities (a rider needed when the maximal class is not a singleton). Teleological theo-

*Here I adopt W. K. Frankena's definition of teleological theories in *Ethics* (Englewood Cliffs, N.J., Prentice Hall, Inc. 1963), p. 13.

ries have a deep intuitive appeal since they seem to embody the idea of rationality. It is natural to think that rationality is maximizing something and that in morals it must be maximizing the good. Indeed, it is tempting to suppose that it is self-evident that things should be arranged so as to lead to the most good.

It is essential to keep in mind that in a teleological theory the good is defined independently from the right. This means two things. First, the theory accounts for our considered judgments as to which things are good (our judgments of value) as a separate class of judgments intuitively distinguishable by common sense, and then proposes the hypothesis that the right is maximizing the good as already specified. Second, the theory enables one to judge the goodness of things without referring to what is right. For example, if pleasure is said to be the sole good, then presumably pleasures can be recognized and ranked in value by criteria that do not presuppose any standards of right, or what we would normally think of as such. Whereas if the distribution of goods is also counted as a good, perhaps a higher order one, and the theory directs us to produce the most good (including the good of distribution among others), we no longer have a teleological view in the classical sense. The problem of distribution falls under the concept of right as one intuitively understands it, and so the theory lacks an independent definition of the good. The clarity and simplicity of classical teleological theories derives largely from the fact that they factor our moral judgments into two classes, the one being characterized separately while the other is then connected with it by a maximizing principle.

Teleological doctrines differ, pretty clearly, according to how the conception of the good is specified. If it is taken as the realization of human excellence in the various forms of culture, we have what may be called perfectionism. This notion is found in Aristotle and Nietzsche, among others. If the good is defined as pleasure, we have hedonism; if as happiness, eudaimonism, and so on. I shall understand the principle of utility in its classical form as defining the good as the satisfaction of desire, or perhaps better, as the satisfaction of rational desire. This accords with the view in all essentials and provides, I believe, a fair interpretation of it. The appropriate terms of social cooperation are settled by whatever in the circumstances will achieve the greatest sum of satisfaction of the rational desires of individuals. It is impossible to deny the initial plausibility and attractiveness of this conception.

The striking feature of the utilitarian view of justice is that it does not matter, except indirectly, how this sum of satisfactions is distributed among individuals any more than it matters, except indirectly, how one man distributes his satisfactions over time. The correct distribution in either case is that which yields the maximum fulfillment. Society must allocate its means of satisfaction whatever these are, rights and duties, opportunities and privileges, and various forms of wealth, so as to achieve this maximum if it can. But in itself no distribution of satisfaction is better than another except that the more equal distribution is to be preferred to break ties.* It is true that certain common sense precepts of justice, particularly those which concern the protection of liberties and rights, or which express the claims of desert, seem to contradict this contention. But from a utili-

---

*On this point see Sidgwick, *The Methods of Ethics,* p. 416f.

tarian standpoint the explanation of these precepts and of their seemingly stringent character is that they are those precepts which experience shows should be strictly respected and departed from only under exceptional circumstances if the sum of advantages is to be maximized.* Yet, as with all other precepts, those of justice are derivative from the one end of attaining the greatest balance of satisfaction. Thus there is no reason in principle why the greater gains of some should not compensate for the lesser losses of others: or more importantly, why the violation of the liberty of a few might not be made right by the greater good shared by many. It simply happens that under most conditions, at least in a reasonably advanced stage of civilization, the greatest sum of advantages is not attained in this way. No doubt the strictness of common sense precepts of justice has a certain usefulness in limiting men's propensities to injustice and to socially injurious actions, but the utilitarian believes that to affirm this strictness as a first principle of morals is a mistake. For just as it is rational for one man to maximize the fulfillment of his system of desires, it is right for a society to maximize the net balance of satisfaction taken over all of its members.

The most natural way, then, of arriving at utilitarianism (although not, of course, the only way of doing so) is to adopt for society as a whole the principle of rational choice for one man. Once this is recognized, the place of the impartial spectator and the emphasis on sympathy in the history of utilitarian thought is readily understood. For it is by the conception of the impartial spectator and the use of sympathetic identification in guiding our imagination that the principle for one man is applied to society. It is this spectator who is conceived as carrying out the required organization of the desires of all persons into one coherent system of desire: it is by this construction that many persons are fused into one. Endowed with ideal powers of sympathy and imagination, the impartial spectator is the perfectly rational individual who identifies with and experiences the desires of others as if these desires were his own. In this way he ascertains the intensity of these desires and assigns them their appropriate weight in the one system of desire the satisfaction of which the ideal legislator then tries to maximize by adjusting the rules of the social system. On this conception of society separate individuals are thought of as so many different lines along which rights and duties are to be assigned and scarce means of satisfaction allocated in accordance with rules so as to give the greatest fulfillment of wants. The nature of the decision made by the ideal legislator is not, therefore, materially different from that of an entrepreneur deciding how to maximize his profit by producing this or that commodity, or that of a consumer deciding how to maximize his satisfaction by the purchase of this or that collection of goods. In each case there is a single person whose system of desires determines the best allocation of limited means. The correct decision is essentially a question of efficient administration. This view of social cooperation is the consequence of extending to society the principle of choice for one man, and then, to make this extension work, conflating all persons into one through the imaginative acts of the impartial sympathetic spectator. Utilitarianism does not take seriously the distinction between persons. . . .

*See J. S. Mill, *Utilitarianism*, ch. V, last two pars.

11. Two Principles of Justice

I shall now state in a provisional form the two principles of justice that I believe would be agreed to in the original position. The first formulation of these principles is tentative. As we go on I shall consider several formulations and approximate step by step the final statement to be given much later. I believe that doing this allows the exposition to proceed in a natural way.

The first statement of the two principles reads as follows.

> First: each person is to have an equal right to the most extensive scheme of equal basic liberties compatible with a similar scheme of liberties for others.
>
> Second: social and economic inequalities are to be arranged so that they are both (a) reasonably expected to be to everyone's advantage, and (b) attached to positions and offices open to all.

There are two ambiguous phrases in the second principle, namely "everyone's advantage" and "open to all." Determining their sense more exactly will lead to a second formulation of the principle in § 13. . . .

These principles primarily apply, as I have said, to the basic structure of society and govern the assignment of rights and duties and regulate the distribution of social and economic advantages. Their formulation presupposes that, for the purposes of a theory of justice, the social structure may be viewed as having two more or less distinct parts, the first principle applying to the one, the second principle to the other. Thus we distinguish between the aspects of the social system that define and secure the equal basic liberties and the aspects that specify and establish social and economic inequalities. Now it is essential to observe that the basic liberties are given by a list of such liberties. Important among these are political liberty (the right to vote and to hold public office) and freedom of speech and assembly; liberty of conscience and freedom of thought; freedom of the person, which includes freedom from psychological oppression and physical assault and dismemberment (integrity of the person); the right to hold personal property and freedom from arbitrary arrest and seizure as defined by the concept of the rule of law. These liberties are to be equal by the first principle.

The second principle applies, in the first approximation, to the distribution of income and wealth and to the design of organizations that make use of differences in authority and responsibility. While the distribution of wealth and income need not be equal, it must be to everyone's advantage, and at the same time, positions of authority and responsibility must be accessible to all. One applies the second principle by holding positions open, and then, subject to this constraint, arranges social and economic inequalities so that everyone benefits.

These principles are to be arranged in a serial order with the first principle prior to the second. This ordering means that infringements of the basic equal liberties protected by the first principle cannot be justified, or compensated for, by greater social and economic advantages. These liberties have a central range of application within which they can be limited and compromised only when they conflict with other basic liberties. Since they may be limited when they clash with one another, none of these liberties is absolute; but however they are adjusted to form one system, this system is to be the same for all. It is difficult, and perhaps impossible, to give a complete specification of these liberties independently from the particular circumstances—social, economic, and technological—of a given society. The hypothesis is that the general form of such a list could be devised with sufficient exactness to sustain this conception of justice. Of course, liberties not on the list, for example, the right to own certain kinds of property (e.g., means of production) and freedom of contract as understood by the doctrine of laissez-faire are not basic: and so they are not protected by the priority of the first principle. Finally, in regard to the second principle, the distribution of wealth and income, and positions of authority and responsibility, are to be consistent with both the basic liberties and equality of opportunity.

The two principles are rather specific in their content, and their acceptance rests on certain assumptions that I must eventually try to explain and justify. For the present, it should be observed that these principles are a special case of a more general conception of justice that can be expressed as follows.

> All social values—liberty and opportunity, income and wealth, and the social bases of self-respect—are to be distributed equally unless an unequal distribution of any, or all, of these values is to everyone's advantage.

Injustice, then, is simply inequalities that are not to the benefit of all. Of course, this conception is extremely vague and requires interpretation.

As a first step, suppose that the basic structure of society distributes certain primary goods, that is, things that every rational man is presumed to want. These goods normally have a use whatever a person's rational plan of life. For simplicity, assume that the chief primary goods at the disposition of society are rights, liberties, and opportunities, and income and wealth. (Later on . . . the primary good of self-respect has a central place.) These are the social primary goods. Other primary goods such as health and vigor, intelligence and imagination, are natural goods; although their possession is influenced by the basic structure, they are not so directly under its control. Imagine, then, a hypothetical initial arrangement in which all the social primary goods are equally distributed: everyone has similar rights and duties, and income and wealth are evenly shared. This state of affairs provides a benchmark for judging improvements. If certain inequalities of wealth and differences in authority would make everyone better off than in this hypothetical starting situation, then they accord with the general conception.

Now it is possible, at least theoretically, that by giving up some of their fundamental liberties men are sufficiently compensated by the resulting social and economic gains. The general conception of justice imposes no restrictions on what sort of inequalities are permissible; it only requires that everyone's position be improved. We need not suppose anything so drastic as consenting to a condition of slavery. Imagine instead that people seem willing to forego certain political rights when the economic returns are significant. It is this kind of exchange which the two principles rule out; being arranged in serial order they do not permit exchanges between basic liberties and economic and social gains except under extenuating circumstances. . . .

The fact that the two principles apply to institutions has certain consequences. First of all, the rights and basic liberties referred to by these principles are those which are defined by the public rules of the basic structure. Whether men are free is determined by the rights and duties established by the major institutions of society. Liberty is a certain pattern of social forms. The first principle simply requires that certain sorts of rules, those defining basic liberties, apply to everyone equally and that they allow the most extensive liberty compatible with a like liberty for all. The only reason for circumscribing basic liberties and making them less extensive is that otherwise they would interfere with one another. . . .

Now the second principle insists that each person benefit from permissible inequalities in the basic structure. This means that it must be reasonable for each relevant representative man defined by this structure, when he views it as a going concern, to prefer his prospects with the inequality to his prospects without it. One is not allowed to justify differences in income or in positions of authority and responsibility on the ground that the disadvantages of those in one position are outweighed by the greater advantages of those in another. Much less can infringements of liberty be counterbalanced in this way. . . .

13. Democratic Equality and the Difference Principle

The democratic interpretation . . . is arrived at by combining the principle of fair equality of opportunity with the difference principle. This principle removes the indeterminateness of the principle of efficiency by singling out a particular position from which the social and economic inequalities of the basic structure are to be judged. Assuming the framework of institutions required by equal liberty and fair equality of opportunity, the higher expectations of those better situated are just if and only if they work as part of a scheme which improves the expectations of the least advantaged members of society. The intuitive idea is that the social order is not to establish and secure the more attractive prospects of those better off unless doing so is to the advantage of those less fortunate. . . .

To illustrate the difference principle, consider the distribution of income among social classes. Let us suppose that the various income groups correlate with representative individuals by reference to whose expectations we can judge the distribution. Now those starting out as members of the entrepreneurial class in property-owning democracy, say, have a better prospect than those who begin in the class of unskilled laborers. It seems likely that this will be true even when the social injustices which now exist are removed. What, then, can possibly justify this kind of initial inequality in life prospects? According to the difference principle, it is justifiable only if the difference in expectation is to the advantage of the representative man who is worse off, in this case the representative unskilled worker. The inequality in expectation is permissible only if lowering it would make the working class even more worse off. Supposedly, given the rider in the second principle concerning open positions, and the principle of liberty generally, the greater expectations allowed to entrepreneurs encourages them to do things which raise the prospects of laboring class. Their better prospects act as incentives so that the economic process is more efficient, innovation proceeds at a faster pace, and so on. I shall not consider how far these things are true. The point is that something of this kind must be argued if these inequalities are to satisfy by the difference principle. . . .

24. The Veil of Ignorance

The idea of the original position is to set up a fair procedure so that any principles agreed to will be just. The aim is to use the notion of pure procedural justice as a basis of theory. Somehow we must nullify the effects of specific contingencies which put men at odds and tempt them to exploit social and natural circumstances to their own advantage. Now in order to do this I assume that the parties are situated behind a veil of ignorance. They do not know how the various alternatives will affect their own particular case and they are obliged to evaluate principles solely on the basis of general considerations.*

It is assumed, then, that the parties do not know certain kinds of particular facts. First of all, no one knows his place in society, his class position or social status; nor does he know his fortune in the distribution of natural assets and abilities, his intelligence and strength, and the like. Nor, again, does anyone know his conception of the good, the particulars of his rational plan of life, or even the special features of his psychology such as his aversion to risk or liability to optimism or pessimism. More than this, I assume that the parties do not know the particular circumstances of their own society. That is, they do not know its economic or political situation, or the level of civilization and culture it has been able to achieve. The persons in the original position have no information as to which generation they belong. These broader restrictions on knowledge are appropriate in part because questions of social justice arise between generations as well as within them, for example, the question of the appropriate rate of capital saving and of the conservation of natural resources and the environment of nature. There is also, theoretically anyway, the question of a reasonable genetic policy. In these cases too, in order to carry through the idea of the original position, the parties must not know the contingencies that set them in opposition. They must choose principles the consequences of which they are prepared to live with whatever generation they turn out to belong to.

As far as possible, then, the only particular facts which the parties know is that their society is subject to the circumstances of justice and whatever this implies. It is taken for granted, however, that they know the general facts about human society. They understand political affairs and the principles of economic theory; they know

---

*The veil of ignorance is so natural a condition that something like it must have occurred to many. The formulation in the text is implicit, I believe, in Kant's doctrine of the categorical imperative, both in the way this procedural criterion is defined and the use Kant makes of it. Thus when Kant tells us to test our maxim by considering what would be the case were it a universal law of nature, he must suppose that we do not know our place within this imagined system of nature. See, for example, his discussion of the topic of practical judgment in *The Critique of Practical Reason*, Academy Edition, vol. 5, pp. 68–72. A similar restriction on information is found in J. C. Harsanyi, "Cardinal Utility in Welfare Economics and in the Theory of Risk-taking," *Journal of Political Economy*, vol. 61 (1953). However, other aspects of Harsanyi's view are quite different, and he uses the restriction to develop a utilitarian theory. See the last paragraph of §27.

the basis of social organization and the laws of human psychology. Indeed, the parties are presumed to know whatever general facts affect the choice of the principles of justice. There are no limitations on general information, that is, on general laws and theories, since conceptions of justice must be adjusted to the characteristics of the systems of social cooperation which they are to regulate, and there is no reason to rule out these facts. It is, for example, a consideration against a conception of justice that, in view of the laws of moral psychology, men would not acquire a desire to act upon it even when the institutions of their society satisfied it. For in this case there would be difficulty in securing the stability of social cooperation. An important feature of a conception of justice is that it should generate its own support. Its principles should be such that when they are embodied in the basic structure of society men tend to acquire the corresponding sense of justice and develop a desire to act in accordance with its principles. In this case a conception of justice is stable. This kind of general information is admissible in the original position.

The notion of the veil of ignorance raises several difficulties. Some may object that the exclusion of nearly all particular information makes it difficult to grasp what is meant by the original position. Thus it may be helpful to observe that one or more persons can at any time enter this position, or perhaps better, simulate the deliberations of this hypothetical situation, simply by reasoning in accordance with the appropriate restrictions. In arguing for a conception of justice we must be sure that it is among the permitted alternatives and satisfies the stipulated formal constraints. No considerations can be advanced in its favor unless they would be rational ones for us to urge were we to lack the kind of knowledge that is excluded. The evaluation of principles must proceed in terms of the general consequences of their public recognition and universal application, it being assumed that they will be complied with by everyone. To say that a certain conception of justice would be chosen in the original position is equivalent to saying that rational deliberation satisfying certain conditions and restrictions would reach a certain conclusion. If necessary, the argument to this result could be set out more formally. I shall, however, speak throughout in terms of the notion of the original position. . . .

26. The Reasoning Leading to the Two Principles of Justice

. . . Now consider the point of view of anyone in the original position. There is no way for him to win special advantages for himself. Nor, on the other hand, are there grounds for his acquiescing in special disadvantages. Since it is not reasonable for him to expect more than an equal share in the division of social primary goods, and since it is not rational for him to agree to less, the sensible thing is to acknowledge as the first step a principle of justice requiring an equal distribution. Indeed, this principle is so obvious given the symmetry of the parties that it would occur to everyone immediately. Thus the parties start with a principle requiring equal basic liberties for all, as well as fair equality of opportunity and equal division of income and wealth.

But even holding firm to the priority of the basic liberties and fair equality of opportunity, there is no reason why this initial acknowledgment should be final. Society should take into account economic efficiency and the requirements of organization and technology. If there are inequalities in income and wealth, and differences in authority and degrees of responsibility, that work to make everyone better off in comparison with the benchmark of equality, why not permit them? One might think that ideally individuals should want to serve one another. But since the parties are assumed to be mutually disinterested, their acceptance of these economic and institutional inequalities is only the recognition of the relations of opposition in which men stand in the circumstances of justice. They have no grounds for complaining of one another's motives. Thus the parties would agree to these differences only if they would be dejected by the bare knowledge or perception that others are better situated; but I suppose that they decide as if they are not moved by envy. Thus the basic structure should allow these inequalities so long as these improve everyone's situation, including that of the least advantaged, provided that they are consistent with equal liberty and fair opportunity. Because the parties start from an equal division of all social primary goods, those who benefit least have, so to speak, a veto. Thus we arrive at the difference principle. Taking equality as the basis of comparison, those who have gained more must do so on terms that are justifiable to those who have gained the least.

By some such reasoning, then, the parties might arrive at the two principles of justice in serial order. I shall not try to justify this ordering here, but the following remarks may convey the intuitive idea. I assume that the parties view themselves as free persons who have fundamental aims and interests in the name of which they think it legitimate for them to make claims on one another concerning the design of the basic structure of society. The religious interest is a familiar historical example; the interest in the integrity of the person is another. In the original position the parties do not know what particular forms these interests take; but they do assume that they have such interests and that the basic liberties necessary for their protection are guaranteed by the first principle. Since they must secure these interests, they rank the first principle prior to the second. The case for the two principles can be strengthened by spelling out in more detail the notion of a free person. Very roughly the parties regard themselves as having a highest-order interest in how all their other interests, including even their fundamental ones, are shaped and regulated by social institutions. They do not think of themselves as inevitably bound to, or as identical with, the pursuit of any particular complex of fundamental interests that they may have at any given time, although they want the right to advance such interests (provided they are admissible). Rather, free persons conceive of themselves as beings who can revise and alter their final ends and who give first priority to preserving their liberty in these matters. Hence, they not only have final ends that they are in principle free to pursue or to reject, but their original allegiance and continued devotion to these ends are to be formed and affirmed under conditions that are free. Since the two principles secure a social form that maintains these conditions, they would be agreed to rather than the principle of utility. Only by this agreement can the parties be sure that their highest-order interest as free persons is guaranteed.

The priority of liberty means that whenever the basic liberties can be effectively established, a lesser or an unequal liberty cannot be exchanged for an improvement in economic well-being. It is only when social circumstances do not allow the effective establishment of these basic rights that one can concede their limitation; and even then these restrictions can be granted only to the extent that

they are necessary to prepare the way for the time when they are no longer justified. The denial of the equal liberties can be defended only when it is essential to
change the conditions of civilization so that in due course these liberties can be enjoyed. Thus in adopting the serial order of the two principles, the parties are assuming that the conditions of their society, whatever they are, admit the effective
realization of the equal liberties. Or that if they do not, circumstances are nevertheless sufficiently favorable so that the priority of the first principle points out the
most urgent changes and identifies the preferred path to the social state in which
all the basic liberties can be fully instituted. The complete realization of the two
principles in serial order is the long-run tendency of this ordering, at least under
reasonably fortunate conditions.

It seems from these remarks that the two principles are at least a plausible conception of justice. . . .

Study Questions

1. Is it true that people's chances in life can be determined by the social position
or social background into which they are born? Is that fair? Why or why not?
2. What does Rawls mean by the "basic structure of society"? Why does he think
that it is "the primary subject of justice"? (Section 2)
3. What does Rawls mean by "the original position"? (Section 4) What role is
played by the "veil of ignorance" in the original position? (Sections 3 and 24) Is
the original position a "fair choice situation" for selecting principles of justice?
4. Does the idea of the "veil of ignorance" make sense? Once the veil of ignorance
is imposed, is it possible for the parties to choose principles of justice? (Section
24)
5. What are Rawls's main criticisms of utilitarianism? (Section 5) How might a
utilitarian reply?
6. What are Rawls's main arguments for accepting his two principles of justice?
Does he succeed in showing that these principles are the most reasonable principles of justice for our society? (Section 26)
7. What does Rawls's second principle of justice require (fair equal opportunity
plus the difference principle), and how would it be applied? In your view, is it
acceptable as a principle of distributive justice? Why or why not?

Selected Bibliography

Arneson, Richard J., ed. "Symposium on Rawlsian Theory of Justice: Recent Develop-
ments." *Ethics* 99:4 (1989). An issue of *Ethics* devoted to Rawls.
Barry, Brian. *A Treatise of Social Justice*, Vol. 1, *Theories of Social Justice* (Berkeley and Los
Angeles: The University of California Press, 1989). Discusses contemporary theories of
social justice.
Daniels, Norman, ed. *Reading Rawls: Critical Studies of A Theory of Justice* (New York:
Basic Books, 1975). An important collection of essays that followed the initial publica-
tion of *A Theory of Justice*.

Freeman, Samuel, ed., *The Cambridge Companion to Rawls* (Cambridge/New York: Cambridge University Press, 2003). Recent essays on Rawls.

Nozick, Robert. *Anarchy, State and Utopia* (New York: Basic Books, 1974), esp. Chap. 7. A libertarian theory of justice, including critical discussion of Rawls.

Rawls, John. *A Theory of Justice* (Cambridge, MA: Harvard University Press, 1971, Revised Edition 1999).

———. *Justice as Fairness: A Restatement* (Cambridge, MA: Harvard University Press, 2001). Restates the theory of justice in light of changes introduced in *Political Liberalism* and responses to critics.

———. *Political Liberalism* (New York: Columbia University Press, 1993, revised paperback edition 1996). A revised presentation of theory that takes better account of value pluralism in modern democratic societies.

———. *The Law of Peoples* (Cambridge, MA: Harvard University Press, 1999). The application of theory to international justice.

Richardson, Henry S., and Paul J. Weithman, eds. *The Philosophy of Rawls: A Collection of Essays*. 5 volumes (New York: Garland, 1999).

21

R. M. HARE

From the early 19th century through the middle of the 20th century the dominant moral theory in the English-speaking world was utilitarianism. Simply put, utilitarians hold that actions, as well as social practices and institutions, are right if they promote the overall

> *. . . objections to utilitarianism . . . are to be answered by recognizing that moral thinking occurs at two levels, the critical and the intuitive . . .*

balance of happiness in the world. The appeal of such theories is clear. Happiness or well-being is a value of obvious importance, and it is plausible to think that right action should aim at producing the most good in the world in some impartial fashion—in particular that it should aim at increasing happiness and well-being and minimizing suffering. However, utilitarianism has always had its critics, who have rejected the theory on the grounds that it has implications that are strongly at odds with ordinary moral thought. Critics have pointed out that because utilitarianism is concerned with maximizing total happiness, it has no intrinsic concern with how happiness is distributed. It seems that utilitarianism must be indifferent between a state of affairs in which a few are well off and many fare poorly and one in which all are equally well off, if the total level of happiness is the same in each. Moreover, isn't the utilitarian forced to permit the sacrifice of the interests of the few if that will benefit a greater number and increase overall happiness? For such reasons critics have thought that utilitarianism is unable to accommodate certain central moral notions, such as the ideas of rights and justice, or certain indefeasible moral rules.

R. M. Hare has been a staunch defender and leading advocate of utilitarianism. Hare argues that utilitarians can respond to these objections by employing a distinction between two levels of moral thinking, the critical and the intuitive. In ordinary circumstances we need to guide our choices by a set of moral rules and precepts that we regard as more or less indefeasible. The rules we should follow are those that would increase general happiness if inculcated and socially reinforced. They are the basis of intuitive moral thought. Critical thinking is needed for reflecting on these rules and deciding which are most socially beneficial, and for making decisions in exceptional circumstances—for example, circumstances in which two ordinary rules conflict. Intuitive rules that are justified by critical thinking for the most part will conform to ordinary moral thought. But where ordinary moral thought is not supported by critical thinking, why accept it? Different contexts call for different kinds of moral thinking, and by combining them in the right way, Hare claims, utilitarianism can address the standard objections.

R. M. Hare (1919–2002) was one of the most important moral philosophers of the 20th century. He was the White's Professor of Moral Philosophy at Oxford University from 1966 to 1983 and graduate research professor at the University of Florida from 1984–1993. His experiences in World War II led him to moral philosophy. He wrote widely on moral philosophy, including on many topics in applied ethics. His many books include *The Language of Morals* (1952), *Freedom and Reason* (1963), *Moral Thinking* (1981), *Essays on Political Morality* (1989), *Essays on Ethical Theory* (1989), *Essays on Bioethics* (1993), and *Objective Prescriptivism and Other Essays* (1999).

———

A Utilitarian Approach to Ethics

1. The main constituents of any utilitarian theory may be called *"consequentialism," "welfarism"* (Sen and Williams 1982: 3), and *"aggregationisin."* Consequentialism can be defined, roughly at first, as the view that the consequences of an act are what make it right or wrong. But this by itself is unclear. There is one sense of "consequences" in which nobody who thinks carefully about the question can help being a consequentialist. That is the sense used here. But there are other senses in which consequentialism is clearly an inadequate theory. We must first explain the sense in which everybody has to be a consequentialist.

A consequentialist is somebody who thinks that what determine the moral quality of an action (that is, determine whether it is right or wrong) are its consequences. An action is the making of some difference to what happens—to the history of the world. If I make no difference to what happens, I have done no action. In the widest sense, even if I do nothing (do not move a finger), I have done an action what is sometimes called an act of omission). It made a difference to the history of the world that I did nothing. We are, in other words, *responsible* for what we fail to do as well as for what we actively do. I can of course be blamed for doing nothing: someone might say "You were to blame for not saving the life of the patient when you could have."

Suppose, then, that my gun is pointing at somebody and I pull the trigger, and he dies. We say "I have killed him." Killing him was what I did—my act. If I did wrong, what made it wrong was the consequence of my pulling the trigger, namely that I killed him. In the light of this example, it is hard to see how people

R. M. Hare, "A Utilitarian Approach to Ethics," from *Objective Prescriptions and Other Essays* (Oxford University Press, 1999); first published in H. Kuhse and P. Singer, eds. *A Companion to Bioethics* (Blackwell Publishing, 1998). Reprinted by permission of Blackwell Publishing Company.

can deny that consequences, in *this* sense, are relevant to moral judgements about actions. So, in this sense, consequentialism is hard to reject. The people who reject it no doubt have some other sense of "consequentialism" in mind; but it is seldom clear what sense.

In this sense of "act" and "consequence," no distinction can be drawn between an act and its consequences. What I do is what I bring about. Of course in some other senses distinctions can be drawn. For example, we might say that the action is the movements of my own body, and the consequences are what happens as a result of these movements. This distinction does not correspond to our normal use of words. We certainly would say in the example that killing the person was an action of mine. Nor will this way of making the distinction divide what is morally relevant from what is not. We do not want to say that it was morally relevant that I moved my finger on the trigger, but morally irrelevant that somebody died in consequence. If the gun had been pointing at the ground, what I did might have been quite all right.

2. There are some other distinctions that the anti-consequentialists might be relying on. One is that between the consequences that make an act right or wrong, and the rest of the consequences. Sometimes people say "Do what is right and damn the consequences." This may be a good thing to say; but, rightly understood, it is not inconsistent with consequentialism as I have been using the word. Suppose that by telling a lie I could make a lot of money. Here there are two consequences of telling it that we have to consider, not just one. The first is that the person to whom I tell the lie is deceived, as was my intention. The second is that I make a lot of money. Someone who says "Do what is right and damn the consequences" is including, in the consequences that we ought to damn, the fact that I do not make the money. He means, "Don't tell the lie, because that's wrong, even if the consequence is that you don't get the money." But he does not mean "Disregard *all* the consequences." You certainly ought not to disregard the consequence that your victim is intentionally deceived. What would be wrong, if you told the lie, would be that very consequence, that he was intentionally deceived by your lie. If you could be sure he would disbelieve you, and that nobody else was in earshot, it would perhaps be perfectly all right to make a false statement to him, because no harm would come of it.

In this case, therefore, what the anti-consequentialists should be saying is, "Pay attention to the morally relevant consequences, and damn the rest." Of course in any decision that we make there will be some consequences that are morally relevant and some that are not; and we have to pay attention to the former, and disregard the latter, even if they are important to us for other reasons (for example, because they will bring in a lot of money). But this is consistent with consequentialism, properly understood. Consequentialism does not say that *all* consequences are morally relevant, only that everything that is morally relevant is some feature of the action, which, as we saw, boils down to the consequences that we are intentionally bringing about by doing it. . . .

3. Another distinction that the anti-consequentialists might have in mind is this. Some of the consequences of our actions are foreseen and some are not. For example, if I tell someone where his wife is, he may go off and kill her. But perhaps I did not know what his relations with his wife were—if I had known I would not have told him.

Here it is very important what sort of moral judgement we are making. If it is about the character of the person who did the act, then the unforeseen consequence is not relevant. I cannot be blamed for his killing his wife, because I could not have known how it was between them. If I had known, I would not have told him where she was. There are cases where I ought to have known what the consequences of my act would, or might, be. For example, if I shoot into a hedge without looking, and therefore do not know that there is a person standing on the other side, and I kill him, I am blamed for not knowing; I ought to have looked before I shot. This is called in law, "negligence." Here I am blamed for an act of omission—for not looking. I am going in what follows to disregard such cases, and say (with this exception) that in judging the moral worth of the agent, as Mill put it (1861: ch. 2), we take into account only the known consequences of his act.

Another important distinction is between the consequences that are *intended* and those that are not. Instead of saying that, in judging the moral worth of the agent, we take into account the consequences known to him when he did it, we could say that we take into account the consequences that he *intended*. But here we have to be very careful. There seem to be two senses of "intend"—at least some philosophers say that there are. In one sense I am said to intend a consequence if I intentionally do something, knowing that that will be a consequence (that is, that that is one of the things I should be doing), even if I do not want for its own sake to bring about that thing. Suppose, to take a well-known example, that I clean my apartment with a noisy vacuum cleaner late at night, knowing that I shall keep my neighbours awake. I do not *want* to keep them awake; my intention in the narrow sense is just to clean my apartment. But I know that I *shall* be keeping them awake. So in the broad sense in which, as the lawyers say, "a man must be presumed to intend the natural consequences of his actions," I could be said to intend to keep them awake.

Jeremy Bentham coined the useful terms "direct intention" and "oblique intention" to mark this distinction. . . . We directly intend a consequence of our action which we both foresee and desire. We obliquely intend a consequence if we foresee it, but do not actually desire it. It is usually held (rightly) that in judging acts and their agents, oblique intentions are relevant as well as direct ones. In the last example, my neighbours will blame me for keeping them awake even if I do not actually *want* to keep them awake (that is not my purpose in using the noisy vacuum cleaner), but simply know that I shall keep them awake, and carry on cleaning regardless.

Another example would be the company which runs a plant that is polluting the environment. It does not *want* to pollute the environment, although it knows that it is polluting it—its purpose is not to do that, but simply to make money running the plant. But all the same it will be blamed for the pollution. In Bentham's terms, it has the oblique intention of polluting, though it does not directly intend this.

4. So far we have been talking about judgements about the moral worth or character of the agent. But there are two other kinds of moral judgements that we make. The first is when, *after* the act has been done and the consequences have become apparent, we ask whether it is what ought to have been done, or whether it had been right to do it. To revert to our previous example: after the man whom I told where his wife was has killed her, I may say that I did wrong, as it turned out, to tell him. I ought not to have told him. I shall not be blamed for telling him, because I could not have known how it was between them. But all the same I ought not to have told him, and if I had known as much as I know now, I would have thought that I ought not to tell him.

That brings us to the other kind of moral judgement that we make which is not about the moral worth of agents. This kind is where we are asking ourselves, *before* we decide whether to do something, whether it is what we ought to do. We are wondering what *to* do, and therefore wondering what we *ought* to do. This is what we call "deliberation." In this situation it is impossible for us to take into account information which we do not have. We can of course take steps to get it, but if we *cannot* get it, we cannot take it into account. It follows that consequences that we simply do not and cannot know about cannot enter into this kind of deliberation. All we can do is estimate the *probabilities* of certain consequences of certain possible decisions. If we have done that, we have done all we can.

This situation is therefore quite different from that in which we are making a moral judgement after the event, with fuller knowledge, about what we, or what someone else, ought to *have* done. If we cannot have the information, we cannot use it. This enables us to sort out a problem that has occupied a lot of pages in the writings of philosophers, sometimes called the problem of "duty and ignorance of tact" (the title of a famous article of Prichard, 1932–1949: ch. 2). Prichard thought that there was a distinction between what he called "objective" and "subjective" duties. Our objective duty is what we would see to be our duty if we had full information and did our moral thinking properly. Our subjective duty is what we *think* to be our duty, when we only have the information that we actually have. In the example I used earlier, the person who told the other man where his wife was had a subjective duty to tell him the truth; but his objective duty was not to tell him. This is because when he actually made the decision he lacked information about the state of their marriage, whereas in the light of the full facts about this he clearly ought not to have told him.

When we do not have full information, the best thing we can do is to act on the information that we have, making the most *rational* decision we can in the light of the probabilities. But it does not follow that it is the *right* decision (Smart 1973: 49). It may turn out to have been sadly wrong. So in one sense our duty *at the time* is to follow the right method of thinking, and act accordingly. But although it was our duty at the time, it may turn out after doing it that we did the wrong thing. Once we understand the distinction between the morally rational act and the morally right act, we shall not be troubled any more by the paradox that sometimes the right decision procedure may lead to the wrong action.

This has a bearing on the first kind of moral judgements I talked about: judgements about the moral worth or character of the agent. We shall not count it against him if he acted in unavoidable ignorance, and did the wrong thing. When this happens, we have to say that clearly what he did was wrong, but it was not his fault; we do not call him a bad person because he did it.

5. I will go on now to *welfarism*, which I said was the second constituent in utilitarianism. Obviously one could be a consequentialist, and think that only con-

sequences were relevant to the morality of actions, but not be a utilitarian. Suppose, to take an extreme example, that I were a consequentialist, and thought that what determined the morality of actions was their consequences (what we were doing in doing them), but that I thought that the relevant consequences were those which conduced to, or impeded, the emergence of a master race. Or suppose that I thought something less extreme than this, which indeed many people have held, that the relevant consequences are those which conduce to or impede my own moral perfection. Perfectionism, as this kind of theory is sometimes called, is obviously inconsistent with utilitarianism as commonly understood. The difference is that the utilitarian thinks that the consequences that are relevant to the morality of actions are consequences that increase, or diminish, the welfare of all those affected. This means, for a utilitarian, the *welfare* of all those affected considered impartially. This makes utilitarianism different from perfectionism, and also from egoism, which in some versions says that the consequences relevant to morality are those which increase or diminish the welfare of the agent, or of the maker of the judgement. Utilitarianism, by contrast, says that what is relevant is welfare, but the welfare of everybody considered impartially.

The difficulty here is to say just what we mean by "welfare." Bentham and Mill said not "welfare" but "happiness," and defined this as "pleasure and the absence of pain." To be fair to them we have to realize that they were using the words "pleasure" and "pain" in extended senses. In Greek the words *hēdonē* and *lypē* may sometimes have had these extended senses. In this wide sense pain includes any kind of suffering, not just physical aches and pains; and pleasure means any state of mind that we like being in. But even so, many people have thought that "pleasure" and "pain" are too narrow notions for what the utilitarians ought to have been after. So, although some of them (for example, Brandt 1989) have gone on talking about happiness, they have not defined it in terms of pleasure and pain. Sometimes the expression "human flourishing" has been used. This was introduced as a translation, better than "happiness," of the Aristotelian word *eudaimoniā*, which Aristotle himself equates with "living well" and "faring well." I do not myself like the expression "*human* flourishing" (although Aristotle also talks about *anthrōpinon agathon* or "human good"), because a utilitarian ought to be thinking about the good of other sentient beings as well as humans.

There are many states of life that we should hesitate to call pleasure," but which we think of as desirable in themselves and constituents of happiness. For example, sailors who get drenched to the skin in freezing weather go on doing it at great expense year after year, so they must on the whole like doing it; but it would be odd to describe their state of mind as "pleasure." At least the word has to be taken in a *very* wide sense. The philosopher T. H. Green was fond of quoting the line from Browning's *Rabbi ben Ezra*, "Be our joys three-parts pain." "Joy" might in some contexts be a better word than "pleasure." But the sailors are not exactly enjoying their sport either. We want some more general word. Perhaps "liking" would do. We shall return to this word.

6. Another problem concerns the time span over which the liking is supposed to extend. Perhaps the sailors like their active and strenuous life as a whole or globally, and the "three parts pain," though in themselves unpleasant, are a necessary constituent of a way of life which on the whole they want or prefer to live. I have now introduced the word "prefer," which is going to be very important. People commonly distinguish between what are called "happiness" versions of utilitarianism and what are called "preference" versions.

The word "preference" is ambiguous. It can be used, and often is by economists, to mean a pattern of behaviour. In this sense we are said to prefer one sort of thing to another if we habitually and intentionally choose the first kind of thing when we have the choice. On the other hand, it can be used to mean an introspectable mental state of liking one thing more than another. Economists tend to use the first sense, because it enables us to determine empirically, by observing people's behaviour, what they prefer to what. The ambiguity normally causes no trouble, because what we prefer in the introspectable sense we normally also prefer in the behavioural sense; but there could be exceptions where the uses diverge. Perhaps my sailors prefer in the behavioural sense to go sailing in cold weather, but not in the introspectable sense.

7. There is also a problem about whether, for a preference utilitarian, *all* preferences have to be counted in when we decide what we ought to do, or only some. For example, suppose that some child now prefers to go on eating sweets, although it will tend to make him fat, which he will later prefer not to be. This is a fairly easy case to deal with: the utilitarian will aim at the child's preference satisfaction as a whole; its enjoyment of the sweets will count for something, but probably its suffering later from the disadvantages that fat people cannot avoid will count for more.

But there are more difficult problems. How about what Ronald Dworkin (1977: 234) has called "external" preferences? These are preferences that states of affairs should obtain which will never enter into the experience of the preferrer. . . . I can now set out an improved version of the distinction between "happiness" and "preference" versions of utilitarianism. It enables us to represent both of these as different kinds of preference utilitarianism, the difference being that one of them excludes from consideration preferences that the other includes (*Moral Thinking* 5.6). Briefly, we have to use the term "preference," as I think it is generally used, to cover both preferences for what is present and preferences for what is absent. If I desire something that I do not now have, I can be said in one sense to prefer having it to not having it in the future. And if I like something (for example some state of mind) that I *do* now have, I can be said to prefer having it to not having it. Thus this convenient word "preference" enables us to cover not only desires, which have to be for something absent, but likings, in the sense in which they have to be for something present.

I can now reformulate a kind of happiness version of utilitarianism in terms of a select set of preferences. Consider the preferences that we have for what should be the case, in our experience, at the time the preference is had . . . i.e., "synchronic preferences." So, for example, I prefer now to be looking now at this beautiful view from the top of the mountain, rather than not to be looking at it. In short, I like looking at the view.

We can make a first shot at reformulating the happiness version of utilitarianism by saying that it is the theory that what we have to maximize is the satisfaction of a certain limited class of preferences, namely those I have called "synchronic non-external preferences." These are preferences for what should happen in our own experience at the time the preference is had. All other preferences—that is, preferences for what should happen at other times, or outside our own experience—are to be disregarded, according to this version of utilitarianism.

This is a plausible rendering of happiness utilitarianism. It is plausible, because one sense of "happiness" could be, "getting, on the whole, more of what one likes than of what one dislikes," that is, "having one's synchronic non-external preferences satisfied on the whole." Thus happiness utilitarianism is reformulated as a kind of preference utilitarianism that disregards all but this limited class of preferences. This is like the theory advocated by Brandt (1989). It is a very plausible theory, though it may have problems.

This kind of happiness or limited-preference utilitarianism has to be contrasted with other more expansive versions of preference utilitarianism, of which there could be many. For example, we might include in our moral reasoning external preferences (that is, preferences for things other than experiences of the preferrer), and asynchronic preferences (that is, preferences, such as now-for-then preferences, which are for times other than that at which the preference is had).

8. We must now leave these matters, on which I have not made up my mind. So far we have as constituents of utilitarianism consequentialism, or the view that it is their consequences that determine the morality of actions, and welfarism, or the view that the consequences that we have to attend to are those that conduce to the welfare of those affected or the opposite. The remaining constituent is a view about the *distribution* of this welfare. It is the view that when, as usually, we have a choice between the welfare of one lot of people and the welfare of another, we should choose the action which maximizes the welfare, that is maximally promotes the interests, of all *in sum,* or *in aggregate.* That is why I call this constituent *"aggregationism."*

Aggregationism implies that we should ignore the *distribution* of the welfare that we are bringing about, and simply maximize its total sum in aggregate. That is, if one outcome will produce more welfare, but distribute it very unequally, but another will produce less, but distribute it more equally, it is, according to aggregationism, the first outcome that we ought to choose. This, as we shall see, often leads to objections to aggregationism, and therefore to utilitarianism itself, by people of an egalitarian bent, who think that equality of distribution matters in itself, as an independent value, and must not be sacrificed to the maximization of the total welfare. To this sort of objection I shall return later.

But before I discuss objections to aggregationism, I must point out that it certainly *seems* to be a simple consequence of a view that is held by many people, including many opponents of utilitarianism, namely the view that in making moral judgements we have to be *impartial* between the interests of the people affected by our judgements. This impartiality is what Bentham was getting at in his famous dictum "Everybody to count for one, nobody for more than one" (Mill 1861: ch. 5, end). It is also what is implied by a requirement, which a great many anti-utilitarians (Dworkin 1977: 180, for example) hold dear, that we should show "equal concern and respect" for all. I cannot see what it would be to show equal concern and respect, if not to respect their interests equally. But if we respect their interests equally, we shall give the same weight to the equal interests of each of them. So, for example, if one of them wants some outcome more than the other wants to avoid it, we shall think we ought to bring that outcome about. But this leads directly to aggregationism.

It is easy to see this. If I give as much weight to the interests of a person *A* as to those of person *B*, and the same weight again to those of person *C*, what happens when the interests of *A* and *B*, taken together, preponderate over the interests of *C*? Obviously, it would seem, the interests of *A* and *B* ought to weigh more with us than those of *C*. If we said anything but this, we should not be giving equal weight to the interests of *A*, *B*, and *C*, and therefore not showing equal concern and respect for *A*, *B*, and *C*. So, if one outcome will promote the interests of *A* and *B*, and the other will promote the interests of *C*, and the interests of each of these individuals are equal, and we cannot produce both outcomes, it is the first outcome that we ought to produce, if we are to show all three equal concern and respect.

I therefore find it surprising that so many anti-utilitarians, who profess to believe that we ought to show equal concern and respect to all those affected, object to aggregationism. The argument I have just set out could be put by saying that if the interests of *A* and *B* are stronger in *aggregate* than those of *C*, we should promote the former rather than the latter. Yet it was based on the requirement to give equal concern and respect to all three.

There is another argument commonly used against aggregationism that is also hard to understand (Rawls 1971: 27). This is the objection that utilitarians "ignore the difference between persons." To explain this objection: it is said that, if we say there is a duty to promote maximal preference satisfaction regardless of its distribution, we are treating a great interest of one as of less weight than the lesser interests of a great many, provided that the latter add up in aggregate to more than the former. For example, if I can save five patients moderate pain at the cost of not saving one patient severe pain, I should do so if the interests of the five in the relief of their pain is greater in aggregate than the interest of the one in the relief of his (or hers).

But to think in the way that utilitarians have to think about this kind of example is *not* to ignore the difference between persons. Why should anybody want to say this? The utilitarian is perfectly well aware that *A*, *B*, and *C* in my example are different people. He is not blind. All he is doing is trying to do *justice* between the interests of these different people. It is hard to see how else one could do this except by showing them all equal respect, and that as we have seen, leads straight to aggregationism (on justice, see *Moral Thinking* 5.6 ff.).

It must be admitted that often utilitarians argue that we should treat other people's interests as if they were all our own interests. This is a way of securing impartiality. It is implied both by the Christian doctrine of *agapē* and by the Kantian categorical imperative, as Kant explicitly says. . . . But this is not to ignore the difference between persons. It is merely to give equal weight to the interests of all persons, as we would do if we gave them all the weight that we give to our own interests; and this is what *agapē*, and treating everybody as ends as Kant says we should, require. This objection belongs to a class of objections to utilitarianism that rest on an appeal to common moral convictions or intuitions. In the case we have just been considering, it seems counterintuitive to say that an enormous harm to one person can be outweighed in moral thinking by a huge number of very small gains to other people.

9. There are a tedious number of other objections to utilitarianism based on appeals to intuition. They are to be answered by recognizing that moral thinking occurs at two levels, the critical and the intuitive, and that intuition operates at the latter level, but utilitarianism at the former level, so that the two do not conflict. Examples are the alleged requirement of utilitarianism that the sheriff should execute the innocent man to prevent a riot; that one should save an important person from an air crash rather than one's own son if one cannot save both; that one should break promises when even the slightest advantage in preference satisfaction is produced thereby: and that one should kidnap one person, kill him, and extract his organs for transplants in order to save the lives of many. I say that these examples are tedious because they are constantly repeated *after* the answer to them has been given in print, as I did in *Moral Thinking* ch. 8.

They are all easily answered once we realize the importance for moral practice of having firm principles or rules that we do not readily depart from. We cannot often predict the future well enough to be sure what act would maximize utility; and even if we have the information, we do not often have time to consider it fully, and without bias in our own favour. These sound general rules form the basis of our general moral convictions and intuitions, and it is unwise to depart from then lightly. If we do, we shall often be in danger of not acting for the best.

These rules have to be general or unspecific enough to be manageable. For one thing, if they are too complicated we shall not be able to teach them to our children or even learn them ourselves. Also, if they are too specific they may not be of much use. The point—or one of the points—of having moral rules is to cover a lot of cases which, though different in detail, resemble one another in important features.

So there is a good case for having simple general rules. We need therefore some way of putting a limit to the specificity that our rules can have. By "specificity" I mean the opposite of "generality." It is important to notice that generality, in the sense in which it is the opposite of specificity, is not the same as universality. . . . But this is not yet a sufficient answer to the objections we have been considering—the objections from counterintuitiveness. What shall we do in unusual cases, where we find ourselves wanting to make exceptions to the rules for good moral reasons, as they seem to us?

The way to get over this difficulty, as we have seen, is to allow two levels of moral thinking. At the intuitive level we have the general rules, which are simple enough to master. But there will be conflicts between these simple rules. These conflicts are really the source of the objections from counterintuitiveness. For example, there is a simple rule which bids doctors do the best they can to cure their patients, and another which forbids them to murder people in order to extract their organs. One rule would bid them murder a person to extract his organs for transplants, and the other would forbid this. To resolve these conflicts, we need a higher level of thinking, which can be much more specific and deal in detail with unusual cases.

It will be found that real cases, such as we might encounter in practice, are not so difficult to handle as the cases in philosophers' examples. The former will generally be much more complex than the latter, and the additional information available will enable us to reconcile our intuitions with utilitarianism. For example, the abandonment of the rule forbidding murder will inevitably have such serious evil consequences that no saving of patients' lives by giving them murdered people's organs will compensate for the harm done. These murders will not long remain secret; and there are better ways of securing organs for transplant. And the sheriff will do well to think what will happen in real life if sheriffs do not maintain the rule of law and justice, and so preserve people's rights. Rights certainly have a place in moral thinking, but it is a place easily preserved for them by consequentialism and utilitarianism. . . . (*Moral Thinking* 9.1 ff.). Similarly, there are utilitarian reasons why a substantial degree of equality in society is good for everybody . . . and why doctors and parents should look after their own patients and children respectively. . . . These partial and egalitarian principles at the intuitive level can be justified by impartial reasoning at the higher or critical level.

It is good enough if utilitarianism tallies with our intuitions in real cases; it does not have to fit cases which are unlikely ever to arise. If such cases do arise in unusual circumstances, most people on reflection will decide that they ought to act for the best (that is, as utilitarianism bids), even if this involves breaking one of the conflicting intuitive rules in order to observe the other.

———

Moral Thinking

"The Archangel and the Prole"*

3.3 . . . the relation between the two kinds of thinking is this. Critical thinking aims to select the best set of prima facie principles for use in intuitive thinking. It can also be employed when principles from the set conflict *per accidens*. Such employment may lead to the improvement of the principles themselves, but it need not; a principle may be overridden without being altered. . . . The best set is that whose acceptance yields actions, dispositions, etc. most nearly approximating to

*Earlier in this chapter of *Moral Thinking*, Hare has defined the "archangel" as an ideal observer who has superhuman powers of thought and the ability to foresee all the consequences of alternative actions and is completely impartial. The "archangel" uses only critical thinking. By contrast, the "prole" (after Orwell's 1984) is capable only of intuitive thinking and must rely on prima facie principles learned from others. [Ed.]

[References in parentheses are to sections of *Moral Thinking*.—Ed.]

those which would be chosen if we were able to use critical thinking all the time. This answer can be given in terms of acceptance-utility, if one is a utilitarian; if one is not a utilitarian but a Kantian, one can say in effect the same thing by advocating the adoption of a set of maxims for general use whose acceptance yields actions, etc., most approximating to those which would be chosen if the categorical imperative were applied direct on each occasion by an archangel. Thus a clear-headed Kantian and a clearheaded utilitarian would find themselves in agreement, once they distinguished between the two kinds of thinking.

But besides the role of *selecting* prima facie principles, critical thinking has also the role of *resolving conflicts* between them. If the principles have been well chosen, conflicts will arise only in exceptional situations; but they will be agonizing in proportion as the principles are deeply held (as they should be). Though in general it is bad policy to question one's prima facie principles in situations of stress, because of the danger of "cooking" . . . the conflicts we are speaking of force us to do this (hence the anguish). There can be different outcomes. In simpler cases we may "feel sure" that some principle or some feature of a situation is *in that situation* more important than others. . . . We shall then be able to sort the matter out intuitively, letting one principle override the other in this case, without recourse to critical thinking. This might well be best in the promise-breaking example with which we started. But though this intuitive sorting out may seem to offer a straw at which intuitionists can clutch, it is obvious that it will not be available in more serious conflicts.

At the other extreme, a conflict may force us to examine the prima facie principles themselves, and perhaps, instead of overriding one, qualify them from then on. People who have been through such crises often think differently thereafter about some fundamental moral questions—a sign that some critical thinking has been done, however inarticulate. This qualification of the principles will have brought with it a resolution of the conflict, because the principles as qualified are no longer inconsistent even *per accidens*. There is also a middle way: the person in the conflict-situation may come to be fairly sure that one or both of the principles ought to be qualified, but not be sure how, except that the qualification would allow such and such an accommodation in this particular case; he can then decide about the particular case, overriding one of the principles, and leave reflection on the principles themselves for another time when he is in a better position to do it rationally. Only when he has done it can he be sure that he was right.

Another version of this middle way is to say "The principles, since they are in conflict, cannot be altogether relied on; I am compelled to depart from one or the other, and do not know which. So let me put the principles aside for the time being and examine carefully the particular case to see what critical thinking would say about it." This is possible for critical thinking, in so far as humans can do it, and it is what the situational ethicists and crude act-utilitarians might recommend in all cases. It is, as we have seen, a dangerous procedure; but sometimes we may be driven to it. Anti-utilitarians make it their business to produce examples in which this is the only recourse, and then charge utilitarians with taking it (which is unavoidable) and with taking it light-heartedly (which is a slander, 8.1 ff.). The good utilitarian will reach such decisions, but reach them with great reluctance because of his ingrained good principles; and he may agonize, and will certainly reflect, about them till he has sorted out by critical thinking, not only what he ought to have done in the particular case, but what his prima facie principles ought to be.

It may be said that one cannot compartmentalize one's moral thinking in the way the two-level account seems to require (Williams, 1976:230). I can only reply by asking whether those who raise this objection have ever faced such situations. I do my own moral thinking in the way described in this book (not like an archangel, for I am not one, nor like a prole, but doing my best to employ critical and intuitive thinking as appropriate). In difficult situations one's intuitions, reinforced by the dispositions that go with them, pull one in different directions, and critical thinking, perhaps, in another. A person with any deep experience of such situations will have acquired some *methodological* prima facie principles which tell him when to launch into critical thinking and when not; they too would be justified by critical thinking in a cool hour. To say that it is impossible to keep intuitive and critical thinking going in the same thought-process is like saying that in a battle a commander cannot at the same time be thinking of the details of tactics, the overall aim of victory, and the principles (economy of force, concentration of force, offensive action, etc.) which he has learnt when learning his trade. Good generals do it. The good general is one who wins his battles, not one who has the best prima facie principles; but the best prima facie principles are those which, on the whole, win battles. . . .

Loyalty and Evil Desires

8.1 The two remaining chapters of this part will be devoted to answering some objections commonly made against utilitarianism, which might also be, and have been, encountered by my own theory. Since nearly all these objections employ the same basic move, originating in the same misunderstanding, it may be helpful if I first explain the move and the answer to it in quite general terms. I shall do this in the form of some simple instructions to students, first on how to manufacture objections of this sort, and then on how to demolish them. I hope thereby to forewarn and forearm them against anybody who tries to waste too much of their time with such objections; the answer to them all is the same, and one exercise in dealing with them is enough.

Suppose then that you are in a disputation with a utilitarian. Your object should be to enlist the sympathies of your audience on your side by showing that the utilitarian is committed to views which nearly everybody finds counterintuitive. What you have to do, therefore, is to find some moral opinion which nearly everybody will agree with, and bring utilitarianism into conflict with it. It is not necessary to choose for this purpose an opinion that can be defended by argument; any widely held prejudice will do. I have heard this kind of objection based on premisses like "Surely any theory is absurd which makes cruelty to animals as wicked as the same degree of cruelty to humans"; and no doubt in earlier centuries "blacks" and "whites" would have done as well. But obviously it is better if the opinion is a defensible one; the objection will then seem even more plausible.

Having selected your favoured received opinion, you can then proceed to bring utilitarianism into conflict with it in the following way. You find some example, rather simply described, in which, on an obvious interpretation of utilitarianism (and nearly all the versions of it can be made susceptible to this treatment, except for some versions of rule-utilitarianism which are highly implausible on other grounds) the utilitarian is committed to prescribing an act which almost everybody will agree is wrong. Give your case as much verisimilitude as you can. Professional opponents of utilitarianism are not always as careful as they should be about this. Sometimes they use extremely jejune examples, thinking the game to be a pushover, so that they need not take too much trouble with them. But it is better if the case is something which your audience can be got to believe really could happen. Thus you will seem to have established a knock-down counterinstance to the utilitarian theory; it will have been shown to require us to say some act is right when we all know it to be wrong.

8.2 Now suppose by contrast that you are on the opposite side in the disputation. How will you answer the objection? First of all you must be quite clear what version of utilitarianism you are defending. Naturally I strongly recommend that you should choose the version defended in this book; for if you have understood what has been said in it so far, especially about the separation of levels, you will not find it hard to see the weaknesses in your opponent's position. Indeed, your first move should be to ask him what level of thinking he is talking about; for on this will depend what moves in the game are permissible, and in particular what examples can properly be adduced. In any case, if he has never heard of the difference between levels, mention of it will put him off his stroke.

Briefly, if he is talking about the critical level, he is allowed to bring up any examples he pleases however fantastic; but at that level no appeals to received intuitions are allowed, because the function of critical thinking is to judge the acceptability of intuitions, and therefore it cannot without circularity invoke intuitions as premisses. If, on the other hand, he is talking about the intuitive level, he is allowed to appeal to any intuitions he thinks the audience will agree with, pending their examination by critical thinking, but must be very careful what examples he uses. For his audience's intuitions are the product of their moral upbringings . . . and, however good these may have been, they were designed to prepare them to deal with moral situations which are likely to be encountered . . . ; there is no guarantee at all that they will be appropriate to unusual cases. Even in the unusual cases, no doubt, the usual moral feelings will be in evidence; but they provide no argument.

The dispute is likely to resolve itself, therefore, into one about the admissibility and the treatment of examples. To illustrate this, suppose that your opponent's case is the following: there are in a hospital two patients, one needing for survival a new heart and the other new kidneys; a down-and-out who is known to nobody and who happens to have the same tissue-type as both the patients strays in out of the cold. Ought they not to kill him, give his heart and kidneys to the patients, and thus save two lives at the expense of one? The utilitarian is supposed to have to say that they ought; the audience is supposed to say that they ought not, because it would be murder. Let us suppose that your opponent manages to get the audience to treat murder as a descriptive, not a secondarily evaluative, word . . . , and thus to call the statement that it would be murder a purely factual one, which can be established prior to any judgement that it would be wrong. I have simplified the case a little from the way it has sometimes been presented in the literature . . . , because the complications will not affect the moves we shall be making.

On this example you have to mount a two-pronged attack. If we are to do intuitive thinking, the matter is fairly simple. It *is* murder, and *would* therefore be wrong. A utilitarian does not have to dissent from this verdict at the intuitive level. If he has been well brought up (and in particular if he has been brought up by a sound critical utilitarian thinker) he will have that intuition, and it is a very good thing, from the utilitarian point of view, that he will have it. For just think what would be the consequences of a moral education which contained no prohibition on murder!

Your opponent will now object that although on the utilitarian view it is a good thing for people to have these intuitions or feelings, it also follows from that view that they ought to overcome and act contrary to them in cases like this, in which, *ex hypothesi*, it is for the best to do so. Let us ask, then, whether the doctors in the hospital ought to do this if they are utilitarians. It will turn upon their estimate of the *probability* of hitting off the act which is for the best by so doing. The crucial words are, of course, "*ex hypothesi*"; for your opponent has constructed his example with the express purpose of making the murder the act which will have the best consequences. You must not allow him simply to *assume* that this is so; he has to convince the audience, not just that it really could be so in a real-life situation, but that it could be known to be so by the doctors with a high degree of probability. For utilitarianism, as a method of choosing the most rational action (the best bet for a utilitarian) in a moral dilemma of this sort, requires them to maximize the *expectation* of utility (i.e., preference-satisfaction); and since, if they get it wrong, the consequences will be pretty catastrophic, the doctors have to be very sure that they are not getting it wrong. There is perhaps no need to go into any technicalities of games-theory to establish this point, though a full account would need to contain a method of weighing combinations of probabilities with utilities against one another, by asking which combination one would prefer, after exposure to logic and the facts.

It is fairly obvious that this high degree of probability will not be forthcoming in many actual situations, if any at all. Have the doctors checked on the down-and-out's connexions or lack of them? (How? By consulting the police records, perhaps! But a colleague of my psychiatrist sister once wrote in his notes, about a dishevelled individual brought in off the streets very late at night by the police, "Has delusion that he is a high-ranking civil servant," and it turned out that he was in fact a *very* high-ranking civil servant.) Have they absolute confidence in the discretion and support of all the nurses, porters, mortuarists, etc., who will know what has happened? Add to this the extreme unlikelihood of there being no other way of saving these patients, if they can be saved at all, and it will be evident that your opponent is not going to get much help out of this example, once it is insisted that it has to be fleshed out and given verisimilitude.

But perhaps that was not his intention. Perhaps, that is to say, he all along intended the example to be a dummy. Is he not allowed, after a brief introduction of the example to give its general shape, to skip the details and simply *posit* that it is a case where murder would be for the best? The audience, which is probably prejudiced against utilitarians anyway, will have no difficulty in imagining that the details could be filled in in a way that would suit his case and damage yours. But you must not let him get away with this. If we are talking about intuitive thinking in a real-life sort of situation, the example needs to be a real-life sort of example.

If, on the other hand, he claims the right to introduce any *logically possible* example, then he is exposed to the other prong of your attack. For then he has put himself beyond the range of intuition and cannot appeal to it. Critical thinking can certainly deal with such cases, and will give a utilitarian answer. If he tailors the case so that the utilitarian answer is that murder is the right solution, then that is the answer he will get. What you have to say to the audience is that this does not in the least matter, because such cases are not going to occur. This has two important consequences for the argument. The first is that allowing that in such a case murder would be justified commits us to no prescription to murder in the actual world, in which we have to live our moral lives. The second is a generalization of the first: the prima facie principles which the critical thinker will select for use in this world can also, and will, include a ban on murder, because for the selection of these principles this peculiar case, since it will not occur, is irrelevant.

Your opponent may say "Are there not some cases occurring in real life, albeit rarely, in which murder is justified on utilitarian grounds?" To which you should reply that he has not produced any, but that if he really did find one, we should have to do some critical thinking on it because it would be clearly so unusual as to be beyond the range of our intuitions. If we then found that murder really was justified in that case, we still should not have shown that the rational moral agent would commit the murder; for he would be unlikely to have sufficient evidential grounds for saying that it was the right act. But, giving your opponent everything that he asks for, if he did actually have sufficient evidence (a very unlikely contingency), murder would *in that case* be justified; though even then the agent in question, if he had been well brought up, might not do it, because it would go so much against all his moral feelings, which in a good man are powerful. So, owing to being a good man, he might fail to do the right act. If he did bring himself to do it, it would haunt him for the rest of his life. But until your opponent produces actual cases, you should not let yourself be troubled overmuch with fictional ones. If the actual cases are produced, you will probably find that the critical discussion of them will leave you and the audience at one, provided that the discussion is serious.

8.3 We are now in a position to apply the same technique to some more genuine problems. Let us take first the objection commonly made to utilitarianism that it does not allow us to give any weight to the duties usually thought to exist towards particular persons, or to ties of affection and loyalty which bind us to them but not to mankind in general. . . . For example, it is usually held that we have special duties to our spouses and children, and ought to have greater affection and loyalty to them than to total strangers, and so seek their good more earnestly. Similar things are said about the relation between a doctor and his patient, or a teacher and his pupil. And similar things *used* to be universally, and are still quite widely, accepted about that between a citizen and his country. I have heard the same argued about the loyalty of a worker to his union.

These last two instances might make us pause before proceeding on the assumption that all commonly upheld loyalties can be used as a stick to beat utilitarians with. They show how palpable, and how dubious, is the appeal to intuition when people say that utilitarianism treats everybody's preferences as of equal weight (e.g., those of my children and other people's children), and therefore has to be rejected as giving no weight to these feelings of special affection which we all think it a good thing to encourage. We have first to be sure that, in a particular example, it is a good thing to encourage these feelings. Even family loyalties provide examples of extremely various intuitions. In some countries it is considered wrong if someone who has obtained a position of power does not use it to advance the interests of the members of his family; in others this is called nepotism and thought corrupt. And even in Britain there is dispute about whether it is right for a well endowed father to try to get the best possible education for his children by sending them to expensive schools which others cannot afford.

This should warn us that even where intuitions are all in agreement, they should not be taken for granted; it needs to be established by critical thought which of them ought, in our present circumstances, to be fostered. Anybody who asks himself whether, and in what sense, he ought to bring up his children to be patriotic will see the force of this question. So let us proceed as before and ask our anti-utilitarian objector what level of thinking he is talking about, intuitive or critical. In order to make it easy for him, let us allow him to choose an example in which nearly everybody will agree that the loyalty in question is a good thing. A mother, say, has a newborn child and her maternal feelings make her provide for this child, but they do not, or not to anything like the same degree, impel her to provide for other people's children. Ought a utilitarian to condemn this partiality?

At the intuitive level we all think that the mother is to be praised, in all normal circumstances (barring a few extreme radical advocates of communes, and Plato). Given our two-level structure, there is nothing in this that a utilitarian need object to. *If* the intuition is one that ought to be inculcated (and this cannot be determined without critical thinking), the most likely way of doing the right thing in normal circumstances will be to follow the intuition. If this were not so, then the intuition would not be the one which ought to be inculcated. If we ascend to the critical level and ask why it ought to be, the answer is fairly obvious. If mothers had the propensity to care equally for all the children in the world, it is unlikely that children would be as well provided for even as they are. The dilution of the responsibility would weaken it out of existence. Our traditional upbringing has taken account of this. And evidently Evolution (if we may personify her) has had the same idea; there are, we are told, a great many of these particular loyalties and affections which are genetically transmitted, and have no doubt favoured the survival of the genes which transmit them (Singer, 1981).

8.4 The general lines of the utilitarian answer to this objection should by now be clear. *In so far* as the intuitions are desirable ones, they can be defended on utilitarian grounds by critical thinking, as having a high acceptance-utility; if they can be so defended, the best bet, even for an act-utilitarian, will be to cultivate them and follow them in all normal cases; if he cultivates them seriously, or has had them cultivated for him by those who brought him up, all the associated moral feelings will be present, but will provide no argument whatever against utilitarianism. Unlike intuitionism, it is actually able to *justify* the intuitions, where they can be justified.

Faced with this argument the anti-utilitarian will produce examples in which we would all have the intuitions, but in which, he asks us to suppose, the utilitarian would have to prescribe that we acted contrary to them. This would be because in the particular cases sufficient information is assumed to be available to show that the intuitively right act would not be for the best. To take a pasteboard example with which I was once confronted by Professor Bernard Williams on television: you are in an air crash and the aircraft catches fire, but you have managed to get out; in the burning plane are, among others, your son and a distinguished surgeon who could, if rescued, save many injured passengers' lives; to say nothing of those whose lives he would save in his subsequent career. You have time to rescue only one person.

It is hard to make Williams' example realistic. How do you know he is so distinguished a surgeon—perhaps he was only shooting a line when you struck up an acquaintance in the departure lounge? Has he got his tools with him, and can he do any more for the injured people than the first aid which the crew are trained to give (which probably prescribes keeping them warm and immobile and giving some common drugs which, we hope, they managed to extract from the aircraft)? How promising is your son's future (he can probably look forward to a greater span of it than the surgeon)? However, setting aside all these minor points, we find that you have a very strong feeling that you ought to rescue your son and let the surgeon burn. But what does this show?

It would take a very hardened intuitionist to think that it shows that to rescue your son is your undoubted duty. You almost certainly will rescue your son. But that is because you have (rightly from the critical utilitarian point of view) been brought up to attach dominant importance to these family loyalties. Of course no upbringing takes into account such rare cases as this (they are not what those who influenced you were preparing you for, nor would evolution be affected by them). To be in an air crash of any sort is, fortunately, a statistically very rare experience; to be in one in which one has the opportunity to rescue anybody is rarer still; to be in one in which one can rescue precisely one person and no more is hardly to be expected. So you come to this unhappy experience entirely unprepared for it. Your intuitions were simply not designed to cope with it. However, you do have the strong moral feelings and will probably act on them in the split second which is all you have in which to decide. And who is to blame you? Probably in a situation of complete uncertainty and panic it is the rational thing to do. The fraudulence of the example consists in suggesting that you can at one and the same time be in this emergency situation, and do the leisured critical thinking which would be necessary in order to justify you in going against your intuitions.

Undoubtedly critics of utilitarianism will go on trying to produce examples which are both fleshed out and reasonably likely to occur, and also support their argument. I am prepared to bet, however, that the nearer they get to realism and

specificity, and the further from playing trains—a sport which has had such a fasci-
nation for them—the more likely the audience is, on reflection, to accept the utilitarian solution. I am thinking of their examples in which trolleys hurtling down
the line out of control have to be shunted into various alternative groups of unfortunate people. I have myself, when helping to build a railway, seen trolleys run out
of control, and therefore find the unrealism of the examples very obvious. The
point is that one has no time to think what to do, and so relies on one's immediate
intuitive reactions; but these give no guide to what critical thinking would prescribe if there were time for it. But, personal experience aside, I have done quite a
lot of work on serious practical problems in medicine, war, politics, urban planning
and the like, and have never come across any actual example in which this kind of
anti-utilitarian argument was in the least convincing. . . .

8.6 Another objection of the sort we are considering in this chapter is based
on our common distinction between good and evil desires. We have, following
Brandt, given some account of how *irrational* preferences might be adjusted in
the light of logic and the facts. . . . But we have done nothing to show that preferences commonly thought to be *immoral* could be similarly treated. A different
move is needed to cope with this problem, which in another form troubled the
classical utilitarians: John Stuart Mill's rather unhappy discussion of higher and
lower pleasures is an instance (1861: ch. 2). But not all the examples adduced are
of the same kind. Here, to start with, is an easy kind to demolish. According to the
utilitarians, it is said, we should have to give as much weight to the pleasures or
preferences of the Marquis de Sade as to those of Mother Teresa. The fact that the
former likes to torture people, and the latter wants nothing so much as to supply
the needs of the poor, should count for nought; a preference is a preference and
weighs in the utilitarian calculation purely in proportion to its strength.

As before, if we are speaking of the intuitive level, we do have the intuitions
which are being appealed to, and the utilitarian could give, at the critical level,
good reasons why they should be encouraged. Obviously, the more people there
are like Mother Teresa (within reason) and the fewer like the Marquis, the better.
So if we have been brought up successfully by thoughtful utilitarians, these are the
intuitions we shall have. If it is alleged that the intuitions and the moral feelings
that go with them should be suppressed in particular cases where this would maximize preference-satisfaction, we have to ask what these cases would be, and how
likely they would be to occur. Professor Amartya Sen (1979:473) has an example
in which a morose and sadistic policeman gets so much pleasure (his only pleasure)
out of torturing another character whom he calls the romantic dreamer that the
latter's pain is more than compensated for in the utilitarian calculation. The
dreamer, it appears, does not all that much mind being tortured (but if so, would
it not be frustrating rather than pleasurable for the policeman to see him lying
there happily on the rack?).

It is fairly obvious that no real case like this will occur. So, as before, nothing
in the real world is going to be affected by having a method of *critical* moral
thinking which allows one to say that *if* it occurred, the torturing should be done;
at least, no harm would come of it unless the existence of this logical possibility
were allowed to weaken our hold upon the prima facie principle which condemns
cruelty. But if this did happen, it would be in contravention of the method, which

forbids us, when selecting prima facie principles, to attend to cases which are not going to occur.

It may now be suggested that the case could be made more difficult for the utilitarian by supposing that there were not one but thousands of sadists, who could be, in sum, given quite a lot of pleasure by torturing some unfortunate victims quite badly. This example is not all that fanciful; the Romans, though probably not many of them were sadists in the narrow sexual sense, actually had this kind of entertainment, and so did our own nearer ancestors, except that the victims were bears not humans. I say nothing of foxhunting and bullfighting and the like which go on to this day. Ought the utilitarian not to commend what happened in the Roman arenas?

The argument is plausible but fallacious. For what ought to be done, on any theory including the utilitarian, depends on the alternatives to doing it. It would be absurd to suggest that there was no other way in which the Roman populace could get its pleasures. The right thing to have done from the utilitarian point of view would have been to have chariot races or football games or other less atrocious sports; modern experience shows that they can generate just as much excitement. Mass sadism does occur, perhaps; but it does not have to. It is in accordance with utilitarian critical thinking to recommend the adoption of prima facie principles which forbid its indulgence and encourage less harmful pleasures. If we all had the right intuitions (the ones which a wise critical thinker would seek to inculcate) we would condemn such practices unhesitatingly. There need therefore be no conflict between utilitarianism and received opinion over this kind of example. . . .

8.8 . . . what are we to say about the pushpin-poetry question that troubled Mill (1861: ch. 2; cf. Bentham, 1825: III, ch. 1)? Are the preferences of those capable of only the grosser (but harmless) pleasures to have the same weight as those of their more refined contemporaries? Can we justify the reservation of funds for opera houses and programmes on television for the better-educated minority, which could have been diverted in order to increase the supply of mass entertainment? The question is a hot one politically, but perhaps a sane utilitarian solution can be found.

We are committed by the formality of our method to a Benthamite answer to the basic question: equal preferences count equally, whatever their content. This is because the only question the method allows us to ask is, What shall we rationally universally prescribe, or from an impartial standpoint prefer, if we are fully informed and make no logical mistakes? There is no place here for discrimination, at the critical level, between pleasures or preferences because of their content. We are not allowed to bring in intuitions that such and such pleasures are more worth while. But it can be argued even so that the "higher pleasures" deserve some protection. To at least a great many people who are able to enjoy them, they afford more enjoyment than the modern equivalents of pushpin, so that the quantity of pleasure is not equal. So these people, at any rate, will prefer the higher pleasures. This step in Mill's argument is correct, and does not require him to disagree with Bentham.

Moreover, if the percentage of such people in the population were to be increased by better education, utility over the foreseeable future would also be increased, on the assumption, not only that the better educated people will get more pleasure, minded as they are, from Bach than from pop music, but that they will get more pleasure from Bach than they would have got if they had never known anything but pop music. I think this a not absurd assumption to make. Such a line of reasoning might lead us to the conclusion that, putting ourselves impartially in the places of all, now and in the future, who would be affected by such a decision, we would prefer to preserve what we have inherited of these civilized arts and try to get a bigger audience for them. This can be done at the cost of an amount of money which, if diverted to mass entertainment instead, would provide no noticeable addition to the present ample supply. Technological improvements (opera and ballet on television, video tapes, etc.) will reduce the cost and increase the market. So we can hope that if those responsible for these matters can hold the philistines off, preference-satisfaction will in the long run be increased overall.

The basic move in all these arguments is to show that, even if preferences are given weight in proportion to their strengths and regardless of their content, a sound critical thinker, in the actual state of the world, will come up with prima facie principles for general use which accord with most of our intuitions. Not all of them, perhaps. Maybe those who think that the desires of homosexuals are inherently evil and should be utterly discounted or given negative weight will have, if they do some careful critical thinking, to abandon this intuition. But in general critical thinking will result in prima facie principles which discriminate quite sharply between good and evil desires, and between higher and lower pleasures, even though at the critical level no discrimination is allowed on grounds of content. This is because, in the world as it is, the encouragement of good desires and higher pleasures will maximize preference-satisfaction as a whole in the long term, even when preference-satisfaction is assessed in an impartial and content-indifferent way.

Rights and Justice

9.5 . . . It should be clear by now how lacking in substance is the common objection to utilitarianism, which might be advanced against my own theory of moral reasoning too, that it can give no place to rights, and can ride rough-shod over them in the interests of utility. We are very reasonably told (Dworkin, 1977:184) that we should "take rights seriously." If we take them seriously enough to inquire what they are and what their status is, we shall discover that they are, indeed, an immensely important element in our moral thinking—important enough to justify, in many cases, the claim that they are "trumps"—but that this provides no argument at all against utilitarians. For utilitarianism is better able to secure them this status than are intuitionist theories.

Let us take any typical conflict between claims to rights. A racist organization seeks to reserve a public hall for a meeting, and it is obvious that, if the meeting is held, there will be incitement to racial hatred and a danger of violence (we need not ask who will start it). The public authority which controls the hall, urged perhaps by the police, refuses to make the hall available. The racist organization then protests that it is being denied its right to free speech. The public authority counters that it has an obligation to preserve the right of minorities not to have hatred preached against them, and that the public has a right to be protected against outbreaks of violence. Here we have a very typical case of conflict between rights, comparable in all respects to the conflicts of duties. . . . Another instance is the well canvassed conflict between the right of a woman to dispose of her own body and the right of the foetus (or of the person whom the foetus would become, H 1975) to life. In such conflicts both rights may be important *in general;* the problem is, which should be overridden in a particular case. Certainly, in the public meeting case, the right to freedom of speech is of great importance; but so are the other rights which conflict with it.

Faced with such situations, how is an intuitionist to decide which right is "trumps"? Different people will have conflicting intuitions. What is needed is a method of critical thinking which will decide which of the rights, or the principles on which they are based, should override the other in this case. Intuitionists provide no method of critical thinking beyond the appeal (perhaps after "reflection") to further intuitions, which have no more authority than the first lot. The most that such a method can achieve is consensus between those who happen to have been similarly educated.

The method I would advocate, by contrast, bases itself on logical considerations established by an understanding of the words used in the questions we are asking, and compelling on anybody who is using the words in the same senses, i.e., asking the same questions. If I am not mistaken in what I have said earlier about the logical character of the moral words, and here about the word "rights," the method to be employed is one which will select moral principles for use at the intuitive level, including principles about rights, on the score of their acceptance-utility, i.e., on the ground that they are the set of principles whose general acceptance in the society in question will do the best, all told, for the interests of the people in the society considered impartially.

In the case we have described it is likely that a principle will be selected which guarantees freedom of speech but qualifies it by restrictions on what may be said. This is not the place to discuss precisely what those restrictions should be; for example, how to draw the line between incitement to violence and the expression of political dissent. What I hope to have made clear is that the method I have been advocating provides a way (and so far as I can see the only secure way) of reasoning about such questions. The use of this method at the critical level to select principles for general use does not in the least stop us entrenching those principles, once selected and inculcated, against too facile appeals to immediate utility; it is sound utilitarian wisdom to think that such appeals can tempt us into actions which are likely to turn out not at all for the best, given our human limitations. So perhaps the intuitionists can be praised for giving an adequate account of intuitive thinking about rights. Would that they had lifted their eyes a bit higher!

———

References

Bentham, Jeremy. (1825). *The Rationale of Reward.*
Brandt, Richard B. (1989). "Fairness to Happiness," *Social Theory and Practice* 15.
Dworkin, Ronald. (1977). *Taking Rights Seriously.* Cambridge, MA: Harvard University Press.
Hare, R. M. (1975). "Abortion and the Golden Rule," *Philosophy and Public Affairs* 4.
Mill, John Stuart. (1861). *Utilitarianism.*

Prichard, H. A. (1949). "Duty and Ignorance of Fact" in *Moral Obligation*. Oxford: Oxford University Press.

Rawls, John. (1971). *A Theory of Justice*. Cambridge, MA: Harvard University Press.

Sen, Amartya. (1979). "Utilitarianism and Welfarism," *Journal of Philosophy* 76.

Sen, Amartya and Bernard Williams. (1982). *Utilitarianism and Beyond*, Cambridge/New York: Cambridge University Press.

Singer, Peter. (1981). *The Expanding Circle: Ethics and Sociobiology*. New York: Farrar, Strauss and Giroux.

Smart, J. J. C. (1973). "An Outline of a System of Utilitarian Ethics," in Smart and Williams, *Utilitarianism: For and Against*. Cambridge/New York: Cambridge University Press.

Williams, Bernard. (1976). "Utilitarianism and Self-Indulgence," in H. D. Lewis, ed. *Contemporary British Philosophy*. London: Allen and Unwin.

Study Questions

1. Hare draws a distinction between a decision or action that is "morally rational" and one that is "morally right." (See Section 4 of "A Utilitarian Approach to Ethics.") What is this distinction? Give an example of a decision that is morally rational but not morally right.

2. How does Hare define "welfare"? (See Section 5 of "A Utilitarian Approach to Ethics.") Do you agree that morality should be concerned with promoting human welfare so understood?

3. Hare claims that the requirement of treating the interests of all people impartially leads directly to "aggregationism"—that is, the idea that right action involves maximizing total welfare or preference satisfaction. (See Section 8 of "A Utilitarian Approach to Ethics.") Why does he think this? Do you agree? Is this a problem for utilitarianism? Explain.

4. What does Hare mean by "critical thinking"? What role does it play in his view and when is it needed?

5. Is intuition a reliable guide to moral decision-making? Why or why not? In your view, do Hare's two levels of moral thinking provide a good framework for assessing our moral intuitions?

6. Hare defends utilitarianism against the common objection that, under certain circumstances, it would permit one to kill one innocent person in order to use that person's organs to save the lives of several others. (See, e.g., *Moral Thinking*, Section 8.2.) What are the main elements of Hare's defense of utilitarianism? Is his defense persuasive?

Selected Bibliography

Brandt, Richard B. *A Theory of the Good and the Right* (Oxford: Clarendon Press, 1979). An important presentation of utilitarianism

Hare. R. M. *Moral Thinking* (Oxford/New York: Oxford University Press, 1981).

———. *Objective Prescriptions and Other Essays* (Oxford/New York: Oxford University Press, 1999). A recent collection of essays by Hare.

Scheffler, Samuel, ed. *Consequentialism and Its Critics* (Oxford/New York: Oxford University Press, 1988). An anthology on the controversy between consequentialism and deontology.

Sen, Amartya and Bernard Williams. *Utilitarianism and Beyond* (Cambridge/New York: Cambridge University Press, 1982). An important anthology, containing defenses of utilitarianism by Hare and John Harsanyi, as well as many critical articles.

Smart, J. J. C. and Bernard Williams. *Utilitarianism: For and Against* (Cambridge/New York: Cambridge University Press, 1973). Criticism and defense of utilitarianism by two prominent philosophers.

22

T. M. SCANLON

John Rawls's theory of justice uses the idea of a hypothetical rational agreement that is fair to all for the limited, but clearly important purpose of supporting principles of justice to govern major social institutions. A natural extension of his

> *An act is wrong if . . . [it] would be disallowed by rules for the general regulation of behavior which no one could reasonably reject. . . .*

theory is to use the idea of fair agreement to support a comprehensive set of moral principles to govern how people should treat each other. We see the outlines of such a theory in the next selection by T. M. Scanlon.

Scanlon calls his theory "contractualism," and he develops it as a philosophical theory of the "subject matter of morality." It is fairly clear that a scientific theory is about some part of the physical world. What, we might ask, is morality about? When we claim that a certain way of acting is wrong, what are we talking about? What might make such claims true or false? A philosophical account of the nature of right and wrong will provide answers to such questions. One such theory is what Scanlon calls "philosophical utilitarianism" (in contrast to utilitarianism as a normative theory), according to which claims about right and wrong are in some way based on facts about human well-being. Scanlon's contractualism develops an alternative that bases right and wrong on principles that it would be reasonable for people to agree to. The theory that he develops here holds that the wrongness of an act is the fact that it would be disallowed by general principles of conduct that no one could reasonably reject, assuming that they have the aim of finding generally acceptable principles that people can cite to justify their actions to each other. An important part of this theory is that it provides an account of why we care about morality and take it as seriously as we do. Scanlon's view is that the basis of moral motivation is a desire to be able to justify our actions to others on grounds they could not reasonably reject.

T. M. Scanlon taught for many years at Princeton University, and is currently professor of philosophy at Harvard University. He has written many influential articles in moral and political philosophy. His book, *What We Owe to Each Other* (1998), develops the contractualist theory first outlined in this article.

Contractualism and Utilitarianism*

Utilitarianism occupies a central place in the moral philosophy of our time. It is not the view which most people hold; certainly there are very few who would claim to be act utilitarians. But for a much wider range of people it is the view towards which they find themselves pressed when they try to give a theoretical account of their moral beliefs. Within moral philosophy it represents a position one must struggle against if one wishes to avoid it. This is so in spite of the fact that the implications of act utilitarianism are wildly at variance with firmly held moral convictions, while rule utilitarianism, the most common alternative formulation, strikes most people as an unstable compromise.

The wide appeal of utilitarianism is due, I think, to philosophical considerations of a more or less sophisticated kind which pull us in a quite different direction than our first order moral beliefs. In particular, utilitarianism derives much of its appeal from alleged difficulties about the foundations of rival views. What a successful alternative to utilitarianism must do, first and foremost, is to sap this source of strength by providing a clear account of the foundations of non-utilitarian moral reasoning. In what follows I will first describe the problem in more detail by setting out the questions which a philosophical account of the foundations of morality must answer. I will then put forward a version of contractualism which, I will argue, offers a better set of responses to these questions than that supplied by straightforward versions of utilitarianism. Finally I will explain why contractualism, as I understand it, does not lead back to some utilitarian formula as its normative outcome.

Contractualism has been proposed as the alternative to utilitarianism before, notably by John Rawls in *A Theory of Justice* (Rawls 1971). Despite the wide discussion which this book has received, however, I think that the appeal of contractualism as a foundational view has been underrated. In particular, it has not been sufficiently appreciated that contractualism offers a particularly plausible account of moral motivation. The version of contractualism that I shall present differs from Rawls' in a number of respects. In particular, it makes no use, or only a different and more limited kind of use, of his notion of choice from behind a veil of ignorance. One result of this difference is to make the contrast between contractualism and utilitarianism stand out more clearly.

*I am greatly indebted to Derek Parfit for patient criticism and enormously helpful discussion of many earlier versions of this paper. Thanks are due also to the many audiences who have heard parts of those versions delivered as lectures and kindly responded with helpful comments. In particular, I am indebted to Marshall Cohen, Ronald Dworkin, Owen Fiss, and Thomas Nagel for valuable criticism.

I

There is such a subject as moral philosophy for much the same reason that there is such a subject as the philosophy of mathematics. In moral judgements, as in mathematical ones, we have a set of putatively objective beliefs in which we are inclined to invest a certain degree of confidence and importance. Yet on reflection it is not at all obvious what, if anything, these judgements can be about, in virtue of which some can be said to be correct or defensible and others not. This question of subject matter, or the grounds of truth, is the first philosophical question about both morality and mathematics. Second, in both morality and mathematics it seems to be possible to discover the truth simply by thinking or reasoning about it. Experience and observation may be helpful, but observation in the normal sense is not the standard means of discovery in either subject. So, given any positive answer to the first question—any specification of the subject matter or ground of truth in mathematics or morality—we need some compatible epistemology explaining how it is possible to discover the facts about this subject matter through something like the means we seem to use.

Given this similarity in the questions giving rise to moral philosophy and to the philosophy of mathematics, it is not surprising that the answers commonly given fall into similar general types. If we were to interview students in a freshman mathematics course many of them would, I think, declare themselves for some kind of conventionalism. They would hold that mathematics proceeds from definitions and principles that are either arbitrary or instrumentally justified, and that mathematical reasoning consists in perceiving what follows from these definitions and principles. A few others, perhaps, would be realists or platonists according to whom mathematical truths are a special kind of non-empirical fact that we can perceive through some form of intuition. Others might be naturalists who hold that mathematics, properly understood, is just the most abstract empirical science. Finally there are, though perhaps not in an average freshman course, those who hold that there are no mathematical facts in the "world outside of us," but that the truths of mathematics are objective truths about the mental constructions of which we are capable. Kant held that pure mathematics was a realm of objective mind-dependent truths, and Brouwer's mathematical Intuitionism is another theory of this type (with the important difference that it offers grounds for the warranted assertability of mathematical judgements rather than for their truth in the classical sense). All of these positions have natural correlates in moral philosophy. Intuitionism of the sort espoused by W. D. Ross is perhaps the closest analogue to mathematical platonism, and Kant's theory is the most familiar version of the thesis that morality is a sphere of objective, mind-dependent truths.

All of the views I have mentioned (with some qualification in the case of conventionalism) give positive (i.e., non-skeptical) answers to the first philosophical question about mathematics. Each identifies some objective, or at least intersubjective, ground of truth for mathematical judgements. Outright skepticism and subjective versions of mind-dependence (analogues of emotivism or prescriptivism) are less appealing as philosophies of mathematics than as moral philosophies. This is so in part simply because of the greater degree of intersubjective agreement in mathematical judgement. But it is also due to the difference in the further questions that philosophical accounts of the two fields must answer.

Neither mathematics nor morality can be taken to describe a realm of facts existing in isolation from the rest of reality. Each is supposed to be connected with other things. Mathematical judgements give rise to predictions about those realms to which mathematics is applied. This connection is something that a philosophical account of mathematical truth must explain, but the fact that we can observe and learn from the correctness of such predictions also gives support to our belief in objective mathematical truth. In the case of morality the main connection is, or is generally supposed to be, with the will. Given any candidate for the role of subject matter of morality we must explain why anyone should care about it, and the need to answer this question of motivation has given strong support to subjectivist views.

But what must an adequate philosophical theory of morality say about moral motivation? It need not, I think, show that the moral truth gives anyone who knows it a reason to act which appeals to that person's present desires or to the advancement of his or her interests. I find it entirely intelligible that moral requirement might correctly apply to a person even though that person had no reason of either of these kinds for complying with it. Whether moral requirements give those to whom they apply reasons for compliance of some third kind is a disputed question which I shall set aside. But what an adequate moral philosophy must do, I think, is to make clearer to us the nature of the reasons that morality does provide, at least to those who are concerned with it. A philosophical theory of morality must offer an account of these reasons that is, on the one hand, compatible with its account of moral truth and moral reasoning and, on the other, supported by a plausible analysis of moral experience. A satisfactory moral philosophy will not leave concern with morality as a simple special preference, like a fetish or a special taste, which some people just happen to have. It must make it understandable why moral reasons are ones that people can take seriously, and why they strike those who are moved by them as reasons of a special stringency and inescapability.

There is also a further question whether susceptibility to such reasons is compatible with a person's good or whether it is, as Nietzsche argued, a psychological disaster for the person who has it. If one is to defend morality one must show that it is not disastrous in this way, but I will not pursue this second motivational question here. I mention it only to distinguish it from the first question, which is my present concern.

The task of giving a philosophical explanation of the subject matter of morality differs both from the task of analysing the meaning of moral terms and from that of finding the most coherent formulation of our first order moral beliefs. A maximally coherent ordering of our first order moral beliefs could provide us with a valuable kind of explanation: it would make clear how various, apparently disparate moral notions, precepts and judgements are related to one another, thus indicating to what degree conflicts between them are fundamental and to what degree, on the other hand, they can be resolved or explained away. But philosophical inquiry into the subject matter of morality takes a more external view. It seeks to explain what kind of truths moral truths are by describing them in relation to other things in the world and in relation to our particular concerns. An explanation of how we can come to know the truth about morality must be based on such an external explanation of the kind of things moral truths are rather than on a list of particular moral truths, even a maximally coherent list. This seems to be true as well about explanations of how moral beliefs can give one a reason to act.*

Coherence among our first-order moral beliefs—what Rawls has called narrow reflective equilibrium**—seems unsatisfying† as an account of moral truth or as an account of the basis of justification in ethics just because, taken by itself, a maximally coherent account of our moral beliefs need not provide us with what I have called a philosophical explanation of the subject matter of morality. However internally coherent our moral beliefs may be rendered, the nagging doubt may remain that there is nothing to them at all. They may be merely a set of socially inculcated reactions, mutually consistent perhaps but not judgements of a kind which can properly be said to be correct or incorrect. A philosophical theory of the nature of morality can contribute to our confidence in our first order moral beliefs chiefly by allaying these natural doubts about the subject. Insofar as it includes an account of moral epistemology, such a theory may guide us towards new forms of moral argument, but it need not do this. Moral argument of more or less the kind we have been familiar with may remain as the only form of justification in ethics. But whether or not it leads to revision in our modes of justification, what a good philosophical theory should do is to give us a clearer understanding of what the best forms of moral argument amount to and what kind of truth it is that they can be a way of arriving at. (Much the same can be said, I believe, about the contribution which philosophy of mathematics makes to our confidence in particular mathematical judgements and particular forms of mathematical reasoning.)

Like any thesis about morality, a philosophical account of the subject matter of morality must have some connection with the meaning of moral terms: it must be plausible to claim that the subject matter described is in fact what these terms refer to at least in much of their normal use. But the current meaning of moral terms is the product of many different moral beliefs held by past and present speakers of the language, and this meaning is surely compatible with a variety of moral views and with a variety of views about the nature of morality. After all, moral terms are used to express many different views of these kinds, and people who express these views are not using moral terms incorrectly, even though what some of them say must be mistaken. Like a first-order moral judgement, a philosophical characterisation of the subject matter of morality is a substantive claim about morality, albeit a claim of a different kind.

While a philosophical characterisation of morality makes a kind of claim that differs from a first-order moral judgement, this does not mean that a philosophical theory of morality will be neutral between competing normative doctrines. The

---

*Though here the ties between the nature of morality and its content are more important. It is not clear that an account of the nature of morality which left its content *entirely* open could be the basis for a plausible account of moral motivation.

**See Rawls 1974–5, p. 8; and Daniels 1979, pp. 257–8. How closely the process of what I am calling philosophical explanation will coincide with the search for "wide reflective equilibrium" as this is understood by Rawls and by Daniels is a further question which I cannot take up here.

†For expression of this dissatisfaction see Singer 1974 and Brandt 1979, pp. 16–21.

adoption of a philosophical thesis about the nature of morality will almost always have some effect on the plausibility of particular moral claims, but philosophical theories of morality vary widely in the extent and directness of their normative implications. At one extreme is intuitionism, understood as the philosophical thesis that morality is concerned with certain non-natural properties. Rightness, for example, is held by Ross* to be the property of "fittingness" or "moral suitability." Intuitionism holds that we can identify occurrences of these properties, and that we can recognise as self-evident certain general truths about them, but that they cannot be further analysed or explained in terms of other notions. So understood, intuitionism is in principle compatible with a wide variety of normative positions. One could, for example, be an intuitionistic utilitarian or an intuitionistic believer in moral rights, depending on the general truths about the property of moral rightness which one took to be self-evident.

The other extreme is represented by philosophical utilitarianism. The term "utilitarianism" is generally used to refer to a family of specific normative doctrines—doctrines which might be held on the basis of a number of different philosophical theses about the nature of morality. In this sense of the term one might, for example, be a utilitarian on intuitionist or on contractualist grounds. But what I will call "philosophical utilitarianism" is a particular philosophical thesis about the subject matter of morality, namely the thesis that the only fundamental moral facts are facts about individual well-being.** I believe that this thesis has a great deal of plausibility for many people, and that, while some people are utilitarians for other reasons, it is the attractiveness of philosophical utilitarianism which accounts for the widespread influence of utilitarian principles.

It seems evident to people that there is such a thing as individuals' being made better or worse off. Such facts have an obvious motivational force; it is quite understandable that people should be moved by them in much the way that they are supposed to be moved by moral considerations. Further, these facts are clearly relevant to morality as we now understand it. Claims about individual well-being are one class of valid starting points for moral argument. But many people find it much harder to see how there could be any other, independent starting points. Substantive moral requirements independent of individual well-being strike people as intuitionist in an objectionable sense. They would represent "moral facts" of a kind it would be difficult to explain. There is no problem about recognising it as a fact that a certain act is, say, an instance of lying or of promise breaking. And a utilitarian can acknowledge that such facts as these often have (derivative) moral significance: they are morally significant because of their consequences for individual well-being. The problems, and the charge of "intuitionism, arise when it is claimed that such acts are wrong in a sense that is not reducible to the fact that they decrease individual well-being. How could this independent property of moral wrongness be understood in a way that would give it the kind of importance and motivational force which moral considerations have been taken to have? If one accepts the idea that there are no moral properties

*Ross 1939 pp. 52–4, 315.
**For purposes of this discussion I leave open the important questions of which individuals are to count and how "well-being" is to be understood. Philosophical utilitarianism will retain the appeal I am concerned with under many different answers to these questions.

having this kind of intrinsic significance, then philosophical utilitarianism may seem to be the only tenable account of morality. And once philosophical utilitarianism is accepted, some form of normative utilitarianism seems to be forced on us as the correct first-order moral theory. Utilitarianism thus has, for many people, something like the status which Hilbert's Formalism and Brouwer's Intuitionism have for their believers. It is a view which seems to be forced on us by the need to give a philosophically defensible account of the subject. But it leaves us with a hard choice: we can either abandon many of our previous first-order beliefs or try to salvage them by showing that they can be obtained as derived truths or explained away as useful and harmless fictions.

It may seem that the appeal of philosophical utilitarianism as I have described it is spurious, since this theory must amount either to a form of intuitionism (differing from others only in that it involves just one appeal to intuition) or else to definitional naturalism of a kind refuted by Moore and others long ago. But I do not think that the doctrine can be disposed of so easily. Philosophical utilitarianism is a philosophical thesis about the nature of morality. As such, it is on a par with intuitionism or with the form of contractualism which I will defend later in this paper. None of these theses need claim to be true as a matter of definition; if one of them is true it does not follow that a person who denies it is misusing the words "right," "wrong" and "ought." Nor are all these theses forms of intuitionism, if intuitionism is understood as the view that moral facts concern special non-natural properties, which we can apprehend by intuitive insight but which do not need or admit of any further analysis. Both contractualism and philosophical utilitarianism are specifically incompatible with this claim. Like other philosophical theses about the nature of morality (including, I would say, intuitionism itself), contractualism and philosophical utilitarianism are to be appraised on the basis of their success in giving an account of moral belief, moral argument and moral motivation that is compatible with our general beliefs about the world: our beliefs about what kinds of things there are in the world, what kinds of observation and reasoning we are capable of, and what kinds of reasons we have for action. A judgement as to which account of the nature of morality (or of mathematics) is most plausible in this general sense is just that: a judgement of overall plausibility. It is not usefully described as an insight into concepts or as a special intuitive insight of some other kind.

If philosophical utilitarianism is accepted then some form of utilitarianism appears to be forced upon us as a normative doctrine, but further argument is required to determine which form we should accept. If all that counts morally is the well-being of individuals, no one of whom is singled out as counting for more than the others, and if all that matters in the case of each individual is the degree to which his or her well-being is affected, then it would seem to follow that the basis of moral appraisal is the goal of maximising the *sum* of individual well-being. Whether this standard is to be applied to the criticism of individual actions, or to the selection of rules or policies, or to the inculcation of habits and dispositions to act is a further question, as is the question of how "well-being" itself is to be understood. Thus the hypothesis that much of the appeal of utilitarianism as a normative doctrine derives from the attractiveness of philosophical utilitarianism explains how people can be convinced that some form of utilitarianism must be correct while yet being quite uncertain as to which form it is, whether it is "direct" or "act" utilitarianism or some form of indirect "rule" or "motive" utilitarianism. What these views have in common, despite their differing normative consequences, is the identification of the same class of fundamental moral facts.

II

If what I have said about the appeal of utilitarianism is correct, then what a rival theory must do is to provide an alternative to philosophical utilitarianism as a conception of the subject matter of morality. This is what the theory which I shall call contractualism seeks to do. Even if it succeeds in this, however, and is judged superior to philosophical utilitarianism as an account of the nature of morality, normative utilitarianism will not have been refuted. The possibility will remain that normative utilitarianism can be established on other grounds, for example as the normative outcome of contractualism itself. But one direct and, I think, influential argument for normative utilitarianism will have been set aside.

To give an example of what I mean by contractualism, a contractualist account of the nature of moral wrongness might be stated as follows.

> An act is wrong if its performance under the circumstances would be disallowed by any system of rules for the general regulation of behaviour which no one could reasonably reject as a basis for informed, unforced general agreement.

This is intended as a characterisation of the kind of property which moral wrongness is. Like philosophical utilitarianism, it will have normative consequences, but it is not my present purpose to explore these in detail. As a contractualist account of one moral notion, what I have set out here is only an approximation, which may need to be modified considerably. Here I can offer a few remarks by way of clarification.

The idea of "informed agreement" is meant to exclude agreement based on superstition or false belief about the consequences of actions, even if these beliefs are ones which it would be reasonable for the person in question to have. The intended force of the qualification "reasonably," on the other hand, is to exclude rejections that would be unreasonable given the aim of finding principles which could be the basis of informed, unforced general agreement. Given this aim, it would be unreasonable, for example, to reject a principle because it imposed a burden on you when every alternative principle would impose much greater burdens on others. I will have more to say about grounds for rejection later in the paper.

The requirement that the hypothetical agreement which is the subject of moral argument be unforced is meant not only to rule out coercion, but also to exclude being forced to accept an agreement by being in a weak bargaining position, for example because others are able to hold out longer and hence to insist on better terms. Moral argument abstracts from such considerations. The only relevant pressure for agreement comes from the desire to find and agree on principles which no one who had this desire could reasonably reject. According to contractualism, moral argument concerns the possibility of agreement among persons who are all moved by this desire, and moved by it to the same degree. But this counter-factual assumption characterises only the agreement with which morality is concerned, not the world to which moral principles are to apply. Those who are concerned with morality look for principles for application to their imperfect world which they could not reasonably reject, and which others in this world, who are not now moved by the desire for agreement, could not reasonably reject should they come to be so moved.*

The contractualist account of moral wrongness refers to principles "which no one could reasonably reject" rather than to principles "which everyone could-reasonably accept" for the following reason.** Consider a principle under which some people will suffer severe hardships, and suppose that these hardships are avoidable. That is, there are alternative principles under which no one would have to bear comparable burdens. It might happen, however, that the people on whom these hardships fall are particularly self-sacrificing, and are willing to accept these burdens for the sake of what they see as the greater good of all. We would not say, I think, that it would be unreasonable of them to do this. On the other hand, it might not be unreasonable for them to refuse these burdens, and, hence, not unreasonable for someone to reject a principle requiring him to bear them. If this rejection would be reasonable, then the principle imposing these burdens is put in doubt, despite the fact that some particularly self-sacrificing people could (reasonably) accept it. Thus it is the reasonableness of rejecting a principle, rather than the reasonableness of accepting it, on which moral argument turns.

It seems likely that many non-equivalent sets of principles will pass the test of non-rejectability. This is suggested, for example, by the fact that there are many different ways of defining important duties, no one of which is more or less "rejectable" than the others. There are, for example, many different systems of agreement-making and many different ways of assigning responsibility to care for others. It does not follow, however, that any action allowed by at least one of these sets of principles cannot be morally wrong according to contractualism. If it is important for us to have *some* duty of a given kind (some duty of fidelity to agreements, or some duty of mutual aid) of which there are many morally acceptable forms, then one of these forms needs to be established by convention. In a setting in which one of these forms *is* conventionally established, acts disallowed by it will be wrong in the sense of the definition given. For, given the need for such conventions, one thing that could not be generally agreed to would be a set of principles allowing one to disregard conventionally established (and morally acceptable) definitions of important duties. This dependence on convention introduces a degree of cultural relativity into contractualist morality. In addition, what a person can reasonably reject will depend on the aims and conditions that are important in his life, and these will also depend on the society in which he lives. The definition given above allows for variation of both of these kinds by making the wrongness of an action depend on the circumstances in which it is performed.

*Here I am indebted to Gilbert Harman for comments which have helped me to clarify my statement of contractualism.
**A point I owe to Derek Parfit.

The partial statement of contractualism which I have given has the abstract character appropriate in an account of the subject matter of morality. On its face, it involves no specific claim as to which principles could be agreed to or even whether there is a unique set of principles which could be the basis of agreement. One way, though not the only way, for a contractualist to arrive at substantive moral claims would be to give a technical definition of the relevant notion of agreement, e.g., by specifying the conditions under which agreement is to be reached, the parties to this agreement and the criteria of reasonableness to be employed. Different contractualists have done this in different ways. What must be claimed for such a definition is that (under the circumstances in which it is to apply) what it describes is indeed the kind of unforced, reasonable agreement at which moral argument aims. But contractualism can also be understood as an informal description of the subject matter of morality on the basis of which ordinary forms of moral reasoning can be understood and appraised without proceeding via a technical notion of agreement.

Who is to be included in the general agreement to which contractualism refers? The scope of morality is a difficult question of substantive morality, but a philosophical theory of the nature of morality should provide some basis for answering it. What an adequate theory should do is to provide a framework within which what seem to be relevant arguments for and against particular interpretations of the moral boundary can be carried out. It is often thought that contractualism can provide no plausible basis for an answer to this question. Critics charge either that contractualism provides no answer at all, because it must begin with some set of contracting parties taken as given, or that contractualism suggests an answer which is obviously too restrictive, since a contract requires parties who are able to make and keep agreements and who are each able to offer the others some benefit in return for their cooperation. Neither of these objections applies to the version of contractualism that I am defending. The general specification of the scope of morality which it implies seems to me to be this: morality applies to a being if the notion of justification to a being of that kind makes sense. What is required in order for this to be the case? Here I can only suggest some necessary conditions. The first is that the being have a good, that is, that there be a clear sense in which things can be said to go better or worse for that being. This gives partial sense to the idea of what it would be reasonable for a trustee to accept on the being's behalf. It would be reasonable for a trustee to accept at least those things that are good, or not bad, for the being in question. Using this idea of trusteeship we can extend the notion of acceptance to apply to beings that are incapable of literally agreeing to anything. But this minimal notion of trusteeship is too weak to provide a basis for morality, according to contractualism. Contractualist morality relies on notions of what it would be reasonable to accept, or reasonable to reject, which are essentially comparative. Whether it would be unreasonable for me to reject a certain principle, given the aim of finding principles which no one with this aim could reasonably reject, depends not only on how much actions allowed by that principle might hurt me in absolute terms but also on how that potential loss compares with other potential losses to others under this principle and alternatives to it. Thus, in order for a being to stand in moral relations with us it is not enough that it have a good, it is also necessary that its good be sufficiently similar to our own to provide a basis for some system of comparability. Only on the basis of such a system can we give the proper kind of sense to the notion of what a trustee could reasonably reject on a being's behalf.

But the range of possible trusteeship is broader than that of morality. One could act as a trustee for a tomato plant, a forest or an ant colony, and such entities are not included in morality. Perhaps this can be explained by appeal to the requirement of comparability: while these entities have a good, it is not comparable to our own in a way that provides a basis for moral argument. Beyond this, however, there is in these cases insufficient foothold for the notion of justification to a being. One further minimum requirement for this notion is that the being constitute a point of view; that is, that there be such a thing as what it is like to be that being, such a thing as what the world seems like to it. Without this, we do not stand in a relation to the being that makes even hypothetical justification *to it* appropriate.

On the basis of what I have said so far contractualism can explain why the capacity to feel pain should have seemed to many to count in favour of moral status: a being which has this capacity seems also to satisfy the three conditions I have just mentioned as necessary for the idea of justification to it to make sense. If a being can feel pain, then it constitutes a centre of consciousness to which justification can be addressed. Feeling pain is a clear way in which the being can be worse off; having its pain alleviated a way in which it can be benefited; and these are forms of weal and woe which seem directly comparable to our own.

It is not clear that the three conditions I have listed as necessary are also sufficient for the idea of justification to a being to make sense. Whether they are, and, if they are not, what more may be required, are difficult and disputed questions. Some would restrict the moral sphere to those to whom justifications could in principle be communicated, or to those who can actually agree to something, or to those who have the capacity to understand moral argument. Contractualism as I have stated it does not settle these issues at once. All I claim is that it provides a basis for argument about them which is at least as plausible as that offered by rival accounts of the nature of morality. These proposed restrictions on the scope of morality are naturally understood as debatable claims about the conditions under which the relevant notion of justification makes sense, and the arguments commonly offered for and against them can also be plausibly understood on this basis.

Some other possible restrictions on the scope of morality are more evidently rejectable. Morality might be restricted to those who have the capacity to observe its constraints, or to those who are able to confer some reciprocal benefit on other participants. But it is extremely implausible to suppose that the beings excluded by these requirements fall entirely outside the protection of morality. Contractualism as I have formulated it can explain why this is so: the absence of these capacities alone does nothing to undermine the possibility of justification to a being. What it may do in some cases, however, is to alter the justifications which are relevant. I suggest that whatever importance the capacities for deliberative control and reciprocal benefit may have is as factors altering the duties which beings have and the duties others have towards them, not as conditions whose absence suspends the moral framework altogether.

III

I have so far said little about the normative content of contractualism. For all I have said, the act utilitarian formula might turn out to be a theorem of contractualism. I do not think that this is the case, but my main thesis is that whatever the normative implications of contractualism may be it still has distinctive content as a philosophical thesis about the nature of morality. This content—the difference, for example, between being a utilitarian because the utilitarian formula is the basis of general agreement and being a utilitarian on other grounds—is shown most clearly in the answer that a contractualist gives to the first motivational question.

Philosophical utilitarianism is a plausible view partly because the facts which it identifies as fundamental to morality—facts about individual well-being—have obvious motivational force. Moral facts can motivate us, on this view, because of our sympathetic identification with the good of others. But as we move from philosophical utilitarianism to a specific utilitarian formula as the standard of right action, the form of motivation that utilitarianism appeals to becomes more abstract. If classical utilitarianism is the correct normative doctrine then the natural source of moral motivation will be a tendency to be moved by changes in aggregate well-being, however these may be composed. We must be moved in the same way by an aggregate gain of the same magnitude whether it is obtained by relieving the acute suffering of a few people or by bringing tiny benefits to a vast number, perhaps at the expense of moderate discomfort for a few. This is very different from sympathy of the familiar kind toward particular individuals, but a utilitarian may argue that this more abstract desire is what natural sympathy becomes when it is corrected by rational reflection. This desire has the same content as sympathy—it is a concern for the good of others—but it is not partial or selective in its choice of objects.

Leaving aside the psychological plausibility of this even-handed sympathy, how good a candidate is it for the role of moral motivation? Certainly sympathy of the usual kind is one of the many motives that can sometimes impel one to do the right thing. It may be the dominant motive, for example when I run to the aid of a suffering child. But when I feel convinced by Peter Singer's article* on famine, and find myself crushed by the recognition of what seems a clear moral requirement, there is something else at work. In addition to the thought of how much good I could do for people in drought-stricken lands, I am overwhelmed by the further, seemingly distinct thought that it would be wrong for me to fail to aid them when I could do so at so little cost to myself. A utilitarian may respond that his account of moral motivation cannot be faulted for not capturing this aspect of moral experience, since it is just a reflection of our non-utilitarian moral upbringing. Moreover, it must be groundless. For what kind of fact could this supposed further fact of moral wrongness be, and how could it give us a further, special reason for acting? The question for contractualism, then, is whether it can provide a satisfactory answer to this challenge.

According to contractualism, the source of motivation that is directly triggered by the belief that an action is wrong is the desire to be able to justify one's

*Singer 1972.

actions to others on grounds they could not reasonably* reject. I find this an extremely plausible account of moral motivation—a better account of at least my moral experience than the natural utilitarian alternative—and it seems to me to constitute a strong point for the contractualist view. We all might like to be in actual agreement with the people around us, but the desire which contractualism identifies as basic to morality does not lead us simply to conform to the standards accepted by others whatever these may be. The desire to be able to justify one's actions to others on grounds they could not reasonably reject will be satisfied when we know that there is adequate justification for our action even though others in fact refuse to accept it (perhaps because they have no interest in finding principles which we and others could not reasonably reject). Similarly, a person moved by this desire will not be satisfied by the fact that others accept a justification for his action if he regards this justification as spurious.

One rough test of whether you regard a justification as sufficient is whether you would accept that justification if you were in another person's position. This connection between the idea of "changing places" and the motivation which underlies morality explains the frequent occurrence of "Golden Rule" arguments within different systems of morality and in the teachings of various religions. But the thought experiment of changing places is only a rough guide; the fundamental question is what would it be unreasonable to reject as a basis for informed, unforced, general agreement. As Kant observed,** our different individual points of view, taken as they are, may in general by simply irreconcilable. "Judgemental harmony" requires the construction of a genuinely interpersonal form of justification which is nonetheless something that each individual could agree to. From this interpersonal standpoint, a certain amount of how things look from another person's point of view, like a certain amount of how they look from my own, will be counted as bias.

I am not claiming that the desire to be able to justify one's actions to others on grounds they could not reasonably reject is universal or "natural." "Moral education" seems to me plausibly understood as a process of cultivating this desire and shaping it, largely by learning what justifications others are in fact willing to accept, by finding which ones you yourself find acceptable as you confront them from a variety of perspectives, and by appraising your own and others' acceptance or rejection of these justifications in the light of greater experience.

In fact it seems to me that the desire to be able to justify one's actions (and institutions) on grounds one takes to be acceptable is quite strong in most people. People are willing to go to considerable lengths, involving quite heavy sacrifices, in order to avoid admitting the unjustifiability of their actions and institutions. The notorious insufficiency of moral motivation as a way of getting people to do the right thing is not due to simple weakness of the underlying motive, but rather to the fact that it is easily deflected by self-interest and self-deception.

It could reasonably be objected here that the source of motivation I have described is not tied exclusively to the contractualist notion of moral truth. The account of moral motivation which I have offered refers to the idea of a justification which it

** Reasonably, that is, given the desire to find principles which others similarly motivated could not reasonably reject.
**Kant 1785, section 2, footnote 14.

would be unreasonable to reject, and this idea is potentially broader than the contractualist notion of agreement. For let M be some non-contractualist account of moral truth. According to M, we may suppose, the wrongness of an action is simply a moral characteristic of that action in virtue of which it ought not to be done. An act which has this characteristic, according to M, has it quite independently of any tendency of informed persons to come to agreement about it. However, since informed persons are presumably in a position to recognise the wrongness of a type of action, it would seem to follow that if an action is wrong then such persons would agree that it is not to be performed. Similarly, if an act is not morally wrong, and there is adequate moral justification to perform it, then there will presumably be a moral justification for it which an informed person would be unreasonable to reject. Thus, even if M, and not contractualism, is the correct account of moral truth, the desire to be able to justify my actions to others on grounds they could not reasonably reject could still serve as a basis for moral motivation.

What this shows is that the appeal of contractualism, like that of utilitarianism, rests in part on a qualified scepticism. A non-contractualist theory of morality can make use of the source of motivation to which contractualism appeals. But a moral argument will trigger this source of motivation only in virtue of being a good justification for acting in a certain way, a justification which others would be unreasonable not to accept. So a non-contractualist theory must claim that there are moral properties which have justificatory force quite independent of their recognition in any ideal agreement. These would represent what John Mackie has called instances of intrinsic "to-be-doneness" and "not-to-be-doneness."* Part of contractualism's appeal rests on the view that, as Mackie puts it, it is puzzling how there could be such properties "in the world." By contrast, contractualism seeks to explain the justificatory status of moral properties, as well as their motivational force, in terms of the notion of reasonable agreement. In some cases the moral properties are themselves to be understood in terms of this notion. This is so, for example, in the case of the property of moral wrongness, considered above. But there are also right- and wrong-making properties which are themselves independent of the contractualist notion of agreement. I take the property of being an act of killing for the pleasure of doing so to be a wrong-making property of this kind. Such properties are wrong-making because it would be reasonable to reject any set of principles which permitted the acts they characterise. Thus, while there are morally relevant properties "in the world" which are independent of the contractualist notion of agreement, these do not constitute instances of intrinsic "to-be-doneness" and "not-to-be-doneness": their moral relevance—their force in justifications as well as their link with motivation—is to be explained on contractualist grounds.

In particular, contractualism can account for the apparent moral significance of facts about individual well-being, which utilitarianism takes to be fundamental. Individual well-being will be morally significant, according to contractualism, not because it is intrinsically valuable or because promoting it is self-evidently a right-making characteristic, but simply because an individual could reasonably reject a form of argument that gave his well-being no weight. This claim of moral significance is, however, only approximate, since it is a further difficult question exactly

*Mackie 1977, p. 42.

how "well-being" is to be understood and in what ways we are required to take account of the well-being of others in deciding what to do. It does not follow from this claim, for example, that a given desire will always and everywhere have the same weight in determining the rightness of an action that would promote its satisfaction, a weight proportional to its strength or "intensity." The right-making force of a person's desires is specified by what might be called a conception of morally legitimate interests. Such a conception is a product of moral argument; it is not given, as the notion of individual well-being may be, simply by the idea of what it is rational for an individual to desire. Not everything for which I have a rational desire will be something in which others need concede me to have a legitimate interest which they undertake to weigh in deciding what to do. The range of things which may be objects of my rational desires is very wide indeed, and the range of claims which others could not reasonably refuse to recognise will almost certainly be narrower than this. There will be a tendency for interests to conform to rational desire—for those conditions making it rational to desire something also to establish a legitimate interest in it—but the two will not always coincide.

One effect of contractualism, then, is to break down the sharp distinction, which arguments for utilitarianism appeal to, between the status of individual well-being and that of other moral notions. A framework of moral argument is required to define our legitimate interests and to account for their moral force. This same contractualist framework can also account for the force of other moral notions such as rights, individual responsibility and procedural fairness. . . .

V

I have described this version of contractualism only in outline. Much more needs to be said to clarify its central notions and to work out its normative implications. I hope that I have said enough to indicate its appeal as a philosophical theory of morality and as an account of moral motivation. I have put forward contractualism as an alternative to utilitarianism, but the characteristic feature of the doctrine can be brought out by contrasting it with a somewhat different view.

It is sometimes said* that morality is a device for our mutual protection. According to contractualism, this view is partly true but in an important way incomplete. Our concern to protect our central interests will have an important effect on what we could reasonably agree to. It will thus have an important effect on the content of morality if contractualism is correct. To the degree that this morality is observed, these interests will gain from it. If we had no desire to be able to justify our actions to others on grounds they could reasonably accept, the hope of gaining this protection would give us reason to try to instill this desire in others, perhaps through mass hypnosis or conditioning, even if this also meant acquiring it ourselves. But given that we have this desire already, our concern with morality is less instrumental.

*In different ways by G. J. Warnock in Warnock 1971, and by J. L. Mackie in Mackie 1977. See also Richard Brandt's remarks on justification in Chapter X of Brandt 1979.

The contrast might be put as follows. On one view, concern with protection is fundamental, and general agreement becomes relevant as a means or a necessary condition for securing this protection. On the other, contractualist view, the desire for protection is an important factor determining the content of morality because it determines what can reasonably be agreed to. But the idea of general agreement does not arise as a means of securing protection. It is, in a more fundamental sense, what morality is about.

———

References

Brandt, R. B. (1979). *A Theory of the Good and the Right*. Oxford/New York: Oxford University Press.

Daniels, Norman. (1979). "Wide Reflective Equilibrium and Theory Acceptance in Ethics," *Journal of Philosophy* 76: 256–282

Kant, Immanuel. (1785). *Foundations of the Metaphysics of Morals*, Tr. Lewis White Beck, Indianapolis: Liberal Arts Press, 1959.

Mackie, J. L. (1977). *Ethics: Inventing Right and Wrong*. Hammondsworth, England: Penguin.

Parfit, Derek. (1976). "On Doing the Best for Our Children," in *Ethics and Population*, ed. M. Bayles. Cambridge, MA: Schenkman Publishing.

Rawls, J. (1971). *A Theory of Justice*. Cambridge, MA: Harvard University Press.

———. (1974). "The Independence of Moral Theory," *Proceedings of the American Philosophical Association, 1974–5*. Reprinted in J. Rawls, *Collected Papers*. Cambridge, MA: Harvard University Press, 2000.

Ross, W. D. (1939). *Foundations of Ethics*. Oxford: Oxford University Press.

Singer, Peter. (1972). "Famine, Affluence and Morality," *Philosophy and Public Affairs* 1: 229–243

———. (1974). "Sidgwick and Reflective Equilibrium," *The Monist* 58: 490–517.

Warnock, G. J. (1971) *The Object of Morality*. London: Methuen & Co.

Study Questions

1. What does Scanlon mean by "philosophical utilitarianism"? (Section I) What, according to him is the appeal of philosophical utilitarianism? How does Scanlon's account of the subject matter of morality differ?

2. What is Scanlon's account of the "nature of moral wrongness"? (Section II) In your view, is this a plausible account of moral wrongness? If not, what would you propose as an alternative?

3. According to Scanlon's theory, the "desire to be able to justify our actions to others on grounds they could not reasonably reject" (Section III) is what leads us to care about morality and the source of moral motivation. Is this a strong desire in most people? Is it a desire that you have? Does it provide a solid basis for morality and moral motivation?

4. Give some examples of general rules for the regulation of conduct that no one could reasonably reject. Can Scanlon's theory be used to derive an adequate set of moral principles?

Selected Bibliography

Freeman, Samuel. "Contractualism and Motivation," *Journal of Philosophy* 88 (1991), 281–303. A useful discussion of Scanlon's article.

Scanlon, T. M. *What We Owe to Each Other* (Cambridge, MA: Harvard University Press, 1998), esp. Chap. 5.

"Special Issue on T. M. Scanlon, *What We Owe to Each Other*," *Social Theory and Practice*, 28, no. 2 (2002).

Watson, Gary. "Some Considerations in Favor of Contractualism," in Jules Coleman and Christopher Morris, eds., *Rational Commitment and Social Justice* (Cambridge/New York: Cambridge University Press, 1998). A general discussion of contractualism.

23

THOMAS NAGEL

———

Consequentialist theories hold that the rightness or wrongness of an action depends on its consequences, so that, for example, the right action in any given situation is the one that produces the most overall good. Deontological moral

> ... we seem to apprehend in each individual case an extremely powerful agent-relative reason not to harm an innocent person.

theories, by contrast, hold that there are principles of right conduct that apply immediately to our actions, requiring or prohibiting certain actions in certain circumstances without reference to any further end beyond the action. They claim that certain ways of acting are right or wrong in themselves, independent of their consequences. W. D. Ross argues, for example, that we should keep a promise simply because we have made it, or that we should show gratitude towards a benefactor simply because of the service we have received, and that the reasons for these actions do not depend on their overall consequences. One role of deontological constraints is to restrict the ends or goals that we may permissibly adopt, or to restrict the means that we may take to our permissible ends.

Ross acknowledged that, according to his theory, an action could be right even though some other action open to an agent might have better overall consequences. This point raises a question for deontology. If there are deontological prohibitions against lying, then it seems that it is wrong for you to lie, even if by telling a lie you can prevent other lies from being told elsewhere. But if lying is wrong, why shouldn't you do whatever you can to prevent lies from occurring—including *tell a lie*? Likewise, deontological constraints make it impermissible to violate the rights of an innocent person—even if violating the rights of one person will somehow prevent violations of the rights of more innocent people elsewhere. But why shouldn't the considerations that support this constraint lead one to do *whatever* will minimize the overall number of rights violations that occur? Many theorists have thought that this puzzle—sometimes called "the paradox of deontology"—presents a challenge that casts doubt on deontological constraints. In this selection, Thomas Nagel addresses this challenge and tries to show that deontological constraints are real.

Nagel's discussion uses a distinction between "agent-neutral" and "agent-relative reasons." Agent-neutral reasons are impersonal reasons for anyone to bring about a state of affairs or to prevent a state of affairs from occurring. For example we might think it a bad thing from an impersonal standpoint if a certain event occurs—for example, that Jane experiences serious physical pain—and that *anyone* in a position to stop it has a reason to. This reason is agent-neutral because it is a reason for anyone. Utilitarianism is often thought to provide agent-neutral reasons to increase general happiness. Agent-relative reasons, on the other hand, are reasons for specific individuals to do or refrain from certain actions. Nagel mentions two kinds of agent-relative reasons. "Reasons of autonomy" are reasons stemming from one's personal goals and values. If my goal is to climb Mt. Kilimanjaro, it gives me a reason to prepare for and to attempt the climb, but offhand it is not clear that it gives anyone else a reason to support my project. Deontological constraints provide another kind of agent-relative reason. If there are deontological constraints against lying, violating rights, harming innocent people, and so on, then I have reason not to do any of these things, as do you and everyone else. These constraints seem to supply personal reasons for each of us not to treat others in certain ways. Nagel wishes to argue that deontological constraints should be understood as agent-relative, and are not reducible to agent-neutral reasons to prevent certain states of affairs or outcomes from occurring.

Thomas Nagel taught for many years at Princeton University and is currently professor of philosophy and law at New York University. He is one of the leading contemporary moral and political philosophers. His many books include *The Possibility of Altruism* (1970), *Mortal Questions* (1979), and *Equality and Partiality* (1991). This selection is taken from *The View from Nowhere* (1986).

———

The View from Nowhere

Deontology

Let me turn now to the obscure topic of deontological constraints. These are agent-relative reasons which depend not on the aims or projects of the agent but on the claims of others. Unlike autonomous reasons, they are not optional. If they exist, they restrict what we may do in the service of either relative or neutral goals.

They complicate an already complicated picture. If there are agent-relative reasons of autonomy that do not give rise to agent-neutral interpersonal claims, then the claims of others must compete with these personal reasons in determining what one should do. Deontological constraints add further agent-relative reasons to the system—reasons not to treat others in certain ways. They are not impersonal claims derived from the interests of others, but personal demands governing one's relations with others.

Whatever their explanation, they are conspicuous among the moral appearances. Here is an example to focus your intuitions.

You have an auto accident one winter night on a lonely road. The other passengers are badly injured, the car is out of commission, and the road is deserted, so you run along it till you find an isolated house. The house turns out to be occupied by an old woman who is looking after her small grandchild. There is no phone, but there is a car in the garage, and you ask desperately to borrow it, and explain the situation. She doesn't believe you. Terrified by your desperation she runs upstairs and locks herself in the bathroom, leaving you alone with the child. You pound ineffectively on the door and search without success for the car keys. Then it occurs to you that she might be persuaded to tell you where they are if you were to twist the child's arm outside the bathroom door. Should you do it?

It is difficult not to see this as a dilemma, even though the child's getting its arm twisted is a minor evil compared with your friends' not getting to the hospital. The dilemma must be due to a special reason against doing such a thing. Otherwise it would be obvious that you should choose the lesser evil and twist the child's arm.

Common moral intuition recognizes several types of deontological reasons—limits on what one may do to people or how one may treat them. There are the special obligations created by promises and agreements; the restrictions against lying and betrayal; the prohibitions against violating various individual rights, rights not to be killed, injured, imprisoned, threatened, tortured, coerced, robbed; the restrictions against imposing certain sacrifices on someone simply as means to an end; and perhaps the special claim of immediacy, which makes distress at a distance so different from distress in the same room. There may also be a deontological requirement of fairness, of evenhandedness or equality in one's treatment of people. (This is to be distinguished from an impersonal value thought to attach to equality in the distribution of benefits, considered as an aspect of the assessment of states of affairs.)

In all these cases it appears that the special reasons, if they exist, cannot be explained simply in terms of neutral values, because the particular relation of the agent to the outcome is essential. Deontological constraints may be overridden by neutral reasons of sufficient strength, but they are not themselves to be understood as the expression of neutral values of any kind. It is clear from the way such reasons work that they cannot be explained by the hypothesis that the violation of a deontological constraint has high negative impersonal value. Deontological reasons have their full force against your doing something—not just against its happening.

For example, if there really are such constraints, the following things seem to be true. It seems that you shouldn't break a promise or tell a lie for the sake of some benefit, even though you would not be required to forgo a comparable benefit in order to prevent someone else from breaking a promise or telling a lie. And it seems that you shouldn't twist the arm of a small child to get its grandmother to do something, even something important enough so that you would not he required to forgo a comparable benefit in order to prevent someone else from twisting a child's arm. And it may be that you shouldn't engage in certain kinds of unfair discriminatory treatment (in an official role, for example) even to produce a good result which you would not be required to forgo in order to prevent similar unfairness by others.

Some may simply deny the plausibility of such moral intuitions. Others may say that their plausibility can be subtly accounted for in terms of impersonal values, and that they appear to involve a fundamentally different type of reason for action only if they are inadequately analyzed. As I have said, I don't want to take up these alternative accounts here. They may provide the best hope of rationally justifying something that has the rough shape of a set of deontological restrictions; but offered as complete accounts they seem to me essentially revisionist. Even if from that point of view they contain a good deal of truth, they do not shed light on the independent deontological conceptions they are intended to replace. Those conceptions still have to be understood, even if they will eventually be rejected.

Sometimes, particularly when institutions and general practices are involved in the case, there is a neutral justification for what looks initially like an agent-relative restriction on action. And it is certainly a help to the acceptance of deontological constraints that general adherence to them does not produce disastrous results in the long run. Rules against the direct infliction of harm and against the violation of widely accepted rights have considerable social utility, and if it ceased to be so, those rules would lose much of their moral attractiveness.

But I am convinced that a less indirect, nonstatistical form of evaluation is also at work in support of deontological constraints, and that it underlies the central, most puzzling intuitions in this area. This is what would produce a sense of dilemma if it turned out that general adherence to deontological restrictions worked consistently contrary to impersonal utility. Right or wrong, it is this type of view that I want to explore and understand. There is no point in trying to show in advance that such dilemmas cannot arise.

One reason for the resistance to deontological constraints is that they are formally puzzling, in a way that the other reasons we have discussed are not. We can understand how autonomous agent-relative reasons might derive from the specific projects and concerns of the agent, and we can understand how neutral reasons might derive from the interests of others, giving each of us reason to take them into account. But how can there be relative reasons to respect the claims of others? How can there be a reason not to twist someone's arm which is not equally a reason to prevent his arm from being twisted by someone else?

The relative character of the reason cannot come simply from the character of the interest that is being respected, for that alone would justify only a neutral reason to protect the interest. And the relative reason does not come from an aim or project of the individual agent, for it is not conditional on what the agent wants. Deontological restrictions, if they exist, apply to everyone: they are mandatory and may not be given up like ambitions or commitments.

It is hard to understand how there could be such a thing. One would expect that reasons stemming from the interests of others would be neutral and not relative. How can a claim based on the interests of others apply to those who may infringe it directly or intentionally in a way that it does not apply to those whose actions may damage that same interest just as much indirectly? After all, it is no worse *for the victim* to be killed or injured deliberately than accidentally, or as an unavoidable side-effect of the dangerous rescue operation. In fact the special features of action that bring these reasons into effect may not add to the impersonal badness of the occurrence at all. To use an example of T. M. Scanlon, if you have to choose between saving someone from being murdered and saving someone else from being killed in a similar manner accidentally, and you have no special relation to either of them, it seems that your choice should depend only on which one you're more likely to succeed in saving. Admittedly the wickedness of a murder is in some sense a bad thing; but when it is a matter of deciding which of them there is more reason to prevent, a murder does not seem to be a significantly worse event, impersonally considered, than an accidental or incidental death. Some entirely different kind of value must be brought in to explain the idea that one should not kill one person even to prevent a number of accidental deaths: murder is not just an evil that everyone has reason to prevent, but an act that everyone has reason to *avoid*.

In any case, even if a murder were a worse event, impersonally considered, than an accidental death, this could not be used to explain the deontological constraint against murder. For that constraint prohibits murder even if it is necessary to prevent other *murders*—not only other deaths.

There is no doubt that ideas of this kind form an important part of common moral phenomenology. Yet their paradoxical flavor tempts one to think that the whole thing is a kind of moral illusion resulting either from innate psychological dispositions or from crude but useful moral indoctrination. Before debunking the intuition, however, we ought to have a better grasp of what it is. No doubt it's a good thing for people to have a deep inhibition against torturing children even for very strong reasons, and the same might be said of other deontological constraints. But that does not explain why we find it almost impossible to regard it as a merely useful inhibition. An illusion involves a judgment or a disposition to judge, and not a mere motivational impulse. The phenomenological fact to be accounted for is that we seem to apprehend in each individual case an extremely powerful agent-relative *reason* not to harm an innocent person. This presents itself as the apprehension of a normative truth, not just as a psychological inhibition. It needs to be analyzed and accounted for, and accepted or rejected according to whether the account gives it an adequate justification.

I believe that the traditional principle of double effect, despite problems of application, provides a rough guide to the extension and character of deontological constraints, and that even after the volumes that have been written on the subject in recent years, this remains the right point of convergence for efforts to capture our intuitions.* The principle says that to violate deontological constraints one must maltreat someone else intentionally. The maltreatment must be something that one does or chooses, either as an end or as a means, rather than something ones actions merely cause or fail to prevent but that one doesn't aim at.

It is also possible to foresee that one's actions will cause or fail to prevent a harm that one does not intend to bring about or permit. In that case it does not come under a deontological constraint, though it may still be objectionable for neutral reasons. The precise way to draw this distinction has been the subject of extensive debate, sometimes involving ingenious examples of a runaway trolley which will kill five people unless you . . . , where the dots are filled in by different ways of saving the five, all of which in some way involve one other person's death. I won't try to draw the exact boundaries of the principle. Though I say it with trepidation, I believe that for my purposes they don't matter too much, and I

---

*A good statement of a view of this type is found in C. Fried [*Right and Wrong* Harvard University Press, 1971].

suspect they can't be drawn more than roughly: my deontological intuitions, at least, begin to fail above a certain level of complexity. But one point worth mentioning is that the constraints apply to intentionally permitting as well as to intentionally doing harm. Thus in our example there would be the same kind of objection if with the same end in view you permitted someone else to twist the child's arm. You would have let it happen intentionally, and that would be different from a failure to prevent such an occurrence because you were too engaged in doing something else, which was more important.

Agents and Victims

So far this is just moral phenomenology: it does not remove the paradox. Why should we consider ourselves far more responsible for what we do (or permit) intentionally than for consequences of action that we foresee and decide to accept but that do not form part of our aims (intermediate or final)? How can the connection of ends and means conduct responsibility so much more effectively than the connection of foresight and avoidability?

It is as if each action produced a unique normative perspective on the world, determined by intention. When I twist the child's arm intentionally I incorporate that evil into what I do: it is my deliberate creation and the reasons stemming from it are magnified and lit up from my point of view. They overshadow reasons stemming from greater evils that are more "faint" from this perspective, because they do not fall within the intensifying beam of my intentions even though they are consequences of what I do.

That is the picture, but can it be correct? Isn't it a normatively distorted picture?

This problem is an instance of the collision between subjective and objective points of view. The issue is whether the special, personal perspective of agency has legitimate significance in determining what people have reason to do—whether, because of this perspective, I can have sufficient reason not to do something which, considered from an external standpoint, it would be better if I did. That is, *things* will be better, what *happens* will be better, if I twist the child's arm than if I do not. But I will have done something worse. If considerations of what I may do, and the correlative claims of my victim against me, can outweigh the substantial impersonal value of what will happen, that can only be because the perspective of the agent has an importance in practical reasoning that resists domination by a conception of the world as a place where good and bad things happen whose value is perspective-free.

I have already claimed that the dominance of this neutral conception of value is not complete. It does not swallow up or overwhelm the relative reasons arising from those individual ambitions, commitments, and attachments that are in some sense chosen. But the admission of what I have called autonomous reasons does not imply the possibility of deontological reasons.* The two are very different. The peculiarity of deontological reasons is that although they are agent-relative,

---

*This is emphasized by Scheffler [*The Rejection of Consequentialism* (Oxford University Press, 1982)], who has a cautiously skeptical discussion of deontological constraints under the heading of "agent-centred restrictions."

they do not express the subjective autonomy of the agent at all. They are demands, not options. The paradox is that this partial, perspectival respect for the interests of others should not give way to an agent-neutral respect free of perspective. The deontological perspective seems primitive, even superstitious, by comparison: merely a stage on the way to full objectivity. How can what we *do* in this narrow sense be so important?

Let me try to say where the strength of the deontological view lies. We may begin by considering a curious feature of deontological reasons on which I have not yet remarked. Intention appears to magnify the importance of evil aims by comparison with evil side-effects in a way that it does not magnify the importance of good aims by comparison with good side-effects. We are supposed to avoid using evil means to produce a good end, even though it would be permissible to produce that good end by neutral means with comparably evil side-effects. On the other hand, given two routes to a legitimate end, one of which involves good means and neutral side-effects and the other of which involves neutral means and equally good side-effects, there is no reason to choose the first route. Deontological reasons tell us only not to aim at evil; they don't tell us to aim at good, as a means. Why should this be? What is the relation between evil and in-tention, or aiming, that makes them clash with such force?

The answer emerges if we ask ourselves what it is to aim at something, what differentiates it from merely producing the result knowingly.

The difference is that action intentionally aimed at a goal is guided by that goal. Whether the goal is an end in itself or only a means, action aimed at it must follow it and be prepared to adjust its pursuit if deflected by altered circum-stances—whereas an act that merely produces an effect does not follow it, is not *guided* by it, even if the effect is foreseen.

What does this mean? It means that to aim at evil, even as a means, is to have one's action guided by evil. One must be prepared to adjust it to insure the pro-duction of evil: a falling-off in the level of the desired evil becomes a reason for al-tering what one does so that the evil is restored and maintained. But the essence of evil is that it should *repel* us. If something is evil, our actions should be guided, if they are guided by it at all, toward its elimination rather than toward its mainte-nance. That is what evil *means*. So when we aim at evil we are swimming head-on against the normative current. Our action is guided by the goal at every point in the direction diametrically opposite to that in which the value of that goal points. To put it another way, if we aim at evil we make what we do in the first instance a positive rather than a negative function of it. At every point, the intentional func-tion is simply the normative function reversed, and from the point of view of the agent, this produces an acute sense of moral dislocation.

If you twist the child's arm, your aim is to produce pain. So when the child cries, "Stop, it hurts!" his objection corresponds in perfect diametrical opposition to your intention. What he is pleading as your reason to stop is precisely your rea-son to go on. If it didn't hurt you would twist harder, or try the other arm. There may be cases (e.g., of justified punishment or obloquy) when pain is not intrinsi-cally evil, but this is not one of them: the victim is innocent. You are pushing directly and essentially against the intrinsic normative force of your goal, for it is the production of his pain that guides you. It seems to me that this is the phenomenological nerve of deontological constraints. What feels peculiarly wrong about doing evil intentionally even that good may come of it is the headlong striving against value that is internal to one's aim.

I have discussed a simple case, but naturally there can be complications. One is the possibility of someone volunteering to be subjected to some kind of pain or damage, either for his own good or for some other end which is important to him. In that case the particular evil that you aim at is swallowed up in the larger aim for deontological purposes. So the evil at which we are constrained not to aim is *our victim's* evil, rather than just a particular bad thing, and each individual has considerable authority in defining what will count as harming him for the purpose of this restriction.*

All this still leaves unsettled the question of justification. For it will be objected that if one aims at evil as a means only, then even if several people's interests are involved one's action is really being guided not by evil but by overall good, which includes a balance of goods and evils. So when you twist the child's arm, you are guided by the aim of rescuing your injured friends, and the good of that aim dominates the evil of the child's pain. The immediacy of the fact that you must try to produce evil as a subsidiary aim is phenomenologically important, but why should it be morally important? Even though it adds to the personal cost to you, why should it result in a prohibition?

I don't believe there is a decisive answer here. The question is whether to disregard the resistance encountered by my immediate pursuit of what is evil for my victim, in favor of the overall value of the results of what I do. When I view my act from outside and think of it as resulting from a choice of the impersonally considered state of the world in which it occurs, this seems rational. In thinking of the matter this way, I abstract my will and its choices from my person, as it were, and even from my actions, and decide directly among states of the world, as if I were taking a multiple choice test. If the choice is determined by what on balance is impersonally best, then I am guided by good and not by evil.

But the self that is so guided is the objective self, which regards the world impersonally, as a place containing TN and his actions, among other things. It is detached from the perspective of TN, for it views the world from nowhere within it. It chooses, and TN, its instrument, or perhaps one could say its agent, carries out the instructions as best he can. *He* may have to aim at evil, for the impersonally best alternative may involve the production of good ends by evil means. But he is only following orders.

To see the matter in this light is to see both the appeal of agent-neutral, consequentialist ethics and the contrary force of agent-relative, deontological ethics. The detached, objective view takes in everything and provides a standpoint of choice from which all choosers can agree about what should happen. But each of us is not only an objective self but a particular person with a particular perspective; we act in the world from that perspective and not only from the point of view of a detached will, selecting and rejecting world-states. So our choices are not merely choices of states of the world, but of actions. Every choice is two choices, and from

*The same seems to apply even when informed consent is impossible, as when we cause suffering or damage to a young child for its own greater good—though here there may be a residual inhibition: if we imagine in the case described that the *child's* safety depends on getting the car keys, it doesn't altogether remove the revulsion against twisting his arm to get them.

the internal point of view, the pursuit of evil in twisting the child's arm looms large. The production of pain is the immediate aim, and the fact that from an external perspective you are choosing a balance of good over evil does not cover up the fact that this is the intrinsic character of your action.

I have concentrated on the point of view of the agent, as seems suitable in the investigation of an agent-relative constraint. But there is also something to be said about the point of view of the victim. There too we encounter problems having to do with the integration of the two standpoints, and further support for the analysis. Moral principles don't simply tell agents what they may and may not do. They also tell victims what sort of treatment they may and may not object to, resist, or demand.

If I were justified in killing one innocent person to save five others, then he would have no right to object, and on a fully consequentialist view he would have no right to resist. The other five, by contrast, would have the right to object if I *didn't* kill him to save them. A thoroughly impersonal morality would require that victims as well as actors be dominated by impersonal, agent-neutral values in their judgments about how others treat them.

But this seems an excessive demand to make of individuals whose perspective on the world is inherently complex and includes a strong subjective component. Of course none of the six people in this dilemma wants to die, but only one of them is faced with me trying to kill him. This person is not permitted, on a purely agent-neutral consequentialist view, to appeal for his life against my deliberate attempt to take it from him. His special position as my victim doesn't give him any special standing to appeal to me.

Of course the deontological position has a parallel feature. On a deontological view, the five people I could save by killing the one cannot appeal to me for their lives, against my refusal to save them. (They may appeal against *their* killers, if that's the nature of the death threat, but not against me.) But this does not make the two positions symmetrical, for there is a difference. The deontological constraint permits a victim always to object to those who aim at his harm, and this relation has the same special character of normative magnification when seen from the personal perspective of the victim that it has when seen from the personal perspective of the agent. Such a constraint expresses the direct appeal to the point of view of the agent from the point of view of the person on whom he is acting. It operates through that relation. The victim feels outrage when he is deliberately harmed even for the greater good of others, not simply because of the quantity of the harm but because of the assault on his value of having my actions guided by his evil. What I do is immediately directed against his good: it doesn't just in fact harm him.

The five people I could save by killing him can't say the same, if I refrain. They can appeal only to my objective acknowledgment of the impersonal value of their lives. That is not trivial, of course, but it still seems less pressing than the protest available to my victim—a protest he can make not to them but to me, as the possessor of the life I am aiming to destroy.

This merely corroborates the importance of the internal perspective in accounting for the content of deontological intuitions. It does not prove the correctness of those intuitions. But it confirms that a purely impersonal morality requires the general suppression of the personal perspective in moral motivation, not only in its rejection of relative reasons of autonomy but also in its refusal to accept agent-relative deontological restrictions. Such restrictions need not be absolute: they can be thought of as relative reasons with a certain weight, that are among the sources of morality but do not exhaust it. When we regard human relations objectively, it does not seem irrational to admit such reasons at the basic level into the perspective of both agents and victims.

Moral Progress

This account of the force of deontological reasons applies with special clarity to the constraint against doing harm as a means to your ends. A fuller deontological theory would have to explain the different types of normative grain against which one acts in breaking promises, lying, discriminating unfairly, and denying immediate emergency aid. It would also have to deal with problems about what exactly is being aimed at, in cases of action that can be described in several different ways. But I believe that the key to understanding any of these moral intuitions is the distinction between the internal viewpoint of the agent or victim and an external, objective viewpoint which both agent and victim can also adopt. Reasons for action look different from the first two points of view than from the third.

We are faced with a choice. For the purposes of ethics, should we identify with the detached, impersonal will that chooses total outcomes, and act on reasons that are determined accordingly? Or is this a denial of what we are really doing and an avoidance of the full range of reasons that apply to creatures like us? This is a true philosophical dilemma; it arises out of our nature, which includes different points of view on the world. When we ask ourselves how to live, the complexity of what we are makes a unified answer difficult. I believe the human duality of perspectives is too deep for us reasonably to hope to overcome it. A fully agent-neutral morality is not a plausible human goal.

On the other hand, it is conceivable that deontological restrictions now widely accepted may be modified under the pressure of conflict with the impersonal standpoint. Some degree of skepticism about our current moral intuitions is not unreasonable, in light of the importance to moral belief of our starting points, the social influences pressing on us, and the confusion of our thought. If we aspire to objective truth in this area—that is, truth that is independent of our beliefs—we would be wise to hold many of our views more tentatively than we are naturally inclined to do. In ethics, even without the benefit of many clear examples, we should be open to the possibility of progress as we are in other areas, with a consequent effect of reduced confidence in the finality of our current understanding.*

It is evident that we are at a primitive stage of moral development. Even the most civilized human beings have only a haphazard understanding of how to live, how to treat others, how to organize their societies. The idea that the basic principles of morality are known, and that the problems all come in their interpretation and application, is one of the most fantastic conceits to which our conceited species has been drawn. (The idea that if we cannot easily know it, there is no

---

*See Parfit [*Reasons and Persons* (Oxford University Press, 1984)], pt. 1, for discussion of some ways commonsense morality might be revised to bring it closer to consequentialism.

truth here is no less conceited.) Not all of our ignorance in these areas is ethical, but a lot of it is. And the idea of the possibility of moral progress is an essential condition of moral progress. None of it is inevitable.

The pursuit of objectivity is only a method of getting closer to the truth. It is not guaranteed to succeed, and there is room for skepticism about its specific results in ethics as elsewhere. How far it can take us from the appearances is not clear. The truth here could not be radically inaccessible in the way that the truth about the physical world might be. It is more closely tied to the human perspective and the human motivational capacity because its point is the regulation of human conduct. It has to be suited to govern our lives day by day, in a way in which theoretical understanding of the physical world does not. And to do its work it must be far more widely accepted and internalized than in areas where the public is willing to defer to expert opinion.

There might be forms of morality incommensurable with our own that are appropriate for Martians but to which we do not have access for the same reason that we do not have access to the minds of such creatures. Unless we can understand their lives, experiences, and motives from inside, we will be unable to appreciate the values to which they respond in a way that allows us to objectify them accurately. Objectivity needs subjective material to work on, and for human morality this is found in human life.

How far outside ourselves we can go without losing contact with this essential material—with the forms of life in which values and justifications are rooted—is not certain. But I believe that ethics, unlike aesthetics, requires more than the purification and intensification of internal human perspectives. It requires a detachment from particular perspectives and transcendence of one's time and place. If we did not have this capacity then there would be no alternative to relativism in ethics. But I believe we do have it, and that it is not inevitably a form of false consciousness.

Even the very primitive stage of moral development we have reached was arrived at only by a long and difficult journey. I assume a much longer one lies ahead of us, if we survive. It would be foolish to try to lay down in advance the outlines of a correct method for ethical progress, but it seems reasonable at present to continue the awkward pursuit of objectivity described here. This does not mean that greater detachment always takes us closer to the truth. Sometimes, to be sure, objectivity will lead us to regard our original inclinations as mistaken, and then we will try to replace them or bracket them as ineliminable but illusory. But it would be a mistake to try to eliminate perspective from our conception of ethics entirely—as much of a mistake as it would be to try to eliminate perspective from the universe. This itself must be objectively recognized. Though it may be equally tempting, it would be no more reasonable to eliminate all those reasons for action that cannot be assimilated to the most external, impersonal system of value than it would be to eliminate all facts that cannot be assimilated to physics.

Yet in defending the legitimacy of agent-relative principles we must guard against self-deception and the escalation of personal claims simply to resist burdensome moral demands. It is not always easy to tell, for example, whether a morality that leaves extensive free space in each individual life for the pursuit of personal interests is not just a disguise for the simplest form of badness: selfishness in the face of the legitimate claims of others. It is hard to be good, as we all know.

I suspect that if we try to develop a system of reasons which harmonizes personal and impersonal claims, then even if it is acknowledged that each of us must live in part from his own point of view, there will be a tendency for the personal components to be altered. As the claims of objectivity are recognized, they may come to form a larger and larger part of each individual's conception of himself, and will influence the range of personal aims and ambitions, and the ideas of his particular relations to others and the claims they justify. I do not think it is utopian to look forward to the gradual development of a greater universality of moral respect, an internalization of moral objectivity analogous to the gradual internalization of scientific progress that seems to be a feature of modern culture.

On the other hand there is no reason to expect progress to be reductive, though here as elsewhere progress is too easily identified with reduction and simplification. Distinct individuals are still the clients of ethics, and their variety guarantees that pluralism will be an essential aspect of any adequate morality, however advanced.

There have to be principles of practical reason that allow us to take into account values that we do not share but whose force for others we must acknowledge. In general, the problem of how to combine the enormous and disparate wealth of reasons that practical objectivity generates, together with the subjective reasons that remain, by a method that will allow us to act and choose in the world, is dauntingly difficult.

This brings us to a final point. There can be no ethics without politics. A theory of how individuals should act requires a theory—an ethical theory, not just an empirical one—of the institutions under which they should live: institutions which substantially determine their starting points, the choices they can make, the consequences of what they do, and their relations to one another. Since the standpoint of political theory is necessarily objective and detached, it offers strong temptations to simplify, which it is important to resist. A society must in some sense be organized in accordance with a single set of principles, even though people are very different.

This is inconvenient: it may seem that political theory must be based on a universal human nature, and that if we cannot discover such a thing we have to invent it, for political theory must exist. To avoid such folly, it is necessary to take on the much more difficult task of devising fair uniform social principles for beings whose nature is not uniform and whose values are legitimately diverse. If they were diverse enough, the task might be impossible—there may be no such thing as intergalactic political theory—but within the human species the variation seems to fall within bounds that do not rule out the possibility of at least a partial solution. This would have to be something acceptable from a standpoint external to that of each particular individual, which at the same time acknowledges the plurality of values and reasons arising within all those perspectives. Even though the morality of politics is rightly more impersonal than the morality of private life, the acknowledgment of personal values and autonomy is essential even at the level that requires the greatest impersonality.

There is no telling what kinds of transcendence of individuality will result over the long term from the combined influence of moral and political progress, or decline. A general takeover of individual life from the perspective of the universe, or even from the perspective of humanity, seems premature—even if some saints or mystics can manage it. Reasons for action have to be reasons for individuals, and individual perspectives can be expected to retain their moral importance so long as diverse human individuals continue to exist.

———

Study Questions

1. You are in the accident situation that Nagel describes at the opening of the selection. May you twist the child's arm if that is the only way to get the car keys from her grandmother so that you can get help for your injured friends? Why or why not?

2. If you twist the child's arm (and succeed in getting help), Nagel claims that "what happens will be better" but that you "will have done something worse." What does he mean by this contrast? Do you agree?

3. Imagine two situations: (1) You can get $500 from someone (which they have no obligation to give you) by lying to them. (2) You are about to win $500, but by giving up the prize you can stop someone else from telling a lie. If it is wrong to lie in (1), should you give up the $500 to stop someone else from lying in (2)? If not, why are these cases not parallel?

4. Can a utilitarian theory give an acceptable account of the kind of rules that Nagel calls deontological constraints?

5. Nagel accounts for deontological constraints by linking them to the idea that we are especially responsible for what we intentionally do or prevent. How does he explain the force of deontological constraints? Is his explanation plausible?

6. Imagine a situation in which an intelligence agent can use torture to get information from someone with knowledge of a planned terrorist attack, thereby foiling the attack and saving thousands of lives. Can a deontologist permit torture in this situation?

7. At the end of the selection, Nagel suggests that, regarding moral knowledge, we are still at a primitive stage of moral development. Do you agree or disagree? Explain.

Selected Bibliography

Dworkin, Ronald. *Life's Dominion* (New York: Knopf, 1993), esp. Chap. 3. Develops a deontological moral view based on equal concern and respect for persons.

Frankena, William. *Ethics* (Engelwood Cliffs, N.J.: Prentice-Hall, 1963), Chap. 1. Discusses the distinction between deontology and teleology (or consequentialism).

Nagel, Thomas. *Mortal Questions* (Cambridge/New York: Cambridge University Press, 1979), Chap. 5 "War and Massacre." An interesting application of deontological principles.

Quinn, Warren. *Morality and Action* (Cambridge/New York: Cambridge University Press, 1993), Chaps. 7 and 8. A sophisticated treatment of deontological principles.

Scheffler, Samuel, ed. *Consequentialism and Its Critics* (Oxford/New York: Oxford University Press, 1988). An anthology on the controversy between consequentialism and deontology.

24

DAVID GAUTHIER

——

One of the oldest concerns of moral philosophy is to explain how moral considerations can have rational force for us. This is an ongoing concern, and an issue over which moral philosophers have divided. The question is particularly acute if one holds that one role of morality is to limit the ends and goals that we may adopt and the means that we may take to our ends—that is, to constrain the pursuit of self-interest. What reason

> *. . . if one benefits more from a constraint on others than one loses by being constrained oneself, one may have a reason to accept a practice requiring everyone, including oneself, to exhibit such a constraint . . . this agreement is the basis of morality.*

do we have for complying with moral requirements, especially in cases where morality imposes significant demands on us, or where it seems that we would do better for ourselves (or for people that we care about) by ignoring or violating some commonly accepted moral principle? The quick version of this question is: "Why be moral?" The question has occupied thinkers as diverse as Plato and Hobbes, both of whom thought, though in quite different ways, that the reasons for complying with moral constraints are based in self-interest. Kant also addressed this issue, although his separation of duty and happiness and his complex views about practical reason precluded any attempt to ground morality in self-interest. Rather, he argued—seemingly paradoxically—that reasons for acting morally and complying with duty come from the fact that in doing so we realize our freedom and autonomy.

The problem has taken on another dimension in the contemporary era. The need to find a place for moral discourse in the scientific worldview, and to square it with a scientifically respectable picture of human action and motivation, has pushed some thinkers to claim that morality must be grounded in rational self-interest—that is, either morality can be grounded in rational self-interest or its hold on us is illusory. This approach is taken by David Gauthier, who develops a modern Hobbesian view. He argues that reasons of long-term self-interest—what maximizes the satisfaction of an individual's preferences over time—are fundamental. Thus, if morality has any rational force, it must be based in rational self-interest. He argues that agreeing to and complying with moral constraints is indeed rational for an individual (assuming that others do the same) because it maximizes the expected satisfaction of one's preferences over time. Agents who accept moral constraints on the pursuit of their interests, who are strongly disposed to comply with such constraints, and who are known by others to have this disposition can expect to do better for themselves in the long run because they will have greater opportunities for productive social cooperation with like-minded others. Morality is a set of constraints that it would be rational to agree to for reasons of mutual advantage.

David Gauthier has taught at the University of Toronto and, since 1980, at the University of Pittsburgh, where he was appointed Distinguished Service Professor in 1986. In 1979 he was elected a Fellow of the Royal Society of Canada. His books include *The Logic of Leviathan* (1969), *Morals by Agreement* (1986), and *Moral Dealing: Contract, Reason and Ethics* (1990).

———

Why Contractarianism?*

I

> As the will to truth thus gains self-consciousness—there can be no doubt of that—
> morality will gradually perish now: this is the great spectacle in a hundred acts reserved
> for the next two centuries in Europe—the most terrible, most questionable, and per-
> haps also the most hopeful of all spectacles.
>
> —Nietzsche**

Morality faces a foundational crisis. Contractarianism offers the only plausible resolution of this crisis. These two propositions state my theme. What follows is elaboration.

Nietzsche may have been the first, but he has not been alone, in recognizing the crisis to which I refer. Consider these recent statements. "The hypothesis which I wish to advance is that in the actual world which we inhabit the language of morality is in . . . [a] state of grave disorder . . . we have—very largely, if not

*Two paragraphs of Section II and most of Section IV are taken from "Morality, Rational Choice, and Semantic Representation—A Reply to My Critics," in E. F. Paul, F. D. Miller, Jr., and J. Paul (eds.), *The New Social Contract: Essays on Gauthier* (Oxford: Blackwell, 1988), pp. 173–4, 179–180, 184–5, 188–9 (this volume appears also as *Social Philosophy and Policy* 5 [1988], same pagination). I am grateful to Annette Baier, Paul Hurley, and Geoffrey Sayre-McCord for comments on an earlier draft. I am also grateful to discussants at Western Washington University, the University of Arkansas, the University of California at Santa Cruz, and the University of East Anglia for comments on a related talk.
** *On the Genealogy of Morals*, trans. by Walter Kaufmann and R. J. Hollingdale (New York: Random House, 1967), third essay, sec. 27, p. 161.
David Gauthier, "Why Contractarianism?," in Peter Vallentyne, ed., *Contractarianism and Rational Choice* (Copyright © Cambridge University Press, 1991). Reprinted with the permission of Cambridge University Press.

entirely—lost our comprehension, both theoretical and practical, of morality"
(Alasdair MacIntyre).* "The resources of most modern moral philosophy are not
well adjusted to the modern world" (Bernard Williams).** "There are no objective values. . . . [But] the main tradition of European moral philosophy includes
the contrary claim" (J. L. Mackie).† "Moral hypotheses do not help explain why
people observe what they observe. So ethics is problematic and nihilism must be
taken seriously. . . . An extreme version of nihilism holds that morality is simply an
illusion. . . . In this version, we should abandon morality, just as an atheist aban-
dons religion after he has decided that religious facts cannot help explain observations" (Gilbert Harman).††

I choose these statements to point to features of the crisis that morality faces.
They suggest that moral language fits a world view that we have abandoned—a
view of the world as purposively ordered. Without this view, we no longer truly
understand the moral claims we continue to make. They suggest that there is a lack
of fit between what morality presupposes—objective values that help explain our
behavior, and the psychological states—desires and beliefs—that, given our present
world view, actually provide the best explanation. This lack of fit threatens to undermine the very idea of a morality as more than an anthropological curiosity. But
how could this be? How could morality *perish*?

II

To proceed, I must offer a minimal characterization of the morality that faces a
foundational crisis. And this is the morality of justified constraint. From the standpoint of the agent, moral considerations present themselves as constraining his
choices and actions, in ways independent of his desires, aims, and interests. Later, I
shall add to this characterization, but for the moment it will suffice. For it reveals
clearly what is in question—the ground of constraint. This ground seems absent
from our present world view. And so we ask, what reason can a person have for
recognizing and accepting a constraint that is independent of his desires and interests? He may agree that such a constraint would be *morally* justified; he would
have a reason for accepting it *if* he had a reason for accepting morality. But what
justifies paying attention to morality, rather than dismissing it as an appendage of
outworn beliefs? We ask, and seem to find no answer. But before proceeding, we
should consider three objections.

The first is to query the idea of constraint. Why should morality be seen as
constraining our choices and actions? Why should we not rather say that the moral
person chooses most freely, because she chooses in the light of a true conception
of herself, rather than in the light of the false conceptions that so often predomi-
nate? Why should we not link morality with self-understanding? Plato and Hume
might be enlisted to support this view, but Hume would be at best a partial ally,
for his representation of "virtue in all her genuine and most engaging charms, . . .

After Virtue (Notre Dame, IN: University of Notre Dame Press, 1981), p. 2.
**Ethics and the Limits of Philosophy* (Cambridge, MA: Harvard University Press, 1985), p. 197.
†*Ethics: Inventing Right and Wrong* (Harmondsworth: Penguin, 1977), pp. 15, 30.
††*The Nature of Morality* (New York: Oxford University Press, 1977), p. 11.

talk[ing] not of useless austerities and rigors, suffering and self-denial," but rather making "her votaries . . . , during every instant of their existence, if possible, cheerful and happy," is rather overcast by his admission that "in the case of justice, . . . a man, taking things in a certain light, may often seem to be a loser by his integrity."* Plato, to be sure, goes further, insisting that only the just man has a healthy soul, but heroic as Socrates' defense of justice may be, we are all too apt to judge that Glaucon and Adeimantus have been charmed rather than reasoned into agreement, and that the unjust man has not been shown necessarily to be the loser.** I do not, in any event, intend to pursue this direction of thought. Morality, as we, heirs to the Christian and Kantian traditions, conceive it, constrains the pursuits to which even our reflective desires would lead us. And this is not simply or entirely a constraint on self-interest; the affections that morality curbs include the social ones of favoritism and partially, to say nothing of cruelty.

The second objection to the view that moral constraint is insufficiently grounded is to query the claim that it operates independently of, rather than through, our desires, interests, and affections. Morality, some may say, concerns the well-being of all persons, or perhaps of all sentient creatures.† And one may then argue, either with Hume, that morality arises in and from our sympathetic identification with our fellows, or that it lies directly in well-being, and that our affections tend to be disposed favorably toward it. But, of course, not all of our affections. And so our sympathetic feelings come into characteristic opposition to other feelings, in relation to which they function as a constraint.

This is a very crude characterization, but it will suffice for the present argument. This view grants that morality, as we understand it, is without purely *rational* foundations, but reminds us that we are not therefore unconcerned about the well-being of our fellows. Morality is founded on the widespread, sympathetic, other-directed concerns that most of us have, and these concerns do curb self-interest, and also the favoritism and partiality with which we often treat others. Nevertheless, if morality depends for its practical relevance and motivational efficacy entirely on our sympathetic feelings, it has no title to the prescriptive grip with which it has been invested in the Christian and Kantian views to which I have referred, and which indeed Glaucon and Adeimantus demanded that Socrates defend to them in the case of justice. For to be reminded that some of the time we do care about our fellows and are willing to curb other desires in order to exhibit that care tells us nothing that can guide us in those cases in which, on the face of it, we do not care, or do not care enough— nothing that will defend the demands that morality makes on us in the hard cases. That not all situations in which concern for others combats self-concern are hard cases is true, but morality, as we ordinarily understand it, speaks to the hard cases, whereas its Humean or naturalistic replacement does not.

These remarks apply to the most sustained recent positive attempt to create a moral theory—that of John Rawls. For the attempt to describe our moral capacity, or more particularly, for Rawls, our sense of justice, in terms of principles, plausible in the light of our more general psychological theory, and coherent with "our

*David Hume, *An Equiry Concerning the Principles of Morals,* 1751, sec. IX, pt. II.
**See Plato, *Republic,* esp. books II and IV.
†Some would extend morality to the nonsentient, but sympathetic as I am to the rights of trolley cars and steam locomotives, I propose to leave this view quite out of consideration.

considered judgements in reflective equilibrium,"* will not yield any answer to why, in those cases in which we have no, or insufficient, interest in being just, we should nevertheless follow the principles. John Harsanyi, whose moral theory is in some respects a utilitarian variant of Rawls' contractarian construction, recognizes this explicitly: "All we can prove by rational arguments is that anybody who wants to serve our common human interests in a rational manner must obey these commands."** But although morality may offer itself in the service of our common human interests, it does not offer itself only to those who want to serve them.

Morality is a constraint that, as Kant recognized, must not be supposed to depend solely on our feelings. And so we may not appeal to feelings to answer the question of its foundation. But the third objection is to dismiss this question directly, rejecting the very idea of a foundational crisis. Nothing justifies morality, for morality needs no justification. We find ourselves, in morality as elsewhere, in mediis rebus. We make, accept and reject, justify and criticize moral judgments. The concern of moral theory is to systematize that practice, and so to give us a deeper understanding of what moral justification is. But there are no extramoral foundations for moral justification, any more than there are extraepistemic foundations for epistemic judgments. In morals as in science, foundationalism is a bankrupt project.

Fortunately, I do not have to defend *normative* foundationalism. One problem with accepting moral justification as part of our ongoing practice is that, as I have suggested, we no longer accept the world view on which it depends. But perhaps a more immediately pressing problem is that we have, ready to hand, an alternative mode for justifying our choices and actions. In its more austere and, in my view, more defensible form, this is to show that choices and actions maximize the agent's expected utility, where utility is a measure of considered preference. In its less austere version, this is to show that choices and actions satisfy, not a subjectively defined requirement such as utility, but meet the agent's objective interests. Since I do not believe that we have objective interests, I shall ignore this latter. But it will not matter. For the idea is clear; we have a mode of justification that does not require the introduction of moral considerations.†

Let me call this alternative nonmoral mode of justification, neutrally, deliberative justification. Now moral and deliberative justification are directed at the same objects—our choices and actions. What if they conflict? And what do we say to the person who offers a deliberative justification of his choices and actions and refuses to offer any other? We can say, of course, that his behavior lacks *moral* justification, but this seems to lack any hold, unless he chooses to enter the moral framework. And such entry, he may insist, lacks any deliberative justification, at least for him.

If morality perishes, the justificatory enterprise, in relation to choice and action, does not perish with it. Rather, one mode of justification perishes, a mode that, it may seem, now hangs unsupported. But not only unsupported, for it is dif-

---

*John Rawls, *A Theory of Justice* (Cambridge, MA: Harvard University Press, 1971), p. 51.
**John C. Harsanyi, "Morality and the Theory of Rational Behavior," in *Utilitarianism and Beyond*, edited by Amartya Sen and Bernard Williams (Cambridge: Cambridge University Press, 1982), p. 62.
†To be sure, if we think of morality as expressed in certain of our affections and/or interests, it will incorporate moral considerations to the extent that they actually are present in our preferences. But this would be to embrace the naturalism that I have put to one side as inadequate.

ficult to deny that deliberative justification is more clearly basic, that it cannot be avoided insofar as we are rational agents, so that if moral justification conflicts with it, morality seems not only unsupported but opposed by what is rationally more fundamental.

Deliberative justification relates to our deep sense of self. What distinguishes human beings from other animals, and provides the basis for rationality, is the capacity for semantic representation. You can, as your dog on the whole cannot, represent a state of affairs to yourself, and consider in particular whether or not it is the case, and whether or not you would want it to be the case. You can represent to yourself the contents of your beliefs, and your desires or preferences. But in representing them, you bring them into relation with one another. You represent to yourself that the Blue Jays will win the World Series, and that a National League team will win the World Series, and that the Blue Jays are not a National League team. And in recognizing a conflict among those beliefs, you find rationality thrust upon you. Note that the first two beliefs could be replaced by preferences, with the same effect.

Since in representing our preferences we become aware of conflict among them, the step from representation to choice becomes complicated. We must, somehow, bring our conflicting desires and preferences into some sort of coherence. And there is only one plausible candidate for a principle of coherence—a maximizing principle. We order our preferences, in relation to decision and action, so that we may choose in a way that maximizes our expectation of preference fulfillment. And in so doing, we show ourselves to be rational agents, engaged in deliberation and deliberative justification. There is simply nothing else for practical rationality to be.

The foundational crisis of morality thus cannot be avoided by pointing to the existence of a practice of justification within the moral framework, and denying that any extramoral foundation is relevant. For an extramoral mode of justification is already present, existing not side by side with moral justification, but in a manner tied to the way in which we unify our beliefs and preferences and so acquire our deep sense of self. We need not suppose that this deliberative justification is itself to be understood foundationally. All that we need suppose is that moral justification does not plausibly survive conflict with it.

III

In explaining why we may not dismiss the idea of a foundational crisis in morality as resulting from a misplaced appeal to a philosophically discredited or suspect idea of foundationalism, I have begun to expose the character and dimensions of the crisis. I have claimed that morality faces an alternative, conflicting, deeper mode of justification, related to our deep sense of self, that applies to the entire realm of choice and action, and that evaluates each *action* in terms of the reflectively held concerns of its *agent*. The relevance of the agent's concerns to practical justification does not seem to me in doubt. The relevance of anything else, except insofar as it bears on the agent's concerns, does seem to me very much in doubt. If the agent's reflectively endorsed concerns, his preferences, desires, and aims, are, with his considered beliefs, constitutive of his self-conception, then I can see no remotely plausible way of arguing from their relevance to that of anything else that is not similarly related to his sense of self. And, indeed, I can see no way of introducing anything as relevant to practical justification except through the agent's self-conception. My assertion of this practical individualism is not a conclusive argument, but the burden of proof is surely on those who would maintain a contrary position. Let them provide the arguments—if they can.

Deliberative justification does not refute morality. Indeed, it does not offer morality the courtesy of a refutation. It ignores morality, and seemingly replaces it. It preempts the arena of justification, apparently leaving morality no room to gain purchase. Let me offer a controversial comparison. Religion faces—indeed, has faced—a comparable foundational crisis. Religion demands the worship of a divine being who purposively orders the universe. But it has confronted an alternative mode of explanation. Although the emergence of a cosmological theory based on efficient, rather than teleological, causation provided warning of what was to come, the supplanting of teleology in biology by the success of evolutionary theory in providing a mode of explanation that accounted in efficient-causal terms for the *appearance* of a purposive order among living beings, may seem to toll the death knell for religion as an intellectually respectable enterprise. But evolutionary biology and, more generally, modern science do not refute religion. Rather they ignore it, replacing its explanations by ontologically simpler ones. Religion, understood as affirming the justifiable worship of a divine being, may be unable to survive its foundational crisis. Can morality, understood as affirming justifiable constraints on choice independent of the agent's concerns, survive?

There would seem to be three ways for morality to escape religion's apparent fate. One would be to find, for moral facts or moral properties, an explanatory role that would entrench them prior to any consideration of justification.* One could then argue that any mode of justification that ignored moral considerations would be ontologically defective. I mention this possibility only to put it to one side. No doubt there are persons who accept moral constraints on their choices and actions, and it would not be possible to explain those choices and actions were we to ignore this. But our explanation of their behavior need not commit us to their view. Here the comparison with religion should be straightforward and uncontroversial. We could not explain many of the practices of the religious without reference to their beliefs. But to characterize what a religious person is doing as, say, an act of worship, does not commit us to supposing that an object of worship actually exists, though it does commit us to supposing that she believes such an object to exist. Similarly, to characterize what a moral agent is doing as, say, fulfilling a duty does not commit us to supposing that there are any duties, though it does commit us to supposing that he believes that there are duties. The skeptic who accepts neither can treat the apparent role of morality in explanation as similar to that of religion. Of course, I do not consider that the parallel can be ultimately sustained, since I agree with the religious skeptic but not with the moral skeptic. But to establish an explanatory role for morality, one most first demonstrate its justificatory credentials. One may not assume that it has a prior explanatory role.

*This would meet the challenge to morality found in my previous quotation from Gilbert Harman.

The second way would be to reinterpret the idea of justification, showing that, more fully understood, deliberative justification is incomplete, and must be supplemented in a way that makes room for morality. There is a long tradition in moral philosophy, deriving primarily from Kant, that is committed to this enterprise. This is not the occasion to embark on a critique of what, in the hope again of achieving a neutral characterization, I shall call universalistic justification. But critique may be out of place. The success of deliberative justification may suffice. For theoretical claims about its incompleteness seem to fail before the simple practical recognition that it works. Of course, on the face of it, deliberative justification does not work to provide a place for morality. But to suppose that it must, if it is to be fully adequate or complete as a mode of justification, would be to assume what is in question, whether moral justification is defensible.

If, independent of one's actual desires, and aims, there were objective values, and if, independent of one's actual purposes, one were part of an objectively purposive order, then we might have reason to insist on the inadequacy of the deliberative framework. An objectively purposive order would introduce considerations relevant to practical justification that did not depend on the agent's self-conception. But the supplanting of teleology in our physical and biological explanations closes this possibility, as it closes the possibility of religious explanation.

I turn then to the third way of resolving morality's foundational crisis. The first step is to embrace deliberative justification, and recognize that morality's place must be found within, and not outside, its framework. Now this will immediately raise two problems. First of all, it will seem that the attempt to establish any constraint on choice and action, within the framework of a deliberation that aims at the maximal fulfillment of the agent's considered preferences, must prove impossible. But even if this be doubted, it will seem that the attempt to establish a constraint *independent of the agent's preferences,* within such a framework, verges on lunacy. Nevertheless, this is precisely the task accepted by my third way. And, unlike its predecessors, I believe that it can be successful; indeed, I believe that my recent book, *Morals by Agreement,* shows how it can succeed.*

I shall not rehearse at length an argument that is now familiar to at least some readers, and, in any event, can be found in that book. But let me sketch briefly those features of deliberative rationality that enable it to constrain maximizing choice. The key idea is that in many situations, if each person chooses what, given the choices of the others, would maximize her expected utility, then the outcome will be mutually disadvantageous in comparison with some alternative—everyone could do better.** Equilibrium, which obtains when each person's action is a best response to the others' actions, is incompatible with (Pareto-)optimality, which obtains when no one could do better without someone else doing worse. Given the ubiquity of such situations, each person can see the benefit, to herself, of participating with her fellows in

---

*See David Gauthier, *Morals by Agreement* (Oxford: Oxford University Press, 1986), especially chaps. V and VI.

**The now-classic example of this type of situation is the Prisoner's Dilemma; see *Morals by Agreement,* pp. 79–80. More generally, such situations may be said, in economists' parlance, to exhibit market failure. See, for example, "Market Contractarianism" in Jules Coleman, *Markets, Morals, and the Law* (Cambridge: Cambridge University Press, 1988), chap. 10.

practices requiring each to refrain from the direct endeavor to maximize her own utility, when such mutual restraint is mutually advantageous. No one, of course, can have
reason to accept any unilateral constraint on her maximizing behavior; each benefits
from, and only from, the constraint accepted by her fellows. But if one benefits more
from a constraint on others than one loses by being constrained oneself, one may
have reason to accept a practice requiring everyone, including oneself, to exhibit such
a constraint. We may represent such a practice as capable of gaining unanimous
agreement among rational persons who were choosing the terms on which they
would interact with each other. And this agreement is the basis of morality.

Consider a simple example of a moral practice that would command rational
agreement. Suppose each of us were to assist her fellows only when either she
could expect to benefit herself from giving assistance, or she took a direct interest
in their well-being. Then, in many situations, persons would not give assistance to
others, even though the benefit to the recipient would greatly exceed the cost to
the giver, because there would be no provision for the giver to share in the benefit.
Everyone would then expect to do better were each to give assistance to her fellows, regardless of her own benefit or interest, whenever the cost of assisting was
low and the benefit of receiving assistance considerable. Each would thereby accept a constraint on the direct pursuit of her own concerns, not unilaterally, but
given a like acceptance by others. Reflection leads us to recognize that those who
belong to groups whose members adhere to such a practice of mutual assistance
enjoy benefits in interaction that are denied to others. We may then represent such
a practice as rationally acceptable to everyone.

This rationale for agreed constraint makes no reference to the content of anyone's preferences. The argument depends simply on the *structure* of interaction, on
the way in which each person's endeavor to fulfill her own preferences affects the fulfillment of everyone else. Thus, each person's reason to accept a mutually constraining practice is independent of her particular desires, aims and interests, although not,
of course, of the fact that she has such concerns. The idea of a purely rational agent,
moved to act by reason alone, is not, I think, an intelligible one. Morality is not to
be understood as a constraint arising from reason alone on the fulfillment of nonra-
tional preferences. Rather, a rational agent is one who acts to achieve the maximal fulfillment of her preferences, and morality is a constraint on the manner in which she
acts, arising from the effects of interaction with other agents.

Hobbes's Foole now makes his familiar entry onto the scene, to insist that however rational it may be for a person to agree with her fellows to practices that hold
out the promise of mutual advantage, yet it is rational to follow such practices only
when so doing directly conduces to her maximal preference fulfillment.* But then
such practices impose no real constraint. The effect of agreeing to or accepting them
can only be to change the expected payoffs of her possible choices, making it rational for her to choose what in the absence of the practice would not be utility maximizing. The practices would offer only true prudence, not true morality.

The Foole is guilty of a twofold error. First, he fails to understand that real acceptance of such moral practices as assisting one's fellows, or keeping one's

---

*See Hobbes, *Leviathan,* London, 1651, chap. 15.

promises, or telling the truth is possible only among those who are disposed to comply with them. If my disposition to comply extends only so far as my interests or concerns at the time of performance, then you will be the real fool if you interact with me in ways that demand a more rigorous compliance. If, for example, it is rational to keep promises only when so doing is directly utility maximizing, then among persons whose rationality is common knowledge, only promises that require such limited compliance will be made. And opportunities for mutual advantage will be thereby forgone.

Consider this example of the way in which promises facilitate mutual benefit. Jones and Smith have adjacent farms. Although neighbors, and not hostile, they are also not friends, so that neither gets satisfaction from assisting the other. Nevertheless, they recognize that, if they harvest their crops together, each does better than if each harvests alone. Next week, Jones's crop will be ready for harvesting; a fortnight hence, Smith's crop will be ready. The harvest in, Jones is retiring, selling his farm, and moving to Florida, where he is unlikely to encounter Smith or other members of their community. Jones would like to promise Smith that, if Smith helps him harvest next week, he will help Smith harvest in a fortnight. But Jones and Smith both know that in a fortnight, helping Smith would be a pure cost to Jones. Even if Smith helps him, he has nothing to gain by returning the assistance, since neither care for Smith nor, in the circumstances, concern for his own reputation, moves him. Hence, if Jones and Smith know that Jones acts straightforwardly to maximize the fulfillment of his preferences, they know that he will not help Smith. Smith, therefore, will not help Jones even if Jones pretends to promise assistance in return. Nevertheless, Jones would do better could he make and keep such a promise—and so would Smith.

The Foole's second error, following on his first, should be clear; he fails to recognize that in plausible circumstances, persons who are genuinely disposed to a more rigorous compliance with moral practices than would follow from their interests at the time of performance can expect to do better than those who are not so disposed. For the former, constrained maximizers as I call them, will be welcome partners in mutually advantageous cooperation, in which each relies on the voluntary adherence of the others, from which the latter, straightforward maximizers, will be excluded. Constrained maximizers may thus expect more favorable opportunities than their fellows. Although in assisting their fellows, keeping their promises, and complying with other moral practices, they forgo preference fulfillment that they might obtain, yet they do better overall than those who always maximize expected utility, because of their superior opportunities.

In identifying morality with those constraints that would obtain agreement among rational persons who were choosing their terms of interaction, I am engaged in rational reconstruction. I do not suppose that we have actually agreed to existent moral practices and principles. Nor do I suppose that all existent moral practices would secure our agreement, were the question to be raised. Not all existent moral practices need be justifiable—need be ones with which we ought willingly to comply. Indeed, I do not even suppose that the practices with which we ought willingly to comply need be those that would secure our present agreement. I suppose that justifiable moral practices are those that would secure our agreement ex ante, in an appropriate premoral situation. They are those to which we should have agreed as constituting the terms of our future interaction, had we been, per impossible, in a position to decide those terms. Hypothetical agreement thus provides a test of the justifiability of our existent moral practices.

IV

Many questions could be raised about this account, but here I want to consider only one. I have claimed that moral practices are rational, even though they constrain each person's attempt to maximize her own utility, insofar as they would be the objects of unanimous ex ante agreement. But to refute the Foole, I must defend not only the rationality of agreement, but also that of compliance, and the defense of compliance threatens to preempt the case for agreement, so that my title should be "Why Constraint?" and not "Why Contractarianism?" It is rational to dispose oneself to accept certain constraints on direct maximization in choosing and acting, if and only if so disposing oneself maximizes one's expected utility. What then is the relevance of agreement, and especially of hypothetical agreement? Why should it be rational to dispose oneself to accept only those constraints that would be the object of mutual agreement in an appropriate premoral situation, rather than those constraints that are found in our existent moral practices? Surely it is acceptance of the latter that makes a person welcome in interaction with his fellows. For compliance with existing morality will be what they expect, and take into account in choosing partners with whom to cooperate.

I began with a challenge to morality—how can it be rational for us to accept its constraints? It may now seem that what I have shown is that it is indeed rational for us to accept constraints, but to accept them whether or not they might be plausibly considered moral. Morality, it may seem, has nothing to do with my argument; what I have shown is that it is rational to be disposed to comply with whatever constraints are generally accepted and expected, regardless of their nature. But this is not my view.

To show the relevance of agreement to the justification of constraints, let us assume an ongoing society in which individuals more or less acknowledge and comply with a given set of practices that constrain their choices in relation to what they would be did they take only their desires, aims, and interests directly into account. Suppose that a disposition to conform to these existing practices is prima facie advantageous, since persons who are not so disposed may expect to be excluded from desirable opportunities by their fellows. However, the practices themselves have, or at least need have, no basis in agreement. And they need satisfy no intuitive standard of fairness or impartiality, characteristics that we may suppose relevant to the identification of the practices with those of a genuine morality. Although we may speak of the practices as constituting the morality of the society in question, we need not consider them morally justified or acceptable. They are simply practices constraining individual behavior in a way that each finds rational to accept.

Suppose now that our persons, as rational maximizers of individual utility, come to reflect on the practices constituting their morality. They will, of course, assess the practices in relation to their own utility, but with the awareness that their fellows will be doing the same. And one question that must arise is: Why these practices? For they will recognize that the set of actual moral practices is not the only possible set of constraining practices that would yield mutually advantageous, optimal outcomes. They will recognize the possibility of alternative moral orders. At this point it will not be enough to say that, as a matter of fact, each person can expect to benefit from a disposition to comply with existing practices. For persons will also ask themselves: Can I benefit more, not from simply abandoning any morality, and recognizing no constraint, but from a partial rejection of existing constraints in favor of an alternative set? Once this question is asked, the situation is transformed; the existing moral order must be assessed, not only against simple noncompliance, but also against what we may call alternative compliance.

To make this assessment, each will compare her prospects under the existing practices with those she would anticipate from a set that, in the existing circumstances, she would expect to result from bargaining with her fellows. If her prospects would be improved by such negotiation, then she will have a real, although not necessarily sufficient, incentive to demand a change in the established moral order. More generally, if there are persons whose prospects would be improved by renegotiation, then the existing order will be recognizably unstable. No doubt those whose prospects would be worsened by renegotiation will have a clear incentive to resist, to appeal to the status quo. But their appeal will be a weak one, especially among persons who are not taken in by spurious ideological considerations, but focus on individual utility maximization. Thus, although in the real world, we begin with an existing set of moral practices as constraints on our maximizing behavior, yet we are led by reflection to the idea of an amended set that would obtain the agreement of everyone, and this amended set has, and will be recognized to have, a stability lacking in existing morality.

The reflective capacity of rational agents leads them from the given to the agreed, from existing practices and principles requiring constraint to those that would receive each person's assent. The same reflective capacity, I claim, leads from those practices that would be agreed to, in existing social circumstances, to those that would receive ex ante agreement, premoral and presocial. As the status quo proves unstable when it comes into conflict with what would be agreed to, so what would be agreed to proves unstable when it comes into conflict with what would have been agreed to in an appropriate presocial context. For as existing practices must seem arbitrary insofar as they do not correspond to what a rational person would agree to, so what such a person would agree to in existing circumstances must seem arbitrary in relation to what she would accept in a presocial condition.

What a rational person would agree to in existing circumstances depends in large part on her negotiating position vis-à-vis her fellows. But her negotiating position is significantly affected by the existing social institutions, and so by the currently accepted moral practices embodied in those institutions. Thus, although agreement may well yield practices differing from those embodied in existing social institutions, yet it will be influenced by those practices, which are not themselves the product of rational agreement. And this must call the rationality of the agreed practices into question. The arbitrariness of existing practices must infect any agreement whose terms are significantly affected by them. Although rational agreement is in itself a source of stability, yet this stability is undermined by the arbitrariness of the circumstances in which it takes place. To escape this arbitrariness, rational persons will revert from actual to hypothetical agreement, considering what practices they would have agreed to from an initial position not structured by existing institutions and the practices they embody.

The content of a hypothetical agreement is determined by an appeal to the equal rationality of persons. Rational persons will voluntarily accept an agreement only insofar as they perceive it to be equally advantageous to each. To be sure, each would be happy to accept an agreement more advantageous to herself than to her fellows, but since no one will accept an agreement perceived to be less advantageous, agents whose nationality is a matter of common knowledge will recognize the futility of aiming at or holding out for more, and minimize their bargaining costs by coordinating at the point of equal advantage. Now the extent of advantage is determined in a twofold way. First, there is advantage internal to an agreement. In this respect, the expectation of equal advantage is assured by procedural fairness. The step from existing moral practices to those resulting from actual agreement takes rational persons to a procedurally fair situation, in which each perceives the agreed practices to be ones that it is equally rational for all to accept, given the circumstances in which agreement is reached. But those circumstances themselves may be called into question insofar as they are perceived to be arbitrary—the result, in part, of compliance with constraining practices that do not themselves ensure the expectation of equal advantage, and so do not reflect the equal rationality of the complying parties. To neutralize this arbitrary element, moral practices to be fully acceptable must be conceived as constituting a possible outcome of a hypothetical agreement under circumstances that are unaffected by social institutions that themselves lack full acceptability. Equal rationality demands consideration of external circumstances as well as internal procedures.

But what is the practical import of this argument? It would be absurd to claim that mere acquaintance with it, or even acceptance of it, will lead to the replacement of existing moral practices by those that would secure presocial agreement. It would be irrational for anyone to give up the benefits of the existing moral order simply because he comes to realize that it affords him more than he could expect from pure rational agreement with his fellows. And it would be irrational for anyone to accept a long-term utility loss by refusing to comply with the existing moral order, simply because she comes to realize that such compliance affords her less than she could expect from pure rational agreement. Nevertheless, these realizations do transform, or perhaps bring to the surface, the character of the relationships between persons that are maintained by the existing constraints, so that some of these relationships come to be recognized as coercive. These realizations constitute the elimination of false consciousness, and they result from a process of rational reflection that brings persons into what, in my theory, is the parallel of Jürgen Habermas's ideal speech situation.* Without an argument to defend them-

*See Raymond Geuss, *The Idea of a Critical Theory: Habermas and the Frankfurt School* (Cambridge: Cambridge University Press, 1981), p. 65ff.

selves in open dialogue with their fellows, those who are more than equally advantaged can hope to maintain their privileged position only if they can coerce their fellows into accepting it. And this, of course, may be possible. But coercion is not agreement, and it lacks any inherent stability.

Stability plays a key role in linking compliance to agreement. Aware of the benefits to be gained from constraining practices, rational persons will seek those that invite stable compliance. Now compliance is stable if it arises from agreement among persons each of whom considers both that the terms of agreement are sufficiently favorable to herself that it is rational for her to accept them, and that they are not so favorable to others that it would be rational for them to accept terms less favorable to them and more favorable to herself. An agreement affording equally favorable terms to all thus invites, as no other can, stable compliance.

V

In defending the claim that moral practices, to obtain the stable voluntary compliance of rational individuals, must be the objects of an appropriate hypothetical agreement, I have added to the initial minimal characterization of morality. Not only does morality constrain our choices and actions, but it does so in an impartial way, reflecting the equal rationality of the persons subject to constraint. Although it is no part of my argument to show that the requirements of contractarian morality will satisfy the Rawlsian test of cohering with our considered judgments in reflective equilibrium, yet it would be misleading to treat rationally agreed constraints on direct utility maximization as constituting a morality at all, rather than as replacing morality, were there no fit between their content and our pretheoretical moral views. The fit lies, I suggest, in the impartiality required for hypothetical agreement.

The foundational crisis of morality is thus resolved by exhibiting the rationality of our compliance with mutual, rationally agreed constraints on the pursuit of our desires, aims, and interests. Although bereft of a basis in objective values or an objectively purposive order, and confronted by a more fundamental mode of justification, morality survives by incorporating itself into that mode. Moral considerations have the same status, and the same role in explaining behavior, as the other reasons acknowledged by a rational deliberator. We are left with a unified account of justification, in which an agent's choices and actions are evaluated in relation to his preferences—to the concerns that are constitutive of his sense of self. But since morality binds the agent independently of the particular content of his preferences, it has the prescriptive grip with which the Christian and Kantian views have invested it.

In incorporating morality into deliberative justification, we recognize a new dimension to the agent's self-conception. For morality requires that a person have the capacity to commit himself, to enter into agreement with his fellows secure in the awareness that he can and will carry out his part of the agreement without regard to many of those considerations that normally and justifiably would enter into his future deliberations. And this is more than the capacity to bring one's desires and interests together with one's beliefs into a single coherent whole. Although this latter unifying capacity must extend its attention to past and future, the unification it achieves may itself be restricted to that extended present within which a person judges and decides. But in committing oneself to future action in accordance with one's agreement, one must fix at least a subset of one's desires and beliefs to hold in that future. The self that agrees and the self that complies must be one. "Man himself must first of all have become *calculable, regular, necessary*, even in his own image of himself, if he is to be able to stand security for *his own future*, which is what one who promises does!"*

In developing *"the right to make promises,"*** we human beings have found a contractarian bulwark against the perishing of morality.

———

Study Questions

1. Gauthier claims that moral considerations present themselves as constraints on our desires and choices. What does he mean by this? (Give examples.) Do you agree?
2. Related question: Can morality demand that you do something that is not in your self-interest? If so, would you have a reason to do it?
3. What does Gauthier mean by "deliberative justification"? (Section II) How does it differ from moral justification?
4. Gauthier writes: "persons who are genuinely disposed to a more rigorous compliance with moral practices than would follow from their interests at the time of performance can expect to do better than those who are not so disposed." (Section III) Explain what he means. How would such a disposition help Smith and Jones to do better, in the example given in the previous paragraph?
5. How does Gauthier's theory try to address the "foundational crisis" to which he refers at the beginning of his article? In your view, does he succeed? Do you agree that morality must be grounded in rational self-interest?

Selected Bibliography

Gauthier, David, ed. *Morality and Rational Self-Interest* (Englewood Cliffs, NJ: Prentice-Hall, 1970). An anthology of essays on egoism and the connection between morality and individual advantage.

Gauthier, David, *Moral Dealing: Contract, Reason and Ethics* (Ithaca, NY: Cornell University Press, 1990). A collection of Gauthier's essays.

———. *Morals by Agreement* (Oxford/New York: Oxford University Press, 1986). Gauthier's major work in which he develops his contractarian theory of morality.

Vallentyne, Peter, ed. *Contractarianism and Rational Choice* (Cambridge/New York: Cambridge University Press, 1991). A collection of essays on Gauthier.

———

*Nietzsche, *On the Genealogy of Morals*, trans. by Walter Kaufmann and R. J. Hollingdale (New York: Random House, 1967), second essay, sec. 1, p. 58.
**Ibid., p. 57.

25

GILBERT HARMAN

—

Is there a single true morality? Since at least the time of the Greek historian Herodotus it has been recognized that different societies have accepted differing codes of conduct, and this has raised the question of whether there is a single true morality. But the word

> It turns out, to my surprise, that the question whether there is a single true morality is an unresolved question in moral philosophy.

"true" is important in this context. The issue is not simply whether different societies or groups of individuals have accepted different moral codes—clearly they have. Rather, the question is whether there are any universally valid principles that apply to all individuals and societies, that all *ought to* accept. Moral absolutists believe that there are universally or objectively valid moral principles. The absolutist need not hold that there is a single moral code that governs all areas of conduct or provides a highly detailed conception of the good life that is objectively valid. It would be enough if there are some fundamental moral principles, or basic moral requirements, that all individuals have reason to accept. The prohibitions on murder and gratuitous harm of innocent people and the principle of assisting others in serious need when one can do so at little cost to oneself are obvious candidates. Moral relativists, by contrast, deny that there are basic universal moral demands that apply to everyone. They hold instead that the moral demands to which individuals are subject depend on the principles, values, and practices accepted in one's society, and that such values and practices can differ from one society or social group to another. Relativists often cite the existence of basic moral disagreement that is rationally unresolvable in support of their position.

Should we be moral absolutists or moral relativists? Gilbert Harman has defended moral relativism in a number of essays. His view is that moralities arise from conventions or tacit agreements among people, and that individuals have reasons to accept the demands of a morality only if they accept or are party to such an agreement. Different people are subject to different moral demands, depending on the conventions and practices that they or their society accept. However, in this essay Harman claims that the issue is not fully decided. For him the question turns on when it makes sense to say that someone has a reason to comply with a principle or requirement. In order to have a reason to comply with a principle, must one actually accept it, display some motivation to comply, or be a party to the agreement, tacit or explicit, by which it is instituted? Or may we say that a person has a reason to comply if they do not appear to accept it, or show any motivation to comply? His primary concern here is not to resolve this question or to defend relativism, but to explain why some thinkers tend towards relativist and others towards absolutist positions in ethics. Philosophers who think that it is important to show how morality fits with the scientific picture of the world tend to be relativists, whereas those who think that we can engage in moral reflection without addressing this question tend to be absolutists.

Gilbert Harman is professor of philosophy at Princeton University, where he has taught for many years. He is an important philosopher who has written on many areas of philosophy. His main writings in moral philosophy are *The Nature of Morality: An Introduction to Ethics* (1977) and the essays collected in *Explaining Value and Other Essays in Moral Philosophy* (2000).

Is There a Single True Morality?

1 Confession

I have always been a moral relativist. As far back as I can remember thinking about it, it has always seemed to me obvious that the dictates of morality arise from some sort of convention or understanding among people, that different people arrive at different understandings, and that there are no basic moral demands that apply to everyone. For many years this seemed so obvious to me that I assumed it was everyone's instinctive view, at least everyone who gave the matter any thought.

When I first studied philosophical ethics, I was not disabused of this opinion. The main issue at the time seemed to be to determine exactly what form of "noncognitivism" was correct. (According to noncognitivism, moral judgements do not function to describe a moral reality, but do something else—express feelings, prescribe a course of action, and so forth.) It is true that many of the philosophers I studied seemed for some reason to want to avoid calling themselves "relativists." This was usually accomplished by defining moral relativism to be an obviously inconsistent position (M. Singer, 1961; Williams, 1972); for example, the view both that there are no universal moral truths and also that everyone ought to follow the dictates of his or her group, where this last claim is taken to be a universal moral truth. I wasn't sure what this verbal manoeuvre was supposed to accomplish. Why would anyone want to give such a definition of moral relativism? Moral relativism was obviously correct, and the philosophers I was studying seemed all to be moral relativists even if they did not want to describe themselves in that way.

From Gilbert Harman, "Is There a Single True Morality?," in *Morality, Truth and Reason: New Essays in the Foundations of Ethics,* ed. D. Copp and D. Zimmerman (Totowa, NJ: Rowman & Allenheld, 1985). Reprinted by permission of Rowman & Littlefield.

Later I was distressed to hear from various people teaching ethics that students in their classes tended to proclaim themselves moral relativists until they had been shown how confused they were about ethics. I suspected that the confusions were not confusions of the students, but were confusions of their teachers, due perhaps to a faulty definition of moral relativism. The obvious solution was to show that moral relativism can be consistently defined as a plausible view and that standard objections to moral relativism are mistaken.

So, I eventually wrote and published an essay about this . . . , thinking it would clear things up and end worries about moral relativism. I was surprised to discover that this did not happen. I was also startled to find that many students in my own ethics courses resisted my attempt to make clear what I thought they instinctively believed. After some study I concluded that in fact only some of the students in my courses were instinctive moral relativists; a significant number of them were instinctive absolutists.

I had known, of course, that there were philosophers and friends of mine who were not moral relativists. For a long time I attributed this to their perversity and love of the bizarre, and attached no significance to it. But then I discovered that some of them thought moral relativism was the perverse view, a kind of philosophical folly like scepticism about other minds or the external world (for example, Nagel, 1980). I was stunned! How could they think that, when they knew so many moral relativists (like me) and no epistemological sceptics (at least none who took such scepticism seriously in ordinary life)? It then occurred to me to wonder how I could think of moral absolutism as such a perverse view, when I knew so many moral absolutists.

2   The Issue

It turns out, to my surprise, that the question whether there is a single true morality is an unresolved issue in moral philosophy. On one side are relativists, sceptics, nihilists, and noncognitivists. On the other side are those who believe in absolute values and a moral law that applies to everyone. Strangely, only a few people seem to be undecided. Almost everyone seems to be firmly on one side or the other, and almost everyone seems to think his or her side is obviously right, the other side representing a kind of ridiculous folly. This is strange, since everyone knows, or ought to know, that many intelligent people are on each side of this issue.

2.1 Two Approaches

In this essay I want to suggest that part of the explanation for this mutual incomprehension is that there are two different ways to do moral philosophy. If one approach is taken, moral relativism, noncognitivism, or scepticism may seem obviously correct and moral absolutism may seem foolish. If the other approach is taken, absolutism may seem clearly right and scepticism, relativism, and noncognitivism may seem foolish.

The difference in approaches is, to put it crudely, a difference in attitude toward science. One side says we must concentrate on finding the place of value and obligation in the world of facts as revealed by science. The other side says we must ignore that problem and concentrate on ethics proper.

Both sides agree that we must begin at the beginning with our initial beliefs, moral and nonmoral, and consider possible modifications that will make these beliefs more coherent with each other and with plausible generalizations and other explanatory principles. Eventually, we hope to arrive at a "reflective equilibrium" (Rawls, 1971) when no further modifications seem called for, at least for the time being. The process will leave some issues unresolved; in particular, we may find ourselves with no account of the place that value and obligation have in the world of facts. This will not dismay someone who is willing to leave that question unanswered. But it will be disturbing to someone who, on the way to reflective equilibrium, has come to think that the basic issue in moral philosophy is precisely how value and obligation fit into the scientific conception of the world.

I will use the term "naturalism" for an approach to ethics that is in this way dominated by a concern with the place of values in the natural world. I will call any approach that is not so dominated an instance of "autonomous ethics," because such an approach allows us to pursue ethics internally. Autonomous ethics allows that science is relevant to ethics in as much as ethical assessment depends on the facts of the case. But unlike naturalism, autonomous ethics does not take the main question of philosophical ethics to be the naturalistic status of values and obligations.

2.2 Naturalism

I hope the terms "naturalism" and "autonomous ethics" are not misleading. The term "naturalism" is sometimes reserved for the thesis that moral judgements can be analysed into or reduced to factual statements of a sort clearly compatible with the scientific world view. I am using the term "naturalism" more broadly. Naturalism in this sense does not have to lead to naturalistic reduction, although that is one possibility. Another possibility is that there is no way in which ethics could fit into the scientific conception of the world. In that case, naturalism leads to moral nihilism, as in Mackie (1977). Mackie supposes that ethics requires absolute values. Such values would have the property that anyone aware of their existence must necessarily be motivated to act morally. Because our scientific conception of the world has no place for entities of this sort, and because there is no way in which we could become aware of such entities, Mackie concludes that ethics must be rejected as resting on a false presupposition. That is a version of naturalism as I am using the term.

Naturalism can also lead one to a noncognitive analysis of moral judgements. In this view, moral judgements do not function to describe the world, but to do something else—to express one's attitudes for and against things, as Stevenson (1963) argues—or to recommend one or another course of action or general policy, as Hare (1952, 1963) proposes. Or a naturalist may decide that moral judgements do make factual claims that fit in with the claims of science. This can be illustrated by some sort of naturalistic reduction. One example would be an analysis that takes moral claims to be claims about the reactions of a hypothetical impartial observer as in Hume (1739) or Firth (1952).

More complex positions are possible. Mackie (1977) argues in chapter 1 that ethics rests on a false presupposition, but then he goes on in later chapters to discuss particular moral issues. It is almost as if he had first demonstrated that God does not exist and had then gone on to consider whether He is wise and loving. Presumably, Mackie believes that ethics as normally conceived must be or can be replaced with something else. But he does not indicate exactly what sort of replacement he has in mind—whether it is an institution of some sort, for example. Nor does he say how moral claims made within this replacement fit in with the claims of science. I suspect he would accept some sort of noncognitivist account of the judgements that are to replace the old moral judgements.

It is possible to be both a naturalist and an absolutist, although this is not very common. Firth (1952) defends an absolutist version of the ideal observer theory and Hare (1963) defends an absolutist version of noncognitivism. But I believe that the most plausible versions of naturalism involve a moral relativism that says different agents are subject to different basic moral requirements depending on the moral conventions in which they participate.

2.3 Autonomous Ethics

Naturalism tends toward relativism. What I am calling autonomous ethics, on the other hand, can have a very different tendency. In this approach, science is relevant, since our moral judgements depend on what we take the facts to be; but we attach no special importance to saying how obligations and values can be part of the world revealed by science. Rather, we do ethics internally. We begin with our initial moral beliefs and search for general principles. Our initial opinions can be changed to some extent so as to come into agreement with appealing general principles and our beliefs about the facts, but an important aspect of the appeal of such principles will be the way in which they account for what we already accept.

The autonomous approach normally (but not always) involves an initial assumption of moral absolutism. In this context, absolutism is of course not the thesis that there are simple moral principles that hold absolutely without exceptions. It is rather the thesis that there are basic moral demands that apply to all moral agents. Autonomous ethics tends to retain that absolutist thesis. It may also involve some sort of intuitionism, claiming that each of us has immediate insight into the truths of certain moral principles. It sometimes leads to a fairly conservative morality, not much different from one's initial starting point. That is not surprising, given the privileged position assigned to our initial moral beliefs.

But let me stress that conservatism is not inevitable, and autonomous ethics can and often does lead to more radical moralities, too. It leads some philosophers to a radical utilitarianism. It leads Rawls (1971) to principles of social justice that appear to be considerably more egalitarian than those most people accept. Nozick (1974), using the same general approach, comes out at a very different place, in which he ends up denying that any sort of egalitarian redistribution by governments is ever morally justified. (However, the moral theory in Nozick, 1981, as contrasted with the political theory in Nozick, 1974, insists on the moral requirement of helping others.) Indeed, there are many different ways in which ethics can be pursued as an autonomous discipline with its own principles that are not reducible to the principles of any science. I can illustrate this variety by mentioning a few of the many other contemporary philosophers who accept some form of autonomous ethics: Baier (1958), Darwall (1983), Donagan (1977), Frankena (1976), Fried (1978), Gewirth (1978), Grice (1967), Nagel (1970, 1980), and Richards (1971). Each of these philosophers has a somewhat different approach, although all are absolutists who rely on some form of autonomous ethics.

I should say that it is possible to believe in autonomous ethics without being an absolutist. One might be impressed by the variety of views held by those who accept autonomous ethics and so be led to allow for relativism while continuing to accept the method of autonomous ethics, believing that naturalism must be rejected. But the tendency of autonomism in ethics is toward absolutism. In what follows I will restrict my discussion to absolutist versions of autonomous ethics and to relativistic versions of naturalism.

2.4 Teachers of Ethics

I might also mention that ethics pursued internally, as in autonomous ethics, is more interesting to many people than ethics as pursued by naturalism. That is because autonomous ethics allows one to spend more of one's time thinking about interesting, complicated moral puzzles than naturalistic ethics does, and many people find moral puzzles more interesting than "abstract" questions about the objectivity of value and its place in nature. Philosophers attracted by naturalism tend not to find ethics as interesting a subject as do philosophers attracted by autonomous ethics. So, relativists tend to be less interested in ethics than absolutists. For example, logicians, philosophers of science, and philosophers of mathematics, who tend toward naturalism, are usually not moral absolutists and are not very interested in ethics as a philosophical subject. Philosophers who are relatively interested in ethics tend to be those who favour autonomous ethics and therefore tend to be absolutists. This is why teachers of ethics tend, more than their students, to be absolutists. It is not merely, as they sometimes suppose, that ethics teachers have seen through confusions that affect their students. A more important factor is that relativists tend not to become teachers of ethics. (I am an exception!)

3 Why Do We Believe What We Believe?

Autonomous ethics and naturalism represent very different attitudes towards the relation between science and ethics. Consider, for example, the question of what explains our believing what we in fact believe. Naturalists see an important difference between our factual beliefs and our moral beliefs. Our ordinary factual beliefs provide us with evidence that there is an independent world of objects, because our having those beliefs cannot be plausibly explained without assuming we interact with an independent world of objects external to ourselves, objects we perceive and manipulate. But our having the moral beliefs we do can be explained entirely in terms of our upbringing and our psychology, without any appeal to an independent realm of values and obligations. So our moral beliefs do not provide us with evidence for such an independent realm of values and obligations, and we must choose between scepticism, noncognitivism, and relativism (Harman, 1977: ch. 1).

Autonomists disagree with this. They claim we often believe that something is good or right or obligatory in part because it is good or right or obligatory. They accuse naturalists of begging the question. When naturalists say that a belief cannot be explained by virtue of something's being right, unless that thing's being right consists in some psychological or sociological fact, they simply assume that all explanatory factors are part of the world revealed by science. But this is the point at issue. Autonomists argue that it is more obvious that we sometimes recognize what is right than that naturalism is correct. True, we may be unable to say how a given "moral fact" and someone's recognition of it fit into the world of facts as revealed by science. But there are always unanswered questions. To jump from our current inability to answer this question to scepticism, relativism, or noncognitivism is to make a more drastic move than this puzzle warrants, from the point of view of autonomous ethics.

3.1 Explanation and Reduction

The naturalist seeks to locate the place of value, justice, right, and wrong, and so forth in the world in a way that makes clear how they might explain what we take them to explain. A naturalist cannot understand how value, justice, right, and wrong might figure in explanations without having some sense of their "location" in the world. We can say that this involves "naturalistic reduction," but it need not involve reductive definitions of a serious sort. Indeed, reduction rarely (if ever) involves serious reductive definitions. We identify tables with clusters of atoms in a way that allows us to understand how tables can hold up the things they hold up without having to suppose the word "table" is definable using only the concepts of physics. Similarly, we identify colours with dispositional properties of objects, namely, their tendency to look in certain ways to certain sorts of observers in certain conditions, without having to suppose there is a satisfactory definition in these terms. Similarly for temperatures, genes, and so on. What a naturalist wants is to be able to locate value, justice, right, wrong, and so forth in the world in the way that tables, colours, genes, temperatures, and so on can be located in the world.

What is at issue here is understanding how moral facts might explain something, how the badness of someone's character might explain why that person acts in a certain way, to take an example from Sturgeon (1985). It is not sufficient that one be prepared to accept the counterfactual judgement that the person would not have acted in that way if the person had not had a bad character, if one does not see how the badness of the person's character could have such an effect. A naturalist believes one can see that only by locating badness of character in aspects of the world that one sees can have the relevant effect.

Notice that a naturalist, as I am here using the term, is not just someone who supposes that all aspects of the world have a naturalistic location in this way, but rather someone who takes it to be of overriding importance in doing moral philosophy actually to attempt to locate moral properties. My claim is that, when one takes this attempt seriously, one will tend to become sceptical or relativistic. Sturgeon is not a naturalist in my sense, despite his insistence that he takes moral facts to be natural facts.

4 Moral Absolutism Defined

I now want to be more specific about what is to count as moral absolutism. Various things might be meant by the claim that there are absolute values and one true morality. Moral absolutists in one sense might not be moral absolutists in other senses. We must be careful not to mix up real issues with purely verbal issues. So let me stipulate that I will take moral absolutism to be a view about the moral reasons people have to do things and to want or hope for things. I will understand a belief about absolute values to be a belief that there are things that everyone has a reason to hope or wish for. To say that there is a moral law that "applies to everyone" is, I hereby stipulate, to say that everyone has sufficient reasons to follow that law.

It is true that many philosophers pursue something that resembles autonomous ethics when they ask what principles an "ideal" moral code of one or another sort would have, quite apart from the question whether people now have any reason to follow that code. Depending on what sort of idealization is being considered, there may or may not be a unique ideal code of that sort. But I am not going to count as a form of moral absolutism the claim that there is a unique ideal moral code of such and such a type. Relativists and absolutists in my sense might very well agree about this claim without that having any effect at all on what I take to be the basic issue that separates them. A claim about ideal codes has no immediate relevance to questions about what reasons people actually have to hope for certain things or to do certain things.

Similarly, I am not going to count as a form of moral absolutism the claim that there is one true morality that applies to everyone in that everyone ought to follow it, if this is not taken to imply that everyone has a sufficient reason to follow it. I am not sure what "ought" is supposed to mean if it is disconnected in this way from reasons to do things. If what is meant is that it ought to be the case that everyone followed the one true morality—in other words, that it would be a good thing if they did—then this is a version of the view that there is a unique ideal moral code. I am not sure what else might be meant, although a great deal more could be said here. . . . Rather than try to say it, however, I simply stipulate that this sort of claim is not a version of what I am counting as moral absolutism.

I should note that, of the contemporary philosophers I have identified as absolutists, Baier, Darwall, Donagan, Frankena, Gewirth, Grice, Nagel, and Richards clearly advocate moral absolutism in this sense. They all think that there are basic moral demands that in some sense every competent adult has reasons to adhere to. I believe the others I mentioned—namely, Rawls, Nozick, and Fried—also agree with this, although they do not explicitly say so in the works I have cited.

5 Does a Single Moral Law Apply to Everyone?

Consider the issue between absolutism and relativism concerning reasons people have for doing things. According to moral absolutism about this, there is a single moral law that applies to everyone; in other words, there are moral demands that everyone has sufficient reasons to follow, and these demands are the source of all moral reasons. Moral relativism denies that there are universal basic moral demands, and says different people are subject to different basic moral demands depending on the social customs, practices, conventions, values, and principles that they accept.

For example, a moral absolutist might suppose there is a basic moral prohibition on causing harm or injury to other people. This prohibition is in one sense not absolute, since it can be overridden by more compelling considerations and since it allows exceptions in order to punish criminals, for instance. But the prohibition is supposed to be universal in the sense that it applies to absolutely all agents and not just to those who happen to participate in certain conventions. The absolutist claims that absolutely everyone has sufficient reasons to observe this prohibition and to act as it and other basic moral requirements dictate.

A moral relativist denies this, and claims that many people have no reasons to observe this prohibition. Many people participate in moralities that sharply distinguish insiders and outsiders and do not prohibit harm or injury to outsiders, except perhaps as this is likely to lead to retaliation against insiders. A person participating in such a morality has no reason to avoid harm or injury to outsiders, according to the relativist, and so the general prohibition does not apply to that person. The person may be a member of some primitive tribal group, but he or she need not be. He or she might also be part of contemporary society, a successful professional criminal who recognizes various obligations to other members of a criminal organization but not to those on the outside. According to the moral relativist, the successful criminal may well have no reason at all not to harm his or her victims.

5.1 An Argument for Relativism

Let us concentrate on this case. The moral absolutist says the demands of the one true morality apply as much to this successful criminal as to anyone else, so this criminal does have a reason not to harm a given victim. The relativist denies the criminal has any such reason, and so denies the relevant moral demand is a universal demand that applies to everyone. Here naturalism tends to support relativism in the following way.

Consider what it is for someone to have a sufficient reason to do something. Naturalism requires that this should be explained in terms congenial to science. We cannot simply treat this as irreducibly normative, saying, for example, that someone has a sufficient reason to do something if and only if he or she ought to do it. Now, presumably, someone has a sufficient reason to do something if and only if there is warranted reasoning that person could do that would lead him or her to decide to do that thing. A naturalist will suppose that a person with a sufficient reason to do something might fail to reason in this way to such a decision only because of some sort of empirically discoverable failure. Such a failure might be inattention, lack of time, failure to consider or appreciate certain arguments, ignorance of certain available evidence, an error in reasoning, some sort of irrationality or unreasonableness, or weakness of will. If the person does not intend to do something and that is not because he or she has failed in some such empirically discoverable way to reason to a decision to do that thing, then according to the naturalist the person cannot have a sufficient reason to do that thing. This is the first premise in a naturalistic argument in support of the relativist.

The other premise is that there are people, such as certain professional criminals, who do not act in accordance with the alleged requirement not to harm or injure others, where this is not due to any these failings. The argument for this is simply that there clearly are people who do not adhere to the requirement in question and who do not seem to have failed in any of the ways mentioned. So, in the absence of special theoretical reasons, for example, deriving from psychology, to think these people must have failed in one of the specified ways, we can conclude they have not done so.

From these two premises it follows that there are people who do not have sufficient reasons, and therefore do not have sufficient moral reasons, to adhere to the general prohibition against harming or injuring others. In particular, a successful criminal may not have a sufficient reason not to harm his or her victims. The moral prohibition against harming others may simply fail to apply to such a person. It may fail to apply in the relevant sense, which is of course not to say that the principle makes an explicit exception for criminals, allowing them but not others to injure and harm people without restraint. Rather, the principle may fail to apply in the sense that the criminal in question may fail to have sufficient reason to act in accordance with the principle.

5.2 An Absolutist Reply

Moral absolutism must reject this argument. It can do so by invoking autonomous ethics at the place at which moral relativism invokes naturalism. Autonomous ethics does not suppose that we must give some sort of naturalistic account of having a sufficient reason to do something. Nor does it suppose that only a science like psychology can discover the conditions under which someone has failed to reason in a certain way because of inattention, irrationality, unreasonableness, or any of the other causes of failure mentioned in the relativistic argument.

Autonomous ethics approaches this issue in the following way. We begin with certain beliefs. Presumably these imply that everyone has a sufficient reason to observe the prohibition against harm to others, including the successful criminal who does not participate in or accept any practice of observing this general prohibition. At the start we therefore believe that the criminal does have sufficient reason not to harm his or her victims. Following autonomous ethics, then, we should continue to believe this unless such continued belief conflicts with generalizations or other theoretical principles internal to ethics that we find attractive because they do a better job at making sense of most of the things we originally believe. Taking this approach, the absolutist must claim that the relativistic argument does not provide sufficient reason to abandon our original absolutism. It is more plausible, according to the absolutist, that at least one of the premises of the relativistic argument is false, than that its conclusion is true.

5.3 Assessing the First Premise

The first premise of the relativistic argument is that for someone to have a sufficient reason to do something, there must be warranted reasoning available to that person that leads to a decision to do that thing. So, if the person fails to intend to do that thing, this must be because of inattention, lack of time, failure to consider or appreciate certain arguments, ignorance of relevant evidence, an error in reasoning, irrationality, unreasonableness, or weakness of will. The absolutist might object that this is oversimplified. If a person with sufficient reason to do something does not do it, then something has gone wrong. It might be one of the things the relativist mentions, but it might be something else as well. There might just be something wrong with the person in question. That person might be immoral. The failure might simply be a failure not to care enough about other people. A person ought to care about others and there is something wrong with a person who does not care, even if that person is not inattentive, ignorant, rushed, or defective in any other of the particular ways the relativist mentions. So, even if some people fail to observe the prohibition against harming others not because of inattention, lack of time, and so forth, but simply because of lack of concern and respect for others, such people still do have sufficient reason not to harm others. (Thomas M. Scanlon suggested this response on behalf of absolutism to me.)

This response to the relativistic argument is a response within autonomous ethics. It does not explain having a sufficient reason to do something in terms that are acceptably factual from a naturalistic perspective. It also appeals to the notion of something's being wrong with someone, where what might be wrong is simply that the person is immoral. It is like saying one has a sufficient reason to do something if and only if one ought to do it, or if and only if it would be wrong not to do it. The relativist claims that the only plausible accounts of these normative notions are relativistic ones. There is no prohibition on harm to outsiders, in the criminals' morality. There is such a prohibition only in some other morality. In that other morality, something is wrong with a person who has no compunction about injuring someone else; but nothing is wrong with such a person with respect to the criminal morality, as long as those injured are outsiders. But how can it be a sufficient reason for the criminal not to harm his or her victims that this is prohibited by somebody else's morality? How can its being bad, immoral, or wrong in this other morality not to care about and respect others give the criminal, who does not accept that morality, a sufficient reason to do anything?

The absolutist responds that failure to respect others is not just wrong according to some morality the criminal does not accept; it is also wrong, period. Something is really wrong with lack of respect and concern for others. It is not just wrong in relation to one or another morality. Of course, the relativist will not be satisfied with this answer and, appealing to naturalism, will ask what it is for something to be wrong in this way. The absolutist supposes that the failure to care about and respect others does involve something the absolutist points to by saying this failure is wrong. But what is this thing that is true of such a failure to care and that can give the criminal a sufficient reason not to harm and injure others? The relativist can see no aspect of such a failure that could provide such a reason. This is because the relativist, as a naturalist, considers only aspects of the failure that are clearly compatible with a scientific world view. The relativist disregards putative aspects that can be specified only in normative terms. But the absolutist, as an autonomist, can specify the relevant aspect of such a failure to care about others: it is bad, immoral, wrong not to care. The criminal ought to have this concern and respect and so ought not to harm and injure others, and therefore has a sufficient reason not to harm and injure them.

5.4 Assessing the Second Premise

We have been discussing an argument for relativism concerning moral reasons. We have seen that naturalism supports the first premise of this argument and that autonomous ethics allows the rejection of this premise. The same thing is true of the second premise, which says that there are people, such as the successful criminal, who do not observe the alleged requirement not to harm or injure others, and this is not due to inattention, failure to consider or appreciate certain arguments, ignorance of relevant evidence, errors in reasoning, irrationality, unreasonableness, or weakness of will. Naturalism supports this, because there do seem to be such people, and no scientifically acceptable grounds exist for thinking this is an illusion. On the other hand, autonomous ethics allows other grounds, not reducible to scientific grounds, for thinking this is an illusion. In autonomous ethics we begin by supposing that we recognize the wrongness of harming others, where this is to recognize a sufficient reason not to harm others. If that is something we recognize, then it must be there to be recognized, so the successful criminal in question must be failing to recognize and appreciate something that is there.

The absolutist might argue that the criminal must be irrational, or at least unreasonable. Seeing that a proposed course of action will probably cause serious injury to some outsider, the criminal does not treat this as a reason not to undertake that course of action. This must be irrational or unreasonable, because such a consideration simply is such a reason and indeed is an obvious reason, a basic reason, not one that has to be derived in some complex way through arcane reasoning. But then it must be irrational, or at least unreasonable, for the criminal not to care sufficiently about others. The criminal's lack of concern for others is what is responsible for the criminal's not taking the likelihood of harm to an outsider to be a reason against a proposed course of action. This is one way an absolutist might argue.

The relativist's reply to such an argument is that, on any plausible characterization of reasonableness and unreasonableness (or rationality and irrationality) as notions that can be part of the scientific conception of the world, the absolutist's claim is just false. Someone can be completely rational without feeling concern and respect for outsiders. But, of course, this reply appeals to naturalism. The absolutist who rejects naturalism in favour of autonomous ethics relies on an unreduced normative characterization of rationality and irrationality (or reasonableness and unreasonableness).

Now the argument continues as before. The relativist argues that, if rationality and irrationality (or reasonableness and unreasonableness) are conceived normatively, they become relative notions. What one morality counts as irrational or unreasonable, another does not. The criminal is not irrational or unreasonable in relation to criminal morality, but only in relation to a morality the criminal rejects. But the fact that it is irrational or unreasonable in relation to this other morality not to have concern and respect for others, does not give the criminal who rejects that morality any reason to avoid harming or injuring others. The absolutist replies that relative irrationality or unreasonableness is not what is in question. The criminal is irrational, or at least unreasonable, period; not just irrational or unreasonable in relation to a morality he or she does accept. Since it is irrational or unreasonable for anyone not to care sufficiently about others, everyone has a sufficient reason not to injure others. This is so, whether he or she recognizes this reason or, through irrationality or unreasonableness, does not recognize it.

The naturalist is unconvinced by this because the naturalist can find no aspect of the criminal the absolutist might be referring to in saying the criminal is "irrational" or "unreasonable," if this aspect is to give the criminal any reason to care about others. This, of course, is because the naturalist is considering only naturalistic aspects of the criminal, whereas the absolutist, as an autonomist, is thinking about an unreduced normative aspect, something the naturalist cannot appeal to.

So, as was true of the first premise of the relativistic argument about reasons, the second premise depends on an assumption of naturalism. By appealing to autonomous ethics, an absolutist can reject this premise.

An absolutist may in fact actually accept one or the other of the premises of the relativistic argument (although, of course, not both). A given absolutist might reject either the first premise, or the second, or both premises. An absolutist might even be undecided, holding merely that one or the other premise must be rejected, without saying which. There is nothing wrong with being undecided about this. Reflective equilibrium leaves many issues unresolved. . . .

7 Naturalism Versus Autonomous Ethics

So the issue between relativism and absolutism comes down to the dispute between naturalism and autonomous ethics. Which is the best approach in moral philosophy? Should we concentrate on the place of values and reasons in the world of scientific fact, as naturalism recommends? Or should we start with our initial moral beliefs and look for general principles and moral theories that will eventually yield a reflective equilibrium, not putting too much weight on the question of the place of value in the world of facts?

7.1 Religious Beliefs

In thinking of the issue between naturalism and autonomous ethics, it is useful to consider analogous issues that arise in other areas. Consider religious beliefs. Our scientific conception of the world has no place for gods, angels, demons, or devils. Naturalists hold that there is no empirical evidence for the existence of such beings, nor for any sort of divine intervention in human history. Naturalists say that people's religious beliefs can be explained in terms of their upbringing and psychology without any supernatural assumptions, so these beliefs provide no evidence whatsoever for the truth of religious claims. Naturalists therefore incline toward scepticism and atheism, although naturalism might also lead to a kind of religious noncognitivism holding that religious language makes no factual claims about a supernatural realm but has a different function, for example, in religious ritual.

Another approach to religion is for a believer to start with his or her initial religious beliefs, including beliefs in the authority of certain writings, and then to develop general principles and theories that would accommodate these beliefs, allowing modifications in the interest of more plausible general principles. This will continue until no further modifications seem useful in improving the organization and coherence of that person's views. Inevitably, many questions will remain unanswered, and these may include issues concerning the relation between that person's religious views and his or her scientific views, for example, as regards creation. But this is not a serious worry for autonomous religion, which will say this shows merely that science is not everything, or at least that there are things we do not know and perhaps never will understand.

Naturalists say there is no reason to accept religious claims, because the fact that people have the religious beliefs they have can be explained without any supernatural assumptions. Religious autonomists say there is reason to accept religious claims, at least for someone who begins with religious beliefs, since the process of generalization, systematization, and theory construction internal to religion will give that person no reason to abandon more than a few, if any, of those religious beliefs. Furthermore, certain supernatural events might be part of the correct explanation of the appearance of sacred texts, the occurrence of miracles, and particular religious experiences. There is at present no way to say how these religious explanations mesh with ordinary scientific conceptions, but that by itself is no more an objection to religion than it is an objection to science.

Naturalists in ethics might urge this religious analogy as an *ad hominem* argument against those defenders of autonomous ethics who are not willing to take the same line with respect to religion.

7.2 Beliefs about the Mind

There is another sort of issue in which an autonomous position comes off looking rather good, namely, the so-called mind–body problem. Here the naturalistic position corresponds to the thesis of physicalism, according to which all real aspects of mind must be features of the physical brain and central nervous system, its atomic or neural structure, or some more complex structure that the brain and nervous system instantiate. This may involve behaviourism or some sort of functionalism that treats the brain as an information-processing system like a computer in a robot. A few defenders of this approach, like Skinner (1974), conclude that there are no mental events, no mind, no consciousness, no sensation. (Rorty, 1965, sympathetically describes a similar view, "eliminative materialism.") But most physicalists suppose that mental events and other aspects of mind do exist and can be identified with certain physical or structural or functional aspects of the brain and central nervous system.

On the other side is autonomous mentalism, which holds that the physicalist hypothesis leaves something out. In this view, we know we are conscious, can initiate action, and have experiences of a distinctive phenomenological character and feeling. The physicalist hypothesis does not account for this knowledge. A computer or robot is not conscious. Although a robot can move, it does not act in the way people can act. And a robot has no sensuous experience. Indeed, something could have exactly the functional structure of the human brain and nervous system without being conscious. Block (1978) describes a case in which one billion people in radio communication with each other model a particular brain for an hour, each person corresponding to a particular neuron in the brain. Block takes it to be absurd to suppose that this vast collection of people would have a group consciousness that was phenomenologically the same as the consciousness of the person whose brain and central nervous system was being modelled. Nagel (1974) observes that we might know everything there was to know about the neurophysiological structure and functioning of the brain and central nervous system of a bat without knowing what the experience of the bat was like. Defenders of autonomous mentalism agree that this leaves a mind–body problem. They agree that they are unable to say how consciousness, free will, and sensory experience can be part of the world described by physics. But they deny that this means we must stop believing in consciousness or must identify it with some aspect of physical or functional structure. For they claim, with considerable plausibility, that it is much more reasonable to believe in consciousness, free will, and sensory experience, and to believe that these are not aspects of neurophysiological functional structure, than it is to believe in physicalism.

I do not say that autonomous mentalism is more plausible than physicalism. After all is said and done, I find a physicalistic functionalism more plausible than autonomous mentalism. My point is that autonomous mentalism is a perfectly respectable philosophical position.

A defender of autonomous ethics might even argue that naturalism in ethics loses much of its plausibility once autonomous mentalism is recognized as plausible. For that casts doubt on the universal applicability of the naturalistic approach and therefore casts doubt on the naturalist's argument that a belief that something is right cannot be explained by that thing's being actually right unless that thing's being right consists in some psychological or sociological fact. The naturalist's only argument for this, it might be said, depends on accepting the general applicability of naturalism. But it is not obvious that this approach is generally applicable, since it is not obviously correct as compared with autonomous mentalism. There is at least some plausibility to the claim that one's awareness of what red looks like is to be explained by appeal to an experience of redness that does not consist entirely in some neurophysiological event. It might be said that the naturalist has no argument against autonomous ethics, since the naturalist cannot take for granted the general applicability of naturalism.

7.3 Ethics

Defenders of autonomous ethics argue that their approach represents the only undogmatic way to proceed. They say that naturalism begs the question in supposing that everything true must fit into a scientific account of the world and by supposing that the central question about morality is how, if at all, morality fits into such a scientific account.

Defenders of naturalism reply that naturalism itself is the result of following the method of reflective equilibrium. Autonomous ethics begs the question by assigning a specially protected status to initial moral beliefs as compared, say, with initial beliefs about the flatness of the earth or the influence of the stars on human history. Naturalists say that, starting with our initial beliefs, we are led to develop a scientific conception of the world as an account of everything there is. In doing so, we also acquire beliefs about how we learn about the world and about how errors can arise in our thinking. We come to see how superstition arises. We begin to worry about our moral views: are they mere superstitions? We note certain sorts of disagreement in morality and extreme differences in moral customs. We observe that some people are not much influenced by what we consider important moral considerations. All this leads us to raise as a central question about morality how morality fits in with our scientific conception of the world. Naturalism is no mere prejudice in favour of science; it is an inevitable consequence of intelligent thought. This, at least, is what a defender of naturalism will say.

A defender of autonomous ethics will reply that moral disagreements, differences in custom, and the behaviour of criminals prove nothing. All these things are compatible with moral absolutism.

The naturalist retorts that any view can be made compatible with the evidence; astrology, for example, is perfectly compatible with the evidence. The issue is not what is compatible with the evidence, but what best accounts for it. The naturalist argues that relativism accounts for the evidence better than absolutism does, since relativism is able to say how reasons and values are part of the world science describes, whereas absolutism is not able to do that.

The defender of autonomous ethics replies that such an argument is no better than the corresponding argument for behaviourism. Behaviourism is able to say how mental states (as it conceives them) are part of the world physics describes, and autonomous mentalism is not able to say how mental states (as it conceives them) are part of the world physics describes. But one should not for this reason alone abandon one's initial view that one is conscious, makes decisions, has feelings, and so on, where this is not just being disposed to act in various ways. Something could have the dispositions without being conscious and could be conscious without having the dispositions. Similarly, one should not accept the naturalistic argument and give up one's belief in absolute values and universal moral reasons.

I see no knockdown argument for either side. A question of judgement is involved: "Which view is more plausible, all things considered?" To me, the relativistic, naturalist position seems more plausible. Others find the absolutist position of autonomous ethics more plausible. In this essay, I have not tried to argue that one side is correct. I have tried to bring out the central issue.

———

References

Baier, K. (1958). *The Moral Point of View.* Ithaca, NY: Cornell University Press.

Block, N. (1978). "Troubles with Functionalism," in C. W. Savage, ed., *Perception and Cognition: Issues in the Foundations of Psychology. Minnesota Studies in the Philosophy of Science 9.* Minneapolis, MN: University of Minnesota Press.

Darwall, S. L. (1983). *Impartial Reason.* Ithaca, NY: Cornell University Press.

Donagan, A. (1977). *The Theory of Morality.* Chicago: University of Chicago Press.

Firth, R. (1952). "Ethical Absolutism and the Ideal Observer," *Philosophy and Phenomenological Research* 12: 317–45.

Frankena, W. (1976). "Obligation and Motivation in Recent Moral Philosophy," in K. E. Goodpaster, ed., *Perspectives on Morality: Essays by William Frankena*. Notre Dame, IN: University of Notre Dame Press.

Fried, C. (1978). *Right and Wrong*. Cambridge, MA: Harvard University Press.

Gewirth, A. (1978). *Reason and Morality*. Chicago: University of Chicago Press.

Grice, G. R. (1967). *The Grounds of Moral Judgment*. Cambridge: Cambridge University Press.

Hare. R. M. (1952). *The Language of Morals*. Oxford: Oxford University Press.

———. (1963). *Freedom and Reason*. Oxford: Oxford University Press.

Harman, G. (1977). *The Nature of Morality: An Introduction to Ethics*. New York: Oxford University Press.

Hume, D. (1739). *Treatise of Human Nature*.

Mackie, J. L. (1977). *Ethics: Inventing Right and Wrong*. Harmondsworth, England: Penguin.

Nagel, T. (1970). *The Possibility of Altruism*. Princeton: Princeton University Press.

———. (1974). "What Is It Like to Be a Bat?" *Philosophical Review* 83: 435–450. Reprinted in Nagel, *Mortal Questions*. Cambridge/New York: Cambridge University Press, 1979

———. (1980). "The Limits of Objectivity," in S. M. McMurrin, ed., *Tanner Lectures on Human Values*. Salt Lake City: University of Utah Press.

Nozick, R. (1974). *Anarchy, State and Utopia*. New York: Basic Books.

———. (1981). *Philosophical Explanations*. Cambridge, MA: Harvard University Press.

Rawls, J. (1971). *A Theory of Justice*. Cambridge, MA: Harvard University Press.

Richards, D. A. J. (1971) *A Theory of Reasons for Action*. Oxford/New York: Oxford University Press.

Rorty, R. (1965). "Mind-Body Identity, Privacy and Categories," *Review of Metaphysics* 19:24–54

Singer, M. (1961). *Generalization in Ethics*. New York: Knopf.

Skinner, B. F. (1974). *About Behaviorism*. New York: Knopf.

Stevenson, C. L. (1963). "The Nature of Ethical Disagreements" in his *Facts and Values*. New Haven: Yale University Press.

Sturgeon, N. (1985). "Moral Explanations." In D. Copp and D. Zimmerman, eds., *Morality, Reason and Truth*. Totowa, NJ: Rowman & Allanheld.

Williams, B. (1972). *Morality: An Introduction to Ethics*. New York: Harper and Row. Reissued by Cambridge University Press, 1993.

Study Questions

1. Harman says that "absolutism is not the thesis that there are simple moral principles that hold absolutely without exception," but "rather the thesis that there are basic moral demands that apply to all agents" (Section 2.3) or that "there are moral demands that everyone has sufficient reason to follow." (Section 5) What is the difference between these two definitions? Why does Harman define moral absolutism in the second way?

2. Naturalists hold that "our having the moral beliefs we do can be explained entirely in terms of our upbringing and our psychology, without any appeal to an independent realm of values and obligations." (Section 3) Do you agree or disagree with the naturalist view? Why?

3. What is the connection that Harman sees between naturalism and moral relativism?

4. Harman mentions the example of a successful criminal who recognizes obligations to other members of his organization, but not to people who are not part of this organization. Does this criminal have a reason not to harm his victims? (For example, is it irrational or unreasonable for the criminal not to care about these people?) Explain. If so, what is the reason? If not, does this lead to relativism?

5. Analyze the arguments in Section 5 between the absolutist and the relativist. Whose argument is more compelling?

6. Do you accept moral absolutism (as defined by Harman) or moral relativism? Explain why.

Selected Bibliography

Harman, Gilbert. *Explaining Value and Other Essays in Moral Philosophy* (Oxford/New York: Oxford University Press, 2000). Chapters 1 through 5 defend moral relativism.

Harman, Gilbert and Judith Jarvis Thomson. *Moral Relativism and Moral Objectivity* (Oxford: Blackwell Press, 1996). Extended essays defending both moral relativism (Harman) and moral objectivity (Thomson).

Krausz, Michael and Jack W. Meiland, eds. *Relativism: Cognitive and Moral* (Notre Dame: University of Notre Dame Press, 1982). Essays on moral relativism by several distinguished philosophers.

Moody-Adams, Michelle. *Fieldwork in Familiar Places: Morality, Culture and Philosophy* (Cambridge, MA: Harvard University Press, 1997). Critical treatment of certain forms of moral relativism.

Moser, Paul K. and Thomas L. Carson. *Moral Relativism: A Reader* (Oxford/New York: Oxford University Press, 2001). An extensive collection of essays.

Scanlon, T. M. *What We Owe to Each Other* (Cambridge, MA: Harvard University Press, 1998), Chap. 8, "Relativism." A sophisticated discussion of relativism.

Wong, David B. *Moral Relativity* (Berkeley: University of California Press, 1984). Defends certain forms of moral relativism.

26

PHILIPPA FOOT

—

Philippa Foot begins her essay by observing that the subject of the virtues and the vices had for many years been "strangely neglected" by contemporary moral philosophers working in the analytic tradition. But that is changing. She sees a re-

> ... *some kinds of difficulty do indeed provide an occasion for much virtue, but ... others rather show that virtue is incomplete.*

vival of interest in the virtues that signals an alternative approach to ethics—one that takes its inspiration from Aristotle and Aquinas. Indeed, a movement in ethical thought that focuses on the virtues has emerged in recent years—due in part to the influence of her essay, among others—as a prominent trend that rivals the broadly Kantian and utilitarian traditions. This approach is known as "virtue ethics" or "virtue theory."

It is difficult to give a precise characterization of what is distinctive about virtue ethics. But to begin, Kantianism and utilitarianism have been regarded as rule- or principle-based moral outlooks that seek to provide criteria of right action. Further, due to the focus on right action—what is permissible, required, prohibited, and so on—these theories give a central place to notions of duty and obligation. In contrast, writers who stress the virtues approach ethical issues from a different angle, where the concept of right action is secondary and duty and obligation have little apparent role. The focus instead is on the qualities and traits of character of the good person, or that make a life good—in short, on the virtues. The point is sometimes made by saying that the primary question for virtue ethics is "How should one live?" or "What kind of person should I be?", rather than "How ought I to act?" Normative discussion tends to consider the nature of the virtues—what constitutes courage or honesty, whether or when a person displays justice or charity, and so on—and how specific virtues are part of the good human life.

In this essay, Philippa Foot develops a number of theses that help elucidate the concept of a moral virtue. Virtues are beneficial characteristics, both to those who possess them and to others, and thus are part of an individual's good. Virtues concern the will, in the sense that whether a person possesses a virtue depends on one's choices and intentions, but also on one's desires and attitudes. (Here recall Aristotle's claim in Book II.3 of the *Nicomachean Ethics* that virtue is concerned with pleasure and pain.) And virtues are "corrective." Finally, she raises the difficult question of whether a bad act may display a virtue.

Philippa Foot is one of the most important and original contemporary moral philosophers. She studied and then taught for many years at Somerville College, Oxford. Beginning in the early 1970s she was a visiting professor at many American universities, including Cornell, MIT, UCLA, Berkeley, and Princeton. In 1976 she accepted a position as professor of philosophy at UCLA, where she remained until her retirement in 1991. She has written many influential articles, some of which are collected in her *Virtues and Vices* (1978). Her most recent books are *Natural Goodness* (2001) and *Moral Dilemmas and Other Topics in Moral Philosophy* (2002).

———

Virtues and Vices

I

For many years the subject of the virtues and vices was strangely neglected by moralists working within the school of analytic philosophy. The tacitly accepted opinion was that a study of the topic would form no part of the fundamental work of ethics; and since this opinion was apparently shared by philosophers such as Hume, Kant, Mill, G. E. Moore, W. D. Ross, and H. A. Prichard, from whom contemporary moral philosophy has mostly been derived, perhaps the neglect was not so surprising after all. However that may be, things have recently been changing. During the past ten or fifteen years several philosophers have turned their attention to the subject; notably G. H. von Wright and Peter Geach. Von Wright devoted a not at all perfunctory chapter to the virtues in his book *The Varieties of Goodness** published in 1963, and Peter Geach's book called *The Virtues*** appeared in 1977. Meanwhile a number of interesting articles on the topic have come out in the journals.

In spite of this recent work, it is best when considering the virtues and vices to go back to Aristotle and Aquinas. I myself have found Plato less helpful, because the individual virtues and vices are not so clearly or consistently distinguished in his work. It is certain, in any case, that the most systematic account is found in Aristotle, and in the blending of Aristotelian and Christian philosophy found in St. Thomas. By and large Aquinas followed Aristotle—sometimes even heroically—where Aristotle gave an opinion, and where St. Thomas is on his own, as in developing the doctrine of the theological virtues of faith, hope and charity, and in his

*G. H. von Wright, *The Varieties of Goodness* (London, 1963).
**Peter Geach, *The Virtues* (Cambridge, 1977).

theocentric doctrine of happiness, he still uses an Aristotelian framework where he can: as for instance in speaking of happiness as man's last end. However, there are different emphases and new elements in Aquinas's ethics: often he works things out in far more detail than Aristotle did, and it is possible to learn a great deal from Aquinas that one could not have got from Aristotle. It is my opinion that the *Summa Theologica* is one of the best sources we have for moral philosophy, and moreover that St. Thomas's ethical writings are as useful to the atheist as to the Catholic or other Christian believer.

There is, however, one minor obstacle to be overcome when one goes back to Aristotle and Aquinas for help in constructing a theory of virtues, namely a lack of coincidence between their terminology and our own. For when we talk about the virtues we are not taking as our subject everything to which Aristotle gave the name *aretē* or Aquinas *virtus,* and consequently not everything called a virtue in translations of these authors. "The virtues" to us are the moral virtues whereas *aretē* and *virtus* refer also to arts, and even to excellences of the speculative intellect whose domain is theory rather than practice. And to make things more confusing we find some dispositions called moral virtues in translations from the Greek and Latin, although the class of virtues that Aristotle calls *aretai ēthikai* and Aquinas *virtutes morales* does not exactly correspond with our class of moral virtues. For us there are four cardinal moral virtues: courage, temperance, wisdom and justice. But Aristotle and Aquinas call only three of these virtues moral virtues; practical wisdom (Aristotle's *phronēsis* and Aquinas's *prudentia*) they class with the intellectual virtues, though they point out the close connections between practical wisdom and what they call moral virtues; and sometimes they even use *aretē* and *virtus* very much as we use "virtue."

I will come back to Aristotle and Aquinas, and shall indeed refer to them frequently in this paper. But I want to start by making some remarks, admittedly fragmentary, about the concept of a moral virtue as we understand the idea.

First of all it seems clear that virtues are, in some general way, beneficial. Human beings do not get on well without them. Nobody can get on well if he lacks courage, and does not have some measure of temperance and wisdom, while communities where justice and charity are lacking are apt to be wretched places to live, as Russia was under the Stalinist terror, or Sicily under the Mafia. But now we must ask to whom the benefit goes, whether to the man who has the virtue or rather to those who have to do with him? In the case of some of the virtues the answer seems clear. Courage, temperance and wisdom benefit both the man who has these dispositions and other people as well; and moral failings such as pride, vanity, worldliness, and avarice harm both their possessor and others, though chiefly perhaps the former. But what about the virtues of charity and justice? These are directly concerned with the welfare of others, and with what is owed to them; and since each may require sacrifice of interest on the part of the virtuous man both may seem to be deleterious to their possessor and beneficial to others. Whether in fact it is so has, of course, been a matter of controversy since Plato's time or earlier. It is a reasonable opinion that on the whole a man is better off for being charitable and just, but this is not to say that circumstances may not arise in which he will have to sacrifice everything for charity or justice.

Nor is this the only problem about the relation between virtue and human good. For one very difficult question concerns the relation between justice and the common good. Justice, in the wide sense in which it is understood in discussions of the cardinal virtues, and in this paper, has to do with that to which someone has a right—that which he is owed in respect of non-interference and positive service—and rights may stand in the way of the pursuit of the common good. Or so at least it seems to those who reject utilitarian doctrines. This dispute cannot be settled here, but I shall treat justice as a virtue independent of charity, and standing as a possible limit on the scope of that virtue.

Let us say then, leaving unsolved problems behind us, that virtues are in general beneficial characteristics, and indeed ones that a human being needs to have, for his own sake and that of his fellows. This will not, however, take us far towards a definition of a virtue, since there are many other qualities of a man that may be similarly beneficial, as for instance bodily characteristics such as health and physical strength, and mental powers such as those of memory and concentration. What is it, we must ask, that differentiates virtues from such things?

As a first approximation to an answer we might say that while health and strength are excellences of the body, and memory and concentration of the mind, it is the will that is good in a man of virtue. But this suggestion is worth only as much as the explanation that follows it. What might we mean by saying that virtue belongs to will?

In the first place we observe that it is primarily by his intentions that a man's moral dispositions are judged. If he does something unintentionally this is usually irrelevant to our estimate of his virtue. But of course this thesis must be qualified, because failures in performance rather than intention may show a lack of virtue. This will be so when, for instance, one man brings harm to another without realizing he is doing it, but where his ignorance is itself culpable. Sometimes in such cases there will be a previous act or omission to which we can point as the source of the ignorance. Charity requires that we take care to find out how to render assistance when we are likely to be called on to do so, and thus, for example, it is contrary to charity to fail to find out about elementary first aid. But in an interesting class of cases in which it seems again to be performance rather than intention that counts in judging a man's virtue there is no possibility of shifting the judgement to previous intentions. For sometimes one man succeeds where another fails not because there is some specific difference in their previous conduct but rather because his heart lies in a different place; and the disposition of the heart is part of virtue.

Thus it seems right to attribute a kind of moral failing to some deeply discouraging and debilitating people who say, without lying, that they mean to be helpful; and on the other side to see virtue *par excellence* in one who is prompt and resourceful in doing good. In his novel *A Single Pebble* John Hersey describes such a man, speaking of a rescue in a swift flowing river:

> It was the head tracker's marvellous swift response that captured my admiration at first, his split second solicitousness when he heard a cry of pain, his finding in mid-air, as it were, the only way to save the injured boy. But there was more to it than that. His ac-

tion, which could not have been mulled over in his mind, showed a deep, instinctive love of life, a compassion, an optimism, which made me feel very good . . .

What this suggests is that a man's virtue may be judged by his innermost desires as well as by his intentions; and this fits with our idea that a virtue such as generosity lies as much in someone's attitude as in his actions. Pleasure in the good fortune of others is, one thinks, the sign of a generous spirit; and small reactions of pleasure and displeasure often the surest signs of a man's moral disposition.

None of this shows that it is wrong to think of virtues as belonging to the will; what it does show is that "will" must here be understood in its widest sense, to cover what is wished for as well as what is sought.

A different set of considerations will, however, force us to give up any simple statement about the relation between virtue and will, and these considerations have to do with the virtue of wisdom. Practical wisdom, we said, was counted by Aristotle among the intellectual virtues, and while our *wisdom* is not quite the same as *phronēsis* or *prudentia* it too might seem to belong to the intellect rather than the will. Is not wisdom a matter of knowledge, and how can knowledge be a matter of intention or desire? The answer is that it isn't, so that there is good reason for thinking of wisdom as an intellectual virtue. But on the other hand wisdom has special connections with the will, meeting it at more than one point.

In order to get this rather complex picture in focus we must pause for a little and ask what it is that we ourselves understand by wisdom: what the wise man knows and what he does. Wisdom, as I see it, has two parts. In the first place the wise man knows the means to certain good ends; and secondly he knows how much particular ends are worth. Wisdom in its first part is relatively easy to understand. It seems that there are some ends belonging to human life in general rather than to particular skills such as medicine or boatbuilding, ends having to do with such matters as friendship, marriage, the bringing up of children, or the choice of ways of life; and it seems that knowledge of how to act well in these matters belongs to some people but not to others. We call those who have this knowledge wise, while those who do not have it are seen as lacking wisdom. So, as both Aristotle and Aquinas insisted, wisdom is to be contrasted with cleverness because cleverness is the ability to take the right steps to any end, whereas wisdom is related only to good ends, and to human life in general rather than to the ends of particular arts.

Moreover, we should add, there belongs to wisdom only that part of knowledge which is within the reach of any ordinary adult human being: knowledge that can be acquired only by someone who is clever or who has access to special training is not counted as part of wisdom, and would not be so counted even if it could serve the ends that wisdom serves. It is therefore quite wrong to suggest that wisdom cannot be a moral virtue because virtue must be within the reach of anyone who really wants it and some people are too stupid to be anything but ignorant even about the most fundamental matters of human life. Some people are wise without being at all clever or well informed: they make good decisions and they know, as we say, "what's what."

In short wisdom, in what we called its first part, is connected with the will in the following ways. To begin with it presupposes good ends: the man who is wise does not merely know *how* to do good things such as looking after his children well, or strengthening someone in trouble, but must also want to do them. And then wisdom, in so far as it consists of knowledge which anyone can gain in the course of an ordinary life, is available to anyone who really wants it. As Aquinas put it, it belongs "to a power under the direction of the will."*

The second part of wisdom, which has to do with values, is much harder to describe, because here we meet ideas which are curiously elusive, such as the thought that some pursuits are more worthwhile than others, and some matters trivial and some important in human life. Since it makes good sense to say that most men waste a lot of their lives in ardent pursuit of what is trivial and unimportant it is not possible to explain the important and the trivial in terms of the amount of attention given to different subjects by the average man. But I have never seen, or been able to think out, a true account of this matter, and I believe that a complete account of wisdom, and of certain other virtues and vices must wait until this gap can be filled. What we can see is that one of the things a wise man knows and a foolish man does not is that such things as social position, and wealth, and the good opinion of the world, are too dearly bought at the cost of health or friendship or family ties. So we may say that a man who lacks wisdom "has false values," and that vices such as vanity and worldliness and avarice are contrary to wisdom in a special way. There is always an element of false judgement about these vices, since the man who is vain for instance sees admiration as more important than it is, while the worldly man is apt to see the good life as one of wealth and power. Adapting Aristotle's distinction between the weak-willed man (the *akratēs*) who follows pleasure though he knows, in some sense, that he should not, and the licentious man (the *akolastos*) who sees the life of pleasure as the good life,** we may say that moral failings such as these are never purely "akratic." It is true that a man may criticize himself for his worldliness or vanity or love of money, but then it is his values that are the subject of his criticism.

Wisdom in this second part is, therefore, partly to be described in terms of apprehension, and even judgement, but since it has to do with a man's attachments it also characterizes his will.

The idea that virtues belong to the will, and that this helps to distinguish them from such things as bodily strength or intellectual ability has, then, survived the consideration of the virtue of wisdom, albeit in a fairly complex and slightly attenuated form. And we shall find this idea useful again if we turn to another important distinction that must be made, namely that between virtues and other practical excellences such as arts and skills.

Aristotle has sometimes been accused, for instance by von Wright, of failing to see how different virtues are from arts or skills;† but in fact one finds, among the many things that Aristotle and Aquinas say about this difference, the observation that seems to go the heart of the matter. In the matter of arts and skills, they say, voluntary error is preferable to involuntary error, while in the matter of virtues

---

*Aquinas, *Summa Theologica*, 1a2ae Q.56 a.3.
**Aristotle, *Nicomachean Ethics*, especially bk. VII.
†von Wright op. cit. chapter VIII.

(what we call virtues) it is the reverse.* The last part of the thesis is actually rather hard to interpret, because it is not clear what is meant by the idea of involuntary viciousness. But we can leave this aside and still have all we need in order to distinguish arts or skills from virtues. If we think, for instance, of someone who deliberately makes a spelling mistake (perhaps when writing on the blackboard in order to explain this particular point) we see that this does not in any way count against his skill as a speller: "I did it deliberately" rebuts an accusation of this kind. And what we can say without running into any difficulties is that there is no comparable rebuttal in the case of an accusation relating to lack of virtue. If a man acts unjustly or uncharitably, or in a cowardly or intemperate manner, "I did it deliberately" cannot on any interpretation lead to exculpation. So, we may say, a virtue is not, like a skill or an art, or mere capacity: it must actually engage the will.

II

I shall now turn to another thesis about the virtues, which I might express by saying that they are *corrective,* each one standing at a point at which there is some temptation to be resisted or deficiency of motivation to be made good. As Aristotle put it, virtues are about what is difficult for men, and I want to see in what sense this is true, and then to consider a problem in Kant's moral philosophy in the light of what has been said.

Let us first think about courage and temperance. Aristotle and Aquinas contrasted these virtues with justice in the following respect. Justice was concerned with operations, and courage and temperance with passions.** What they meant by this seems to have been, primarily, that the man of courage does not fear immoderately nor the man of temperance have immoderate desires for pleasure, and that there was no corresponding moderation of a passion implied in the idea of justice. This particular account of courage and temperance might be disputed on the ground that a man's courage is measured by his action and not by anything as uncontrollable as fear; and similarly that the temperate man who must on occasion refuse pleasure need not *desire* them any less than the intemperate man. Be that as it may (and something will be said about it later) it is obviously true that courage and temperance have to do with particular springs of action as justice does not. Almost any desire can lead a man to act unjustly, not even excluding the desire to help a friend or to save a life, whereas a cowardly act must be motivated by fear or a desire for safety, and an act of intemperance by a desire for pleasure, perhaps even for a particular range of pleasure such as those of eating or drinking or sex. And now, going back to the idea of virtues as correctives, one may say that it is only because fear and the desire for pleasure often operate as temptations that courage and temperance exist as virtues at all. As things are we often want to run away not only where that is the right thing to do but also where we should stand firm; and we want pleasure not only where we should seek pleasure but also where we should

*Aristotle op. cit. 1140 b 22–25. Aquinas op. cit. 1a2ae Q.57 a.4.
**Aristotle op. cit. 1106 b 15 and 1129 a.4 have this implication; but Aquinas is more explicit in op. cit. 1a2ae Q.60 a.2.

not. If human nature had been different there would have been no need of a corrective disposition in either place, as fear and pleasure would have been good guides to conduct throughout life. So Aquinas says, about the passions

> They may incite us to something against reason, and so we need a curb, which we name *temperance*. Or they make us shirk a course of action dictated by reason, through fear of dangers or hardships. Then a person needs to be steadfast and not run away from what is right; and for this *courage* is named.*

As with courage and temperance so with many other virtues: there is, for instance, a virtue of industriousness only because idleness is a temptation; and of humility only because men tend to think too well of themselves. Hope is a virtue because despair too is a temptation; it might have been that no one cried that all was lost except where he could really see it to be so, and in this case there would have been no virtue of hope.

With virtues such as justice and charity it is a little different, because they correspond not to any particular desire or tendency that has to be kept in check but rather to a deficiency of motivation; and it is this that they must make good. If people were as much attached to the good of others as they are to their own good there would no more be a general virtue of benevolence than there is a general virtue of self-love. And if people cared about the rights of others as they care about their own rights no virtue of justice would be needed to look after the matter, and rules about such things as contracts and promises would only need to be made public, like the rules of a game that everyone was eager to play.

On this view of the virtues and vices everything is seen to depend on what human nature is like, and the traditional catalogue of the two kinds of dispositions is not hard to understand. Nevertheless it may be defective, and anyone who accepts the thesis that I am putting forward will feel free to ask himself where the temptations and deficiencies that need correcting are really to be found. It is possible, for example, that the theory of human nature lying behind the traditional list of the virtues and vices puts too much emphasis on hedonistic and sensual impulses, and does not sufficiently take account of less straightforward inclinations such as the desire to be put upon and dissatisfied, or the unwillingness to accept good things as they come along.

It should now be clear why I said that virtues should be seen as correctives; and part of what is meant by saying that virtue is about things that are difficult for men should also have appeared. The further application of this idea is, however, controversial, and the following difficulty presents itself: that we both are and are not inclined to think that the harder a man finds it to act virtuously the more virtue he shows if he does act well. For on the one hand great virtue is needed where it is particularly hard to act virtuously; yet on the other it could be argued that difficulty in acting virtuously shows that the agent is imperfect in virtue: according to Aristotle, to take pleasure in virtuous action is the mark of true virtue, with the self-mastery of the one who finds virtue difficult only a second best. How then is this conflict to be decided? Who shows most courage, the one who wants

*Aquinas op. cit. 1a2ae Q.61 a.3.

to run away but does not, or the one who does not even want to run away? Who shows most charity, the one who finds it easy to make the good of others his object, or the one who finds it hard?

What is certain is that the thought that virtues are corrective does not constrain us to relate virtue to difficulty in each individual man. Since men in general find it hard to face great danger or evils, and even small ones, we may count as courageous those few who without blindness or indifference are nevertheless fearless even in terrible circumstances. And when someone has a natural charity or generosity it is at least part of the virtue that he has; if natural virtue cannot be the whole of virtue this is because a kindly or fearless disposition could be disastrous without justice and wisdom, and because these virtues have to be learned, not because natural virtue is too easily acquired. I have argued that the virtues can be seen as correctives in relation to human nature in general but not that each virtue must present a difficulty to each and every man.

Nevertheless many people feel strongly inclined to say that it is for moral effort that moral praise is to be bestowed, and that in proportion as a man finds it easy to be virtuous so much the less is he to be morally admired for his good actions. The dilemma can be resolved only when we stop talking about difficulties standing in the way of virtuous action as if they were of only one kind. The fact is that some kinds of difficulties do indeed provide an occasion for much virtue, but that others rather show that virtue is incomplete.

To illustrate this point I shall first consider an example of honest action. We may suppose for instance that a man has an opportunity to steal, in circumstances where stealing is not morally permissible, but that he refrains. And now let us ask our old question. For one man it is hard to refrain from stealing and for another man it is not: which shows the greater virtue in acting as he should? It is not difficult to see in this case that it makes all the difference whether the difficulty comes from circumstances, as that a man is poor, or that his theft is unlikely to be detected, or whether it comes from something that belongs to his own character. The fact that a man is *tempted* to steal is something about him that shows a certain lack of honesty: of the thoroughly honest man we say that it "never entered his head," meaning that it was never a real possibility for him. But the fact that he is poor is something that makes the occasion more *tempting,* and difficulties of this kind make honest action all the more virtuous.

A similar distinction can be made between different obstacles standing in the way of charitable action. Some circumstances, as that great sacrifice is needed, or that the one to be helped is a rival, give an occasion on which a man's charity is severely tested. Yet in given circumstances of this kind it is the man who acts easily rather than the one who finds it hard who shows the most charity. Charity is a virtue of attachment, and that sympathy for others which makes it easier to help them is part of the virtue itself.

These are fairly simple cases, but I am not supposing that it is always easy to say where the relevant distinction is to be drawn. What, for instance, should we say about the emotion of fear as an obstacle to action? Is a man more courageous if he fears much and nevertheless acts, or if he is relatively fearless? Several things must be said about this. In the first place it seems that the emotion of fear is not a necessary condition for the display of courage; in face of a great evil such as death or injury a man may show courage even if he does not tremble. On the other hand even irrational fears may give an occasion for courage: if someone suffers from claustrophobia or a dread of heights he may require courage to do that which would not be a courageous action for others. But not all fears belong from this point of view to the circumstances rather than to a man's character. For while we do not think of claustrophobia or a dread of heights as features of character, a general timorousness may be. Thus, although pathological fears are not the result of a man's choices and values some fears may be. The fears that count against a man's courage are those that we think he could overcome, and among them, in a special class, those that reflect the fact that he values safety too much.

In spite of problems such as these, which have certainly not all been solved, both the distinction between different kinds of obstacles to virtuous action and the general idea that virtues are correctives will be useful in resolving a difficulty in Kant's moral philosophy closely related to the issues discussed in the preceding paragraphs. In a passage in the first section of the *Groundwork of the Metaphysics of Morals* Kant notoriously tied himself into a knot in trying to give an account of those actions which have as he put it "positive moral worth." Arguing that only actions done out of a sense of duty have this worth he contrasts a philanthropist who "takes pleasure in spreading happiness around him" with one who acts out of respect for duty, saying that the actions of the latter but not the former have moral worth. Much scorn has been poured on Kant for this curious doctrine, and indeed it does seem that something has gone wrong, but perhaps we are not in a position to scoff unless we can give our own account of the idea on which Kant is working. After all it does seem that he is right in saying that some actions are in accordance with duty, and even required by duty, without being the subjects of moral praise, like those of the honest trader who deals honestly in a situation in which it is in his interest to do so.

It was this kind of example that drove Kant to his strange conclusion. He added another example, however, in discussing acts of self-preservation; these he said, while they normally have no positive moral worth, may have it when a man preserves his life not from inclination but without inclination and from a sense of duty. Is he not right in saying that acts of self-preservation normally have no moral significance but that they may have it, and how do we ourselves explain this fact?

To anyone who approaches this topic from a consideration of the virtues the solution readily suggests itself. Some actions are in accordance with virtue without requiring virtue for their performance, whereas others are both in accordance with virtue and such as to show possession of a virtue. So Kant's trader was dealing honestly in a situation in which the virtue of honesty is not required for honest dealing, and it is for this reason that his action did not have "positive moral worth." Similarly, the care that one ordinarily takes for one's life, as for instance on some ordinary morning in eating one's breakfast and keeping out of the way of a car on the road, is something for which no virtue is required. As we said earlier there is no general virtue of self-love as there is a virtue of benevolence or charity, because men are generally attached sufficiently to their own good. Nevertheless in special circumstances virtues such as temperance, courage, fortitude, and hope may be needed if someone is to preserve his life. Are these circumstances in which the preservation of one's own life is a duty? Sometimes it is so, for sometimes it is what is owed to others that should keep a man from destroying himself, and then he may act out of a sense of duty. But not all cases in which acts of self-preservation show virtue are like this. For a man may display each of the virtues just listed even where he does not do any harm to others if he kills himself or fails to preserve his life. And it is this that explains why there may be a moral aspect to suicide which does not depend on possible injury to other people. It is not that suicide is "always wrong," whatever that would mean, but that suicide is *sometimes* contrary to virtues such as courage and hope.

Let us now return to Kant's philanthropists, with the thought that it is action that is in accordance with virtue and also displays a virtue that has moral worth. We see at once that Kant's difficulties are avoided, and the happy philanthropist re-instated in the position which belongs to him. For charity is, as we said, a virtue of attachment as well as action, and the sympathy that makes it easier to act with charity is part of the virtue. The man who acts charitably out of a sense of duty is not to be undervalued, but it is the other who most shows virtue and therefore to the other that most moral worth is attributed. Only a detail of Kant's presentation of the case of the dutiful philanthropist tells on the other side. For what he actually said was that this man felt no sympathy and took no pleasure in the good of others because "his mind was clouded by some sorrow of his own," and this is the kind of circumstance that increases the virtue that is needed if a man is to act well.

III

It was suggested above that an action with "positive moral worth," or as we might say a positively good action, was to be seen as one which was in accordance with virtue, by which I mean contrary to no virtue, and moreover one for which a virtue was required. Nothing has so far been said about another case, excluded by the for-mula, in which it might seem that an act displaying one virtue was nevertheless con-trary to another. In giving this last description I am thinking not of two virtues with competing claims, as if what were required by justice could nevertheless be demanded by charity, or something of that kind, but rather of the possibility that a virtue such as courage or temperance or industry which overcomes a special temptation, might be displayed in an act of folly or villainy. Is this something that we must allow for, or is it only good or innocent actions which can be acts of these virtues? Aquinas, in his definition of virtue, said that virtues can produce only good actions, and that they are dispositions "of which no one can make bad use,"* except when they are treated as objects, as in being the subject of hatred or pride. The common opinion nowadays is, however, quite different. With the notable exception of Peter Geach hardly any-one sees any difficulty in the thought that virtues may sometimes be displayed in bad actions. Von Wright, for instance, speaks of the courage of the villain as if this were a quite unproblematic idea, and most people take it for granted that the virtues of courage and temperance may aid a bad man in his evil work. It is also supposed that charity may lead a man to act badly, as when someone does what he has no right to do, but does it for the sake of a friend.

*Aquinas op. cit. 1a2a3 Q.56 a.5.

There are, however, reasons for thinking that the matter is not so simple as this. If a man who is willing to do an act of injustice to help a friend, or for the common good, is supposed to act out of charity, and he so acts where a just man will not, it should be said that the unjust man has more charity than the just man. But do we not think that someone not ready to act unjustly may yet be perfect in charity, the virtue having done its whole work in prompting him to do the acts that are permissible? And is there not more difficulty than might appear in the idea of an act of injustice which is nevertheless an act of courage? Suppose for instance that a sordid murder were in question, say a murder done for gain or to get an inconvenient person out of the way, but that this murder had to be done in alarming circumstances or in the face of real danger; should we be happy to say that such an action was an act of courage or a courageous act? Did the murderer, who certainly acted boldly, or with intrepidity, if he did the murder, also act courageously? Some people insist that they are ready to say this, but I have noticed that they like to move over to a murder for the sake of conscience, or to some other act done in the course of a villainous enterprise but whose immediate end is innocent or positively good. On their hypothesis, which is that bad acts can easily be seen as courageous acts or acts of courage, my original example should be just as good.

What are we to say about this difficult matter? There is no doubt that the murderer who murdered for gain was *not a coward*: he did not have a second moral defect which another villain might have had. There is no difficulty about this because it is clear that one defect may neutralize another. As Aquinas remarked, it is better for a blind horse if it is slow.* It does not follow, however, that an act of villainy can be courageous; we are inclined to say that it "took courage," and yet it seems wrong to think of courage as equally connected with good actions and bad.

One way out of this difficulty might be to say that the man who is ready to pursue bad ends does indeed have courage, and shows courage in his action, but that in him courage is not a virtue. Later I shall consider some cases in which this might seem to be the right thing to say, but in this instance it does not seem to be. For unless the murderer consistently pursues bad ends his courage will often result in good; it may enable him to do many innocent or positively good things for himself or for his family and friends. On the strength of an individual bad action we can hardly say that in him courage is not a virtue. Nevertheless there is something to be said even about the individual action to distinguish it from one that would readily be called an act of courage or a courageous act. Perhaps the following analogy may help us to see what it is. We might think of words such as "courage" as naming characteristics of human beings in respect of a certain power, as words such as "poison" and "solvent" and "corrosive" so name the properties of physical things. The power to which virtue-words are so related is the power of producing good action, and good desires. But just as poisons, solvents and corrosives do not always operate characteristically, so it could be with virtues. If P (say arsenic) is a poison it does not follow that P acts as a poison wherever it is found. It is quite natural to say on occasion "P does not act as a poison here" though P is a poison

*Aquinas op. cit. 1a2ae Q.58 a.4.

and it is P that is acting here. Similarly courage is not operating as a virtue when the murder turns his courage, which is a virtue, to bad ends. Not surprisingly the resistance that some of us registered was not to the expression "the courage of the murderer" or to the assertion that what he did "took courage" but rather to the description of that action as an act of courage or a courageous act. It is not that the action *could* not be so described, but that the fact that courage does not here have its characteristic operation is a reason for finding the description strange.

In this example we were considering an action in which courage was not operating as a virtue, without suggesting that in that agent it generally failed to do so. But the latter is also a possibility. If someone is both wicked and foolhardy this may be the case with courage, and it is even easier to find examples of a general connection with evil rather than good in the case of some other virtues. Suppose, for instance, that we think of someone who is over-industrious, or too ready to refuse pleasure, and this is characteristic of him rather than something we find on one particular occasion. In this case the virtue of industry, or the virtue of temperance, has a systematic connection with defective action rather than good action; and it might be said in either case that the virtue did not operate as a virtue in this man. Just as we might say in a certain setting "P is not a poison here" although P is a poison and P is here, so we might say that industriousness, or temperance, is not a virtue in some. Similarly in a man habitually given to wishful thinking, who clings to false hopes, hope does not operate as a virtue and we may say that it is not a virtue in him.

The thought developed in the last paragraph, to the effect that not every man who has a virtue has something that is virtue in him, may help to explain a certain discomfort that one may feel when discussing the virtues. It is not easy to put one's finger on what is wrong, but it has something to do with a disparity between the moral ideals that may seem to be implied in our talk about the virtues, and the moral judgements that we actually make. Someone reading the foregoing pages might, for instance, think that the author of this paper always admired most those people who had all the virtues, being wise and temperate as well as courageous, charitable, and just. And indeed it is sometimes so. There are some people who do possess all these virtues and who are loved and admired by all the world, as Pope John XXIII was loved and admired. Yet the fact is that many of us look up to some people whose chaotic lives contain rather little of wisdom or temperance, rather than to some others who possess these virtues. And while it may be that this is just romantic nonsense I suspect that it is not. For while wisdom always operates as a virtue, its close relation prudence does not, and it is prudence rather than wisdom that inspires many a careful life. Prudence is not a virtue in everyone, any more than industriousness is, for in some it is rather an over-anxious concern for safety and propriety, and a determination to keep away from people or situations which are apt to bring trouble with them; and by such defensiveness much good is lost. It is the same with temperance. Intemperance can be an appalling thing, as it was with Henry VIII of whom Wolsey remarked that

> rather than he will either miss or want any part of his will or appetite, he will put the loss of one half of his realm in danger.

Nevertheless in some people temperance is not a virtue, but is rather connected with timidity or with a grudging attitude to the acceptance of good things. Of course what is best is to live boldly yet without imprudence or intemperance, but the fact is that rather few can manage that.

Postscript 2002

In my introduction to the book named from this article and written over 25 years ago I said that a sound moral philosophy should "start from" a theory of the virtues, but I should no longer like to say quite that because it, and perhaps other things that I wrote in the article have given the false impression that I am now, or ever was, a believer in "virtue ethics" as that is nowadays understood. I write this postscript to explain why I am not a "virtue ethicist" as is, for instance Michael Slote, Rosalind Hursthouse, or Christine Swanton. I want to emphasise the distance between their beliefs and my own.

   This can best be done by considering the topic of acts of injustice which Hursthouse, in her interesting book *Virtue Ethics*, described with characteristic honesty as presenting difficulties to a position such as hers, and awaiting further developments before it could be dealt with within "virtue ethics." I find no such difficulty in the ethics to which I subscribe, and recently expounded in my book *Natural Goodness*, where I insisted that the wrongness of acts such as murder, theft, and promise-breaking is based on the need that human societies have for a ban on such *actions*, rather than on facts about the soul of one who acts unjustly. (What matters is that these things *should not be done*.)

   We can therefore distinguish two different "moments" in moral judgements concerning justice and injustice. There is first the question of whether an action is contrary to justice because of what the agent (by intention) *does*, and if it is contrary to justice then it is ipso facto a bad action. That settles *this* matter, *with no reference to psychological factors such as the agent's motives, feelings, or habitual ways of acting*. The relevance of the latter is in determining whether the individual agent's action can be called an act of the virtue of justice, because there are further tests for *that*. For even an action positively required by justice, such as the keeping of a contract on a particular occasion, may yet be bad as done by a particular agent at a particular time because done maliciously, or in contravention of this person's (erroneous) conscience. It can be called an *act of the virtue* of justice only when these further tests are passed. This is where we do indeed need to think about what it is to attribute a virtue to an agent, because we are now concerned with something that goes beyond the *raison d'etre* for considering *certain classes of actions* to be just or unjust.

———

Study Questions

1. Foot writes: "For us there are four cardinal moral virtues: courage, temperance, wisdom and justice." Is her list complete? How does one decide which qualities belong in this list?

2. In what ways does virtue belong to the will? Foot suggests that a person's virtue "may be judged by his innermost desires as well as by his intentions." May we hold people responsible for and evaluate them on the basis of their desires, rather than their actions? Why or why not?

3. According to Foot, what does wisdom involve? What do you think it involves?

4. What does Foot mean by saying that virtues are "corrective"? How does this tie the virtues to human nature? Give examples.

5. Foot asks: "Who shows most courage, the one who wants to run away but does not, or the one who does not even want to run away? Who shows most charity, the one who finds it easy to make the good of others his object, or the one who finds it hard?" What is your answer?

6. Can a virtue lead to a bad action? To take Foot's example, can an act of injustice, such as a murder done for gain, show courage, or be considered a courageous act?

Selected Bibliography

Anscombe, G. E. M. "Modern Moral Philosophy," in *The Collected Philosophical Papers of G.E.M. Anscombe* (Minneapolis: University of Minnesota Press, 1981). A seminal article critical of obligation-based approaches to ethics.

Crisp, Roger. *How Should One Live?: Essays on the Virtues* (Oxford/New York: Oxford University Press, 1996). A collection that explores several issues in virtue ethics.

Crisp, Roger and Michael Slote. *Virtue Ethics* (Oxford/New York: Oxford University Press, 1997). A collection of important essays on virtue ethics.

Foot, Philippa. *Moral Dilemmas and Other Topics in Moral Philosophy* (Oxford/New York: Oxford University Press, 2002).

———. *Natural Goodness* (Oxford/New York: Oxford University Press, 2001).

———. *Virtues and Vices* (Berkeley: University of California Press, 1978. Reissued by Oxford University Press, 2003).

McDowell, John. "Virtue and Reason," *Monist* 62 (1979): 331–350. Reprinted in Crisp and Slote. Difficult but significant essay on the concept of a virtue.

MacIntyre, Alisdair. *After Virtue*, 2nd edition (Notre Dame, IN: University of Notre Dame Press, 1984). An influential book advocating a return to virtue ethics.

von Wright, G. H. *The Varieties of Goodness* (London: Routledge & Kegan Paul, 1964), esp. Chap. 7, "Virtue." An important discussion of the concept of virtue.

27

ROSALIND HURSTHOUSE

—

An issue that has arisen for virtue-based approaches to ethics is whether they can provide guidance about how to act in specific circumstances. Virtue ethics does not

> An action is right iff it is what a virtuous agent would characteristically . . . do in the circumstances

focus primarily on the criteria of right action. Its concern, instead, is the nature and content of the virtues—those traits of character and intellect possessed by the good person, or that are part of the good human life. This focus on good agents rather than right action has led many philosophers to ask whether virtue ethics can tell us how to act in specific situations. Furthermore, the criterion of right action that does emerge from virtue ethics, going back to Aristotle, is this: the right thing to do is just what the virtuous person would do in that situation. But, critics press, that is precisely the problem: Isn't that formula completely empty? In this essay, Rosalind Hursthouse takes on this challenge. She argues that virtue ethics is action guiding and is on the same footing as rival consequentialist and deontological approaches.

Rosalind Hursthouse is a professor of philosophy at the Open University. She has written several important essays on virtue ethics, and recently published *On Virtue Ethics* (2000).

—

Normative Virtue Ethics

A common belief concerning virtue ethics is that it does not tell us what we should do. This belief is something manifested merely in the expressed assumption that virtue ethics, in being "agent-centered" rather than "act-centered," is concerned with Being rather than Doing, with good (and bad) character rather than right (and wrong) action, with the question "What sort of person should I be?" rather than the question "What should I do?" On this assumption, "virtue ethics" so-called does not figure as a normative rival to utilitarian and deontological ethics; rather, its (fairly) recent revival is seen as having served the useful purpose of reminding moral philosophers that the elaboration of a normative theory may fall short of giving a full account of our moral life. Thus prompted, deontologists have turned to Kant's long neglected "Doctrine of Virtue," and utilitarians, largely abandoning the old debated about rule- and act-utilitarianism, are showing interest in the general-happiness-maximizing consequences of inculcating such virtues as friendship, honesty, and loyalty.

On this assumption, it seems that philosophers who "do virtue ethics," having served this purpose, must realize that they have been doing no more than supplementing normative theory, and should now decide which of the two standard views they espouse. Or, if they find that too difficult, perhaps they should confine themselves to writing detailed studies of particular virtues and vices, indicating where appropriate that "a deontologist would say that an agent with virtue X will characteristically . . . , whereas a utilitarian would say that she will characteristically. . . . " But anyone who wants to espouse virtue ethics as a rival to deontological or utilitarian ethics (finding it distinctly bizarre to suppose that Aristotle espoused either of the latter) will find this common belief voiced against her as an objection: "Virtue ethics does not, because it cannot, tell us what we should do. Hence it cannot be a normative rival to deontology and utilitarianism."

This paper is devoted to defending virtue ethics against this objection.

I. Right Action

What grounds might someone have for believing that virtue ethics cannot tell us what we should do? It seems that sometimes the ground is no more than the claim that virtue ethics is concerned with good (and bad) character rather than right (and wrong) action. But that claim does no more than highlight an interesting contrast between virtue ethics on the one hand, and deontology and utilitarianism on the other; the former is agent-centered, the latter (it is said) are act-centered.*
It does not entail that virtue ethics has nothing to say about the concept of right action, nor about which actions are right and which wrong. Wishing to highlight a different contrast, the one between utilitarianism and deontology, we might equally well say, "Utilitarianism is concerned with good (and bad) states of affairs rather than right (and wrong) action," and no one would take that to mean that utilitarianism, unlike deontology, had nothing to say about right action, for what utilitarianism does say is so familiar.

Suppose an act-utilitarian laid out her account of right action as follows:

U1. An action is right if it promotes the best consequences.

---

*Kant is standardly taken as the paradigm deontologist, but Stephen Hudson argues he is much closer to Aristotle on the act/agent-centered point than is usually supposed. See "What Is Morality All About?," *Philosophia* 20 (1990), 3–13.

This premise provides a specification of right action, forging the familiar utilitarian link between the concepts of *right action* and *best consequences,* but gives one no guidance about how to act until one knows what to count as the best consequences. So these must be specified in a second premise, for example:

U2. The best consequences are those in which happiness is maximized,

which forges the familiar utilitarian link between the concepts of *best consequences* and *happiness.**

Many different versions of deontology can be laid out in a way that displays the same basic structure. They being with a premise providing a specification of right action:

D1. An action is right if it is in accordance with a correct moral rule or principle.

Like the first premise of act-utilitarianism, this gives one no guidance about how to act until, in this case, one knows what to count as a correct moral rule (or principle). So this must be specified in a second premise which begins

D2. A correct moral rule (principle) is one that . . . ,

and this may be completed in a variety of ways, for example:

(i) is on the following list (and then a list does follow)

or

(ii) is laid on us by God

or

(iii) is universalizable

or

(iv) would be the object of choice of all rational beings

and so on.

Although this way of laying out fairly familiar versions of utilitarianism and deontology is hardly controversial, it is worth noting that it suggests some infelicity in the slogan "Utilitarianism begins with (or takes as its fundamental concept etc.)

*Variations on utilitarianism are not my concern here. I am ignoring rule-utilitarianism, and assuming my reader to be well aware of the fact that different utilitarians may specify *best consequences* in different ways. See the introduction to A. Sen and B. Williams (eds.), *Utilitarianism and Beyond* (Cambridge, 1982), from which I have (basically) taken the characterization of utilitarianism given here.

the Good, whereas deontology begins with the Right." If the concept a normative ethics "begins with" is the one it uses to specify right action, then utilitarianism might be said to begin with the Good (if we take this to be the "same" concept as that of the *best*), but we should surely hasten to add "but only in relation to consequences; not, for instance, in relation to *good* agents, or to living *well*." And even then, we shall not be able to go on to say that most versions of deontology "begin with" the Right, for they use the concept of moral rule or principle to specify right action. The only versions which, in this sense, "begin with" the Right would have to be versions of what Frankena calls "extreme act-deontology*," which (I suppose) specify a right action as one which just *is* right.

And if the dictum is supposed to single out, rather vaguely, the concept which is "most important," then the concepts of *consequences* or *happiness* seem as deserving of mention as the concept of the Good for utilitarianism, and what counts as most important(if any one concept does) for deontologists would surely vary from case to case. For some it would be God, for others universalizability, for others the Categorical Imperative, for others rational acceptance, and so on.

It is possible that too slavish an acceptance of this slogan, and the inevitable difficulty of finding a completion of "a virtue ethics begins with . . ." which does not reveal its inadequacy, has contributed to the belief that virtue ethics cannot provide a specification of right action. I have heard people say, "Utilitarianism defines the Right in terms of the Good, and deontology defines the Good in terms of the Right; but how can virtue ethics possibility define both in terms of the (virtuous) Agent?," and indeed, with no answer forthcoming to the questions "Good *what*? Right *what*?," I have no idea. But if the question is "How can virtue ethics specify right action?," the answer is easy:

V1. An action is right if it is what a virtuous agent would characteristically (i.e., acting in character) do in the circumstances.

This specification rarely, if ever, silences those who maintain that virtue ethics cannot tell us what we should do. On the contrary, it tends to provoke irritable laughter and scorn. "*That*'s no use," the objectors say. "It gives us no guidance whatsoever. Who are the virtuous agents?" But if the failure of the first premise of a normative ethics which forges a link between the concept of right action and a concept distinctive of that ethics may provoke scorn because it provides no practical guidance, why not direct a similar scorn at the first premises of act-utilitarianism and deontology in the form in which I have given them? Of each of them I remarked, apparently *en passant* but with intent, that they gave us no guidance. Utilitarianism must specify what are to count as the best consequences, and deontology what is to count as a correct moral rule, producing a second premise, before any guidance is given. And similarly, virtue ethics must specify who is to count as a virtuous agent. So far, all three are all in the same position.

Of course, if the virtuous agent can only be specified as an agent disposed to act in accordance with moral rules, as some have assumed, then virtue ethics collapses

*W. Frankena, *Ethics,* 2nd edn. (Englewood Cliffs, NJ, 1973), 16.

back into deontology and is no rival to it. So let us add a subsidiary premise to this skeletal outline, with the intention of making it clear that virtue ethics aims to provide a non-deontological specification of the virtuous agent via a specification of the virtues, which will be given in its second premise:

> **V1a.** A virtuous agent is one who acts virtuously, that is, one who has an exercises the virtues.
>
> **V2.** A virtue is a character trait that . . .*

This second premise of virtue ethics might, like the second premise of some versions of deontology, be completed simply by enumeration ("a virtue is one of the following," and then the list is given).** Or we might, not implausibly, interpret the Hume of the second *Enquiry* as espousing virtue ethics. According to him, a virtue is a character trait (of human beings) that is useful or agreeable to its possessor or to others (inclusive "or" both times). The standard neo-Aristotelian completion claims that a virtue is a character trait a human being needs for *eudaimonia*, to flourish or live well.

Here, then, we have a specification of right action, whose structure closely resembles those of act-utilitarianism and many forms of deontology. Given that virtue ethics can come up with such a specification, can it still be maintained that it, unlike utilitarianism and deontology, cannot tell us what we should do? Does the specification somehow fail to provide guidance in a way that the other two do not?

At this point, the difficulty of identifying the virtuous agent in a way that makes V1 action-guiding tends to be brought forward again. Suppose it is granted that deontology has just as much difficulty in identifying the correct moral rules as virtue ethics has in identifying the virtues and hence the virtuous agent. Then the following objection may be made.

"All the same," it may be said, "if we imagine that that has been achieved—perhaps simply by enumeration—deontology yields a set of clear prescriptions which are readily applicable ('Do not lie,' 'do not steal,' 'do not inflict evil or harm on others,' 'Do help others,' 'Do keep promises,' etc.). But virtue ethics yields only the prescription 'Do what the virtuous agent (the one who is honest, charitable, just, etc.) would do in these circumstances.' And this gives me no guidance unless I am (and know I am) a virtuous agent myself (in which case I am hardly in need of it). If I am less than fully virtuous, I shall have no idea what a virtuous

---

*It might be said that V1a does not make it clear that virtue ethics aims to provide a non-deontological specification of the virtuous agent, since it does not rule out the possibility that the virtues themselves are no more than dispositions to act in accordance with moral rules. And indeed, it does seem that the belief that the virtuous agent is nothing but the agent disposed to act in accordance with moral rules is often based on that assumption about the virtues. (See, for example, Frankena, *Ethics*, 65 and A. Gewirth, "Rights and Virtues," *Review of Metaphysics* 38 (1985), 739–62.) Then we must say that V2 aims to clear that up by saying that the virtues are character traits, assuming it to be obvious that someone's being of a certain character is not merely a matter of her being disposed to do certain sorts of acts in accordance with a rule.

**"Enumeration" may connote something more explicit than is required. Deontologists and virtue ethicists actually engaged in normative ethics may well do no more than take it as obvious in the course of what they say that such-and-such is a correct moral rule or virtue, neither stipulating this explicitly, nor attempting to list other rules/virtues which have no bearing on whatever issue is under discussion.

agent would do, and hence cannot apply the only prescription that virtue ethics has given me. (Of course, act-utilitarianism also yields a single prescription, 'Do what maximizes happiness,' but there are no *parallel* difficulties in applying that.) So there is the way in which V1 fails to be action-guiding where deontology and utilitarianism succeed."

It is worth pointing out that, if I acknowledge that I am far from perfect, and am quite unclear what a virtuous agent would do in the circumstances in which I find myself, the obvious thing to do is to go and ask one, should this be possible. This is far from being a trivial point, for it gives a straightforward explanation of an aspect of our moral life which should not be ignored, namely the fact that we do seek moral guidance from people who we think are morally better than ourselves. When I am looking for an excuse to do something I have a horrid suspicion is wrong, I ask my moral inferiors (or peers if I am bad enough), "Wouldn't you do such and such if you were in my shoes?" But when I am anxious to do what is right, and do not see my way clear, I go to people I respect and admire—people who I think are kinder, more honest, more just, wiser, than I am myself—and ask them what they would do in my circumstances. How utilitarianism and deontology would explain this fact, I do not know; but, as I said, the explanation within the terms of virtue ethics is straightforward. If you want to do what is right, and doing what is right is doing what a virtuous agent would do in the circumstances, then you should find out what she would do if you do not already know.

Moreover, seeking advice from virtuous people is not the only thing an imperfect agent trying to apply the single prescription of virtue ethics can do. For it is simply false that, in general, "if I am less than fully virtuous, then I shall have no idea what a virtuous agent would do," as the objection claims. Recall that we are assuming that the virtues have been enumerated, as the deontologist's rules have been. The latter have been enumerated as, say, honesty, charity, justice, etc. So, *ex hypothesi*, a virtuous agent is one who is honest, charitable, just, etc. So what she characteristically does is act honestly, charitably, justly, etc., and not dishonestly, uncharitably, unjustly. So given an enumeration of the virtues, I may well have a perfectly good idea of what the virtuous person would do in my circumstances despite my own imperfection. Would she lie in her teeth to acquire an unmerited advantage? No, for that would be to act both dishonestly and unjustly. Would she help the naked man by the roadside or pass by on the other side? The former, for she acts charitably. Might she keep a deathbed promise even though living people would benefit from its being broken? Yes, for she acts justly.* and so on.

2. Moral Rules

The above response to the objection that V1 fails to be action-guiding clearly amounts to a denial of the oft-repeated claim that virtue ethics does not come up with any rules (another version of the thought that it is concerned with Being rather than Doing and needs to be supplemented with rules). We can now see that

---

*I follow tradition here in taking the virtue of fidelity, or faithfulness to one's word, to be part of the virtue of justice, thereby avoiding a clumsy attempt to manufacture an adverbial phrase corresponding to "fidelity." But nothing hangs on this.

it comes up with a large number; not only does each virtue generate a prescription—act honestly, charitably, justly—but each vice a prohibition—do not act dishonestly, uncharitably, unjustly. Once this point about virtue ethics is grasped (and it is remarkable how often it is overlooked), can there remain any reason for thinking that virtue ethics cannot tell us what we should do? Yes. The reason given is, roughly, that rules such as "Act honestly," "Do not act uncharitably," etc. are, like the rule "Do what the virtuous agent would do," still the wrong sort of rule, still somehow doomed to fail to provide the action guidance supplied by the rules (or rule) of deontology and utilitarianism.

But how so? It is true that these rules of virtue ethics (henceforth "v-rules") are couched in terms, or concepts, which are certainly "evaluative" in *some* sense, or senses, of that difficult word. Is it this which dooms them to failure? Surely not, unless many forms of deontology fail too.* If we concentrate on the single example of lying, defining lying to be "asserting what you believe to be untrue, with the intention of deceiving your hearer(s)," then we might, for a moment, preserve the illusion that a deontologist's rules do not contain "evaluative" terms.** But as soon as we remember that few deontologists will want to forego principles of nonmaleficence or beneficence, the illusion vanishes. For those principles, and their corresponding rules ("Do no evil or harm to others," "Help others," "Promote their well-being"), rely on terms or concepts which are at least as "evaluative" as those employed in the v-rules.† Few deontologists rest content with the simple quasi-biological "Do not kill," but more refined versions of that rule such as "Do not murder," or "Do not kill the innocent," once again employ "evaluative" terms, and "Do not kill unjustly" is itself a particular instantiation of a v-rule.

Supposing this point were granted, a deontologist might still claim that the v-rules are markedly inferior to deontological rules as far as providing guidance for

---

*Forms of utilitarianism which aim to be entirely value-free or empirical, such as those which define happiness in terms of the satisfaction of actual desires or preferences, regardless of their content, or as a mental state whose presence is definitively established by introspection, seem to me the least plausible, but I accept that anyone who embraces them may consistently complain that v-rules give inferior action-guidance in virtue of containing "evaluative" terms. But any utilitarian who wishes to employ any distinction between the higher and lower pleasures, or rely on some list of goods (such as autonomy, friendship, knowledge of important matters) in defining happiness, must grant that even her single rule is implicitly "evaluative."

**It might be thought that the example of promises provided an equally straightforward example. This would not substantially affect my argument, but in any case, I do not think that this is so. The *Shorter Oxford* defines the verb "to promise" as "to undertake or . . . , by word or . . . , to do or refrain . . . , or to give . . . : usu. to the *advantage* of the person concerned" (my italics), and the qualification containing the word I have italicized seems to me essential. Its significance has been highlighted in the many stories and myths whose tragic point turns on someone wicked doing what they literally undertook to do, to the horror and despair of "the person concerned." ("Promise me you will fearfully punish the one who has done so and so," the person concerned says, not realizing that the one in question is her long-lost son.)

†I cannot resist pointing out that this reveals a further inadequacy in the slogan "Utilitarianism begins with the Good, deontology with the Right" when this is taken as committing deontology to making the concept of the Good (and presumably the Bad or Evil) somehow derivative from the concept of the Right (and Wrong). A "utilitarian" who relied on the concept of *morally right*, or *virtuous*, action in specifying his concept of happiness would find it hard to shrug off the scare quotes, but no one expects a deontologist to be able to state each of her rules without employing a concept of *good* which is not simply the concept of *right action for its own sake*, or without any mention of *evil* or *harm*.

children is concerned. Granted, adult deontologists must think hard about what really constitutes harming someone, or promoting their well-being, or respecting their autonomy, or murder, but surely the simple rules we learnt at our mother's knee are indispensable? How could virtue ethics plausibly seek to dispense with these and expect toddlers to grasp "Act charitably, honestly, and kindly," "Don't act unjustly," and so on? Rightly are these concepts described as "thick"!* Far too thick for a child to grasp.

Strictly speaking, this claim about learning does not really support the *general* claim that v-rules fail to provide action-guidance, but the claim about learning, arising naturally as it does in the context of the general claim, is one I am more than happy to address. For it pinpoints a condition of adequacy that any normative ethics must meet, namely that such an ethics must not only come up with action-guidance for a clever rational adult but also generate some account of moral education, of how one generation teaches the next what they should do. But an ethics inspired by Aristotle is unlikely to have forgotten the question of moral education, and the objection fails to hit home. First, the implicit empirical claim that toddlers are taught *only* the deontologist's rules, not the "thick" concepts, is false. Sentences such as "Don't do that, it hurts, you mustn't be *cruel*," "Be *kind* to your brother, he's only little," "Don't be so *mean*, so *greedy*" are commonly addressed to toddlers. Secondly, why should a proponent of virtue ethics deny the significance of such mother's-knee rules as "Don't lie," "Keep promises," "Don't take more than your fair share," "Help others"? Although it is a mistake, I have claimed, to define a virtuous agent simply as one disposed to act in accordance with moral rules, it is a very understandable mistake, given the obvious connection between, for example, the exercise of the virtue of honesty and refraining from lying. Virtue ethicists want to emphasize the fact that, if children are to be taught to be honest, they must be taught to prize the truth, and that *merely* teaching them not to lie will not achieve this end. But they need not deny that to achieve this end teaching them not to lie is useful, even indispensable.

So we can see that virtue ethics not only comes up with rules (the v-rules, couched in terms derived from the virtues and vices), but further, does not exclude the more familiar deontologists' rules. The theoretical distinction between the two is that the familiar rules, and their applications in particular cases, are given entirely different backings. According to virtue ethics, I must not tell this lie, since it would be dishonest, and dishonesty is a vice; must not break this promise, since it would be unjust, or a betrayal of friendship, or, perhaps (for the available virtue and vice terms do not neatly cover every contingency), simply because no virtuous person would.

However, the distinction is not merely theoretical. It is, indeed, the case that, with respect to a number of familiar examples, virtue ethicists and deontologists tend to stand shoulder to shoulder against utilitarians, denying that, for example, this lie can be told, this promise broken, this human being killed because the consequences of so doing will be generally happiness-maximizing. But, despite a fair amount of coincidence in action-guidance between deontology and virtue ethics, the latter has its own distinctive approach to the practical problems involved in dilemmas.

*See B. Williams, *Ethics and the Limits of Philosophy* (London, 1985), 129–30.

3. The Conflict Problem

It is a noteworthy fact that, in support of the general claim that virtue ethics cannot tell us what we should do, what is often cited is the "conflict problem." The requirements of different virtues, it is said, can point us in opposed directions. Charity prompts me to kill the person who would (truly) be better off dead, but justice forbids it. Honesty points to telling the hurtful truth, kindness and compassion to remaining silent or even lying. And so on. So virtue ethics lets us down just at the point where we need it, where we are faced with the really difficult dilemmas and do not know what to do.

In the mouth of a utilitarian, this may be a comprehensible criticism, for, as is well known, the only conflict that classical utilitarianism's one rule can generate is the tiresome logical one between the two occurrences of "greatest" in its classical statement. But it is strange to find the very same criticism coming from deontologists, who are notoriously faced with the same problem "Don't kill," "Respect autonomy," "Tell the truth," "Keep promises" may all conflict with "Prevent suffering" or "Do no harm," which is precisely why deontologists so often reject utilitarianism's deliverances on various dilemmas. Presumably, they must think that deontology can solve the "conflict problem" and, further, that virtue ethics cannot. Are they right?

With respect to a number of cases, the deontologist's strategy is to argue that the "conflict" is merely apparent, or *prima facie*. The proponent of virtue ethics employs the same strategy: according to her, many of the putative conflicts are merely apparent, resulting from a misapplication of the virtue or vice terms. Does kindness require not telling hurtful truths? Sometimes, but in *this* case, what has to be understood is that one does people no kindness by concealing this sort of truth from them, hurtful as it may be. Or, in a different case, the importance of the truth in question puts the consideration of hurt feelings out of court, and the agent does not show herself to be unkind, or callous, by speaking out. Does charity require that I kill the person who would be better off dead but who wants to stay alive, thereby conflicting with justice? Not if, in Foot's words, "[a] man does not lack charity because he refrains from an act of injustice which would have been for someone's good."*

One does not have to agree with the three judgements expressed here to recognize this as a *strategy* available to virtue ethics, any more than one has to agree with the particular judgements of deontologists who, for example, may claim that one rule outranks another, or that a certain rule has a certain exception clause built in, when they argue that a putative case of conflict is resolvable. Whether an individual has resolved a putative moral conflict or dilemma rightly is one question; whether a normative ethics has the wherewithal to resolve it is an entirely different question, and it is the latter with which we are concerned here.

The form the strategy takes within virtue ethics provides what may plausibly be claimed to be the deep explanation of why, in some cases, agents do not know the answer to "What should I do in these circumstances?" despite the fact that

---

*P. Foot, *Virtues and Vices* (Oxford, 1978), p. 60, n. 12.

there *is* an answer. Trivially, the explanation is that they lack moral knowledge of what to do in this situation; but why? In what way? The lack, according to virtue ethics' strategy, arises from lack of moral wisdom, from an inadequate grasp of what is involved in acting *kindly* (unkindly) or *charitably* (uncharitably), in being *honest*, or *just*, or *lacking in charity*, or, in general, of how the virtue (and vice) terms are to be correctly applied.

Here we come to an interesting defense of the v-rules, often criticized as being too difficult to apply for the agent who lacks moral wisdom.* The defense relies on an (insufficiently acknowledged) insight of Aristotle's—namely that moral knowledge, unlike mathematical knowledge, cannot be acquired merely by attending lectures and is not characteristically to be found in people too young to have much experience of life.** Now *if* right action were determined by rules that any clever adolescent could apply correctly, how could this be so? Why are there not moral whiz-kids, the way there are mathematical (or quasi-mathematical) whiz-kids? But if the rules that determine right action are, like the v-rules, very difficult to apply correctly, involving, for instance, a grasp of the *sort* of truth that one does people no kindness by concealing, the explanation is readily to hand. Clever adolescents do not, in general, have a good grasp of that sort of thing.† And *of course* I have to say "the sort of truth that . . ." and "that sort of thing," relying on my readers' knowledgeable uptake. For if I could define either sort, then, once again, clever adolescents could acquire moral wisdom from textbooks.

So far, I have described one strategy available to virtue ethics for coping with the "conflict problem," a strategy that consists in arguing that the conflict is merely apparent, and can be resolved. According to one—only one of many—versions of "the doctrine of the unity of the virtues," this is the only possible strategy (and ultimately successful), but this is not a claim I want to defend. One general reason is that I still do not know what I think about "the unity of the virtues" (all those different versions!); a more particular, albeit related, reason is that, even if I were (somehow) sure that the requirements of the particular virtues could never conflict, I suspect that I would still believe in the possibility of moral dilemmas. I have been talking so far as though examples of putative dilemmas and examples of putative conflict between the requirements of different virtues (or deontologists' rules) coincided. But it may seem to many, as it does to me, that there are certain (putative) dilemmas which can only be described in terms of (putative) conflict with much artifice and loss of relevant detail.

Let us, therefore, consider the problem of moral dilemmas without bothering about whether they can be described in the simple terms of a conflict between the requirements of two virtues (or two deontologists' rules). Most of us, it may be

---

*This could well be regarded as another version of the criticism discussed earlier, that the v-rules somehow fail to provide action-guidance.

** *Nicomachean Ethics* (= *NE*) 1142³12–16.

†In defending the thesis that virtue ethics is a normative *rival* to utilitarianism and deontology, I am not simultaneously aiming to establish the far more ambitious thesis that it beats its rivals hollow. Utilitarians and deontologists may well take the Aristotelian point on board and provide an account, appropriate to their ethics, of why we should not consult whiz-kids about difficult moral decisions. For example, Onora O'Neill's sophisticated version of Kantian "maxims" rules out their application by (merely) clever adolescents.

supposed, have our own favored example(s), either real or imaginary, of the case (or cases) where we see the decision about whether to do A or B as a very grave matter, have thought a great deal about what can be said for and against doing A, and doing B, and have still not managed to reach a conclusion which we think is the right one.* How, if at all, does virtue ethics direct us to think about such cases?

4. Dilemmas and Normative Theory

As a preliminary to answering that question, we should consider a much more general one, namely "How should any normative ethics direct us to think about such cases?" This brings us to the topic of normative theory.

It is possible to detect a new movement in moral philosophy, a movement which has already attracted the name "anti-theory in ethics."** Its various representatives have as a common theme the rejection of normative ethical theory; but amongst them are numbered several philosophers usually associated with virtue ethics, such as Baier, McDowell, MacIntyre, and Nussbaum. This does not mean that they maintain what I have been denying, namely that virtue ethics is not normative; rather, they assume that it does not constitute a normative *theory* (and, mindful of this fact, I have been careful to avoid describing virtue ethics as one). What is meant by a "normative theory" in this context is not easy to pin down, but, roughly, a normative theory is taken to be a set (possibly one-membered in the case of utilitarianism) of general principles which provide a *decision procedure* for all questions about how to act morally.

Part of the point of distinguishing a normative ethics by calling it a normative "theory" is that a decent theory, as we know from science, enables us to answer questions that we could not answer before we had it. It is supposed to resolve those difficult dilemmas in which, it is said, our moral intuitions clash, and, prior to our grasp of the theory, we do not know what we should do.[†] And a large part of the motivation

*I have chosen this description of the sort of dilemmas with which I am concerned deliberately, mindful of Philippa Foot's paper, "Moral Realism and Moral Dilemma." *The Journal of Philosophy* 80 (1983), 379–98. As she points out, some cases that are discussed as "conflicts" or "dilemmas" are taken to be resolvable, that is, taken to be cases in which we do reach a conclusion we think is the right one; these are my cases of "apparent" conflict. Commenting on Wiggins . . . , she also points out that undecidability may exist "in small moral matters, or where the choice is between goods rather than evils, only it doesn't worry us" (395); I am concentrating on the ones that worry us.

**See S. Clarke and E. Simpson (eds.), *Anti-Theory in Ethics and Moral Conservatism* (New York, 1989), containing, *inter alia*, articles by Baier, McDowell, MacIntyre, and Nussbaum, as well as Cheryl N. Noble's seminal "Normative Ethical Theories" (49–64). It is noteworthy that, in the latter, Noble explicitly denies that she is attacking the idea of normative *ethics*. Her criticisms of the idea of normative ethical *theory*, she says, "are aimed at a particular conception of what normative ethics should be" (62, n. 1).

[†]As Noble points out, a normative theory may also be expected to say something about cases "where we have no intuitions on where our intuitions are inchoate or weak" (ibid. 61): and, to some of us, it is indeed one of the oddities of utilitarianism that certain states of affairs, concerning which we may have no moral intuitions at all, emerge from it as so definitively "morally better" than others. I would like to argue for the incoherence of the idea that a theory could attach a truth-value to a sentence (employing a moral term) which lacked a sense outside the theory, but space does not permit. See, however, P. Foot, "Utilitarianism and the Virtues," *Mind* 94 (1985), 196–209.

for subscribing to "anti-theory in ethics" is the belief that we should not be looking to science to provide us with our model of moral knowledge. Our "intuitions" in ethics do not play the same role *vis-à-vis* the systematic articulation of moral knowledge as our "observations" play *vis-à-vis* the systematic articulation of scientific knowledge; many of the goals appropriate to scientific knowledge—universality, consistency, completeness, simplicity—are not appropriate to moral knowledge; the acquisition of moral knowledge involves the training of the emotions in a way that the acquisition of scientific knowledge does not; and so on.

Clearly, many different issues are involved in the question of the extent to which moral knowledge should be modeled on scientific knowledge. The one I want to focus on here is the issue of whether a normative ethics should provide a decision procedure which enables us to resolve all moral dilemmas. Should it, to rephrase the question I asked above, (1) direct us to think about moral dilemmas in the belief that they *must* have a resolution, and that it is the business of the normative ethics in question to provide one? Or should it (2) have built into it the possibility of there being, as David Wiggins puts it, some "absolutely undecidable questions—e.g. cases where . . . nothing could count as *the* reasonable practical answer,"* counting questions about dilemmas of the sort described as amongst them? Or should it (3) be sufficiently flexible to allow for a comprehensible disagreement on this issue between to proponents of the normative ethics in question?

If we are to avoid modeling normative ethics mindlessly on scientific theory, we should not simply assume that the first position is the correct one. But rejection of such a model is not enough to justify the second position either. Someone might believe that for *any* dilemma there must be something that counts as the right way out of it, without believing that normative ethics remotely resembles scientific theory, perhaps because they subscribe to a version of realism (in Dummett's sense of "realism").** More particularly, someone might believe on religious grounds that if I find myself, through no fault of my own, confronted with a dilemma (of the sort described), there must be something that counts as the right way out of it.[†] The belief in God's providence does indeed involve, as Geach says, the thought that "God does not require of a faithful servant the desperate choice between sin and sin."[††] Should a normative ethics be such that it cannot be shared by a realist and an anti-realist (again in Dummett's sense)? Or by an atheist and a theist? It seems to me that a normative ethics should be able to accommodate such differences, and so I subscribe to the third position outlined above.

---

*D. Wiggins, "Truth, Invention and the Meaning of Life," *Proceedings of the British Academy* 62 (1976), 371, my italics. I have omitted the phrase that attracted Foot's criticism (see above, n. 15), in which Wiggins seems to imply that undecidable questions are undecidable *because* the alternatives are particularly terrible.

**M. Dummett, *Truth and Other Enigmas* (London, 1978), 1–24 and 145–65. For a brief helpful discussion of the distinction between Dummett-type realism and cognitivism in ethics, see Foot, "Moral Realism and Moral Dilemma," 397–8.

[†]I am assuming that the qualification "through no fault of my own" is all-important, since I cannot imagine why anyone should think (except through oversight) that there must always be a right action I can do to get myself out of any mess that I have got myself into through previous wrongdoing.

[††]P. Geach, *The Virtues* (Cambridge, 1977), 155.

Which position utilitarians and deontologists might espouse is not my concern here; I want to make clear how it is that virtue ethics is able to accommodate the third.*

Let us return to V1—"An action is right if it is what a virtuous agent would characteristically do in the circumstances." This makes it clear that if two people disagree about the possibility of irresolvable moral dilemmas, their disagreement will manifest itself in what they say about the virtue of agents. So let us suppose that two candidates for being virtuous agents are each faced with their own case of the same dilemma. (I do not want to defend the view that each situation is unique in such a way that nothing would count as two agents being in the same circumstances and faced with the same dilemma.) And, after much thought, one does A and the other does B.

Now, those who believe that there cannot be irresolvable dilemmas (of the sort described) can say that, in the particular case, at least one agent, say the one who did A, thereby showed themselves to be lacking in virtue, perhaps in that practical wisdom which is an essential aspect of each of the "non-intellectual" virtues. ("If you can *see* no way out but a lie, the lie may be the least wicked of the alternatives you can discern: it is still wicked, and you should blame yourself that you lacked the wisdom of St. Joan or St. Athanasius, to extricate yourself without lying. It is not a matter of foxy cleverness; "the testimony of the Lord is sure and giveth wisdom to the simple."** Thus Geach, discussing the absolute prohibition against lying in the context of the claim that God "does not require of any man a choice between sin and sin.") Or they can say that a least one agent must have been lacking in virtue, without claiming to know which.

But those who believe that there are, or may be, irresolvable dilemmas can suppose that both agents are not merely candidates for being, but actually are, virtuous agents. For to believe in such dilemmas is to believe in cases in which even the perfect practical wisdom that the most idealized virtuous agent has does not direct her to do, say, A rather than B. And then the fact that these virtuous agents acted differently, despite being in the same circumstances, *determines* the fact that there is no answer to the question "What is *the* right thing to do in these circumstances?" For if it is true both that *a* virtuous agent would do A, and that *a* virtuous agent would do B (as it is, since, *ex hypothesi*, one did do A and the other B), then both A and B are, in the circumstances, right, according to V1.

The acceptance of this should not be taken as a counsel of despair, nor as an excuse for moral irresponsibility. It does not license coin-tossing when one is faced

*I had hitherto overlooked the possibility of this third position, and hence had emphasized the fact that virtue ethics could occupy the second. But I subsequently heard Philippa Foot point out that Aquinas, Anscombe, and Geach should surely be classified as virtue ethicists, notwithstanding their absolutist stance on many of the familiar deontological rules; and, given their consequent stance on the clear resolvability of some dilemmas that others find irresolvable, this prompted me to look at what a commitment to resolvability (with respect to dilemmas *as described*) might look like within virtue ethics. I am grateful to the editor for reminding me of the further possibility of his own "realist" position. (Aristotle is clearly an absolutist too, at least with respect to "adultery" (*moikheia*), theft, and murder (see *NE* 1107^a11–12), but where he stands (or should stand, to be consistent) on irresolvable dilemmas of the sort described is, I think, entirely unclear.)

**Geach, *The Virtues*, 121.

with a putative dilemma, for the moral choices we find most difficult do not come to us conveniently labeled as "resolvable" or "irresolvable." I was careful to specify that the two candidates for being virtuous agents acted only "after much thought." It will always be necessary to think very hard before accepting the idea that a particular moral decision does not have one right issue, and, even on the rare occasions on which she eventually reached the conclusion that this is such a case, would the virtuous agent toss a coin? Of course not.

No doubt someone will say, "Well, if she really thinks the dilemma is irresolvable, why not, according to virtue ethics?," and the answer must, I think, be *ad hominem*. If their conception of the virtuous agent—of someone with the character traits of justice, honesty, compassion, kindness, loyalty, wisdom, etc.—really is of someone who would resort to coin-tossing when confronted with what she believed to be an irresolvable dilemma, then that is the bizarre conception they bring to virtue ethics, and they must, presumably, think that there is nothing morally irresponsible or light-minded about coin-tossing in such cases. So they should not want virtue ethics to explain "why not." But if their conception of the virtuous agent does not admit of her acting thus—if they think such coin-tossing would be irresponsible, or light-minded, or indeed simply insane—then they have no need to ask the question. *My* question was, "Would the virtuous agent toss a coin?"; they agree that of course she would not. Why not? Because it would be irresponsible, or light-minded, or the height of folly.

The acceptance of the possibility of irresolvable dilemmas within virtue ethics (by those of us who do accept it) should not be seen in itself as conceding much to "pluralism." If I say that I can imagine a case in which two virtuous agents are faced with a dilemma, and one does A while the other does B, I am not saying that I am imagining a case in which the two virtuous agents each think that what the other does is wrong (vicious, contrary to virtue) because they have radically different views about what is required by a certain virtue, or about whether something is to be greatly valued or of little importance. I am imagining a case in which my two virtuous agents have the same "moral views" about everything, up to and including the view that, in this particular case, neither decision is *the* right one, and hence neither is wrong. Each recognizes the propriety of the other's reason for doing what she did—say, "To avoid *that* evil," "To secure *this* good"—for her recognition of the fact that this is as good a moral reason as her own (say, "To avoid *this* evil," "To secure *that* good") is what forced each to accept the idea that the dilemma was irresolvable in the first place. Though each can give such a reason for what they did (A in one case, B in the other), neither attempts to give "the moral reason" why they did one *rather than* the other. The "reason" for or explanation of *that* would be, if available at all, in terms of psychological autobiography ("I decided to sleep on it, and when I woke up I just found myself thinking in terms of doing A," or "I just felt terrified at the thought of doing A: I'm sure this was totally irrational, but I did, so I did B").*

---

*It must be remembered that, *ex hypothesi*, these are things said by virtuous agents about what they did when confronted with an irresolvable dilemma. Of course they would be very irresponsible accounts of why one had done A rather than B in a resolvable case.

The topic of this chapter has been the view that virtue ethics cannot be a normative rival to utilitarianism and deontology because "it cannot tell us what we should do." In defending the existence of normative virtue ethics I have not attempted to argue that it can "tell us what we should do" in such a way that the difficult business of acting well is made easy for us. I have not only admitted but welcomed the fact that, in some cases, moral wisdom is required if the v-rules are to be applied correctly and apparent dilemmas thereby resolved (or indeed identified, since a choice that may seem quite straightforward to the foolish or wicked may rightly appear difficult, calling for much thought, to the wise). Nor have I attempted to show that virtue ethics is guaranteed to be able to resolve every dilemma. It seems bizarre to insist that a normative ethics must be able to do this prior to forming a reasonable belief that there cannot be irresolvable dilemmas, but those who have formed such a belief may share a normative ethics with those who have different views concerning realism, or the existence of God. A normative ethics, I suggested, should be able to accommodate both views on this question, as virtue ethics does, not model itself mindlessly on scientific theory.*

Study Questions

1. How, according to Hursthouse, does virtue ethics provide guidance about how to act in particular situations? How is virtue ethics in this respect different from (or similar to) Kantian or other deontological approaches and utilitarian approaches?
2. Why is moral education important for virtue ethics? Is this a strength or a weakness of the view? Is, or should moral education be equally important for deontological and utilitarian approaches?
3. Construct a situation in which a person is confronted with a difficult moral conflict. Then compare the respective ways in which virtue ethics, a deontological view, and a utilitarian view would try to resolve the conflict.
4. In your view can there be unresolvable moral dilemmas (i.e., moral conflicts in which there is no right response, or even moral conflicts in which one cannot avoid doing wrong, or acting contrary to a virtue, no matter what one chooses)? Explain.

Selected Bibliography

Hursthouse, Rosalind. *On Virtue Ethics* (Oxford/New York: Oxford University Press, 2000). An exposition of virtue ethics.

*At the request of the editor, I have repeated here several points I have made in two other papers, "Virtue Theory and Abortion," *Philosophy and Public Affairs* 20 (1991), 223–46, and "Applying Virtue Ethics," in *Virtues and Reasons: Phillipa Foot and Moral Theory,* ed. R. Hurthouse, G. Lawrence, and W. S. Quinn (Oxford, 1995), 57–75.

————. "Applying Virtue Ethics," in Rosalind Hursthouse, Gavin Lawrence, and Warren Quinn, eds. *Virtues and Reasons: Philippa Foot and Moral Theory* (Oxford/New York: Oxford University Press, 1995).

————. "Virtue Theory and Abortion," *Philosophy and Public Affairs* 20 (1991): 223–246.

Other readings on virtue ethics are given following the essay by Philippa Foot.

28

SUSAN WOLF

———

Is it always better to be morally better? Should one be as morally good as possible? These questions are raised by Susan Wolf in the next essay. At issue is the role that moral

> *. . . there seems to be a limit to how much morality we can stand.*

commitments and ideals should play in our lives, and the relation between moral values and nonmoral values. Wolf depicts examples of people whom she calls "moral saints"—individuals who are as morally good as possible, and fully devoted to pursuing what is morally valuable. Do such individuals represent reasonable and attractive personal ideals that we should strive to realize? Wolf suggests not, because their commitment to moral value will prevent them from realizing important non-moral values and excellences that make a life admirable and worth living. If so, there appears to be a tension between moral values and other kinds of values that go into the good and worthwhile life.

One way to see how this question arises is to think about the role that moral reasons play in our thinking about how to act. On common understandings of morality, moral reasons have a special priority—at least from within the moral point of view. Moral reasons can set limits to the pursuit of personal goals and other kinds of value. In cases of conflict between moral reasons and nonmoral reasons, many people think that moral reasons should be overriding. This is a feature of Kant's moral view—as seen in his claim that a good will has absolute value, and is the condition of the value of any other thing—as well as many versions of utilitarianism. Furthermore, the world in which we live seems to present endless opportunity for action directed at moral improvement. It may seem that there should be no limit to our commitment to morality if moral values have this special priority. But there are also many nonmoral values and activities that play a role in the worthwhile life. Is there a danger that deep commitment to morality will crowd out other kinds of values and worthwhile activities? Or can the moral point of view leave room for all reasonable nonmoral values? Are there limits to the demands that morality can make on our lives? And if so, are these limits drawn from within the moral point of view? Or are they drawn from outside the moral point of view? How are we to accommodate the competing claims of moral and nonmoral value? Susan Wolf's essay addresses these and other issues.

Susan Wolf has taught at Harvard University, the University of Maryland, and the Johns Hopkins University. She is currently professor of philosophy at the University of North Carolina, Chapel Hill. She is the author of *Freedom Within Reason* (1990), and many articles in moral philosophy.

———

Moral Saints*

I don't know whether there are any moral saints. But if there are, I am glad that neither I nor those about whom I care most are among them. By *moral saint* I mean a person whose every action is as morally good as possible, a person, that is, who is as morally worthy as can be. Though I shall in a moment acknowledge the variety of types of person that might be thought to satisfy this description, it seems to me that none of these types serve as unequivocally compelling personal ideals. In other words, I believe that moral perfection, in the sense of moral saintliness, does not constitute a model of personal well-being toward which it would be particularly rational or good or desirable for a human being to strive.

Outside the context of moral discussion, this will strike many as an obvious point. But, within that context, the point, if it be granted, will be granted with some discomfort. For within that context it is generally assumed that one ought to be as morally good as possible and that what limits there are to morality's hold on us are set by features of human nature of which we ought not to be proud. If, as I believe, the ideas that are derivable from common sense and philosophically popular moral theories do not support these assumptions, then something has to change. Either we must change our moral theories in ways that will make them yield more palatable ideals, or, as I shall argue, we must change our conception of what is involved in affirming a moral theory.

In this paper, I wish to examine the notion of a moral saint, first, to understand what a moral saint would be like and why such a being would be unattractive, and, second, to raise some questions about the significance of this paradoxical figure for moral philosophy. I shall look first at the model(s) of moral sainthood that might be extrapolated from the morality or moralities of common sense. Then I shall consider what relations these have to conclusions that can be drawn from utilitarian and Kantian moral theories. Finally, I shall speculate on the implications of these considerations for moral philosophy.

*I have benefited from the comments of many people who have heard or read an earlier draft of this paper. I wish particularly to thank Douglas MacLean, Robert Nozick, Martha Nussbaum, and the Society for Ethics and Legal Philosophy.

Moral Saints and Common Sense

Consider first what, pretheoretically, would count for us—contemporary members of Western culture—as a moral saint. A necessary condition of moral sainthood would be that one's life be dominated by a commitment to improving the welfare of others or of society as a whole. As to what role this commitment must play in the individual's motivational system, two contrasting accounts suggest themselves to me which might equally be thought to quality a person for moral sainthood.

First, a moral saint might be someone whose concern for others plays the role that is played in most of our lives by more selfish, or, at any rate, less morally worthy concerns. For the moral saint, the promotion of the welfare of others might play the role that is played for most of us by the enjoyment of material comforts, the opportunity to engage in the intellectual and physical activities of our choice, and the love, respect, and companionship of people whom we love, respect, and enjoy. The happiness of the moral saint, then, would truly lie in the happiness of others, and so he would devote himself to others gladly, and with a whole and open heart.

On the other hand, a moral saint might be someone for whom the basic ingredients of happiness are not unlike those of most of the rest of us. What makes him a moral saint is rather that he pays little or no attention to his own happiness in light of the overriding importance he gives to the wider concerns of morality. In other words, this person sacrifices his own interests to the interests of others, and feels the sacrifice as such.

Roughly, these two models may be distinguished according to whether one thinks of the moral saint as being a saint out of love or one thinks of the moral saint as being a saint out of duty (or some other intellectual appreciation and recognition of moral principles). We may refer to the first model as the model of the Loving Saint; to the second, as the model of the Rational Saint

The two models differ considerably with respect to the qualities of the motives of the individuals who conform to them. But this difference would have limited effect on the saints' respective public personalities. The shared content of what these individuals are motivated to be—namely, as morally good as possible—would play the dominant role in the determination of their characters. Of course, just as a variety of larger-scale projects, from tending the sick to political campaigning, may be equally and maximally morally worthy, so a variety of characters are compatible with the ideal of moral sainthood. One moral saint may be more or less jovial, more of less garrulous, more or less athletic than another. But, above all, a moral saint must have and cultivate those qualities which are apt to allow him to treat others as justly and kindly as possible. He will have the standard moral virtues to a nonstandard degree. He will be patient, considerate, even-tempered, hospitable, charitable in thought as well as in deed. He will be very reluctant to make negative judgments of other people. He will be careful not to favor some people over others on the basis of properties they could not help but have.

Perhaps what I have already said is enough to make some people begin to regard the absence of moral saints in their lives as a blessing. For there comes a point in the listing of virtues that a moral saint is likely to have where one might naturally begin to wonder whether the moral saint isn't, after all, too good—if not too good for his own good, at least too good for his own well-being. For the moral virtues, given that they are, by hypothesis, *all* present in the same individual, and to an extreme degree, are apt to crowd out the nonmoral virtues, as well as many of the interests and personal characteristics that we generally think contribute to a healthy, well-rounded, richly developed character.

In other words, if the moral saint is devoting all his time to feeding the hungry or healing the sick or raising money for Oxfam, then necessarily he is not reading Victorian novels, playing the oboe, or improving his backhand. Although no one of the interests or tastes in the category containing these latter activities could be claimed to be a necessary element in a life well lived, a life in which *none* of these possible aspects of character are developed may seem to be a life strangely barren.

The reasons why a moral saint cannot, in general, encourage the discovery and development of significant nonmoral interests and skills are not logical but practical reasons. There are, in addition, a class of nonmoral characteristics that a moral saint cannot encourage in himself for reasons that are not just practical. There is a more substantial tension between having any of these qualities unashamedly and being a moral saint. These qualities might be described as going against the moral grain. For example, a cynical or sarcastic wit, or a sense of humor that appreciates this kind of wit in others, requires that one take an attitude of resignation and pessimism toward the flaws and vices to be found in the world. A moral saint, on the other hand, has reason to take an attitude in opposition to this—he should try to look for the best in people, give them the benefit of the doubt as long as possible, try to improve regrettable situations as long as there is any hope of success. This suggests that, although a moral saint might well enjoy a good episode of *Father Knows Best*, he may not in good conscience be able to laugh at a Marx Brothers movie or enjoy a play by George Bernard Shaw.

An interest in something like gourmet cooking will be, for different reasons, difficult for a moral saint to rest easy with. For it seems to me that no plausible argument can justify the use of human resources involved in producing a *paté de canard en croute* against possible alternative beneficent ends to which these resources might be put. If there is a justification for the institution of haute cuisine, it is one which rests on the decision *not* to justify every activity against morally beneficial alternatives, and this is a decision a moral saint will never make. Presumably, an interest in high fashion or interior design will fare much the same, as will, very possibly, a cultivation of the finer arts as well.

A moral saint will have to be very, very nice. It is important that he not be offensive. The worry is that, as a result, he will have to be dull-witted or humorless or bland.

This worry is confirmed when we consider what sorts of characters, taken and refined both from life and from fiction, typically form our ideals. One would hope they would be figures who are morally good—and by this I mean more than just not morally bad—but one would hope, too, that they are not *just* morally good, but talented or accomplished or attractive in nonmoral ways as well. We may make ideals out of athletes, scholars, artists—more frivolously, out of cowboys, private eyes, and rock stars. We may strive for Katharine Hepburn's grace, Paul Newman's "cool"; we are attracted to the high-spirited passionate nature of Natasha Rostov; we admire the keen perceptiveness of Lambert Strether.* Though there is certainly nothing immoral about the ideal characters or traits I have in mind, they cannot be superimposed upon the ideal of a moral saint. For although it is a part of many of these ideals that the characters set high, and not merely acceptable, moral standards for themselves, it is also essential to their power and attractiveness that the moral strengths go, so to speak, alongside of specific, independently admirable, nonmoral ground projects and dominant personal traits.

When one does finally turn one's eyes toward lives that are dominated by explicitly moral commitments, moreover, one finds oneself relieved at the discovery of idiosyncrasies or eccentricities not quite in line with the picture of moral perfection. One prefers the blunt, tactless, and opinionated Betsy Trotwood to the unfailingly kind and patient Agnes Copperfield;** one prefers the mischievousness and the sense of irony in Chesterton's Father Brown to the innocence and undiscriminating love of St. Francis.

It seems that, as we look in our ideals for people who achieve nonmoral varieties of personal excellence in conjunction with or colored by some version of high moral tone, we look in our paragons of moral excellence for people whose moral achievements occur in conjunction with or colored by some interests or traits that have low moral tone. In other words, there seems to be a limit to how much morality we can stand.

One might suspect that the essence of the problem is simply that there is a limit to how much of *any* single value, or any single type of value, we can stand. Our objection then would not be specific to a life in which one's dominant concern is morality, but would apply to any life that can be so completely characterized by an extraordinarily dominant concern. The objection in that case would reduce to the recognition that such a life is incompatible with well-roundedness. If that were the objection, one would fairly reply that well-roundedness is no more supreme a virtue than the totality of moral virtues embodied by the idea it is being used to criticize. But I think this misidentifies the objection. For the way in which a concern for morality may dominate a life, or, more to the point, the way in which it may dominate an ideal of life, is not easily imagined by analogy to the dominance an aspiration to become an Olympic swimmer or a concert pianist might have.

A person who is passionately committed to one of these latter concerns might decide that her attachment to it is strong enough to be worth the sacrifice of her ability to maintain and pursue a significant portion of what else life might offer which a proper devotion to her dominant passion would require. But a desire to be as morally good as possible is not likely to take the form of one desire among others which, because of its peculiar psychological strength, requires one to forego the pursuit of other weaker and separately less demanding desires. Rather, the desire to be as morally good as possible is apt to have the character not just of a

*Lambert Strether is the main character in Henry James's novel *The Ambassadors*. Natasha Rostove is a character in Leo Tolstoy's *War and Peace*.—[Ed.]
**Betsy Trotwood and Agnes Copperfield are characters in Charles Dickens's novel *David Copperfield*.—[Ed.]

stronger, but of a higher desire, which does not merely successfully compete with one's other desires but which rather subsumes or demotes them. The sacrifice of other interests for the interest in morality, then, will have the character, not of a choice, but of an imperative.

Moreover, there is something odd about the idea of morality itself, or moral goodness, serving as the object of a dominant passion in the way that a more concrete and specific vision of a goal (even a concrete *moral* goal) might be imagined to serve. Morality itself does not seem to be a suitable object of passion. Thus, when one reflects, for example, on the Loving Saint easily and gladly giving us his fishing trip or his stereo or his hot fudge sundae at the drop of the moral hat, one is apt to wonder not at how much he loves morality, but at how little he loves these other things. One thinks that, if he can give these up so easily, he does not know what it *is* to truly love them. There seems, in other words, to be a kind of joy which the Loving Saint, either by nature or by practice, is incapable of experiencing. The Rational Saint, on the other hand, might retain strong nonmoral and concrete desires—he simply denies himself the opportunity to act on them. But this is no less troubling. The Loving Saint one might suspect of missing a piece of perceptual machinery, of being blind to some of what the world has to offer. The Rational Saint, who sees it but foregoes it, one suspects of having a different problem—a pathological fear of damnation, perhaps, or an extreme form of self-hatred that interferes with his ability to enjoy the enjoyable in life.

In other words, the ideal of a life of moral sainthood disturbs not simply because it is an ideal of a life in which morality unduly dominates. The normal person's direct and specific desires for objects, activities, and events that conflict with the attainment of moral perfection are not simply sacrificed but removed, suppressed, or subsumed. The way in which morality, unlike other possible goals, is apt to dominate is particularly disturbing, for it seems to require either the lack or the denial of the existence of an identifiable, personal self.

This distinctively troubling feature is not, I think, absolutely unique to the ideal of the moral saint, as I have been using that phrase. It is shared by the conception of the pure aesthete, by a certain kind of religious ideal, and, somewhat paradoxically, by the model of the thorough-going, self-conscious egoist. It is not a coincidence that the ways of comprehending the world of which these ideals are the extreme embodiments are sometimes described as "moralities" themselves. At any rate, they compete with what we ordinarily mean by "morality." Nor is it a coincidence that these ideals are naturally described as fanatical. But it is easy to see that these other types of perfection cannot serve as satisfactory personal ideals; for the realization of these ideals would be straightforwardly immoral. It may come as a surprise to some that there may in addition be such a thing as a *moral* fanatic.

Some will object that I am being unfair to "common-sense morality"—that it does not really require a moral saint to be either a disgustingly goody-goody or an obsessive ascetic. Admittedly, there is no logical inconsistency between having any of the personal characteristics I have mentioned and being a moral saint. It is not morally wrong to notice the faults and shortcomings of others or to recognize and appreciate nonmoral talents and skills. Nor is it immoral to be an avid Celtics fan or to have a passion for caviar or to be an excellent cellist. With enough imagination, we can always contrive a suitable history and set of circumstances that will embrace such characteristics in one or another specific fictional story of a perfect moral saint.

If one turned onto the path of moral sainthood relatively late in life, one may have already developed interests that can be turned to moral purposes. It may be that a good golf game is just what is needed to secure that big donation to Oxfam. Perhaps the cultivation of one's exceptional artistic talent will turn out to be the way one can make one's greatest contribution to society. Furthermore, one might stumble upon joys and skills in the very service of morality. If, because the children are short a ninth player for the team, one's generous offer to serve reveals a natural fielding arm or if one's part in the campaign against nuclear power requires accepting a lobbyist's invitation to lunch at Le Lion d'Or, there is no moral gain in denying the satisfaction one gets from these activities. The moral saint, then, may, by happy accident, find himself with nonmoral virtues on which he can capitalize morally or which make psychological demands to which he has no choice but to attend. The point is that, for a moral saint, the existence of these interests and skills can be given at best the status of happy accidents—they cannot be encouraged for their own sakes as distinct, independent aspects of the realization of human good.

It must be remembered that from the fact that there is a tension between having any of these qualities and being a moral saint it does not follow that having any of these qualities is immoral. For it is not part of common-sense morality that one ought to be a moral saint. Still, if someone just happened to want to be a moral saint, he or she would not have or encourage these qualities, and, on the basis of our common-sense values, this counts as a reason *not* to want to be a moral saint.

One might still wonder what kind of reason this is, and what kind of conclusion this properly allows us to draw. For the fact that the models of moral saints are unattractive does not necessarily mean that they are unsuitable ideals. Perhaps they are unattractive because they make us feel uncomfortable—they highlight our own weaknesses, vices, and flaws. If so, the fault lies not in the characters of the saints, but in those of our unsaintly selves.

To be sure, some of the reasons behind the disaffection we feel for the model of moral sainthood have to do with a reluctance to criticize ourselves and a reluctance to committing ourselves to trying to give up activities and interests that we heartily enjoy. These considerations might provide an *excuse* for the fact that we are not moral saints, but they do not provide a basis for criticizing sainthood as a possible ideal. Since these considerations rely on an appeal to the egoistic, hedonistic side of our natures, to use them as a basis for criticizing the ideal of the moral saint would be at best to beg the question and at worst to glorify features of ourselves that ought to be condemned.

The fact that the moral saint would be without qualities which we have and which, indeed, we like to have, does not in itself provide reason to condemn the ideal of the moral saint. The fact that some of these qualities are good qualities, however, and that they are qualities we *ought* to like, does provide reason to discourage this ideal and to offer other ideals in its place. In other words, some of the qualities the moral saint necessarily lacks are virtues, albeit nonmoral virtues, in the unsaintly characters who have them. The feats of Groucho Marx, Reggie Jackson, and the head chef at Lutèce are impressive accomplishments that it is not only permissible but positively appropriate to recognize as such. In general, the admiration of and striving toward achieving any of a great variety of forms of personal excellence are character traits it is valuable and desirable for people to have. In advocating the development of these varieties of excellence, we advocate nonmoral reasons for acting, and in thinking that it is good for a person to strive for an ideal that gives a substantial role to the interests and values that correspond to these virtues, we implicitly acknowledge the goodness of ideals incompatible with that of the moral saint. Finally, if we think that it is *as* good, or even better for a person to strive for one of these ideals than it is for him or her to strive for and realize the ideal of the moral saint, we express a conviction that it is good not to be a moral saint.

Moral Saints and Moral Theories

I have tried so far to paint a picture—or, rather, two pictures—of what a moral saint might be like, drawing on what I take to be the attitudes and beliefs about morality prevalent in contemporary, common-sense thought. To my suggestion that common-sense morality generates conceptions of moral saints that are unattractive or otherwise unacceptable, it is open to someone to reply, "so much the worse for common-sense morality." After all, it is often claimed that the goal of moral philosophy is to correct and improve upon common-sense morality, and I have as yet given no attention to the question of what conceptions of moral sainthood, if any, are generated from the leading moral theories of our time.

A quick, breezy reading of utilitarian and Kantian writings will suggest the images, respectively, of the Loving Saint and the Rational Saint. A utilitarian, with his emphasis on happiness, will certainly prefer the Loving Saint to the Rational one, since the Loving Saint will himself be a happier person than the Rational Saint. A Kantian, with his emphasis on reason, on the other hand, will find at least as much to praise in the latter as in the former. Still, both models, drawn as they are from common sense, appeal to an impure mixture of utilitarian and Kantian intuitions. A more careful examination of these moral theories raises questions about whether either model of moral sainthood would really be advocated by a believer in the explicit doctrines associated with either of these views.

Certainly, the utilitarian in no way denies the value of self-realization. He in no way disparages the development of interests, talents, and other personally attractive traits that I have claimed the moral saint would be without. Indeed, since just these features enhance the happiness both of the individuals who possess them and of those with whom they associate, the ability to promote these features both in oneself and in others will have considerable positive weight in utilitarian calculations.

This implies that the utilitarian would not support moral sainthood as a universal ideal. A world in which everyone, or even a large number of people, achieved moral sainthood—even a world in which they *strove* to achieve it—would probably contain less happiness than a world in which people realized a diversity of ideals involving a variety of personal and perfectionist values. More pragmatic considerations also suggest that, if the utilitarian wants to influence more people to achieve more good, then he would do better to encourage them to pursue happiness-producing goals that are more attractive and more within a normal person's reach.

These considerations still leave open, however, the question of what kind of an ideal the committed utilitarian should privately aspire to himself. Utilitarianism requires him to want to achieve the greatest general happiness, and this would seem to commit him to the ideal of the moral saint.

One might try to use the claims I made earlier as a basis for an argument that a utilitarian should choose to give up utilitarianism. If, as I have said, a moral saint would be a less happy person both to be and to be around than many other possible ideals, perhaps one could create more total happiness by not trying too hard to promote the total happiness. But this argument is simply unconvincing in light of the empirical circumstances of our world. The gain in happiness that would accrue to oneself and one's neighbors by a more well-rounded, richer life than that of the moral saint would be pathetically small in comparison to the amount by which one could increase the general happiness if one devoted oneself explicitly to the care of the sick, the downtrodden, the starving, and the homeless. Of course, there may be psychological limits to the extent to which a person can devote himself to such things without going crazy. But the utilitarian's individual limitations would not thereby become a positive feature of his personal ideals.

The unattractiveness of the moral saint, then, ought not rationally convince the utilitarian to abandon his utilitarianism. It may, however, convince him to take efforts not to wear his saintly moral aspirations on his sleeve. If it is not too difficult, the utilitarian will try not to make those around him uncomfortable. He will not want to appear "holier than thou"; he will not want to inhibit others' ability to enjoy themselves. In practice, this might make the perfect utilitarian a less nauseating companion than the moral saint I earlier portrayed. But insofar as this kind of reasoning produces a more bearable public personality, it is at the cost of giving him a personality that must be evaluated as hypocritical and condescending when his private thoughts and attitudes are taken into account.

Still, the criticisms I have realized against the saint of common-sense morality should make some difference to the utilitarian's conception of an ideal which neither requires him to abandon his utilitarian principles nor forces him to fake an interest he does not have or a judgment he does not make. For it may be that a limited and carefully monitored allotment of time and energy to be devoted to the pursuit of some nonmoral interests or to the development of some nonmoral talents would make a person a better contributor to the general welfare than he would be if he allowed himself no indulgences of this sort. The enjoyment of such activities in no way compromises a commitment to utilitarian principles as long as the involvement with these activities is conditioned by a willingness to give them up whenever it is recognized that they cease to be in the general interest.

This will go some way in mitigating the picture of the loving saint that an understanding of utilitarianism will on first impression suggest. But I think it will not go very far. For the limitations on time and energy will have to be rather severe, and the need to monitor will restrict not only the extent but also the quality of one's attachment to these interests and traits. They are only weak and somewhat peculiar sorts of passions to which one can consciously remain so conditionally committed. Moreover, the way in which the utilitarian can enjoy these "extra-curricular" aspects of his life is simply not the way in which these aspects are to be enjoyed insofar as they figure into our less saintly ideals.

The problem is not exactly that the utilitarian values these aspects of his life only as a means to an end, for the enjoyment he and others get from these aspects are not a means to, but a part of, the general happiness. Nonetheless, he values these things only because of and insofar as they *are* a part of the general happiness. He values them, as it were, under the description "a contribution to the general happiness." This is to be contrasted with the various ways in which these aspects of life may be valued by nonutilitarians. A person might love literature because of the insights into human nature literature affords. Another might love the cultivation of roses because roses are things of great beauty and delicacy. It may be true that these features of the respective activities also explain why these activities are happiness-producing. But, to the nonutilitarian, this may not be the point. For if one values these activities in these more direct ways, one may not be willing to exchange them for others that produce an equal, or even a greater amount of happiness. From that point of view, it is not because they produce happiness that these activities are valuable; it is because these activities are valuable in more direct and specific ways that they produce happiness.

To adopt a phrase of Bernard Williams', the utilitarian's manner of valuing the not explicitly moral aspects of his life "provides (him) with one thought too many."* The requirement that the utilitarian have this thought—periodically, at least—is indicative of not only a weakness but a shallowness in his appreciation of the aspects in question. Thus, the ideals toward which a utilitarian could acceptably strive would remain too close to the model of the common-sense moral saint to escape the criticisms of that model which I earlier suggested. Whether a Kantian would be similarly committed to so restrictive and unattractive a range of possible ideals is a somewhat more difficult question.

The Kantian believes that being morally worthy consists in always acting from maxims that one could will to be universal law, and doing this not out of any pathological desire but out of reverence for the moral law as such. Or, to take a different formulation of the categorical imperative, the Kantian believes that moral action consists in treating other persons always as ends and never as means only. Presumably, and according to Kant himself, the Kantian thereby commits himself to some degree of benevolence as well as to the rules of fair play. But we surely would not will that *every* person become a moral saint, and treating others as ends hardly requires bending over backwards to protect and promote their interests. On one interpretation of Kantian doctrine, then, moral perfection would be achieved simply by unerring obedience to a limited set of side-constraints. On this interpretation, Kantian theory simply does not yield an ideal conception of a person of any fullness comparable to that of the moral saints I have so far been portraying.

On the other hand, Kant does say explicitly that we have a duty of benevolence, a duty not only to allow others to pursue their ends, but to take up their ends as our own. In addition, we have positive duties to ourselves, duties to increase our natural as well as our moral perfection. These duties are unlimited in the degree to which they *may* dominate a life. If action in accordance with and motivated by the thought of these duties is considered virtuous, it is natural to assume that the more one

*"Persons, Character and Morality" in Amelie Rorty, ed., *The Identities of Persons* (Berkeley: Univ. of California Press, 1976), p. 214.

performs such actions, the more virtuous one is. Moreover, of virtue in general Kant says, "it is an ideal which is unattainable while yet our duty is constantly to approximate to it."* On this interpretation, then, the Kantian moral saint, like the other moral saints I have been considering, is dominated by the motivation to be moral.

Which of these interpretations of Kant one prefers will depend on the interpretation and the importance one gives to the role of the imperfect duties in Kant's over-all system. Rather than choose between them here, I shall consider each briefly in turn.

On the second interpretation of Kant, the Kantian moral saint is, not surprisingly, subject to many of the same objections I have been raising against other versions of moral sainthood. Though the Kantian saint may differ from the utilitarian saint as to *which* actions he is bound to perform and which he is bound to refrain from performing, I suspect that the range of activities acceptable to the Kantian saint will remain objectionably restrictive. Moreover, the manner in which the Kantian saint must think about and justify the activities he pursues and the character traits he develops will strike us, as it did with the utilitarian saint, as containing "one thought too many." As the utilitarian could value his activities and character traits only insofar as they fell under the description of "contributions to the general happiness," the Kantian would have to value his activities and character traits insofar as they were manifestations of respect for the moral law. If the development of our powers to achieve physical, intellectual, or artistic excellence, or the activities directed toward making others happy are to have any moral worth, they must arise from a reverence for the dignity that members of our species have as a result of being endowed with pure practical reason. This is a good and noble motivation, to be sure. But it is hardly what one expects to be dominantly behind a person's aspirations to dance as well as Fred Astaire, to paint as well as Picasso, or to solve some outstanding problem in abstract algebra, and it is hardly what one hopes to find lying dominantly behind a father's action on behalf of his son or a lover's on behalf of her beloved.

Since the basic problem with any of the models of moral sainthood we have been considering is that they are dominated by a single, all-important value under which all other possible values must be subsumed, it may seem that the alternative interpretation of Kant, as providing a stringent but finite set of obligations and constraints, might provide a more acceptable morality. According to this interpretation of Kant, one is as morally good as can be so long as one devotes some limited portion of one's energies toward altruism and the maintenance of one's physical and spiritual health, and otherwise pursues one's independently motivated interests and values in such a way as to avoid overstepping certain bounds. Certainly, if it be a requirement of an acceptable moral theory that perfect obedience to its laws and maximal devotion to its interests and concerns be something we can wholeheartedly strive for in ourselves and wish for in those around us, it will count in favor of this brand of Kantianism that its commands can be fulfilled without swallowing up the perfect moral agent's entire personality.

Even this more limited understanding of morality, if its connection to Kant's views is to be taken at all seriously, is not likely to give an unqualified seal of approval to the nonmorally directed ideals I have been advocating. For Kant is ex-

---

*Immanuel Kant, *The Doctrine of Virtue*, Mary J. Gregor, trans. (New York: Harper & Row, 1964), p. 71.

plicit about what he calls "duties of apathy and self-mastery" (69/70)—duties to ensure that our passions are never so strong as to interfere with calm, practical deliberation, or so deep as to wrest control from the more disinterested, rational parts of ourselves. The tight and self-conscious rein we are thus obliged to keep on our commitments to specific individuals and causes will doubtless restrict our value in these things, assigning them a necessarily attenuated place.

A more interesting objection to this brand of Kantianism, however, comes when we consider the implications of placing the kind of upper bound on moral worthiness which seemed to count in favor of this conception of morality. For to put such a limit on one's capacity to be moral is effectively to deny, not just the moral necessity, but the moral goodness of a devotion to benevolence and the maintenance of justice that passes beyond a certain, required point. It is to deny the possibility of going morally above and beyond the call of a restricted set of duties. Despite my claim that all-consuming moral saintliness is not a particularly healthy and desirable ideal, it seems perverse to insist that, were moral saints to exist, they would not, in their way, be remarkably noble and admirable figures. Despite my conviction that it is as rational and as good for a person to take Katharine Hepburn or Jane Austen as her role model instead of Mother Theresa, it would be absurd to deny that Mother Theresa is a morally better person.

I can think of two ways of viewing morality as having an upper bound. First, we can think that altruism and impartiality are indeed positive moral interests, but that they are moral only if the degree to which these interests are actively pursued remains within certain fixed limits. Second, we can think that these positive interests are only incidentally related to morality and that the essence of morality lies elsewhere, in, say, an implicit social contract or in the recognition of our own dignified rationality. According to the first conception of morality, there is a cut-off line to the amount of altruism or to the extent of devotion to justice and fairness that is worthy of moral praise. But to draw this line earlier than the line that brings the altruist in question into a worse-off position than all those to whom he devotes himself seems unacceptably artificial and gratuitous. According to the second conception, these positive interests are not essentially related to morality at all. But then we are unable to regard a more affectionate and generous expression of good will toward others as a natural and reasonable extension of morality, and we encourage a cold and unduly self-centered approach to the development and evaluation of our motivations and concerns.

A moral theory that does not contain the seeds of an all-consuming ideal of moral sainthood thus seems to place false and unnatural limits on our opportunity to do moral good and our potential to deserve moral praise. Yet the main thrust of the arguments of this paper has been leading to the conclusion that, when such ideals are present, they are not ideals to which it is particularly reasonable or healthy or desirable for human beings to aspire. These claims, taken together, have the appearance of a dilemma from which there is no obvious escape. In a moment, I shall argue that, despite appearances, these claims should not be understood as constituting a dilemma. But, before I do, let me briefly describe another path which those who are convinced by my above remarks may feel inclined to take.

If the above remarks are understood to be implicitly critical of the views on the content of morality which seem most popular today, an alternative that naturally suggests itself is that we revise our views about the content of morality. More specifically, my remarks may be taken to support a more Aristotelian, or even a more Nietzschean, approach to moral philosophy. Such a change in approach involves substantially broadening or replacing our contemporary intuitions about which character traits constitute moral virtues and vices and which interests constitute moral interests. If, for example, we include personal bearing, or creativity, or sense of style, as features that contribute to one's *moral* personality, then we can create moral ideals which are incompatible with and probably more attractive than the Kantian and utilitarian ideals I have discussed. Given such an alteration of our conception of morality, the figures with which I have been concerned above might, far from being considered to be moral saints, be seen as morally inferior to other more appealing or more interesting models of individuals.

This approach seems unlikely to succeed, if for no other reason, because it is doubtful that any single, or even any reasonably small number of substantial personal ideals could capture the full range of possible ways of realizing human potential or achieving human good which deserve encouragement and praise. Even if we could provide a sufficiently broad characterization of the range of positive ways for human beings to live, however, I think there are strong reasons not to want to incorporate such a characterization more centrally into the framework of morality itself. For, in claiming that a character trait or activity is morally good, one claims that there is a certain kind of reason for developing that trait or engaging in that activity. Yet, lying behind our criticism of more conventional conceptions of moral sainthood, there seems to be a recognition that among the immensely valuable traits and activities that a human life might positively embrace are some of which we hope that, if a person does embrace them, he does so *not* for moral reasons. In other words, no matter how flexible we make the guide to conduct which we choose to label "morality," no matter how rich we make the life in which perfect obedience to this guide would result, we will have reason to hope that a person does not wholly rule and direct his life by the abstract and impersonal consideration that such a life would be morally good.

Once it is recognized that morality itself should not serve as a comprehensive guide to conduct, moreover, we can see reasons to retain the admittedly vague contemporary intuitions about what the classification of moral and nonmoral virtues, interests, and the like should be. That is, there seem to be important differences between the aspects of a person's life which are currently considered appropriate objects of moral evaluation and the aspects that might be included under the altered conception of morality we are now considering, which the latter approach would tend wrongly to blur or to neglect. Moral evaluation now is focused primarily on features of a person's life over which that person has control; it is largely restricted to aspects of his life which are likely to have considerable effect on other people. These restrictions seem as they should be. Even if responsible people could reach agreement as to what constituted good taste or a healthy degree of well-roundedness, for example, it seems wrong to insist that everyone try to achieve these things or to blame someone who fails or refuses to conform.

If we are not to respond to the unattractiveness of the moral ideals that contemporary theories yield either by offering alternative theories with more palatable ideals or by understanding these theories in such a way as to prevent them from yielding ideals at all, how, then, are we to respond? Simply, I think, by admitting that moral ideals do not, and need not, make the best personal ideals. Earlier, I mentioned one of the consequences of regarding as a test of an adequate moral theory that perfect obedience to its laws and maximal devotion to its interests be something we can wholeheartedly strive for in ourselves and wish for in those around us. Drawing out the consequences somewhat further should, I think, make us more doubtful of the proposed test than of the theories which, on this test, would fail. Given the empirical circumstances of our world, it seems to be an ethical fact that we have unlimited potential to be morally good, and endless opportunity to promote moral interests. But this is not incompatible with the not-so-ethical fact that we have sound, compelling, and not particularly selfish reasons to choose not to devote ourselves univocally to realizing this potential or to taking up this opportunity.

Thus, in one sense at least, I am not really criticizing either Kantianism or utilitarianism. Insofar as the point of view I am offering bears directly on recent work in moral philosophy, in fact, it bears on critics of these theories who, in a spirit not unlike the spirit of most of this paper, point out that the perfect utilitarian would be flawed in this way or the perfect Kantian flawed in that.* The assumption lying behind these claims, implicitly or explicitly, has been that the recognition of these flaws shows us something wrong with utilitarianism as opposed to Kantianism, or something wrong with Kantianism as opposed to utilitarianism, or something wrong with both of these theories as opposed to some nameless third alternative. The claims of this paper suggest, however, that this assumption is unwarranted. The flaws of a perfect master of a moral theory need not reflect flaws in the intramoral content of the theory itself.

Moral Saints and Moral Philosophy

In pointing out the regrettable features and the necessary absence of some desirable features in a moral saint, I have not meant to condemn the moral saint or the person who aspires to become one. Rather, I have meant to insist that the ideal of moral sainthood should not be held as a standard against which any other ideal must be judged or justified, and that the posture we take in response to the recognition that our lives are not as morally good as they might be need not be defensive.** It is misleading to insist that one is *permitted* to live a life in which the

---

*See, e.g., Williams, *op. cit.* and J. J. C. Smart and Bernard Williams, *Utilitarianism: For and Against* (New York: Cambridge, 1973). Also, Michael Stocker, "The Schizophrenia of Modern Ethical Theories," . . . [*The Journal of Philosophy*], LXIII, 14 (Aug. 12, 1976): 453–466.

**George Orwell makes a similar point in "Reflections on Gandhi," in *A Collection of Essays by George Orwell* (New York: Harcourt Brace Jovanovich, 1945), p. 176: "sainthood is . . . a thing that human beings must avoid . . . It is too readily assumed that . . . the ordinary man only rejects it because it is too difficult; in other words, that the average human being is a failed saint. It is doubtful whether this is true. Many people genuinely do not wish to be saints, and it is probable that some who achieve or aspire to sainthood have never felt much temptation to be human beings."

goals, relationships, activities, and interests that one pursues are not maximally morally good. For our lives are not so comprehensively subject to the requirement that we apply for permission, and our nonmoral reasons for the goals we set ourselves are not excuses, but may rather be positive, good reasons which do not exist *despite* any reasons that might threaten to outweigh them. In other words, a person may be *perfectly wonderful* without being *perfectly moral*.

Recognizing this requires a perspective which contemporary moral philosophy has generally ignored. This perspective yields judgments of a type that is neither moral nor egoistic. Like moral judgments, judgments about what it would be good for a person to be are made from a point of view outside the limits set by the values, interests, and desires that the person might actually have. And, like moral judgments, these judgments claim for themselves a kind of objectivity or grounding in a perspective which any rational and perceptive being can take up. Unlike moral judgments, however, the good with which these judgments are concerned is not the good of anyone or any group other than the individual himself.

Nonetheless, it would be equally misleading to say that these judgments are made for the sake of the individual himself. For these judgments are not concerned with what kind of life it is in a person's interest to lead, but with what kind of interests it would be good for a person to have, and it need not be in a person's interest that he acquire or maintain objectively good interests. Indeed, the model of the Loving Saint, whose interests are identified with the interests of morality, is a model of a person for whom dictates of rational self-interest and the dictates of morality coincide. Yet, I have urged that we have reason not to aspire to this ideal and that some of us would have reason to be sorry if our children aspired to and achieved it.

The moral point of view, we might say, is the point of view one takes up insofar as one takes the recognition of the fact that one is just one person among others equally real and deserving of the good things in life as a fact with practical consequences, a fact the recognition of which demands expression in one's actions and in the form of one's practical deliberations. Competing moral theories offer alternative answers to the question of what the most correct or the best way to express this fact is. In doing so, they offer alternative ways to evaluate and to compare the variety of actions, states of affairs, and so on that appear good and bad to agents from other, nonmoral points of view. But it seems that alternative interpretations of the moral point of view do not exhaust the ways in which our actions, characters, and their consequences can be comprehensively and objectively evaluated. Let us call the point of view from which we consider what kinds of lives are good lives, and what kinds of persons it would be good for ourselves and others to be, the *point of view of individual perfection*.

Since either point of view provides a way of comprehensively evaluating a person's life, each point of view takes account of, and, in a sense, subsumes the other. From the moral point of view, the perfection of an individual life will have some, but limited, value—for each individual remains, after all, just one person among others. From the perfectionist point of view, the moral worth of an individual's relation to his world will likewise have some, but limited, value—for, as I have argued, the (perfectionist) goodness of an individual's life does not vary proportionally with the degree to which it exemplifies moral goodness.

It may not be the case that the perfectionist point of view is like the moral point of view in being a point of view we are ever *obliged* to take up and express in our actions. Nonetheless, it provides us with reasons that are independent of moral reasons for wanting ourselves and others to develop our characters and live our lives in certain ways. When we take up this point of view and ask how much it would be good for an individual to act from the moral point of view, we do not find an obvious answer.*

The considerations of this paper suggest, at any rate, that the answer is not "as much as possible." This has implications both for the continued development of moral theories and for the development of metamoral views and for our conception of moral philosophy more generally. From the moral point of view, we have reasons to want people to live lives that seem good from outside that point of view. If, as I have argued, this means that we have reason to want people to live lives that are not morally perfect, then any plausible moral theory must make use of some conception of supererogation.**

If moral philosophers are to address themselves at the most basic level to the question of how people should live, however, they must do more than adjust the content of their moral theories in ways that leave room for the affirmation of nonmoral values. They must examine explicitly the range and nature of these nonmoral values, and, in light of this examination, they must ask how the acceptance of a moral theory is to be understood and acted upon. For the claims of this paper do not so much conflict with the content of any particular currently popular moral theory as they call into question a metamoral assumption that implicitly surrounds discussions of moral theory more generally. Specifically, they call into question the assumption that it is always better to be morally better.

The role morality plays in the development of our characters and the shape of our practical deliberations need be neither that of a universal medium into which all other values must be translated nor that of an ever-present filter through which all other values must pass. This is not to say that moral value should not be an important, even the most important, kind of value we attend to in evaluating and improving ourselves and our world. It is to say that our values cannot be fully comprehended on the model of a hierarchical system with morality at the top.

---

*A similar view, which has strongly influenced mine, is expressed by Thomas Nagel in "The Fragmentation of Value," in *Mortal Questions* (New York: Cambridge, 1979), pp. 128–141. Nagel focuses on the difficulties such apparently incommensurable points of view create for specific, isolable practical decisions that must be made both by individuals and by societies. In focusing on the way in which these points of view figure into the development of individual personal ideals, the questions with which I am concerned are more likely to lurk in the background of any individual's life.

**The variety of forms that a conception of supererogation might take, however, has not generally been noticed. Moral theories that make use of this notion typically do so by identifying some specific set of principles as universal moral requirements and supplement this list with a further set of directives which it is morally praiseworthy but not required for an agent to follow. [See, e.g., Charles Fried, *Right and Wrong* (Cambridge, Mass.: Harvard, 1979).] But it is possible that the ability to live a morally blameless life cannot be so easily or definitely secured as this type of theory would suggest. The fact that there are some situations in which an agent is morally required to do something and other situations in which it would be good but not required for an agent to do something does not imply that there are specific principles such that, in any situation, an agent is required to act in accordance with these principles and other specific principles such that, in any situation, it would be good but not required for an agent to act in accordance with those principles.

The philosophical temperament will naturally incline, at this point, toward asking, "What, then, *is* at the top—or, if there is no top, how *are* we to decide when and how much to be moral?" In other words, there is a temptation to seek a metamoral—though not, in the standard sense, metaethical—theory that will give us principles, or, at least, informal directives on the basis of which we can develop and evaluate more comprehensive personal ideals. Perhaps a theory that distinguishes among the various roles a person is expected to play within a life—as professional, as citizen, as friend, and so on—might give us some rules that would offer us, if nothing else, a better framework in which to think about and discuss these questions. I am pessimistic, however, about the chances of such a theory to yield substantial and satisfying results. For I do not see how a metamoral theory could be constructed which would not be subject to considerations parallel to those which seem inherently to limit the appropriateness of regarding moral theories as ultimate comprehensive guides for action.

This suggests that, at some point, both in our philosophizing and in our lives, we must be willing to raise normative questions from a perspective that is unattached to a commitment to any particular well-ordered system of values. It must be admitted that, in doing so, we run the risk of finding normative answers that diverge from the answers given by whatever moral theory one accepts. This, I take it, is the grain of truth in G. E. Moore's "open question" argument. In the background of this paper, then, there lurks a commitment to what seems to me to be a healthy form of intuitionism. It is a form of intuitionism which is not intended to take the place of more rigorous, systematically developed, moral theories—rather, it is intended to put these more rigorous and systematic moral theories in their place.

———

Study Questions

1. Explain Susan Wolf's distinction between the "loving saint" and the "rational saint." How (if at all) are these ideals related to some of the theories that you have studied? Are they generated by any of these theories? Is one of these figures more morally admirable than the other? Explain.
2. Do you know any people who come close to fitting either description? If so, are their lives to be emulated?
3. What are Wolf's reasons for thinking that the life of a moral saint would be empty in various ways? Do you accept her claim that moral perfection is not an ideal "to which it is particularly reasonable or healthy or desirable for human beings to aspire"? If you do, what are the implications for morality?
4. Wolf suggests that complete devotion to what is morally valuable will prevent a person from realizing important nonmoral values. Is there a tension between moral value and nonmoral value? Can nonmoral value be accommodated in the right way within the moral point of view?
5. In the last section, Wolf distinguishes the "point of view of individual perfection" from the "moral point of view"? What is the difference? (Here consider

whether the point of view of individual perfection is the same as or different from the "point of view of self-interest.") How do we adjudicate between these points of view?

Selected Bibliography

Adams, Robert M. "Saints," *The Journal of Philosophy* 81 (1984): 392–401. Discusses differences between the religious conception of sainthood and the idea of moral saints.

Baron, Marcia. "On Admirable Immorality," *Ethics* 96 (1986): 557–566. Defends the Kantian ideal of moral perfection.

Boonin-Vale, David. "A Sheep in Wolf's Clothing," *Pacific Philosophical Quarterly* 74 (1993): 175–195. Defends the ideals of moral sainthood.

Louden, Robert B. "Can We Be Too Moral?" *Ethics* 98 (1988): 361–378. Argues that virtue ethics can combine well-roundedness with moral sainthood.

Nagel, Thomas. "The Fragmentation of Value," in *Mortal Questions* (Cambridge/New York: Cambridge University Press, 1979). Discusses the issue of incommensurable values.

Slote, Michael. *Goods and Virtues* (Oxford: Clarendon Press, 1983), Chap. 4. Argues for tensions between moral values and other goods.

Urmson, J. O. "Saints and Heroes," in A. I. Melden, ed. *Essays in Moral Philosophy*, (Seattle: University of Washington Press, 1958). Argues that moral theories must leave room for the idea of supererogation.

29

CHRISTINE M. KORSGAARD

——

Christine Korsgaard is concerned with a basic foundational question in moral philosophy: What justifies the claims that morality makes on us? What is the ground of moral obligation? She calls this "the normative question." The Hobbesian tradition grounds moral obligation in rational self-interest. Humeans trace morality back to certain features of our psychology, such as the capacity for sympathetic identification with others. Korsgaard gives a different answer that draws heavily on Kant. Like Kant, she argues that moral obligation is based on our nature as rational and reflective creatures with the capacity to choose for ourselves laws and principles to govern our actions; that is, moral obligation is grounded on autonomy—our capacity to be a law to ourselves.

> *The reflective structure of human consciousness requires that you identify yourself with some law or principle. . . . It requires you to be a law to yourself. And that is the source of normativity.*

Korsgaard begins by considering what she calls "the reflective structure of human consciousness." That is a formidable phrase, but the idea is fairly simple. We are reflective creatures with the ability to stand back from and assess our desires and impulses. Because of this we need reasons to act—we cannot act on a desire unless we decide that it is a good reason to act, and that requires, if not a decision, at least a judgment on our part. What we take as reasons for action are tied to our conceptions of who we are, what Korsgaard terms a "practical identity." That is, our practical identities are sources of reasons for action. And since there are certain things that one cannot do and still think of oneself under a certain practical identity, some of these reasons are obligations that we cannot escape without giving up that identity. Because we cannot act without reasons, because reasons are based in practical identities, and because some of these reasons are obligations, our identities are laws that we make for ourselves.

Korsgaard's account of moral obligations is a variant on Kant's argument that humanity is an end in itself. She bases moral obligation on a higher order practical identity that stands behind our particular identities. This is an identity that is necessarily true of us, and moreover, one that we share with all human beings. We are creatures who need practical identities to give us reasons for acting and to make things worth doing. Accordingly we must value our capacity to construct a practical identity—our capacity for rational choice. That means that our humanity—our shared human identity—has objective value, and thus is the source of obligations.

Christine Korsgaard has taught at Yale,, the University of California at Santa Barbara, the University of Chicago, and since 1991 at Harvard University. This essay is taken from the Tanner Lectures on Human Value that she gave at Cambridge University in 1992, which became the *Sources of Normativity* (1996). That same year she published a collection of essays, *Creating the Kingdom of Ends*.

———

The Authority of Reflection

1. Introduction

Over the course of the last two lectures I have sketched the way in which the normative question took shape in the debates of modern moral philosophy. Voluntarism tries to explain normativity in what is in some sense the most natural way: we are subject to laws, including the laws of morality, because we are subject to lawgivers. But when we ask why we should be subject to those lawgivers, an infinite regress threatens. Realism tries to block that regress by postulating the existence of entities—objective values, reasons, or obligations—whose intrinsic normativity forbids further questioning. But why should we believe in these entities? In the end, it seems we will be prepared to assert that such entities exist only because—and only if—we are already confident that the claims of morality are justified.

The reflective endorsement theorist tries a new tack. Morality is grounded in human nature. Obligations and values are projections of our own moral sentiments and dispositions. To say that these sentiments and dispositions are justified is not to say that they track the truth, but rather to say that they are good. We are the better for having them, for they perfect our social nature and promote our self-interest.

But the normative question is one that arises in the heat of action. So it is not just our dispositions, but rather the particular motives and impulses that spring from them, that must seem to us to be normative. It is this line of thought that presses us toward Kant. Kant, like the realist, thinks we must show that particular actions are right and particular ends are good. Each impulse as it offers itself to the will must pass a kind of test for normativity before we can adopt it as a reason for action. But the test that it must pass is not the test of knowledge or truth. For Kant, like Hume and Williams, thinks that morality is grounded in human nature and that moral properties are projections of human dispositions. So the test is one of reflective endorsement.

From Christine M. Korsgaard, *The Sources of Normativity*, Lecture III: "The Authority of Reflection," *The Tanner Lectures on Human Values*, vol. 15, ed. Grethe Peterson (University of Utah Press, 1994). Copyright © the University of Utah Press, 1994. Used with permission of the University of Utah Press and the Trustees of the Tanner Lectures on Human Values.

In what follows I will lay out the elements of a theory of normativity. This theory derives its main inspiration from Kant, but with some modifications that I have come to think are needed. What I say will necessarily be sketchy, and sketchily argued. My attention here will be focused on four points: first, that autonomy is the source of obligation, and in particular of our ability to obligate ourselves; second, that we have *moral* obligations, by which I mean obligations to humanity as such; third, that since we can obligate ourselves, we can also be obligated by other people; and fourth, that we have obligations to other living things. I will have little to say about the content of any of these obligations. And it will be no part of my argument to suggest either that all obligations are moral or that obligations can never conflict. My aim is to show you where obligation comes from. Exactly which obligations we have and how to negotiate among them is a topic for another day.

2. The Problem

The human mind is self-conscious. Some philosophers have supposed that this means that our minds are internally luminous, that their contents are completely accessible to us, that we always can be certain what we are thinking and feeling and wanting, and so that introspection yields certain knowledge of the self. Like Kant, and many philosophers nowadays, I do not think that this is true. Our knowledge of our own mental states and activities is no more certain than anything else.

But the human mind *is* self-conscious in the sense that it is essentially reflective. I'm not talking about being *thoughtful*, which of course is an individual property, but about the structure of our minds that makes thoughtfulness possible. A lower animal's attention is fixed on the world. Its perceptions are its beliefs and its desires are its will. It is engaged in conscious activities, but it is not conscious of them. That is, they are not the objects of its attention. But we human animals turn our attention on to our perceptions and desires themselves, and we are conscious *of* them. That is why we can think *about* them.

And this sets us a problem no other animal has. It is the problem of the normative. For our capacity to turn our attention onto our own mental activities is also a capacity to distance ourselves from them and to call them into question. I perceive, and I find myself with a powerful impulse to believe. But I back up and bring that impulse into view and then I have a certain distance. Now the impulse doesn't dominate me and now I have a problem. Shall I believe? Is this perception really a *reason* to believe? I desire and I find myself with a powerful impulse to act. But I back up and bring that impulse into view and then I have a certain distance. Now the impulse doesn't dominate me and now I have a problem. Shall I act? Is this desire really a *reason* to act? The reflective mind cannot settle for perception and desire, not just as such. It needs a *reason*. Otherwise, at least as long as it reflects, it cannot commit itself or go forward.

If the problem springs from reflection then the solution must do so as well. If the problem is that our perceptions and desires might not withstand reflective scrutiny, then the solution is that they might. We need reasons because our impulses must be able to withstand reflective scrutiny. We have reasons if they do. The normative word "reason" refers to a kind of reflective success. If "good" and "right" are also taken to be intrinsically normative words then they too must refer to reflective success. And they do. Think of what they mean when we use them as *exclamations:* "Good!" "Right!" There they mean: I'm satisfied, I'm happy, I'm committed, you've convinced me, let's go. They mean the work of reflection is done.

"Reason" then means reflective success. So if I decide that my desire is a reason to act, I must decide that on reflection I endorse that desire. And here we find the problem. For how do I decide that? Is the claim that I look at the desire and see that it is intrinsically normative or that its object is? Then all of the arguments against realism await us. Does the desire or its object inherit its normativity from something else? Then we must ask what makes that other thing normative, what makes it the source of a reason. And now of course the usual regress threatens. So what brings reflection to an end?

Kant described this same problem in terms of freedom. It is because of the reflective structure of the mind that we must act, as he puts it, under the idea of freedom. He says, "We cannot conceive of a reason which consciously responds to a bidding from the outside with respect to its judgments."* If the bidding from outside is desire, then his point is that the reflective mind must endorse the desire before it can act on it—it must say to itself that the desire is a reason. We must, as he puts it, *make it our maxim* to act on the desire. And this is something we must do of our own free will.

Kant defines a free will as a rational causality that is effective without being determined by any alien cause. Anything outside of the will counts as an alien cause, including the desires and inclinations of the person. The free will must be entirely self-determining. Yet, because the will is a causality, it must act according to some law or other. Kant says, "Since the concept of a causality entails that of laws . . . it follows that freedom is by no means lawless. . . ."** Alternatively, we may say that since the will is practical reason, it cannot be conceived as acting and choosing for no reason. Since reasons are derived from principles, the free will must have a principle. But because the will is free, no law or principle can be imposed on it from outside. Kant concludes that the will must be autonomous: that is, it must have its *own* law or principle. And here again we arrive at the problem. For where is this law to come from? If it is imposed on the will from outside then the will is not free. So the will must adopt the law for itself. But until the will has a law or principle, there is nothing from which it can derive a reason. So how can it have any reason for adopting one law rather than another?

Well, here is Kant's answer. The categorical imperative tells us to act only on a maxim that we could will to be a law. And *this*, according to Kant, *is* the law of a free will. To see why, we need only compare the problem faced by the free will with the content of the categorical imperative. The problem faced by the free will is this: the will must have a law, but because the will is free, it must be its own law. And *nothing determines what that law must be. All that it has to be is a law.* Now consider the content of the categorical imperative. The categorical imperative simply tells us to choose a law. Its only constraint on our choice is that it have the form of a law. And nothing determines what that law must be. *All that it has to be is a law.*

*Kant, *Foundations of the Metaphysics of Morals,* p. 448; in Beck's translation, p. 66.

**Ibid., p. 446; in Beck's translation, p. 65.

Therefore the categorical imperative is the law of a free will. It does not impose any external constraint on the free will's activities, but simply arises from the nature of the will. It describes what a free will must do in order to be what it is. It must choose a maxim it can regard as a law.*

Now I'm going to make a distinction that Kant doesn't make. I am going to call the law of acting only on maxims you can will to be laws "the categorical imperative." And I am going to distinguish it from what I will call "the moral law." The moral law, in the Kantian system, is the law of what Kant calls the Kingdom of Ends, the republic of all rational beings. The moral law tells us to act only on maxims that all rational beings could agree to act on together in a workable cooperative system. Now the Kantian argument that I have just described establishes that *the categorical imperative* is the law of a free will. But it does not establish that *the moral law* is the law of a free will. Any law is universal, but the argument doesn't settle the question of the *domain* over which the law of the free will must range. And there are various possibilities here. If the law is the law of acting on the desire of the moment, then the agent will treat each desire as it arises as a reason, and her conduct will be that of a wanton.** If the law ranges over the interests of an agent's whole life, then the agent will be some sort of egoist. It is only if the law ranges over every rational being that the resulting law will be the moral law, the law of the Kingdom of Ends.

Because of this, it has sometimes been claimed that the categorical imperative is an empty formalism. And this in turn has been conflated with another claim, that the moral law is an empty formalism. Now that second claim is false.[†] But it is true that the argument that shows that we are bound by the categorical imperative does not show that we are bound by the moral law. For that we need another step. The agent must think of herself as a Citizen of the Kingdom of Ends.

3. The Solution

Those who think that the human mind is internally luminous and transparent to itself think that the term "self-consciousness" is appropriate because what we get in human consciousness is a direct encounter with the self. Those who think that

---

*This is a reading of the argument Kant gives in ibid., pp. 446–48; in Beck's translation, pp. 64–67; and in *The Critique of Practical Reason* under the heading "Problem II," p. 29; in Beck's translation, pp. 28–29. It is explained in greater detail in my "Morality as Freedom," in *Creating the Kingdom of Ends* (Cambridge University Press, 1996) [hereafter abbreviated *CKE*].

**I have a reason for saying that her behavior will be that of a wanton rather than simply saying that she will be a wanton. Harry Frankfurt, from whom I am borrowing the term, defines a wanton as someone who has no second-order volitions. An animal, whose desire is its will, is a wanton. I am arguing here that a person cannot be like that, because of the reflective structure of human consciousness. A person must act on a reason, and so the person who acts like a wanton must be treating the desire of the moment as a reason. That commits her to the principle that the desire of the moment is a reason, and her commitment to that principle counts as a second-order volition. See Frankfurt, "Freedom of the Will and the Concept of a Person," [in *The Importance of What We Care About* (Cambridge University Press, 1988)] especially the discussion on pp. 16–19. The affinity of my account with Frankfurt's will be evident.

[†]Bradley and others understood Hegel's famous objection this way, and if it is taken this way it is a mistake. I argue for this in my paper "Kant's Formula of Universal Law" [*CKE*]. In that paper, however, I do not distinguish the categorical imperative from the moral law, and my arguments there actually only show that the moral law has content.

the human mind has a reflective structure use the term too, but for a different reason. The reflective structure of the mind is a source of "self-consciousness" because it forces us to have a *conception* of ourselves. As Kant argues, this is a fact about what it is *like* to be reflectively conscious and it does not prove the existence of a metaphysical self. From a third person point of view, outside of the deliberative standpoint, it may look as if what happens when someone makes a choice is that the strongest of his conflicting desires wins. But that isn't the way it is *for you* when you deliberate. When you deliberate, it is as if there were something over and above all of your desires, something that is *you*, and that *chooses* which desire to act on. This means that the principle or law by which you determine your actions is one that you regard as being expressive of *yourself*. To identify with such a principle or law is to be, in St. Paul's famous phrase, a law to yourself.*

An agent might think of herself as a Citizen in the Kingdom of Ends. Or she might think of herself as a member of a family or an ethnic group or a nation. She might think of herself as the steward of her own interests, and then she will be an egoist. Or she might think of herself as the slave of her passions, and then she will be a wanton. And how she thinks of herself will determine whether it is the law of the Kingdom of Ends, or the law of some smaller group, or the law of the egoist, or the law of the wanton that is the law that she is to herself.

The conception of one's identity in question here is not a theoretical one, a view about what as a matter of inescapable scientific fact you are. It is better understood as a description under which you value yourself, a description under which you find your life to be worth living and your actions to be worth undertaking. So I will call this a conception of your practical identity. Practical identity is a complex matter and for the average person there will be a jumble of such conceptions. You are a human being, a woman or a man, an adherent of a certain religion, a member of an ethnic group, someone's friend, and so on. And all of these identities give rise to reasons and obligations. Your reasons express your identity, your nature; your obligations spring from what that identity forbids.

Our ordinary ways of talking about obligation reflect this connection to identity. A century ago a European could admonish another to civilized behavior by telling him to act like a Christian. It is still true in many quarters that courage is urged on males by the injunction "Be a man!" Duties more obviously connected with social roles are of course enforced in this way. "A psychiatrist doesn't violate the confidence of her patients." No "ought" is needed here because the normativity is built right into the role. But it isn't only in the case of social roles that the idea of obligation invokes the conception of practical identity. Consider the astonishing but familiar "I couldn't live with myself if I did that." Clearly there are two selves here, me and the one I must live with and so must not fail. Or consider the protest against obligation ignored: "Just who do you think you are?"

The connection is also present in the concept of integrity. Etymologically, integrity is oneness, integration is what makes something one. To be a thing, one thing, a unity, an entity; to be anything at all: in the metaphysical sense, that is what it means to have integrity. But we use the term for someone who lives up to his own standards. And that is because we think that living up to them is what makes him one, and so what makes him a person at all.

*Romans 11:14.

It is the conceptions of ourselves that are most important to us that give rise to unconditional obligations. For to violate them is to lose your integrity and so your identity, and no longer to be who you are. That is, it is no longer to be able to think of yourself under the description under which you value yourself and find your life worth living and your actions worth undertaking. That is to be for all practical purposes dead or worse than dead. When an action cannot be performed without loss of some fundamental part of one's identity, and an agent would rather be dead, then the obligation not to do it is unconditional and complete. If reasons arise from reflective endorsement, then obligation arises from reflective *rejection*.

But the question how exactly an agent *should* conceive her practical identity, the question which law she should be to herself, is not settled by the arguments I have given. So moral obligation is not yet on the table. To that extent the argument is formal, and in one sense empty.

But in another sense it is not empty at all. What we have established is this. The reflective structure of human consciousness requires that you identify yourself with some law or principle that will govern your choices. It requires you to be a law to yourself. And that is the source of normativity. So the argument shows just what Kant said that it did: that our autonomy is the source of obligation.

It will help to put the point in Joseph Butler's terms, in terms of the distinction between power and authority. We do not always do what upon reflection we would do or even what upon reflection we have already decided to do. Reflection does not have irresistible power over us. But when we do reflect we cannot but think that we ought to do what on reflection we conclude we have reason to do. And when we don't do that we punish ourselves, by guilt and regret and repentance and remorse. We might say that the acting self concedes to the thinking self its right to government. And the thinking self, in turn, tries to govern as well as it can. So the reflective structure of human consciousness establishes a relation here, a relation that we have to ourselves. And it is a relation not of mere power but rather of *authority*. And *that* is the authority that is the source of obligation.

Notice that this means that voluntarism is true after all. The source of obligation is a legislator, one whose authority is beyond question and does not need to be established. But there is only one such authority and it is the authority of your own mind and will.* So Pufendorf and Hobbes were right. It is not the bare fact that it would be a good idea to perform a certain action that obligates us to perform it. It is the fact that we *command ourselves* to do what we find it would be a good idea to do.

One more step is necessary. The acting self concedes to the thinking self its right to govern. But the thinking self in turn must try to govern well. It is its job to make what is in any case a good idea into law. How do we know what is a good idea or what should be a law? Kant proposes that we can tell whether our maxims should be laws by attending not to their matter but to their form.

*This remark needs a qualification, which springs from the fact that we can unite our wills with the wills of others. In Kant's theory, this happens when we are citizens who together form a general will or when we make friends or get married. In those cases it is sometimes the united will that has authority over our conduct. For further discussion, see my "Creating the Kingdom of Ends: Reciprocity and Responsibility in Personal Relations" [in *CKE*].

To understand this idea, we need to return to its origins, which are in Aristotle. According to Aristotle, a thing is composed of a form and a matter. The matter is the material, the parts, from which it is made. The form of a thing is its functional arrangement. That is, it is the arrangement of the matter or of the parts that enables the thing to serve its purpose, to do whatever it does. For example, the purpose of a house is to be a shelter, so the form of a house is the way the arrangement of the parts—the walls and the roof—enables it to serve as a shelter. "Join the walls at the corner, put the roof on top, and that's how we keep the weather out." That is the form of a house.*

Next consider the maxim of an action. Since every human action is done for an end, a maxim has two parts, the act and the end. The form of the maxim is the arrangement of its parts. Take, for instance, Plato's famous example of the three maxims.**

1. I will keep my weapon, because I want it for myself.

2. I will refuse to return your weapon, because I want it for myself.

3. I will refuse to return your weapon, because you have gone mad and may hurt someone.

Maxims 1 and 3 are good; maxim 2 is bad. What makes them so? Not the actions, for maxims 2 and 3 have the same actions; not the purposes, for maxims 1 and 2 have the same purposes. The goodness does not rest in the parts; but rather in the way the parts are combined and related; so the goodness does not rest in the matter, but rather in the form of the maxim. But form is not merely the arrangement of the parts; it is the *functional* arrangement—the arrangement that enables the thing to do what it does. If the walls are joined and roof placed on top *so that* the building can keep the weather out, then the building has the form of a house. So: if the action and the purpose are related to one another *so that* the maxim can be willed as a law, then the maxim is good.

Notice what this establishes. A good maxim is good in virtue of its internal structure. Its internal structure, its form, makes it fit to be willed as a law. A good maxim is therefore an *intrinsically normative entity*. So realism is true after all, and Nagel, in particular, was right. When an impulse presents itself to us, as a kind of candidate for being a reason, we look to see whether it really is a reason, whether its claim to normativity is true.

But this isn't an exercise of intuition or a discovery about what is out there in the world. The test for determining whether an impulse is a reason is whether *we* can will the maxim of acting on that impulse as law. So the test is a test of endorsement.

This completes the first part of my argument, so let me sum up what I've said. What I have shown so far is why there is such a thing as obligation. The reflective structure of human consciousness forces us to act for reasons. At the same time, and relatedly, it forces us to have a conception of our own identity, a conception that identifies us with the source of our reasons. In this way, it makes us laws to

---

*These views are found throughout Aristotle's writings, but centrally discussed in books VII–IX of the *Metaphysics* and in *On the Soul*.

**Plato, *Republic*, I, 331c.

ourselves. When an impulse presents itself to us we ask whether it could be a reason. We answer that question by seeing whether the maxim of acting on it can be willed as a law by a being with the identity in question. If it can be willed as a law, it is a reason, for it has an intrinsically normative structure. If it cannot be willed as a law, we must reject it, and in that case we get obligation.

A moment ago I said that realism is true after all. But that could be misleading. That we obligate ourselves is simply a fact about human nature. But whether a maxim can serve as a law still depends upon the way that we think of our identities. So there is still an element of relativism in the system. In order to establish that there are *moral* obligations we will need another step.

4. Moral Obligation

There is another way to make the points I have been making, and in approaching the problem of relativism it will be helpful to employ it. We can take as our model the way Rawls employs the concept/conception distinction in *A Theory of Justice*. There, the concept of justice refers to a problem, the problem of how the benefits of social cooperation are to be distributed. A *conception* of justice is a principle that is proposed as a solution to that problem.*

In the same way, the most general normative concepts, the right and the good, are names for problems—for the normative problems that spring from our reflective nature. "Good" names the problem of what we are to strive for, aim for, and care about in our lives. "Right" names the more specific problem of what we are to do. The "thinness" of these terms, to use Bernard Williams's language, comes from the fact that they are only concepts, names for whatever it is that solves the problems in question.

How do we get from concepts to conceptions? What mediates is a conception of practical identity. In Rawls's argument, we move from concept to conception by taking up the standpoint of the pure citizen and asking what principles such a citizen would have reason to adopt. In Kant's argument, we move from concept to conception by taking up the standpoint of a Citizen in the Kingdom of Ends and asking what principles that citizen would have reason to adopt.

Because they are normative, thick ethical concepts stand to thin ones as conceptions to concepts. They represent solutions, or at least reasons that will be weighed in arriving at solutions, to the problems that are set by reflection. And that means that they embody a view about what is right or good. . . .

But this does not eliminate the element of relativism that Williams has sought to preserve. The mediation between concepts and conceptions comes by way of practical identity. And human identity has been differently constituted in different social worlds. Sin, dishonor, and moral wrongness all represent conceptions of what one cannot do without being diminished or disfigured, without loss of identity, and therefore conceptions of what one must not do. But they belong to different worlds in which human beings thought of themselves and of what made them themselves in very different ways. Where sin is the conception, my identity is my soul and it exists in the eyes of my God. Where dishonor is the conception,

---

*Rawls, *A Theory of Justice* [Harvard University Press, 1971], p. 5.

my identity is my reputation, my position in some small and knowable social world. The conception of moral wrongness as we now understand it belongs to the world we live in, the one brought about by the Enlightenment, where one's identity is one's relation to humanity itself. Hume said at the height of the Enlightenment that to be virtuous is to think of yourself as a member of the "party of humankind, against vice or disorder, its common enemy."* And that is now true. But we coherently can grant that it was not always so.

But this is not to say that there is nothing to be said in favor of the Enlightenment conception. This sort of relativism has its limits, and they come from two different but related lines of thought.

We have already seen one of them set forward by Bernard Williams. We could, with the resources of a knowledge of human nature, rank different sets of values according to their tendency to promote human flourishing. If values are associated with ways of thinking of what we most fundamentally are, then the point will be that some ways of conceiving one's identity are healthier and better for us than others.

But it is also important to remember that no argument can preserve any form of relativism without on another level eradicating it. This is one of the main faults with one well-known criticism of liberalism, that the conception of the person that is employed in its arguments is an "empty self."** It is urged by communitarians that people need to conceive themselves as members of smaller communities, essentially tied to particular others and traditions. This is an argument about how human beings need to constitute our practical identities, and if it is successful what it establishes is a *universal* fact, namely that our practical identities must be constituted in part by particular ties and commitments. And the communitarian who has reflected and reached this conclusion now has a conception of his own identity that is universal: he is an animal that needs to live in community.

And there is a further implication of this that is important. Once the communitarian sees himself this way, his particular ties and commitments will remain normative for him only if this more fundamental conception of his identity is one that he can see as normative as well. A further stretch of reflection requires a further stretch of endorsement. So he must endorse this new view of his identity. He is an animal that needs to live in community, and he now takes *this* to be a normative identity. He treats it as a source of reasons, for he argues that it matters that he gets what he needs. And this further stretch of endorsement is exactly what occurs. Someone who is moved to urge the value of *having* particular ties and commitments has discovered that part of their normativity comes from the fact that human beings need to have them. He urges that our lives are meaningless without them. That is not a reason that *springs from* one of his own particular ties and commitments. It is a plea on behalf of all human beings. And that means that he is no longer immersed in a normative world of particular ties and commitments. Philosophical reflection does not leave everything just where it was.

This is just a fancy new model of an argument that first appeared in a much simpler form, Kant's argument for his Formula of Humanity. The form of relativism with

---

*Hume, *Enquiry Concerning the Principles of Morals*, p. 275.
**See, for instance, Michael Sandel, *Liberalism and the Limits of Justice* [Cambridge University Press, 1982].

which Kant began was the most elementary one we encounter—the relativity of value to human desires and interests. He started from the fact that when we make a choice we must regard its object as good. His point is the one I have been making—that being human we must endorse our impulses before we can act on them. Kant asked what it is that makes these objects good, and, rejecting one form of realism, he decided that the goodness was not in the objects themselves. Were it not for our desires and inclinations, we would not find their objects good. Kant saw that we take things to be important because they are important to us—and he concluded that we must therefore take ourselves to be important. In this way, the value of humanity itself is implicit in every human choice.* If normative skepticism is to be avoided—if there is any such thing as a reason for action—then humanity as the source of all reasons and values must be valued for its own sake.**

The point I want to make now is the same. In this lecture I have offered an account of the source of normativity. I have argued that a human being is an animal who needs a practical conception of her own identity, a conception of who she is that is normative for her. Otherwise she could have no reasons to act, and since she is reflective she needs reasons to act. But you are a human being and so if you believe my argument you can now see that this is your identity. You are an animal of the sort I have just described. And that is not merely a contingent conception of your identity, which you have constructed or chosen for yourself or could conceivably reject. It is simply the truth. Now that you see that your need to have a normative conception of yourself comes from the sort of animal you are, you can ask whether it really matters whether animals of this kind conform to their normative practical identities. Does it really matter what human beings do? And here you have no option but to say yes. Since you are human you *must* take something to be normative, that is, some conception of practical identity must be normative for you. If you had no normative conception of your identity, you could have no reasons for action, and because your consciousness is reflective, you could then not act at all. Since you cannot act without reasons and your humanity is the source of your reasons, you must endorse your own humanity if you are to act at all.

It follows from this argument that human beings are valuable. Enlightenment morality is true.

5. Obligating One Another

So far I have argued that the reflective structure of human consciousness gives us legislative authority over ourselves. That is why we are able to obligate ourselves. And just now I argued that once we understand how all of this works, we must concede

---

*Kant, *Foundations of the Metaphysics of Morals,* pp. 427–28; in Beck's translation, pp. 45–47. I am here summarizing the interpretation of this argument I give in "Kant's Formula of Humanity" [in *CKE*].
**This implies that you must accept the laws that arise from this more fundamental view of your identity, the laws of morality. But it does not imply that the less fundamental laws no longer exist or that the more fundamental ones always trump them. The view I have as I have spelled it out so far leaves room for conflict. Some account of how such conflicts might be negotiated is desirable, but I do not mean to be giving or implying any such account here.

that our humanity is an end in itself, that human nature as the source of our values is itself a value. This, I should add, is what gives rise to *moral* obligation.

You might suppose that I am claiming that this settles the question of our obligations to others. Since I regard my humanity as a source of value, I must in the name of consistency regard your humanity that way as well. So I must value the things that you value. Or, to put it another way, since I think my humanity is what makes my desires into normative reasons, I must suppose that the humanity of others makes their desires into normative reasons as well.

This is a familiar form of argument. Versions of it appear in Thomas Nagel's book *The Possibility of Altruism,* and in Alan Gewirth's book *Reason and Morality.* And the criticism of this form of argument is always the same. Consistency can force me to grant that your humanity is normative for you just as mine is normative for me. It can force me to acknowledge that your desires have the status of reasons for you, in exactly the same way that mine do for me. But it does not force me to share in your reasons or make *your* humanity normative for me.* It could still be true that I have my reasons and you have yours, and indeed that they leave us eternally at odds.** Human beings might be egoistic, not in the sense of being concerned only about themselves, but in the sense defined by Nagel in *The Possibility of Altruism.* The egoist thinks that reasons are a kind of private property. We each act on our own private reasons, and we need some special reason, like friendship or contract, for taking the reasons of others into account.

In one sense this objection is correct. Consistency is not what forces us to share our reasons. And even if these arguments did work, they would work in the wrong way. They would show that I have an obligation *to myself* to treat you in ways that respect the value that I place on you. But they would not show that I have obligations *to you.* So we need something more.

As we have seen, I can obligate myself because I am conscious of myself. So if you are going to obligate me I must be conscious of you. You must be able to intrude on my reflections—you must be able to get under my skin. People suppose that practical reasons are private because they suppose that reflection is a private activity. And they suppose that, in turn, because they believe in the privacy of consciousness. So what we need at this point is some help from Wittgenstein.

Consider the private language argument. As Wittgenstein defines it, a private language would be a language that referred to something essentially private and incommunicable, say for instance a sensation that is yours alone, and cannot be described in any other way than by a name that you give to it. You can't even call it a tickle or an itch, for then it would be communicable. So you just call it "S." And whenever you experience it, you say to yourself, "That was S."†

Wittgenstein argues that there couldn't be any such language. One way to understand his argument goes like this: Meaning is relational because it is a *normative* notion: to say that X means Y is to say that one ought to take X for Y; and this

---

*See for instance Williams's criticism of Gewirth in chapter 4 of *Ethics and the Limits of Philosophy* [Harvard University Press, 1985].

**In contemporary jargon, the objection is that the reasons the argument reveals are "agent-relative" rather than "agent-neutral."

†See Wittgenstein, *Philosophical Investigations,* §§243ff., pp. 88ff.

requires two, a legislator to lay it down that one ought to take X for Y and a citizen to obey. And the relation between these two is not merely causal because the citizen can disobey: there must be a possibility of misunderstanding or mistake. Since it is a relation in which one gives a law to another, it takes two to make a meaning. So you cannot peer inwardly at an essentially private and incommunicable sensation and say, "That is what I mean by S" and so in that way mean something. For if that is what you mean by S, then when you call something S it must be that, and if you call something else S you must be wrong. But if what you call S is just that sensation that makes you feel like saying "S," and it cannot be identified in any other way, then you cannot be wrong.* The idea of a private language is inconsistent with the normativity of meaning.

If we read Wittgenstein that way, there is an obvious similarity between the kind of normativity that he thinks characterizes language and the kind of normativity that I have been attributing to practical reasons. We could make a parallel argument against private reasons: Reasons are relational because reason is a normative notion: to say that R is a reason for A is to say that one should do A because of R; and this requires two, a legislator to lay it down and a citizen to obey. And the relation between them is not just causal because the citizen can disobey: there must be a possibility of irrationality or wrongdoing. Since it is a relation in which one gives a law to another, it takes two to make a reason. And here the two are the two elements of reflective consciousness, the thinking self and the active self: what I have been talking about all along is how you can make laws and reasons for your self.**

There are two important points here. The first point is that the mistake involved in thinking that a meaning is a mental entity is exactly like that involved in thinking that a reason or a value is a mental entity. To talk about reasons and meanings is not to talk about entities, but to talk in a shorthand way about relations we have with ourselves and one another. The normative demands of meaning and reason are not demands that are made on us by objects, but are demands that we make on ourselves and each other.

The second point concerns privacy. The private language argument does not show that I could not have my own personal language. It shows that I could not have a language that is in principle incommunicable to anybody else. When I make a language, I make its meanings normative for me. As Wittgenstein puts it, I *undertake* to use words in certain ways.† And however I go about binding myself to those meanings, it must be possible for me to bind another in exactly the same way.

If I say to you, "Picture a yellow spot!" you will. What exactly is happening? Are you simply cooperating with me? No, because at least without a certain active

---

*See especially ibid., §258, p. 92: "But 'I impress it on myself' can only mean: this process brings it about that I remember the connection *right* in the future. But in the present case I have no criterion of correctness. One would like to say: whatever is going to seem right to me is right. And that only means that here we cannot talk about 'right.'"

**It may look as if there is a disanalogy here. The private language argument shows that you cannot mean a certain sensation by "S" just now and never again, because then you could not be wrong. The remark I just made makes it look as if you could have a reason just now and never again—the thinking self could bind the acting self to act a certain way just now. Actually, however, I do not think that is a possibility, since the acting self cannot coherently be taken to exist just at a particular moment. See my "Personal Identity and the Unity of Agency: A Kantian Response to Parfit," pp. 113–14 [*CKE*].

†Wittgenstein, *Philosophical Investigations*, §262, p. 93.

resistance you will not be able to help it. Is it a causal connection then? No, or at least not merely that, for if you picture a *pink* spot you will be mistaken, wrong. Causal connections cannot be wrong. What kind of necessity is this, both normative and compulsive? It is *obligation*.

Philosophers have been concerned for a long time about how we understand the meanings of words, but we have not paid enough attention to the fact that it is so hard not to. It is nearly impossible to hear the words of a language you know as mere noise. And this has implications for the supposed privacy of human consciousness. For it means that I can always intrude myself into your consciousness. All I have to do is talk to you in the words of a language you know, and in this way I can force you to think. The space of linguistic consciousness is essentially public, like a town square. You might happen to be alone in yours, but I can get in anytime. Wittgenstein says, "Think in this connection how singular is the use of a person's name to *call* him."*

If I call out your name, I make you stop in your tracks. (If you love me, I make you come running.) Now you cannot proceed as you did before. Oh, you can proceed, all right, but not just as you did before. For now if you walk on, you will be ignoring me and slighting me. It will probably be difficult for you, and you will have to muster a certain active resistance, a sense of rebellion. But why should you have to rebel against me? It is because I am a law to you. By calling out your name, I have obligated you. I have given you a reason to stop.**

Of course you might not stop. You have reasons of your own, and you might decide, rightly or wrongly, that they outweigh the one I have given you. But that I have given you a reason is clear from the fact that, in ordinary circumstances, you will feel like giving me one back. "Sorry, I must run, I'm late for an appointment." We all know that reasons must be met with reasons, and that is why we are always exchanging them.

We do not seem to need a reason to take the reasons of others into account. We seem to need a reason not to. Certainly we do things because others want us to, ask us to, tell us to, all the time. We give each other the time and directions, open doors and step aside, warn each other of imminent perils large and small. We respond with the alacrity of obedient soldiers to telephones and doorbells and cries for help. You could say that it is because we want to be cooperative, but that is like saying that you understand my words because you want to be cooperative. It ignores the same essential point, which is that it is so hard not to.

Now the egoist may reply that this does not establish that other people's reasons are reasons for me. He'll say that I am merely describing a deep psychological fact—that human beings are very susceptible to one another's pressure. We tend to cave in to the demands of others. But nothing I have said so far shows that we have to treat the demands of others as *reasons*. It is at this point that Thomas Nagel's argument, from *The Possibility of Altruism*, comes into its own.

Suppose that we are strangers and that you are tormenting me, and suppose that I call upon you to stop. I say, "How would you like it if someone did that to

*Ibid., §27, p. 13.
**More strictly speaking, the needs and demands of others present us with what Kant calls "incentives," just as our own inclinations do. Incentives come up for automatic consideration as candidates for being reasons. I thank Ulrike Heuer for prompting me to be clearer on this point.

you?" Now you cannot proceed as you did before. Oh, you can proceed all right, but not just as you did before. For I have obligated you to stop.

How does the obligation come about? Just the way that Nagel says that it does. I invite you to consider how you would like it if someone did that to you. You realize that you would not merely dislike it, you would resent it. You would think that the other has a reason to stop—more, that he has an obligation to stop. And that obligation would spring from your own objection to what he does to you. You make yourself an end for others; you make yourself a law to them. But if you are a law to others insofar as you are just a person, just *someone,* then others are also laws to you.*
By making you think these thoughts, I force you to acknowledge the value of my humanity, and I obligate you to act in a way that respects it.

As Nagel observes, the argument does not go through if you fail to see yourself, to identify yourself, as just someone, a person, one person among others who are equally real.** The argument invites you to change places with the other, and you cannot do this if you fail to see what you and the other have in common. Suppose you could say, "Someone doing that to me, why that would be terrible! But then I am *me,* after all." Then the argument would fail of its effect; it would not find a foothold in you. But the argument never really fails in *that* way.

For it to fail in that way, I would have to hear your words as mere noise, not as intelligible speech. And it is impossible to hear the words of a language you know as mere noise. In hearing your words as *words,* I acknowledge that you are *someone.* In acknowledging that I can hear them, I acknowledge that I am *someone.* If I listen to the argument at all, I have already admitted that each of us is *someone.*

Consider an exchange of reasons. A student comes to your office door and says, "I need to talk to you. Are you free now?" You say, "No, I've got to finish this letter right now and then I've got to go home. Could you possibly come around tomorrow, say about three?" And your student says, "Yes, that will be fine. I'll see you tomorrow at three then."

What is happening here? On my view, the two of you are reasoning together, to arrive at a decision, a single shared decision, about what to do. And I take that to be the natural view. But if egoism is true, and reasons cannot be shared, then that is not what is happening. Instead, each of you backs into the privacy of his practical consciousness, reviews his own reasons, comes up with a decision, and then reemerges to announce the result to the other. And the process stops when the results happen to coincide, and the agents know it, because of the announcements they have made to each other.

Now consider an exchange of ideas, rather than an exchange of practical reasons. Here we do not find these two possibilities. If meanings could not be shared, there would be no point in announcing the results of one's private thinking to anybody else. If they can be shared, then it is in principle possible to think the issues through together, and that is what people do when they talk. But if we have to grant that meanings can be shared, why not grant that practical reasons can be shared too?

---

*See Nagel, *The Possibility of Altruism* [Princeton University Press, 1970], pp. 82–84.
**Ibid., chapter 9.

The egoist may reply that I am leaving out an option. The student/teacher re-lation is a personal one. People who enter into particular personal relationships have special reasons to take each other's reasons into account. So the exchange I've just described takes place against a background agreement that the parties in-volved will take each other's reasons into account. The egoist is someone who only acts on his own reasons, not someone who has no concern for others. So you and your student reason together because you have tacitly agreed to, but this does not show that this is what usually happens.

But the objection reemerges within this framework. How are we to under-stand this personal relationship? If reasons are still private then it goes like this: each of you has a private reason to take the reasons of the other into account. A personal relationship is an interest in one another's interests.* This doesn't change the shape of the deliberation—you still back into your private deliberative spaces and then reemerge to announce the results. This only shows why you think there's a point in the exercise at all, why you hope to reach a convergence. But if you are really reasoning together, if you have joined your wills to arrive at a single deci-sion—well, then that can happen, can't it? And why shouldn't it be what usually happens? Why shouldn't language force us to reason practically together, in just the same way that it forces us to think together?

I believe that the myth of egoism will die with the myth of the privacy of con-sciousness. Now you may object that the way in which I have argued against the privacy of consciousness—by arguing that we can think and reason together—has nothing to do with what philosophers mean when they discuss that privacy. What they mean by privacy is that you don't always know what someone else is thinking or feeling. The way in which you have access to the contents of another person's mind—through words and expressions and other such forms of evidence—doesn't allow you to look around in it freely, and make sure that you know what's there and what's not.

But that's not an issue about privacy. If you accept the thesis that conscious-ness is reflective rather than internally luminous, then you must admit that you don't have access to your *own* mind in *that* way. So that doesn't mark a difference between the kind of relationship you have to yourself and the kind that you have to other people. All we've got here is a matter of degree. You know some people better than others; if you're honest and lucky, you know yourself pretty well.

Human beings are social animals in a deep way. It is not just that we go in for friendship or prefer to live in swarms or packs. The space of linguistic consciousness—the space in which meanings and reasons exist—is a space that we occupy together.

———

Study Questions

1. Korsgaard claims that the fact that we are self-conscious and reflective creatures "sets us a problem that no other animal has." (Section 2) What is this problem? Do you agree with her claims?

*And that's not what a personal relationship is. . . .

2. Do all of your desires give you reasons for action? (Think of examples here.) If not, how do you decide whether you have a reason to act on a desire?
3. What does Korsgaard mean by a "practical identity" (or "normative identity") and how do they function in people's lives? (Section 3) What are examples of practical identities that might apply to you? What is the connection that she sees between practical identities and obligation? In particular, how do the former give rise to the latter?
4. In addition to our several particular practical identities, Korsgaard thinks that we have an identity as a human being that we share with all other people. (Section 4) How does she characterize this identity? Do you agree with her claim that it is true of all of us? What, in her view, is its connection with moral obligation?
5. Must each person value his or her humanity, or capacity for rational choice? If so, does that commit each of us to valuing the humanity of others? Of *all* others?
6. Imagine that as you are walking down the street, someone that you do not know calls out to you and asks you to stop. Korsgaard seems to claim that by calling out to you, that person has obligated you. (Section 5) What does she mean by this and what is it supposed to show? Are you persuaded?
7. In her example of the student and teacher setting up an appointment (Section 5), Korsgaard considers two different analyses of how they reach an agreement, her own view and the view that she attributes to egoism. Explain and contrast these two analyses. Which do you find more compelling?

Selected Bibliography

Cohon, Rachel. "The Roots of Reasons," *The Philosophical Review* 109, no. 1 (2000). A critical discussion of Korsgaard's views.

Frankfurt, Harry G. "Freedom of the Will and the Concept of the Person," in his *The Importance of What We Care About* (Cambridge/New York: Cambridge University Press, 1988). A seminal essay on the nature of free agency.

Korsgaard, Christine M. *Creating the Kingdom of Ends* (Cambridge/New York: Cambridge University Press, 1996). A collection of her essays on both Kant and contemporary moral theory.

———. *The Sources of Normativity* (Cambridge/New York: Cambridge University Press, 1996). An expanded and final version of her Tanner Lectures, with critical comments by several philosophers and her replies.

———. "Self-Constitution in the Ethics of Plato and Kant," *The Journal of Ethics* 3 (1999).

Nagel, Thomas, *The Possibility of Altruism* (Princeton: Princeton University Press, 1970). An influential defense of the idea that morality is a requirement of reason.

30

ANNETTE C. BAIER

—

An issue raised by some feminist writers is whether there are significant differences in the ways in which women and men tend to think about moral issues. This issue came to prominence in the early

> *Is justice blind to important social values, or at least only one-eyed?*

1980s due to the work of psychologist Carol Gilligan. Her research on moral development suggested the existence of two distinct moral perspectives, the perspective of justice and the perspective of care. The first perspective tends to characterize the thinking of men, whereas the second tends to characterize the thinking of women. The perspective of justice employs abstract, universal, and impersonal principles that apply to persons as such. It is associated with Kantian and neo-Kantian theories, though it would seem to apply equally to utilitarianism. Care, by contrast, is a moral attitude of direct concern for the well-being of another; it is particularistic and based on emotional connection between one person and another. Gilligan's work is controversial. Do justice and care represent distinctly male and female perspectives? If so, is the explanation biological or social? These questions remain subjects of debate.

A further dimension of this issue is whether care as a moral attitude or perspective has been given insufficient recognition and has been marginalized by mainstream moral theory, which has been dominated by a concern with justice, rights, and impersonal principles. Some feminist writers accept the view that care is a predominantly female perspective, and argue that the lack of recognition by mainstream moral theory is due to the fact that moral philosophy has traditionally been dominated by men—at least until recently. If they are right—and again, this is subject to debate—the emphasis on justice, rights, and impersonal principles in mainstream moral philosophy may represent a form of male theoretical bias. However, it is important to point out that a number of writers have argued that care and other forms of direct, felt concern for and emotional attachment with others are important moral attitudes that have not been given sufficient attention by theorists, and have done so without claiming that these are gender-specific attitudes. Many writers think that care and related attitudes are important virtues displayed by both men and women, and that they are needed to supplement a morality of abstract general principles.

In the next selection, Annette Baier develops a feminist critique of the primacy assigned to justice and impersonal principles by contemporary Kantian approaches to ethics. While acknowledging that justice and universal human rights are clearly important moral notions, she explores the shortcomings that she finds in a moral outlook based exclusively on these notions. Annette Baier was Distinguished Service Professor of Philosophy at the University of Pittsburgh until her retirement. She has written widely in moral philosophy, the philosophy of mind, and the history of philosophy. Her books include *Postures of Mind: Essays on Mind and Morals* (1985), *A Progress of Sentiments: Reflections on Hume's Treatise* (1991), *Moral Prejudices: Essays on Ethics* (1994), and *The Commons of the Mind* (1997).

———

The Need for More than Justice

In recent decades in North American social and moral philosophy, alongside the development and discussion of widely influential theories of justice, taken as Rawls takes it as the "first virtue of social institutions,"[1] there has been a counter-movement gathering strength, one coming from some interesting sources. For some of the most outspoken of the diverse group who have in a variety of ways been challenging the assumed supremacy of justice among the moral and social virtues are members of those sections of society whom one might have expected to be especially aware of the supreme importance of justice, namely blacks and women. Those who have only recently won recognition of their equal rights, who have only recently seen the correction or partial correction of longstanding racist and sexist injustices to their race and sex, are among the philosophers now suggesting that justice is only one virtue among many, and one that may need the presence of the others in order to deliver its own undenied value. Among these philosophers of the philosophical counterculture, as it were—but an increasingly large counterculture—include Alasdair MacIntyre,[2] Michael Stocker,[3] Lawrence Blum,[4] Michael Slote,[5] Laurence Thomas,[6] Claudia Card,[7] Alison Jaggar,[8] Susan Wolf[9] and a

[1]John Rawls, *A Theory of Justice* (Cambridge: Harvard University Press 1970).

[2]Alasdair MacIntyre, *After Virtue* (Notre Dame: Notre Dame University Press 1981).

[3]Michael Stocker, "The Schizophrenia of Modern Ethical Theories," *Journal of Philosophy* 73, 14, 453–66, and "Agent and Other: Against Ethical Universalism," *Australasian Journal of Philosophy* 54, 206–20.

[4]Lawrence Blum, *Friendship, Altruism and Morality* (London: Routledge & Kegan Paul 1980).

[5]Michael Slote, *Goods and Virtues* (Oxford: Oxford University Press 1983).

[6]Laurence Thomas, "Love and Morality," in *Epistemology and Sociobiology,* James Fetzer, ed. (1985); and "Justice, Happiness and Self Knowledge," *Canadian Journal of Philosophy* (March 1986). Also "Beliefs and the Motivation to Be Just," *American Philosophical Quarterly* 22 (4), 347–52.

[7]Claudia Card, "Mercy," *Philosophical Review* 81, 1, and "Gender and Moral Luck," in *Identity, Character, and Morality,* ed. Owen Flanagan and Amélie O. Rorty (Cambridge: MIT Press 1990).

Annette Baier, "The Need for More than Justice," in Marsha Haren and Kai Nelson, eds., *Science, Morality and Feminist Theory* (University of Calgary Press, 1987). Copyright © University of Calgary Press 1987. Reprinted with permission of the publisher.

whole group of men and women, myself included, who have been influenced by the writings of Harvard educational psychologist Carol Gilligan, whose book *In a Different Voice* (Harvard 1982; hereafter D. V.) caused a considerable stir both in the popular press and, more slowly, in the philosophical journals.[10]

Let me say quite clearly at this early point that there is little disagreement that justice is a social value of very great importance, and injustice an evil. Nor would those who have worked on theories of justice want to deny that other things matter besides justice. Rawls, for example, incorporates the value of freedom into his account of justice, so that denial of basic freedoms counts as injustice. Rawls also leaves room for a wider theory of the right, of which the theory of justice is just a part. Still, he does claim that justice is the "first" virtue of social institutions, and it is only that claim about priority that I think has been challenged. It is easy to exaggerate the differences of view that exist, and I want to avoid that. The differences are as much in emphasis as in substance, or we can say that they are differences in tone of voice. But these differences do tend to make a difference in approaches to a wide range of topics not just in moral theory but in areas like medical ethics, where the discussion used to be conducted in terms of patients' rights, of informed consent, and so on, but now tends to get conducted in an enlarged moral vocabulary, which draws on what Gilligan calls the ethics of *care* as well as that of *justice*.

For "care" is the new buzz-word. It is not, as Shakespeare's Portia demanded, mercy that is to season justice, but a less authoritarian humanitarian supplement, a felt concern for the good of others and for community with them. The "cold jealous virtue of justice" (Hume) is found to be too cold, and it is "warmer" more communitarian virtues and social ideals that are being called in to supplement it. One might say that liberty and equality are being found inadequate without fraternity, except that "fraternity" will be quite the wrong word, if as Gilligan initially suggested, it is *women* who perceive this value most easily. ("Sorority" will do no better, since it is too exclusive, and English has no gender-neuter word for the mutual concern of siblings.) She has since modified this claim, allowing that there are two perspectives on moral and social issues that we all tend to alternate between, and which are not always easy to combine, one of them what she called the justice perspective, the other the care perspective. It is increasingly obvious that there are many male philosophical spokespersons for the care perspective (Laurence Thomas, Lawrence Blum, Michael Stocker) so that it cannot be the prerogative of women. Nevertheless Gilligan still wants to claim that women are the most unlikely to take *only* the justice perspective, as some men are claimed to, at least until some mid-life crisis jolts them into "bifocal" moral vision (see D. V., ch. 6).

Gilligan in her book did not offer any explanatory theory of why there should be any difference between female and male moral outlook, but she did tend to link the naturalness to women of the care perspective with their role as primary caretakers of young children, that is with their parental and specifically maternal role.

[8]Alison Jaggar, *Feminist Politics and Human Nature* (London: Rowman and Allanheld 1983).
[9]Susan Wolf, "Moral Saints," *Journal of Philosophy* 79 (August 1982), 419–39.
[10]For a helpful survey article see Owen Flanagan and Kathryn Jackson, "Justice Care & Gender: The Kohlberg-Gilligan Debate Revisited," *Ethics* 97, 3 (April 1987).

She avoided the question of whether it is their biological or their social parental role that is relevant, and some of those who dislike her book are worried precisely by this uncertainty. Some find it retrograde to hail as a special sort of moral wisdom an outlook that may be the product of the socially enforced restriction of women to domestic roles (and the reservation of such roles for them alone). For that might seem to play into the hands of those who still favor such restriction. (Marxists, presumably, will not find it so surprising that moral truths might depend for their initial clear voicing on the social oppression, and memory of it, of those who voice the truths.) Gilligan did in the first chapter of D. V. cite the theory of Nancy Chodorow (as presented in *The Reproduction of Mothering* [Berkeley 1978]) which traces what appears as gender differences in personality to early social development, in particular to the effects of the child's primary caretaker being or not being of the same gender as the child. Later, both in "The Conquistador and the Dark Continent: Reflections on the Nature of Love" (*Daedalus* [Summer 1984]), and "The Origins of Morality in Early Childhood" [in J. Kagan and S. Lamb, eds., *The Emergence of Morality in Early Childhood*, (Chicago: University of Chicago Press, 1987)], she develops this explanation. She postulates two evils that any infant may become aware of, the evil of detachment or isolation from others whose love one needs, and the evil of relative powerlessness and weakness. Two dimensions of moral development are thereby set—one aimed at achieving satisfying community with others, the other aimed at autonomy or equality of power. The relative predominance of one over the other development will depend both upon the relative salience of the two evils in early childhood, and on early and later reinforcement or discouragement in attempts made to guard against these two evils. This provides the germs of a theory about *why*, given current customs of childrearing, it should be mainly women who are not content with only the moral outlook that she calls the justice perspective, necessary though that was and is seen by them to have been to their hard won liberation from sexist oppression. They, like the blacks, used the language of rights and justice to change their own social position, but nevertheless see limitations in that language, according to Gilligan's findings as a moral psychologist. She reports their discontent with the individualist more or less Kantian moral framework that dominates Western moral theory and which influenced moral psychologists such as Lawrence Kohlberg,[11] to whose conception of moral maturity she seeks an alternative. Since the target of Gilligan's criticism is the dominant Kantian tradition, and since that has been the target also of moral philosophers as diverse in their own views as Bernard Williams,[12] Alasdair MacIntyre, Philippa Foot,[13] Susan Wolf, [and] Claudia Card, her book is of interest as much for its attempt to articulate an alternative to the Kantian justice perspective as for its implicit raising of the question of male bias in Western moral theory, especially liberal-democratic theory. For whether the supposed blind spots of that outlook are due to male bias, or to non-parental bias, or to early traumas of powerlessness or to early resignation to "detachment" from others, we need first

---

[11]Lawrence Kohlberg, *Essays in Moral Development*, vols. I & II (New York: Harper and Row 1981, 1984).
[12]Bernard Williams, *Ethics and the Limits of Philosophy* (Cambridge: Cambridge University Press 1985).
[13]Philippa Foot, *Virtues and Vices* (Berkeley: University of California Press 1978).

to be persuaded that they *are* blind spots before we will have any interest in their cause and cure. Is justice blind to important social values, or at least only one-eyed? What is it that comes into view from the "care perspective" that is not seen from the "justice perspective"?

Gilligan's position here is most easily described by contrasting it with that of Kohlberg, against which she developed it. Kohlberg, influenced by Piaget and the Kantian philosophical tradition as developed by John Rawls, developed a theory about typical moral development which saw it to progress from a preconventional level, where what is seen to matter is pleasing or not offending parental authority-figures, through a conventional level in which the child tries to fit in with a group, such as a school community, and conform to its standards and rules, to a post-conventional critical level, in which such conventional rules are subjected to tests, and where those tests are of a Utilitarian, or, eventually, a Kantian sort—namely ones that require respect for each person's individual rational will, or autonomy, and conformity to any implicit social contract such wills are deemed to have made, or to any hypothetical ones they would make if thinking clearly. What was found when Kohlberg's questionnaires (mostly by verbal response to verbally sketched moral dilemmas) were applied to female as well as male subjects, Gilligan reports, is that the girls and women not only scored generally lower than the boys and men, but tended to *revert* to the lower stage of the conventional level even after briefly (usually in adolescence) attaining the post-conventional level. Piaget's finding that girls were deficient in "the legal sense" was confirmed.

These results led Gilligan to wonder if there might not be a quite different pattern of development to be discerned, at least in female subjects. She therefore conducted interviews designed to elicit not just how far advanced the subjects were towards an appreciation of the nature and importance of Kantian autonomy, but also to find out what the subjects themselves saw as progress or lack of it, what conceptions of moral maturity they came to possess by the time they were adults. She found that although the Kohlberg version of moral maturity as respect for fellow persons, and for their rights as equals (rights including that of free association), did seem shared by many young men, the women tended to speak in a different voice about morality itself and about moral maturity. To quote Gilligan, "Since the reality of interconnection is experienced by women as given rather than freely contracted, they arrive at an understanding of life that reflects the limits of autonomy and control. As a result, women's development delineates the path not only to a less violent life but also to a maturity realized by interdependence and taking care" (D. V., 172). She writes that there is evidence that "women perceive and construe social reality differently from men, and that these differences center around experiences of attachment and separation . . . because women's sense of integrity appears to be intertwined with an ethics of care, so that to see themselves as women is to see themselves in a relationship of connection, the major changes in women's lives would seem to involve changes in the understanding and activities of care" (D. V., 171). She contrasts this progressive understanding of care, from merely pleasing others to helping and nurturing, with the sort of progression that is involved in Kohlberg's stages, a progression in the understanding, not of mutual care, but of mutual *respect*, where this has its Kantian overtones of distance, even of

510 Annette C. Baier

some fear for the respected, and where personal autonomy and *in*dependence, rather than more satisfactory interdependence, are the paramount values.

This contrast, one cannot but feel, is one which Gilligan might have used the Marxist language of alienation to make. For the main complaint about the Kantian version of a society with its first virtue justice, construed as respect for equal rights to formal goods such as having contracts kept, due process, equal opportunity including opportunity to participate in political activities leading to policy and law-making, to basic liberties of speech, free association and assembly, religious worship, is that none of these goods do much to ensure that the people who have and mutually respect such rights will have any other relationships to one another than the minimal relationship needed to keep such a "civil society" going. They may well be lonely, driven to suicide, apathetic about their work and about participation in political processes, find their lives meaningless and have no wish to leave offspring to face the same meaningless existence. Their rights, and respect for rights, are quite compatible with very great misery, and misery whose causes are not just individual misfortunes and psychic sickness, but social and moral impoverishment.

What Gilligan's older male subjects complain of is precisely this sort of alienation from some dimly glimpsed better possibility for human beings, some richer sort of network of relationships. As one of Gilligan's male subjects put it, "People have real emotional needs to be attached to something, and equality does not give you attachment. Equality fractures society and places on every person the burden of standing on his own two feet" (D. V., 167). It is not just the difficulty of self-reliance which is complained of, but its socially "fracturing" effect. Whereas the younger men, in their college years, had seen morality as a matter of reciprocal non-interference, this older man begins to see it as reciprocal attachment. "Morality is . . . essential . . . for creating the kind of environment, interaction between people, that is a prerequisite to the fulfillment of individual goals. If you want other people not to interfere with your pursuit of whatever you are into, you have to play the game," says the spokesman for traditional liberalism (D. V., 98). But if what one is "into" is interconnection, interdependence rather than an individual autonomy that may involve "detachment," such a version of morality will come to seem inadequate. And Gilligan stresses that the interconnection that her mature women subjects, and some men, wanted to sustain was not merely freely chosen interconnection, nor interconnection between equals, but also the sort of interconnection that can obtain between a child and her unchosen mother and father, or between a child and her unchosen older and younger siblings, or indeed between most workers and their unchosen fellow workers, or most citizens and their unchosen fellow citizens.

A model of a decent community different from the liberal one is involved in the version of moral maturity that Gilligan voices. It has in many ways more in common with the older religion-linked versions of morality and a good society than with the modern Western liberal ideal. That perhaps is why some find it so dangerous and retrograde. Yet it seems clear that it also has much in common with what we call Hegelian versions of moral maturity and of social health and malaise, both with Marxist versions and with so-called right-Hegelian views.

Let me try to summarize the main differences, as I see them, between on the one hand Gilligan's version of moral maturity and the sort of social structures that would encourage, express and protect it, and on the other the orthodoxy she sees herself to be challenging. I shall from now on be giving my own interpretation of the significance of her challenges, not merely reporting them.[14] The most obvious point is the challenge to the individualism of the Western tradition, to the fairly entrenched belief in the possibility and desirability of each person pursuing his own good in his own way, constrained only by a minimal formal common good namely a working legal apparatus that enforces contracts and protects individuals from undue interference by others. Gilligan reminds us that noninterference can, especially for the relatively powerless, such as the very young, amount to neglect, and even between equals can be isolating and alienating. On her less individualist version of individuality, it becomes defined by responses to dependency and to patterns of interconnection, both chosen and unchosen. It is not something a person *has*, and which she then chooses relationships to suit, but something that develops out of a series of dependencies and interdependencies, and responses to them. This conception of individuality is not flatly at odds with, say, Rawls's Kantian one, but there is at least a difference of tone of voice between speaking as Rawls does of each of us having our own rational life plan, which a just society's moral traffic rules will allow us to follow, and which may or may not include close association with other persons, and speaking as Gilligan does of a satisfactory life as involving "progress of affiliative relationship" (D. V., 170) where "the concept of identity expands to include the experience of interconnection" (D. V., 173). Rawls can allow that progress to Gilligan-style moral maturity may be *a* rational life plan, but not a moral constraint on every life-pattern. The trouble is that it will not do just to say "let this version of morality be an optional extra. Let us agree on the essential minimum, that is on justice and rights, and let whoever wants to go further and cultivate this more demanding ideal of responsibility and care." For, first, it cannot be satisfactorily cultivated without closer cooperation from others than respect for rights and justice will ensure, and, second, the encouragement of some to cultivate it while others do not could easily lead to exploitation of those who do. It obviously *has* suited some in most societies well enough that others take on the responsibilities of care (for the sick, the helpless, the young) leaving them free to pursue their own less altruistic goods. Volunteer forces of those who accept an ethic of care, operating within a society where the power is exercised and the institutions designed, redesigned, or maintained by those who accept a less communal ethic of minimally constrained self-advancement, will not be the solution. The liberal individualists may be able to "tolerate" the more communally minded, if they keep the liberals' rules, but it is not so clear that the more communally minded can be content with just those rules, nor be content to be tolerated and possibly exploited.

For the moral tradition which developed the concept of rights, autonomy and justice is the same tradition that provided "justifications" of the oppression of

[14]I have previously written about the significance of her findings for moral philosophy in "What Do Women Want in a Moral Theory?" *Nous* 19 (March 1985), "Trust and Antitrust," *Ethics* 96 (1986), and in "Hume the Women's Moral Theorist?" in *Women and Moral Theory*, E. Kittay and D. Meyers, ed. [Totowa, NJ: Rowman and Littlefield 1987].

those whom the primary right-holders depended on to do the sort of work they themselves preferred not to do. The domestic work was left to women and slaves, and the liberal morality for right-holders was surreptitiously supplemented by a different set of demands made on domestic workers. As long as women could be got to assume responsibility for the care of home and children, and to train their children to continue the sexist system, the liberal morality could continue to be the official morality, by turning its eyes away from the contribution made by those it excluded. The long-unnoticed moral proletariat were the domestic workers, mostly female. Rights have usually been for the privileged. Talking about laws, and the rights those laws recognize and protect, does not in itself ensure that the group of legislators and rights-holders will not be restricted to some elite. Bills of rights have usually been proclamations of the rights of some in-group, barons, land-owners, males, whites, non-foreigners. The "justice perspective," and the legal sense that goes with it, are shadowed by their patriarchal past. What did Kant, the great prophet of autonomy, say in his moral theory about women? He said they were incapable of legislation, not fit to vote, that they needed the guidance of more "rational" males.[15] Autonomy was not for them, only for first-class, really rational persons. It is ironic that Gilligan's original findings in a way confirm Kant's views—it seems that autonomy really may not be for women. Many of them reject that ideal (D. V., 48), and have been found not as good at making rules as are men. But where Kant concludes—"so much the worse for women," we can conclude—"so much the worse for the male fixation on the special skill of drafting legislation, for the bureaucratic mentality of rule worship, and for the male exaggeration of the importance of independence over mutual interdependence."

It is however also true that the moral theories that made the concept of a person's right central were not just the instruments for excluding some persons, but also the instruments used by those who demanded that more and more persons be included in the favored group. Abolitionists, reformers, women, used the language of rights to assert their claims to inclusion in the group of full members of a community. The tradition of liberal moral theory has in fact developed so as to include the women it had so long excluded, to include the poor as well as rich, blacks and whites, and so on. Women like Mary Wollstonecraft used the male moral theories to good purpose. So we should not be wholly ungrateful for those male moral theories, for all their objectionable earlier content. They were undoubtedly patriarchal, but they also contained the seeds of the challenge, or antidote, to this patriarchal poison.

But when we transcend the values of the Kantians, we should not forget the facts of history—that those values were the values of the oppressors of women. The Christian church, whose version of the moral law Aquinas codified, in his very legalistic moral theory, still insists on the maleness of the God it worships, and jealously reserves for males all the most powerful positions in its hierarchy. Its patriarchal prejudice is open and avowed. In the secular moral theories of men, the sexist patriarchal prejudice is today often less open, not as blatant as it is in Aquinas, in the later natural law tradition, and in Kant and Hegel, but is often still there. No moral theorist today would say that women are unfit to vote, to make laws, or to rule a nation without powerful male advisors (as most queens had), but the old doctrines

---

[15]Immanuel Kant, *Metaphysics of Morals*, sec. 46.

die hard. In one of the best male theories we have, John Rawls's theory, a key role is played by the idea of the "head of a household." It is heads of households who are to deliberate behind a "veil of ignorance" of historical details, and of details of their own special situation, to arrive at the "just" constitution for a society. Now of course Rawls does not think or say that these "heads" are fathers rather than mothers. But if we have really given up the age-old myth of women needing, as Grotius put it, to be under the "eye" of a more "rational" male protector and master, then how do families come to have any one "head," except by the death or desertion of one parent? They will either be two-headed, or headless. Traces of the old patriarchal poison still remain in even the best contemporary moral theorizing. Few may actually say that women's place is in the home, but there is much muttering, when unemployment figures rise, about how the relatively recent flood of women into the work force complicates the problem, as if it would be a good thing if women just went back home whenever unemployment rises, to leave the available jobs for the men. We still do not really have a wide acceptance of the equal rights of women to employment outside the home. Nor do we have wide acceptance of the equal duty of men to perform those domestic tasks which in no way depend on special female anatomy, namely cooking, cleaning, and the care of weaned children. All sorts of stories (maybe true stories), about children's need for one "primary" parent, who must be the mother if the mother breast feeds the child, shore up the unequal division of domestic responsibility between mothers and fathers, wives and husbands. If we are really to transvalue the values of our patriarchal past, we need to rethink all of those assumptions, really test those psychological theories. And how will men ever develop an understanding of the "ethics of care" if they continue to be shielded or kept from that experience of caring for a dependent child, which complements the experience we all have had of being cared for as dependent children? These experiences form the natural background for the development of moral maturity as Gilligan's women saw it.

Exploitation aside, why would women, once liberated, not be content to have their version of morality merely tolerated? Why should they not see themselves as voluntarily, for their own reasons, taking on *more* than the liberal rules demand, while having no quarrel with the content of those rules themselves, nor with their remaining the only ones that are expected to be generally obeyed? To see why, we need to move on to three more differences between the Kantian liberals (usually contractarians) and their critics. These concern the relative weight put on relationships between equals, and the relative weight put on freedom of choice, and on the authority of intellect over emotions. It is a typical feature of the dominant moral theories and traditions, since Kant, or perhaps since Hobbes, that relationships between equals, or those who are deemed equal in some important sense, have been the relations that morality is concerned primarily to regulate. Relationships between those who are clearly unequal in power, such as parents and children, earlier and later generations in relation to one another, states and citizens, doctors and patients, the well and the ill, large states and small states, have had to be shunted to the bottom of the agenda, and then dealt with by some sort of "promotion" of the weaker so that an appearance of virtual equality is achieved. Citizens collectively become equal to states, children are treated as adults-to-be, the ill and dying are treated as continuers of their earlier more potent selves, so that their "rights" could be seen as the rights of equals. This pretence of an equality that is in fact absent may often lead to desirable protection of the weaker, or more dependent. But it somewhat masks the question of what our moral relationships *are* to those who are our superiors or our inferiors in power. A more realistic acceptance of the fact that we begin as helpless children, that at almost every point of our lives we deal with both the more and the less helpless, that equality of power and interdependency, between two persons or groups, is rare and hard to recognize when it does occur, might lead us to a more direct approach to questions concerning the design of institutions structuring these relationships between unequals (families, schools, hospitals, armies) and of the morality of our dealings with the more and the less powerful. One reason why those who agree with the Gilligan version of what morality is about will not want to agree that the liberals' rules are a good minimal set, the only ones we need pressure *everyone* to obey, is that these rules do little to protect the young or the dying or the starving or any of the relatively powerless against neglect, or to ensure an education that will form persons to be *capable* of conforming to an ethics of care and responsibility. Put badly, and in a way Gilligan certain has not put it, the liberal morality, if unsupplemented, may *unfit* people to be anything other than what its justifying theories suppose them to be, ones who have no interest in each others' interests. Yet some must take an interest in the next generation's interests. Women's traditional work, of caring for the less powerful, especially for the young, is obviously socially vital. One cannot regard any version of morality that does not ensure that it gets well done as an adequate "minimal morality," any more than we could so regard one that left any concern for more distant future generations an optional extra. A moral theory, it can plausibly be claimed, cannot regard concern for new and future persons as an optional charity left for those with a taste for it. If the morality the theory endorses is to sustain itself, it must provide for its own continuers, not just take out a loan on a carefully encouraged maternal instinct or on the enthusiasm of a self-selected group of environmentalists, who make it their business or hobby to be concerned with what we are doing to mother earth.

The recognition of the importance of all parties of relations between those who are and cannot but be unequal, both of these relations in themselves and for their effect on personality formation and so on other relationships, goes along with a recognition of the plain fact that not all morally important relationships can or should be freely chosen. So far I have discussed three reasons women have not to be content to pursue their own values within the framework of the liberal morality. The first was its dubious record. The second was its inattention to relations of inequality or its pretence of equality. The third reason is its exaggeration of the scope of choice, or its inattention to unchosen relations. Showing up the partial myth of equality among actual members of a community, and of the undesirability of trying to pretend that we are treating all of them as equals, tends to go along with an exposure of the companion myth that moral obligations arise from freely *chosen* associations between such equals. Vulnerable future generations do not choose its place in a family or nation, nor is it treated as free to do as it likes until some association is freely entered into. Nor do its parents always choose their parental role, or freely assume their parental responsibilities any more than we choose our power to affect the conditions in which later generations will live. Gilligan's attention to the version of morality and moral maturity found in women, many of whom had faced choice of whether or not to have an abortion, and who had at some point become mothers, is attention to the perceived inadequacy of the language of rights to help in such choices or to guide them in their parental role. It would not be much of an exaggeration to call the Gilligan "different voice" the voice of the potential parents. The emphasis on care goes with a recognition of the often unchosen nature of the responsibilities of those who give care, both of children who care for their aged or infirm parents, and of parents who care for the children they in fact have. Contract soon ceases to seem the paradigm source of moral obligation once we attend to parental responsibility, and justice as a virtue of social institutions will come to seem at best only first equal with the virtue, whatever its name, that ensures that each new generation is made appropriately welcome and prepared for their adult lives.

This all constitutes a belated reminder to Western moral theorists of a fact they have always known, that as Adam Ferguson, and David Hume before him emphasized, we are born into families, and the first society we belong to, one that fits or misfits us for later ones, is the small society of parents (or some sort of child-attendants) and children, exhibiting as it may both relationships of near equality and of inequality in power. This simple reminder, with the fairly considerable implications it can have for the plausibility of contractarian moral theory, is at the same time a reminder of the role of human emotions as much as human reason and will in moral development as it actually comes about. The fourth feature of the Gilligan challenge to liberal orthodoxy is a challenge to its typical *rationalism,* or intellectualism, to its assumption that we need not worry what passions persons have, as long as their rational wills can control them. This Kantian picture of a controlling reason dictating to possibly unruly passions also tends to seem less useful when we are led to consider what sort of person we need to fill the role of parent, or indeed want in any close relationship. It might be important for father figures to have rational control over their violent urges to beat to death the children whose screams enrage them, but more than control of such nasty passions seems needed in the mother or primary parent, or parent-substitute, by most psychological theories. They need to love their children, not just to control their irritation. So the emphasis in Kantian theories on rational control of emotions, rather than on cultivating desirable forms of emotion, is challenged by Gilligan, along with the challenge to the assumption of the centrality of autonomy, or relations between equals, and of freely chosen relations.

The same set of challenges to "orthodox" liberal moral theory has come not just from Gilligan and other women, who are reminding other moral theorists of the role of the family as a social institution and as an influence on the other relationships people want to or are capable of sustaining, but also, as I noted at the start, from an otherwise fairly diverse group of men, ranging from those influenced by both Hegelian and Christian traditions (MacIntyre) to all varieties of other backgrounds. From this group I want to draw attention to the work of one philosopher in particular, namely Laurence Thomas, the author of a fairly remarkable article[16] in

---

[16]Laurence Thomas, "Sexism and Racism: Some Conceptual Differences," *Ethics* 90 (1980), 239–50; republished in *Philosophy, Sex and Language,* Vetterling-Braggin, ed. (Totowa, NJ: Littlefield Adams 1980).

which he finds sexism to be a more intractable social evil than racism. In a series of articles and a book,[17] Thomas makes a strong case for the importance of supplementing a concern for justice and respect for rights with an emphasis on equally needed virtues, and on virtues seen as appropriate *emotional* as well as rational capacities. Like Gilligan (and unlike MacIntyre) Thomas gives a lot of attention to the childhood beginnings of moral and social capacities, to the role of parental love in making that possible, and to the emotional as well as the cognitive development we have reason to think both possible and desirable in human persons.

It is clear, I think that the best moral theory has to be a cooperative product of women and men, has to harmonize justice and care. The morality it theorizes about is after all for all persons, for men and for women, and will need their combined insights. As Gilligan said (D. V., 174), what we need now is a "marriage" of the old male and the newly articulated female insights. If she is right about the special moral aptitudes of women, it will most likely be the women who propose the marriage, since they are the ones with more natural empathy, with the better diplomatic skills, the ones more likely to shoulder responsibility and take moral initiative, and the ones who find it easiest to empathize and care about how the other party feels. Then, once there is this union of male and female moral wisdom, we maybe can teach each other the moral skills each gender currently lacks, so that the gender difference in moral outlook that Gilligan found will slowly become less marked.

Study Questions

1. Baier discusses Carol Gilligan's work suggesting the existence of two different perspectives on moral thought, the "justice perspective" and the "care perspective," which lead to different models of moral maturity and moral community. What are the main differences between these two perspectives or models of moral maturity?
2. In your experience, do men and women display different approaches to moral thinking? If so, how would you characterize these differences? What do you think explains these differences (if they exist)?
3. Baier makes it clear that justice is important, but she also suggests that liberal conceptions of justice are not adequate even as a minimal social morality. What are the main shortcomings that she finds in liberal moralities that focus on justice and rights? Do you agree or disagree with her claims?
4. In your view which is most important to the moral point of view, reason or emotion? Why?

Selected Bibliography

Baier, Annette, "Hume, the Women's Moral Theorist?" in E. F. Kittay and D. T. Meyers, eds. *Women and Moral Theory* (Totowa, NJ: Rowman and Littlefield, 1987).

[17]See articles listed in note 6, above. [Laurence Thomas, *Living Morally: A Psychology of Moral Character* (Philadelphia: Temple University Press 1989).]

———. "What Do Women Want in a Moral Theory?" *Nous* 19 (1985).

———. *Moral Prejudices: Essays on Ethics* (Cambridge, MA: Harvard University Press, 1994)

Gilligan, Carol. *In a Different Voice* (Cambridge, MA: Harvard University Press, 1982). An influential book arguing that justice and care represent distinct, gendered moral perspectives.

———. "Moral Orientation and Moral Development," in Kittay and Meyers, ed. *Women and Moral Theory*. Reprinted in Held, ed. *Justice and Care: Essential Readings in Feminists Ethics*. Further development of Gilligan's views.

Held, Virginia, ed. *Justice and Care: Essential Readings in Feminists Ethics* (Boulder, CO: Westview Press, 1995). A collection of essays by several leading feminist writers.

Kittay, E. F. and D. T. Meyers, eds. *Women and Moral Theory* (Totowa, NJ: Rowman and Littlefield, 1987).

Noddings, Nel, *Caring: A Feminine Approach to Ethics* (Berkeley: University of California Press, 1984). Develops an ethic of care.

Okin, Susan. "Feminism: Moral Development and the Virtues," in Roger Crisp, ed., *How Should One Live? Essays on the Virtues* (Oxford/New York: Oxford University Press, 1996).

———. *Justice, Gender and the Family* (New York: Basic Books, 1989). Assesses the existence of gender bias in contemporary theories of justice.

Pearsall, M. ed. *Women and Moral Values*, 3rd edition (Belmont, CA: Wadsworth, 1999).

Young, Iris Marion. *Moral Understanding: A Feminist Study of Ethics* (London: Routledge, 1998).

31

MARTHA NUSSBAUM

———

A number of feminist writers have charged that liberal moral and political thought, in spite of its emphasis on equality and individual rights, is inadequate to the aims of feminism. They have argued that the dominant moral theories of the western tradition, including those of the contemporary era, having

> *Liberalism . . . is centrally about the protection of spheres of choice—not . . . in a purely negative way . . . but rather in a way closely tied to the norm of equal respect for personhood.*

been developed for the most part by men, show a degree of male bias. As a result, they do not adequately reflect the point of view and needs of women, or do not properly represent the barriers to full social equality of women. Feminists have asked whether what are represented as universal features of human nature or human agency in fact reflect a male point of view. They have wondered whether some of the basic theoretical presuppositions of liberal normative theories have prevented them from recognizing certain kinds of gender injustice. Some have worried that a moral perspective distinctive of women has been ignored or devalued, and thus is not fully reflected in liberal moral outlooks. These charges are given some support by the fact that many of the most important philosophers in the western tradition—despite the fact that they developed the theoretical basis for universal human equality—held strikingly inegalitarian views about women.

Martha Nussbaum defends modern liberalism against three objections that some feminist writers have leveled against it—that it is too individualistic, and thus does not sufficiently acknowledge the value of community; that its ideal of equality is too abstract, so that it ignores important realities of history and social context that sustain gender inequality; and that by focusing on reason, it undervalues the roles of emotion and care. Nussbaum's assessment of these objections is complex. She argues that certain objections are based on misunderstandings, and that liberalism can accommodate the feminist concerns when it is properly understood. In other cases, she argues that liberal positions are more defensible than the proposed feminist alternatives. But she also believes that liberal theories have much to learn from feminist thought, and indicates a number of points at which liberalism needs modification. Overall she thinks that liberalism is a powerful tool that strengthens feminism.

Martha Nussbaum received her doctorate from Harvard, where she was the first woman to be accepted into Harvard's Society of Fellows. She has taught at Harvard and Brown, and is currently professor of philosophy and law at the University of Chicago. She has written on many areas of philosophy, including Aristotle, moral philosophy, philosophy of literature, and political philosophy. Her many books include *The Fragility of Goodness* (1986), *Love's Knowledge* (1990), *The Therapy of Desire* (1994), *Poetic Justice* (1996), *Sex and Social Justice* (1999), *Women and Human Development: The Capabilities Approach* (2000), and *Upheavals of Thought: The Intelligence of Emotions* (2001).

The Feminist Critique of Liberalism

Women around the world are using the language of liberalism. Consider some representative examples from recent publications:

1. Roop Rekha Verma, philosopher and grass-roots activist from Lucknow, India, speaks about the many ways in which Indian religious traditions have devalued women. She concludes that the largest problem with these traditions is that they deprive women of "full personhood." "What is personhood?" Verma asks. "To me three things seem essential for [full personhood]: autonomy, self-respect, and a sense of fulfillment and achievement."[1]

2. Nahid Toubia, the first woman surgeon in the Sudan and woman's health activist, writes of the urgent needs to mobilize international opposition to the practice of female genital mutilation (FGM), especially when it is performed on young girls without their consent. "International human rights bodies and organizations," she concludes, "must declare FGM to be violence against women and children and a violation of their rights. . . . If women are to be considered as equal and responsible members of society, no aspect of their physical, psychological, or sexual integrity can be compromised."[2]

3. Describing a meeting at the Indian Institute of Management in Gangalore that brought together widows from all over India for a discussion of their living conditions *The Hindu Magazine* reports as follows:

[1]Roop Rekha Verma, "Femininity, Equality, and Personhood," in *Women, Culture, and Development* (hereafter WCD), ed. M. Nussbaum and J. Glover (Oxford: Clarendon Press, 1995(, 433–43.
[2]Nahid Toubia, "Female Genital Mutilation," in *Women's Rights, Human Rights* (hereafter WRHR), ed. Julie Peters and Andrea Wolpher (New York and London: Routledge, 1995), 224–37, at 235, reprinted from Toubia, *Female Genital Mutilation: A Call for Global Action* (New York: Women, Ink., 1993).

Throughout the week they came to realize many things about themselves and their lives—especially how much they had internalized society's perceptions of them as daughters, wives, mothers and widows (their identity invariably defined in some of their relationship to men). . . . They were encouraged to see themselves as persons who had a right to exist even if their husbands were dead, and as citizens who had a right to resources—such as land, housing, employment, credit and ration cards—which would enable them to live and bring up their children (if any) with dignity and self-respect.[3]

Personhood, autonomy, rights, dignity, self-respect: These are the terms of the liberal Enlightenment. Women are using them, and teaching other women to use them when they did not use them before. They treat these terms as though they matter, as though they are the best terms in which to conduct a radical critique of society, as though using them is crucial to women's quality of life.

This situation looks in some respects deeply paradoxical, because liberalism has been thought by many feminists to be a political approach that is totally inadequate to the needs and aims of women, and in some ways profoundly subversive of these aims. Over the past twenty years, feminist political thinkers have put forward many reasons to reject liberalism and to define feminism to some extent in opposition to liberalism. In 1983, in *Feminist Politics and Human Nature,* one of the most influential works of feminist political theory, Alison Jaggar concluded that "the liberal conception of human nature and of political philosophy cannot constitute the philosophical foundation for an adequate theory of women's liberation."[4] Many influential feminist thinkers have agreed with Jaggar, treating liberalism as at best negligent of women's concerns and at worst an active enemy of women's progress.

But liberalism has not died in feminist politics; if anything, with the dramatic growth of the movement to recognize various women's rights as central human rights under international law, its radical feminist potential is just beginning to be realized. So it is time to reassess the charges most commonly made in the feminist critique.

Why should this reassessment matter? It is obvious that the activists from whom I have quoted have gone about their business undaunted by the feminist critique, and they will not be daunted now, if feminists once again tell them that autonomy and personhood are bad notions for feminists to use. In that sense a philosophical investigation could be seen as beside the point. But the international political situation is volatile, and the liberal discourse of personhood and rights has come under attack from many directions, some of them practical and influential. Looking at the case for the defense is therefore not simply a scholarly exercise but also a contribution to practical politics.

---

[3] *The Hindu,* April 24, 1994.
[4] Alison Jaggar, *Feminist Politics and Human Nature* (Totowa, NJ: Rowman and Allanheld, 1983, repr. 1988), 47–8. For related views, see also Carole Pateman, *The Problem of Political Obligation: A Critique of Liberal Theory* (Berkeley: University of California Press, 1979); Nancy C. M. Hartsock, *Money, Sex, and Power* (Boston: Northeastern University Press, 1983). An interesting response to some of the criticisms is found in Marilyn Friedman, "Feminism and Modern Friendship," *Ethics* 99 (1989), 304–19.

In general, I shall argue, liberalism of a kind can be defended against the charges that have been made. The deepest and most central ideas of the liberal tradition are ideas of radical force and great theoretical and practical value. These ideas can be formulated in ways that incorporate what is most valuable in the feminist critique—although liberalism needs to learn from feminism if it is to formulate its own central insights in a fully adequate manner. Taking on board the insight of feminism will not leave liberalism unchanged, and liberalism needs to change to respond adequately to those insights: But it will be changed in ways that make it more deeply consistent with its own foundational ideas. Another way of putting this is to say that there have been many strands within liberalism; thinking about the feminist critique proves important in choosing among these because feminism shows defects in some forms of liberalism that continue to be influential. Some feminist proposals do resist incorporation even into a reformulated liberalism, but I shall argue that these are proposals that should be resisted by anyone who seeks justice for the world's women.

There is danger in speaking so generally about "liberalism," a danger that has often plagued feminist debates. "Liberalism" is not a single position but a family of positions; Kantian liberalism is profoundly different from classical Utilitarian liberalism, and both of these from the Utilitarianism currently dominant in neoclassical economics. Many critiques of liberalism are really critiques of economic Utilitarianism, and would not hold against the views of Kant or Mill. Some feminist attacks oversimplify the tradition, and in responding to them I run a grave risk of oversimplification myself. When I speak of "liberalism," then, I shall have in mind, above all, the tradition of Kantian liberalism represented today in the political thought of John Rawls, and also the classical Utilitarian liberal tradition, especially as exemplified in the work of John Stuart Mill. I shall also refer frequently to some major precursors, namely, Rousseau,[5] Hume, and Adam Smith. It seems reasonable to assess the feminist critique by holding it up against the best examples of liberal political thought; any critique of liberalism that cannot be taken seriously as a criticism of Kant or Mill probably is not worth discussing.

The thinkers I have chosen are not in agreement on many important matters, but a core of common commitments can be scrutinized with the interests of feminism in mind. At the heart of this tradition is a twofold intuition about human beings: namely, that all, just by being human, are of equal dignity and worth, no matter where they are situated in society, and that the primary source of this worth is a power of moral choice within them, a power that consists in the ability to plan a life in accordance with one's own evaluations of ends.[6] To these two

---

[5]Rousseau is, of course, in crucial ways not a liberal, but I shall be referring to those portions of his thought that influenced portions of the liberal tradition.

[6]Of course, this power needs development, but the basis for human equality is the possession of the potentiality for that development. Even if individuals possess differing degrees of this basic potentiality, we can say that a sufficient condition for equal moral personality is the possession of a certain basic minimum. See "The Basis of Equality," sec. 77 in John Rawls, *A Theory of Justice* (hereafter TJ) (Cambridge, MA: Harvard University Press, 1970), 504–12; and also the discussion of "basic capabilities," in Martha C. Nussbaum, "Human Capabilities, Female Human Beings," in WCD. This was also the view of the ancient Stoics.

intuitions—which link liberalism at its core to the thought of the Greek and Roman Stoics—the liberal tradition adds one more, which the Stoics did not emphasize: that the moral equality of persons gives them a fair claim to certain types of treatment at the hands of society and politics. What this treatment is will be a subject of debate within the tradition, but the shared starting point is that this treatment must do two closely related things. It must respect and promote the liberty of choice, and it must respect and promote the equal worth of persons as choosers. . . .

Feminists have made three salient charges against this liberal tradition as a philosophy that might be used to promote women's goals. They have charged, first, that it is too "individualistic": that its focus on the dignity and worth of the individual slights and unfairly subordinates the value to be attached to community and to collective social entities such as families, groups, and classes. They have charged, second, that its ideal of equality is too abstract and formal, that it errs through lack of immersion in the concrete realities of power in different social situations. Finally, they have charged that liberalism errs through its focus on reason, unfairly slighting the role we should give to emotion and care in the moral and political life. All these alleged failings in liberalism are linked to specific failings in the tradition's handling of women's issues. It has frequently been claimed that liberalism cannot atone for these defects without changing utterly, and that feminists interested in progress beyond the status quo would be better off choosing a different political philosophy—whether a form of socialism or Marxism or a form of communitarian or care-based political theory. Let us examine these charges.

Individual and Community

The most common feminist charge against liberalism is that it is too "individualistic." By taking the individual to be the basic unit for political thought, it treats the individual as prior to society, as capable, in theory if not in fact, of existing outside all social ties. "Logically if not empirically," writes Jaggar of the liberal view, "human individuals could exist outside a social context; their essential characteristics, their needs and interests, their capacities and desires, are given independently of their social context and are not created or even fundamentally altered by that context" (29).[7] Jaggar later restates this liberal "metaphysical assumption" in an even stronger form: "[E]ach human individual has desires, interests, etc. that in principle can be fulfilled quite separately from the desires and interests of other people" (30). Jaggar later describes this as the liberal assumption of "political solipsism, the assumption that human individuals are essentially self-sufficient entities" (40). She holds that this starting point makes liberals characterize "community and cooperation . . . as phenomena whose existence and even possibility is puzzling," if not downright "impossible" (41).

Described this way, liberal individualism lies perilously close to two positions most feminists agree in rejecting: *egoism* and *normative self-sufficiency*. . . .

[7]Jaggar, see p. 520, n. 4.

More initially plausible is the suggestion that liberalism, by conceiving the human being in a way that imagines her cut off from all others and yet thriving, encourages normative projects of self-sufficiency—urges people, that is, to minimize their needs for one another and to depend on themselves alone. This, I think, is what Jaggar is really worried about when she speaks of "political solipsism." This is certainly one of the charges feminists commonly think true of liberalism, and one of the ways in which feminists have connected liberalism with common male attitudes and concerns. Feminists hold that by encouraging self-sufficiency as a goal, liberalism subverts the values of family and community, ends that feminists rightly prize. What should we say about this charge?

First, we should note that the normative goal of self-sufficiency is not one that feminists should dismiss without argument. The figures in the Western philosophical tradition who have defended some form of detachment and self-sufficiency as goals—in particular, the Stoics and Spinoza—have done so using powerful arguments, in particular arguments that connect the aim of self-sufficiency with the elimination of anger and revenge and the creation of a just and merciful society. Even if feminists want to reject those arguments, they need to grapple with them rather than viewing them as so many signs of heedless maleness.[8] They also need to grapple with the fact that some feminists, especially in the developing world, endorse self-sufficiency as an appropriate goal. To give just one example, the Self-Employed Women's Association in India (SEWA), one of the most successful feminist employment and credit projects worldwide, makes self-sufficiency one of its ten normative points for women, following Gandhi's use of this concept in the struggle against Britain.[9] These feminists do not take self-sufficiency to entail neglect of others, but they do hold that women care for others best when they are economically situated so that they can survive on their own.

Second, we should observe that the ethical aim of self-sufficiency and detachment is not strongly linked to individualism, that is, to the view that the primary focus of ethical and political thought should be the individual, understood as a separate unit. Indeed, in its most influential world form, in the Buddhist and to some extent also Hindu traditions, the normative doctrine of self-sufficiency and detachment presupposes the recognition that individuals as such do not really exist; it is precisely this recognition that grounds indifference to events, such as deaths of loved ones, that might be thought to matter deeply. Individualism, with its focus on what happens here and now in one's very own life, would seem to have an uphill battle in order to cultivate detachment from such external events.

Next, even if the psychology of liberalism were as described, that is, even if liberals did hold that our most basic desires can be satisfied independently of relationships to others, the normative conclusions about self-sufficiency would not follow. For moral theories frequently demand of people things that go against the

---

[8]On these arguments, see Martha C. Nussbaum, *The Therapy of Desire: Theory and Practice in Hellenistic Ethics* (Princeton, NJ: Princeton University Press, 1994), especially chaps. 11–13.
[9]Personal communication, Ela Bhatt, March 1997 on a visit to SEWA in Ahmedabad. For a history of the SEWA movement, see Kalima Rose, *Where Women Are Leaders: The SEWA Movement in India* (New Delhi: Vistaar, 1992).

grain, and we could demand great concern for others from people to whom such concern does not seem to come naturally. Such appears to have been the enterprise of Jeremy Bentham, who combined an extremely self-centered psychology with an exigent normative altruism. Kant too was ready to demand of agents that they disregard their most powerful desires; he famously holds that even a man in whose heart nature has placed little sympathy for others can still be expected to be absolutely committed to their good. Kant certainly believes that all altruistic commitment and loving concern in marriage goes against the grain, given the extremely solipsistic tendencies he imputes to sexual desire, but he expected individuals to live up to those commitments, rather than to seek self-sufficiency. Liberals, then, can and do highly value benevolence, family concern, and social/political involvement, even if they should hold that individuals must control strong selfish inclinations. And, as I have argued, liberalism typically endows individuals with powerful other-regarding motives also.

Liberal individualism, then, does not entail either egoism or normative self-sufficiency. What does it really mean, then, to make the individual the basic unit for political thought? It means, first of all, that liberalism responds sharply to the basic fact that each person has a course from birth to death that is not precisely the same as that of any other person; that each person is one and not more than one, that each feels pain in his or her own body, that the food given to A does not arrive in the stomach of B. The separateness of persons is a basic fact of human life; in stressing it, liberalism stresses something experientially true and fundamentally important. In stressing this fact, the liberal takes her stand squarely in the camp of this worldly experience and rejects forms of revisionary metaphysics (e.g., forms of Buddhism or Platonism) that would deny the reality of our separateness and our substantial embodied character. It rejects the Buddhist picture of persons as mere whorls in the ceaseless flux of world energy and the feudal picture of persons as fundamentally characterized by a set of hierarchical relations. It says that the fundamental entity for politics is a living body that goes from here to there, from birth to death, never fused with any other—that we are hungry and joyful and loving and needy one by one, however closely we may embrace one another. In normative terms, this commitment to the recognition of individual separateness means, for the liberal, that the demands of a collectivity or a relation should not as such be made the basic goal of politics: collectivities, such as the state and even the family, are composed of individuals, who never do fuse, who always continue to have their separate brains and voices and stomachs, however much they love one another. Each of these is separate, and each of these is an end. Liberalism holds that the flourishing of human beings taken one by one is both analytically and normatively prior to the flourishing of the state or the nation or the religious group: analytically, because such unities do not really efface the separate reality of individual lives; normatively because the recognition of that separateness is held to be a fundamental fact for ethics, which should recognize each separate entity as an end not as a means to the ends of others. . . .

Put this way, liberal individualism seems to be a good view for feminists to embrace. For it is clear that women have too rarely been treated as ends in themselves, and too frequently treated as means to the ends of others. Women's individual well-being has far too rarely been taken into account in political and economic planning and measurement. Women have very often been treated as parts of a larger unit, especially the family, and valued primarily for their contribution as reproducers and caregivers rather than as sources of agency and worth in their own right. In connection with this nonindividualistic way of valuing women, questions about families have been asked without asking how well each of its individual members are doing. But conflicts for resources and opportunities are ubiquitous in families around the world, and women are often the victims of these conflicts. When food is scarce in families, it is frequently women, and especially girls, who get less, who become malnourished and die. When there is an illness and only some children can be taken to the doctor, it is frequently girls who are neglected. When only some children can go to school, it is frequently the girls who are kept at home.

Again, when there is violence in the family, women and girls are overwhelmingly likely to be its victims. Sexual abuse during childhood and adolescence, forced prostitution (again, often in childhood), domestic violence and marital rape, and genital mutilation all are extremely common parts of women's lives. Many of the world's women do not have the right to consent to a marriage, and few have any recourse from ill treatment within it. Divorce, even if legally available, is commonly not a practical option given women's economic dependency and lack of educational and employment opportunities.

To people who live in the midst of such facts, it is important to say, I am a separate person and an individual. I count for something as such, and my pain is not wiped out by someone else's satisfaction. When we reflect that a large number of the world's women inhabit traditions that value women primarily for the care they give to others rather than as ends, we have all the more reason to insist that liberal individualism is good for women.

There is no doubt that liberalism deserves feminist criticism on this point. For, as many feminists have long pointed out, where women and the family are concerned, liberal political thought has not been nearly individualist enough. Liberal thinkers tended to segment the private from the public sphere, considering the public sphere to be the sphere of individual rights and contractual arrangements, the family to be a private sphere of love and comfort into which the state should not meddle. This tendency grew, no doubt, out of a legitimate concern for the protection of choice—but too few questions were asked about whose choices were thereby protected. This meant that liberals often failed to notice the extent to which law and institutions shape the family and determine the privileges and rights of its members. Having failed to notice this, they all too frequently failed to ask whether there were legal deficiencies in this sphere that urgently needed addressing. In 1869, John Stuart Mill already urged British law to address the problem of marital rape, which, he said, made the lot of women lower than that of slaves:

Hardly any slave . . . is a slave at all hours and all minutes. . . . But it cannot be so with the wife. Above all, a female slave has (in Christian countries) an admitted right, and is considered under a moral obligation, to refuse to her master the last familiarity. Not so the wife: however brutal a tyrant she may unfortunately be chained to—though she may know that he hates her, though it may be his daily pleasure to torture her, and though she may feel it impossible not to loathe him—he can claim from her and enforce the lowest degradation of a human being, that of being made the instrument of an animal function contrary to her inclinations.[10]

Though Mill seems excessively sanguine here about the female slave,[11] he is right on target about the wife, and he sees what a deep violation of basic liberal tenets is involved in the failure to legislate against marital rape. Again, in the same passage, he argues that the laws that deny the wife equal legal rights over children are also a profound violation of personhood and autonomy.[12] In a similar way, he diagnoses other distortions of the family structure caused by male power and the laws that express it, arguing for women's full equality in all that relates to citizenship and therefore for many changes in disabling family laws.

Mill supports his argument in part by appeal to consistency, saying that liberalism cannot plausibly deny women the rights it vindicates for men. But he also argues that *male* citizenship in a liberal regime is ill served by a mode of family organization based on subordination. For such a family order is a vestige of monarchical power and raises up despots who are ill prepared to respect the rights of their fellow citizens.

> Think what it is to a boy, to grow up to manhood in the belief that without any merit or any exertion of his own, though he may be the most frivolous and empty or the most ignorant and stolid of mankind, by the mere fact of being born a male he is by right the superior of all and every one of an entire half of the human race: including probably some whose real superiority to himself he has daily or hourly occasion to feel. . . . Is it imagined that all this does not pervert the whole manner of existence of the man, both as an individual and as a social being? It is an exact parallel to the feeling of an hereditary king that he is excellent above others by being born a king, or a noble by being born a noble. The relation between husband and wife is very like that between lord and vassal, except that the wife is held to more unlimited obedience than the vassal was. However the vassal's character may have been affected, for better or worse, by his subordination, who can help seeing that the lord's was affected greatly for the worse? . . . The self-worship of the monarch, or of the feudal superior, is matched by the self-worship of the male. Human beings do not grow up from childhood in the possession of unearned distinctions, without pluming themselves upon them.

In short, Mill argues, the stability of a liberal regime demands legal reform of the family. All liberals should and must seek the "advantage of having the most universal and pervading of all human relations regulated by justice instead of injustice."[13] . . .

---

[10]J. S. Mill, *The Subjection of Women,* ed. S. M. Okin (Indianapolis, IN: Hackett, 1988), 33.

[11]Mill's reference to *Uncle Tom's Cabin* in this passage makes it clear that he is thinking about America, yet he appears to be ignorant of the sexual situation of American slaves.

[12]Mill, *Subjection,* 33–4. Mill here discusses the Infant Custody Act of 1839, which allowed the Court of Chancery to award mothers custody of children under the age of seven and access to those under the age of sixteen; this small beginning shows graphically how bad the legal situation of mothers was previously.

[13]Ibid., 86–8. Compare *Considerations on Republican Government,* where Mill observes that a man who takes no pleasure in his wife's pleasure is "stunted." Similar claims are made by Verma. In the context of contemporary India: Verma argues that in this sense, feminism is "the struggle for the liberation of humanity as a whole" (44).

A deep strategic question arises at this point. When liberal people and states prove obtuse, refusing women's legitimate demands to be treated as ends, at what point should women—in pursuit of that liberal end—prefer revolutionary strategies that depart from liberal politics? Many feminists have discovered that Mill is correct: "The generality of the male sex cannot yet tolerate the idea of living with an equal." In consequence, legitimate arguments are met, again and again, not with rational engagement but with a resistance that keeps "throwing up fresh intrenchments of argument to repair any breach made in the old" but is in actuality quite impervious to reason.[14] This sort of thing makes revolutionary collective action deeply attractive to many women. And indeed, in many parts of the world, women have to at least some extent advanced their well-being through alliance with Marxist movements. It is beyond my scope here to give an account of when it is acceptable to use illiberal means for liberal ends, or to give advice to women who are faced with real choices between obtuse liberalism and pro-feminist collectivism. Even in the United States and Europe, the repeated experience of male irrationality may legitimately cause many feminists to find liberal politics insufficiently radical. In the long run, however, it is unlikely that liberal ends will be effectively served by collectivist means. Any noble ideal, furthermore, can be used as a screen by those who wish to do harm. The right response is to expose the abusers, not to discard the ideal.

Abstraction and Concrete Reality

Closely related to the feminist critique of liberal individualism is the criticism that liberalism's vision of persons is too abstract. By thinking of individuals in ways that sever them from their history and their social context, liberal thinkers have deprived themselves of crucial insights. I believe that there are two different criticisms here. The first has great power but can be addressed within liberalism; the second is a genuine attack upon liberalism but does not have great power.

The first attack is pressed by Catharine MacKinnon, Alison Jaggar, and a number of other feminist thinkers.[15] Their claim is that liberalism's disregard of differences between persons that are a product of history and social setting makes it adopt an unacceptably formal conception of equality, one that cannot in the end treat individuals as equals given the reality of social hierarchy and unequal power. Notice that if this were so, it would be an extremely serious *internal* criticism of liberalism, whose central goal is to show equal respect for persons despite actual differences of power. What do these feminist critics have in mind?

[14]Mill notes that when an opinion is grounded in reason, a good counter-argument will shake its solidity; when it is grounded in irrational desires and fears, good counterarguments merely intensify the resistance: "The worse it fares in argumentative contest, the more persuaded its adherents are that their feeling must have some deeper ground, which the arguments do not reach; and while the feeling remains, it is always throwing up fresh intrenchments of argument to repair any breach made in the old" (1–2).

[15]See Catharine MacKinnon, *Toward a Feminist Theory of the State* (Cambridge, MA: Harvard University Press, 1989), 40–47; "Reflections on Sex Equality Under Law," *Yale Law Journal* 100 (1991), 1281–1328; Jaggar, *Feminist Politics,* 181–85 (noting that liberal feminists have been gradually led to abandon the excessively formal approach).

It seems plausible that the liberal principle of formally equal treatment, equality under the law, may, if it is applied in an excessively abstract or remote manner, end up failing to show equal respect for persons. For example, one might use basically liberal language to justify schooling children of different races in separate schools: As long as the schools are equal, the children have been treated as equal; and if any disadvantage attaches to the separation, it is an equal disadvantage to them both. This, in fact, was the reasoning of Herbert Wechsler in a famous article critical of the reasoning in *Brown v. Board of Education,* the landmark school-desegregation case.[16] Insisting on abstraction for reasons of liberal equality and neutrality, Wechsler held that the introduction into evidence of the history of racial stigmatization and inequality was illegitimate and could only result in a biased judgment "tailored to the immediate result." Similar reasoning has been used in cases involving gender. In the Indiana sexual harassment case . . . , the lower court judge insisted on abstracting from the asymmetry of power between Mary Carr and her male coworkers, holding that the continual use of obscenities toward Carr by the male workers was exactly the same as the occasional use of a four-letter word by Carr. Judge Posner, overruling the lower court judge on the findings of fact, held that the asymmetry of power—including its social meaning in historical terms—was a crucial part of the facts of the case.[17] Their use of language was harassing and intimidating in a way that hers could not be. If liberal neutrality forbade one to recognize such facts, this would indeed be a difficulty for liberalism.

In general, liberalism has sometimes been taken to require that the law be "sex blind," behaving as if the social reality before us were a neutral starting point and refusing to recognize ways in which the status quo embodies historical asymmetries of power. Feminists have worried, for example, that this sort of neutrality will prevent them from demanding pregnancy and maternity leaves as parts of women's equality of opportunity. Again, if liberal feminism would prevent the government of Bangladesh from investing its money disproportionately in literacy programs aimed at women, this would lose liberalism the regard of most feminists in international politics.

It seems mistaken, however, to think that liberalism has ever been committed to this type of unrealistic and ahistorical abstraction. MacKinnon is correct that some liberal legal thinkers and some important Supreme Court decisions have been guilty of this error; her critique of liberal equality theory is a valuable critique of positions that have been influential in the law. But liberal philosophers have, on the whole, seen more deeply—and, I would say, more consistently—when they have rejected the purely formal notion of equality. Liberals standardly grant that the equality of opportunity that individuals have a right to demand from their governments has material prerequisites, and that these prerequisites may vary depending on one's situation in society. My own preferred way of expressing this is to say that liberalism aims at equality *of capabilities*. The aim is not just to distribute some resources around but also to see that they truly go to work in promoting the ca-

---

[16]"Toward Neutral Principles of Constitutional Law," *Harvard Law Review* 73 (1959). I discuss Wechsler's argument in detail in *Poetic Justice: The Literary Imagination and Public Life* (hereafter *Poetic Justice*) (Boston: Beacon Press, 1996), chap. 4.
[17]See ibid.

pacity of people to choose a life in accordance with their own thinking.[18] Even Rawls, with his somewhat greater abstemiousness about the role played by a view of the good in society's basic structure, nonetheless provides political thought with ample resources to think well about difference and hierarchy. He emphasizes a distinction between merely formal equal liberty and what he calls the "equal worth of liberty" and also between formal equality and opportunity and truly fair equality of opportunity; the latter members of each pair have material prerequisites that are likely to involve redistribution.[19]

One very good example of a liberal appeal to the worth of equality, used to oppose purely formal equality, is in the 1983 Indian case . . . , which declared unconstitutional the portion of the Hindu Marriage Act that mandated the restitution of conjugal rights. Judge Choudary noted that the remedy of restitution is available to both men and women—but, given the asymmetries of power in Indian society, the remedy is likely to be used only by males against females, and the resulting burdens (including nonconsensual pregnancy) borne only by females. He concludes:

> Thus the use of remedy of restitution of conjugal rights in reality becomes partial and one-sided and available only to the husband. The pledge of equal protection of laws is thus inherently incapable of being fulfilled by this matrimonial remedy in our Hindu society. As a result this remedy works in practice only as an oppression, to be operated by the husband for the husband against the wife. By treating the wife and the husband who are inherently unequal as equals, Section 9 of the Act offends the rule of equal protection of laws.[20]

One could not have a better expression of MacKinnon's critique—in the context of a liberal legal conception, in which the right of all citizens to autonomy and privacy is the central issue in question.

Liberals will continue to differ about the topic of differential treatment, especially in the area of affirmative action. Libertarian liberals allow wide latitude for advantages that individuals derive from morally irrelevant attributes of birth and social location but are strict on the rules that should govern benefits, insisting on a type of neutrality in which morally irrelevant characteristics play no role in the design of distributive policies and programs. Rawlsian liberals, noting that individuals arrive in society with many advantages that they have already derived from morally irrelevant characteristics, think it not just reasonable but morally required to readjust things in order that individuals should not be kings and princes; they therefore permit themselves a more extensive scrutiny of the history of group hierarchy and subordination, rejecting abstractness at this point as incompatible with a fully equal treatment. Feminist liberals have typically followed this strand of liberal

---

[18]This is brought out by Amartya Sen, "Freedoms and Needs," *The New Republic*, January 10/17, 1994, and by Martha C. Nussbaum, "The Good as Discipline, the Good as Freedom," in *The Ethics of Consumption and Global Stewardship*, ed. D. Crocker (Lanham, MD: Rowman and Littlefield, 1998), 312–41; also "Capabilities and Human Rights," *Fordham Law Review* 66 (1997), 273–300.

[19]See TJ, 83–9, 203–4.

[20]*T. Sareetha v. T. Venkata Subbaiah*, AIR 1983 Andhra Pradesh 356.

thinking, and their criticisms of other ideas of neutrality have been very important in generating legal change.

The criticism, then, is a serious criticism of some parts of the liberal political and legal tradition and of the obtusely remote language this tradition has sometimes chosen to characterize human affairs, but it can be and frequently has been accommodated within liberalism. To address it well, however, liberalism needs to pay close attention to history and to the narratives of people who are in situations of inequality. This it will do best if, in the spirit of Rousseau's *Emile,* it allows a generous role for the imagination in the formation and the writing of liberal theory.

Another criticism of liberal abstractness cuts deeper.[21] Many communitarian thinkers, among them some feminists, have held that liberalism's determination to think of persons in abstraction from allegedly moral irrelevant features, such as birth, class, ethnicity, gender, religion, and race, entails a pernicious form of "essentialism" that disregards the extent to which people are deeply identified with their religious heritage, their ethnicity, and so forth, and the extent to which these social and historical differences shape people. In one sense, we could say again that this is just a mistake: Liberalism is very interested in knowing these historical facts of difference in order to ensure fair equality of opportunity. But there is a deep point that is correct: Liberalism does think that the core of rational and moral personhood is something all human beings share, shaped though it may be in different ways by their differing social circumstances. And it does give this core a special salience in political thought, defining the public realm in terms of it, purposefully refusing the same salience in the public political conception to differences of gender and rank and class and religion. This, of course, does not mean that people may not choose to identify themselves with their religion or ethnicity or gender and to make that identification absolutely central in their lives. But for the liberal, choice is the essential issue; politics can take these features into account only in ways that respect it. This does not mean treating these features of people's lives as unimportant; indeed, in the case of religion it is because they are regarded as so important that any imposition on a person's conscience on these matters is seen as inappropriate in the public political conception.

At this point deep conflicts arise between liberalism and various religious and traditional views of life, insofar as the latter hold that freedom of choice is not a central ethical goal. Even if those views are accommodated respectfully within a liberal polity, their adherents may feel that respectful accommodation within a regime of toleration and free choice is not accommodation enough. Many delicate legal and political issues arise at this point. . . .

The more urgent question for our purposes is, what values prized by feminists are likely to be slighted in this liberal emphasis on choice? If women are understood to be, first and foremost, members of families, or members of religious traditions, or even members of ethnic groups—rather than, first and foremost, as human centers of choice and freedom—is this likely to be in any way better for women than is

---

[21]See the discussion of this second criticism in Onora O'Neill, "Justice, Gender, and International Boundaries," in *The Quality of Life,* ed. M. Nussbaum and A. Sen (Oxford: Clarendon Press, 1993), 279–323. The feminists criticized by O'Neill include Carol Gilligan, Eva Kittay, Genevieve Lloyd, Sara Ruddick, and Nel Noddings.

the "abstract individualism" of liberalism? Better in whose terms, we have to ask, and of course we encounter at this point many religious women who sincerely hold that the account of their identity given in the Laws of Manu, or the *analects*, or the *Koran*, is superior to the account given in Kant and Mill. We cannot follow out all those lines of argument here, except to note that a political type of liberalism . . . strives to leave space for other identities.

But we can ask how wise antiliberal feminists are to jettison the liberal account of the human essence in favor of an account that gives more centrality to "accidental" features of religion or class or even gender. These features are especially likely not to have been chosen by the women themselves and to embody views of life that devalue and subordinate them. Even feminists who are themselves communitarians should be skeptical about accepting uncritically this feature of communitarian thought. Communitarianism need not be altogether uncritical of the status quo, as many traditions have an internal critical strand. But feminists who are generally critical of tradition should still be skeptical of communitarian antiessentialism. The idea that all human beings have a core of moral personhood that exerts claims on government no matter what the world has done to it is an idea that the women of the world badly need to vindicate their equality and to argue for change. It is the disparity between humanity and its social deformation that gives rise to claims of justice. And the communitarian vision of persons, in which we are at heart and essentially what our traditions have made us, is a vision that leaves reduced scope for feminist critique.

We can make one further reply to feminists who stress the importance of recognizing differences of race and class. The liberal approach is a principled approach that address itself to issues of human dignity in a fully general way. As a liberal feminist, one is also, by the entailment of one's very feminist position, also an antiracist, a defender of religious toleration, and a supporter of fair equality of opportunity across classes. One's feminism is not mere identity politics, putting the interests of women as such above the interests of other marginalized groups. It is part of a systematic and justifiable program that addresses hierarchy across the board in the name of human dignity. To that extent, the liberal feminist is in a better position than are many other to show her fellow women that she has not neglected claims that are peculiar to their own class-, religion-, or race-based identities.

Feminism needs to operate with a general notion of the human core, without forgetting that this core has been differently situated and also shaped in different times and places. We should not overlook the questions raised by these differences, and we cannot formulate a just social policy if we do. But insofar as feminism denies the value of the whole idea of a human core, it gives up something vital to the most powerful feminist arguments.

Reason and Emotion

Liberalism traditionally holds that human beings are above all reasoning beings, and that the dignity of reason is the primary source of human equality. As Jaggar puts it, "Liberal political theory is grounded on the conception of human beings as essentially rational agents."[22] Here liberal thinkers are not alone: They owe much to their forebears in the Western philosophical tradition, in particular the Greek and Roman Stoics, whose conception of the dignity of reason as a source of equal human worth profoundly influenced Kant, Adam Smith, and others. Continuing the Stoic heritage, liberalism typically holds that the relevant type of reason is practical reason, the capacity for understanding moral distinctions, evaluating options, selecting means to ends, and planning a life. Thinkers differ in the relative weight they assign to these different components, but not in the choice of practical over theoretical reasoning power as the essential mark of humanity.

Modern feminist thinkers usually grant that this liberal move has had at least some value for women in seeking to secure their equality. They point out that earlier feminists from Cartesian philosopher Mary Astell to Mary Wollstonecraft, were able to appeal to women's rational capacity as a ground for claims to full political and moral equality. (They could indeed go much further back in history to support this claim: for Astell's arguments are closely related to the arguments of the Greek and Roman Stoics.) And they could reflect that the decision to base moral and political claims on an innate capacity of persons, rather than on social endowments or relations, is one that opens the door to radical claims of empowerment for the disempowered.

On the other hand, feminists have worried that liberalism is far too rationalist: that by placing all emphasis on reason as a mark of humanity, it has emphasized a trait that males traditionally prize and denigrated traits, such as emotion and imagination, that females traditionally prize. This emphasis has permitted men to denigrate women for their emotional natures and to marginalize them on account of their alleged lack of reason. This would not have been possible, the argument goes, had political philosophy been grounded in a conception that gave, at least, equal weight to reason and to emotion.

Most feminists who make such claims do not argue for innate differences between the sexes, although some do.[23] Their argument is, more frequently, that women, as a result of their experiences of mothering and of family love, have rightly valued some important elements in human life that men often undervalue.[24] Liberal philosophy is accused of making that male error in a way that contributes to the denigration of women.

This is a complicated issue. Grappling with it fully would require us to argue for an account of what emotions are. The objection, as I have stated it, drawing a strong contrast between reason and emotion, suggests that emotions are not forms of thought or reasoning. But is this true? Both the history of philosophy and contemporary psychology debate the issue. On the whole, the dominant view, both in the Western philosophical tradition and in recent cognitive psychology, is that emotions such as fear, anger, compassion, and grief involve evaluative appraisals, in

---

[22]Jaggar, *Feminist Politics,* 28.

[23]See Nussbaum, "Emotions and Women's Capabilities," in WCD; also Anne Fausto-Sterling, *Myths of Gender,* 2nd ed. (New York: Basic Books, 1992).

[24]Some examples include Carol Gilligan, *In a Different Voice* (Cambridge, MA: Harvard University Press, 1982); Nancy Chodorow, *The Reproduction of Mothering* (Berkeley: University of California Press, 1978); Virginia Held, *Feminist Morality* (Chicago: University of Chicago Press, 1993).

which people (or animals) survey objects in the world with an eye to how important goals and projects are doing. If one holds some such view of what emotions involve, the entire distinction between reason and emotion begins to be called into question, and one can no longer assume that a thinker who focuses on reason is by that move excluding emotion.[25] So we must proceed cautiously, looking both at the view of the emotion-reason contrast a thinker holds and also at the normative judgments the thinker makes about how good or valuable emotions are. This is tricky, because in the liberal tradition these positions cut across one another: Thinkers who hold a strong form of the emotion-reason contrast disagree about the value they attach to emotions, as do thinkers who consider emotions to involve thought and evaluation. By trying to keep these distinctions straight we can make some progress in understanding the force of feminist objections.

First, then, we do discover in the liberal tradition some philosophers who conceive of emotions as impulses distinct from reason, unintelligent forces that push the person around. On this basis, they endorse a contrast between reason and emotion. Kant and Hume (to some extent) are very different examples of this tendency. A strong feminist objection to such elements in the liberal tradition is that this is an indefensible picture of what emotions are.[26] To put a complex issue very briefly, it is implausible because it neglects the extent to which perceptions of an object and beliefs about the object are an intrinsic part of the experience of a complex emotion such as grief or fear. Grief, for example, is not simply a tug at the heartstrings: It involves the recognition that an object of great importance has been lost. Emotions involve ways of seeing.[27] This objection has been made by many philosophers and psychologists independently of feminist concerns, but the fact that the oversimple pictures were not criticized sooner may be explained in part by a cultural suspiciousness of emotions as female.[28]

But even Kant and Hume, whatever the deficiencies in their analysis of emotions, are far from dismissing emotions from their normative picture of the moral life. Kant is guarded about the contribution of emotions to moral motivation, but even he sees a necessary role for pity in motivating benevolence. Hume sees the emotions as the source of all the ends that morality pursues. Modern feminist Annette Baier has recently defended Hume's conception of the passions as the one feminists ought to use.[29] Although I am far from agreeing with Baier, because I think Hume's conception indefensible,[30] I think she is right to acknowledge the

[25]For criticisms of the reason-emotion contrast, see Martha Minow and Elizabeth Spelman, "Passions Within Reason," *Cardazo Law Review* 10 (1998), 37–76.
[26]See, for example, Catherine Lutz, *Unnatural Emotions: Everyday Sentiments on a Micronesian Atoll and their Challenge to Western Theory* (Chicago: University of Chicago Press, 1988); Helen Longino, "To See Feelingly: Reason, Passion, and Dialogue in Feminist Philosophy," in *Feminisms in the Academy*, ed. D. Stanton and A. Stewart (Ann Arbor: University of Michigan Press, 1995), 19–45.
[27]This is the theme of my Gifford Lectures at the University of Edinburgh 1993, now entitled *Upheavals of Thought: A Theory of the Emotions* (Cambridge: Cambridge University Press, 2001).
[28]See Genevieve Lloyd, *The Man of Reason* (Minneapolis: University of Minnesota Press, 1984); Lutz, *Unnatural Emotions.*
[29]Annette Baier, "Hume: The Reflective Woman's Epistemologist," in *A Mind of One's Own.*
[30]For a trenchant critique that has not been displaced, see Anthony Kenny, *Action, Emotion, and Will* (London: Macmillan, 1963).

central place Hume gives to passion in his account of human nature. So even if major liberal thinkers have failed to appreciate sufficiently the amount of intelligence involved in emotion, it has not altogether stopped them from valuing the contribution of emotion to our moral choices.

Let me now turn to the cognitive conceptions of emotion. . . . The position that many feminists would favor as doing most justice to women's experience of the value of emotional attachment would be a position that first analyzes emotions as containing cognition and then evaluates them positively, as having at least some value in the ethical life. This position is powerfully represented in the liberal tradition—to some extent under the influence of Aristotle. Both Jean-Jacques Rousseau and Adam Smith seem to have held that emotions involve thought and imagination; they also hold that the capacity for sympathy is a central mark of both private and public rationality, and indeed of humanity as such. Rousseau holds that a person who has no capacity for feeling pain at the distress of others is not fully human, that this capacity for imaginative response is the essential thing that draws us together in community and makes political thought possible in the first place. Smith's entire account of the "judicious spectator"—his model of good public judgment—is preoccupied with ascertaining the correct balance in the passions of anger and sympathy and love that such a public actor will feel; he explicitly criticizes his Stoic forebears for their normative doctrine of self-sufficiency and passionlessness. These thinkers hold conventional and nonprogressive views of women, but their positions on emotion offer what feminists have demanded. To this pair we may add Mill, whose *Autobiography* provides a moving testament to barrenness of a rationality starved of emotional attachment and imaginative stimulation.

What, then, is the issue? What does this liberal tradition assert about emotions, that feminist thinkers might still wish to deny? The liberal tradition holds that emotions should not be trusted as guides to life without being subjected to some sort of critical scrutiny. Emotions are only as reliable as the evaluations they contain, and because such evaluations of objects are frequently absorbed from society, they will be only as reliable as those social norms. To naturalize them would be to naturalize the status quo. In general, emotions, like other forms of thought and imagination, should be valued as elements in a life governed by critical reasoning.

Some feminists, however, hold that this entire idea of subjecting emotion to rational appraisal is mistaken, an imposition of a male norm of cool rationality on the natural vigor of the passions. Unlike other feminist objections to liberal views of reason and emotion—which, as I have argued, inaccurately characterize the strongest liberal positions—this one directly assails a central tenet of liberalism. In her influential book *Caring*,[31] Nel Noddings holds that women's experience of mothering reveals a rich terrain of emotional experience into which judgment and appraisal do not and should not enter. For example, the primitive bond of joy and love between mother and child would be sullied by reflection, and this primitive unscrutinized love should be the model for our social attachments. From the per-

[31]Nel Noddings, *Caring: A Feminine Approach to Ethics and Moral Education* (Berkeley: University of California Press, 1984). I do not discuss the even more influential views of Carol Gilligan because it is very unclear what Gilligan's normative view is and also what analysis she gives to emotions of love and care (to what extent she connects them with thought).

spective of a moral view such as Noddings's, liberalism, by urging people to ask whether their emotions are appropriate, robs moral life of a spontaneous movement toward others that is at the very core of morality.[32] Unless we give ourselves away to others without asking questions, we have not behaved in a fully moral way. It is the very unreasoning and unjudicious character of maternal love and care that make it a fitting paradigm for social life.

Noddings appeals, here, to images of selfless giving that lie deep in the Jewish and Christian traditions, though her view would certainly be controversial in both. She holds that her maternal paradigm of care is incompatible with norms of reflective caring that are preferred by liberalism. And she is correct. The liberal tradition is profoundly opposed to the idea that people should spontaneously give themselves away without reflection, judgment, or reciprocity. We have finally identified a position about the emotional life that is truly opposed to liberalism; it puts itself forward as a feminist position because it appeals to maternal experience as a paradigm for all human concern. Liberalism says to let them give themselves away to others—provided that they so choose in all freedom. Noddings says that this is one thought too many: Love based on reflection lacks some of the spontaneity and moral value of true maternal love.

What should feminists say about this? First of all, we should ask some questions about Noddings's claim that maternal love and joy can and should be innocent of appraisal and judgment. She gives an example that makes at least one mother doubt.

> There is the joy that unaccountably floods over me as I walk into the house and see my daughter asleep on the sofa. She is exhausted from basketball playing, and her hair lies curled on a damp forehead. The joy I feel is immediate. . . . There is a feeling of connectedness in my joy, but no awareness of particular belief and, certainly, no conscious assessment.[33]

Noddings concludes that such moments in which consciousness is emptied of focus and the personality flows toward another in a condition of fusion lie at the core of morality.

Let us consider this allegedly thoughtless and objectionless joy. Noddings thinks nothing; she simply basks in the fused experience of maternal caring.[34] But can it really be the case that she has no thought at all? Doesn't Noddings have to

---

[32]Noddings's general position is that the notions of "justification, fairness, justice" are "the language of the father," and that the primary defect in contemporary ethical thought is that it focuses on his voice rather than on the "mother's voice," *passim*.

[33]Noddings, 137.

[34]Perhaps I am handicapped by the fact that I simply do not recognize my own experience of motherhood in Noddings's descriptions of fusing and bonding. My first sharp impression of Rachel Nussbaum was as a pair of feet drumming on my diaphragm with a certain distinct separateness, a pair of arms flexing their muscles against my bladder. Before even her hair got into the world a separate voice could be heard inside, proclaiming its individuality or even individualism, and it has not stopped arguing yet, 23 years later. I am sure RN would be quite outraged by the suggestion that her own well-being was at any time merged with that of her mother, and her mother would never dare to make such an overweening suggestion. This liberal experience of maternity as the give and take of argument has equipped me ill to understand the larger mysteries of Noddings's text.

have, in fact, the belief that her daughter is alive and asleep on the couch, rather than dead? Change that belief and her emotion would change from joy to devastating grief. She may not have to stop to ponder such a fact, but when her daughter was a baby she probably did.[35] Again, doesn't her joy presuppose the recognition that it is her daughter there on the couch rather than, say, a burglar? Doesn't its intensity also presuppose a recognition of the importance of her daughter in her life? To some extent, then, the view seems just wrong of the case as characterized.

But to the extent to which Noddings does give in to a joy without thought, how wise is she to do so? It does not occur to her, for example, to ask whether her daughter is sleeping from a drug or alcohol overdose, or following risky sex with a boyfriend, or sexual abuse from a relative. Assuming things are as she thinks, her joy is fine, and her maternal reactions appropriate. But aren't there circumstances in which the erasure of thought (which, as we see, is not complete even in the example) could be pushed too far? If her daughter really is unconscious from an overdose, or from sexual abuse, Noddings's joy would be inappropriate and her maternal responses harmful. Such heedless caring is dangerous in a world where many of the forces affecting children are malign. Noddings may live in a world in which she may safely bracket those concerns, but most mothers do not.

As Nietzsche wrote in a related connection: Blessed are the sleepy ones—for they shall soon nod off.[36]

A child is not an arm or a leg or a wish but a separate person. This person lives in a world full of both delight and danger. Therefore, the mother had better think, and she had better teach her child how to think. And she had better think critically, asking whether the norms and traditions embodied in the emotions of fear and shame and honor in her society—and in her own emotions as well—are reasonable or unreasonable norms. What shall she teach her child to fear, and what not to fear? How shall she urge her child to see the stranger who offers her an ice cream, or the teacher who caresses her, or the friend who says that people with black skin are bad? Unless society is perfect, as it probably is not, critical thought needs to inform emotional development and response. This liberal idea seems a better recipe for maternal care than Noddings's emphasis on thoughtless giving. . . .

In fact, the most powerful feminist criticism of liberal views of reason and emotion points in the opposite direction to Noddings's. Made most influentially by Catharine MacKinnon and Andrea Dworkin, and by now commonly accepted in at least some form, the argument is that emotion, desire, and preference are not given or "natural" but shaped by social norms and appraisals—and that many emotions of both men and women are shaped by norms that subordinate women to men.[37] MacKinnon has argued that not only male aggression and female timidity but also the character of both male and female sexual desire are shaped by the social norm that women ought to be the subordinates of men. Men eroticize dom-

[35]See the acute criticism of Noddings in Diana Fritz Cates, *Compassion for Friends in Fellowship with God* (Notre Dame: Notre Dame University Press, 1997).
[36]Nietzsche, *Thus Spoke Zarathustra*, Part I, "On the Teachers of Virtue." (Kaufmann translates *einnicken* as "drop off," but I have substituted a moral literal rendering.)
[37]See Catharine MacKinnon, *Feminism Unmodified* (Cambridge, MA: Harvard University Press, 1987); Andrea Dworkin, *Intercourse* (New York: The Free Press, 1988).

ination and learn to achieve sexual satisfaction in connection with its assertion. Women eroticize submission and learn to find satisfaction in giving themselves away. This, MacKinnon has argued, harms both individuals and society.

MacKinnon's insistence on criticizing socially deformed preferences goes against one strand in contemporary liberalism, namely, the part of economic utilitarianism that sees preferences as given, a bedrock to which law and politics respond rather than material that is itself shaped by law and politics. Economics is increasingly calling these views into question. They have always been at odds with the Kantian liberal tradition, which insists that individuals' desires are frequently distorted by self-interest. They are even more clearly at odds with Smith and Rousseau, both of whom were highly critical of diseased emotions and desires and blamed bad social arrangements for those diseases. Rousseau vividly shows how differences of rank corrupt human sympathy, preventing nobles from seeing their own pain in the pain they inflict on a peasant.[38] Smith shows how society, attaching importance to money and status, corrupts anger and sympathy, producing bad citizens.[39] Both follow the ancient Stoic tradition, according to which human beings are born good and envy and malice result from social deformation.[40]

Nor are such insights foreign to the utilitarian tradition. Mill recognized that gender hierarchy deformed the desires of both men and women. Women, he held, internalize their inferior status in ways that shape their desires and choice, and many of these ways are very damaging to them and to society. He held that "what is now called the nature of women is an eminently artificial thing—the result of forced repression in some directions, unnatural stimulation in others." It is, he says, as if one had grown a tree half in a vapor bath and half in the snow, and then, noting that one part of it is withered and another part luxuriant, had held that it was the nature of the tree to be that way.[41] Mill draws special attention to the way in which society eroticizes female "meekness, submissiveness and resignation of all individual will" as "an essential part of sexual attractiveness," whereas strength of will is eroticized in the case of men (16). Given the upbringing of women, it would be "a miracle if the object of being attractive to men had not become the polar star of feminine education and formation of character" (16), and equally miraculous if this object had not been understood to entail subordination. Here again, Mill makes a judicious comparison to feudalism: To both nobles and vassals, domination and subordination seemed natural, and the desires of both were shaped by this sense of the natural. Equality always seems unnatural to the dominator; this is why any departure from women's subjection

---

[38] J.-J. Rousseau, *Emile*, Book IV.

[39] Adam Smith, *The Theory of Moral Sentiments* (rep. Liberty Press, 1976), Parts I and III. The remarks especially critical of greed and competition are primarily from the later editions.

[40] On Rousseau, see Joshua Cohen, "The Natural Goodness of Humanity," in *Reclaiming the History of Ethics*, ed. Christine Korsgaard, Barbara Herman, and Andrews Reath (Cambridge: Cambridge University Press, 1997).

[41] The judgment of naturalness is said by Mill to be made "with that inability to recognize their own work which distinguishes the unanalytic mind" (22–3); see also "Was there ever any domination which did not appear natural to those who possessed it?" (12); and "How rarely it is that even men complain of the general order of society; and how much rarer still would such complaint be, if they did not know of any different order existing anywhere else" (84).

to men appears unnatural. "But how entirely, even in this case, the feeling is dependent on custom, appears by ample experience" (12–13).

What is new and remarkable in the work of MacKinnon and Dworkin is the insight that even sexual desire—which has often been thought to be natural and presocial, even by thinkers who would not hold this of envy and fear and anger—is socially shaped, and that this shaping is often far from benign. Their central idea is already in Mill, but they have developed it much further, given that they can discuss sexual matters with a candor unavailable to Mill. One may differ with many of their analyses and conclusions, but it seems hard to avoid granting that they have identified a phenomenon of immense human importance, one that lies at the heart of a great deal of human misery. Insofar as liberalism has left the private sphere unexamined, this critique of desire is a critique of liberalism. It challenges liberalism to do for desire what it has often done with greed and anger and envy—that is, to conduct a rigorous examination of its social formation and to think of the moral education of children with these aims in mind. As Mill shows us, such scrutiny of desire is right in line with liberalism's deepest aspirations.

Doesn't this ruin sex? As in the case of maternal caring, so here: Doesn't the liberal ask women to have "one thought too many"? Doesn't sex at its best involve a heedless giving away of oneself to the other, an erasing of conscious reflection? Yes and no. Liberal feminism—and here I believe it is right to treat MacKinnon as a kind of Kantian liberal, inspired by a deep vision of personhood and autonomy—does not ask women not to abandon themselves to and in pleasure, any more than it asks them not to invest themselves deeply in caring for children and loved ones. Once again, however, it says: Fine, so long as you think first. Abandon yourself, as long as you do so within a context of equality and noninstrumental respect. In some areas of life, perhaps, noninstrumental respect can be taken for granted. In this one, because of its history of distortion, it cannot be, and so you must think. If, as Mill plausibly suggests, "the generality of the male sex cannot yet tolerate the idea of living with an equal" (53), this thinking may cause pain. The liberal holds that this pain should be risked rather than endure the hidden pain that arises from subordination.

In short, wherever you most mistrust habit, there you have the most need for reason. Women have lots of grounds to mistrust most habits people have had through the centuries, just as poor people have had reason to mistrust the moral emotions of kings. This means that women have an especially great need for reason. Males can at least take consolation from the thought that the habits they live by have been formed by them, whether for good or for ill. Women should recognize that where the voice of tradition speaks, that voice is most often male, and it has even invented a little squeaky voice for women to speak in, a voice that may be far from being their own true voice, whatever precise content we attach to that idea.

In an age skeptical of reason, as Mill rightly argues, we have a hard time unmasking such deeply habitual fictions. Thus the romantic reaction against reason that he saw in his own time seemed to him profoundly subversive of any critique of established custom, "For the apotheosis of Reason," he concludes, "we have substituted that of Instinct; and we call everything instinct which we find in ourselves

and for which we cannot trace any rational foundation." Contemporary feminism should beware of making the same error.

Two things fill the mind with ever-increasing awe, wrote Kant: "the starry sky above me, and the moral law within me."[42] In that famous statement we see the radical vision of liberalism. Think what real people usually hold in awe: money, power, success, nice clothes, fancy cars, the dignity of kings, the wealth of corporations, the authority of despots of all sorts—and, perhaps most important of all, the authority of custom and tradition. Think what real women frequently hold in awe, or at least in fear: the physical power of men, the authority of men in the workplace, the sexual allure of male power, the alleged maleness of the deity, the control males have over work and shelter and food. The liberal holds none of these things in awe. She feels reverence for the world, its mystery and its wonder. And she reveres the capacity of persons to choose and fashion a life. That capacity has no gender, so the liberal does not revere established distinctions of gender any more than the dazzling equipment of kings. Some liberal thinkers have in fact revered established distinctions of gender. But, insofar as they did, they did not follow the vision of liberalism far enough. It is the vision of a beautiful, rich, and difficult world, in which a community of persons regard one another as free and equal but also as finite and needy—and therefore strive to arrange their relations on terms of justice and liberty. In a world governed by hierarchies of power and fashion, this is still, as it was from the first, a radical vision, a vision that can and should lead to social revolution. It is always radical to make the demand to see and to be seen as human rather than as someone's lord or someone's subject. I believe it is best for women to embrace this vision and make this demand.

———

Study Questions

1. What does Nussbaum identify as the core value commitments of liberalism?
2. How does Nussbaum address the charge that liberalism is "too individualistic"? Do you find her arguments on this point persuasive?
3. In your view, can gender equality be achieved under current conditions by policies that are "sex blind," or does it require policies that look at gender and take gender differences into account (for example, affirmative action programs, policies that permit pregnancy leaves from work, etc)?
4. Nussbaum writes: "Liberalism does think that the core of rational and moral personhood is something that all human beings share, shaped though it may be in differing ways by their differing circumstances." Comment.
5. How does Nussbaum address the objection that "liberalism is far too rationalist: that by placing all emphasis on reason as a mark of humanity, it has emphasized a trait that males traditionally prize and denigrated traits, such as emotion and imagination, that females traditionally prize"? What is your view on this issue?

[42]Kant, *Critique of Practical Reason,* Conclusion. The origin of this passage is probably in Seneca, *Moral Epistle* 40: see Martha C. Nussbaum, "Kant and Stoic Cosmopolitanism," *Journal of Political Philosophy* 5 (1997), 1–25.

Selected Bibliography

Antony, L., and C. Witt, eds. *A Mind of One's Own: Feminist Essays on Reason and Objectivity* (Boulder, CO: Westview Press, 1993).

Mill, John Stuart. *The Subjection of Women* (1869).

Nussbaum, Martha. "The Future of Feminist Liberalism," *Proceedings and Addresses of the American Philosophical Association* 75, no. 2 (2001).

———. "Rawls and Feminism," in Samuel Freeman, ed. *The Cambridge Companion to Rawls* (Cambridge/New York: Cambridge University Press, 2002).

———. *Sex and Social Justice* (Oxford/New York: Oxford University Press, 1999).

———. *Women and Human Development: The Capabilities Approach* (Cambridge/New York: Cambridge University Press, 2000).

"Symposium on Martha Nussbaum's Political Philosophy," *Ethics* 111, no. 1 (2000).

GLOSSARY

The glossary consists of short definitions and explanations of a number of important ethical terms, most of which appear in this book, either in the introductions or in the selections. When a term being defined is closely associated with a particular writer, the writer's name is given in parentheses.

Absolutism, moral or ethical The theory that there are objective, universally valid moral principles or moral truths. Opposed to *moral relativism.*

Agent-relative vs. agent-neutral reasons *Agent-relative* reasons are reasons for a specific person to do or refrain from certain actions. Reasons stemming from one's personal goals and reasons based on deontological constraints are considered agent-relative. *Agent-neutral* reasons are reasons for anyone to bring about or prevent a state of affairs that is impersonally good or bad. Utilitarianism is sometimes regarded as providing agent-neutral reasons for doing what will increase overall human well-being. (Nagel)

Aesthetics The philosophy of art, in all its forms.

Alienation The estrangement of the worker in modern capitalistic society from labor, the world of nature, other people, and him or herself. (Marx)

Altruism Action aimed at the good or well-being of someone other than the agent. Contrasted with *egoism.*

Amoralism Complete indifference to and lack of concern for moral principles. Not the same as *immoralism,* which is the deliberate breaking of moral rules.

A posteriori Describes a claim whose truth is based on appeal to evidence or facts. Science is a posteriori.

Appetite Desire or inclination. A psychological state of wanting something.

A priori Describes a claim whose truth is independent of any particular experience, based on reason alone. Mathematics is a priori. According to Kant, ethics is a priori as well.

Arête Commonly translated as "virtue," although *arête* has broader connotations than modern understandings of virtue. "Excellence" is a more ac-

curate translation. An *arête* is any state that enables a thing or being to perform its function well. For Aristotle, an *arête,* or virtue, is a state of the human being that is conducive to achieving the human good. Aristotle distinguishes two kinds of virtue: moral and intellectual.

Asceticism A way of life from which all pleasures have been banished.

Atheism Denial of the existence of God. (Sartre)

Autonomy The capacity of the will to follow a law that it imposes on itself. Moral action is always autonomous action. (Kant)

Basic structure of society The major social institutions (such as the constitution and political system, economy, structure of the family) that determine how rights, duties, and opportunity are distributed to individuals. (Rawls)

Care A moral attitude of direct concern for the well-being of another person, based on emotional connection with that person. The perspective of care is contrasted with the perspective of justice by some feminist writers.

Categorical imperative A requirement that binds or obligates an agent unconditionally, independently of the agent's desires and personal interests (for example, that one ought not to lie to advance one's own self-interest). According to Kant, all moral requirements are categorical imperatives. The categorical imperative is Kant's supreme moral principle, which applies to humans simply as rational beings, without regard to empirically given desires and interests.

Cognitivism The theory that moral claims can be true or false and that there can be moral knowledge. Opposed to *noncognitivism* or *skepticism.*

Conscience A special faculty or capacity to judge between right and wrong action, which condemns us when we violate its dictates. (Butler)

Consequentialism   A moral theory that holds that the rightness or wrongness of an action depends on its consequences. The right action is that which produces the most overall good. Utilitarianism is a form of consequentialism. See also *teleology*. (Bentham, Mill, Moore, Hare)

Contemplation   The life devoted to contemplation or theoretical knowledge of the nature of reality, identified as the highest good for human beings. (Aristotle)

Contractarianism   An approach to moral or political philosophy that bases moral or political principles in rational agreement, either hypothetical or actual. An offshoot of social contract theory. (Rawls, Gauthier)

Contractualism   The theory that the wrongness of an act is the fact that it would be disallowed by general principles of conduct that no one could reasonably reject, as a basis for informed, unforced agreement. Related to *contractarianism*. (Scanlon)

Deontological constraints or restrictions   Rules that prohibit or constrain individuals from actions that are wrong in themselves—for example, deontological rules against lying, harming innocent people, violating rights, and so on. Deontological theories hold that such rules constrain the pursuit of desirable ends and consequences. (Ross, Nagel)

Deontology   The view that certain ways of acting can be right or wrong in themselves, and that the rightness or wrongness of an action is not based simply on its good or bad consequences. (Kant, Ross, Rawls, Nagel)

Determinism   The theory that all events, including human actions, are causally necessitated. Determinism denies that a person could have done otherwise in any given situation and thus seems incompatible with free will.

Difference principle   One part of Rawls's second principle of justice: a principle of distributive justice holding that inequalities in the distribution of certain social goods are permissible if they benefit the least advantaged members of society.

Distributive justice   Area of justice concerned with the proper distribution of the benefits of social cooperation (such as opportunity, authority, wealth, and so on). Sometimes contrasted with *retributive justice*, which is concerned with just punishment.

Duty   An act that a person morally ought or is obliged to do.

Egalitarianism   Any theory holding that opportunity, wealth, and other social resources should be distributed more or less equally.

Egoism, ethical   The view that an action is rational only if it is directed at self-interest or some good for oneself; in other words, that one ought always act in ways conducive to one's self-interest.

Egoism, psychological   The psychological thesis that all human action is motivated by self-interest. Associated with *ethical egoism*. (Hobbes)

Emotivism   The theory that the function of moral claims, such as "lying is wrong," is to express a speaker's emotional attitudes (such as feelings of approval or disapproval) and to influence others to share these attitudes.

End   A goal or aim of action. A final end is an end that is desired for its own sake and not for the sake of anything beyond itself. Final ends are contrasted with *means* or *instrumental goods*.

End in itself   Something that has absolute and incomparable value. Kant claimed that "humanity" or "rational nature," by which he meant our capacities for rational choice, is an end in itself. (Kant)

Essence   The real nature of a thing, that which makes it what it is.

Eternal law   The law of God. Sometimes called "natural law." (Aquinas)

Ethical objectivism   The theory that there are objective and universally valid moral truths. Used interchangeably with *absolutism*.

Eudaimonia   Often translated as "happiness," but sometimes as "human flourishing." Not the same as pleasure, *eudaimonia* is sometimes proposed as the highest good in life. (Aristotle)

Existentialism   A literary and philosophical outlook, primarily from the 20th century, that ascribes to human beings the freedom and the responsibility for choosing their own values and creating themselves in a world in which there are no preexisting, objective values. (Sartre)

Faculty   A capacity, such as the ability to think, feel, choose, or the like.

Fatalism   The theory that an individual's destiny is fixed and that the individual can do nothing to alter it. Not the same as *determinism*.

Feminist ethics   Approaches to ethics that are particularly concerned with the equality of women and with uncovering ways in which women have been subordinated to men. On a theoretical level, feminist ethics aims at correcting male bias in ethics and fully representing women's moral experiences.

Final end   See *end*.

Free will   The idea that we have the capacity to choose between alternative courses of action. Opposed to *determinism*.

Friendship "Those who wish for their friends' good for their friends' sake are friends in the truest sense, since their attitude is determined by what their friends are and not by incidental considerations." (Aristotle)

Good will A will that is motivated to action by duty or respect for the moral law. (Kant)

Hedonism, ethical The theory that pleasure is the only thing that is intrinsically good or good in itself. (Epicurus, Bentham, Mill)

Hedonism, psychological The psychological thesis that the desire for pleasure is the fundamental motive of all human action. Associated with *ethical hedonism*. (Epicurus, Bentham)

Hedonistic calculus A method for estimating the total amount of pleasure and pain resulting from a course of action that involves weighing such factors as the intensity and duration of pleasures or pains, the certainty (probability) with which they are likely to occur, the number of people who will experience pleasure or pain, and so on. (Bentham)

Heteronomy The character of a will that is moved to act by forces or sources of authority outside itself, particularly desires. Opposed to *autonomy*. (Kant)

Hypothetical imperative An imperative stating that one ought to take a certain action as a means to a desired end. Hypothetical imperatives are conditional (rather than unconditional or categorical), because they apply on the condition that one desires a certain end. The hypothetical imperative is the general principle of rationality that one ought to take the means to one's ends or abandon the end. Contrasted with *categorical imperatives*. (Kant)

Ideal utilitarianism The theory that we ought always to act in such a way as to produce the greatest total amount of good possible, in which the good is not limited to pleasure (as in Bentham and Mill) but includes other intrinsic goods as well. (Moore)

Imperative A statement claiming that one ought to act in a certain way. Kant distinguishes two basic kinds of imperatives: hypothetical imperatives and categorical imperatives.

Inclination A desire or feeling that is a motive to action. Opposed to *motivation by duty*. (Kant)

Indeterminism The theory that at least some events, in particular human actions that result from choices or decisions, are not causally determined by antecedent conditions. Opposed to *determinism*.

Instrumental good Something that is valued as a means to an end beyond itself. Contrasted with *intrinsic good*. See also *means*.

Intellectual virtue A virtue or excellence of the intellect as opposed to a virtue of character or of the will (i.e., moral virtue). Intellectual virtues include wisdom, prudence, good judgment, and so on. (Aristotle)

Intrinsic good Something that is good in itself or good as an end—that is, something desired for its own sake and not for the sake of anything beyond itself. Contrasted with *instrumental good*. See also *final end*.

Intuitionism The theory that the truth of some moral claims (e.g., about the rightness or wrongness of certain kinds of action) can be apprehended or grasped noninferentially by a direct act of moral insight or intuition. (Ross, Moore)

Justice as fairness The theory of social justice developed by John Rawls that derives principles of justice from a hypothetical fair agreement between free and equal persons. "Justice as fairness" refers both to Rawls's method of deriving the principles of justice and to the principles that Rawls derives.

Libertarianism (a) A theory of free will, according to which human choices are undetermined by antecedent conditions. (b) In political philosophy, the theory that individuals should have the widest possible range of freedoms and that the power of the state to restrict individual freedom should be minimized.

Logical positivism A philosophical view from the early to mid 20th century that held that a substantive proposition, to be cognitively meaningful, must be verifiable by sense observation. Since ethical propositions cannot be verified in this way, they were judged to be meaningless.

Master morality The value system of the powerful individuals of the aristocratic or ruling class, which celebrates the character traits that they value in themselves. Opposed to *slave morality*. (Nietzsche)

Maxim A subjective principle of volition or action—in other words, the principle on which a person actually acts in some situation, which expresses that person's reasons or motives for action. (Kant)

Mean, doctrine of the The theory that a virtue is an intermediate state between extremes of excess and deficiency, both of which are vices. For example, courage is a mean between excess of fear and brashness or overconfidence. (Aristotle)

Means Something that serves as a way to achieve an end and is valued for the end to which it leads. See also *instrumental good*.

Meta-ethics A second-order discipline that takes normative ethics as its object of study.

Meta-ethics is concerned with such questions as the meaning of ethical concepts, the nature of moral properties and their relation to the natural world, the distinction between fact and value, the ways in which ethical claims can be justified, and so on.

Moral law The supreme principle of morality, also called the categorical imperative." Distinguished from law in the legal or political sense. (Kant)

Moral sense A special feeling, which is a part of our emotional nature or psychology, through which we are led to view some situations and actions with approval and others with disapproval. (Hume)

Moral virtue A virtue of character, such as courage, temperance, justice, generosity, and so on. The excellence possessed by the individual who is disposed to act well, according to a rational standard (the "mean"). Moral virtues are acquired by habituation and include the disposition to take pleasure in good action. (Aristotle)

Naturalism The theory that all normative ethical concepts can be defined in terms of empirical concepts.

Naturalistic fallacy The attempt to give a definition of "good," in particular to define "good" in naturalistic terms—a fallacy because "good" is indefinable (Moore). However, other theorists disagree, claiming that "good" can be defined and that there is therefore no naturalistic fallacy.

Natural law Law of nature. A set of moral standards, embedded in the nature of things or ordained by God, to which positive laws, as well as the actions of human beings, ought to conform. First emphasized by the Stoic philosophers, natural law occupies a prominent role in the views of Thomas Aquinas, the later social contract theorists, and Butler. Hobbes, however, gives a reinterpretation of the concept.

Normative Concerning norms or standards—for example, standards governing how one ought to act. Ethics is a normative discipline. Contrasted with *descriptive*.

Normative ethics The branch of ethics concerned with substantive questions about right and wrong, good and bad.

Original position The "original position of equality" (corresponding to the state of nature in social contract theory) from which principles of justice are derived in Rawls's theory of justice. The original position is a theoretical construct designed to represent a fair choice between citizens, all of whom are represented equally. In Rawls's construct, the parties are behind a "veil of ignorance."

Passion The 17th- and 18th-century term for feeling or emotion. (Butler, Hume)

Perfectionism A teleological theory holding that the good is perfection and that human action should be directed at increasing perfection in the world.

Pleasure, higher vs. lower A qualitative distinction between two kinds of pleasures. Lower pleasures are pleasures of sensation. Higher pleasures come from activities that engage the intellect, imagination, and moral sentiments. Higher pleasures are more valuable than lower pleasures and are preferred by those with experience of both. (Mill)

Practical reason Reasoning concerned with how we ought to act and to lead our lives. Normally practical reason is regarded as having motivational force. (Aristotle and Kant)

Precept A rule to be followed.

Prima facie duty An action whose characteristics tend to make it a duty, unless it is outweighed by a stronger duty. A prima facie duty is distinguished from an actual (or all things considered) duty, which is the action that ought to be performed in some situation after weighing all the morally significant features. (Ross)

Realm of ends An ideal society governed by moral principles in which each individual treats every other as an end and not merely as a means. (Kant)

Relativism, moral or ethical The view that there are no universally valid moral principles; rather, different people are subject to different moral requirements depending on the principles or conventions that their societies accept.

Sanction A form of pressure (such as the threat of punishment or social disapproval) that provides incentives for individuals to perform acts they would not perform of their own accord. (Bentham)

Self-realization The theory that the good for human beings lies in the realization of their highest potential. (Aristotle)

Slave morality The morality of the masses or the herd, which is formed in reaction to the master morality. Includes such traits as humility, sympathy, kindness, and self-denial and is exemplified in the institutions of Christianity and democracy. Opposed to *master morality*. (Nietzsche)

Social contract A theory that attempts to justify civil society and political institutions through the idea of an implicit agreement among citizens to support social institutions and abide by the laws in order to enjoy the benefits of an ordered social life. Most social contracts view the agreement as hypothetical—as an agreement that it would be rational to enter into, rather than an agreement that has actually occurred. (Hobbes)

State of nature   A hypothetical situation in which there is no government or law. (Hobbes)

Stoicism   An important school of ethical thought that flourished in the ancient Greek and Roman eras. One basic tenet is that the good is a life in agreement with nature. (Epictetus)

Subjectivism   The theory that moral standards depend on the feelings of the individual, so that there are no objective standards of right and wrong. Related to *moral relativism.*

Summum bonum   Literally, "highest good." The good most worth seeking in life, at which rational action should be directed.

Teleology   From the Greek *telos,* "goal" or "end." A kind of ethical theory that holds that good or right action is directed at an overarching final end. Ancient and medieval ethical theories, such as those of Aristotle and Aquinas, are teleological because they define a final end, or *summum bonum,* at which individuals should direct their actions—*eudaimonia* (Aristotle) or contemplation of God (Aquinas). In the modern sense, teleological theories define right action as what maximizes overall good; they are forms of consequentialism. (Bentham, Mill, Moore, Hare)

Theodicy   Any attempt to account for the existence of evil in a world created by an omnipotent, perfect God or to give a vindication of divine providence in relation to the existence of evil. (Augustine)

Theoretical reason   Reason as used in the acquisition of knowledge—for example, in science or philosophy. (Aristotle, Kant)

Universalisability   A criterion of right action that assesses an action by asking whether one can rationally and without inconsistency will that everyone adopt the underlying principle of action. (Kant)

Utilitarianism   A moral theory that defines the right as what maximizes total happiness, or utility. For example, an action or social institution is right if it produces more overall happiness than the alternatives. (Bentham, Mill, Hare)

Utility   The utilitarian conception of the good, defined variously as happiness, desire satisfaction, or preference satisfaction.

Veil of ignorance   A feature of Rawls's "original position"—that is, the parties in the original position have no information about their social position, natural abilities, conception of the good, special features of their psychology, or particular facts about their society (such as level of economic, cultural or technological development). The veil of ignorance is intended to exclude information that is morally irrelevant and to ensure fairness and equality in the choice of principles of justice.

Vice   Any form of bad action or wrongdoing, or a state of character that is conducive to bad action.

Virtue   An acquired, desirable state of character. See also *arête.* (Aristotle, Foot)

Virtue theory or virtue ethics   An approach to ethics that gives a central role to the virtues and their role in the good human life and only a secondary role to the concepts of duty and obligation. Ancient and medieval theories (such as those of Plato, Aristotle, and Aquinas) tend to stress the virtues. Virtue ethics is also now an important trend in contemporary moral theory. (Foot, Hursthouse)

Volition   An act of will or choice.

Welfarism   A form of consequentialism that measures the goodness or badness of the consequences of action by their tendency to increase human well-being. Utilitarianism is a welfarist form of consequentialism. (Hare)

Will   The capacity for choice, or the faculty that moves us to act.

Will to power   The basic drive to exert one's force or strength and to exercise power. According to Nietzsche, values are an expression of the will to power. (Nietzsche)

INDEX

absolutism, moral: defined, 428; single true morality debate and, 421–436; virtue ethics and, 466

Academy (of Athens), 27, 56

action(s): consequentialism and, 353–362; deontological approach to, 277–279; ends of, 5–9; good as aim of, 57–58, 64–65; happiness as activity, 89–90; Korsgaard's discussion of, 490, 494–496; moral theory and, 6–9; Nagel's discussion of, 395–405; Ross on rightness of, 294–309; utilitarian view of, 239–252; virtue ethics and, 71–72, 447–452, 455–459

affection, 79–80, 83–85, 102. *See also* love; social relationships

affirmative action, 529–531

agape, 360–361

agents (agency): contractarianism and, 411–420; end as intention of, 123–125; goodness and acts of, 125–126; moral obligation and, 493–503; Nagel's agent-neutral/agent-relative reason, 393–405; victims and, 398–405

aggregationism, 353, 359–362

agreement, contractarianism and, 416–420

Albertus Magnus, 121

Alexander the Great, 56

alienation, Marx's concept of, 227–236, 510

Ambrose, Saint, 115

amoralism, Williams's discussion of, 320–326

Anscombe, G. E. M., 466

anthropology, ethics and, 1–2, 326–328

anti-theory ethics, 464–468

appetite, 148, 172–177. *See also* desire

Aquinas, St. Thomas, 7, 13–15, 121–122; care ethics and, 512–513; contemporary philos-

ophy and, 278; *Summa Contra Gentiles* of, 122–132; *Summa Theologica* of, 132–139, 142; virtue theory of, 440–441, 444–446, 450, 466

Aristotle: belief in rationality, 14; contemporary philosophy and, 278; impact of, 56–57, 123; Korsgaard's discussion of, 495; liberalism and, 534; on nature of good, 7; *Nicomachean Ethics*, 15, 57–93; Rawls's discussion of, 342–343; Ross's translation of, 293–294; virtue theory and, 439–441, 444–446, 463, 466

Astell, Mary, 532

atheism, existentialism and, 310–318

Augustine, St.: *Enchiridion*, 119–120; on eternal law, 132–133; on immortality, 14–15; on morality and Catholic Church, 115–118, 123

authority, *vs.* power, 172–173, 494

autonomous ethics, 425–436

autonomy: care ethics and, 510–516; Kant and, 214–216; obligation and, 489–503

Bacon, Francis, 147

Baier, Annette, 278, 407; care ethics and, 505–516; Hume defended by, 533–534

behavior, conduct *vs.*, 1–2

beliefs, moral relativism and, 426–427

Bentham, Jeremy: Hare's discussion of, 355, 357, 359, 371; Hobbes and, 143–144; liberalism and, 524; Mill and, 238, 260–261; Moore and, 281, 293; utilitarianism and, 8–9, 96, 218–226

Beyond Good and Evil, 264

Block, N., 434–435

Blum, Lawrence, 506–507

body: Aquinas' discussion of, 128–129; Epictetus' discussion of, 102–113; goods of, 64–65

Bradley, F. H., 492

Brandt, Richard B., 357, 359, 390

Brouwer, L. G. J., 378, 382

Browning, Robert, 357

Brown v. Board of Education, 528

Butler, Joseph, 7, 143–144, 161–177, 494

Calvin, John, 115, 141

Camus, Albert, 321

Capital, 227–228

Card, Claudia, 506, 508

care ethics, 505–516, 534–536

Caring, 534–536

Carlyle, Thomas, 243

Carr, Mary, 528

categorical imperative, 193–216, 347, 360–365, 491–492

Catholic Church, ethics and, 116–118, 141–145

causality, Kant's concept of, 491–492

Cave, allegory of, 28, 51–54

character, natural virtues and vices and, 189–191, 457–458

children, ethics and, 507–516, 534–536

Chodorow, Nancy, 508, 532

Christian ethics: Aquinas' work in, 122–139; Augustine's work in, 115–120; Butler's discussion of, 161–177; care ethics and, 512–513; contractarianism and, 409, 419–420; existentialism and, 310–318; history of, 13–15; Nietzsche's discussion of, 264–273; Reformation and, 141–145; utilitarianism and, 250–252; virtue theory and, 440–441

Chryssipus, 112

claims, Ross's discussion of, 296–297